D0984463

THE THEORY OF WAGES

THE
THEORY OF WAGES

By

PAUL H. DOUGLAS

NEW YORK

KELLEY & MILLMAN, INC.

1957

FIRST PUBLISHED IN 1934

TO MY FRIENDS AND ASSOCIATES

CHARLES W. COBB

SIDNEY W. WILCOX

ERIKA SCHOENBERG

TO WHOM THIS WORK OWES MUCH

"If we wish to make ourselves acquainted with the economy and arrangements by which the different nations of the earth produce or distribute their revenue, I really know of but one way to attain our object, and that is *to look and see.*"

Richard Jones. *Introductory Lecture on Political Economy.* 1833, p. 31

"In good sooth, my masters, this is no door. Yet it is a little window, that looketh upon a great world."

Quoted in Risley, *The People of India*

FOREWORD TO 1957 EDITION

I am naturally greatly pleased that the present publishers have rescued the *Theory of Wages* from the limbo of out-of-print and half-forgotten books. This book was first published in 1934 and represented a decade of inductive work on my part in the field of wage theory and an attempt to determine the basic quantitative laws of production and distribution. In the years which followed, I sought to develop this line of inquiry still further. With a group of able associates I published a series of studies which brought together a large mass of statistical evidence on the probable relative influence of changes in the quantities of labor and capital upon production and the relation of these changes to the distributive shares received by labor and capital.

These studies were interrupted during the years 1942-46 by other engagements. But in 1947, with the help of Miss Grace Gunn, I largely finished the manuscript of a book on these topics and gave a summary of the results in my presidential address before the American Economic Association in December, 1947. This address, entitled *Are There Laws of Production?*, which was originally published in the American Economic Review for March 1948, is reprinted in the front of this volume preceding *The Theory of Wages* because I believe it is a good summary of the more mature and extensive treatment of the subject, and is therefore an appropriate introduction to the longer and earlier work.

I had intended to bring out the new and detailed study on the theory of production in 1948. But on the very night on which I read my presidential address, I was selected by my party to run for my present position and since then my energies have necessarily been directed into other channels. While I still hope to finish the task I began so long ago, the immediate prospects for doing so are not bright. I therefore welcome this opportunity to present in a coherent manner some aspects of the quantitative effect of the factors of production upon production itself and then upon the distribution of the product.

I must confess, however, that in addition to the need for more quantitative studies along the lines which I have suggested in my article, there is also need to explore the economic meaning of b in the formula $P = bl^k c7$, and the role of technology or what was formerly termed "the state of the industrial arts" in affecting production. The intangible, but real influence of morale should also be considered. I can only hope that the present volume may serve as a challenge for such further research.

PAUL H. DOUGLAS
United States Senate
Washington, D. C.
April 18, 1957

ARE THERE LAWS OF PRODUCTION?*

By PAUL H. DOUGLAS

I. *Introduction*

A century and a third ago, in 1815, Malthus[1] and Sir Edward West[2] simultaneously pointed out that if successive combined doses of labor and capital were applied to a given piece of land, the amount of the product would increase by diminishing increments. Two years later this principle was adopted by Ricardo in his *Principles of Political Economy* as the basis for his theory of distribution. The joint return to labor and capital was declared by Ricardo to be governed by and to be equal to the amount of product added by the last combined dose of labor and capital, while the owners of land received as rent all sums in excess of these amounts. Since the quantities of labor and capital were not supposed to vary in relation to each other but were instead bound together in fixed and unvarying proportions, there was no way of isolating the specific contributions of these two factors as a means of determining the rates of wages and of interest. These rates were instead presumed to be regulated by cost-of-supply factors, namely, the Malthusian forces governing population which would keep wages down to a fixed minimum which was at least close to basic subsistence and the low minimum needed to compensate savers and investors. Such was the classical theory of distribution which dominated economic thinking for over sixty years.

Meanwhile, in Germany, during the 1840's, Von Thünen had theoretically broken up the combined dose of labor and capital and had pointed out that when each of the factors was separately increased but the others held constant, the product increased by diminishing

* Presidential address delivered at the Sixtieth Annual Meeting of the American Economic Association, Chicago, Illinois, December 29, 1947.   Reprinted By Permission

[1] T. R. Malthus, *Nature and Progress of Rent*, p. 61.

[2] Edward West, *The Application of Capital to Land* (Hollander ed., 1815) p. 54. Prior to Malthus and West, Turgot had pointed out in 1768 that successive applications of labor to land yielded diminishing increments to product. Turgot, *Oeuvres* (1844 ed.), pp. 420-21.

increments.[3] Von Thünen went on to state that the rates of wages and of interest were equal to the amounts of the product added by the last increments of each. He was thus the real discoverer of marginal productivity. Nor was this all. He reasoned that the product added by each equal increment of a factor was a constant fraction of the preceding increment of product, namely two-thirds, in the case of labor and nine-tenths, in the case of capital. This meant that it would be necessary to increase a factor in a given geometric ratio in order to increase the product by equal arithmetic amounts. This is precisely the law of the soil which Mitscherlich and W. J. Spillman later discovered,[4] and it is strikingly similar to the so-called Weber-Fechner law of physiological response. It would be most interesting to find out whether these conclusions of Von Thünen were merely happy hypotheses or whether, like so much of his work, they were based upon experimentation. Von Thünen's work, unfortunately, never had the influence which it deserved. The British, with their customary insularity of thought, virtually ignored it. The Germans, dominated by the fact-grubbing historical school, while lavishing attention upon Von Thünen's theory of location and his advocacy of $\sqrt{ap}$ as a just wage, almost completely neglected his discovery of the curve of the diminishing increment as the guiding principle for both production and distribution. Indeed, schooled as they were to believe in the relativity of economic principles, they naturally averted their gaze from what gave every evidence of being an economic law, which was independent of time and place.

It is to the glory of American economics that it was one of our own number, John Bates Clark, who at a meeting of our Association in 1888, fifty-nine years ago tonight, announced what was in effect the rediscovery of the marginal productivity principle. Clark, who had studied in Germany, had possibly been unconsciously influenced by Von Thünen, but certainly he was not consciously following him when he stated:[5]

An increasing amount of labor applied to a fixed amount of pure capital goods yields a smaller and smaller rate of return. . . . Let there be ten thousnd dollars worth of productive instruments and ten men to use them. Let each man be supposed to create by the operation a product worth three dollars

[3] J. H. Von Thünen, *Der Isolirte Staat; Zweiter Teil,* pp. 507-557-59.

[4] W. J. Spillman, *The Law of Diminishing Returns* (1924).

[5] John Bates Clark, "The Possibility of a Scientific Law of Wages," *Publications, American Economic Association,* Vol. IV (March, 1889). pp. 39-63. It was at this same session that Stuart Wood, the economist-businessman, also developed the marginal productivity theory of wages and interest and indeed went somewhat further by developing the principle of elasticity of substitution. Stuart Wood, "The Theory of Wages," *op. cit.,* pp. 5-35.

a day. Raise now the number of workmen to twenty and let the capital remain the same and each man will create less than before. A day's product will be 3 — X dollars. Each successive unit of labor employed in connection with a fixed amount of pure capital produces less than any of its predecessors. . . . General wages tend to be equal to the actual product created by the last laborer that is added to the social working force.[6]
The earnings of capital are subject to identically the same law as those of labor; they are fixed by the product of the last increment that is brought into the field. . . . Let the labor supply remain fixed and let capital increase and each increment of the latter, as it enters the productive field finds that it can create less than any of its predecessors. The general law of diminishing returns is two-sided.[7]

During the next decade Clark completed his theory in a series of subtle articles, and in 1899 gave it final expression in his book *The Distribution of Wealth.*

In the meantime, in 1894, the extraordinarily gifted Philip Wicksteed showed in his pathbreaking little essay, *The Coordination of the Laws of Distribution,* that if production were characterized by a homogeneous linear function of the first degree (that is, if when each and all of the factors of production were doubled or tripled, product would increase in the same proportion), then with each factor receiving its marginal product, the total product would be absorbed in payments to the factors without either surplus or deficit. This essay of Wicksteed's fluttered the mathematical dovecotes. Edgeworth, who in his *Mathematical Psychics,* had attempted to prove, by quotations from Owen Meredith's *Lucille,* that men should receive larger incomes than women, now dismissed with elegant irony the theory that production followed a homogeneous linear function. Pareto's attempted refutation was almost pure sophistry in which, by limiting the market, he sought to prove that product would not increase in proportion to the factors. It remained for Wicksell to give the most sensible treatment of this subject when he pointed out that while the homogeneous production function could not be expected to apply over the whole range of output within a plant, nevertheless under perfect competition, each firm would tend to carry its scale of output to the point where neither increasing nor decreasing returns prevailed but where instead the rate of return was constant.[8] Since industries were merely aggregates of firms and the economy as a whole was an aggregate of industries, it was presumed that the linear function tended, therefore, to be true of society

[6] *Publications, American Economic Association* (Mar., 1889), p. 49.
[7] *Ibid.,* p. 53.
[8] Knut Wicksell, *Lectures on Political Economy,* Vol. I, pp. 101-33.

as a whole at its growing points. Under these conditions, Wicksteed's conclusion held that the payment of the marginal products to each unit of the respective factors of production exactly distributed the product.

At this point, the theoretical discussion of marginal productivity was largely allowed to lapse, except for the clarifications and refinements which were introduced by our chairman, Professor Carver and by F. M. Taylor.

Over the course of the decades which followed, two tendencies in economic teaching became fairly evident. The first was a form of split personality or scientific schizophrenia, which developed in our economics departments. In the classes in economic theory, the principles of pure marginal productivity were taught, uncontaminated by any idea that there might be imperfect competition in either the product or the factor markets, or that there might be unemployment for reasons other than a wage rate in excess of social marginal productivity. This group taught that labor received the amount which its last unit added to the total product multiplied by the number of workers, while the return to capital was similarly determined. Neither trade union nor governmental action was needed to give to labor its own marginal product under conditions of full employment. All that was required was for the employers to bid competitively against each other for labor and this condition was commonly assumed to exist. But if government and unions disturbed the system of *laissez-faire* by raising wage rates above the social margin, this could only be effected by decreasing the numbers employed and hence creating unemployment.

In the classes which dealt with labor economics, however, a different doctrine was taught. Here marginal productivity was muted and the theory of the Webbs, as developed in *Industrial Democracy,* was stressed. It was the pressure of the market competition for lower prices which, weighing more heavily upon the successive levels of sellers because of their heavier overhead costs, tended to drive down wages and to worsen working conditions. Unions and governmental legislation operating through the imposition of common rules, could not only protect the workers from this competition but could raise the general standard of living.

It would be a fascinating task to analyze the differences between these two sets of theories; one dealing primarily with real and the other, with money wages; one assuming the relative absence and the other, the presence of unemployment; one postulating free and perfect competition between employers and between workers; the other absorbed by the power struggles of combinations of employers and workers. But such is not our present task. It is enough to point out that both of these two widely conflicting doctrines have been taught within our economics departments with little effort made by either set of protagonists to determine the relative truth of either, or their compatability. So far has this confusion of doctrine gone, that I have known professors, who teaching both theory and labor economics, have instilled the pure doctrine of John Bates Clark during one hour, and then during the next hour have taught as economic gospel the bargain theories of Sidney and Beatrice Webb!

The effect upon our students of this dualism in the winds of doctrine has been most unfortunate. It has caused some to shrug their shoulders and to dismiss all economic teaching with the words of Omar, so beloved by sophomores,

> Myself when young, did eagerly frequent
> Doctor and Saint, and heard great argument
> About it and about; but evermore
> Came out by the same door where in I went.

Others, like chameleons, have given diametrically different answers to identical questions, depending on which instructor asked them. But to every candidate for the Ph.D. degree, there has loomed the nightmare of that dreaded hour when in his oral examination, he must face both sets of teachers and know that the answers which would be judged right by one school would be judged wrong by the other. Such a state of affairs is at once both ridiculous and scandalous, and as long as it continues, there is little hope for scientific progress or even sound mental health among economists.

But within the ranks of the theorists themselves, a serious intellectual slovenliness, unfortunately, set in. Convinced that the marginal productivity curves of the factors were negatively inclined, they contented themselves with drawing the curves as sloping downwards and to the right, but took apparently little interest in trying to determine what the positions and slopes of these curves actually were. Thus I have seen an experienced instructor on successive days draw widely differing marginal productivity curves for labor, one declining very gradually, one at an angle of 45°, and the third plunging sharply downward. Moreover, this instructor gave every evidence of not realizing that there was any significant difference between these curves nor did he indicate whether he was drawing the curves upon an arithmetic or a double logarithmic scale. Indeed, the slope of the curve seemed to be determined partly by chance, partly by the stance of the instructor, and partly by the degree to which he happened to bend his arm!

The orthodox theorists may urge in self defense that they do not have the statistical information which would permit them to approximate the production function, the elasticities of the marginal productivity curves, or to determine the degree to which the actual distribution of the product conforms to what one would expect from the nature of the production function itself. But the sad truth of the matter is that they have made little effort to find out and have instead turned their backs upon inductive research and have, in effect, been school men living within ivy-clad towers.

II. *The Early Studies of the Cobb-Douglas Production Function*

It was twenty years ago last spring that, having computed indexes for American manufacturing of the numbers of workers employed by years from 1899 to 1922, as well as indexes of the amounts of fixed capital in manufacturing deflated to dollars of approximately constant purchasing power, and then plotting these on a log scale together with the Day index of physical production for manufacturing, I observed that the product curve lay consistently between the two curves for the factors of production and tended to be approximately a quarter of the relative distance between the curve of the index for labor, which showed the least increase over the period, and that of the index for capital which showed the most. Since I was lecturing at Amherst College at the time, I suggested to my friend, Charles W. Cobb, that we seek to develop a formula which would measure the relative effect of labor and capital upon product during this period. We were both familiar with the Wicksteed analysis and Cobb was, of course, well versed in the history of the Euler theorem. At his suggestion, therefore, the sum of the exponents was tentatively made equal to unity in the formula

$$P = bL^k C^{1-k} \tag{1}$$

Here it was only necessary to find the values of b and k. This was done by the method of least squares and the value of k was found to be .75. This was almost precisely what we had expected because of the relative distance of the product curve from those of the two factors. The value of the capital exponent, or $1-k$, was, of course, then taken as .25. Using these values, we then computed indexes of what we would theoretically have expected the product to be in each of the years had it conformed precisely to the formula. We found that the divergencies between the actual and theoretical product were not great since in only one year did they amount to more than 11 per cent, and that except for two years, the deviation of the differences was precisely what we would expect from the imperfect nature of the indexes of capital and labor. Since our index of capital measured the quantities which were *available for*, rather than their relative *degree of use*, it did not make allowance for the idle capital in periods of depression nor for the more intensive use of capital during years of prosperity. Similarly, our index of labor did not make allowance for failures to work full time in the bad years, nor for overtime hours which were worked in the good years. It was, therefore, to be expected that the actual product (P) would exceed the theoretical product (P') in years of prosperity and would fall below it in years of depression. So in fact it did in every year except the war years of 1918 and 1919. Professor Cobb and I, therefore, regarded these deviations as additional evidence of the general validity of the formula for normal times.

Still another striking bit of evidence was found in the fact that under perfect competition with a production formula of this type we would expect a factor to receive as its share of the product, the proportion indicated by its exponent. From the income studies of the National Bureau of Economic Research, we found that labor's share of the net value product of manufacturing during the decade 1909-1918, was estimated at 74.1 per cent, or almost precisely the value of the exponent for labor.

Professor Cobb and I embodied the results of our inquiries in a paper which we read before this Association exactly twenty years ago tonight.[9] We then determined to analyze more of such time series. Cobb computed indexes of labor, capital, and product in Massachusetts manufacturing for the period 1890-1926, and found the value of k to be .743. Interestingly enough, it was also found that the average of labor's share of the net value of the product in that state for that period was .74, or a virtual identity with the value of k.[10] A similar study, which was made in Chicago by Mr. Director for New South Wales manufacturing for the period 1901-1927, found k to have a value of .65.

There the matter more or less rested when my book, *The Theory of Wages*, appeared in 1934. Three years later, with the aid of Mrs. Marjorie Handsaker, I resumed our analysis of time series, and after working up data for Victorian manufacturing for the period 1907-1929, we found the value of k under the k and $1-k$ formula to be .71.[11] Labor's share of the net product or W/P was found to be .61 for this period.

We then introduced two important new features into our investiga-

[9] C. W. Cobb and Paul H. Douglas, "A Theory of Production," *Am. Econ. Rev.*, Suppl., Vol. XVIII (Mar., 1928), pp. 139-65.

[10] See Douglas, *The Theory of Wages*, pp. 159-66.

[11] Handsaker and Douglas, "The Theory of Marginal Productivity as Tested by Data for Manufacturing in Victoria," *Quart. Jour. Econ.*, Vols. LII and LIII (Nov., 1937 and Feb., 1938), pp. 1-36 and 215-54.

tions. An able young American scholar, David Durand,[12] had published in 1937, an excellent critical article of the earlier material, and had urged that the restricted function of

$$P = bL^kC^{1-k} \qquad (1)$$

be abandoned for one in which the exponent for capital was independently determined. As he correctly pointed out, the use of the k and $1-k$ function assumed the existence of an economic law which it should be one of the tasks of science to test, namely, the assumption of true constant returns. If we permitted the exponent for capital to be independently determined, it would then be possible for the sum of the exponents to be either greater or less than unity and hence to show true increasing and decreasing as well as constant returns to scale. We therefore decided that Durand's suggestion should be adopted and that we should try to find the values in terms of the formula:

$$P = bL^kC^j \qquad (2)$$

The second change was to broaden our fields of investigation. Hitherto, we had dealt only with time studies and had found the values of our exponents from index numbers of labor, capital, and product within a given economy, with each year serving as a separate observation. Here we measured the effect upon total physical product, of changes in the physical quantities of labor and of capital and from these we derived curves of diminishing incremental physical productivity of the classical type. We now determined to open up another field for investigation and to make cross-section analyses between industries in a given economy for specific years. Thus the annual statistics of manufacturing for the British Dominions (although not the British Census of Production itself) and the decennial and quinquennial *Censuses for Manufacturing* for the United States up until 1921 showed aggregates for each of a wide variety of industries from which it was possible to compute: (1) aggregates of the average numbers employed, including wage earners, clerical and salaried employees, officials and generally firm members and working proprietors (L), (2) aggregates of capital (C) expressed in terms of dollars including both fixed and working capital, and (3) aggregates of the *net* value of product added by manufacturing expressed in terms of dollars (P).

In these studies, differences between industries in the quantities of their net value product were presumed to be a function of the total

[12] David Durand, "Some Thoughts on Marginal Productivity with Special Reference to Professor Douglas' Analysis," *Jour. Pol. Econ.*, Vol. XLV (Dec., 1937), pp. 740-58.

number of employees and of the total quantities of fixed and working capital with each industry serving as a separate observation. This is obviously a somewhat different production function from that which is based on the time series. The quantities of labor used are physical quantities and though capital is expressed in value terms, these are also rough measurements of relative physical amounts. But since product is also expressed in value terms, this is the result not only of: (a) changes in the increments to the total physical product but also of (b) changes in the exchange value, or the relative price per unit of the products of an industry. The net values turned out by the respective industries will, therefore, be affected in these cases not only by the quantities produced but also by the respective demand curves for the products. Changes in each of these variables will affect the total exchange value produced.

Some critics will, of course, object that this second type of study, since it includes both quantities and prices, does not measure production at all and is in no sense a test of marginal productivity theory. It is certainly a somewhat different type of production function from that which is based on index numbers of quantities. But marginal productivity theory has always implicitly dealt in terms of values as well as of physical quantities since it assumes that the supplies of labor and capital in each of the various industries are regulated by the principle that the respective marginal laborers will produce equal amounts of value as will the marginal units of capital. In the apportionment of resources within an economy, therefore, the principle of diminishing incremental value productivity is an essential part of economic theory and is worthy of consideration. There is no reason why a production function which deals with it should not also be worthy of consideration and treatment.

Although interrupted by the war, we now have completed six cross-section or inter-industry studies for American manufacturing, namely, for the years 1889, 1899, 1904, 1909, 1914, and 1919; four cross-section studies for Canada covering the years 1923, 1927, 1935, and 1937; three studies for Victoria for the years 1910-11, 1923-24, and 1927-28; one study for New South Wales for 1933-34, and five studies for the Commonwealth of Australia, namely, 1912, 1922-23, 1926-27, 1934-35, and 1936-37. Two of my students, Messrs. G. Brinegar and K. O. Campbell, have just finished such a study for Queensland for 1937-38, and two more, Messrs. B. Solomon and N. A. Deif, are completing another study for New Zealand for 1926-27. In all, therefore, twenty-one cross-section studies have been carried through by our Chicago group to add to our previous four time studies, namely, for the United States, Massachusetts, New South Wales, and Victoria. In addition, two New Zealand economists, Max Brown[13] and J. W. Williams,[14] have carried through two time studies for New Zealand while the latter has also carried through a cross-section study for that country, as has G. W. G. Browne[15] for South Africa. We have, therefore, records for a total of twenty-nine inductive studies of the production function instead of the three which were reported upon thirteen years ago in *The Theory of Wages*.

In these investigations which have been carried out over the last two decades, we have had the assistance of a devoted and, I believe, competent group of associates, and in the aggregate many tens of thousands of hours have been spent upon the work. I am deeply indebted to this group, and while I am solely responsible for any errors which may lie within the work, my associates are chiefly entitled to any credit which may be forthcoming.[16]

Since these studies were carried out over a period of many years and since there were differences between countries and between years within a country in the basic data used, and since we were also constantly trying to improve our methods, it was inevitable that some dissimilarities should have developed in the precise content of the categories used and in the methods of attack. We have now ironed out a great many of these differences, and I believe that with a few exceptions which will be later noted, the results have now been made roughly comparable. It is hoped that in the next few months they may be made completely so.

III. *The Main Results of the Study of the Production Function in Manufacturing*

We can summarize the main results of these studies in three tables. Table I brings together the main results for manufacturing in the

[13] See an unpublished Ph.D. thesis at Cambridge by Max Brown, *The Relation Between Capital and Labour in New Zealand.*

[14] J. W. Williams, "Professor Douglas' Production Function," *Econ. Record*, Vol. XXV (1945), pp. 55-63.

[15] G. W. G. Browne, "The Production Function for the South African Manufacturing Industry," *So. African Jour. Econ.*, Vol. XI (Dec., 1943), pp. 258-68.

[16] First, of course, I am indebted to my chief associate during this period, namely, Grace Gunn, and after her to Marjorie L. Handsaker, Patricia Ogburn, Martin Bronfenbrenner, Ernest Olson, and Estelle Mass. But we have also had the faithful aid of numerous research assistants, computers, and draftsmen, among whom have been Yetta Abend, Helen Butcher, Julia Elliott Lewis, Oscar Seltzer, K. Sanow, H. Minsky, B. Nimer, William L. Slayton, Betty Roth, Donna Allen, Mitchell Locks, Y. K. Wong and Margaret Labadie. My colleague H. G. Lewis has also been most helpful in his criticisms and suggestions, as have John H. Smith and Colin Clark.

United States, as does Table II, for Australia; while Table III covers the investigations for the three British Dominions of New Zealand, South Africa, and Canada.

We may properly begin with a consideration of the American results, which include four time series studies for the period 1899-1922, and six cross-section or inter-industry investigations for the various census years from 1889 to 1919. It is unfortunate that the statistics of capital were omitted from the *United State Census of Manufactures* after 1919 and that we have been unable to continue our analysis of American data beyond the dates stated. Fortunately, the British Dominions in their admirable annual *Censuses of Production* have continued to collect statistics on the amounts of capital invested and this has permitted us to carry on studies for these countries in more recent times.

The four sets of time studies for the United States show somewhat differing results because of the differences which exist between the series of index numbers for labor and product. The precise nature of these series is described in the footnotes to Table I. It is believed that Series II, III, and IV, are appreciable improvements over the original Cobb-Douglas series or Series I. It will be observed that Series II and III, which use total man years (including clerical employees as well as wage earners) and total standard man hours respectively, as the measure of labor, show k's with values of .78 and .73 respectively. Series IV, which eliminates secular trends from each of the three basic series and expresses each observation as a percentage of its respective trend, gives k a value of .63. The value of j varies from .15 under Series II to .30 under Series IV. On the whole, Series II is the one in which the definition of the factors of production is most comparable to that of the cross-section or inter-industry studies, but Series IV avoids the dangers connected with the downward bias of the index of production and also eliminates the factor of time.

Five of the six inter-industries studies show lower values for k than do Series I, II, and III of the time studies. The k's average .63 for the six cross-section years with the average of the j's amounting to .34. The values of k and j for the initial and terminal years of 1889 and 1919, however, deviate appreciably from this average. Those for the earlier years have lower values of k and higher values of j, while in 1919 this tendency is reversed. The values of the exponents during the four middle years of 1899, 1904, 1909, and 1914, however, do exhibit a marked stability around the general average, with the k's ranging between .61 and .65, and the j's between .31 and .37.

It will be observed that in three cross-section studies, the values of k and j are many times their respective standard errors, the k's from

TABLE I.—THE VALUES OF THE PRODUCTION FUNCTION FOR AMERICAN
MANUFACTURING 1889–1922

Years		$P=bL^kC^j$						$P=bL^kC^{1-k}$	
		k	σ_k	j	σ_j	$k+j$	b	k	σ_k
A. Time series									
Series I[a]	1899–1922	.81	±.15	.23	±.06	1.04	.84	.75	±.04
Series II[b]	1899–1922	.78	±.14	.15	±.08	.93	1.38	.90	±.04
Series III[c]	1899–1922	.73	±.12	.25	±.05	.98	1.12	.76	±.04
Series IV[d]	1899–1922	.63	±.15	.30	±.05	.93	1.35	.69	±.05
B. Cross-section or inter-industry studies based on industry aggregates[e]									
Year	N								
1889	363	.51	±.03	.43	±.03	.94	58.34	.53	±.03
1899	332	.62	±.02	.33	±.02	.95	106.43	.66	±.02
1904	336	.65	±.02	.31	±.02	.96	107.40	.68	±.21
1909	258	.63	±.02	.34	±.02	.97	90.99	.66	±.02
1914	340	.61	±.03	.37	±.02	.98	81.66	.63	±.02
1919	556	.76	±.02	.25	±.02	1.01	244.21	.75	±.02
Average		.63		.34		.97		.65	

[a] The original Cobb-Douglas series of Labor, Capital, and Product as published in the original paper in 1927, were as follows: (1) Labor (L) = average number of employed wage earners only. Salaried employees, officials, working proprietors, etc., were *not* included; (2) Capital (C) = value of plant, buildings, and tools and machinery reduced to dollars of constant purchasing power with annual increments of investment divided by a specially constructed index of the relative cost of capital goods in which the wholesale prices of metals and metal products, of building materials, and of wages were given the respective weights of 4, 2, and 3; (3) Product (P) = the original Day index of physical production as published in the *Review of Economic Statistics*, Vol. II (1920), pp. 328–29, and Vol. VI (1923), p. 201. For a fuller description see Cobb and Douglas, "A Theory of Production," *Am. Econ. Rev.*, Vol. XVIII, Suppl. (Mar., 1928), pp. 139–65.

[b] The basic data used in Series II differ from those in Series I in that (1) labor now includes clerical and salaried workers as well as wage earners; (2) The basic index of physical production used was the Day-Thomas revision as it appeared in *The Growth of Manufactures, 1899–1923*, Census Monograph VIII, instead of the earlier Day study which was used in Series I. Values for the intercensal years were interpolated by the use of the earlier Day series, while I constructed a new index for leather. See Douglas, *The Theory of Wages*, pp. 174–76. The Day-Thomas index gave slightly lower values for P for the terminal years than the earlier index.

[c] The main difference which distinguishes Series III from Series II is that Labor (L) is defined to be the *relative total standard man hours* worked in the various years by the combined force of wage earners and clerical and salaried employees. This was obtained by multiplying (a) the indexes of employment for the various years by (b) the indexes of the length in manufacturing of the standard working week. For data and methods see Douglas, *Real Wages in the United States*, pp. 546–47.

[d] The essential distinguishing feature of Series IV is that the factor of time was eliminated from the basic data, not from the logs of data. This was done by fitting trends to each of the three series and expressing each index for a given year as a percentage of its trend. The basic data themselves were, however, identical with those used in Series II.

[e] The series of Labor, Capital, and Product in the six cross-section studies have now been reduced to an almost completely comparable basis: (1) Labor (L) = average number of wage

17 to 38 times their standard errors and the j's from 12 to 18 times as great as their standard errors.

On the whole, we should not be surprised by the fact that we obtain higher values for k and lower values for j in our first three time series studies than we do for the cross-section studies. For as we have pointed out, the two functions are, in fact, somewhat different and we should not necessarily expect identical results. Moreover, in the time studies, there tends to be a systematic downward bias to the index of production which keeps it closer to the index of labor than it should be in reality and hence gives an excessive value to k. This downward bias is caused by two factors: (1) Since the indexes are primarily based on the quantities of raw material produced, they do not include the increased fabrication and reworking of these materials which is a pronounced, although not a universal, tendency of industry. (2) It is in practice not possible to include with sufficient rapidity the new products which are continually pushing themselves forward, nor to drop in adequate time the products which are becoming obsolete. The net result is to keep the index numbers of Product (P), particularly during the latter years of a given period, closer to Labor (L) than in reality they should be and hence k is raised above and j is depressed below their "true" values.

This weakness is absent from the cross-section or inter-industry studies, which are made for a given year, and we would, therefore, expect the k's to be lower and the j's to be higher in this group of studies. Such is, in fact, exactly the case.

It may be of some significance that when the factor of time is eliminated from each of the three basic series of Labor, Capital, and Product, and the deviations from the trends are studied (as in Series IV), that the true value of k for the period of 1899-1922 is reduced to .63. This is identical with the average value of k for the six years for which inter-industry studies were made.

It may also be of some significance that in three of the four time

earners, salaried employees, supervisory officials, firm members, and working proprietors; (2) Capital (C) = total fixed and working capital; (3) Product (P) = gross sales value minus (a) cost of raw materials, (b) cost of fuel, heat, power, and rent, (c) taxes and insurance payments, (d) amounts paid to contractors, (e) cost of repairs, (f) sundries. No deduction has been made for the depreciation of fixed capital except that included under the heading of "repairs." For earlier studies on four of these years see Gunn and Douglas, "The Production Function for American Manufacturing for 1919," *Am. Econ. Rev.*, Vol. XXXI (Mar., 1941) pp. 67–80; Gunn and Douglas, "The Production Function for American Manufacturing for 1914," *Jour. Pol. Econ.*, Vol. L (Aug., 1942), pp. 595–602; Bronfenbrenner and Douglas, "Cross-Section Studies in the Cobb-Douglas Function," *Jour. Pol. Econ.*, Vol. XLVII (Dec., 1939), pp. 761–85; Daly, Olson and Douglas, "The Production Function for Manufacturing in the United States in 1904," *Jour. Pol. Econ.*, Vol. LI (Feb., 1943), pp. 61–65. A more complete description of the methods and results for 1889 will shortly be published by Miss Estelle Mass.

studies and in five of the six cross-section studies, the sum of k and j is slightly less than unity. While this by no means establishes the reality of true diminishing returns, since the differences between $k + j$ and unity are well within the range of the standard errors, there is at least a faint suggestion to that effect. It is possible that American manufacturing industry during this period may have exceeded the optimum size and that the desire for the power and prestige which is attached to bigness may have caused firms to be conducted on a larger scale than that which was justified by the most efficient combination of the factors of production.

While all due caution in drawing conclusions should be observed, it would seem that the most likely long-run norm for k during the period covered was between .63 and .64; and for j was approximately .34. This would mean that a change of one per cent in the quantity of labor (unaccompanied by any change in the quantity of capital) would normally result during this period in a change in the same direction of about sixty-three or sixty-four hundredths of one per cent in the quantity of product, and that similarly a change of one per cent in quantity of capital (unaccompanied by any change in the quantity of labor) would normally result, during this period, in a change in the same direction of about thirty-four hundredths of one per cent. If both factors of production were increased by one per cent, then the total product would normally increase during this period by from ninety-seven to ninety-eight hundredths of one per cent.

If we disregard the slight suggestion of decreasing returns and treat the most probable sum of the exponents as equal to unity, then an increase of one per cent in the quantities of both labor and capital would normally result in a corresponding increase of one per cent in product. A one per cent increase in the quantity of labor alone would normally be accompanied, during this period, by an increase of approximately two-thirds of one per cent in product and an increase of one per cent in the quantity of capital alone would normally be accompanied by an approximate increase of one-third of one per cent in the product. Perhaps this is as close a tentative conclusion as we should draw for this period although further studies may lead to some revision of these results.

Since under these conditions (*i.e.*, $k + j = 1.0$) the elasticity of the marginal productivity curves for a given factor is equal to the reciprocal of the exponent for the other factors, that is $e_L = \dfrac{1}{1\text{-}k}$ and $e_C = \dfrac{1}{1\text{-}j}$, it follows that the approximate elasticity of the normal marginal productivity curve for labor during this period would seem to be not far from 3.0, and for capital, to be around 1.5[17]

Let us now turn to the examination of the two time series and nine cross-section studies which have been made for Australia, and which are summarized in Table II, with its accompanying notes. In the Victorian time study, k has a value of .84 and j of .23, while in the New South Wales study, the value of k is .78, and that of j is .20. It should be noticed, however, that the respective standard errors of k and j are quite high and that the values of k under the original formula $(P = bL^kC^{1-k})$ vary somewhat from those obtained under the second formula.

As we would expect from the reasons which have been given, the values of k in the nine cross-section studies for Australia are somewhat lower. The combined average of the k's was .60 and of the j's was .37. Their average sum was, therefore, .97. Here it will be observed that we get identical results with either formula since the average of the k's under formula (1) is also .60. It should also be noted that the values of k are from 8 to 14 times and the j's from 3 to 10 times their standard errors.

The results for the five Commonwealth studies differ somewhat from those for the separate states, having somewhat lower k's and higher j's. Thus, in the Commonwealth, the average of the k's is .55, with a spread in individual years between .49 and .64, while the average for the four state studies is .65. On the other hand, the j's average .43 in the Commonwealth, as contrasted with .20 in the state studies.[18] After the text

[17] The marginal productivity of labor is

$$\frac{\partial P}{\partial L} = \frac{k}{L}P = \frac{k}{L}bL\,^kC^j = MP_L.$$

The elasticity of the marginal productivity curve for labor is then defined as

$$\eta = \frac{1}{\dfrac{(MP_l)}{L}} \cdot \frac{MP_L}{L} = \frac{1}{\dfrac{k(k-1)P}{L^2}} \cdot \frac{k\,\dfrac{P}{L}}{L},$$

then

$$\eta = \frac{1}{k-1}.$$

The flexibility of the marginal productivity curve for labor is defined as the reciprocal of the elasticity of this curve or

$$\phi_I = \frac{1}{\eta} = k - 1.$$

[18] The values of k and j are each relatively large in relation to their standard errors.

TABLE II.—THE VALUES OF THE PRODUCTION FUNCTION FOR MANUFACTURING IN AUSTRALIA

Years		N	$P=bL^kC^j$						$P=bL^kC^{1-k}$	
			k	σ_k	j	σ_j	$k+j$	b	k	σ_k
A. Time series								.71		
Victoria[a]	1907–29	22	.84	±.34	.23	±.17	1.07	.71	.71	±.07
New South Wales[b]	1901–27	26	.78	±.12	.20	±.08	.98	1.14	.86	±.05
B. Cross-section or inter-industry studies										
Australia[c]	1912	85	.52	±.05	.47	±.05	.99	15.87	.52	±.04
Australia[c]	1922–23	87	.53	±.05	.49	±.05	1.02	16.49	.52	±.05
Australia[c]	1926–27	85	.59	±.05	.34	±.04	.93	77.26	.64	±.05
Australia[c]	1934–35	138	.64	±.04	.36	±.04	1.00	39.79	.64	±.04
Australia[c]	1936–37	87	.49	±.04	.49	±.04	.98	21.57	.50	±.04
Victoria[d]	1910–11	34	.74	±.08	.25	±.11	.99	42.87	.75	±.08
Victoria[d]	1923–24	38	.62	±.08	.31	±.10	.93	96.93	.61	±.08
Victoria[d]	1927–28	35	.59	±.07	.27	±.09	.86	207.49	.60	±.05
New South Wales[d]	1933–34	125	.65	±.04	.34	±.03	.99	53.70	.66	±.03
Average all Commonwealth and state studies			.60		.37		.97		.60	
Average Commonwealth studies only			.55		.43		.98		.56	
Average state studies only			.65		.29		.94		.66	

[a] The Victorian index numbers for Labor, Capital, and Product from which the results were computed, were constituted as follows: (1) Labor (L) = average number of persons employed including wage earners, salaried employees, supervisory officials, and working employers; (2) Capital (C) = fixed capital reduced to dollars of constant purchasing power but excluding land values and working capital; (3) Product (P) = index of physical production using 1911 value weights. See Handsaker and Douglas, "The Theory of Marginal Productivity Tested by Data for Manufacturing in Victoria," *Quart. Jour. Econ.*, Vol. LII (Nov., 1937), pp. 1–36.

[b] The New South Wales study is based on series for Labor, Capital, and Product, which are virtually identical in their definition with those of Victoria. The capital index differs from that constructed earlier by Mr. Director in that it does not provide for the replacement at differing price levels for the estimated depreciation on capital. For the Director study, see Douglas, *The Theory of Wages*, pp. 167–172.

[c] In the Commonwealth cross-section studies, the terms are defined as follows: (1) Labor (L) = average number employed of wage earners and salaried employees but generally excluding working proprietors (except in 1934–35); (2) Capital (C) = value of plant and machinery, buildings, and land, but excluding working capital. The exclusion of working capital is the chief dissimilarity between this series and the definition of total capital used in the case of the United States and Canadian cross-section studies. We will try to revise the Australian capital figures to include working capital but this may be difficult. (3) Product (P) = value added by manufacturing. For all the years except 1934–35, this was defined as gross sales value minus (a) cost of materials used, (b) cost of fuel and light, and (c) cost of replacing tools and repairs to plants. In the 1934–35 study estimated deductions were made for fire insurance and workmen's compensation premiums, and also for estimated depreciation rates on the various types of capital goods used based on the rates estimated in the Production Bulletin, No. 29, *Commonwealth Bureau of Census and Statistics*. For a further discussion of these issues, see Gunn

for this article had been prepared, Keith Campbell and George Brinegar, in their Queensland study for 1937-38, found k to have a value of .58 and j one of .45.[19]

Since the sum of the exponents tends to be slightly less than unity, there is an added slight suggestion of true diminishing returns. But here again, since the difference is less than the standard errors of estimate, we should be chary about drawing definite conclusions.

If we choose .60 as the most probable "normal" value of k and .37 as the corresponding value of j, this would mean that the approximate elasticity of the marginal productivity curve in Australia for labor was somewhere around 2.7 and for capital of about 1.7.

The third set of results which we should consider are those for New Zealand, Canada, and South Africa. These are shown in Table III. Using the formula of k and 1-k, Max Brown found for New Zealand a value of .51 for k for the period 1915-1935,[20] and when we reworked the Brown series with the second formula, we found values of .42 for k and .49 for j. It is interesting that in the single cross-section study which has been made for New Zealand, namely, that made by Williams for 1938-39, k has a value of .46 and j of .51.[20a] In the four Canadian studies which we made for so-called "normal" years, the k's range between .43 and .50, with an average of .47, and the j's between .48 and .58, with an average of slightly more than .52. There is a considerable degree of steadiness in these results, which seem to indicate an elasticity of the marginal productivity curve for labor in that country as slightly less than 2.0 for the years studied and of capital as slightly more than that figure.

One of the most interesting studies which has been made is that by G. W. G. Browne for South Africa for 1937-38. Taking the seventeen main groups of industry and treating all labor as homogeneous, Browne

---

and Douglas, "The Production Function for Australian Manufacturing," *Quart. Jour. Econ.*, Vol. LVI (Nov., 1941), pp. 108–129.

d The definitions of terms in the studies for the separate Australian states were substantially similar to those in the four Commonwealth studies, except that (1) working proprietors were included in the definition of labor; (2) the estimated value of land was deducted from the capital figures; (3) deductions were made from the value of product for (a) the estimated cost of local and state and federal taxes, (b) estimated fire insurance and workmen's compensation premiums, and (c) allowances for depreciation upon buildings, plant, and machinery. These were also the methods used in the Commonwealth Study of 1934–35. See Gunn and Douglas, "Further Measurements of Marginal Productivity," *Quart. Jour. Econ.*, Vol. LIV (May 1940), pp. 399–428.

[19] See an unpublished manuscript study by Keith O. Campbell and George K. Brinegar, *The Production Function for Queensland Manufacturing in 1937-38* (1947).

[20] Brown omitted the war years of 1916-17 and 1917-18.

[20a] In the cross-section study just completed for New Zealand, 1926-27, k has a value of .48 and j of .53.

TABLE III.—THE VALUES OF THE PRODUCTION FUNCTION FOR MANUFACTURING IN
NEW ZEALAND, CANADA, AND SOUTH AFRICA

Years		N	$P = bL^kC^j$						$P = bL^kC^{1-k}$	
			k	σ_k	j	σ_j	$k+j$	b	k	σ_k
A. Time studies										
New Zealand[a]	1915–16	18	.42	±.11	.49	±.03	.91	2.03	.51	±.03
(Brown)	1918–35									
New Zealand[b]										
(Williams)	1923–40	18	—	—	—	—	—	—	.54	±.02
B. Cross-section or inter-										
industry studies										
South Africa[c]										
(Browne)	1937–38	17	.66	±.08	.32	±.08	.98	54.48	—	—
South Africa[d]										
(Browne)	1937–38	85	.65	—	.37	±.08	1.02	55.25	—	—
Canada[e]	1923	167	.48	±.04	.48	±.04	.96	48.53	.52	±.04
Canada[e]	1927	163	.46	±.04	.52	±.04	.98	33.04	.48	±.04
Canada[e]	1935	165	.50	±.04	.52	±.04	1.02	22.23	.48	±.04
Canada[e]	1937	164	.43	±.04	.58	±.04	1.01	15.42	.42	±.04
New Zealand[f]										
(Williams)	1938–39	61	.46	—	.51	—	.97	.73	—	—

[a] Dr. Max Brown, in his study, *The Relation Between Capital and Labour in New Zealand* (an unpublished doctoral dissertation at Cambridge University), defined Product (P) as the total money value of production divided by the price index of locally produced goods. His index of Labor (L) was one of total *man-hours* worked., *i.e.*, numbers employed multiplied by the length of the standard working week plus or minus the hours of overtime worked or short time suffered in the various years. The index of Capital (C) was the value of buildings, plant, and machinery (*i.e.*, fixed capital) with the annual increments of investment deflated by a price index of the cost of capital goods. We have fitted the function $P = bL^kC^j$ to the Brown data as well as the $P = bL^kC^{1-k}$ formula which Brown originally used.

[b] Professor Williams computed his indexes as follows: (1) Product (P) = (a) value added by manufacturing (*i.e.*, gross value minus cost of materials, fuel, and power), divided by (b) the price index of locally produced goods; (2) Capital (C) = initial value (1919–20) of land, buildings, machinery, and plant *minus* depreciation actually written off each year, and *plus* the money value of additions to capital in each year adjusted for changes in the index, number of prices for buildings and construction; (3) Labor (L) = number of persons employed. See J. W. Williams, "Professor Douglas' Production Function," *Econ. Record*, Vol. XXI (1945), pp. 55–63.

[c] Professor Browne defined his units as follows: (1) Product (P) = net value added by manufacturing or the gross value of output minus cost of materials, fuel, light, and power; (2) Labor (L) = average number of employees, including wage earners, salaried staff, managers, accountants, working proprietors, and persons regularly employed in their homes; (3) Capital (C) = the value of land, buildings, machinery, plant, and tools (*i.e.*, *fixed* capital only, with working capital excluded). See G. W. G. Browne, "The Production Function for South African Manufacturing Industry," *South African Jour. Econ.*, Vol. XI (1943), p. 259.

[d] This study differed from the former in that it was based on a more minute classification of industries and that it also separated white and black laborers and treated each as a separate factor of production. The value of k given is the sum of the k for white labor (.45) and for native labor (.20). See Browne, *op. cit.*, pp. 260–61. The value of σ_k could not be obtained by adding the σ_k of the exponents for native and white labor.

[e] The statistical series used were: (1) Labor (L) = average number of employed wage earn-

found the value of k was .66, and that for j, .32. When he made white and black labor separate factors of production and broke manufacturing down into eighty-five industries, the sum of the two exponents for labor amounted to .65. While we cannot rely too much upon only one study, it is of interest that his results were substantially the same as those which we obtained on the average for the United States for the period 1889-1919 and not far from the Australian results. This would be equivalent to an elasticity of approximately 3.0 for the marginal productivity curve for labor and of 1.5 for the marginal productivity curve for capital.

If we try to summarize our results, we do find a relatively close agreement between the values of k and j which we obtain from the cross-section studies for the United States, Australia, and South Africa. But we also find differences in the values of k and j (1) between Canada and New Zealand, on the one hand, and the United States, upon the other, with the former having lower k's and higher j's than the United States, and (2) between years within the same country. This is to be expected, as I pointed out long ago in a section of my *Theory of Wages*.[21] But underneath all these differences, it is submitted that there has been *for the periods studied*, a substantial core of stability within countries and that differences in technique, differences in the relative importance of given industries, and differences in the ratios of capital to labor may account for such deviations in the values of the exponents as exist.[22]

[21] Douglas, *The Theory of wages*, pp. 203-4.

[22] The economic and statistical meaning of b deserves to be considered.

A. In the four time series for the United States, the values of b under formula (1) are closely approximate to unity. For the United States the values are the same for each of the four series.

	b		b
Series I	1.01	Series III	1.01
Series II	1.01	Series IV	1.01

(Footnote 22 continued on next page)

ers, salaried workers, etc.; (2) Capital (C) = total capital used, *i.e.*, (a) fixed capital in the form of land, buildings, plant, tools, and machinery plus (b) working capital including materials, goods in process, and goods in storage. The inclusion of working capital makes the results comparable with the cross-section studies for the United States but differentiates them from the series used in Australia, New Zealand, and South Africa. (3) Product (P) = gross sales value *minus* cost of materials, fuel, electricity, etc., used. See Patricia Daly (Ogburn) and Paul H. Douglas, "The Production Function for Canadian Manufactures," *Jour. Am. Stat. Assoc.*, Vol. XXXVIII (1943), pp. 178–86.

† Professor Williams defined his terms as follows: (1) Labor (L) = number of persons engaged; (2) Capital (C) = value of land, buildings, plant, and machinery, *i.e.*, *fixed* capital. (3) Product (P) = gross sales value of product minus cost of materials, fuel, and power. See J. W. Williams, *op. cit.*, p. 59.

It is submitted that the results are, on the whole, corroborative. If they were purely accidental, as some have charged, they would show widely varying results. The fact that on the basis of fairly wide studies there is an appreciable degree of uniformity, and that the sum of the

For Victoria, the value of b was .97 and for New South Wales, 1.02. In all these cases, b represents the value of the intercept with the functional plane of theoretical product merely moved up or down by the small difference between the values of b and unity. In the time series, of course, we are dealing with index numbers which show relative changes, not absolute values.

B. Under formula (2) (*i.e.*, $P = bL^kC^j$) b deviates in a greater degree from unity because of the greater degree of freedom given to the exponent for capital. Here the values for the United States are:

	b		b
Series I	.84	Series III	1.12
Series II	1.38	Series IV	1.35

For Victoria b is .71 and for New South Wales, .97.

C. In the cross-section or inter-industry studies, b still represents the intercept but it is also a conversion factor which translates the number of employees and dollars of invested capital into *dollars* of net value product. As in the case of the time series based on index numbers, b is generally higher under formula (2) when the values of j are independently determined than under formula (1). It also tends to move in some direct ratio with changes in the general price level, being generally higher in those years when the price level is higher and *vice versa*. There are, however, occasional exceptions to this rule. These tendencies are shown in the following tables for the United States:

Year	Values of b	
	Formula (1)	Formula (2)
1889	28.58	58.34
1899	69.66	106.43
1904	79.62	120.23
1909	98.63	90.99
1914	66.22	81.66
1919	258.82	244.21

For the Commonwealth of Australia the corresponding values are

Year	Values of b	
	Formula (1)	Formula (2)
1912	14.79	15.87
1922-23	19.72	16.49
1926-27	41.50	77.26
1934-35	37.15	39.79
1936-37	17.99	21.57

It will, of course, be remembered that Australian prices and values are expressed in terms of pounds.

For Canada, the values are

Year	Values of b	
	Formula (1)	Formula (2)
1923	38.55	48.53
1927	28.51	33.04
1935	24.38	22.23
1937	16.48	15.42

I hope to give a fuller treatment of the significance of the b term in the regression equations in a book on *The Theory of Production* which I hope shortly to publish with Miss Grace Gunn.

exponents approximates unity, fairly clearly suggests that there are laws of production which can be approximated by inductive studies and that we are at least approaching them.

And yet it is proper to chronicle the fact that we have obtained some negative results. One persistent area of difficulty in these last months has been the Massachusetts time series. We tried to improve on Professor Cobb's series of capital and product with the result that the more we refined the basic series, the more nonsensical the results became. We are still working on this problem, but at the moment we certainly do not see the light. Secondly, it is disconcerting to observe that if we shorten our time periods by dropping off a number of terminal years, we appreciably alter our results. We observed this fact earlier, as did Professor Williams in New Zealand, but this paradox has been most manifest when we omit the war years from 1916 on, in our United States time series. Finally, we have attempted various inter-spatial studies in which we use individual states as separate observations. We have personally had no success with these attempts. The most ambitious study of this latter nature has, however, been made by my friend and former associate, Ernest Olson, and will be presented to this Association later in these meetings. I do not wish to anticipate the results of his paper, but I think it is proper to say that Mr. Olson has been able to develop a formula which makes differences between countries in their *real* national income a mathematical function of (1) the total energy used, (2) the numbers of the working population, (3) the quantity of livestock reduced to comparable units, and (4) the amount of land—and he has derived exponents which indicate the comparative importance of each. There is still much to be done in this direction and some hard puzzles remain to be solved, but Mr. Olson's comparative success offers us some hope that we may not face a completely blank wall in working with this third method for deriving the laws of production.

Finally, I should like to point out that in the case of the United States, we were compelled because of lack of capital figures, to stop with 1922 in our time series and with 1919 in our cross-section studies. We have, therefore, not been able to cover the very perplexing period of 1920-40. I am doubtful for two reasons whether we can develop a satisfactory production function for the United States during this period: (a) In spite of the excellent work of the National Bureau of Economic Research, we still lack adequate data for this period on the capital *available* for use; and (b) there was wide variation between the decades in the degree to which the available capital was *actually used*. During the 'twenties, capital was quite fully employed, but during the 'thirties a large proportion of this equipment lay idle. Variations in the degree to which available capital was utilized created some difficulties within the ordinary business cycles which prevailed between 1899 and 1919 when each of the four phases of the cycle did not last for more than one or two years. But the period between the two wars was quite extraordinary in that we had high prosperity from 1922 to the fall of 1929 and that we did not fully recover from the collapse which then set in until 1941. It was this fundamental difficulty which prevented one of my students, Mr. Leonard Felsenthal, from developing a satisfactory production function for Germany in the inter-war period. I shall, therefore, await with sympathetic interest the paper on this subject which Mr. Burton Wall is to give tomorrow.

IV. *The Production Function as Based on Plant Averages Rather than Industry Aggregates*

The inductive values which have thus far been developed in the cross-section or inter-industry studies have been based on industry aggregates, namely the totals of workers, capital, and net values added by manufacturing in each industry. This method is somewhat disconcerting to those who are accustomed in their *a priori* reasoning to start with the theory of production for the individual firm and who then move to a model for a given industry but who shy away from developing a theory of production for the economy as a whole or from the manufacturing sector of that economy. Such theorists probably believe that we are starting at the wrong end and that we should begin instead with the individual firm rather than the whole manufacturing sector of the economy and that we should consider the production function within these units rather than deal with inter-industry and aggregate functions.

There are two answers to this position. The first is that I should be very glad indeed to make studies of individual firms if the necessary data were available. But statistics on the changing quantities of labor and capital which are used over a period of time by individual firms, and the amounts of product which are thus turned out by them, are some of the most carefully guarded secrets of business. I am reluctant to believe that we should stop all our investigations until all of these facts are forthcoming for a multitude of firms.

Secondly, I personally see no reason why we cannot approach this problem from either end and study the macrocosm as well as the microcosm. No one, for example, in the physical sciences would propose that we give up using the telescope because the microscope had not yielded all its secrets. Why should we not, therefore, study the economy as a whole as well as speculate about the individual firm, particularly since a knowledge of the former throws a great deal of light upon the problems of the latter?

In the meantime, however, we should all welcome such brilliant studies of the production function for individual firms as that which will shortly be published by my friend and colleague, Professor William H. Nicholls, for a meat-packing plant.[22a] Moreover, if we could get the figures for specific firms and plants *within* given industries for a specific year, we would then be able to develop production functions for each of the main industries with each firm serving as an observation. But the census has always been obligated to conceal the identity of the specific firms which report to it and can only publish totals by industries and geographical subdivisions. This fact prevents us, at present, from developing such studies, although it is barely possible that either the Census Bureau itself or employers' associations could carry them on, were they once convinced of their value. This cannot, however, be done at present.

To my mind, therefore, we are at present forced to work primarily with industry aggregates. But there is one important refinement which we can and should introduce. That is to divide the total number of workers, the aggregate amounts of capital, and the total net value of the product in each of the various industries by the number of plants in that industry. This will give us *plant averages* for given industries rather than industry aggregates as the individual observations[23] and from these we can derive another variant of the production function.

We have made such studies for each of the six years which were covered for American manufacturing and for two of the Australian studies and these results are embodied in Table IV.

It will thus be seen that while we obtained closely similar results in Australia by the two methods, nevertheless, clear differences developed in the case of the United States. In every year the value of k in our American studies was substantially less under the method of plant averages than it was under the method of industry aggregates. The amount of this difference ranged between 5 and 6 points, as in 1904 and 1909, to 15 points in 1889. On the other hand, the values of j were always higher under the methods of plant averages than under that of industry aggregates but the amounts of these differences were much less. As a result, the combined values of $k + j$ are less by from 3 to 8 points

---

[22a] William H. Nicholls, *Labor Productivity Functions in Meat Packing*, to be published by University of Chicago Press, 1948.

[23] This is not quite the same as the so-called "representative" firm because many firms operate multiple plants.

on the plant average basis than they are when industry aggregates are used and, indeed, average only .92. This gives an unmistakable indication of true diminishing returns so far as the size of individual

TABLE IV.—A COMPARISON OF THE VALUES OF k AND j OBTAINED BY THE METHOD OF PLANT AVERAGES WITH THOSE OBTAINED BY THE METHOD OF INDUSTRY AGGREGATES
$(P = bL^kC^j)$[a]

Year	Values According to Method of Plant Averages			Difference (In Points) from Those Obtained by Methods of Industry Aggregates		
	k	j	$k+j$	k	j	$k+j$
United States						
1889	.36	.50	.86	−.15	+.07	−.08
1899	.52	.36	.88	−.10	+.03	−.07
1904	.60	.32	.92	−.05	+.01	−.04
1909	.57	.37	.94	−.06	+.03	−.03
1914	.52	.41	.93	−.09	+.04	−.05
1919	.66	.32	.98	−.10	+.07	−.03
Australia Commonwealth						
1934–35[b]	.60	.38	.98	+.04	−.04	.00
Victoria						
1910–11	.76	.26	1.02	+.02	+.01	+.03

[a] The formula, $P = bL^kC^{1-k}$, gives identical results using aggregate and per plant data.

(1) $$P = bL^kC^{1-k}$$

(2) $$\frac{P}{N} = b\left(\frac{L}{N}\right)^k\left(\frac{C}{N}\right)^{1-k} = b\frac{L^k}{N^k}\frac{C^{1-k}}{N^{1-k}}$$

$$\frac{P}{N} = \frac{b}{N}L^kC^{1-k}.$$

Multiplying both sides by N, we get formula (1).

[b] Figures refer to Commonwealth of Australia 1934-35 A, which used the studies of C. H. Wickens, "The Commonwealth Statistical Allocation of Factory Output," *Econ. Record* (1929), pp. 226-33. The values of k and j for the industry aggregates were .56 and .42, respectively. The results of the plant averages for the Commonwealth for the years 1912, 1922-23, 1926-27, 1936-37 were previously published. It was found that the values of k and j did not change greatly. Only one value of k, that for 1922-23, differed from the aggregate k, by an amount greater than σ_k. For further discussion, see Gunn and Douglas, "The Production Function for Australian Manufacturing," *Quart. Jour. Econ.*, Vol. LVI (Nov., 1941), pp. 108-29.

plants is concerned. While much more study is needed to develop and to clarify this point, it is suggested that quite possibly American plants during this period were in practice developed beyond the point of maximum efficiency. Whether or not the differences between the respective $k + j$'s can be taken as a coefficient of managerial megalomania, I shall have to leave to the psychiatrists.[24]

[24] If this is a psychiatric problem, we can take consolation in the fact that the disease was apparently less acute in 1919 than in 1889.

V. *Do the Deviations of the Actual Products from Those Which We Would Theoretically Expect from the Formula Tend to Strengthen or Weaken Belief in the Validity of the Production Function?*

An important test of our function is the degree to which the values of the product which we would expect from the quantities of labor

CHART I—DEVIATIONS OF ACTUAL FROM THEORETICAL VALUES OF LOG P
UNITED STATES MANUFACTURING 1889

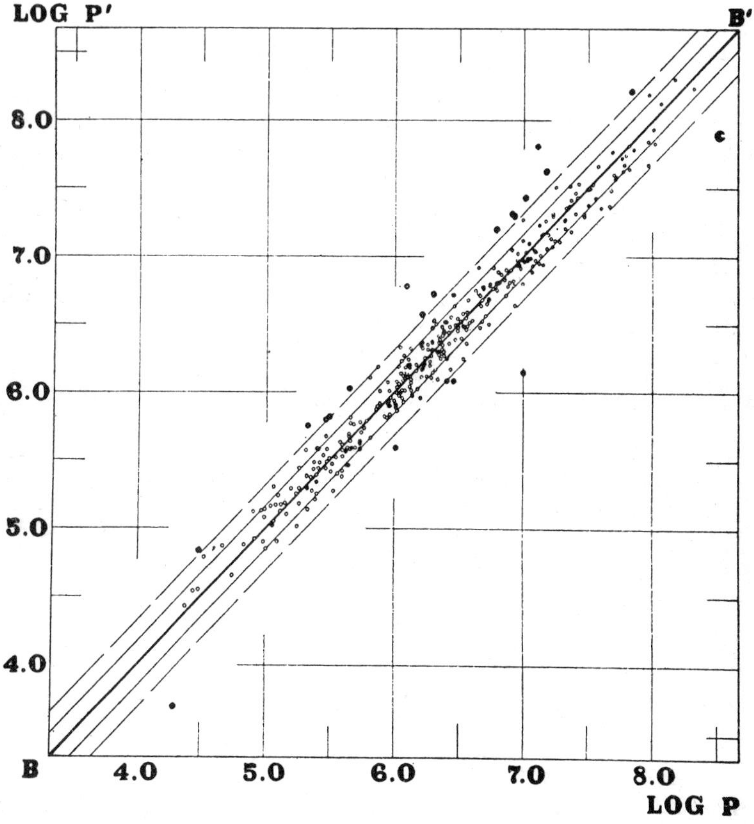

and capital available, tend in practice to be realized in terms of actual product in each of the various industries during the given years. We have made these tests and I should like to present our results in a series of charts and summary tables. As a first step, we computed the standard errors of estimate (S) for each study. Under a normal distribution of cases with the only departures of the actual from theoretical values being those caused by random errors of measurement and of sampling, we would expect that in 68.3 per cent of the cases

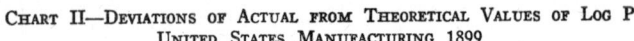

CHART II—DEVIATIONS OF ACTUAL FROM THEORETICAL VALUES OF LOG P
UNITED STATES MANUFACTURING 1899

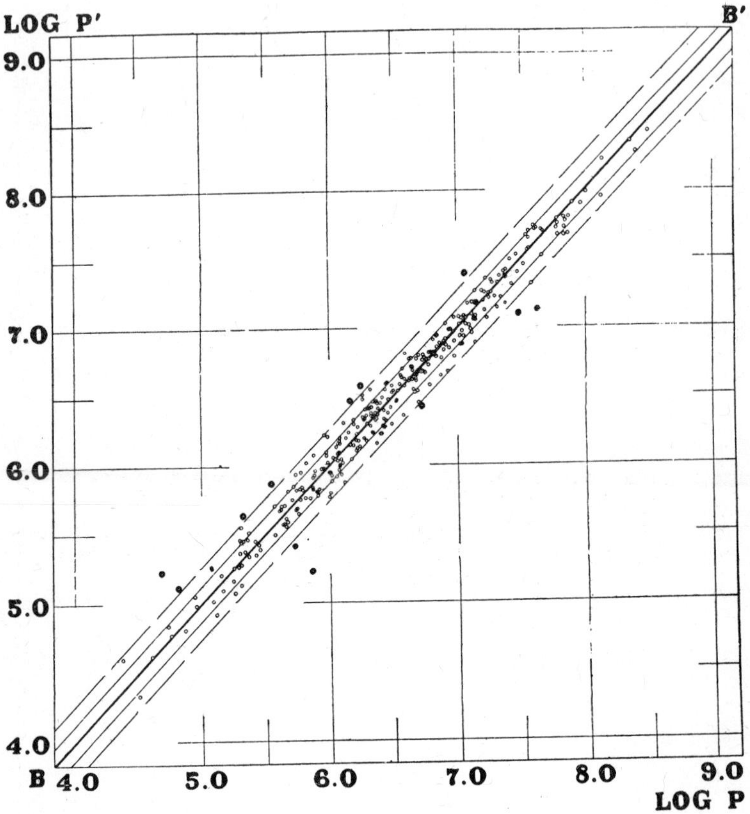

the actual values would deviate from the theoretical values by less than one standard error of estimate, and that in 95 per cent of the cases the actual values would deviate from the theoretical values by less than two such standard errors. In only one per cent of the cases would the actual values deviate by more than three standard errors of estimate. Then in our charts of the cross-section or inter-industry studies, we have plotted the logs of the theoretical or expected products on the vertical scale and of the actual products on the horizontal scale. Since the values of scale are the same on both axes, the line BB′ (with a slope of unity) is the locus of all those points for which the theoretical

CHART III—DEVIATIONS OF ACTUAL FROM THEORETICAL VALUES OF LOG P
UNITED STATES MANUFACTURING 1904

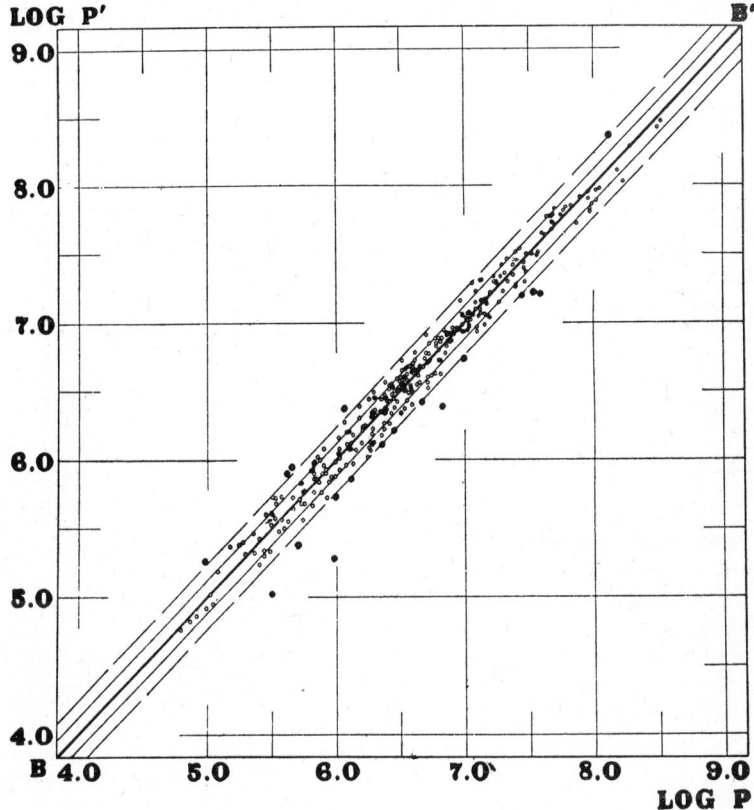

values of the product are identical with the actual values. In these studies for a given year, it will be remembered that each industry constitutes a separate observation.

The degree of departure of the actual from the theoretical values is, therefore, shown by either the horizontal or the vertical distance of a given point from the line BB′. We have, therefore, marked out on each side of the **line BB′** two other pairs of lines at the respective distances of one and two standard errors of estimate. An inspection of these charts for American manufacturing for the years 1889, 1899, 1904, 1909, 1914, and 1919, (Charts I, II, III, IV, V, and VI) show that in practice the actual values tend to be close to the line BB′, and a statistical analysis of these variations is given in Table V. Here it will be seen that in every year more than 70 per cent of the actual values were within one standard error of estimate of the values which we would

TABLE V.—DEGREE OF DEVIATION OF ACTUAL FROM THEORETICAL VALUES OF PRODUCT IN AMERICAN MANUFACTURING INDUSTRIES 1889–1919

Census Year	Number of Industries or Observations—N	Deviation of Actual Product (P) from Theoretical Product (P') in Terms of Standard Errors of Estimate					
		Number			Per Cent		
		Less than 1σ	1–2 σ	Over 2σ	Less than 1σ	1–2 σ	Over 2σ
1889	363	280	63	20	77.0	17.0	6.0
1899	332	250	70	12	75.0	21.0	4.0
1904	336	236	82	18	70.0	25.0	5.0
1909	258	215	38	5	83.0	15.0	2.0
1914	340	243	83	14	72.0	24.0	4.0
1919	556	453	85	18	82.0	15.0	3.0
Total	2185	1677	421	87	—	—	—
Averages	—	—	—	—	76.5	19.5	4.0

theoretically expect under the formula and that in two of the six years, over 80 per cent of the cases were within this range.

Taking the 2185 industry observations in the United States as a whole, we find that in 76.5 per cent of the cases, the actual products were within one standard error of estimate of the theoretical products, whereas under a normal distribution we would only expect a little over 68 per cent of the cases to lie within this range. Moreover, in only one year did the number of observations whose actual products varied from the theoretical values by more than two standard errors of estimate come to as much as 6 per cent of the total while the average for all 2185 observations was 4 per cent as compared with the 5 per cent which we would normally expect.[25]

In our American studies, the distribution of the actual values about

[25] Incidentally, instead of 22 cases or 1.0 per cent of the total, which would normally expect to deviate by more than three standard errors of estimate, we find only 16 observations or three-quarters of one per cent in this class.

the theoretical values is, therefore, somewhat *closer* than what we would normally expect on the basis of random errors of sampling and of measurement. Belief in the reliability of the formula as a description of production during this period is, therefore, strengthened, rather than weakened.

TABLE VI.—DEGREE OF DEVIATION OF ACTUAL FROM THEORETICAL VALUES OF PRODUCT IN MANUFACTURING INDUSTRIES OF BRITISH DOMINIONS FOR SPECIFIC YEARS

Country and Year	Number of Industries (N)	Deviation of Actual Product (P) from Theoretical Product (P') in Terms of Standard Errors of Estimate (σ)					
		Number			Per Cent		
		Less than 1σ	1–2 σ	More than 2σ	Less than 1σ	1–2 σ	More than 2σ
Canada							
1923	167	116	41	10	69.0	25.0	6.0
1927	163	115	40	8	71.0	24.0	5.0
1935	165	113	45	7	69.0	27.0	4.0
1937	164	122	33	9	74.0	20.0	6.0
Commonwealth of Australia							
1912	85	66	13	6	78.0	15.0	7.0
1922–23	87	66	15	6	76.0	17.0	7.0
1926–27	85	65	17	3	76.0	20.0	4.0
1934–35	138	110	23	5	80.0	17.0	3.0
1936–37	87	70	9	8	81.0	10.0	9.0
Australian States New South Wales							
1933–34	125	98	22	5	78.0	18.0	4.0
Victoria 1910–11	34	26	7	1	76.0	21.0	3.0
Victoria 1923–24	38	32	4	2	84.0	11.0	5.0
Victoria 1927–28	35	26	6	3	74.0	17.0	9.0
Total	1373	1025	275	73	—	—	—
Average	—	—	—	—	74.7	20.0	5.3

Let us see from Table VI if these results are confirmed by an analysis of the deviations of the actual from the theoretical values in the thirteen cross-section studies which we have thus far made for the Dominions within the British Commonwealth of Nations. It will be noticed that out of the total of 1373 observations, 1025, or over 74 per cent deviated by less than one standard error of estimate from the theoretical values, and that between 94 and 95 per cent deviated by less than two standard errors of estimate. The distribution of the observations in this sample is, therefore, somewhat better than that which we would expect

CHART IV—DEVIATIONS OF ACTUAL FROM THEORETICAL VALUES OF LOG P
UNITED STATES MANUFACTURING 1909

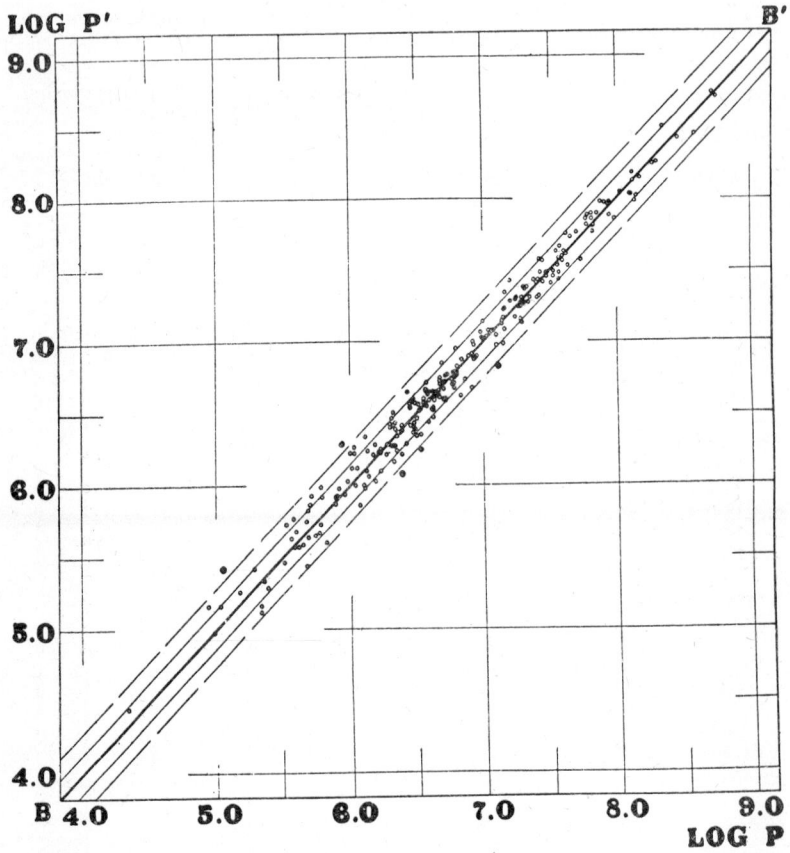

under normal conditions of random error. Credence in the production function would seem to be further reinforced.[25a]

The fact that we have, therefore, in practice, a somewhat closer distribution of the actual values about the line of the theoretical values

[25a] While charts showing the distribution of the individual products about the line of theoretical relationship have been prepared for the British Dominion, these are not published in this article because of considerations of space and expense. They were, however, shown in connection with the address.

under the formula than we would normally expect, is all the more striking in view of the fact that the values of the production function need not be the same within all industries or allied groups of industries.

CHART V—DEVIATIONS OF ACTUAL FROM THEORETICAL VALUES OF LOG P
UNITED STATES MANUFACTURING 1914

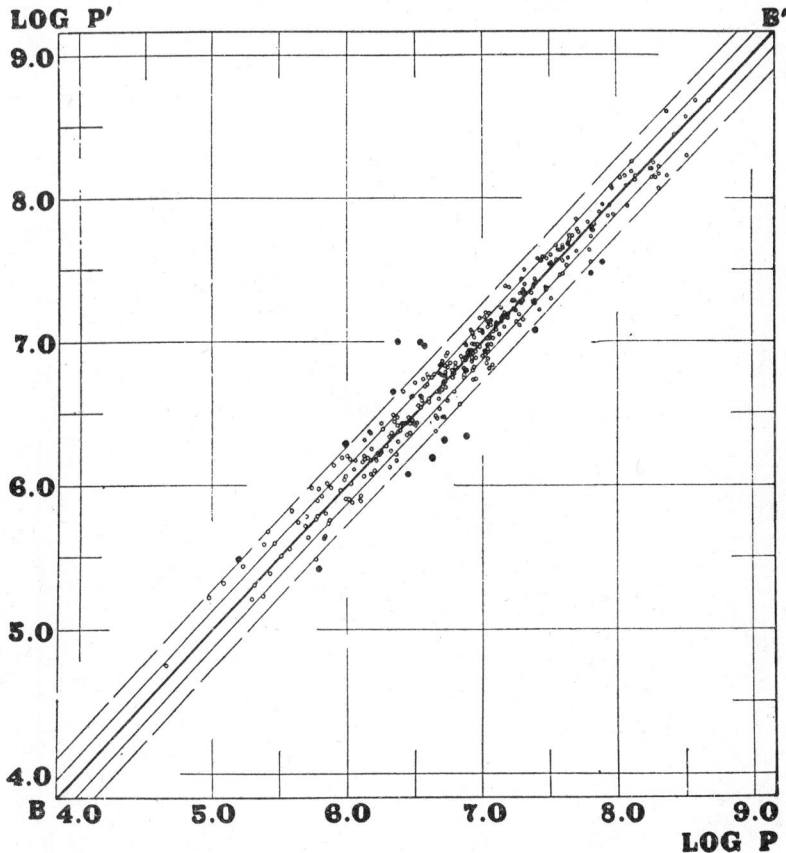

As I have constantly pointed out during the last twenty years, there is no reason why the exponents of capital and labor should be constant for all periods and economies. As a matter of fact, we have already seen that they are not and that there is some variation between countries and years in the values of k and j. We would similarly expect some variation to exist as between groups of industries within a country at any given time. Thus the values of the production function for the textile industries need not be the same as for the clothing group, while these might well differ from those prevailing in the food industries and be appreciably different from those in the iron and steel and heavy metals industries, etc. If, therefore, we could compute separate values

CHART VI—DEVIATIONS OF ACTUAL FROM THEORETICAL VALUES OF LOG P
UNITED STATES MANUFACTURING 1919

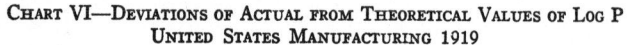

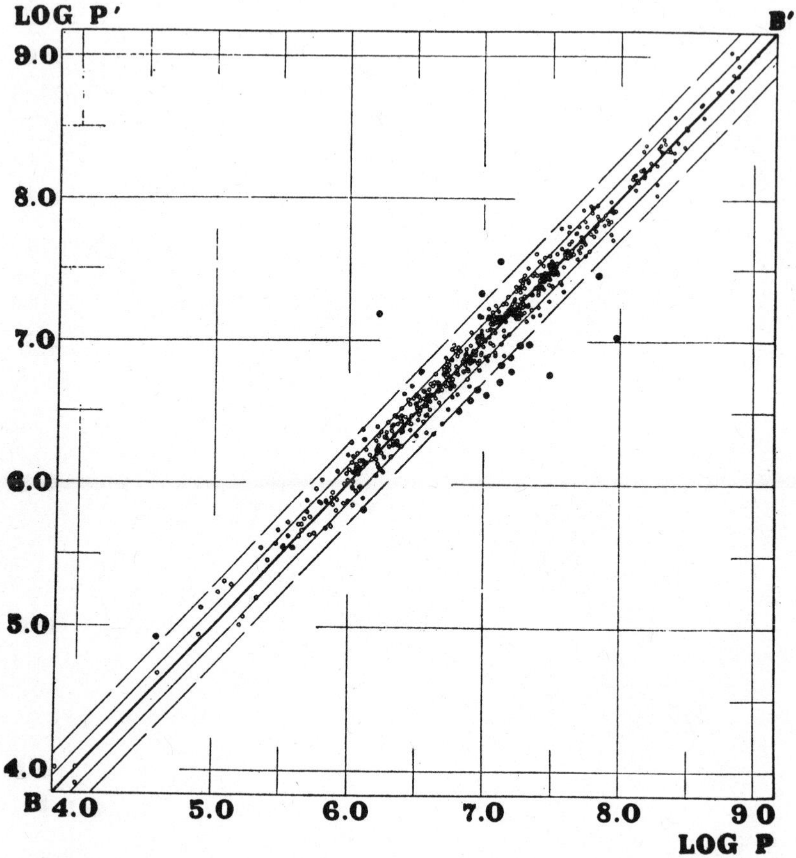

of k and j for each of the various main groups of manufacturing and compare the actual with the resulting theoretical products, we could doubtless find the resulting deviations to be appreciably less than those obtained when we treat all manufacturing as a whole. The fact that we do get such a good fit when we treat all of the industries as homogeneous is, therefore, all the more remarkable. It seems, further, to suggest that to the degree that the values of k and j do differ between groups of industries, such differences tend to be more or less symmetrically distributed around the "normal" values which we have found in the given years for manufacturing as a whole.

A further analysis of the plus and minus deviations offers interesting suggestions. We would expect industries characterized by monopoly and by highly imperfect competition to have a value product which would be appreciably greater than that which we would expect from the production formula itself, and from the quantities of labor and capital which are available. This would be caused by the control over supplies and prices exercised by the dominant firms and by their ability to control or to limit entrance into the monopolized industries. Conversely, in the industries which may be characterized by "excessive" competition into which large numbers of workers and also in some cases, relatively large quantities of capital are forced and which consequently lower the marginal productivity of one or both factors appreciably below their general levels, we would expect the value product per unit of labor and possibly also of capital, to be below the general average for society as a whole.

Similarly, we would expect that the industries which are rapidly expanding because of an increase in demand or in the disposition of consumers income, or because of great technical progress, will have value products which are in excess of those derived from the formula. Conversely, again, we would expect that the contracting industries, which are suffering from a decrease in demand and an obsolescence of technique, would produce less value product than that which our formula would predict.

There are, moreover, a considerable number of industries which probably can best be described as "sweated." These are industries which have had large supplies of cheap labor, sometimes caused, as in the past, by an influx of immigrants or by the presence of a large number of women and juveniles who are forced to seek work because of the low earnings of the male heads of households. The average earnings in these industries tends to be appreciably below the national average, and if there is a normal degree of competition at work, these low earnings will commonly be translated into a lower sales price for the product than would normally be the case. The value product in these industries will, therefore, tend to be less than what would be shown under the formula for manufacturing as a whole.

We can test the relative truth of these hypotheses both by statistical analysis and also by identifying the specific industries where the deviations of the actual from the theoretical values are great. In analyzing the American deviations by years, as in Table VII, certain marked differences appear between the results for the earliest year of 1889 and the years from 1904 on. From 1904 on, and particularly in 1914 and 1919, the big deviations were predominantly on the plus, and the minor deviations on the minus, side. Thus, in 1919, of the 18 industries where the deviations amounted to more than two standard errors of

TABLE VII.—AN ANALYSIS OF THE COMPARATIVE DEGREES OF PLUS AND MINUS DEVIATIONS OF ACTUAL FROM THEORETICAL PRODUCTS IN AMERICAN MANUFACTURING INDUSTRIES 1889–1919

Year	Number of Industries with Deviations of Less Than Two Standard Errors of Estimate		Number of Industries with Deviations of More Than Two Standard Errors of Estimate	
	Plus	Minus	Plus	Minus
1889	190	153	4	16
1899	166	154	5	7
1904	144	174	11	7
1909	122	131	3	2
1914	152	174	10	4
1919	230	308	16	2

estimate, 16 had their actual products in excess of the theoretical values, while in only two cases did they fall below. On the other hand, of the 538 industries in 1919 where the deviations amounted to less than two standard errors, 308 or nearly three-fifths, were below what would have been expected under the formula. For the three census years of 1909, 1914, and 1919, there were 29 industry observations where the actual products were more than two standard errors of estimate greater than the theoretical values and only 10 industry observations which were more than two standard errors less. Conversely, in these three years there were only 504 industries which had actual products which exceeded the theoretical values up to two standard errors as contrasted with 613 industries where the actual products fell below the theoretical by these amounts.

The general framework of these later results is approximately what we would expect on theoretical grounds. The monopolistic and expanding industries tend to absorb large quantities of purchasing power at the expense of the rest of the economy. They would, therefore, be expected to show wider profit margins than the general average and each combined dose of labor and capital would consequently tend to yield a greater dollar value than would normally be the case. The withdrawal of this purchasing power would, moreover, exert a slight depressing influence upon each of the remaining industries so that we would expect the number of industries where the actual product fell below the theoretical to exceed in number those where it was greater. This was exactly what happened from 1904 to 1919. Why the opposite result should have occurred in 1889 and to a much lesser degree in 1899, however, merits further study.

Even more important, however, is an analysis of each of the 87 American cases where the deviations were more than two standard errors of estimate from the theoretical values and I only regret that lack of time prevents a full analysis of these instances. Let us first consider the forty in which the deviations were of a minus nature. In no less than ten cases, these were in the flax, hemp, linen, jute and oakum family of industries, which has always been one of the most "sweated" groups in all industrial countries. Two were in allied "sweated" industries, namely nets and seines (1904) and hammocks (1889), while three more were connected with cotton which has generally been a sub-standard industry. Three more, charcoal, waste, and canning oysters, have been distinctly disagreeable and badly "sweated" industries, while several others, such as grindstones, millstones, hooks and eyes, etc., were instances of contracting demand.

On the other hand, the vast majority of the plus deviations which amounted to more than two standard errors of estimate can be explained as caused by (1) some form of quasi-monopoly or imperfect competition, or (2) by expanding demand, or (3) by both factors. Examples of the first are wood engraving, gold and silver reducing, lapidary work, music publishing, glucose, starch, linseed oil, patent medicines, tin plate, brass, and lead. These in themselves accounted for nineteen of the markedly plus deviations.

Illustrations of the second group, namely those caused by an expanding demand, were cordials and flavoring syrups (1909, 1914, 1919), oleomargarine (1914), perfumery (1919), and washing machines (1919).

There is also a third class of plus deviations which was probably affected both by imperfect competition and by expanding demand. Illustrations of this group are airplanes (1914), chewing gum (1919), cigars and cigarettes (1919), fountain pens (1914), photographic supplies and equipment (1904, 1909, 1914), cash registers (1889), smelting and refining copper (1899, 1904), typewriters and supplies (1889).

A very large majority of the major deviations so far as the United States is concerned, were, therefore, precisely what we would expect on a priori grounds. Belief in the function as a description of "normal" relationships is, therefore, still further strengthened.

VI. *To What Degree Do the Shares Which Labor and Capital Receive of the Product Approximate the Proportions Which We Would Expect from the Values of the Production Function?*

We now come to one of the most important features of the theory of production and of distribution, namely, the relative degree to which the actual shares received by labor and capital approximate those

TABLE VIII.—A COMPARISON BY YEARS OF THE VALUES OF THE EXPONENTS OF LABOR AND CAPITAL IN THE PRODUCTION FUNCTION FOR AMERICAN MANUFACTURING (k AND j) WITH THE UNWEIGHTED AVERAGE OF THE SHARES OF THE NET VALUE PRODUCT RECEIVED BY LABOR (W/P)

Year	N	k		$\dfrac{k}{k+j}$	$\dfrac{W}{P}$	Degree to which W/P differs from k and $\dfrac{k}{k+j}$ in terms of standard errors	
						$\dfrac{\dfrac{W}{P}-k}{\sigma_k}$	$\dfrac{\dfrac{W}{P}-\dfrac{k}{k+j}}{\sigma_k}$
1889	363	.51	.43	.54	.60	+ 3	+ 2
1899	332	.62	.33	.65	.58	− 2	−3–4
1904	336	.65	.31	.68	.64	−0–1	− 2
1909	258	.63	.34	.65	.63	0	− 1
1914	340	.61	.37	.62	.59	−0–1	− 1
1919	556	.76	.25	.75	.59	−8–9	− 8
Average	—	.63	.34	.65	.605	—	—

which we would expect from the values of the production function. As my associates and I have demonstrated mathematically a number of times, we would expect, under conditions of (1) true constant returns where the sum of the exponents is equal to unity and (2) perfect competition, that each factor of production would receive that fraction of the total product which is indicated by its exponent.[26]

[26] The share which labor receives:

Let W = the amount of wages received.

Marginal productivity of labor = $k\dfrac{P}{L}$

$W = L\,k\,\dfrac{P}{L} = kP$

$W = kP$

$k = W/P$

Similarly, for capital.

Let us, therefore, compare the actual share which wages and salaries formed of the net value product (*i.e.*, W/P) in the various years with the values of k. It will also be instructive to compare W/P with the ratio of $\dfrac{k}{k+j}$ since the latter is a rough measure of what we would approximately expect to occur if the total product were to be divided between labor and capital so as to eliminate either net residual profits or losses.

This is shown for the United States cross-section studies in Table VIII. From an examination of this table, it will be seen that in five of the six years there was a very close agreement between the values of k and of W/P. In one year (1909), there was precise agreement between the two; in two of the years (1904 and 1914), the differences were approximately only one standard error, while in two more (1889 and 1899), they amounted to two to three standard errors. The biggest difference was in 1919 when W/P was less than k by over eight standard errors.[27]

Taking the average for the six years as a whole, we find that k averages .63, $\dfrac{k}{k+j}$ equals .65, and labor's actual share or W/P was .605. There was, therefore, a close average agreement for the period between what we would have theoretically expected the distribution of the product to be under conditions of perfect competition and that which actually occurred. It should be remembered, moreover, that due to our inability to deduct allowances for depreciation in specific industries, the true values of W/P are probably understated by approximately 3 percentage points,[28] and that, therefore, the average

---

[27] The year 1919 was one in which prices rose with great rapidity. It would be expected, therefore, that wages would lag behind in such a period.

[28] On the basis of Dr. Fabricant's estimate of depreciation totals for manufacturing as a whole in 1919, it appears that these amounted to approximately five per cent of the value added by manufacturing in that year. If this had been deducted, labor's share would, therefore, have been raised in 1919 by about three percentage points, or to approximately .62. Thus, Fabricant's careful allowance for depreciation in 1919 was 1151 millions of dollars. (Solomon Fabricant, *Capital Consumption and Adjustment,* pp. 260-61.) The total value added by manufacturing in that year, (*i.e.*, value of product minus cost of raw material minus rent and taxes minus cost of contract work) was 22,486 millions of dollars. This comes to a depreciation rate in terms of net value of product of 5.1 per cent. If we deduct such estimated charges, we would raise labor's share by almost precisely 3 points (*i.e.*, $^{59}\!\!/_{95} = .62$). Due to the smaller quantity of capital used per unit of product, in the earlier years the additional "loading" required to approximate labor's share would then have been somewhat less, and for 1889 and 1899 would probably have been nearer two percentage points.

ratio of W/P was probably very close to .63 or the exact average value of k.

I submit, therefore, that the degree of agreement between the values of k and of W/P is most striking and that the results conform to what normally would be expected to occur under competitive productivity theory. Hence, this constitutes a still further reinforcement to the productivity function itself.

It should, however, be frankly recognized that there is a further problem of reconciling these results with the known facts of imperfect competition, oligopoly and monopoly. Such conditions, as has been abundantly developed in our meetings, do exist, and, in fact, characterize a large sector of our economy. It is, therefore, puzzling to find labor's share approximately equal to that which we would expect under conditions of perfect competition. A further investigation of this subject is much needed. In the meantime, I would merely suggest that perhaps one answer to the paradox may be that the quasi-monopolies and oligopolies may have shared with their workers the excess gains which they have made at the expense of the consumers.

We can make a further test of the degree to which W/P approximates k and $\dfrac{k}{k+j}$ by examining the results for the British Dominions of Australia, New Zealand, and Canada. This is done in Table IX.

Taken in the large, the agreement in the cross-section studies for Australia between the values of W/P and k are indeed striking. In each and all of the five inter-industry studies for the Commonwealth, the differences never exceeded one standard error of k. For the five years as a whole, the average value of k and W/P were both .55. The average value of $\dfrac{k}{k+j}$ was .56. It would scarcely be possible to have a closer agreement than this.

In the case of the four studies for the Australian states, the differences in the case of Victoria were not great, never exceeding two standard errors of k and being slightly reduced if the comparisons are made between W/P and $\dfrac{k}{k+j}$.[29] For the three years as a whole, the differences are largely ironed out since the average values of k are .65 and of W/P .66. The average value of $\dfrac{k}{k+j}$ was .70.

---

[29] In the Queensland study the value of W/P was .614 or less than one standard error more than the value of k.

TABLE IX.—A COMPARISON BY YEARS OF THE VALUES OF THE EXPONENTS OF LABOR AND CAPITAL IN THE PRODUCTION FUNCTION FOR THE BRITISH DOMINIONS (k AND j) WITH THE UNWEIGHTED AVERAGE OF THE SHARES OF THE NET VALUE PRODUCT RECEIVED BY LABOR (W/P)

Dominion and Year	N	k	j	$\dfrac{k}{k+j}$	$\dfrac{W}{P}$	Differences between W/P and k in terms of standard error	
						$\dfrac{\dfrac{W}{P}-k}{\sigma_k}$	$\dfrac{\dfrac{W}{P}-\dfrac{k}{k+j}}{\sigma_k}$
I. Australian time series							
Victoria 1907–1929	22	.84	.23	.79	—	—	—
New Zealand (Brown) (1915–16)–(1934–35)	18	.42	.49	.46	.52[a]	+0–1	+0–1
New Zealand (Williams) 1923–1940[b]	18	.54	—	—	.54	—	—
II. Cross-section studies							
Australia 1912	85	.52	.47	.53	.54	+0–1	+0–1
Australia 1922–23	87	.53	.49	.52	.54	+0–1	+0–1
Australia 1926–27	85	.59	.34	.63	.57	−0–1	−1–2
Australia 1934–35	138	.64	.36	.64	.61	+0–1	−0–1
Australia 1936–37	87	.49	.49	.50	.51	+0–1	+0–1
Victoria 1910–11	34	.74	.25	.75	.64	−1–2	−1–2
Victoria 1923–24	38	.62	.31	.67	.65	+0–1	−0–1
Victoria 1927–28	35	.59	.27	.69	.68	+1–2	−0–1
New South Wales 1933–34	125	.65	.34	.66	.51	−3–4	−3–4
Average All Commonwealth and State Studies		.60	.37	.62	.58		
Average Commonwealth Studies Only		.55	.43	.56	.55		
New Zealand 1938–39	61	.46	.51	.47	.57	—	—
Canada 1923	167	.48	.48	.50	.50	+0–1	0
Canada 1927	163	.46	.52	.47	.48	+0–1	+0–1
Canada 1935	165	.50	.52	.49	.40	−2–3	−2–3
Canada 1937	164	.43	.58	.43	.52	+2–3	+2–3
Average Canadian Studies	—	.47	.52	.47	.48	—	—

[a] For the years 1924–1935 only.

[b] In the Williams study, the values of k were computed using formula (1). All other values were computed under formula (2).

In the one cross-section study which was carried through for New South Wales, the differences were greater, amounting to between 3 and 4 standard errors of estimate. In the case of Canada, however, the *average* degree of agreement was very close. The average value of k for the four years was .47, and similarly, $\dfrac{k}{k+j}$ was .47; while the average ratio of W/P was .48. This is an almost precise agreement. This agreement was also true of the years 1923 and 1927 when they are considered individually. The years 1935 and 1937, however, exhibit opposing tendencies. In the former year, k exceeded W/P by an appreciable amount; in the latter year, which was marked by great wage advances in the United States, which were reflected to some degree in Canada, this situation was exactly reversed. The two differences, however, almost precisely offset each other. The case of South Africa does, however, merit special mention. As I have pointed out, Professor Browne found that the combined exponents for black and white labor in 1937-38 were .65, but he also found that both groups of labor received only a total of .46 per cent of the net value added. While Professor Browne does not draw such a conclusion, perhaps this is a case where a highly monopolized set of industries which are largely run by foreign employers or by men whose cultural interests are elsewhere, do not give to the laborers that which in a competitive society they would obtain.

VII. *Summary*

After working on this problem for the better part of twenty years, I think I am aware of the many difficulties which are involved. In a few cases, the method apparently breaks down and in other cases incongruous results are obtained. I should like to suggest, however, that the following tentative conclusions seem justified.

1. That within a given country for the periods studied, there is a substantial and indeed a surprising degree of agreement in the values of k and of j which we obtain for various years.

2. There is also a surprising degree of agreement between the results for the United States, Australia, and South Africa.

3. It is hard to believe that these results can be purely accidental, as some critics have maintained.[30] Time studies for the period between

---

[30] It would be interesting to work out the mathematical possibility that these results are purely accidental. I believe that it would only be one out of many millions. It is theoretically possible, as Bertrand Russell has pointed out, that all the books in the British Museum were written by monkeys pounding typewriters at random. But we know that they were not!

the two great wars are, however, likely to present difficulties.

4. The deviations of the actual or observed values from those which we would theoretically expect to prevail under the formula are not large and indeed are slightly less than we would expect under the random distribution of errors of sampling and of measurement. It is submitted that the total number of observations, namely over 3,500, is sufficiently large so that if the results had been purely accidental, this degree of agreement would not have occurred.

5. The instances of large deviations of the actual from the theoretical values can in most cases be explained as being caused by imperfect competition and by expanding demand in the case of the plus deviations and by contracting demand, "sweating," and possibly "excessive" competition in the case of the minus industries. This would indicate that if these complications could be eliminated, the agreement between the actual and theoretical products would be greater.

6. That, taken in the large, there is an almost precise degree of agreement between the actual share received by labor and that which, according to the theory of marginal productivity, we would expect labor to obtain.

In conclusion, may I emphasize again that there is much work which remains to be done on this question and that a lifetime would be all too short to probe the many problems which present themselves. Is it too much to hope that the succeeding twenty years may see further progress along this line and that if the older generation finds it impossible to carry on such studies, the younger economists may find such lines of inquiry a challenge to their ingenuity and abilities?[31] I have always been struck by the old Hindu saying, "This is no door but only a little window that opens out upon a great world." Since this is peculiarly applicable to the studies which I have attempted, upon that note I shall end.

[31] Some of the studies which badly need to be carried out are (1) to develop the production function for each and every year over a long period, say 1910-1940, for Australia, New Zealand, and Canada; (2) to carry on studies of the production function for a large number of specific firms and *within* specific industries and hence connect the theory of the firm and of the industry with that of the economy; (3) to carry on further studies, along the lines of Mr. Olson, on inter-spatial variations in real income and the factors affecting them; and (4) to develop production functions for agriculture, mining, and public utilities.

In order to bring our analysis down to date in the larger countries, it is highly desirable that statistics on the quantities of capital be collected for Great Britain, Sweden, and the United States.

PREFACE

WHEN this manuscript was submitted for the Hart, Schaffner and Marx international competition in 1926 it really consisted of three parts, namely, (1) a history of past wage theories, (2) a more or less original explanation of general wages drawn in terms of relative elasticities of supply, and (3) the theory of occupational and geographical differences in wage rates. The manuscript thus contained the material for no less than three volumes and was much too long for publication in its existent form.

In 1927, in cooperation with my friend Professor Charles W. Cobb of Amherst College, I began to explore the possibility of measuring inductively the marginal productivities of labor and capital in recent times. This line of approach gradually began to produce results which crystallized in Part Two of the present volume.

In the following year, with the initial aid of Mr. Harold Glasser, I pushed additional inductive investigations into the short-run supply curve of labor and these studies have been continued in more recent years with the assistance of Mrs. Erika Schoenberg. A great deal of additional work was also done on the long-time supply curve of labor and the supply curve of capital.

As the inductive material thus developed over the years, it became apparent that the form of the work would have to be radically altered and compressed. Accordingly the last portion on differences in wages was completely omitted and the first portion on the history of wage theory was confined strictly to the development of the theory of production and the principle of diminishing incremental yields of the factors. The book as a whole, as the result of almost continuous revision during a period of seven years has therefore come to be an attempt at an inductive study of both the productivity and supply curves of labor and capital, and from these, certain tentative results have been obtained which the author at least believes to be important. The book is therefore somewhat less inclusive than its title may indicate but this was necessary if the subjects considered were to be treated with any adequacy within the necessary limitations of space. Even as it is the book is perhaps too bulky.

It has long seemed to me that the inductive, statistical, and quasi-mathematical method must be used if we are ever to make economics a truly fruitful and progressive science. The neo-classical school has constructed a valuable theoretical scaffolding according to which the value of commodities and the rates of return to land, labor and capital are fixed at the intersections of the various supply and the demand curves. This is a beginning but only a beginning. For in order to make the analysis precise, to forecast, and to detect interactions in economic society it is plainly necessary to determine the slopes of the demand and supply curves of the various commodities. An excellent beginning has been made in this direction during the last twenty years by such scholars as Henry L. Moore, Schultz, Ezekiel, Bean, Working and Marschak and in this development the United States has reason to be proud of the part which her investigators have played. The victory of these men is not yet won for there are still those who sneer at all attempts to introduce greater precision and who at times seem to take a perverse pleasure in muddying the waters. But the skill of these pioneers and their followers is growing and they are using ever more powerful techniques with a resultant narrowing of the margin of error and uncertainty. This line of attack has, therefore, more than justified itself in dealing with the problem of the prices and the values of commodities. The younger generation of economists has indeed shown their recognition of this fact in the way they are increasingly turning on the one hand from the sterile shadow-boxing which has characterized so much of dialectical economics and on the other from the theoretical blind alley of the purely historical and institutional methods.

There is need for a similar approach to the problems of distribution. We need to know whether the assumed curves of diminishing incremental productivity are merely imaginative myths or whether they are real, and if the latter, what their slopes are. We need to know more about the supply functions of the factors of production and whether the actual processes of distribution furnish any degree of corroboration to the inductive tendencies discovered. This book is an attempt to do just that. Since it is a pioneering study and since I certainly am not a mathematician, it undoubtedly has many lacunae and defects. But it is hoped that it at least furnishes a fruitful method of attack and that its results have some significance.

PREFACE

Even its weaknesses may perhaps be pardoned if they stimulate others to remedy them and to launch out further upon the trail. As one of the mottoes of the book indicates, the author realizes that it "is no door yet it is a little window that opens out upon a great world."

The passion of Americans for statistics is as a matter of fact accumulating vast quantities of data which almost cry aloud for analysis if they are to be rendered intelligible and significant. The patient accumulation of facts will in itself avail us little unless these facts are subjected to mathematical and statistical analysis to determine their inner relationships. It is however one of the amusing and at times irritating ironies of the present state of economic science that many modern statisticians, or economic arithmeticians, seem resolved to maintain the innocence of their beloved figures by keeping them unsullied from intelligent analysis. They apparently want to cherish these facts as ends in themselves and are commonly ready to give battle to the death against anyone who seeks to use them as a means of obtaining significant and interpretative results. The author is well aware that he will probably arouse the emotional opposition of these devotees by his attempt to use such statistical series as raw material with which to work but he feels that the sooner economists come to use facts as means rather than as ends, the more rapid will be the progress of economic science. It is of course true that there is a certain margin of error in most of our economic data but there are many series which are sufficiently close approximations to the facts to permit of more refined analysis. In short while we should try to improve our existing statistics, we can wring far more meaning than we have from those which are now available.

This is perhaps enough for the general history of the work and for the spirit in which it has been carried out. There are however perhaps further comments which should be made.

1. The inductive evidence of the book, as well as the deductive reasoning, is drawn from modern economies which have been characterized by competitive or quasi-competitive capitalism. Some of the principles developed might, therefore, not apply in an authoritarian or a monopolistic capitalism, in a rationed communism or a liberal socialism. If society is passing out from the stage of competitive capitalism, this study may, therefore, in part become obsolescent. Even then however some of the principles such as diminishing incremental productivity

and the importance of supply functions will still apply. The way in which economic theory may be adapted to a state of partial or complete monopolies has been well illustrated by a recent brilliant book by Mrs. Joan Robinson of Cambridge University on *The Economics of Imperfect Competition* which seems to me to be very illuminating in its treatment of a set of problems which the economists who are accustomed to deal with the problems of pure competition have tended to neglect.

2. The forces connected with the determination of wages are so inter-related with those which determine interest and rent that it is impossible to consider the theory of wages by itself. Wages, interest, and rent are instead determined by mutually interacting forces. This accounts for the fact that the present volume treats the theory of distribution as a whole and considers the productivity and supply curves of capital as well as those of labor. If less attention has been given to land, it is due to the lack of sufficient homogeneous data.

3. It may be objected that instead of trying to find an explanation of the general rate of wages, interest and rent, I should have abandoned this attempt because of the lack of homogeneity in each of the factors. According to this criticism, the lack of transferability between different sections of each factor is such as to compel the abandonment of this attempt. Instead of a basic rate of wages for labor as a whole, it is argued that there should be basic rates for an indefinite series of labor groups and similarly in the case of capital and land. Instead of three factors there would, according to this contention, be an almost infinite number. This criticism is not only considered in the text but a theoretical explanation of how this may be treated from the standpoint of marginal productivity is also given. The difficulty with proceeding inductively upon this hypothesis is however at least three-fold. First, capital funds are sufficiently fluid and ultimately sufficiently homogeneous as to prevent great differences in true yields from cumulating and instead operate towards rather than away from uniformity. Urban land can be shifted from one use to another fairly readily and this is true to a very considerable degree of agricultural land. There is also a very large degree of transferability in the field of labor. Secondly, differences from the basic rate of wages for unskilled labor and the pure rate of interest may be explained by other methods. The theory of wages and of interest may, in fact, also be built up from an analysis of (a) the basic rate and (b) differentials from this basic rate. In the third

place, I have been unable as yet to determine any way by which the various separate sub-groups of labor, capital and land could be segregated and measured. It would be almost impossible to measure the incremental productivities of this infinite series of sub-groups or to determine their supply curves. In view of the present inability to test the validity of this great sub-division of the factors, I can only consider this suggestion to be at present, in the words of Professor Bridgman, a non-operational concept. From the standpoint of scientific progress, we should primarily concern ourselves with problems which we can solve. We have sufficient statistics to permit a beginning at least in the attempt to determine the theory of distribution from three variable factors. We do not have enough material to try to work with from twenty to a hundred. If and when we do, the task should be attempted but the time for this is apparently not yet.

4. It will be noticed that I have treated the marginal productivity and supply curves for labor and capital in society as a whole and not for particular industries and plants. This has been done in part because as Willard Gibbs once remarked "the whole is simpler than its parts" and because it has seemed to me to be the more significant problem. When we deal with separate industries and enterprises we are involved in the whole problem of increasing and decreasing costs, technical factors determining the ratios of labor and capital, the elasticity of substitution of labor for capital and vice-versa. This whole range of problems has been very acutely treated by Mrs. Robinson and there is need for further studies along this line. At the same time, the forces at work in society as a whole need to be analyzed. For surely general results are at once more significant than are those for particular branches of industry and in turn are conditioning forces upon these sub-groups.

5. While most of the logical analysis is carried through on the assumption that men act rationally in economic matters, the statistical material is based on a somewhat broader approach, namely to detect patterns of influence and response whether or not these be logical. There is much in life and even in the economic phases of life which does not spring from a rational pursuit of individual or group ends but which arises instead from passion, prejudice, stupidity and even blind physiological and psychological reaction. There are indeed "more things on heaven and earth than are dreamt of" in the Hedonistic psychology. But statistics takes these other responses into account as well as those which are purely rational and it is consequently

not so circumscribed as is most of deductive reasoning.

May I now turn to the very grateful duty of recording my indebtedness to various friends and co-workers? My greatest obligations are to the three associates to whom I have dedicated this book. Professor Cobb first brought mathematical order out of the relationship between the series for labor, capital, and production and the general theory of production which has been developed would have been impossible without his pioneering work and his unfailing generosity. Mr. Wilcox was of great help in the early stages of the study and I have profited from his advice in the later period as well, while Mrs. Schoenberg has been literally invaluable in the later years. Her patience, accuracy, and ability have greatly improved the whole work. Mr. Aaron Director was responsible for the material for New South Wales and has aided in many other ways while Mr. Harold Glasser also shared in the work. I have also had the faithful and devoted service of a staff of computers among whom should be mentioned Mr. Stanley Posner, Miss Mabel Byrd, Mr. Harold Weber and Mr. A. D. Battey. My friend and former colleague, Professor J. M. Clark, was kind enough to read the manuscript and I have profited greatly from his criticism. Without these associates, I could never have finished this work and I am deeply appreciative of all they have done. From my students and my colleagues I have also received many fruitful suggestions and criticisms which though not always easy for me to identify have been no less real. Professor Henry Schultz has been especially generous in the aid which he has given in the field of statistical method. Some of the devices which he developed after prolonged study for checking and systematizing the computations used in computing the elasticities have been used in this study at the saving of great labor and expense. Mae Shiffman and A. W. Keith have drawn the charts while Agnes Jacques, Janet Murray and Mrs. Helen Parsons have helped with the proof. Erika Schoenberg in addition to all her other aid has read the proofs with great care and with her husband, Walter Schoenberg, has prepared the index.

Finally had it not been for the unfailing support which the administration of the University of Chicago and in particular its President, Robert M. Hutchins, has given to the maintenance of a free and fearless pursuit of truth, I could never have completed this book.

Chapter V originally appeared in much of its present form in the Supplement to the American Economic Review for March,

PREFACE

1928, and Chapter X in the volume of Economic Essays Contributed in Honor of John Bates Clark. The editors of these publications have been good enough to permit the use of these chapters in substantially their original form. A. A. Knopf, Inc., and The Macmillan Company have also kindly permitted me to reproduce certain charts from Raymond Pearl's *The Biology of Population Growth* and J. B. Clark's *The Distribution of Wealth*.

May I add that both Hart, Schaffner and Marx itself and its Committee of Award were extraordinarily patient and understanding during the delay which necessarily occurred. Another group of men would have become disgusted at the seven years of apparent delay during which the manuscript was being revised and re-written on an average of at least once a year while extensive further studies were being constantly carried on. If such were the feelings of these gentlemen, they generously refrained from giving expression to them and I only hope that the result justifies their forbearance.

Every effort has been made to make the statistical work as accurate as possible and all data have been carefully checked. Many millions of computations have however been made and it is possible there may still be some undetected errors. It is not believed however that these can be of any appreciable magnitude.[1]

PAUL H. DOUGLAS

Addendum

It may perhaps be added that Professor Pigou's recent book on the *Theory of Unemployment* did not appear until after the galley proofs of this book had been corrected. It is interesting and to my mind significant that he should have estimated by purely deductive methods that the probable elasticity of de-

CHICAGO, DECEMBER 9, 1933

---

[1] It may perhaps not be presumptious to indicate how this volume fits into the program for the investigation of wages which I have set myself. In my *Real Wages in the United States, 1890–1926,* and the *Movement of Money and Real Wages 1926–1928,* I studied the movement in this country for nearly forty years of wage rates, earnings, unemployment and the cost of living in order to obtain an index of the material progress of the American wage-earning and salaried classes. In my *Wages and the Family,* I developed a method of wage payment to take account of family responsibilities. In the future I hope, if permitted adequate leisure and resources, (1) to carry down to date and improve my indexes of money and real wages for this country (2) to prepare

PREFACE

mand for labor as a whole during periods of depression is not less than —3.0 (*Ibid.*, p. 97). My own estimates, based upon an inductive study, indicate a "normal" elasticity of between —3.0 and —4.0. Pigou's work therefore lends some corroboration to my "normal" results. It remains to be seen, however, whether Professor Pigou's sharp distinction between the elasticity of demand for labor during periods of prosperity and periods of depression is fundamentally valid. His conclusion, however, that during the periods of boom "it is impossible for the real demand for labour . . . to be other than highly inelastic" (i.e., less than —1.0) seems to me to be incorrect. On the contrary, my results indicate that as a direct consequence of the equation of production, which Pigou apparently does not consider, the elasticity of demand in "normal" times is, as stated, not far from —3.0.

---

indexes of money and real wages for the more important European countries (3) to investigate the problems of wages and the business cycle (4) to study wage and salary differences between localities, industries and crafts and to offer an analysis of the reasons for these differences (5) to continue the present set of studies and find for other countries and for divergent periods of time the probable marginal productivity curves of labor and capital and the supply curves of these factors in order to work out inductively and with more precision the forces governing the competitive equilibrium of distribution (6) to carry on similar studies for specific industries and plants and to deal more definitively with the problems presented by complete or partial monopoly and (7) finally to prepare a history of wage theories.

CONTENTS

CONTENTS

PART I

*The Development of the Theory of Production
and the Problem of Distribution*

CHAPTER I

WAGES AND THE GENERAL PROBLEM OF DISTRIBUTION

1. The Development of the Problem of Distribution from That of Production

The development of economic life has at once increased the volume of goods which man can produce with his labor, and has made infinitely more complicated the forces which determine the share of this product which the various classes in society receive. In the household stage, producer and consumer are one. The more that is produced, the more the worker can enjoy. The only economic problem is, therefore, one of production. Early economic writing, such as that of Hesiod, concerned itself, therefore, with how this output of goods might be increased, and virtually with that subject alone.

With the development of the handicraft stage, however, a division of labor sets in where men specialize in particular products and exchange these for the products produced by other specialists which they want. This not only creates the necessity for the institution of money, but it also alters the problem of prosperity for the worker. The return to the craftsman now depends not only on the quantity of the goods which he produces, but also on the ratio at which these goods exchange for the other commodities which he obtains in exchange. If the group of craftsmen in one industry now produces more than it did before while the craftsmen in other industries are producing no more than previously, then the greater plentifulness of the first article lowers its exchange value. At the very least, therefore, the real income of those craftsmen who have produced more will not rise in the same proportion as their output. Their real income may, as a matter of fact, be actually reduced. This will be the case if the exchange value per unit falls by a greater relative proportion than the quantity produced increases.[1]

---

[1] This, of course, is the case when the elasticity of demand for this commodity is, in the language of the economist, less than unity. The flexibility of prices is the reciprocal of this and consequently would be greater than unity. Agricultural products fall within this class, and it is well-known how farmers suffer collectively from a general increase in their output.

A decrease in output will, on the other hand, cause the unit value of the article to rise, and this will at least tend to mitigate the diminution in real income suffered by the craftsmen. Here again in some cases, when the relative increase in unit values has been greater than the reduction in output, the real income of the craftsmen will rise. When the outputs of each of the various commodities are changing, but at divergent rates of speed, the problem is much more complicated; but the relative prosperity of the craftsman will still depend on the ratio at which his product exchanges for others, as well as upon the quantity of the product which he produces.[2] The economic problem now becomes one of value as well as of production.

There is, of course, a problem of distribution in such a society, as the struggles within the medieval cities well illustrate, but the distribution of the social product is in the main either between individuals or between groups organized on a commodity basis. The processes of distribution operate in terms of quantities produced and their respective exchange values; they do not operate in terms of the shares which the factors of production receive, since the ownership of these factors is not separated but rather united in the same individuals.

In the early days of the handicraft system the craftsman was worker, manager, capitalist, and merchant rolled in one. As industry developed, distinct classes began to form which performed one instead of all of these functions. As the amount of capital needed in an enterprise increased, the line of division between the groups which owned the materials, tools, and machines and those which furnished only labor became increasingly distinct. The return in a given industry to those who furnished the capital and to those who gave their labor came to depend, therefore, not only on the quantity produced by the industry and the ratio at which its products exchanged for others, but also on the relative share which was received by the other and by the owners of the land and on the natural resources which were utilized. The real income of each class came to depend, therefore, upon the forces determining the distribution of the product among the factors as well as upon those affecting production and value.

During the Middle Ages, the gildsmen of the towns were united in their efforts to raise the prices of manufactured goods at the expense of agricultural commodities. They were divided, however, on the relative prices of the manufactured commodities in relation to each other. Each gild, naturally, tried to increase the exchange value of its product.

2. Distribution Is Inter-related in Turn with Value and Production

But while distribution comes to join value and production as one of the central problems of our present economic life, it retains a close connection with them both.

On the one hand, if we view the production of goods as a whole, with an eye to determining the amounts obtained by those who furnish respectively labor, land, capital, and business direction, and why they are what they are, the problem of distribution merges, in a sense, with that of value. The services of all of these factors are offered for sale, and hence their prices are matters of supreme importance not only to those who immediately receive them, but to all the others as well. Indeed, the ultimate slopes of the supply or cost curves of commodities, which furnish one of the determinants of value, depend primarily on the prices which it is necessary to pay for the services of labor, capital, and natural resources. The problem of value can, therefore, neither be understood nor solved, apart from the forces governing distribution. But while workers and capitalists in individual industries will be interested in the ratios at which the products they help to produce exchange for others, this will not be the primary concern for either the wage-earning or capitalistic classes as a whole. They will each instead be concerned with the amount which its respective factor as a whole receives. The relative exchange ratio which is attached to a unit of labor as contrasted with a unit of land and a unit of capital is, therefore, essentially a problem of value. It differs only in that it views the problem of distribution from the standpoint of a horizontal cleavage between the factors of production rather than from the standpoint of a vertical cleavage between commodities. An adequate theory of distribution must, therefore, be cast in much the same pattern as an adequate theory of value.

On the other hand, the distribution of the product among the owners of land and capital and the active providers of labor and managerial ability still remains also tied to the problem of production. If one man, working with tools which he owns, makes two pairs of shoes a day which sell for $4 a pair, we may say that he "produces" $8 a day minus, of course, such payments as may be necessary for the leather, nails, and thread. And this is what he will tend to receive. But if one set of persons owns the tools and buildings which are utilized in making the shoes and another set furnishes the immediate labor which helps to make them, on what basis will the relative contributions which each makes to the final product be appraised, and what will determine the relative amounts received by them? The issue is still further complicated when we consider the contributions and claims of the owners of the land and of those who furnish the directing ability and who take the risk.

Some will immediately object that since the product is a joint product, the share of each in its attainment cannot be measured, and, consequently, the reward of each will be determined by forces other than those of their relative influence on production. Many varied explanations of the precise nature of these other forces which are said to be the real determinants are offered by such sceptics. To some, only the relative bargaining strength of the various claimants determines the relative share which each receives. The field of distribution is viewed by these writers as

> "A darkling plain
> Swept by confused alarms of struggle and flight,
> Where ignorant armies clash by night."

and where the victory falls only to the strong.

Others have thought that they have solved the problem of distribution by finding some alleged force which determines the amounts paid to one or two of the factors, and then have concluded that the remaining factor merely receives what is left. Nearly every theory of distribution save those of the marginal productivity and mathematical schools has employed this residual method. Thus to Ricardo and his followers rent was the differential between the costs on the better land and at the margin. At the latter point, after deducting a fixed day-wage for the worker which was scaled down close to a subsistence basis, capital received the residual. To Walker[3] and Taussig[4] wages in turn are the residual. The former assumed a rate of interest determined by "competent causes" which was deducted

---

[3] *Cf.* Francis A. Walker, *Political Economy* (3rd Ed., 1887), pp. 236–55; "The Source of Business Profits," *Quarterly Journal of Economics,* Vol. 1 (1887), pp. 265–88; "A Reply to Mr. MacVane On the Source of Business Profits," *Ibid.,* Vol. II (1888), pp. 263–96; "The Doctrine of Rent and the Residual Claimant Theory of Wages," *Ibid.,* Vol. IV, pp. 408–33.

[4] *Cf.* Frank W. Taussig, *Principles of Economics* (1912 Ed.), Vol. II, pp. 192–208; "Outlines of a Theory of Wages," *Publications American Economic Association,* 3rd Series, Vol. XI (1910), pp. 136–56; "Capital, Interest and Diminishing Returns," *Quarterly Journal of Economics,* Vol. XXII, pp. 333–63.

from the net product on no-rent land, and after this was paid, and profits provided for differences in natural ability, wages alone were left. Taussig declared his belief in a single "effective rate of interest" which was believed to be remarkably steady through time and which resulted from the almost indefinite tendency of savings to expand at that rate. The joint product of labor and capital was then discounted by this "effective rate of accumulation," and again the residue was left for wages.

But clearly the amount which is paid in wages for labor and in interest for the use of capital must depend in some measure, at least, upon the amounts which they each respectively add to the total product. The business man buys both, and within limits he can alter the proportions of each which he uses. What will determine the quantities which he uses and the rates which he will pay? To all save those whose observation has been blinded by closet theorizing, it would seem evident that the business man considers that the returns from the added quantities of labor and capital will be at least one factor in determining what he will offer for them.

It may be objected that the individual producer can no more alter the rate of wages or of interest than he can the price of the commodity which he sells, and that he must take each of these as he finds them and merely seek to make the most effective combination of them that he can. The general rate of wages and of interest must, therefore, it is alleged, be determined by other forces. But while for any one individual wages and interest may indeed be fixed, and the only question which remains is to determine the quantities of each which shall be used and how they shall be employed, yet the effect which both labor and capital have upon the output in all of the businesses taken as a whole clearly must help to determine what these rates of wages and of interest must be. What may be fixed, therefore, for the individual is nevertheless determined by the group.

Viewed in this light, it is, therefore, an inadequate view to regard the distributive process as merely a ring in which force and craft fight it out for supremacy. It is almost equally inadequate to ascribe a given reason for the return to one or more of the factors and then to walk away from the rest of the problem with the airy comment that the remaining factor gets what is left. It would seem instead that there are positive factors determining the return which each and every one of the factors receives.

3. The Problem of Distribution Is, However, a Mutually Interdependent One in Which the Determination of Wages, Interest, and Rent Are Interlocked

The amounts received by each of the factors are not, however, completely independent of each other but are, instead, dependent in part upon what each of the other factors receives. If the rate of wages is high, for example, it will not pay to cultivate some land which would be cultivated were wages to be lower. Some land, for instance, is cultivated in China, where wages are low, which would not be farmed in America, where wages are high. The amounts of differential rent, or the difference between what is earned on the best and on the poorest land used, will, therefore, be affected by the rate of wages. Similarly, if, in consequence of a small quantity of capital, the rate of interest is high, then labor will work with less effective tools and machinery, and its wages will be lower than would be the case were the quantity of capital greater in proportion to that of labor. Not only is the productivity of each factor dependent in part upon the quantities of the other factors which are present, but the supplies of each which are utilized are in part affected by the amounts which are paid to the others. A fuller proof of these statements will be evidenced when the data on production and supply, which will be given later, are studied, but in the meantime a general appreciation of the interlocking nature of these forces can perhaps be gained.

The problem of distribution is, therefore, an interdependent one. While the separate influences playing upon wages, rent, interest, and profits must be recognized, it is not possible, as we shall see, to frame an explanation of wages which does not also explain the determination of interest and of rent. While we shall concentrate in this book upon the theory of wages, we shall of necessity be forced at times to consider the theory both of interest and of rent. We shall indeed try to approach each of these problems with the same method of attack, namely, (1) to measure the approximate effect upon production of each, (2) to measure the degree, if any, to which the supply of each factor varies with its rate of remuneration, (3) to take into account the complicating historical, psychological, and institutional influences which play upon the factors, and (4) to determine the degree to which the actual course of wages, of interest, and, if possible, of rent has in practice borne out what would theoretically be expected to be true of each.

4. The Return to Labor: Contract Wages and the Return for Effort

For what then are wages paid? The answer is at first thought simple. They are paid for labor. But the labor furnished tends to be of two kinds: namely, that by wage-earners who receive a money wage for their services and that by self-employed workers who are paid from the prices of products which they sell rather than for the price of services alone. Both receive an income from their labor, but this return is much more distinguishable in the first case than in the second.

As has been intimated, we mean by wage-earners those who do not own individually the product upon which they labor, but those who are instead paid a money price for their services and who, therefore, abandon any title to the finished product. Such wage-earners generally do not own the machines or tools with which they work, although this is not strictly true among some of the building tradesmen and some of the other highly skilled crafts. As workers, therefore, they draw their immediate income from their labor alone and not from the sale of their product. This income, which we shall call *contract wages,* is clearly evident and can be easily identified. The English classical school from Ricardo down, as a matter of fact, regarded this type of wages as synonomous with wages as a whole.

There is another class of workers, however, who are not wage-earners. These are the self-employed and independent proprietors, and they include such groups as the farmers, the small store-keepers, the independent handicraftsmen, and such professional men as the main run of doctors, lawyers, dentists, etc. These men sell directly or indirectly to the public either their services or the material products upon which they have worked. Unlike the wage-earner, they hold title to their products and derive their income from prices. They are interested in prices rather than in wages, and their income is indeed composite. They furnish labor, capital, managerial ability, and sometimes land as well, and hence, wages, interest, profits, and frequently rent are all component parts of the same price and of the same income. But, while wages do form a real part of this joint income, it is very difficult to disentangle them from the other shares and to determine how much they are.

One way of measuring them is to assume that the return for the labor share is the contract wage which the self-employed person would be able to obtain were he to give up his business and hire himself out to someone else as a wage-earner. The amount of the total income which is attributed as interest is generally found in a similar way by computing the amount which his capital could earn in the form of contract interest, if it were invested in other enterprises.

This method meets an apparent refutation in the well-known fact that the net income of the American farmer, even before the present depression, was rarely sufficient to meet the total amounts thus attributed to the value both of his labor and his capital. If the average farmer were to put both his services and his capital at the hire of others, he would apparently even in the period prior to 1929 have obtained more than he did by combining them together under his own direction. But this apparent paradox largely resulted from the fact that the farmers' investment was primarily in the form of land rather than in capital. The price of American farm lands has notoriously been based not only upon the capitalization of existing rentals, but also upon that of expected future increases. It cannot be expected, therefore, that the farmers' investment should yield in the present the market rate of return. A second factor which would compensate the farmer for a somewhat lower labor return than he could secure as a wage-earner is the sense of psychic satisfaction which comes from being one's own master and from enjoying the real attractions of country life.

It is fairly safe to assume, therefore, that contract wages tend to measure with some accuracy the amount of the composite incomes which properly can be ascribed to labor.[5] We can, therefore, center our attention upon the earnings from labor of the wage-earning class.

We are justified in speaking of the wage-earners as a separate class since the owners, or capitalistic classes, are in the main composed of different persons from the wage-earners. Many wage-earners, however, still own stock in the concerns where they are employed, while others have invested their savings either in other enterprises or in banks which have in turn invested them.[6] But even though the gross income of the wage-earners is in some cases composed of interest and rent as well as of wages, it is, of course, true that wages still comprise the vast proportion of their receipts, and that such other shares as they received

---

[5] This in a sense may involve the assumption that contract wages reflect economic wages. This point will be developed later.

[6] The workers never had the savings which were claimed for them in the golden days of the twenties and they have far less now.

are secured from different and clearly distinguishable sources.

Wages can, therefore, be identified fairly clearly, and upon their height depends the economic well-being of many millions of people. This group includes not merely the manual workers who are generally paid by the hour, the day, or the piece, but also the lower-grade salaried workers who are paid by the week or month. Both of these groups are fundamentally wage-earners although the members of the salaried group, because of their desire to maintain a fancied social superiority, are generally not anxious to acknowledge the similarity. The salaried managers of a business which they do not own are in some ways also wage-earners, although it is generally true that they share in one way or another in the profits which their business makes, and that consequently they tend, perhaps, to be more concerned with profits than with salaries.

5. Some Needed Distinctions in the Field of Wages [7]

The economic well-being of the wage-earners depends, of course, primarily upon the amount of commodities and services which they can purchase, or their *real wages*, rather than upon the amount of money which they receive. These real wages depend upon the relationship between money wages, on the one hand, and the prices of the commodities which they consume, on the other. If the former increase more rapidly than the latter, then the real wages will, of course, rise. If the opposite occurs, they will fall.

Another distinction which should be observed is that between wage rates and earnings. The former refers to the amount paid for a given unit of work, such as an hour or a full-time week, if measured in terms of time, or a piece, if measured in units of product. Earnings, on the other hand, refer to the actual amounts of money received during a week or a year. The difference between rates and earnings is primarily, although not solely, caused by differences in the volume of employment. Thus wage rates do not take into account how many hours a worker is employed during a week, or the number of days he is employed during a year. Consequently, they do not make any allowance for short time, absenteeism, overtime, or unemployment. Weekly earnings, on the other hand, or the average annual earnings of employed workers, do include the relative amounts of time worked by those who are employed and hence

---

[7] For a more complete discussion of the various ways in which wages can be measured see my book *Real Wages in the United States, 1890–1926,* Chapter I.

vary not merely according to the rate per hour, but also according to the amount of lost time and according to the amount of overtime worked, fines imposed, and bonuses paid. In the case of piece-work, earnings consist of rates per piece multiplied by the units of output.

Since statistics of earnings include only those who are on the payroll of business concerns, they do not cover those who are unemployed. In order to determine the average income of the wage-earning class as a whole, it is necessary, therefore, to add the unemployed and to divide the total amount paid out in wages not by the average number actually employed, but by the number of those in the wage-earning class as a whole.

But both wage rates and earnings refer to the amounts paid to workers. They are not identical with the amounts received by members of wage-earners' families. A community of employed bachelors will be able to enjoy more commodities and services than will a community of working-class families where there are children and other dependents who must be maintained out of the earnings of those who are gainfully employed. The working-class may enjoy more commodities, even though individual workingmen are not able to purchase as much with a week's or with a year's work as they could a decade before. This apparent paradox may be caused either by a relative increase in the number of members of a family who are gainfully employed or by a decrease in the number who are dependent. Thus an increase in the percentage of workmen who are gainfully employed will raise the family's money income and possibly also its real income. Against the increased money income which the family secures should, however, be set the fact that less care and attention is generally given to the duties of a home, and hence the gain in welfare is not as great as might at first be thought. A reduction in the birth-rate will mean that a worker will have fewer children to support and that consequently each child can be given more comforts and conveniences.

6. Wages as a Share in the Product of Industry

Hitherto we have been discussing wages from the standpoint of the individual wage-worker or his family. They should also, however, be considered from the standpoint of the working-class as a whole. Thus some writers, when they speak of an increase or decrease in wages, refer to the total or aggregate amount paid out in wages. It is, of course, possible for this total to increase because of an increase in the number employed or in the population as a whole, but for the wage of the average worker to decrease.

Still another way of looking at wages is to view them in their relationship to the returns paid to the other factors of production, such as capital, land, and business management. Sometimes wages per capita are compared with the rate of interest, and if the former has increased more rapidly than the latter, then it is said that wages have risen relatively to interest. But this is clearly not identical with the *relative share* which labor receives of the total product of industry. It was with this meaning of wages that Ricardo, for example, was concerned. Although the rate of interest may not increase as rapidly as the rate of earnings, the amount of capital may increase so much more rapidly than the quantity of labor that interest may come to claim a larger share of the total product than before. An increase in return per unit is, therefore, perfectly compatible with a decrease in the share which the factor as a whole receives.

7. Can the "Value" of Labor Rise and Fall?

A further distinction concerning the meaning of the value of labor, the value of capital, and the value of land should be made. Following Jevons, economists have almost universally declared that value is a relative and not an absolute concept. The value of commodity *A*, for example, consists of the amount of commodities *B, C, D,* etc., which it can command. The value of *B* in turn is dependent upon the quantities of *A, C,* and *D,* for which it can be exchanged. If the value of one commodity rises, those of the others must consequently fall. It is accordingly said that there can be no such thing as a general rise or fall in values.[8]

If we are considering the value of commodities at any one time this statement is probably correct, but if we change our point of approach and consider the factors of production over a period of time it will be seen to be wide of the mark. It is not only theoretically possible for the exchange value of land, labor, and capital as a whole to rise or fall, but, as a matter of fact, they are nearly always doing so. What, for example, is the meaning of a rise in real wages per unit of labor? Does not this mean that a given unit of work will exchange for more commodities and services than before? This increase may be purchased, to be sure, at the expense of the other factors of

[8] For an attack upon this position see B. M. Anderson's, *Social Value* and *The Value of Money.*

production, but it need not necessarily be. The increase in productivity may be such that the owners of each unit of physical capital may also secure an increased return, and the owners of land may profit likewise. The exchange value of every unit of all the factors may thus increase. Conversely, of course, they may all fall. Even when the units of one factor rise in value while those of another fall, it would be only a coincidence should the two precisely offset each other. The more likely possibility would be that there would be gains or losses for the units of production as a whole.

If we turn from a consideration of the units which form the factors of production to the factors as a whole, it is, of course, still clearer that there may be a total increase or decrease in values. Thus, in this sense, if the total amounts received by the wage-workers, by the capitalists, and by the landlords, all increase, then the total exchange value of the factors of production as a whole will have increased.

Thus if we look at the claims which the factors of production have upon the stream of goods and services turned out by modern industry, it is evident that the amounts received by individual units of the factors and by the factors as a whole may vary from time to time. It is proper, therefore, to speak of the value of a unit of labor or of all labor rising over a period of time, and this does not mean that the value of the units of the other factors must fall correspondingly.

8. What Is a Unit of Labor?

But what precisely do we mean by a unit of labor? The simplest unit is, of course, the labor hour, and it is this which was used by the various labor exchanges which were established during the second quarter of the nineteenth century.[9] But, as Adam Smith, Ricardo, and Marx observed, laborers work with varying degrees of intensity and skill. An hour's labor of an indolent and unskilled worker cannot be said to equal that of an energetic artisan who has spent some years in acquiring his skill. Neither Ricardo nor Marx attempted seriously to explain how these three dimensions of time, intensity, and skill were reduced to a common basis, but instead contented themselves with merely remarking that "it comes soon to be adjusted in the market"[10] and "behind the backs of the producers."[11]

---

[9] See Josiah Warren's, *Equitable Commerce.*
[10] Ricardo, *Principles of Political Economy* (Gonner Edition), p. 15.
[11] Marx, *Capital* (Kerr Edition), Vol. 1, p. 52.

Later writers of the classical school, most notably Cairnes, returned to the unit which Adam Smith [12] had set up, namely, that of a given amount of sacrifice or pain experienced in working. Labor was, therefore, reduced to common units of pain or sacrifice.

Such a unit, however, did not allow for differences in natural talents. When it was seen that the man of great capacities could accomplish more with less pain than inferior workers, economists, who were anxious to maintain that there was a correspondence between labor expended and relative exchange value found it difficult to maintain that he had performed less labor. Others also contended that since people differed so widely it was impossible to reduce the amount of psychic loss which they experienced in working to a common unit.

One group of economists turned, therefore, to the contention that work could only be measured by output. Labor, like electricity, they said, could not be measured in terms of what it was, but only in terms of what it *did*. Factory managers had been trying, of course, for a long time to follow this principle in fixing the relative earnings of the wage-earners. Piece-rates furnished an automatic means of accomplishing this within a factory, while attempts at least were made to pay the more efficient time workers higher hourly rates than their fellows. There can be little doubt that the business world, when comparing the relative worth of individuals, does primarily tend to base its comparison upon the relative amount of work which it believes each individual can perform and that it fixes its bid accordingly. Relative output is, therefore, an important factor in determining differences in wages.

But while the differences between men may perhaps be measured and paid in terms of output, the basic quantities of labor which are common to all cannot be appraised in any such fashion. Thus, if we place at work ten men of equal ability and energy for equal lengths of time in China and in the United States, the product of the former group will be much less than that of the latter. Will this be because they have not put in as many "units of labor," or will it be because they have worked

---

[12] Adam Smith had said of the laborer, "In his ordinary state of health, strength and spirits; in the ordinary degree of his skill and dexterity, he must always lay down the same portion of his ease, his liberty and his happiness. The price which he pays must always be the same, whatever may be the quantity of goods which he receives in return for it." *Wealth of Nations* (Cannan Edition), Vol. 1, p. 35.

with inadequate tools and equipment in a country where there is a much more severe pressure upon each acre of cultivable land than there is here? Does, moreover, the fact that a year of work now will produce vastly more than it could a century ago mean that the modern worker expends commensurately more "units of labor" during the year than his fellow of 1833? Finally, does the fact that the output added by each day's labor tends, after a time, to decrease as more days of labor are expended upon a given acreage of land mean that these added days of labor are of inferior quality, or does it mean that land is subject to diminishing physical returns?

If we define labor in terms of output, we are indeed driven to ascribe these differences in output to differences in labor, and in effect to deny the enhancement of productivity by machinery as well as to deny the diminishing yield of land. We would thus conceal two of the most important forces in our whole economic life, and in trying to simplify our problem we would, instead, have confused and falsified it.

However useful differences in output may therefore be in measuring differences in the economic merits of men, we cannot accept output as the unit by which to measure those basic performances of men which are characteristic of all labor. However heroic the abstraction, we shall have to assume as our unit an hour of work which is characterized by at least a minimum of intensity, skill, and ability. In common practice business men deal with such units of labor when they contract for the average run of unskilled labor, and the rate for this class furnishes in turn the basing point upon which the differentials for the other classes of labor are erected.

It is then with such units of labor that we shall deal in the chapters which follow. We shall try to see what is the effect upon production of changing the quantities of labor and in turn the effect, if any, of changes in wages upon the quantities of labor supplied. But before we proceed to attack these problems inductively, it is worth while to sharpen our concepts of what we are really looking for by reviewing how economists have gradually come to recognize the problem of the effect of changes in the factors of labor, capital, and land upon product, and some of the problems which arise out of this functional relationship. This we shall attempt to do in the three succeeding chapters.

CHAPTER II

THE DEVELOPMENT OF THE THEORY
OF PRODUCTION

If one reads the *Wealth of Nations* with a critical eye, one is struck with the fact that save for Smith's chapters on the advantages of the occupational and territorial division of labor, he virtually slights the problem of production. Labor is regarded as producing all wealth but as suffering deductions at the hands of the owners of capital and of land.[1] The forces which according to Smith determined the rates of wages and of interest (or in Smith's language, profits) had no relationship to any effect which the quantities of labor and capital might have had upon production. Wages and "profits" were instead fixed by the relationship between working capital, which was the amount available for the maintenance of the laborers, on the one hand, and the number of these laborers on the other. It was working capital, moreover, upon which interest was received, and virtually no explanation was offered for the return upon fixed capital. When the size of the working population was great and the relative quantity of working capital small, the rate of wages would be low and the rate of interest or "profits" high, and vice versa. But this result merely followed from demand and supply relationships, whereby the price of the factor which was becoming relatively less plentiful through time would advance, because the demand for it would be increasing. It was not based in any way upon the amounts of production which could be attributed to each.

The appreciation of the influence of production upon distribution has, therefore, been a post-Smithian development. This

---

[1] Smith, *The Wealth of Nations* (Cannan Edition). "In this state of things, the whole produce of labour does not always belong to the labourer. He must in most cases share it with the owner of the stock which employs him." Vol. I, p. 51.

And again: "As soon as the land becomes private property, the landlord demands a share of almost all the produce which the labourer can either raise or collect from it." *Ibid.*, Vol. I, p. 67.

For other passages see Vol. I, pp. 49, 66, and 68. I have given a more complete discussion of the whole problem in my essay, "Smith's Theory of Value and Distribution," in the volume, *Adam Smith, 1776–1926*, pp. 77–115.

development has indeed been so beautiful an illustration of the gradual unfolding of men's understanding of the problem that its chronological sequence can, with some exceptions, serve at the same time as the pattern for logical analysis. But before this treatment is given, it is worth while to attempt to plumb the possible consequences which follow from a simultaneous and equal change in all of the factors before proceeding to investigate what is the effect of only changing some factors and holding the others constant.

1. The General Problem of the Forces Affecting the Volume of Production

The amount which can be received by those who furnish labor and capital and those who own land and natural resources is limited by the total volume of production. If this increases, the total amounts which can be distributed increase, and if it diminishes, the amounts decrease. In order to determine, therefore, the wages of labor, as well as the interest on capital and the rent of land, we must ascertain, if possible, as one of the elements, the forces which cause the total production of commodities to increase or to decrease.

These are fundamentally of two main kinds: (1) A change in technical knowledge, or what Adam Smith termed "the state of the arts." New inventions, new processes, new methods of business organization and management may so increase the effectiveness of a day's labor at a machine or on a piece of land that more goods will be produced with the same quantity of labor, capital, and natural resources than before. This improvement is, moreover, not always external to those factors of production; they may be such as to change the quality of the factors themselves. Thus education, both general and technical, has made of the American farmer a far more efficient workman than he was a half-century ago, and improvements in the quality of seed and of agricultural implements have endowed each unit of capital with more productive power.

A retrogression in the arts is today far less frequent. Due to our system of recording knowledge, there are few improvements which have once justified themselves in progress which are now given up or forgotten. The growth of what the anthropologists term "material culture" is thus a cumulative process and, in the realm of the economic branches of knowledge at least, the pendulum theory of history, with its assumption that society must ultimately reverse any forward swing, is quite clearly false.

This is not to say, however, that a deterioration in human qualities and in social organization cannot occur. A great war, for example, by its disorganization of production, its breaking up of the international division of labor, and the post-war feeling of lassitude, hatred, and hopelessness which it almost invariably engenders, may well operate to decrease appreciably the quantity of physical product which can be produced from a given combination of land, labor, and capital. But while these dynamic changes are important elements in determining the relative prosperity of a country, we shall for the present ignore them and concentrate our attention upon the other main source of increase in the total product.

(2) The second way in which the total quantity of the product may be altered is from a change in the quantities of the three essential factors of labor, capital, and natural resources. An increase in any one of these factors will result, even though the state of the industrial arts remains constant, in some increase in the total product. Just how much of an increase, however, this will be and what relation it will bear to the relative increase of the given factor is a question which few economists or business men have hitherto been able competently to answer and upon which it is the purpose of this book to throw as much light as possible.

Perhaps the best way to try to deal with this question of the rate at which the quantity of the product changes as the quantity of the factors change is to see just what will happen (1) if all the factors change in equal proportions, (2) if the quantity of one factor remains constant, but the two other factors change at equal proportionate rates, (3) if in dealing with only two factors the quantity of one is constant and the quantity of the other changing, or if in dealing with all three factors, two remain constant and only one changes, and finally (4) if the quantities of all the factors are changing but at unequal rates.

We may begin with the first of these main types of conditions, both because of its relative simplicity and because of the fact that any conclusions which may be drawn concerning the three later types of cases largely rest upon what is either assumed or ascertained to be true of it. It should be understood, moreover, that we are throughout assuming that the state of the arts is constant.

2. What Will Be the Most Probable Relative Effect Upon Total Production of Equal Changes in All of the Factors?

Let us now assume that in a given year the number of factories of equal size and quality on the average with those which existed in the previous year should increase by 5 per cent, and at the same time the active working force of the society should through immigration and the natural increase of population also advance by 5 per cent. Let us assume, moreover, to make this illustration complete, that an untapped supply of land and natural resources equal in quality to the average previously utilized becomes available so that land also increases in quantity at the same rate as the two other factors.

What then will be the effect upon the total volume of production? Will it increase by more than 5 per cent, by less than 5 per cent, or by precisely this proportion? The common sense assumption would seem to be that if we take society as a whole, the increase in total product would be proportionate to the relative increase in the three factors of production or by 5 per cent, no more and no less. Thus for every new machine or factory there would be the same quota of new workers as before, and these would be furnished with the same ratio of natural resources. In effect, new units of production would be set up, staffed, and equipped by the three factors of production mixed in the same proportions as before. Under these conditions, with the state of technical knowledge and of the industrial arts the same as before, the common-sense conclusion would seem to follow that total production would normally tend to increase in precisely the ratio as that which the new production units bore to the old.

Similarly if each of the factors were to suffer the same relative decrease in their quantities, production might also normally be supposed to decrease in the same ratio.

If all this were true, total production might be described as being a homogeneous linear function of the first degree of magnitude [2] and as conforming to Euler's theorem. The legitimacy

---

[2] A function may be said to be homogeneous if, when each of the variables is multiplied by the same quantity, the function is multiplied by a power of this quantity. And it is of the first degree if equal proportionate changes in the variables will result in equal proportionate changes in the function. This may be written, according to the notation of Leon Walras, as follows:

$Q = F(T, P, K)$

If we have a homogeneous function of the first degree, then

$M Q = F(M T, M P, M K)$

of this assumption has been questioned by the distinguished Italian economist, Vilfredo Pareto, who in arguing against its use by Walras [3] and Wicksteed [4] declared

Some authors assume that if *all* the factors of production are doubled the product will also double. This may be true approximately, in a certain case, but not rigorously and in general. Some expenses vary with the importance of the business (enterprise). It is certain that if we could assume another business under conditions exactly resembling those of the first, we might double all the factors and the product. But this assumption is not, in general, admissible. If, for example, one were engaged in the transportation business in Paris, it would be necessary to assume another business and another Paris. But as this other Paris does not exist, we must consider two businesses in the same Paris, and then, we cannot assume that, when the quantities of the factors of production are doubled, the product will also be doubled.[5]

This criticism by Pareto does not, however, seem to be well taken, and his attempted refutation by analogy is singularly inconclusive. Doubling the number of transportation lines in and about Paris is not really analogous to doubling all the factors of production, for Paris remains the same, and the total number of persons to be transported is no greater than before. The quantity of transportation demanded is relatively constant and is not appreciably increased by a further spreading out of transportation facilities. Here demand is limited by a constant population, and while there are more lines there are not more persons to ride on them. In manufacturing and in other branches of production, however, the production of goods and services constitutes the real demand for the goods and services, and since the two are identical as production increases, demand increases *pari-passu*. To make the analogy really comparable, Pareto should explicitly have assumed that another Paris with a similar net of railways had come into existence. To assume this, how-

---

where Q = total output, T = quantity of land, P = quantity of labor and K = quantity of capital. On this whole matter see the very able article by Henry Schultz, "Marginal Productivity and the General Pricing Process," *Journal of Political Economy*, Vol. XXXVII, Oct., 1929, pp. 511–55, especially pp. 511–3 and 542–5.

[3] Leon Walras, *Éléments d'Économie Politique Pure* (4th edit., 1900), pp. 375–6.

[4] P. H. Wicksteed, *An Essay on the Coördination of the Laws of Distribution*, London, 1894, p. 32. For a later and what the author termed a more mature view of the matter in which the necessity of the Euler theorem was abandoned as a result of the criticisms of Pareto and Edgeworth, and in my opinion unnecessarily, see his *The Commonsense of Political Economy*, pp. 358 ff.

[5] Pareto, Vilfredo, *Cours d'Économie Politique*, Vol. II., 1897, pp. 82–3.

ever, would necessarily mean that the total traffic on the roads would double, and Euler's theorem would be confirmed in matters of production instead of being refuted, as ostensibly appeared to be the case.

The question as to whether production will increase in the same proportion as an equal relative increase in the quantity of all the factors tends as a matter of fact to resolve itself into the question whether industry as a whole tends to be characterized by constant, increasing, or decreasing returns. If constant returns prevail, then production will increase in the same ratio as the factors while under decreasing returns it will increase less rapidly and under increasing returns more rapidly.

Textbook writers have tended to resolve this problem by the facile answer that constant returns characterize the handicrafts, diminishing returns agriculture, and increasing returns manufacturing and transportation. Decreasing returns in agriculture, however, primarily result when the quantity of land is not increased as rapidly as that of labor and capital. This is simply a further illustration of the principle of diminishing incremental productivity. It does not prove that if the quantity of land of the same quality were increased as rapidly as that of labor and capital, the quantity of produce would not increase in the same ratio. On the contrary, it would seem as though if land were increased in the same ratio as labor and capital that product would tend to increase by that ratio as well. This would mean constant rather than decreasing returns.

Two further comments may be made on the question as to whether diminishing returns prevail when all three factors are increased proportionately. The first is that if this were so, then the larger the business the higher would be the marginal average unit costs, while the smaller the business, the lower would be the costs. This would mean as Wicksell [5a] has pointed out that workmen would do better when they employed themselves than when they were employees. The wage system would thus be dissolved into a series of individual enterprises. The fact that this does not happen should be proof that the principle of diminishing returns is not commonly applicable when all the factors are varied.

The second comment which should be made is that the so-called curve of increasing money costs which is supposed to

---

[5a] Knut Wicksell, *Vorlesungen über Nationalökonomie*, Erster Band (1913), p. 189.

characterize agriculture and to be proof of the supposed tendency towards diminishing returns is only true if we consider the payments for labor and capital as the sole costs. If we include rent as a cost, which from a monetary standpoint, it most certainly is, then this makes the supposed increasing cost curve really a constant cost curve. For rent would be the difference between the gross receipts and the total combined expenditures for labor and capital with the result that the average money cost per unit of product would be constant.

Now let us turn to the question whether equal relative increases in land, labor and capital would yield a *more than proportionate increase* in total product. Those who reason as though they would, tend to assume that there are latent and unfolding advantages in the form of inventions, technique, machinery, and administrative devices which can only be taken advantage of by progressively larger and larger concerns. This contention, however, tends to be refuted by four separate lines of evidence and logic. (1) In Western civilizations there is commonly sufficient labor and capital for the utilization of such practicable inventions, techniques, and devices as have been developed. Even if these called for more costly machines, the existing capital can be readjusted so as to provide for them even though this program would call for fewer separate plants and machines. There is no reason to believe that the addition of more land, labor, and capital would cause qualitatively better machines, etc., to be provided. On the contrary, it would merely permit more of such instruments to be used. This would operate towards constant rather than increasing returns.

(2) So far as the state of the technical arts is concerned, it seems probable that their development is largely conditioned by the quantities of land, labor, and capital which are available. For industrial mankind tends to work only at problems which it can solve, and the existing quantities of the factors furnish conditioning forces upon invention.

(3) If increasing returns and their ultimate corollary, decreasing costs, were really to apply, then competition would be impossible as Cournot demonstrated nearly a century ago [5b] and

<hr>

[5b] Cournot, *Recherches sur les principes mathématiques de la théorie des richesses*, (1838). This followed from the fact that if the supply (average cost) curve cut the demand curve from above and continued below it, average costs for the industry were decreased more rapidly by an expansion of output than was unit price and there was no limit to output as long as this continued. If on the other hand the supply curve cut the demand curve from below and continued above the latter although inclined downward, then each individual plant

monopoly would become the general rule. This even yet is not the case in most areas of business such as agriculture, commerce, building, coal mining, amusements, the professions, and such manufacturing industries as textiles, clothing, boots and shoes, food products, etc. This persistence of competition is therefore presumptive proof that increasing returns is not the primary characteristic of industry.

(4) Finally, even so far as decreasing money costs are concerned these tend primarily to prevail only so long as an existing plant is not utilized to full capacity. When output is added beyond this in a given concern, a great addition in fixed capital is required and the marginal cost curve shoots sharply upwards. Under these circumstances the marginal cost function is more of a saw-tooth curve, the downward drift of which is far less than is commonly conceived. It is probable indeed that the desire of big bankers for profits from floating the securities of giant consolidations is more responsible for these combines than their strictly economic advantages [5c] and what is commonly treated as the downward movement of costs tends in practice to be the historical lowering of the level of costs through improved technique rather than the fact of decreasing marginal and average costs at any one moment and under given conditions.

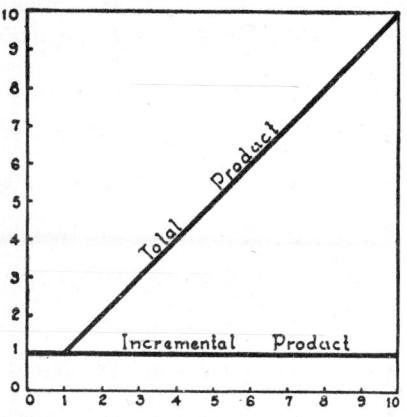

Chart 1. The Normal Increase in Total Product with Equal Increases in All of the Factors of Production.

The most probable of all assumptions seems, therefore, to be that production can be described as a simple homogeneous linear function of the first degree and that if *all* the factors are

under atomistic competition could reduce its costs more by expanding output than it would lower price because of its infinitesimal additions to the total supply. But while this would be true of each individual plant, the combined effect of all adopting it would be that prices would fall more rapidly than costs. General bankruptcy would, therefore, be the result under competition and monopoly would tend inevitably to follow.

[5c] See an article on this point by A. S. Dewing, "A Statistical Text of the Success of Consolidations." *Quarterly Journal of Economics*, Vol. 36 (1921), pp. 84–101.

increased or decreased by a given per cent, product will increase or decrease by that per cent. This relationship is shown in Chart 1 and may in any event be used as a first approximation. It may incidentally be mentioned that the inductive studies by the author and others for certain periods of time seem to indicate that this condition may very well be the case even for historical periods.

This definition of the normal course of industry enables us in turn to detect qualitative changes in economic progress. When output rises at a faster rate than that which would follow under the Euler theorem, we may define this period as one characterized by progress, but when output fails to rise as rapidly, the reverse applies.

3. The Effect Upon Production of Holding One Factor Constant and Increasing the Other Two—The Law of Rent

From all this, it follows as another commonsense deduction that if all factors contribute toward production, then holding any one factor constant and increasing the others will result in an increase in the total product but at a smaller ratio than that by which the two factors were themselves increased. This would be caused by the fact that one of the factors which had contributed to the proportional increase in output was not expanding in quantity. The proportional increase in factors A and B alone could not, therefore, cause the same relative increase in output which would result from a proportional increase in all three of the factors. This is indicated graphically in Chart 2.

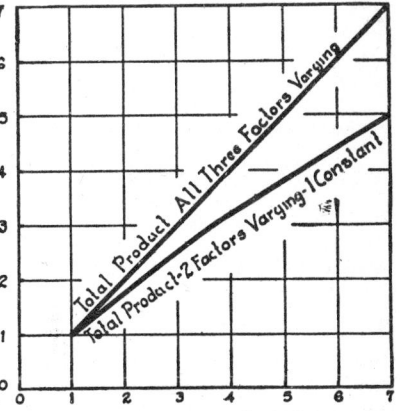

Chart 2. Comparison of the Effects upon Total Product When (1) All Three Factors Vary, and (2) Two Factors Vary and One Is Held Constant.

But the increase of two factors alone, with the third held constant, not only results in a less than proportionate addition to the total product as factors A and B are increased, but it also results in a gradual diminution of the absolute amounts of the successive increments to the total product. This can be demonstrated by the following example. Let us assume that one unit each of factors A, B, and C will yield one unit of product. A proportional increase in A and B, as we have seen, will not result in a corresponding increase in product but in a somewhat smaller rate of increase, which we may assume to be eight-tenths. Then as the quantities of A and B are increased, the total product will expand at eight-tenths of this rate, and these increments will be of a continuously smaller magnitude. This general type of relation between factor and product is the one which agrees best with manufacturing experience and will be used in our later studies of manufacturing.[6]

TABLE 1

INCREMENTAL INCREASE IN THE TOTAL PRODUCT WITH QUANTITY OF ONE FACTOR CONSTANT AND WITH TWO FACTORS VARYING

Quantity of Factors		Percentage Increase of AB as Compared with Previous Quantity	Percentage Increase of Product (80% of Percentage Increase in AB)	Amount of Increase of Product	Total Product
C	A & B				
(1)	(2)	(3)	(4)	(5) (Col. 4 applied to preceding item in Col. 6)	(6)
1	1				1.00
1	2	100.0	80.0	(.80 × 1.0) = .80	1.80
1	3	50.0	40.0	(.40 × 1.80) = .72	2.52
1	4	33.3	26.7	(.267 × 2.52) = .67	3.19
1	5	25.0	20.0	(.20 × 3.19) = .64	3.83
1	6	20.0	16.0	(.16 × 3.83) = .61	4.44
1	7	16.7	13.3	(.133 × 4.44) = .59	5.03

Thus in the illustration given above and shown in Chart 3, a doubling in A and B will result in an increase of 80 per cent or .8 of a unit of product. An increase of another unit of A and B to a total of three each, is equivalent to a 50 per cent increase. Product, maintaining its eight-tenths ratio, will increase by 40 per cent. But 40 per cent of 1.80 is .72, and this will be the second increment. This, however, is .08 units less than the first increment. When we increase A and B to four, the percentage rise in their quantity is 33.3. Product will, therefore, increase by 26.7 per cent or by 33.3 × .80. The absolute amount of the increase will then be .673 units, which would be .047 less than the second increment.

As the units of A and B rise successively to 5, 6, and 7, the

---

[6] See Chapters V–VII, below.

percentage addition to the total product will be 20.0, 16.0, and 13.3 respectively. The amounts of the successive increments would in turn be .64, .61, and .59.

It follows, therefore, that if one factor is held constant and the others increased, with each addition of a combined unit of the other two factors, the amount by which the total product is increased will diminish with each successive increase of the variable factors A and B. This diminution of the increment is, therefore, a logical corollary of the economic application of Euler's theorem, as long as the relative addition to the product is equal to eighttenths (or to any constant proportion) of the percentage increase in the factors which are varied. The diminution of the increment is, therefore, a general and natural trend, although at some points it need not always be true.

If only one factor were to be increased and the other two

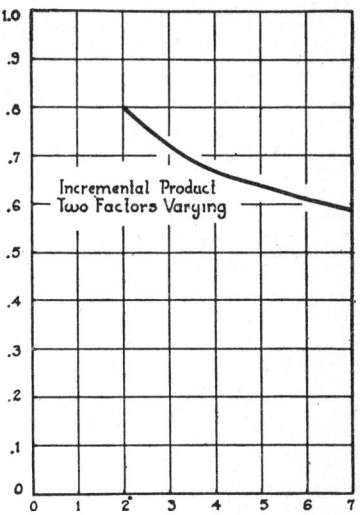

Chart 3. Incremental Increases in the Total Product with the Quantity of One Factor Constant and with Two Factors Increasing.

were held constant, then product would increase less rapidly than it would were another factor to increase along with this one, and only one factor to remain constant. Thus in the illustration which has been given in Table 1 if only A were to increase while B as well as C remained constant, then the product would not advance at the rate of 80 per cent of the proportionate increase in A which prevailed when the quantity of B as well as A was augmented. This is illustrated by Chart 4, and it follows from this that the amounts of the increments to the total product would be less than those indicated in Chart 3.

It was this law in reality, although disguised under its special applications, which was somewhat unwittingly discovered by Sir Edward West in 1815 and elaborated by Ricardo in 1817 when they enunciated the principle of diminishing returns on land, and from this deduced the law of rent. West, for example, pointed out "that each additional quantity of work bestowed on agriculture yields an actually diminished return;"[7] and in another place he reasoned that "the necessity of having recourse to land inferior to that already in tillage, or of cultivating the same land more expensively tends to make labour in agriculture less productive in the progress of improvement."[8] While West's language might lead one to believe that he was varying only one factor, labor, a study of the context of his essay indicates that he was also increasing the quantity of capital as well as that of labor.

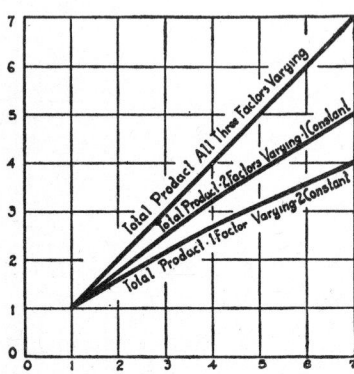

Ricardo, drawing his clue from West, showed how as the population increased it was necessary to resort to poorer soils where the yield, with an equal employment of capital and labor, would be less than on the best grade of land, or in his illustration, 90 and 80 quarters of wheat respectively instead of 100 quarters, and continued:

Chart 4. Comparison of the Effects upon Total Product When (1) All Three Factors Vary, (2) Two Factors Vary and One Is Held Constant, and (3) One Varies and Two Are Held Constant.

It often and, indeed, commonly happens, that before No. 2, 3, 4, or 5, or the inferior lands are cultivated, capital can be employed more productively on those lands which are already in cultivation. It may perhaps be found, that by doubling the original capital employed on No. 1, though the produce will not be doubled, will not be increased by 100 quarters, it may be increased by eighty-five quarters, and that this quantity exceeds what could be obtained by employing the same capital, on land No. 3.[9]

That Ricardo had clearly grasped the fact of the diminishing increment is evidenced by the fact that after explaining what determined the amount of rent, he wrote, "If capital could be indefinitely employed without a diminished return on the old land, there could be no rise of rent; for rent, invariably, proceeds from the employment of an additional quantity of labour with a proportionally less return."[10]

---

[7] Sir Edward West, *The Application of Capital to Land* (Hollander Edition), 1815, p. 12.
[8] *Ibid.*, pp. 23–4.
[9] Ricardo, David, *Principles of Political Economy* (Gonner Edition), p. 48.
[10] *Ibid.*, p. 49.

Rent, or the amount attributed to the use of the land, was made 'the residual or the difference between the number of bushels which could be raised with a given quantity of labor and capital with the earlier applications on the better soils and that which could be raised with the last application of labor and capital. Since at the margin no rent would be paid, but only a return to labor and capital, tenants would compete to secure the differential on the better soils and consequently would force their bids up to a point which would approximately equal this differential. "Rent," declared Ricardo, "is always the difference between the produce obtained by the employment of two equal quantities of capital and labour."

It is interesting to note, however, that Ricardo did not vary the proportions between capital and labor, and a proportionate addition to the one was accompanied by a proportionate addition to the other. Only their combined ratio to land was altered, but they were bound to each other at least so far as agriculture was concerned in fixed and unvarying proportions. This assumption was continued by the followers of Ricardo in the English classical tradition, and it was one of these, James Mill, who gave the happy term of "a dose of labor and capital" to the application on land of another composite unit of the other two factors.

The principle of the diminishing increment was, therefore, established in so far as the application of increasing quantities of labor and capital to it was concerned, and from this, the law of rent emerged as the natural consequence.

But it was not so clear what determined the quantity of labor and capital which would be applied to the land, or hence to what point the margin would be carried. In the case of any individual farmer, it was, of course, determined at the point where the cost of the labor and capital applied was precisely equal to the price of the commodities produced. But while the individual enterpriser had to accept the rate of wages and the rate of interest as given, and govern himself accordingly, the question clearly presented itself as to how these rates were determined in the economic society as a whole. Ricardo found the answer for labor at a relatively constant rate of wages which was certainly close to the minimum of subsistence; if wages went above this point, population, in true Malthusian fashion, expanded. The diminished incremental yield of the added units of labor would in turn reduce the sums available for wages.

When the wage reached the level which Ricardo assumed as relatively constant over considerable periods of time at a point close to the subsistence level, and when "profits," or what we would now term "interest plus profits," had reached their minimum, an equilibrium would be reached. This minimum of profits was not zero, as might be supposed from Ricardo's failure to deal explicitly with the forces necessitating interest. For Ricardo declared, "long indeed before this period (the disappearance of profits), the very low rate of profits will have arrested all accumulation." Ricardo, however, as we shall see, did not deal with the question at what point this probable minimum would be.

Ricardo made a most significant contribution to an understanding of the laws of production when he grasped the idea of a diminishing increment of product as successive doses of labor and capital were applied, but neither he nor his followers realized that they had stumbled upon only one phase of a universal tendency. Nor did they carry out the two next steps which logically should have followed from his analysis, namely, (1) the inductive determination of the precise rate at which the rate of growth of total output, or the incremental output, diminished as the doses of labor and capital were applied, and (2) the determination, both by deductive reasoning and by inductive experiments, of the effect upon production of a more flexible variation of the factors. Thus instead of holding labor and capital together in fixed doses, labor could be varied with land, and capital could be constant or vice versa.

4. The Breaking-up of the Combined "Dose" of Labor and Capital and the Variation of Each in Comparison with Land and Natural Resources

The writer who first broke up the combined dose of labor and of capital in which the two were mixed in fixed proportions was apparently the acute German thinker, T. H. von Thünen. Working independently of Ricardo and as a result of his experiments as a scientific farmer, in the first part of his *Der Isolierte Staat* published in 1826, he showed what the effects upon the total agricultural product were when: (1) the quantity of labor was varied with land held constant, and with capital disregarded; and (2) the quantity of capital varied while land was held constant, and labor was virtually disregarded. In both cases he found that incremental additions to the total product diminished as successive units of each of the factors were added.

In recent years an extraordinarily interesting relationship between the addition of successive units of capital in the form of fertilizer, etc., and of product has been independently discovered by Mitscherlich, of Königsberg, Germany, and the American economist, W. J. Spillman.[11] It is that the amount of the increment of product added as the result of successive units of fertilizer tends to decrease according to given ratios. That is, if the addition of the second unit of fertilizer, amounting let us say to 200 pounds, gives an increment which is 80 per cent of that added by the first 200 pounds of fertilizer, then the third unit of fertilizer will add approximately only 80 per cent of what the second had added and the fourth will in turn add 80 per cent of the increment of the third, and so on. The same principle has also been found to apply in the feeding of animals, the amount of weight added in a given period of time by successive increments of the same type of feed declining in a geometrical series as the animal increases in size and as the amount of feed increases.

This principle can be described in another way by saying that in order to increase output in an arithmetical ratio it is necessary to increase the application of the independent variable, capital, as represented by fertilizer and by feed, in a somewhat complex ratio of the geometrical type. This is essentially analogous to the so-called Weber-Fechner law of physiological reaction. Here it has been found that the amount of added sensation received is an approximate logarithmic function of the stimulus applied, and that it, therefore, depends not solely on the amount of the *added* stimulus, but also on the quantity of stimulus which has gone before. Equal relative increases in stimulus will give approximately equal absolute increases in sensation.

But two qualifications should be interjected at this point concerning the nature of this tendency of output to follow a logarithmic curve. (1) In the first place, the tendency is approxi-

---

[11] A statement of Spillman's theory is given in his *The Law of the Diminishing Increment*, which is Part I, pp. 1–77 of his *The Law of Diminishing Returns*. Mitscherlich's results are well stated by Dr. Emil Lang in an article entitled "Der Ertragsverlauf in der Landwirtschaft bei steigendem Aufwand. Ein Beitrag zur Lehre vom Bodengesetz." *Landwirtschaftliche Jahrbücher*, Vol. LV, 1920, and a translation of this under the title of *The Law of the Soil*, is published as Part II, of *The Law of Diminishing Returns*. This formula differs from the one we have found typical for manufacturing, in that product per acre or weight per animal approaches a fixed maximum limit, while under our manufacturing formula, product per worker (for example) could be indefinitely increased by the aid of greater increases in capital. This difference is natural in view of the technical facts of the two types of production.

mate rather than precise, and the actual yields frequently vary by a few per cent from what the computations would lead one to expect. (2) The constants which fix the ratio by which the increments of output diminish apparently vary quite widely according to the nature of the crop, the nature of the fertilizer, and the nature of the land. It is, therefore, not possible as yet to frame a mathematical equation which describes the effect upon product of added doses of more or less abstract "capital" upon agricultural land as a whole.

5. Longfield's Attempt at Varying the Quantities of Capital to Labor and Thus Deducing the Rate of Interest and Wages

One of the first gropings toward determining wages and interest through varying the respective quantities of capital and labor was that of Longfield.[12] During the 1820's it began to be seen in England that supplies of labor and capital might increase at unequal rates of speed, but the contention was commonly advanced that an increase of capital, unaccompanied by any increase in population, would not reduce the rate of interest or, in the term then used, profits.[13] These writers believed that the last unit of capital would be as productive as the first. Longfield went beyond this group in grasping the fact that were other things equal such an increase in the quantity of capital unaccompanied by an increase in the size of the population would necessarily result in a lowering of the rate of interest. Interest or profits, to him, were not only limited but determined by the difference between what a worker could produce working by himself alone and what he could produce when he worked with tools and machines of any given value. Longfield declared that this difference grew less as the ratio of capital to labor in-

---

[12] *Lectures on Political Economy*, by Mountifort Longfield, Dublin, 1834. This has recently been reprinted by the London School of Economics. Longfield's contributions were little appreciated at the time, but in recent years his worth has been more and more recognized. For his contributions to the theory of utility and price, see Seligman, "Some Neglected British Economists," *Economic Journal*, Vol. 13, 1903, pp. 335–63; 511–35. Lauderdale as early as 1804 had thrown out the statement that there "must be at all times, a point determined by the existing state of knowledge in the art of supplanting and performing labour with capital, beyond which capital cannot profitably be increased, and beyond which it will not naturally increase because the quantity, when it exceeds that point, must increase in proportion to the demand for it." Lord Lauderdale, *An Inquiry into the Nature and Origin of Public Wealth* (1st edition), p. 228; 2nd edition (1819), p. 225. It is regrettable that Ricardo did not expand this hint into a universal tendency towards diminishing incremental yields instead of confining this principle merely to the combined application of labor and capital upon land and thus only giving it a partial and incomplete application.

[13] Longfield, *ibid.*, p. 184.

creased. This conclusion, of course, clearly rested on the implicit assumption that the product added by capital increased at a diminishing rate as further capital was added, and that consequently the increments of product attributable to the additional units of capital decreased.

It could hardly be expected at so early a period that even a writer who had made so penetrating an observation could fully follow it up by assigning only the correct reasons for this diminution of the increment. Longfield did not. Groping for a solution, he found two wrong explanations as well as the right one. Thus, the first explanation was [14] that "as the number of such instruments (spades) increases in the hands of the same or different capitalists, other and inferior labourers must be employed to use them." [15] Since "the rate of profits must be determined by those cases in which the efficiency of capital is least, the profits of a single tool will be equal to the difference of the quantities of work which the feeblest labourer could execute with and without its use."

Here Longfield depends upon a deterioration in the quality of the workers using the successive additions of tools as the cause of the diminution of the increment rather than upon the natural tendency for added tools of the same quality to fail to increase output proportionately to their added expense.

A second reason which Longfield advanced for the necessity of a fall in the rate of profits was that articles which men "produced partly by means of capital, will overstock the market for them, and must be sold cheaper." [16] Here Longfield confuses value production with what he has been previously discussing, namely, physical production. The primary question is what will be the ratio of the added increments of total physical product to those which have gone before, and not what happens to the total exchange value of any one commodity belonging to the general group. Value product, as we have seen, applies only to individual commodities or groups of commodities, while for commodities as a whole, total physical product is the vital reality.[17]

Finally, in a somewhat clumsy and elliptical manner, Long-

---

[14] *Ibid.*, p. 191.
[15] *Ibid.*, p. 192.
[16] Longfield, *op. cit.*, p. 197.
[17] That these value differences do alter the index number of production depending upon whether base or end-year weights are used, has been pointed out by N. A. Tolles and myself in our article, "A Measure of British Industrial Production," *Journal of Political Economy*, February, 1930, pp. 1–27.

field did adumbrate the principle of diminishing incremental yields as an explanation of interest when he wrote, "In order to find employment for all the increased capital, machinery must be resorted to, of greater value in proportion to its efficiency, when labourers are not numerous enough to create a demand for all the instruments of the more efficacious kind that can be procured for them." [18]   The full implications which underlay this passage if it were to have validity, namely, that there must be a diminishing *physical* increment as well as a declining value increment, were neither explicitly stated nor worked out. The clue which Longfield offered in this somewhat concealed form passed, therefore, relatively unnoticed.

Longfield did not attempt to obtain the wages of labor by even a similar procedure but contented himself by saying that wages would consist of the residue left after rent and interest had been paid. He, therefore, merely determined independently the return to two of the factors of production, land and capital, and ascribed to labor what was left. He was thus the forerunner of Jevons who used an almost identical method for determining interest and wages, and, in a sense, also, of Taussig who recognizes a joint productivity of labor and of capital and arrives at the rate of wages by deducting the rate of interest from the joint marginal product.[19]

6. Von Thünen and the Origin of Marginal Productivity

The first writer to deduce both the rate of interest and the rate of wages from the additions to the total product which were made by the last units of capital and labor respectively was again Von Thünen. Whereas in the first part of his *Der Isolierte Staat,* he had varied merely the quantity of labor and of capital directly against land, and hence had treated only of agriculture, in the second part he varied these quantities directly against each other in the field of manufacturing as well. Thus, dealing with a marginal situation where no rent was paid, he increased the number of persons employed with a given quantity of capital, and pointed out that product would not increase proportionately and that in fact the actual quantity of the increment

---

[18] *Ibid.*, p. 197. A similar passage is found on pp. 192–3, which states that owners of capital as they become "more plentiful, must sustain a reduction of profits"—among other reasons because they will be "furnishing their labourers with tools which, though more effective than those hitherto used, are expensive in a still greater proportion."

[19] With Taussig, however, "the" rate of interest is not determined by marginal productivity but by "the effective rate of accumulation."

would diminish. The following table was indeed used by him.[20]

Number of Workers	Units of Product	Number of Units Added by the Last Worker
4	80.0	
5	86.6	6.6
6	91.0	4.4
7	94.0	3.0
8	96.0	2.0
9	97.3	1.3
10	98.2	.9
11	98.8	.6
12	99.2	.4

In a similar fashion Von Thünen increased the quantity of capital used by a given number of workers and pointed out that the product increased in diminishing quantities.[21]

He then declared that the rate of wages was fixed by the addition of the product which was made by the last unit of labor, and the rate of interest by the addition to the product made by the last unit of capital. Thus he wrote, "The use of the last small unit of capital applied determines the height of the rate of interest." [22] And similarly, "the wage of labor is likewise the increment which results in a large business from the last laborer." [23] The rate of return to the earlier units of labor and capital was brought down to a level with the incremental additions of the last because of the operation of what was later named the "law of indifference." "The wage which the last added laborer obtains must normally determine the wage for all workers of equal skill and industry, *since there cannot be unequal wages for equal services*." [24]

If the last unit of labor would receive, therefore, the amount which it added to the product, the other units, since they were identical in quality, would of necessity receive the same sum. A similar equalization of return would take place in the case of capital.

---

[20] J. H. von Thünen, *Der Isolierte Staat*, Zweiter Teil, 3 Aufl. (1930 Edition), p. 570.

[21] *Ibid.*, pp. 557 ff.

[22] "Die Nutzung des zuletzt angelegten Kapitalteilchens bestimmt die Höhe des Zinsfusses." *Ibid.*, p. 557.

[23] "Der Arbeitslohn ist gleich dem Mehrerzeugniss was durch den, in einem grossen Betrieb, zuletzt angestellten Arbeiter hervorgebracht wird." *Ibid.*, p. 569.

[24] "Der Lohn aber, den der zuletzt angestellte Arbeiter erhält, muss normierend für alle Arbeiter von gleicher Geschicklichkeit und Tüchtigkeit sein; denn für gleiche Leistungen kann nicht ungleicher Lohn gezahlt werden." *Ibid.*, p. 577.

If anything else were needed to prove that Von Thünen's theory of wages and interest was identical with what was later termed marginal productivity, the two following brief para-

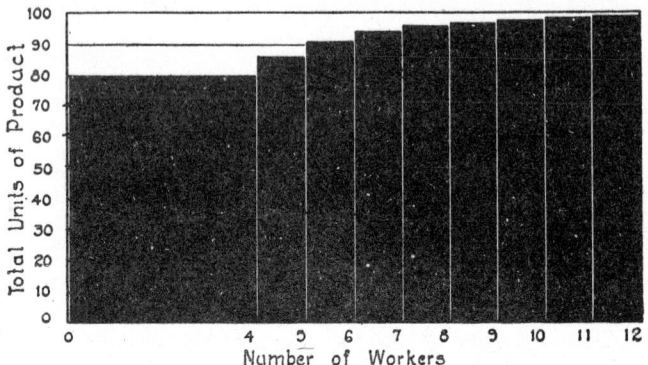

Chart 5. Increase in Total Product with Increase in Labor Alone. (From Numerical Illustration of J. H. von Thünen)

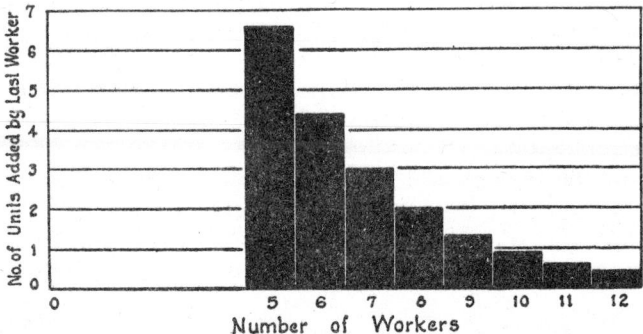

Chart 6. Number of Units Added to Total Product by Additions of Successive Laborers. (From the Numerical Illustration of J. H. von Thünen)

graphs in which he summarizes his theory should finally clinch the point.[25]

The significance of capital we have measured by the increase in the product of the labor of a man which results from an increase of

[25] "Die Wirksamkeit des Kapitals haben wir ermessen an dem Zuwachs, den das Arbeitsprodukt eines Mannes durch Vergrösserung des Kapitals, womit er arbeitet, erlangt. Hier ist die Arbeit eine konstante, das Kapital aber eine veränderliche Grösse. Wenn wir dies Verfahren beibehalten, aber umgekehrt das Kapital als gleichbleibend, die Arbeiterzahl als wachsend betrachten, so muss auch bei einem Betrieb im grossen die Wirksamkeit der Arbeit durch den Zuwachs, den das Gesamtprodukt durch die Vermehrung der Arbeiter um einen erhält, der Anteil des Arbeiters an dem Produkt, zu unserer Kenntnis gelangen." *Ibid.*, p. 584.

the capital with which he works. Here labor is a constant, capital a varying magnitude.

When, on the other hand, we consider capital as remaining constant and the number of workers as varying, we realize in a large business that the significance of labor and the share of labor in the product is determined by the increase in the product which results from the addition of another laborer.

It was indeed Von Thünen's understanding of some of the implications resulting from the fact that it was the product added by the last laborer, which led him to develop his celebrated "just wage." He was troubled by the fact that the wages of the earlier workers were diminished by the smaller increments resulting from the addition of the later laborers, although they continued to work as hard as before. He rightly felt that there was no necessary ethical justification for this result and set himself the task of determining a better method by which the workers would obtain a larger share of the total product. The solution which he believed he found and which he regarded as his greatest contribution was that the rate of wages should be the geometric average of the product of the amount required to maintain the workers on a minimum of subsistence and the total product. This would be written $\sqrt{ap}$ where a represented the minimum of subsistence and p the total product.

It is indeed something of a pity that economists have so engrossed themselves with Von Thünen's attempts to arrive at a "just" wage and with the logical and mathematical slips which he made in attempting to deduce it, that they have ignored the finished and elegant statement of the diminishing increments which resulted when the quantities of either labor or capital were varied in terms of the other and of how the increments added by the last unit of these factors determined the rates of interest and of wages.[26]

7. J. B. Clark and the Modern Re-Discovery of Marginal Productivity

By one of those curious coincidences which so frequently occur in science, the theory of diminishing incremental productiv-

---

[26] The way in which the essential features of Von Thünen's theory of distribution were in fact neglected by the economic world which at the same time was loud in its lip-service to the power of his thought is a melancholy reflection on the slowness with which economists have grasped fundamental types of analysis. Thus see G. F. Knapp, *Zur Prüfung der Untersuchungen über Lohn und Zinsfluss im Isolierten Staate* (1865); the article by Dr. Carl Grünberg on Von Thünen in the *Handwörterbuch der Staatswissenschaften*, (edited by Elster, Weber and Wieser), 4th edition, and the article on Von Thünen by Dr. Mithoff in Schönbergs, *Handbuch der Politischen Oekonomie*, pp. 636–40.

ity and the marginal determination of wages and interest which had been worked out by Von Thünen was again adumbrated by Jevons [27] and finally rediscovered independently towards the end of the nineteenth century by a group of economists which included Leon Walras,[28] Philip H. Wicksteed,[29] Enrico Barone,[30] and in America, Stuart Wood [31] and John Bates Clark.[32] Since the writings of the latter have been by far the most influential of the group, we shall center our attention on his reasoning and consider the others only in so far as they may modify or expand his development of the theory.

Thus in his reasoning concerning agriculture, Professor Clark [33] stated: "Imagine men placed in a field, one at a time, till there are twenty of them at work. Each of them is thus seen to add less to the crop than did his predecessor. The product that can be attributed to any one man grows steadily less, as the force is thus built up to its full complement; and the amount that is due to the twentieth man is least of all. If all men must accept as pay what this man produces, we have the solution of the problem of wages."

The same principle applies in manufacturing and in society as a whole. "Give to this isolated community a hundred million dollars worth of capital and introduce gradually a corresponding

---

[27] W. S. Jevons. "The ratio which this increment (of produce) bears to the increment of the investment of capital will determine the rate of interest." *The Theory of Political Economy* (1871), p. 244. Wages were not, however, independently determined in Jevon's theory but were merely the residue left after the marginal increment of product resulting from the last unit of capital had been multiplied by the number of units of capital.

[28] Leon Walras, *Éléments d'Économie Politique Pure,* especially, 4th Edition, pp. 254–80; 297–380.

[29] Philip H. Wicksteed, *An Essay on the Coördination of the Theory of Distribution.* 56 pp. (1894).

[30] Enrico Barone, "Studi Sulla Distribuzione," *Giornale degli Economisti,* Vol. XII (Feb. and March, 1896), pp. 107–55; 235–52.

[31] Stuart Wood, *"The Theory of Wages,"* *Publications American Economic Association,* Vol. IV, 1889, pp. 5–35. "The price of all labor is regulated . . . by its final utility, that is of the portion which comes into use last." Wood emphasized (1) the diminishing utility of successive units of labor and (2) the equivalence at the margin between capital and labor for which equal sums were paid rather than (3) the diminishing physical increment resulting from the addition of successive units of labor and capital.

See also Wood's article, "A New View of the Theory of Wages," *Quarterly Journal of Economics,* Vol. III, pp. 60–86; 462–80.

[32] See especially his *Distribution of Wealth* and *Essentials of Economic Theory.* See also his articles, "The Possibility of a Scientific Law- of Wages," *Publications American Economic Association,* Vol. IV (1889), pp. 39–63, where the statement is made: "The returns of each agent are fixed in identically the same manner. Each gets an amount gauged by the product of its final increment," p. 61; and "Distribution as Determined by a Law of Rent," *Quarterly Journal of Economics,* Vol. V (1891), pp. 289–318.

[33] J. B. Clark, *The Distribution of Wealth,* pp. 165–6.

force of workers. Put a thousand laborers into the rich environment that these conditions afford and their product *per capita* will be enormous. Their work will be aided by capital to the extent of a hundred thousand dollars per man. This sum will take such forms as the workers can best use and a profusion of the available tools, machines, etc. will be at every laborer's disposal. . . . Add, now, a second thousand workers to the force and, with the appliances at their service changed in form—as they must be—to adapt them to the uses of the larger number of men, the output per man will be smaller than before. This second increment of labor has at its disposal capital amounting to only half a hundred thousand dollars per man, and this it has taken from the men who were formerly using it. Where one of the original workers had an elaborate machine, he now has a cheaper and less efficient one; and the new workers by his side also have machines of the cheaper variety. This reduction in the efficiency of the instrument that the original worker used must be taken into account in estimating how much the new worker can add to the product of industry." [34] His advent, in brief, has caused both the original worker and himself to work with poorer tools than those in the first group, and he "therefore brings into existence less wealth than did one of the first division of laborers." [35] We must, however, says Professor Clark, "be careful as to the nature of this change. The product that can be attributed to this second increment of labor is, of course, not all that it creates by the aid of the capital that the earlier division of workers has surrendered to it; it is only what its presence adds to the product previously created. With a thousand workers using the whole capital, the product was four units of value; with two thousand, it is four, plus; and the plus quantity, whatever it is, measures the product that is attributable to the second increment of labor only." [36]

Additional increments of labor were then assumed to have been added to the working force but with no increase in the total amount of capital, although its form naturally changed with each fresh addition to labor. If the hundredth increment of labor represented all of the available supply, then "we have the law of wages. The last composite unit of labor—the final division of a thousand men—has created its own distinguishable product. This is less than the product that was attributable to

[34] J. B. Clark, *The Distribution of Wealth,* pp. 174-5.
[35] *Ibid.,* p. 175.
[36] *Ibid.,* p. 176.

any of the earlier divisions; but, now that this section of the laboring force is in the field, no division is effectively worth any more than is this one." [37]

It will be noticed that in the above illustration Professor Clark assumed that, as more labor was added, the forms of capital were changed so that each worker was provided with a cheaper and less effective machine. This resulted in a drop in per capita productivity and a lessened addition to the total product than that which attended the labors of the first group. This assumes, of course, a flexibility of capital and an ability to change its forms, which is certainly not present in the short run, although given a period of years it may be approximated. The same general result, however, can be secured by assuming the addition of further increments of labor to the existing apparatus of tools and machinery. Two men may be employed at a given printing press instead of one, and an additional five men may be provided to keep up steam, etc. The total product will increase but not at as rapid a rate as that which resulted from the efforts of the first group of workers.

But it may be queried, how does this fact of diminishing productivity determine the rate of wages? The answer is: in the same logical manner that diminishing and marginal demand prices determine the prices of products.

As Professor Clark says: "if any earlier section of the working force were to demand more than the last one produces, the employer could discharge it and put into its place the last section of men. What he would lose by the departure of any body of a thousand men is measured by the product that was brought into existence by the last body that was set working.[38] Workers who demanded more than that which the marginal laborers added would, therefore, be thrown out of work and, in time, would be willing to work for the amount added by the marginal laborer. It would, moreover, be impossible for employers long to pay different rates of wages for identical workers, because should certain of them pay more than the marginal product, the other workers would offer their services for less, and the wage would hence be reduced back to the marginal limit.

If, on the other hand, a given employer were to pay a worker less than what he could add to the product elsewhere, other employers, if competition were free, would offer more for his

---

[37] Clark, *op. cit.*, p. 177.
[38] J. B. Clark, *The Distribution of Wealth*, p. 177.

services. Competition between employers would thus force wages up to the point of marginal productivity.

The same point can perhaps be still more simply stated by saying that only when the rate of wages (or the price of labor) is equal to marginal productivity will the quantity of labor demanded equal the quantity supplied and equilibrium be established. For at any wage higher than marginal productivity, less labor will be demanded by the employers than is available for employment since the employers will not normally pay to workers more than they add to the product. There will then be unemployment amongst the laborers and those unemployed will offer to work for less than the previous rate rather than earn nothing. Wage rates in excess of the marginal yields are therefore always tending to decrease. If the rate of wages on the other hand is less than the marginal productivity, more labor will be demanded than is available. At this rate of wages some employers will have to go without workers whom they would like to hire. In order to employ them they will therefore raise their wages. Any wage below marginal productivity is therefore tending to increase. Wages tend to move towards marginal productivity as the point where the market is "cleared" because the quantity demanded is equal to the quantity supplied. And this is true of the rate of interest as well. The marginal productivity of labor can be written as $\frac{\partial P}{\partial L}$, or the change in product with respect to a change in the quantity of labor.

Clark's interest theory is of an almost identical nature. To add more units of capital to a given amount of labor causes the total product to increase but at less than a proportionate rate. The marginal productivity of capital is, therefore, determined by the amount which the addition of the last unit of capital adds to the total previous output. Competition among entrepreneurs for capital and capitalists for investment causes this specific and marginal productivity to constitute the rate of interest. If less is offered by an enterpriser than this amount, the capital will be attracted elsewhere by the offers of other enterprisers who will bid the rate of interest up to the point of marginal yield rather than lose the services of the capital entirely. The owner of capital, on the other hand, will not be able to secure more than this sum since the enterprisers will naturally refuse to pay more than such a unit of capital would yield to them. The marginal productivity of capital can, therefore, be written as $\frac{\partial P}{\partial C}$ or the change in product with respect to a change in capital.[38a]

It should be noted, however, that Clark, in his discussion of capital and interest, almost invariably refers to capital in terms of fixed capital, i.e., of machinery, plant, buildings, power houses, railroads, steamships, and the like. Interest is paid because these capital goods aid in turning out more material goods (and hence more utilities) than could be produced without them, and the amount of interest which is paid for their services is determined by the amount of goods (or utilities) which are added by the last unit of capital. This explanation of interest is drawn in terms of those capital instruments which transform and shape material objects, but it does not by itself explain why interest

---

[38a] One of the most interesting of problems in the history of the evolution of economic doctrine and one which will probably always be unsolved is that of what influence, if any, von Thünen had upon Clark. Clark studied economics at Heidelberg and Zurich during the seventies, after his graduation from Amherst College, when there was a great revival of interest in von Thünen. In his preface to the *Distribution of Wealth* (p. vii), he states, however, that he did not read the essential passages in von Thünen bearing on final productivity until many years afterward when he had already developed and published his own theory. The up-rightness of Clark's character has always been such as to make this disavowal proof of the lack of any conscious influence of von Thünen upon Clark.

It is possible, however, that the seed of von Thünen's theory of final productivity may have been dropped in Clark's mind through lectures and economic discussion in Germany and Switzerland, and that it may later have sprouted from the sub-conscious without his being aware of its origin. It is certainly true that German teachers and students of economics have never appreciated the real significance of von Thünen's principle of final productivity as the regulation of the rate of wages and of interest, and that if this principle was mentioned, it would probably have been in a somewhat cloudy and misty form.

Clark in a lengthy note (*Distribution of Wealth*, pp. 321–4) sought to distinguish his theory from that of von Thünen on the ground that the latter believed the principle of final productivity involved the exploitation of the earlier units because their return was reduced by the addition of further units. Clark objected to this implication of exploitation and insisted that his theory recognized that labor and capital each received their "specific" product since "at any one time all units of labor tend to be equally productive." (p. 323). And there is "imputed" to the preceding units according to the Austrian theory of Wieser, what the last unit adds. Clark therefore declared (p. 324) "as von Thünen did not suspect, the natural law of wages gives a result that would satisfy his own requirement, as being *reasonable and morally* justifiable." (italics mine). The difference between Clark's theory and von Thünen's lay, therefore, in the ethical conclusions which each drew from the fact that final productivity in a competitive and capitalistic society governed the rates of wages and of interest rather than in the fact itself. And on this point, Clark, as will be seen from the subsequent discussion in the text, certainly erred in identifying marginal productivity as necessarily identical with what was "desirable and morally justifiable."

For Marshall's great debt to von Thünen see his *Principles*, p. xv and *Memorials to Alfred Marshall* (edited by Pigou), p. 100.

should be paid on circulating capital such as raw materials in the process of manufacture and the wages advanced to the laborers before the product is sold. Clark does not state whether or not he would regard such forms of capital as productive, and indeed ignores them. Yet interest is of course paid upon them as well as upon fixed capital. Why then is this interest paid, and what determines it?

The probable answer which a follower of Clark would tend to give is that the added goods (or utilities) produced or added by the units of fixed capital in a society are distributed over all of the units of capital equally.[39]

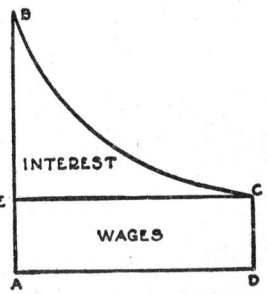

Chart 7. The Distribution of the Joint Product Attributable to Labor and Capital between Wages and Interest. (After J. B. Clark)

Not being a mathematician, Clark resorted in part to a simple graphic device to prove that the marginal product of each factor multiplied by the number of units of each would equal the total product. Thus he illustrated the diminishing increments of product added by successive units of labor, as in Chart 7. The marginal product DC became the wage received by the number of workers AD so that the total amount paid out in wages was the rectangle $ADCE$ while the triangle EBC above this was assigned to interest. Similarly, in measuring the increments of product added by successive units of capital, as in Chart 8, the area representing interest was the rectangle $ADCE$ and that representing wages, the residual triangle EBC. Then Clark declared that the triangle of each chart was equal to the rectangle of the other. Now it is of course true that when rent is not considered, whatever is not wages is interest, and what is not interest is wages. Unless one explicitly assumes however that total product increases proportionately with equal percentage

[39] This would be an interesting parallelism to the Marxian theory of profits. As is well known, Marx held that constant capital (fixed capital plus raw materials) did not yield any surplus value. Only variable capital, or the amount advanced in wages, did this. But it was evident that enterprises with widely differing proportions of constant and variable capital did, nevertheless, give equal rates of interest upon the total capital invested. In the third volume of *Capital*, Marx attempted to explain this by saying that the profits which had been drawn from the variable capital were generalized through the process of competition over all capital as a whole. For a critique of this theory see Böhm-Bawerk, *Karl Marx and the Close of His System;* and W. B. Horace Joseph, *The Labor Theory of Value in Karl Marx.*

increases in all the factors, it is somewhat begging the question to assume that the areas obtained by treating interest both as a determinate share and as a residual should be identical and that the same should also apply in the case of wages. If the assumption mentioned above is not true, then this consequence need not follow.

8. Some Implications of the Marginal Productivity Theory of Distribution

It is important to recognize that Clark's analysis involves a tendency towards equality in the various productive enterprises of the added productivity of the last units of labor and capital. This can be shown by a simple illustration of a community of two farms and five wage-earners of equal ability. On farm A, eight bushels per acre are added by the first worker, seven by the second, six by the third. On Farm B, the respective amounts of added product are seven, six, and five bushels. In bidding for labor, Farm A will be able to secure three of the hired men and Farm B two; the marginal product on both farms will be six bushels, which will be the wage. If farmer B were to try to secure a third worker, he would not find it profitable to offer more than five bushels, and for this amount he would not be able to entice the laborer from Farm A where he could secure six bushels. This may be expressed in agricultural terms by saying that the intensive and extensive margins will tend to coincide.

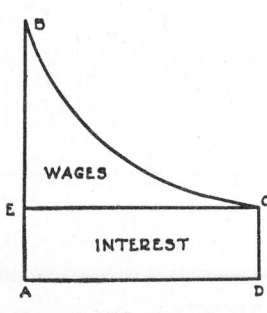

Chart 8. The Distribution of the Joint Product Attributable to Labor and Capital between Interest and Wages. (After J. B. Clark)

In the above illustration we have measured productivity in terms of similar physical units. But how does this tendency of production, to be carried to a common margin, work itself out in industries which produce dissimilar products? The answer is simple, although many eminent economists have missed it. The margin is one of an equal production of *value*. Thus, if a worker in a New England textile mill daily adds an amount of cloth which is equal to four dollars command over economic goods and services, while a worker on a barren hillside farm can only raise a quantity of hay which gives but two dollars command over goods, then to the extent that the farm-hand is an economic man and is not deterred by sentimental considerations, he will enter the textile mills or some such similar enterprise. The margin of production in the mills falls but that on the farm rises, and this readjustment tends to continue until the productivity of the workers in the various industries in terms of the amount of purchasing power over other commodities which they add is approximately equal. The productivity of the workers is, therefore, fundamentally measured in terms of value rather than in terms of physical product.

From this it follows that wages, according to the productivity theory, are fixed at a margin which runs through society as a whole. The relative productivity of the workers of any given plant has but comparatively little influence on this general margin. Thus if the productivity of the major industries were to increase so that the laborers in these industries were each to turn out more products with greater value than before, then wages for farm-hands in New England would also rise (as they have) even though no increase in their relative productivity has taken place. More workers would leave the farms for industry, the margin of cultivation would recede, and the farmers would have to pay more for the laborers whom they retained.

This process would go on until an equalized marginal product in terms of value was established in both lines of industry. This tendency towards an equality of the margin would operate through a dual set of forces. On the one hand, the movement of labor from the farms to the mills would, by diminishing the number of farm workers, increase the marginal physical product on the farms at the same time that the increase in the factory force lowered the marginal physical product in manufacturing. Added to this equilibrating tendency would be the further force of a relative rise in the prices and hence of the exchange value of each unit of farm products and a fall in the prices and exchange values of each unit of manufactured goods. This would necessarily result from the diminution in the quantity of the former which would follow the withdrawal of labor from it and the increase in the quantity of the latter which would result from the expansion of its working force. The increase in the number of physical units produced on the agricultural margin together with the increased exchange value of each unit would then raise the marginal productivity of labor nearer the point of equalized return, while the fall in the number of physical units on the manufacturing margin together with the reduction in the exchange value of each unit would similarly operate to pull down the marginal productivity of labor nearer the general social margin. In a frictionless society this process would go on until returns at the margin were equalized in all industries.[40] It is therefore, not a disproof of the marginal productivity theory, if wages should advance in industries where there has been little improvement in production. This is, on the contrary, precisely what would be expected to occur, if and when the marginal productivity of the country as a whole were to advance. The exchange value of a unit of the product of the backward industry would rise because, *relative to the other commodities* this product would now be more scarce. If this were not sufficient in itself to produce an equality in the production of value at the margin, the flow of labor out of these industrially retarded industries into others would tend to create such an equality.

It might indeed even happen that because of the general increase in production, the relative increase in the demand for the products of the backward industry might so raise their unit values as to elevate the marginal value product of those workers above the general social average and lead to a migration of labor into rather than out of the technically retarded industry.

This tendency for wages to be determined by the social margin of production has been strikingly demonstrated in a recent study of differences in wages between states by Dr. Maurice Leven.[41] When the average annual earnings in agriculture in each state were compared with those in manufacturing, a striking degree of correlation was found. In those states where manufacturing wages were high, agricultural wages were also relatively high, while in those where the manufacturing wage level was low, that for agriculture was low as well. When the averages for mining and manufacturing together are taken, the correlation is even more impressive. The correlation between the wages of males in agriculture and in power laundries is, indeed, almost perfect. This furnishes a strong proof that within any one market there is a tendency for the margin to be approximately the same in all industries. Differences in remuneration

---

[40] One of the most valuable inductive studies which could be made would be to measure (1) the relative changes from time to time in the relative quantities of the various commodities, (2) the relative changes in the *unit* exchange values of these commodities, (3) the changes in the relative total value of these commodities, i.e. the product of (1) multiplied by (2), (4) the net ebb and flow of labor out of and into given industries in the tendency towards an equalized return in the various occupations.

[41] Maurice Leven, *Income in the Various States. Its Sources and Distribution, 1919, 1920, 1921,* Number 7 of the *Publications of the National Bureau of Economic Research,* pp. 84–90.

between different sections of the country can only result from an incomplete mobility of labor which prevents the equalizing process from being carried out to its final limits.

In recent years certain cost accounting studies have, however, shown great differences in *average* cost between enterprises within a given industry. These have been interpreted by some to prove that there is not one margin which runs through all the plants in a given industry, but that production stops at different points in different establishments. These statistics do not in themselves demonstrate any such aberrant tendency, since they merely measure average costs for each particular establishment and not incremental costs within each establishment. It would be possible for firms to have differing average costs, but for the cost of the last unit of the product in each to be identical. This is, indeed, a much more probable interpretation.

In some establishments, for example, costs may begin at a relatively high point, and the margin be soon reached. Average costs will consequently be high. In another firm costs may begin at a low point, may decrease for a time, and then increase but slowly so that a large output will be forthcoming before the margin is reached. In such a plant average costs will be relatively low. The last units of product in both plants will, however, have been produced at the margin.

The same line of reasoning may also explain differences between industries in the average rates of interest and of profits.

It may have been noticed that the marginal analysis which has just been outlined above is primarily in terms of *cost* and not of *output*. If wages were the sole or vastly predominating manufacturing cost, then the process of diminishing returns in terms of physical product would, at the same time, be one of increasing cost in money terms. Wages would be fixed at the margin for society and would consequently be relatively constant for each unit of labor within the individual establishment. Since output per added unit of labor would go down, money costs would necessarily go up.

But this does not necessarily follow in enterprises where the proportion of fixed capital is high and where overhead charges are relatively heavy. If increased output can be obtained even though physical output per worker remains constant, the fixed overhead charges will be distributed over more units, and hence the combined unit cost for labor and overhead will be reduced.

Similarly, this reduction in fixed costs per unit may be more than sufficient to offset the increased labor cost caused by the diminishing physical output per unit of labor. This indicates the error which many writers of text-books have committed in identifying diminishing returns with increasing cost. But the relative advantages from a reduction in overhead charges decline steadily as the output of a plant more and more approaches its maximum capacity and as the relative effect of diminishing physical product and of increasing labor cost becomes more and more important. In these later stages of production, therefore, diminishing physical productivity will come to carry with it, although not in the same ratio, increasing money costs per unit.

A further implication of the productivity analysis which many have been reluctant to admit is that, under the present organization of society, the relative worth of an individual to his employer is measured in terms of the money addition which he makes to the income of the concern rather than in terms of the amount of benefit which he creates for society. Thus, the process of reasoning by which a saloon-keeper decides whether it would be profitable to hire another bartender is precisely the same as that by which a dairyman decides whether he should employ another milkmaid. Each worker will yield less profit to his employer than his predecessor, although, in the one case, the profits will come from producing milk for children and in the other from distributing a beverage which is on the whole socially disadvantageous. There are many men, moreover, who are employed in business who do not even add to the quantity of goods which the public consumes, but who merely enable their employers to maintain or improve their competitive position in comparison with their fellows.[42] A great deal, although not all, of modern advertising is of this nature. Effort is frequently expended in enticing customers away from one's competitors rather than in increasing output [43] or enhancing the real satisfaction of the consumers, and the men who succeed in thus diverting business have a high market value. Added units of advertising ability yield, however, after a time, fewer competitive gains, and the universal law of diminishing returns applies in such activities

[42] See Thorstein Veblen's original paper on *Industrial and Pecuniary Employment*, Publications American Economic Association, reprinted in *The Place of Science in Modern Civilization*. See also Stuart Chase, *The Tragedy of Waste*.

[43] Except in so far as advertising: (1) effects economies through stimulating large scale production and (2) induces men to work longer or harder to satisfy the added wants which it creates.

as well as in farming and in manufacturing.[44] The manager will decide whether he should add an additional advertising man to the staff, and the remuneration of the latter will tend to be fixed by the amount of profit over manufacturing cost which his labor will create. Such a marginal productivity will of course tend to be identical with that in the manufacturing end of the business, for if it were higher than the latter, relatively more money would be spent in advertising, while if it were less, more money would be expended upon hiring workers for manufactures.

Fundamentally, therefore, men are valued according to their ability to produce profits for their employers, and they may do this at the expense of the size and the quality of the national dividend. In the very process of decreasing the total amount to be shared, a worker may enhance his individual portion of that product.

9. The Inclusion of Rent under the Marginal Productivity Theory of Distribution.

According to the classical interpretation of rent, as developed by Ricardo,[45] the return to land was made a differential between the yield of a "dose" of labor and capital on a given unit of land and that on the poorest or marginal land where the yield was just sufficient to pay for the cost' of the labor and capital used. A no-rent margin was therefore assumed, and rent was measured from it by the greater yields of the same quantity of labor and capital. As population and capital increased, the added application of those two factors produced on the already utilized land a less than proportionate return and one which was subject to diminishing physical increments. This forced poorer lands to be utilized where the joint return to the combined "dose" of labor and capital was less. The differences in yield between labor and capital on the new no-rent margin and on the already utilized land became greater, and economic rent therefore increased.[46] Since men would under competition tend to bid for the use of the land up to this differential yield, contract rent was presumed, if a sufficiently long period of time were taken, to approximate economic rent.

---

[44] Because of the over-stimulation of attention, which presumably is another expression of the Weber-Fechner law.

[45] Ricardo, *Principles of Political Economy*, Chapter II.

[46] According to Ricardo rent increased in a double relationship since both (1) the number of bushels of differential yield in comparison with the lower margin increased, and (2) each bushel now had a higher exchange value because of the greater quantity of labor expended upon it at the new, as compared with the old, margin.

Such is the theory of rent which has dominated economic thought for over a century. Although misunderstood by H. C. Carey and by most of the early American school, it never purported to be a historical law. The fact, therefore, that in opening up new continents better land was developed than the average in England and in Europe, did not disprove the analysis. All that the theory stated was that with an available stock of land whose capacities were relatively known, the better land would be used first, and as long as the technique of farming or of urban life did not change the poorer lands would be used subsequently as population rose and capital increased.

If one, however, probes both the theory and the facts of rent somewhat more closely, certain disconcerting difficulties appear. Perhaps the most important of these is the fact that in settled countries true no-rent land is virtually impossible to find. Even the poorest land which is utilized seems normally to "earn" some rent and therefore to have a money value. It is true that part of its money value may be due to the capitalization of rents which are expected to accrue in the future. But this explanation does not seem to be sufficient, and instead there does not seem to be any truly no-rent land. The disappearance of this extensive margin from which rent can be solely measured naturally raises the question whether rent can be said to be wholly a differential when at the supposed no-rent margin it is found to exist. How, it may be asked, can the Ricardian theory explain this basic amount of rent which even the poorest land yields and which to this extent at least is therefore also present in the rent of the better pieces of land?

The advocates of the classical theory reply to this that the differential theory is still adequate if we measure rent from the intensive rather than from the extensive margin. On the poorest land, they assert, the last dose of labor and capital will yield a return which will just meet the cost of those factors and leave no surplus for land as such. There is, therefore, they assert, a no-rent use of labor and capital. This intensive no-rent margin will, as a matter of fact, exist on all types of land as well, although it will naturally occur with much later doses on the better land than on the poorer. As the extensive margin is pushed out so will the intensive margin follow. It will coincide with the extensive margin until, when the latter disappears, the intensive margin will still exist although it may be reached with the second dose of labor and capital on the poorest land, with the tenth on moderately good land, and with the fortieth on the best land of all.

But this apology is a little far-fetched and unnecessary. It is similar to Professor Clark's attempt to find no-rent capital where labor produced all of the product. One might equally well try to find no-rent workers whose entire product could be entirely attributed to capital. This type of analysis then presents such humorists as Professor Stephen Leacock with the opportunity of picturing a no-rent worker with full beard, tottering steps, and palsied arm, swinging a no-rent marginal hammer upon a no-rent anvil as he stands on no-rent barren land far out on the margin of settlement, where the winds are sharp and the outlook bleak and dreary. But unless the output in this lonely outpost were absolutely zero, there would still be the problem of how whatever yield there was could be divided according to the respective contributions of no-rent land, no-rent capital, and no-rent labor! For this would involve the miracle as to how three separate factors, which could contribute nothing when each was taken by itself, could, when combined, produce something. The only sensible answer to this conundrum is, therefore, to deny its major premise, namely, that each of the factors is a no-rent one, and instead to believe that each has probably made some contribution to the product.

The way is then open to explain the basic quantity of rent which runs through all land at a given time on the same principles of marginal productivity which have been used to explain the basic rate of wages and the basic rate of interest. Land is not the only factor, when as it is held constant, the incremental yield will decrease as the other two factors increase. If we hold labor constant and increase land and capital, or hold capital constant and increase land and labor, the same thing will happen. It would, therefore, be almost as foolish to attempt to explain rent only in terms of differences between land, as it would be to explain wages and interest exclusively in this fashion.

The principle of marginal productivity can instead, as Walras, Pareto and Wicksteed [46a] saw, explain this basic rent of land. Thus, if there were 100 acres of land of a uniform quality, 200 man-days of labor, and $4000 worth of farm machinery, horses and equipment, which taken together yielded 2000 bushels of wheat, then the amount which would be attributed to any one acre of land would be the amount by which the product would

---

[46a] See Wicksteed, *An Essay on the Coördination of Distribution*, pp. 20–2.

be diminished by the withdrawal of an acre and the use of the same quantity of labor and capital upon 99 instead of 100 acres of land. If the total yield were now 1996 bushels, then the decrease would be 4 bushels, and the total amount attributed to land and, therefore, ultimately payable in rent would be 396 bushels (i.e. 4×99).[47]

It is now possible to combine both the marginal productivity and the differential theories of rent. The former will determine the return on the poorest type of land used, and, on the proportion which this poorest and basic quality forms of the qualities of the more superior land. The Ricardian or differential theory explains the differences between the rent of this land and of the other and superior varieties.

This bi-furcation of the theory of rent into a dualistic form, in which one branch explains the basic rent and the other the differential, is after all precisely similar to an earlier development in the theory of wages and a somewhat later development in the theory of interest. Adam Smith, for example, saw that it was not only necessary to explain both the basic rate of wages, but also the differences in the rates of wages. Today we may explain both the basic rate of wages and of rent by the principle of marginal productivity, and then frame explanations for the differences from these rates. In the case of rent these differences in return will be caused by differences in productivity. In the case of wages they will tend to be of a triple character, namely, (1) equalizing differences such as those which Smith described, (2) differences caused by imperfect mobility and monopoly privileges such as those which Mill and Cairnes pointed out in connection with non-competing groups, and (3) differences in return resulting from differences in natural ability. In a similar fashion differences in the rates of interest for different types of loans may also be largely explained by differences in risk, together with such impediments to complete mobility as may exist not merely between industries and localities, but perhaps to an even greater degree between short-term and long-term funds.[48]

The theory of rent may, therefore, be brought into a common theory of distribution, namely, that of marginal productivity, instead of being isolated under a differential form of treatment, while wages and interest are explained in terms of marginal

---

[47] For an excellent statement of the marginal productivity theory as applied to land, see Garver and Hansen, *Principles of Economics*, pp. 454–6.
[48] See Riefler, *Money Rates and Money Markets in the United States;* Kock, *A Study of Interest Rates.*

productivity.[49]   The whole problem of different varieties of land as well as of labor can also be approached from an extension of the productivity analysis, as is shown in Section 12 of this chapter.

10. The Coördination of the Theory of Distribution.

Various writers have set themselves to prove not only that the rate of remuneration for each of the factors of production was equal to their respective marginal productivities but also that the whole quantity of the product was exhausted by the payment of these marginal productivities to all of the units of each factor.[50]   Wicksteed,[51] Walras,[52] and Wicksell[53] worked this proof out with precision on the assumption that if all the factors were increased in the same proportion, production would increase in that ratio.   This assumption that production can be described by a simple homogeneous function of the first degree is basic to the reasoning which follows.

Thus if we take all three factors then in order that the payment of marginal productivities should exhaust the total product with no surplus or deficit the following condition will hold, namely:

(1) The marginal productivity of labor multiplied by the number of units of labor plus

(2) the marginal productivity of capital multiplied by the number of units of capital plus

(3) the marginal productivity of land multiplied by the number of units of land would equal

(4) the total product.

This may be written in the form of an equation as follows. Let P represent the total volume of output, $T = $ land, $L = $ labor

---

[49] There still remains in connection with rent the puzzling problem of opportunity cost which Davenport and Knight have treated so suggestively. Is the amount which could be realized from an alternative use of a piece of land a real basic cost which has to be met from the price of the given product? If it is, then rent tends to be even more a marginal cost. If we take each commodity as a separate unit, this argument is exceedingly strong. If we view the process of production as a whole, however, as one which produces utilities, then it is not necessary to have a series of separate margins for the various industries but, instead, a lower basic margin for all industry. This diminishes the marginal element in rent and increases the differential.

[50] It was this which H. M. Thompson was attempting to solve in his *The Theory of Wages* (1892).

[51] P. H. Wicksteed, *The Coördination of the Theory of Distribution* (1894) especially pp. 18–30.

[52] Leon Walras, *Elements d'Economie Politique Pure* (4th edition), 1900, pp. 375–6.

[53] Knut Wicksell, *Vorlesungen über Nationalökonomie*, Erster Band (1913), especially pp. 184–95.

and C = capital. Then $\dfrac{\partial P}{\partial L}$ = the marginal productivity of labor or the change of product with respect to a change in labor. Also $\dfrac{\partial P}{\partial C}$ = the marginal productivity of capital and $\dfrac{\partial P}{\partial T}$ = the marginal productivity of land. Then

$$P = \frac{\partial P}{\partial L} \cdot L + \frac{\partial P}{\partial C} \cdot C + \frac{\partial P}{\partial T} \cdot T. [54]$$

Mathematical proofs for this formula have been developed amongst the economists [55] by Walras, Wicksteed, and Schultz.[56] Wicksell has expressed this formula in a very simple fashion by dealing with production as though it were a function of only two factors, namely, land and labor.[57] The same principles would of course hold if the third factor, capital, were added. Wicksell starts with an illustration of where 100 laborers are employed on 100 acres of land. Then if one laborer and one acre of land are each added so that we now have 101 of each, the product is, under a homogeneous linear function of the first degree also increased by one per cent. These additions are apparently taken as roughly equivalent to infinitesimal increments. Now let l = the marginal productivity of labor $\left(\text{i.e. } \dfrac{\partial P}{\partial L} \right)$ and r, the marginal productivity of land $\left(\text{i.e. } \dfrac{\partial P}{\partial T} \right)$ with P equalling the total product then

$$l + r = \frac{1}{100} P$$

$$l + r = \frac{P}{100}$$

$$P = 100\, l + 100\, r$$

Here, therefore, is expressed again the condition that the payment to all the units of each factor of the marginal productivity

---

[54] If one wished to deal with separate commodities which we may designate by a, b, c, etc., and designate the product of each as P_a, P_b, P_c, etc., then

$$P_a = \frac{\partial P_a}{\partial L} \cdot L + \frac{\partial P_a}{\partial C} \cdot C + \frac{\partial P_a}{\partial T} \cdot T$$

$$P_b = \frac{\partial P_b}{\partial L} \cdot L + \frac{\partial P_b}{\partial C} \cdot C + \frac{\partial P_b}{\partial T} \cdot T, \textit{etc.}$$

[55] For those who would like to see the generalized proof under Euler's theorem see for example E. B. Wilson, *Advanced Calculus*, pp. 107–08.

[56] Henry Schultz, "Marginal Productivity and the General Pricing Process," *Journal of Political Economy*, Vol. XXXVII (October, 1929), pp. 542–45.

[57] Wicksell, *Vorlesungen über Nationalökonomie*, pp. 187–88.

of the last unit results in the precise exhaustion of the total product.

All this is however based upon the assumption that production is carried on under constant returns if all factors change in an equal ratio and that it can be described as a simple homogeneous function of the first degree. This we already have seen is the most probable condition if we abstract from a change in the industrial arts. Under these conditions the sum of the exponents for land (T) and labor (L) would be equal to unity or 1.0. For the moment these can be designated as k and 1 — k.

If production is not a homogeneous linear function of the first degree then the summation of (a) the marginal productivities of each factor when multiplied by (b) the number of units of that factor will not equal the total product.[58]

If, for example, production should be characterized by increasing returns so that the added units of land and labor (and capital) would yield larger proportionate quantities of product, then under these conditions the marginal productivities of each factor multiplied by the number of units would when summated exceed the total product and the sum of the exponents would exceed 1.0 or unity.

This may be written as follows:

$$\frac{\partial P}{\partial L} \cdot L + \frac{\partial P}{\partial T} \cdot T > P$$

Here, however, there would be distributed to the factors of production more than was produced. It is hard to attach definite economic meaning to this, and it certainly cannot be a permanent condition. It would mean heavy losses to the enterprises and as Wicksell points out, following Cournot, would lead to the disappearance of competition and the coming of monopoly. This would be capitalistic chaos.

If the production equation were such that decreasing returns prevailed when all of the factors were increased and production did not increase as rapidly as these factors, then the sum of the exponents would be less than 1.0 or unity. Under these conditions

$$\frac{\partial P}{\partial L} \cdot L + \frac{\partial P}{\partial T} \cdot T <. P$$

The whole product would therefore not be distributed to the factors, and there would be large surplus profits. Everyone

---

[58] Wicksell, *op. cit.*, p. 189.

would want to obtain these, and this, as Wicksell pointed out, would lead to the break-up of industry into many small units and individual enterprises. This also would follow from the principle of increasing costs.

It is thus seen again then that there is no occasion for any violent scorn, such as Edgeworth once displayed, about the principle that if all the factors are increased in a given proportion, production will increase in that proportion. On the contrary that seems to be by far the most probable relationship, if we keep technical change constant. Under these conditions, the total product will, as we have shown, be precisely exhausted by the free working of the principle of marginal productivity.

11. The Substitution of One Factor For Another.

A final step in the coördination of the theory of distribution was effected when it was shown that business could and did substitute one factor for another.[59] If a dollar expended in wages for labor yielded a smaller increment to the product than a dollar spent for the use of capital instruments, then more of the latter would be used and less of the former, and this process would continue until the productive effects of the last units of money spent for labor and for capital were equal. In a similar fashion the last unit of money spent for the use of natural resources would have the same influence on production as the marginal units expended on the other two factors.

This equivalence at the margin of the productive powers of monetary units is indeed comparable to the tendency for the last units of money which a consumer spends on various commodities to yield equal utilities to him, and that if they do not do so, he will so apportion his expenditures in his effort to maximize his satisfactions that they will come to give him equality of satisfaction.[60]

The fact that there is an equality in the productive work effected by the marginal dollars expended for the various factors does not mean, however, that there is any necessary equality in the amount of output obtained by the earlier dollars which were spent for these purposes. Even though the curves of output in relation to expenditure upon the factors are equal at their respective terminal points, it does not follow that their points of origin or their previous course were identical.

Nor does it follow that because the marginal effectiveness of

[59] Stuart Wood and Alfred Marshall were among the first to point this out.
[60] This, of course, does not mean that there is any necessary equivalence *between* individuals in the amounts of satisfaction which they obtain.

the last units of money expenditures upon each of the three factors is equal, the amount of sacrifice embodied in the quantities of land, labor, and capital for which equal sums were paid must be equal. Natural resources in themselves entail no sacrifices, and the savings of the wealthy probably do not require as much sacrifice as the continuing labor through time of unskilled laborers.[61]

Recently two able English economists in the person of J. R. Hicks[62] and Joan Robinson[63] have given greater precision to the measurement of the tendency to substitute one factor for another. This has been done through the concept of the relative elasticity of substitution. By this is meant the degree to which a relative change in the rate of remuneration of one factor will lead to a given alteration of the relative quantities which will be combined with the other factors. Thus if the same ratios of labor and capital, for example, are combined together irrespective of the rate of return to either, the elasticity of substitution of one for the other is equal to zero. If, on the other hand, "the smallest fall in wages (the cost of capital remaining the same) were to cause the whole output to be produced by labour alone, the elasticity of substitution would be infinite."[64] Should a given fall in wages such as 1 per cent cause the quantity of labor which is mixed with capital to be increased in the same proportion or by 1 per cent and if a rise in wages results in an equal proportionate decline in the quantity of labor which is thus mixed, then we can say that the elasticity of substitution is equal to 1.0 or unity. If such a change in wages is accompanied by a more than proportionate change in the quantity of labor substituted for the other factors then the elasticity of substitution is greater than 1.0 or unity, and if by a less than proportionate change in its quantity the elasticity is less than unity.

Mr. Hicks points out that if the elasticity of substitution is greater than unity, then a fall in its unit return will cause proportionately more units to be utilized and will hence increase the aggregate returns to that factor and also its relative share in the total national income. This last point would however only invariably follow if the number of units of the other

[61] Thus Cairnes was demonstrably wrong in asserting that the average "pain cost" to savers for each dollar of interest received was necessarily equal to the average "pain cost" to workers for each dollar of wages paid. See Cairnes, *Leading Principles of Political Economy Newly Expounded*, p. 87.
[62] J. R. Hicks, *The Theory of Wages*, pp. 117–20.
[63] Joan Robinson, *The Economics of Imperfect Competition*, pp. 256, 330.
[64] Robinson, *op. cit.*, p. 257.

factor were so decreased at the same time as to make the total product (national income) the same as before. Under these conditions an increase in the supply of such a factor would, by causing a reduction in its unit price, lead to such a substitution of the factor in question for the other factors, as to send up its relative share in the total product.

When the elasticity of substitution is however equal to unity, then since changes in wages will merely give rise to equal proportionate substitutions of quantities, the aggregate return of labor will be the same and if the total produce remained constant, then the share of labor would also be constant. Hicks has developed this point further by pointing out [65] that in this case "the increase in one factor will raise the marginal product of all other factors taken together in the same proportion as the total product is raised."

When the elasticity of substitution is less than unity, a lowering in unit return by not calling forth an equal proportionate substitution will entail a smaller aggregate and with a fixed total product, a decreased relative share. The effect of an increased supply of the factor under these conditions would be to decrease the relative share of that factor and to increase the marginal productivities of the other factors by more than the increase in the total product to raise their shares.

This concept and the method of measuring the substitution of one factor for another undoubtedly gives greater precision to the theory of marginal productivity. Those who have developed it seem however to have neglected certain very important points which at once limit its applicability and make its real measurement more complicated than it seems at first sight.

(1) In the first place, the total quantities of labor and capital available at any one time, while not absolutely fixed, are comparatively so and this as we shall see is particularly the case with capital. While therefore there is a great possibility in any particular enterprise or industry of substituting one factor for another, this possibility is, under conditions of full employment, not great for industry as a whole. If there is appreciable unemployment of labor or large quantities of unemployed capital, then to be sure business can pick and choose by substituting one for the other. But when both factors are employed fairly fully then the choice of alternatives is greatly lessened. At

[65] Hicks, *op. cit.*, p. 117.

any one time therefore the general elasticity of substitution is not as great as Mr. Hicks' writings would seem to imply.

(2) Second, the question as to the effect which the increase of a factor will have upon its unit, its aggregate, and its relative return as well as upon those phases of the return to the other factors will not depend solely or perhaps even primarily upon the relative elasticities of substitution. On the contrary the elasticities of the curves of diminishing incremental product and the relative elasticities of supply would seem to be the more decisive influences. For clearly when a factor increases, the rate at which the unit returns fall will be primarily determined by the elasticity of its marginal productivity curve. If this is elastic then the decrease in the return per unit will be less than the relative increase in the number of units and the total received by the factor will be greater, while the opposite will hold if the elasticity of the marginal productivity curve is less than unity.

Similarly changes in the return per unit may give rise to changes in the quantities of the factors which are supplied and this will affect both the total quantities produced and the ratios at which the factors are combined. We can therefore no more neglect the respective elasticities of supply than we can those of marginal productivity. Not only is the concept of the elasticity of substitution, therefore, only one of the forces determining the relative returns to the factors, but it would also seem to involve in itself some consideration of these other two elasticities.

12. How Can the Theory of Marginal Productivity Be Broadened to Include Various Kinds of Labor, Capital, and Land?

Some will object to the way in which the theory of production has been developed on the ground that it has treated labor, capital, and land as though each were composed of homogeneous and mutually interchangeable units. In practise the qualities of different groups of laborers differ widely, and it is not possible completely to interchange one unit with another both because of innate differences and because of social and economic stratification which impedes the free movement of labor. Similarly the qualities of land differ and though there are not social barriers in the way of transfer and interchange, there are the differences of fertility and location. Capital is the most interchangeable of all and while the different forms in which it is embodied differ widely there is a tendency through depreciation, replacement, and fresh investment, to bring the various capital instruments up to a common level of effectiveness.

Now there are two ways of dealing with these differences in quality, lack of homogeneity, and interchangeableness. One is that outlined in section 9 of this chapter, namely, to explain basic returns to the factors according to the principles of marginal productivity and then to explain the differences in wages, interest, and rent in terms of such forces as lack of mobility, differences in risk, and differences in quality.

Another way is to apply the principles of marginal productivity to these sub-groups. Instead of treating Labor (L) as an entity we could divide this into as many sub-divisions, such as L_1, L_2, L_3, $\ldots\ldots L_n$, as there were separate sub-groups. Each of these sub-groups would, however, be homogeneous within itself, and its units would be interchangeable. The same could be done for land, and instead of T we would have T_1, T_2, T_3, T_4, $\ldots\ldots T_n$. Whether or not it would be necessary to sub-divide Capital (C) into such groups is not certain. Marginal productivities of labor would thus be the change of product with respect to the changes in these various groups of labor (i.e., $\dfrac{\partial P}{\partial L_1}$, $\dfrac{\partial P}{\partial L_2}$, $\dfrac{\partial P}{\partial L_3}$, $\dfrac{\partial P}{\partial L_4}$), and the same would be true of land. Then if each one of these various groups were to increase by 1 per cent, product would tend to increase by 1 per cent just as would be the case if we were dealing with only three factors. In this case the sum of (a) the marginal productivities multiplied by (b) the number of units in each of the sub-groups would exhaust the total product. Thus

$$\frac{\partial P}{\partial L_1} L_1 + \frac{\partial P}{\partial L_2} L_2 + \cdots\cdots + \frac{\partial P}{\partial L_n} L_n + \frac{\partial P}{\partial C_1} C_1 + \frac{\partial P}{\partial C_2} C_2 + \cdots\cdots$$

$$+ \frac{\partial P}{\partial C_n} C_n + \frac{\partial P}{\partial T_1} T_1 + \frac{\partial P}{\partial T_2} T_2 + \cdots\cdots + \frac{\partial P}{\partial T_n} T_n = P$$

This is a convenient way of dealing with the theoretical issues involved. In practise, it would at present be almost impossible to differentiate between the various classes of labor and to mark out the bounds of each, and there would be similar difficulty with land. For the present, therefore, this concept does not seem promising as a practical method of attack upon concrete sets of data. This line of approach is therefore at the moment "non-operational." If and when the statistical data can be classified in those terms, it should be experimented with as a more refined type of analysis.

13. Some Criticisms of the Productivity Theory Answered

One of the finest spirits in modern life, in the person of Mr. J. A. Hobson, has attacked the marginal productivity theory on the ground that it assumes an almost infinite divisibility of labor, whereas in practice men are hired in groups.[66] Hobson concludes from this that the doctrine cannot hold. Yet even if workers are engaged in groups, such a group would be only an infinitesimal increment for a corporation such as the United States Steel Company and certainly would only be such in all society as a whole. And as I have pointed out, it is precisely in industry as a whole that the margin is fixed. No sensible advocate of the theory claims that it applies with absolute precision, but merely that there is a pronounced tendency for wages to adjust themselves in fairly close proximity to the margin.

Another criticism which is commonly advanced is the contention that all production is carried on by the co-operation of labor, capital, and management and that this is as true of the last unit of labor as of the first. Since the marginal laborer works with capital, the product cannot be apportioned to labor alone. Similarly, since the last unit of capital also operates in conjunction with labor, it is said to be incorrect to ascribe the net addition of product to capital alone. All of the product is joint; that of the marginal units of labor and capital as well as of the non-marginal units. It is said, therefore, that it is as futile to attempt to find the specific productivity of any one factor of production as it is to determine which leg of a three legged stool supports the stool.[67] There is a certain surface merit to this criticism since the factors of production are irretrievably bound together, and it is perhaps impossible to determine with absolute accuracy just what the precise cause for the product may be. But the real problem which is raised by the marginal productivity theory is not that of determining which of the factors produces the product when all work together, but rather what would happen if a unit of any one were taken away.

It was this very difficulty which in all probability led Clark

---

[66] J. A. Hobson, *The Industrial System*, pp. 106–14 and *Work and Wealth*, pp. 172–4.

[67] See Hobson, "The Marginal Theory of Distribution. A Reply to Professor Carver," *Journal of Political Economy*, Vol. 13 (1905), pp. 587–90.

to introduce the celebrated "zone of indifference" into his theory. Carrying over the suggestion of Ricardo and Henry George of a no-rent margin of land, the product upon which furnished the basis for measuring the product of labor and of fixing wages, Clark declared that there was such a "marginal region" [68] in manufacturing industry as well. "There are," he declared, in a famous passage,[69] "mills and furnaces so antiquated, so nearly worn out, or so badly located, that their owners get nothing from them, and yet they run so long as superintendents can earn their salaries and ordinary workers their natural wages. There are machines that have outlived their usefulness to their owners, but still do their work and give the entire product that they help to create to the men who operate them. Everywhere, in indefinite variety and extent, are no-rent instruments, and, if labor uses them, it gets the entire product of the operation." Clark then goes on to state that such no-rent instruments are numerous because "every tool, machine, building, vehicle or other auxiliary of labor that wears out by use must, in the course of its deterioration, necessarily reach a point at which it yields no net gain to its owner." [70]

But there is an intensive "no-rent" zone of indifference as well as the extensive zone which has been described. "If, in each of the general groups into which society is organized for the purposes of production, as many men as one for every hundred can be added to the working force or taken from it, without necessistating any change in the outfit of tools, machines, materials, etc., that they use, this fact is sufficient to furnish a certain theoretical basis for a law of wages. Any one man in a force of a hundred may, then, leave his own employer without injuring or benefiting the employer. There is, it thus appears, what we may call a zone of indifference in the field of employment that each entrepreneur controls." [71]

Thus the course of diminishing returns in Professor Clark's concept does not continue to slope steadily downward but after a given point its progress is arrested and it then extends parallel to the base for an appreciable distance before it again moves downward. This rather broad plateau is the zone of indifference. That Professor Clark believed this plateau was of considerable extent is evidenced by the other terms, such as "area" and

[68] *The Distribution of Wealth*, p. 92.
[69] *Ibid.*, p. 96.
[70] *The Distribution of Wealth*, p. 97.
[71] *The Distribution of Wealth*, pp. 101–2.

"field," which he suggested for it.[72] On this plateau any product that was produced was the result of labor's efforts alone and was received by labor alone. The value product is not joint for the worthless capital instruments make no contribution and hence receive no return. The specific productivity of labor can, therefore, here be isolated without contamination from the other factors of production.

The existence of such a zone has been challenged by later writers. Why, it is asked, will an employer continue to use such relatively worthless tools which are not earning any return and why will he employ laborers upon whose labor no profit is made?

Clark's answer to the first query is that such no-rent capital instruments do exist and to the second that "it is of no appreciable importance to him (the employer) whether such men work or not." [73] Once a worker is hired, humanitarian considerations plus the natural inertia of mankind are sufficient to retain the worker in this zone, although no surplus is being made from his toil.

It may well be doubted whether, in such a frictionless economic society as Professor Clark posits for his theory as a whole, any such broad zone would exist. If, in such a society, a capital instrument yielded absolutely nothing, would it not be discarded? Would laborers be hired or retained if the entire product which they added were turned over to them? Such reasoning would seem to be conclusive that in the society which Professor Clark posits there would be no such wide area, and would seem to indicate that such a margin would be a "point" rather than a "zone." Below this point, production would not logically go, and above it, the productive instruments would be used.

Yet it may be argued that in practice such a "zone" does exist. As Alfred Marshall has pointed out, the return upon capital which has once been invested is determined by price rather than, itself, determining price. The returns upon some investments, therefore, do not equal the market rate of return which, at the time of investment, was expected as the minimum yield. Such return as the owners secure is in the nature of a quasi-rent and may fall so low as actually to reach zero in some

---

[72] The fact that he declared the no-rent instruments existed "in indefinite variety and extent" (*Distribution of Wealth*, p. 96), is a further indication that he thought the "zone of indifference" was in fact a zone and not a point.

[73] *The Distribution of Wealth*, p. 105.

years and to give a negative return in others. Investors and entrepreneurs may endure this for a time in the hope that a surplus will ultimately be secured. But it is difficult to conceive businesses continuing or machines perpetuated, which over any reasonable space of time yield absolutely no returns to their owners. Sooner or later they will be forced out, and either specific machines will be installed which will turn over some surplus, however small, or the machinery will be allowed to wear out and will not be replaced. If the machines while yielding no surplus do provide for depreciation (as Clark seems to assume) then these sums will tend to be transferred to other industries. In any event, that particular class of no-rent machines would not continue to exist for long, except as a reserve to meet "peak" loads. For all these reasons, therefore, it does not seem probable that there is any large area in which labor normally operates without the aid of capital. Consequently, Clark's attempt to escape from the problem of the joint creation of product by both labor and capital and to establish an absolute separate identity for the product of labor as distinguished from that of capital has largely failed.

But the validity of the marginal productivity theory is not dependent upon identifying the precise commodities which are produced by the unaided efforts of labor. This has always been seen by the mathematical school, as well as by such literary economists as Professor Carver. Thus Carver, in describing the effect which added "doses" of nitrogen might have upon the total product, deals with this objection as follows:[74] "The essential thing to consider is how much could a farmer afford to pay for a given quantity of nitrogen to be used in a given combination? It is obvious that this must depend on the way it would affect the crop. How much more wheat could he grow by using more nitrogen or how much less would he grow by using less? There is no question more practical than that."

Such reasoning, of course, holds good for labor as well as for capital, as Professor Carver later goes on to show: "When it is suggested," he writes, "that each factor of production should be paid for in proportion to its contribution to the product, any student who does not understand the law of variable proportions is likely to say that there is no way of finding out what each factor contributes. He will say, for example, that it is like trying to find out how much of the cutting is done by the

---

[74] T. N. Carver, *Principles of Political Economy*, pp. 376-7.

upper and how much by the lower blade of the scissors. To use this comparison is to show that one does not understand the problem. If one blade of the scissors were a little longer than the other, it would not require any so-called metaphysical or theoretical reasoning to see that the scissors might be improved by lengthening the shorter blade. If two workmen were to offer their services, one to lengthen the longer blade and one to lengthen the shorter blade, it would not take much of a theoretician to decide which workman it would be better to hire. The workman who would lengthen the shorter blade would add somewhat more to the cutting power of the scissors than the workman who would lengthen the longer blade." [75]

In practice, therefore, all that it is necessary to maintain is that the employer will: (1) "Impute," as Wieser has said,[76] to the last unit of labor the addition in the product which has resulted from its presence, (2) "impute" to all previous units of labor the amount of value which this added equal unit of labor has added for him.

The productivity of capital is "imputed" in a similar fashion by attributing to each of the homogeneous units the amount added to the total product by the last unit.

A further caution is, however, needed here. The amount which is imputed is not the amount by which the total product would be decreased if all of the units of the factor in question were entirely withdrawn, but only the quantity which would be lost if a given increment were withdrawn. This error lies behind much of Hobson's [77] criticism of the theory and leads to grotesque results when such persons as W. H. Mallock, for example, declare that one factor, such as ability, should receive the difference between what is produced with it and what could be produced without it. In a similar fashion both labor and capital could each claim, as their advocates frequently have done, virtually the entire product!

Another objection which is frequently advanced against the

[75] Carver, *op. cit.*, p. 383.

[76] F. von Wieser, *Natural Value,* especially pp. 74–5; 92–3; 161–2.

[77] See his query: "Put the experiment upon its broadest footing. . . . Take the labor, capital, and land as consisting of single doses each; now withdraw the dose of labour and the whole service of capital and land disappears. Is the destruction of the whole product a right measure of the productivity of the labour-dose alone?" *The Economics of Distribution,* p. 147. Professor Edgeworth retorts to this: "Imagine an analogous application of the differential calculus in physics 'put upon its broadest footing' an objector substituting X whenever a mathematician had used dx or $\Delta x!$" F. Y. Edgeworth, *Papers Relating to Political Economy,* Vol. 1, pp. 19–20.

productivity theory is that wages in specific occupations tend to be fixed by custom and pressure rather than by the relative increments of product added by the last worker. That there is a great deal of truth in this contention is obvious. But what these objectors largely ignore is the fact that when once the wages are fixed, marginal productivity tends to determine the number of workers who will be employed. If the wage is above the previous marginal productivity, some workers will tend either to be dropped or not replaced so that under the new adjustment, the marginal productivity will tend, over a period of time, to equal the wage. Conversely, if the rate of wages were fixed at a point below the marginal productivity of the last worker, there would be a real profit in hiring more workers and this would tend to continue until the marginal productivity had been lowered to the level of the wage rate. Therefore, even when forces other than marginal productivity fix the initial wage, marginal productivity would tend to determine the number who would be employed at these wages.[78]

There then remains the question whether these wages varying from occupation to occupation and from industry to industry because of habit and relative pressures will tend to be brought into uniformity with each other. Custom and force are of course powerful barriers to overcome, but to the degree to which labor is uniform in quality and transferable, there is a strong tendency towards the establishment of a uniform marginal productivity for society as a whole. For workers will tend to move out of regions, crafts, and industries where the marginal productivity is relatively low into the lines of work where it is relatively high. This will operate towards bringing the respective marginal productivities into relative correspondence with each other. Complete coincidence will of course not be established everywhere because of ignorance and inertia, unduly long periods of preparation, and, in a few cases, outright force; but this tendency will still always be present and at work.

It is also sometimes asked how we know that the productivity of the preceding workers has declined merely because of the addition of the last laborer. There are two answers which can be given to this query: (1) that since the quantity of labor has increased and that of capital has remained constant, each

---

[78] For some pertinent comments on this point see D. H. Robertson's essay on "Wage Grumbles," in his *Economic Fragments*, pp. 42–57. I have also profited from suggestions made by Aaron Director.

unit of labor will now have less capital with which to work than before and that consequently while it may be laboring as hard as before, it is only proper to hold that its "productivity" has declined because it is joined with less capital. (2) But the query may still be raised as to how we know that the productivity of the preceding units fell simultaneously by the exact amount of the difference between the old and the new margin. Here we can say that it is only logical to assume that of units which are interchangeable one for another, one is no more "productive" than any other, and that the product which depends upon the presence or absence of *any* worker of similar quality is no more than the product of the marginal man. And if this be objected to as being merely an act of faith, then one can only rejoin that in practice employers will tend to "pay" to the preceding units of labor the amount added by the last labor, and they will not "pay" any more.

The marginal productivity theory is in fact merely an explanation of the way in which wages and interest are determined in a competitive and capitalistic society. It is not an ethical justification of what distribution "ought" to be. Many of its advocates have done it a disservice by erecting it into a moral apology for things as they are and have thereby aroused an understandable emotional revulsion against its validity as an analysis of how things happen. But these false claims on its behalf should not blind us to the power of its analysis.

CHAPTER III

THE POSTULATES OF THE MARGINAL PRODUCTIVITY THEORY

1. The Explicit Assumptions of the Marginal Productivity Theory

The marginal productivity theory requires a number of conditions for its complete working out, and much of its value as an explanation of the actual course of wages, interest, and rent depends indeed upon the degree to which these assumed conditions are actually present. Some of these assumptions are explicitly stated by Clark and his fellow-proponents of the theory, while others are more unconsciously implicit than openly formulated in the doctrine.

Clark, himself, took great pains to point out that the theory which he advanced was applicable in its pure form only in a static society. This static state was one where, (1) population was neither increasing nor decreasing, (2) where capital was constant, (3) where there was no change in the industrial arts, (4) where the existing forms of industrial establishments were maintained without alteration, and finally (5) where there was no change in demand.[1] Such a static state is strikingly similar to the concept of the stationary state adumbrated by Ricardo and envisaged by John Stuart Mill as the terminus of economic development. It is indeed a state in which there is no motion or change and where the future but repeats the past.[2]

Such abstractions are more rigid than is necessary, for the theory would have validity under less heroic restrictions. Thus, a change in the relative demand for products would readjust the margins in specific industries, but it is doubtful whether it would affect to any appreciable degree the general margin of

[1] See J. B. Clark, *The Distribution of Wealth*, p. 56. *Essentials of Economic Theory*, pp. 132–3.
[2] Economics has, I believe, been done a disservice by the tendency on the part of many theorists to identify a state of equilibrium with the absence of motion. The real essence, it seems to me, lies in the tendency towards equalized return in the several fields, and this force will be one of the governors even though the quantities of the factors and of commodities may be changing and the nature of wants altering. It is possible, in other words, to have a moving equilibrium.

the production of values or of utilities to the consumer. The keeping of both the labor force and the fund of capital constant is also unnecessarily cautious. The neo-classical economists, led by Marshall and Taussig, have adopted the method of concomitant variation which J. S. Mill described in his *Logic*. One factor may with propriety be increased or decreased if only the other factors are held constant. With the general abandonment of the "zone of indifference" by modern productivity theorists, this is indeed the only method that can be used to impute productivity either to labor or to capital. Moreover, marginal productivity may be measured when the quantities of both labor and capital are increasing, but at divergent rates.

2. **The Implicit Assumptions of the Marginal Productivity Theory**

There are other assumptions, however, in the productivity theory which deserve to be considered at some length. The most important of these are:

(1) That employers are able to measure and to estimate in advance the added productivity which will accompany the application of further units of labor.

(2) That there is free and complete competition among the employers for labor. Even though the marginal productivity of labor can be measured, laborers may be paid less than this margin if there is not competition among the employers for their services.

(3) That labor knows its marginal productivity. The productivity theorists sometimes seem to assume that the laborers as well as the employers know what they can produce at the margin and consequently will ask for it. It may, however, be contended that the implications of the productivity analysis would be satisfied if the employers alone knew approximately what were the actual increments added by labor and were then to bid against each other for the services of the laborers.

(4) That there is free and complete competition among the wage-earners for work. This is one of the forces depended upon to bring wages down to the point of marginal productivity. If some of the workers are paid more than this sum, others will offer their services at a figure which will be less than this higher wage, although still above that of the margin. But if the workers combine together to demand a wage higher than that secured at the margin and if they adhere to their demands,

those who continue to be employed may well be successful in obtaining it. According to the productivity theory, however, this would cause the employers to lay off that number of men, the value of whose product would be less than the wage paid. These unemployed workers, it is then said, will, by offering themselves in the labor market, bring wages back to the point of original marginal productivity.

(5) That capital is mobile and able to be transferred from industry to industry and from place to place.[3]

(6) That labor is freely mobile and able to transfer itself from industry to industry and from place to place.

(7) That all labor finds employment. One of the most remarkable features about the theoretical work of both the classical and neo-classical schools has been their failure to recognize the possibility of unemployment. In their desire to disprove the "heresy" of overproduction, they have tended to ignore the fact which the advocates of overproduction have sought to explain, namely, that of unemployment. Intent upon demonstrating that the production of goods constitutes the demand for goods (which under a barter economy is the case) they have tended to satisfy themselves by showing that it is, therefore, impossible for widespread unemployment to exist. Until the last decade, the business cycle has been viewed by the "orthodox" economists as an excrescence upon business activity rather than as a tendency which is organically a part of it.[4]

The productivity theorists and the neo-classical school have treated unemployment as resulting solely from the attempt of labor to secure a higher wage than their product at the margin, and as only operating as the mechanism by which the workers' demands were forced down to the point where the employers would be justified in hiring them. The possibility that it might lead to the workers offering their services for less than their marginal product was seldom considered.

Whatever, therefore, may be the condition in the real world of affairs, the productivity theory is based upon the assumption that there is work for all, and that all who really want work and are able to perform it and who are willing to work for the marginal wage are employed. Thus the marginal productivity of labor is made identical with the marginal productivity of

---

[3] See Walter Bagehot, *The Postulates of Political Economy*, especially the essay on "The Transferability of Capital."

[4] See for example the cursory treatment given this subject by so great an economist as Alfred Marshall. *Principles of Economics* (6th Edition), pp. 710–11.

employed labor. There is no idle fringe of labor whose productivity is nil.

(8) That all capital is employed. In orthodox theory there is no more room for unemployed capital than for unemployed labor. All capital is actively at work in production, save that which has been discarded or lost and has consequently ceased to be capital, or that which is temporarily out of use because of the attempt to secure a higher rate of interest than its marginal unit adds. There is indeed in the classical theory no realistic explanation as to why capital instruments which are in good repair should be employed at one time and should be idle at another. The fact that many industries are so over-equipped with fixed capital that a large proportion lies idle even in periods of prosperity has been similarly ignored by the main theorists of the orthodox tradition. In consequence of all this the main stream of marginal productivity theory has made the marginal productivity of capital virtually synonymous with the marginal productivity of employed capital.

(9) That the bargaining powers of labor are equal to those of the owners of "capital" and those of the entrepreneurs. Much of this equality results from the previous assumptions. A world in which laborers would have full and complete knowledge of market and production processes, where they would be completely mobile, where they need not fear unemployment, and where their employers were actively competing for labor would be indeed a world in which they could bargain on relatively even terms with their employers. A final and added factor, however, which might well be of some importance would be the relative amount of financial reserves which the two parties to the bargain possessed. This would be of importance when the two groups dealt with each other collectively, as well as when individual members of their respective groups contracted with each other.

(10) That conditions in the labor market and the terms of the wage agreement are left to the mutual decisions of laborers and employers. Laissez-faire is, in other words, assumed as the normal condition, and the state as a body with compulsory powers is not presumed to interfere.[5]

3. Dynamic Possibilities

Such are the assumptions which lie behind the productivity theory. But since the primary purpose of economic theory

---

[5] Save possibly to restore or maintain the conditions of freedom which have been assumed for the other factors.

should be to explain actual life, it is appropriate to ask how correct these assumptions are as a description of the economic forces which are at work in the United States and Canada, in Great Britain and in western Europe? If they do not afford a correct picture of reality, by how much are they out of focus and to what degree are the results of the productivity theory thereby invalidated? To a consideration of the relative truth or falsity of these assumptions, we now turn.

Let us consider, in the first place, the degree to which dynamic changes resulting from changes in wages may invalidate the static assumptions which are basic in Professor Clark's theory.

(1) An increase in wages may increase the efficiency of labor. This theory has been ably expounded by Brentano,[6] Schultze-Gaevernitz,[7] and by Schoenhof.[8] Higher wages, it is urged, will enable the worker to secure more nourishing food and hence give out more work. For those who are close to the subsistence point this is probably true. The marginal productivity theorist would probably reply to such an argument by saying that such an increase in wages could only have been made permanent by an increase in productivity. The remuneration per unit of work has not ultimately increased, but the workers are now merely capable of turning out more units. But while this might be true, it should be remembered that the increase in wages would have come first and would have initiated the dynamic changes which made the higher daily wage permanently possible.

It is doubtful, however, whether an increase in wages would serve to increase the output of those workers who had already secured a fairly comfortable standard of living. Physical and mental efficiency would already have been attained by this group, and while an increase would add to their enjoyments it would not add materially, if at all, to their yearly output. It might indeed even lessen it. They would be able to earn the same amount of income in less time than before and, if their standard of life were relatively stationary, they would be likely, as we shall see, to work fewer days and to absent themselves more. They would be tempted to take their increased income in the form of leisure rather than in that of more economic goods

[6] Lujo Brentano, *Hours and Wages in Their Relation to Production.*
[7] G. von Schultze-Gaevernitz, *Der Grossbetrieb* (1892).
[8] Jacob Schoenhof, *The Economy of High Wages.*

and services. Thus per capita yearly productivity would decrease. But though fewer hours would probably be worked during each year, the productivity per hour might well rise so that yearly output would by no means necessarily decrease in the same proportion as working time.

(2) An increase in wages may increase the efficiency of industry. Few or no businesses are conducted at the maximum efficiency which they can attain, or that which is postulated by rigid productivity theorists. An increase in wages may stimulate employers to reduce waste and to install more efficient methods in order to avert the increase in cost which would otherwise follow. Those skeptical of such a possibility may inquire why these improvements had not taken place before. Would not the businesses, they urge, previously have profited by making these changes, and would not this incentive have been sufficient to have already led to their adoption?

Such reasoning, however, is based upon the concept of the omniscient and untiring economic man. In practice, most business men have a considerable amount of inertia and are loath to disturb old methods save under pressure. Competition with other business firms is, of course, one such type of pressure, but only one. If one's competitors are in the main also lethargic and are also wedded to antiquated methods of management and production, then such an impetus is not great. The imposition of a higher wage may give a galvanic shock to many businesses and supply a *vis a tergo* which will spur many employers to elimination of waste which they would not effect under the more general stimulation of possible greater profits. A menace to survival, in other words, will serve as a greater stimulant to many business men than the possibility of greater prosperity.[9]

It is indeed probable that the remarkable increase in the efficiency of American industry in 1922 and 1923 was due in part to this very factor. During the depression of 1921 to 1923 hourly wage rates were in general not cut as severely as wholesale prices.[10] If these wage-levels were to be maintained during the succeeding years, which in the main they were, the efficiency of the manufacturing plants had to be increased. This was so

---

[9] See J. S. Nicholson, *Effects of Machinery upon Wages* (London, 1877, 2nd Edition, 1893), pp. 53–4.

[10] For corroborating and detailed material on this point see my *Real Wages in the United States, 1890–1926*, pp. 95–133 and Bulletin 440 of the United States Bureau of Labor Statistics, *Wholesale Prices, 1890 to 1926*, pp. 8–9.

effectively accomplished that the annual physical output of the average wage-earner in manufacturing establishments in 1923 had increased by nearly twenty per cent over its 1921 average.[11]

Relative Index of Physical Production 1890 = 100		Relative Index of Wage-Earners 1890 = 100	Relative Product per Wage-Earners 1890 = 100
1921	181	144	126
1923	260	176	148

The theory that high wages will stimulate industrial efficiency has, in one respect been somewhat over-stressed. This is the common belief that an increase in wages will cause an increased use of machinery, which will in turn lower costs. Where and when wages are low, it is said, business will find it profitable not to introduce expensive though efficient machinery. It will be cheaper to use labor and economize on the machinery. When wages are increased it will then be profitable to economize on the expensive factor, labor, by introducing more machinery. This will increase efficiency. Thus not only are high wages the result of the use of machinery, but they are also a cause.

A weakness in this argument has been exposed by Professor H. G. Hayes.[12] If all wages are increased then, as he points out, the wages of workers in industries which manufacture machines will rise, as well as the wages in the industries which use machines to turn out consumers goods. This will necessarily mean an increase in the price of machinery, and it is implied that there will be no greater relative incentive to use machinery than before. This contention of Professor Hayes is well-grounded in so far as labor costs are concerned and, if the price of machinery were made up solely of labor costs, would be completely true. For then a rise in wages, unaccompanied by an increase in output, would mean a corresponding increase in the prices of the machines. There would then be no greater relative inducement to substitute machines for men than before.

But the price of machinery is not composed solely of wage payments. Part of the payments have instead gone for the interest on capital and for the use of land. A rise in the rate of wages would not increase the rate of interest or the rent of land. Consequently, the price of machines would not rise commensurately with the increase in the rate of wages. There would, therefore, be a slight added inducement for entrepreneurs

---

[11] For the computations see Chapter VIII, Table 24 and Table 27.
[12] H. G. Hayes, "The Rate of Wages and Use of Machinery," *American Economic Review*, Vol. XIII (1923), pp. 461-5.

to substitute machines in which relatively much waiting (capital) and natural resources were embodied for the pure and unassisted exercise of labor alone, or for implements in which the proportion of labor embodied was large and the proportion of capital and natural resources low. It is, for example, precisely to such a situation as this that the concept of elasticity of substitution refers.

To the degree, however, to which wages form a part of the costs of machinery, Hayes' reasoning about the mutually compensatory effects of a general increase in wages is correct. However, it is of course true that were the increases in wages to be greater in the industries which use machines than in the industries which manufacture them a very real inducement would be furnished to reduce costs by substituting machines for direct labor. Such apparently has been the effect in many instances of increasing wages in specific trades and industries.

The establishment by the English trade boards of minimum wages in low wage industries has apparently had such results. Miss Sells, in her competent study, states [13] that "hardly a shop or factory was visited among Trade Board trades where at least one machine had not been installed or where the manager did not proudly explain some bit of reorganization which had increased his output." The statements by a number of these managers lend corroborative force to this generalization. Thus the active head of an aerated water company replied to the inquiry as to the effect of the rulings upon output,[14] by stating that "our firm has reorganized from A to Z and we have put in all new machinery. The result is that we shall be able to double our pre-war volume of output when business picks up." The manager of a twine factory also reported [15] that they had "installed a large amount of new machinery since the war and have extended our plant. We get a much greater output per unit and could entirely offset the increase in wages if we were running at full capacity."

These reports corroborate those made by Tawney [16] and Miss Bulkly [17] of the early operation of the trade board rulings in

[13] D. M. Sells, *The British Trade Board System*, p. 226.

[14] Sells, *op. cit.*, p. 227.

[15] *Ibid.*, p. 228. Many other illustrations are given in the following pages.

[16] R. H. Tawney, *The Establishment of Minimum Rates in the Chain Making Industry under the Trade Boards Act of 1909* (1914). *The Establishment of Minimum Rates in the Tailoring Industry under the Trade Boards Act of 1909* (1914).

[17] M. E. Bulkly, *The Establishment of Minimum Rates in the Box-making Industry under the Trade Boards Act of 1909* (1915).

England and by Ernest Aves of the effects in Australasia and New Zealand.

(3) An increase in wages might increase the efficiency of industry by transferring labor from poorly managed to better managed plants. In virtually every industry there are enterprises which although inefficiently managed are nevertheless able to compete because of their ability to drive down the wages of their employees. To raise the wages in these plants to a level equal to that paid by their efficient competitors would either force these inefficient firms to increase their efficiency or to go out of business. If this latter event were to occur, as in many cases it would, the business of the inefficient plants would gradually be transferred to the more productive firms, and their contributions to the physical product of the industry would be greater in their new location than they were in their old.

4. The Relative Validity of the Static Assumptions

Let us turn now to the second set of assumptions which lie behind the productivity theory, namely, those based upon the concept of the perfectness of competition and of the absence of "friction," and examine their relative validity as a description of economic life.

(1) While it may be impossible for employers to determine with great exactitude precisely what the marginal product is, it is nevertheless probable that the main run of employers will tend over a period of years to make fairly close approximations. The modern science of cost accounting is making this more and more possible, while the pressure of competition tends moreover to eliminate those who over-estimate the amount of the marginal product. Such men find themselves unable to compete, and they are forced to conform to the margin (or to go below it) if they are to survive. If they do not, they then make way for others who will presumably have better judgment in appraising the margin. The selective process, therefore, tends to prevent employers from over-estimating the amount of the marginal product.

These forces do not operate as intensely on those who habitually tend to under-estimate the amount of the marginal product. There are, however, correctives which tend to prevent this bias from becoming predominant. These are the tendency of employers to compete with each other and the assumed mobility of labor. If some business men do not estimate the margin correctly, those who do will be able to hire the more valuable members of the working force away from them. Such men will gradually tend, therefore, either to correct their errors of judgment or will fail to obtain any large share of the business.

At any one time, however, the judgments of the business world may be somewhat at variance from the true marginal product. But this does not seriously impair the validity of the theory. No one who understands the productivity theory claims that it works with mathematical precision. It is enough if it is a broad and powerful tendency which brings wages into some degree of close conformity to it.

(2) Tacit or organized combinations among employers to depress wages or to prevent their being advanced are common. These may range all the way from a rather inarticulate general sentiment on the part of employers that they should not bid against each other for laborers, such as tends to be characteristic for example of middle-class house-wives, to highly compact and organized employers' associations.

Even where no formal organization exists a fear of social disapproval by one's class may frequently be sufficient to deter employers from raising wages. There is also sometimes a fear that if one begins to increase wages other employers will be driven to increase wages still more, so that the individual employer will not ultimately make any more profit. These fears operate to depress wages or to prevent their being increased in much the same fashion that the fear of retaliation or loss of social prestige tend to lessen the degree to which prices are now cut by manufacturers.

But one of the characteristics of the day is for employers of similar industries or localities to band themselves together in a multitude of associations and this tendency has been greatly increased and nearly universalized by the National Recovery Act.[18] These associations have many diverse purposes, but they frequently operate to reassure employers that they will not bid up the rate of wages. Sometimes there is a formal agreement backed by financial guarantees, that no more than a given rate will be paid.[19] It is, moreover, a common practice among many employers' associations in giving employment to discriminate against those workmen who in the past have shown great

[18] See C. E. Bonnett, *Employers' Associations in the United States* and the bulletin of the National Industrial Conference Board on Trade Associations for descriptive material concerning many of these organizations.

[19] Such agreements have existed in retail trade and in the building trades of several cities. It seems probable that the practice is more widespread than is generally admitted.

activity in trying to increase the wages of the workers.[20] This has had an indirect effect in tending to reduce wages below the point at which they would otherwise have been fixed.

It should also be remembered that the relative growth in the importance of large scale enterprises has necessarily decreased the number of separate units which compete for labor and has made agreement upon the basic wage scales between these large concerns easier to effect. Thus most of the independents in the iron and steel industry of the country tend to follow the lead of the United States Steel Corporation in the fixation of wage-rates for unskilled labor, as they do in the matter of prices for the finished product. Combinations of employers engaged in different industries do not, however, depress wages to the same extent as combinations within any given industry. The market for unskilled labor, particularly in the larger cities, is, therefore, one in which there is almost perfect competition.

(3) The workers do not, of course, know the value which the marginal worker adds. They seldom know with any exactness the financial condition of the enterprise or industry. It is on the whole indisputable that the average worker does not possess the knowledge of market conditions and of his economic worth to his prospective employer that the latter possesses. He stands, therefore, at a distinct disadvantage in bargaining, unless there is such brisk bidding for his services as characterized American industry during the war and immediate post-war period.

(4) As has been remarked by economic writers from the time of Adam Smith, competition among laborers for work is undoubtedly more keen than is competition amongst employers for laborers. Yet with the growth of unionism the severity of this competition has been greatly reduced. In 1920, according to Wolman,[21] approximately 21 per cent of the eligible industrial wage-earners in the United States were organized in unions, while in England [22] and Germany the percentages organized were 40 and 50 respectively. At the present time, of course, these percentages have been appreciably reduced and probably not more than 16 per cent of the eligible workers are today organized in unions in this country. The highest percentage of organiza-

---

[20] P. F. Brissenden, *The Employment System of the Lake Carriers Association,* Bulletin 235, Bureau of Labor Statistics; also, "The Butte Miners and the Rustling Card," *American Economic Review,* Vol. X, pp. 755–75.

[21] Leo Wolman, *Growth of American Trade Unionism, 1880–1923,* p. 85.

[22] Excluding those employed in agriculture, commerce and finance, public administration and defense, professions, entertainments, personal service, etc.

tion is in Soviet Russia where no less than 92 per cent of the wage-earners and salaried workers are unionized.[23]

Such a degree of organization produces a profound change in the processes of bargaining. Those unions which have compelled the employers to recognize the principle of collective bargaining fix minimum wages and other standards by this means. To work for less than the union scale is to be guilty in the eyes of one's fellow-unionists of what is on the whole regarded as the worst of offenses. The almost religious devotion which the ardent unionist feels towards the union rate plus the enormous social pressure which is put upon the members not to undercut each other in seeking jobs gives a greater solidarity to the bargaining of labor than is posited in the assumptions of the productivity theory. The productivity theory, as has been stated, assumes that labor is composed of relatively minute units which are distinct from and independent of each other. They feel no more loyalty to each other than do particles of water, and, like the water, they move in such a way as to restore the equilibrium wherever and whenever it may be disturbed. Trade-Unionism, on the other hand, combines these workers in large groups and declares that they must be taken or left as a group.

But does this appreciably modify the ultimate conclusions of the productivity theory? Let us suppose that the wage which is fixed as a result of trade-union pressure is higher than the value productivity which the last worker would add.[24] Will not the employers, as we have seen, then lay off workers to a number equal to those whose wage rates exceed the additional contributions which they would make to the net social value of the product? Since the net profit of the employers is being reduced by the employment of these men and since trade-union agreements seldom provide that a minimum number of men shall be employed, it would seem that an increase in unemployment will necessarily result. These unemployed workers, it is said, will after a time offer their services for less than the union rate,

---

[23] For more details about the Russian system see Robert W. Dunn, *Soviet Trade Unions* (1928), and the chapter by Dunn and the present writer in *Soviet Russia in the Second Decade*.

[24] Professor Pigou's interesting analysis of the forces which determine wage-rates in agreements between unions and employers' associations (*The Economics of Welfare*, pp. 416–26) refers after all to the fixation of the original rate. He does not refer to the question of whether such a rate, once fixed, can be maintained if it is higher than the marginal value productivity of the present staff of workers? He does not consider the possible slow attrition upon the rate resulting from unemployment.

and wages will hence ultimately move back to the point of marginal productivity.

The extent to which these tendencies will work out in practice depends primarily upon two considerations: First, the degree to which the demand for the products of labor is relatively elastic or inelastic. Many factors will, of course, affect this relative elasticity, but one will certainly be as to whether we are considering all labor as a whole or merely those laborers in specific industries; and the other will be the degree of provision which the unions, the employers, or the state are led to make for those who are out of work.

In those industries, such as salt, where the demand for the product is relatively inelastic, an increase in wages, even though it should result in a *commensurate* increase in price, would not cause a proportional falling off in the quantity demanded. The total price and wage area would, in consequence, be greater than before. This would follow from the fact that the amount by which earnings would decrease through unemployment would be less than the amount by which they would increase through the higher wage-rates for those who continued to be employed. It would, therefore, be possible for such a union to provide liberal out-of-work-benefits which might exceed the original marginal product to those of the members who were thus thrown out of work on the condition, of course, that the unemployed would not work for less than the union rate. The entire group of workers would thus be enabled to enjoy the increase in wages which had resulted, and by providing for the unemployed out of the surplus they would be freed from the peril of a reduction in the wage-rate which would carry them back to the original and true marginal level.

As Alfred Marshall has pointed out, the possibilities of thus raising wages are particularly great in those cases of joint production where an appreciable increase in the wages of one trade or industry, such as glazing, will have but a slight effect upon the price of the joint product itself, such as houses.[25] The quantity of housing demanded would, in consequence, decrease but slightly, and hence there would be only a very slight reduction in the number of glaziers employed. This amount of unemployment would be much more than compensated for by the increase in the wage-rates of the glaziers who continued to be employed. If the unemployed were protected, an appreciable

[25] Marshall, *Principles of Economics* (6th Edition), pp. 385–6.

net surplus over and above the marginal product could be secured, for at least a considerable period of time for all those in the trade.[26]

The same result would not occur in those industries where the demand for the product is relatively elastic. In such cases, if an increase in wages were accompanied by a corresponding increase in price, a more than commensurate decrease in the quantity demanded would result. The total price area and therefore presumably the wage area would be less than it was previously. The loss of earnings through the increase in unemployment would exceed the gains made by those who were retained. There would be no net surplus, therefore, out of which to indemnify the unemployed, and they would be likely to underbid the others in order to secure work. Loyalty to the principle of trade-unionism would, however, serve to offset this tendency in some measure even though the benefits which the unemployed received were much less than what they could earn at the marginal rates.

Will, however, the workers in the trades and industries characterized by an inelastic demand be able permanently to enjoy gains in excess of marginal productivity? The rise in the price and in the exchange value of the article in question will necessarily produce a fall in the exchange value of other commodities and consequently in the marginal value productivity of those who are engaged in these other industries. There will, therefore, be a disparity between the marginal productivity of labor as a whole and the remuneration of labor in the unionized industries with an inelastic demand. Would there not, therefore, be a decided tendency for workers to move towards these industries and for the pressure of this movement to bring wages back to a point where they would equal the margin of value productivity which runs through society as a whole?

That such a tendency would exist is undeniable, although it might in part be impeded by the loyalty of the workers outside the given industry to the rates of the union in question. Such

---

[26] The possibility of combinations between unions and employers' organizations in industries with an inelastic demand which will force up prices and wages by restricting output is very real. Noteworthy examples of this have been the agreements in New York City where some unions pledged themselves not to furnish labor to any employer who was not a member of the employers' association. This with other practices had the effect of forcing up the price of buildings. Somewhat similar agreements exist in the photo-engraving industry. The way in which the glassworkers "stabilized" prices and wages in the glass industry by inducing the employers to close their plants for half of the year is well known.

loyalty would, of course, be opposed to the real economic interest of these workers, but it might nevertheless be strong. Such a tendency, moreover, would be effective only to the degree to which labor was actually mobile. If the workers in the given industry could exclude others by excessive apprenticeship requirements and assessments they might be able permanently to enjoy these excess gains. Even if such methods were not employed, if the industry required a considerable degree of skill, there would necessarily be a considerable period of time before wages were brought back to the level of the marginal social product.

The question as to whether trade-union action can increase the wages of all labor is, however, of greater theoretical interest than that as to whether it can raise wages in any particular trade. This is becoming of more than theoretical interest in western Europe because of the great increase in union membership and because of the efforts which are being made on the part of labor for a greater unity of action. First, it should be remarked that if we take the nation as the unit in countries which have large exports of commodities subject to inelastic demand, it is of course possible for labor as a whole to make gains at the expense of consumers in other countries. A trade-union movement in the British East Indian possessions could, for example, raise wages in the rubber industry and compel the consumers, who are predominantly Americans, to pay for the advance.

What, however, would be the situation in a self-sufficing country or closed economy? The productivity analysis would declare that if real wages as a whole were temporarily to be pushed up above the social margin of value productivity, then the employers would be compelled to lay off such a number of workers as to prevent them from suffering any loss upon the labor of individual laborers. These unemployed workers, it is argued, would soon bring wages back to the social margin. But this defense does not differentiate between the possible proportions of the working class which might thus be thrown out of employment. The productivity theorists apparently believe in general that the creation of a small percentage of unemployment and the consequent competition for jobs would be sufficient to restore wages to their original level. Yet this would be inevitable only where the marginal productivity curve of labor had an elasticity greater than unity. For then if wages were increased 10 per cent above their marginal productivity and if all were employed, the employers would lay off more than 10 per cent of the workers [27] so that the total amount distributed in wages would be less than before. Even though those who still had jobs were to subsidize those thrown out of work, they would not be able to pay them as much as they could get if they were employed. Unless there were great loyalty to the trade-union rate, the tendency would be for the unemployed to offer themselves at less than the union rate. Wages would, therefore, move back towards the point of social marginal productivity.

The case might, however, be very different if the productivity curve of labor had an elasticity of less than unity. For then if wages were increased to a point 10 per cent above that of their former marginal productivity when all were employed, the number of workers who would be laid off would be less than 10 per cent. The total amount received in wages would, therefore, be greater than before. It would be possible then for those employed to pay out-of-work benefits to those thrown out of a job, which would be more than they could obtain by getting work at the old wages. If those who continued to be employed were, therefore, to take such care of their unemployed brethren, they could by forcing wages up beyond their former point of marginal productivity, reap a surplus for the laboring class as such.

In practice, however, as we shall see from later chapters, it appears almost certain that the slope of the productivity curve of labor is almost certainly quite elastic and very much greater than unity. The total amount paid out in wages would, therefore, in all probability be less than before were wages raised above their marginal social productivity.

If part of the maintenance of those thrown out of work were to be borne by other classes in the community through the form of poor relief or unemployment benefits and not by employed labor, then, of course, it would be possible, even with an elastic productivity curve, for the net income of the working classes to be greater than before. Were this so, it would still be possible to maintain the wage above its point of social marginal productivity. The loyalty of the unemployed to the union rate would, of course, be another factor which might keep up the rate for the employed.

---

[27] In strict accuracy, of course, unit elasticity would call for a decrease of 9.1 per cent in the numbers employed.

(5) Capital is not of course completely mobile, but through the complicated media of banks, financial institutions, and stock exchanges, it is, on the whole, the most liquid of all our economic factors. There are, of course, barriers of ignorance and inertia which impede its flow to localities which are distant from the main centers of savings, but these are rapidly decreasing. So too, certain monopolies and favored enterprises are able to enjoy larger earnings than the average, and it is not always possible for newcomers either to set up in competition or to buy into the business on equal terms with the original owners. It is also true that the fluidity of capital applies after all to the annual increments of new savings and to depreciation funds. It does not apply to investments which have already crystallized into capital goods. In the main, however, the assumption is valid.

(6) Labor is far from being completely mobile. "Man," remarked Adam Smith,[28] "is of all sorts of luggage the most difficult to be transported." The attachment to localities and the reluctance to change is a barrier against geographical equality in marginal productivity. Perhaps even more important are the barriers which prevent complete occupational mobility. Some occupations can be entered only after a long and costly training which is virtually impossible for the children of those with slender means. Artificial barriers are erected by some unions, particularly by those in the building trades, in the form of exorbitant initiation dues and excessive apprenticeship restrictions. All these tend to cause the marginal social productivity and hence wages to be higher in some groups than in others, yet within each group marginal productivity may still set the standard of remuneration.

(7) Not all labor is successful in finding employment. I have computed an index of unemployment for the United States which includes manufacturing, transportation, mining, and the building trades for the thirty-year period from 1897 to 1926 inclusive and find that the average proportion of unemployment for the period was 10.5 per cent.[29] In the summer even of 1929 before the depression began, the following percentages of unemployment were reported for the countries listed below: [30]

[28] Adam Smith, *Wealth of Nations* (Cannan Edition), Vol. 1, p. 77.
[29] Paul H. Douglas, *Real Wages in the United States*, Chapters XXV and XXVI. This included those not on the payrolls because of illness.
[30] *International Labour Review*, October, 1929, (Vol. XX, No. 4), pp. 577-8.

Germany	8.6	Great Britain	7.9
Australia	9.3	Norway	11.3
Denmark	9.8	New Zealand	9.3
		Sweden	6.5

In addition to these numbers who were completely unemployed, there were others who were partially unemployed, which in Germany amounted to no less than 6.9 per cent of the total number of workers.

What effect then does the existence of this body of unemployed workers, whose presence has generally been ignored by the productivity theorists, have upon the validity of the productivity theory?

In the first place, it should be noted that the economic productivity of this group of workers is nil. From the social standpoint, these are the marginal workers. No laborer will normally wish to be one of them, for the necessary expenses of personal and family maintenance will continue without any income with which to meet them. Individual workers will be willing to work for less than what they would ordinarily demand and secure, because of their fear that if they hold out for such a figure, they will be discharged and preference in employment will be given to those who are willing to accept a lower rate. In such an event they would receive nothing at all. In order to avoid this possibility they will frequently be willing to reduce their rates to a point even below that which those who originally undercut them had offered. This would in turn throw the incidence of unemployment upon the group which had previously offered themselves at a lower wage.[31] But this group would not be quiescent under such a situation and would tend to reduce their offers still further.

The result among the unskilled workers, at least, will tend to be similar to that type of cut-throat competition which prevailed for years between many railroads and in many industries. The anxiety of the workers to secure something to apply to their "fixed" costs of maintenance rather than join the unemployed and thus obtain nothing, will lead them to accept extremely low wages, and a progressive reduction of rates will ensue.[32] This may well be less than the marginal product of those workers

---

[31] In order to simplify the problem, the competing workers have been divided into two groups. In reality of course they are many, and this magnifies the tendency towards a reduction of the rate.

[32] For an elaboration of the theory of the overhead costs of labor see J. M. Clark's acute analysis in his *The Economics of Overhead Cost*, pp. 357–85.

who continue to be employed. It will suffice for the workers, if in such a "spoiled market" they can secure more than those out of work can obtain. Theoretically, therefore, wages in such a situation may approach zero, which is the product of the marginal group wishing employment but not able to secure it, plus whatever added or "variable" costs, such as an increased consumption of food, are necessitated by the fact that the labor is employed rather than idle.

That wages do not fall to so low a point is largely due to the fear on the part of labor that the lower rates once established will continue as the standard when business revives. They are very loath, therefore, to cut their rates, and if they are strongly organized in unions and financially buttressed by individual and collective savings, they will be very likely to refuse to accept a cut and, instead, to live upon their savings. A precisely similar policy is followed in a declining market by many industrial combinations such as the United States Steel Corporation. Rather than cut prices greatly they choose instead to close down plants and to reduce supply, and pay dividends to stockholders out of previously accumulated surpluses.[33] Such a practice cannot, of course, be adopted by organizations which do not control the supply, for to do so would be to deprive oneself completely of income and yet not affect appreciably either supply or price.

It follows, therefore, that unskilled workers, whose savings are at best scanty and who generally do not belong to unions, will tend to have their wage rates cut more than other groups. The tendency towards cut-throat competition for jobs in times of business depression is, therefore, strong among them.[34]

It should, moreover, be recognized that a reduction in the wage rate per unit of effort may take place even without a reduction in the hourly rate of pay. A day's labor is not a constant quantity, and the existence of so large a force of unemployed leads those who are retained to work harder in order to continue to hold their positions. Output per man-hour, therefore, tends to increase. The depression period of 1920–1921 furnished abundant evidence of this tendency. Thus when the Ford Company resumed operations after its shut-down of 1922,

---

[33] Thus the cut in the price of steel rails did not occur until the autumn of 1932 when it was lowered from $43 to $40 a ton.

[34] It may be asked how and by whom are the fixed costs of maintaining the workers and their families borne, if not by industry? A retrenchment is in part made at the expense of the previous standard of life and in many cases of the health and vitality of the family. Charitable relief from the public and private agencies accounts also for part.

it was able to produce with 40,000 employees as many automobiles (and many more parts) as it had previously been able
to turn out with a force of 57,000.[35] This was an increased output per man-hour of over 42 per cent. A large part of this in-
increase, although not all, was attributable to the increased
effort of those who were employed. Thus wages per unit of
"work" done may fall below the marginal productivity of the
value of that work, even when the change in hourly wage-rates
may seem to be only moderate.[36]

(8) Available capital is, on the whole, more unemployed
than is labor itself. The United States Census of Manufactures
in 1921 asked manufacturers to estimate "the percentage which
its actual output constituted of its maximum possible output."[37]
No attempt was made to define what was meant by "maximum
possible output" and the returns cannot, therefore, be relied upon
too implicitly. Presumably, however, this term did not include
output which could be achieved by working more shifts than
was the prevailing practice in the industry, but rather referred
to maximum output within the existing utilization of the day.

For all manufacturing industry as a whole, the actual output
formed only 57 per cent of what was estimated as the maximum
output.[38] This proportion naturally varied from industry to industry, being only 35 and 43 per cent respectively in the manufacturing of agricultural implements and in steel works and rolling mills. In virtually none of the industries, however, did it
exceed 75 per cent. A part of this failure to reach the estimated
maximum may have been due to faulty production methods, but
it is probable that the major part of the estimated discrepancy
was due to the existence of idle capacity which, if utilized, would
have increased output.

Was this unemployment of capital caused by the business depression which prevailed in that year and to what degree would
the results have been different in 1919 and in 1923? The decline
in employment from 1919 to 1921 was one of approximately 25
per cent, so that this would have meant that output in 1919,

---

[35] Paul H. Douglas, "Personnel Problems and the Business Cycle," *Administration* (July, 1922), Vol. IV, p. 22.

[36] The fact that wage-rates and earnings fell less rapidly than wholesale prices
during the 1920–22 depression as shown in Prof. A. H. Hansen's paper, "The Outlook for Wages and Employment" (Supplement, *American Economic Review*,
March 1923, especially pp. 35–6) does not fully show that the pay per unit of
"work" done declined less rapidly.

[37] *Biennial Census of Manufactures*, 1921. United States Department of
Commerce, p. 1337.

[38] *Ibid.*, p. 1338.

which was a prosperous year, could not have been more than 76 per cent of maximum capacity. Even after allowing for idleness caused by archaic and obsolescent equipment maintained only to meet peak loads, and by technological necessities, it seems probable that there is a considerable proportion of the capital which is not utilized even in the busiest years. If all the idle men were to be put to work, there would, therefore, probably be some surplus of unemployed capital equipment for which workers could not be found.

What then are the consequences of these facts? The presence of this idle and unutilized capital naturally creates in and of itself a desire on the part of employers to attract sufficient business to keep it employed. Where the overhead cost of such capital forms a large proportion of the expenses of the business, as is conspicuously true of the railroads and to a lesser degree of sugar refining, oil-distilling, etc., there will be a temptation for the business men to cut prices in order to get something to apply to these overhead charges. This has been the cause for the rate and price wars of the past to which we have alluded.

Two queries, however, may be interposed at this point: First, is it possible for this rate war to take place at any one time in all industries or in the vast majority of industries, or is it necessarily confined to a few? Second, if it is confined to a few industries, will not conditions right themselves after a time?

It is theoretically quite possible for all businesses, in a time of economic depression when excess capacity is particularly great, to cut rates in order to stimulate sales. This would result in a lower money return to capital. But since prices would be falling, it might not mean any less return in value. If labor, for example, were also cutting its rates to the same degree in order to find employment, the general result would be that the unemployed labor and at least a major part of the unemployed capital would come together and production would be at the very least materially increased. Less credit would be needed and created to carry on business, and in terms of money units the national product would be less than before. If measured in terms of goods, however, it need not necessarily have decreased.[39] Hence if cut-throat competition were universal and

---

[39] The one barrier to this would be the difficulty caused by the fact that the raw products would have been purchased at a higher price level and sold at a lower. This is the most effective obstacle in the way of industry doing business effectively under a falling price level. For an able exposition of this point of view which has in general not been appreciated by the critics, see Foster and Catchings, *Profits*. I have tried to work out the implications of these forces in

were carried out equally by all, the theory of marginal productivity would still be valid.

If, however, one factor of production such as labor were to cut its rate and the others were either not to do so at all or were not to do so to the same degree, then the relative return to the factors would be altered from the original basis of division and adversely to the factor which made the cut. The factor, therefore, which is most hard pressed, which is most anxious to secure something on its overhead, and to which the fear of complete unemployment is most vivid, will, therefore, cut its rate more severely. It will consequently lose in comparison with the others.

The same principle applies between industries as between classes. If there are uneven rates of price-cutting between industries, then those industries which have cut most will of course suffer in comparison with the others. This uneven rate of price decline was especially noticeable during the depression of 1920–22 and during the first three and a half years of the present depression when the price of agricultural products at the farm fell much more rapidly than those of manufactured products. The value productivity of the marginal units of labor and capital employed in such industries during the period is, of course, lower than that in society as a whole. But time will normally bring a readjustment. Some labor will probably move out of the depressed industries, and new labor will cease to enter at the former rate. Some of the capital in these industries will be allowed to deteriorate and the depreciation funds will, instead, be invested elsewhere. New capital will be slow in entering. As a result, the relative prices of these commodities will rise and with them the value product of labor and capital. An equivalence between the industries will tend ultimately to be established, although this will take time. In the long run, therefore, we may expect those industries where the "excess" capacity is above the average to grow less rapidly than other lines of effort. Ultimately, therefore, the secular growth of population and of total demand resulting from the increase in total product, which Americans in the past at least have always been able confidently to rely upon, may absorb most of this excess capacity. Whether or not this can be relied upon in the future is much

"The Modern Technique of Mass Production and its Relation to Wages," *Proceedings Academy of Political Science*, April 1927, pp. 37–41 and in my paper, "The World Unemployment Problem" delivered in Geneva in 1931 and printed by the British League of Nations Union and also in *Problems of Peace*.

more dubious in view of the rapid dampening off of the rate of population growth.

Precisely such a dampening off was characteristic of the railway industry between 1900 and 1925. The United States was then growing up to its web of communication. With this increased business, the railways were less tempted to indulge in traffic wars. During the interval before this happened, however, many investors received less than the social marginal return upon their investment.

If most industries, even in prosperous times, have a considerable amount of unused capacity, why does not price cutting then, instead of being always characteristic of only a few industries and only existing for all industry when business is in the throes of a depression, become endemic for all industry at all times? The answer in part lies in the general practice of charging the overhead costs of idle equipment to the product turned out. The fact that this is so almost universally done, serves to make the idle capacity less of a source of positive loss [40] and lessens the temptation to price-cutting. Since most firms follow this practice, a given firm can do so without exposing itself to great competitive pressure. Individual enterprises are, moreover, deterred from reducing prices and temporarily attracting more business by the fear of reprisals on the part of those larger firms [41] whose average costs may well be lower and who would be able to win out in a struggle for survival. The general spirit of business associations and of the business community with its opposition to those who thus "spoil" the market also furnishes an informal but fairly effective means of control. Outright agreements or understandings between the members of the various trade associations are also probably much more common than is ordinarily known.

(9) The bargaining powers of labor and capital are not equal. This follows not only from the lesser mobility and knowledge of labor as compared with capital but also from the great disparities in the reception of income. From the study of the National Bureau of Economic Research it appears that in the United States in 1918, the 2 per cent of the income recipients whose incomes were in excess of $5,000 a year received approximately 18 per cent of the total national income, or a total

---

[40] For an arraignment of current practice in this respect, see H. L. Gantt's, *Organizing for Work.*

[41] As is well known, this is what prevents the independents in the steel industry from reducing the prices of steel.

sum equal to that received by the poorest 40 per cent of income recipients.[42] What is even more significant is the distribution of surplus income. If we count only those dollars received in excess of $2,000 a year as surplus, then the fortunate 2 per cent received no less than 71 per cent of this surplus.[43] Fifty per cent of the total surplus was received by only two-thirds of 1 per cent of the income recipients. In Great Britain the distribution of income is still more unequal. In 1914, 8 per cent of the total income fell into the hands of less than one-tenth of 1 per cent of the income receivers and 22 per cent more into the pockets of 1 per cent.[44] Thus 30 per cent of the national income was received by only slightly over 1 per cent of the income receivers. In all, no less than 45 per cent of the total income was secured by 5½ per cent of those with separate incomes. This means that in Great Britain virtually all of the social surplus was in the hands of 5 per cent of the income recipients and the preponderating part in the hands of only 1 per cent.

Since the large incomes are in the main derived from the ownership of property while the smaller incomes are secured primarily from labor,[45] this means that the owners of capital are provided with far more abundant reserve funds than are the wage-earners. In a trial of strength between an employers' association and a trade-union, therefore, the former would not suffer as much as the latter from the failure to conclude an agreement and from the consequent stoppage of work. It might, therefore, well be possible for the associated employers to beat wages down below the point of marginal productivity. The tendency for individual employers then to try to secure more labor and to increase wages surreptitiously in order to do so, might be checked (as it has been frequently checked in practice) by a compact on the part of the various members not to pay more, with secret and veiled penalties for a breach of the contract.

The possibility that employers in other industries would then hire the workers away from the particular group of associated employers would be, of course, more difficult for the given

---

[42] *Income in the United States,* pp. 134–5.

[43] See an interesting note by Homer Hoyt, "The Inequality in the Distribution of Wealth and Income in the United States," *Journal American Statistical Association,* Vol. XVIII, pp. 650–1. It seems probable that Mr. Hoyt fixed the point at which the surplus began at too high a figure. Single men, for example, do not absolutely need $2,000 a year.

[44] See J. C. Stamp, *Wealth and Taxable Capacity,* p. 87.

[45] The Annual Volumes on *Statistics of Income* published by the United States Bureau of Internal Revenue show this.

group of employers to guard against. This follows from the fact that the bond of unity between the employers in different industries is generally weak. But in certain localities in the United States a substantial unity of action has already been achieved and this bids fair to be greatly increased by the National Industrial Recovery Act.

Where labor and capital are each combined in massed groups, the original fixation of wages will tend to depend upon the relative strength of the two sides rather than upon the marginal productivity of each, and in this struggle labor, because of its relative lack of reserves, is distinctly handicapped.

(10) The state, instead of maintaining complete neutrality concerning the wage contract agreed upon by labor and capital, frequently intervenes. Taking Europe at least as a whole, it is increasingly doing so in the interest of the wage-earners. We have already referred to the way in which unemployment insurance laws may assist the worker to secure more than the added productivity which the last available worker would cause. The state, moreover, may fix minimum wages in given industries instead of allowing them to be determined by competitive forces. This is illustrated by the compulsory arbitration laws of New Zealand and of most of the Australian states, and by the minimum wage acts of Victoria and of Great Britain.

Until the passage of the National Industrial Recovery Act, the United States was overwhelmingly a land of laissez-faire. That act however and the methods of its administration are greatly changing and largely reversing this attitude. For not only are minimum wages and maximum hours being fixed under specific industrial codes for such industries as lumber, oil, coal, textiles, clothes, boots and shoes, steel, electrical machinery, and automobiles, but the blanket code issued by the President is probably sweeping the majority of workers into the scope of the act. As this book goes to press it is still uncertain as to whether or not this regulation will be permanent. The turn of events in many countries away from the competitive market about which economists have reasoned suggests however that pure laissez-faire will, at the very least, not return for some time to come and that society bids fair to try its hand, at a partially controlled society. The question as to by whom and for whom this society is to be controlled is still far from clear but if this were determined by the present balance of power there can be scant doubt that it would be the owners of capital rather than the laborers. But what the future holds is extraordinarily uncertain.

In arbitration decisions, to be sure, the wage which is fixed is generally in rough consonance with the economic strength of the respective sides and will tend to approximate what the two sides would probably have ultimately arrived at by mutual agreement had their *amour propre* permitted them to continue negotiations. If the decision is indeed too greatly at variance with the economic "realities" of the situation or what the respective parties could secure by independent action, it will tend not to be respected by that side which secured appreciably less than it would have been able to secure by dealing directly with the other party.

Yet there is a margin within which the arbitral body may fix rates which differ from those which would have been established without it. This results from the fact that if the award is to be disregarded, recourse will have to be taken in the form of a strike or lockout which will reduce the net gains which the stronger party could secure. Thus if the probable increase in earnings which would result from a strike were to be $6 weekly, but if $2 of this would be absorbed by the expenses of conducting the strike, then the arbitrators would tend to maintain peace by granting an increase of only $4. The cost of strikes and lockouts, therefore, furnishes a zone within which the arbitral board may operate.[46] A further influence is the fact that public opinion will tend to be hostile to any group that refuses to obey a decision of a public body if that body has previously been invested with jurisdiction either by the two parties themselves or by the state. The relative strength of the party that refuses to obey the decision is, therefore, less under such conditions than it would be in the absence of this machinery, and a further margin of discretion is consequently given to the arbitrators which they can use to alter their decisions from those which would be determined competitively.

The foregoing discussion should have tended to show that none of the assumptions which the advocates of the specific productivity theory have made are completely true and none are completely false. Some, of course, are closer approximations to reality than others, and the following classification perhaps best

---

[46] For an elaboration of this point, see Pigou, *Principles and Methods of Industrial Peace.*

shows their relative validity, at least in so far as the United States is concerned.

1. Largely valid but not wholly so
   A. Knowledge by business men of relative productiveness of labor and capital.
   B. Mobility of capital.
   C. (Prior to the passage of the National Recovery Act.) Non-interference by the Government in terms of the wage contract.
2. Primarily valid but with a strong opposing tendency
   A. Competition between laborers for work.
   B. Mobility of Labor.
   C. Competition between employers for laborers.
3. Partially true but on the whole not true
   A. All capital is employed.
   B. All labor is employed.
   C. Laborers know their productivity.
   D. The bargaining powers of labor and capital are equal.
   E. (Since the passage of the National Industrial Recovery Act.) Non-interference by the Government in terms of the wage contract.

It will be seen from the above classification that the assumptions which depart most from reality are those which ascribe more power to the workers than they actually possess. The assumptions which serve to increase the bargaining power of the employers, such as the mobility of capital, and the knowledge of relative productiveness, are far more valid than are the similar assumptions which have been made in the case of labor. Moreover, in the case of those assumptions which are less valid, such as the supposed absence of combination between workers and between capitalists, and that of full employment of the factors, the real situation is one which still further weakens labor's bargaining power. Thus employers' combinations are today in America stronger on the whole than combinations of wage-earners, and the unemployment of capital, while probably greater in amount than the unemployment of labor, leads to less severe competition. It can thus be said that up until the summer of 1933 the forces which operated against labor's receiving its marginal product were stronger than those which tend to prevent capital from securing its margin. An increased activity by the state in behalf of labor, or further unionization on the part of the wage-earners themselves, would have helped to redress this balance. These forces might indeed conceivably become so strong as to turn the scales the other way. Whether the National Recovery Act will permanently strengthen the position of labor still remains to be seen. Thus far it most certainly has increased the strength of labor.

Many, who have seen the degree of variance between real life and the assumptions of the productivity school, have in their impatience declared that because of this defective basis, the conclusions which have been drawn from the productivity theory are not worthy of credence and hence should be disregarded. But such an attitude as this ignores the fact that the assumptions do represent real tendencies which in the aggregate are probably more powerful than those of a conflicting nature. Thus, there is a tendency towards competition between laborers and between employers not only when there are no combinations between the members of each group but also when there are. There is a tendency for wage-rates which are lower than marginal productivity to be raised by the competition of the business men, and there is a tendency for wages in excess of the marginal product to be lowered by the competition of the laborers. Such tendencies may be prevented from working out to their logical conclusion by group pressure and by penalties, but they are not thereby rendered absolutely powerless. Most combinations will, as a matter of fact, take such tendencies into consideration and make some modifications in their policy because of them.

The forces upon which the productivity school built their theories are, therefore, not fictitious, but are instead powerful. To the extent that they are operative, the conclusions which are drawn from them are valid, and the results are modified but not vitiated by the presence of other forces which are at work as well.[47]

The method of the marginal productivity school, as indeed of the entire school of orthodox economists, has described a portion of reality. Within the walls of their assumptions they have tried to trace the results of a change in this factor or in that.

---

[47] The critics of the marginal productivity theory have frequently betrayed their ignorance of the nature of scientific law. The law of gravitation, for example, has not been rendered invalid by the development of heavier than air airplanes. The designers of such airplanes have to take this law into account. It operates. But they have utilized other tendencies which, as long as they are operative, prevent the law of gravitation from working out as it would if unhindered.

This attempt in the field of logic has been precisely similar to the efforts of the physical scientists in their laboratories to eliminate disturbing elements and variables from their experiments and by isolation to secure "controlled" results.

This is a valid method of approach, and its application has been responsible for much scientific advance. It enables the thinker to trace out to its logical end the chain of results flowing from the change in some one factor in a manner which would be almost impossible if a number of other variables were also admitted.

At the same time, it is dangerous to assume that the neat tidy world of the syllogism is in fact a picture of the real world. This caution is applicable to physical science, but it is even more true in economic and social life. Here a multitude of variables are inherently bound up with every situation. They also influence the result. If economics is then to attempt to analyze reality, it must take such factors into consideration. It is difficult and perhaps impossible to handle so many variables by such a necessarily simplified method of analysis as that of the ordinary type of economic theory. The development of quantitative methods of measurement, however, seems to furnish both data and types of analyses which, when extended and refined, may enable us to measure wages objectively and to determine with some accuracy the causes and consequences of such movements as have taken place.

CHAPTER IV

PRELUDE TO THE INDUCTIVE STUDY OF THE IN-
CREMENTAL PRODUCTIVITY AND THE SUPPLY
CURVES OF THE FACTORS OF PRODUCTION

**1. The Need for Inductive Studies into the Productivity
and Supply Curves of the Factors of Production**
The theory of distribution is sadly in need of inductive
studies similar in purpose to those which have recently so clari-
fied the theory of value. The similarities between the development of the theories of distribution and of value are indeed
striking. J. B. Clark left the problem of distribution in about
the same status as the Austrian school had left the problem of
value.[1] Just as the latter assumed the supply of a commodity
to be fixed so did Clark assume the quantities of the factors to
be fixed. As they had pointed out that the value of a commodity was determined by the utility of the last unit consumed
(Grenznutzen) or in price terms, the marginal demand price, so
Clark demonstrated that the amount paid to each unit of a
factor was determined by the amount of product added by the
last unit of that factor.

But just as the Austrians did not explain how the given
quantity of a commodity came to be produced or whether it
would continue to be produced in the future, so did Clark not
explain how the quantities of the factors came to be what they
were or whether these quantities could be expected to remain
constant or whether they would change, and if so in what direction and to what amount.

Marshall and the neo-classicists have shown how inadequate it is to base a theory of value upon the demand curve
alone.[2] The supply curve must also be considered, and the

---

[1] See Jevons, *The Theory of Political Economy;* Menger, *Grundsätze der
Volkswirtschaftslehre,* 1871; Böhm-Bawerk, *Positive Theory of Capital;* Smart,
An Introduction to the Theory of Value.

[2] Böhm-Bawerk and others have sought to make the subjective valuations
of the sellers the factor which limits supply. But since in modern industry
goods are produced for sale and not for personal consumption, the seller has
ultimately no alternative but to sell. He cannot take his goods home, as
Böhm-Bawerk had his hypothetical sellers take their horses. The immediate

equilibrium under competition is normally reached at the intersection of the two curves.[2a] Whether any given quantity or price will equilibrate the quantities supplied and demanded depends, it is needless to say, upon the relationship between the price and the various costs of production. If the short-run price with a given supply yields a surplus to all the competing producers, then more units will be produced, and an ultimate equilibrium will be established where the cost of the final unit will be approximately equal to the amount which will be paid for it in terms of money. If, on the contrary, the price is insufficient to meet the expenses involved in turning out certain units, the supply in the future will tend to decrease, and the ultimate equilibrium will be at a higher price.

What then was needed to determine long-run price was a knowledge of the relative slopes of the demand and supply curves. Excellent progress in measuring the elasticity of demand has been made for several commodities by Moore,[3] Schultz,[4] Ezekiel,[5] Warren and Pearson,[6] Working,[7] and Staehle,[8]

---

limiting factor to the supply of commodities, however, is whether the money income which a seller secures is sufficient to enable him to meet the money costs of production and to continue in business. The number of units he will produce will be determined by the added cost of specific units as compared with the price at which they will sell.

[2a] Except in the case of decreasing costs where under atomistic competition there is no equilibrium.

[3] H. L. Moore, *Forecasting the Yield and Price of Cotton*, and *Synthetic Economics*.

[4] Henry Schultz, *Statistical Laws of Supply and Demand with Special Reference to Sugar*, Chicago, University of Chicago Press. *The Meaning of Statistical Demand Curves*, written for the Veröffentlichungen der Frankfurter Gesellschaft für Konjunkturforschung and an earlier study, "The Statistical Measurement of the Elasticity of Demand for Beef," *Journal of Farm Economics*, June 1924, pp. 254–78. See also "The Shifting Demand for Selected Agricultural Products, 1875–1929." *Journal of Farm Economics*, Vol. XIV (1932), pp. 201–27.

[5] Mordecai Ezekiel "Factors Related to Lamb Prices," *Journal of Political Economy*, Vol. XXXV, pp. 233–60. "Statistical Analysis and the Laws of Price." *Quarterly Journal of Economics*, Vol. 42 (1928), pp. 199–227. (With G. C. Haas) *Factors Affecting the Price of Hogs*, Bulletin 1440 of the United States Department of Agriculture (1926). "A Statistical Examination of the Problem of Handling Annual Surpluses of Non-Perishable Farm Products." *Journal of Farm Economics*, Vol. XI (1929), pp. 193–226.

[6] G. F. Warren and F. A. Pearson, *Interrelationships of Supply and Price*, Bulletin 466, Cornell University Agricultural Experiment Station (1928).

[7] Holbrook Working, "The Statistical Determination of Demand Curves." *Quarterly Journal of Economics*, Vol. XXXIX, pp. 503–43; *Factors Determining the Price of Potatoes in St. Paul and Minneapolis*, Technical Bulletin 10, University of Minnesota Agricultural Experiment Station (1922).

[8] Hans Staehle. *Die Analyse von Nachfragekurven in ihrer Bedeutung für Konjunkturforschung.* Veröffentlichungen der Frankfurter Gesellschaft für Konjunkturforschung.

while the cost studies of the Federal Trade Commission,[9] the War Industries Board,[10] Secrist,[11] and Schultz,[12] together with Viner's [13] keen theoretical analysis, have also thrown some light upon the cost curves of a number of commodities.[14] Schultz has, moreover, furnished in the case of sugar a measurement of how supply changes with price and has thus carried the analysis of supply to a still more definite basis. Such studies as these give concreteness to the neo-classical analysis of the mutual influences of cost and demand. What would otherwise be purely suppositious demand and supply curves, have become in part known,[15] and the approach to the theory of value is being transformed from a philosophical to a quantitative point of view, with the methods and results partaking of the exactitude of the physical sciences. From an analysis of these demand and supply curves, it is possible to forecast with some degree of accuracy what the price of a given product is likely to be with a given volume of output, and whether such a price, barring changes in the general price level, will establish a long-run equilibrium.

---

[9] See Kemper Simpson, "A Statistical Analysis of the Relationship Between Cost and Price," *Quarterly Journal of Economics*, Vol. XXXV (1921), pp. 264–87; "Further Evidence on the Relation between Price, Cost and Profit." *Ibid.* Vol. XXXVII (1923), pp. 476–90.

[10] F. W. Taussig, "Price Fixing as Seen by a Price Fixer," *Quarterly Journal of Economics*, Vol. XXXIII, pp. 205–41.

[11] Horace Secrist, *Expense Levels in Retailing; Competition in the Retail Distribution of Clothing.*

[12] Henry Schultz, "Cost of Production, Supply and Demand and the Tariff," *Journal of Farm Economics* (1927), pp. 192–209. *Statistical Laws of Demand and Supply*, Chapters IV–VI.

[13] Jacob Viner, "Cost Curves and Supply Curves." *Zeitschrift für Nationalökonomie* Wien, III. Band (1931), pp. 23–46.

[14] The value of most of these cost studies as a measurement of the supply curve is seriously impaired by the fact that they (1) do not include interest or profits as cost and (2) measure only the *average* costs for individual firms. Since the cost of additional units must vary appreciably within a given firm, such a curve does not necessarily picture the cost attached to each unit. For a clear statement of this defect see J. M. Clark, "Further Discussion of Three Dimensional Price Diagrams," *American Economic Review*, Vol. XV (1925), pp. 717–9.

[15] Although Marshall and Pigou, the leaders of the Cambridge School of Economists, have also been leaders in the theoretical statement of the laws of demand, Marshall actually discouraged the use of mathematical methods to determine relative elasticities. (Cf. Marshall, *Principles of Economics*, pp. 109–14.) While Pigou had written an early article in 1910 on budgetary elasticities it was not until 1930 that he, in an article "The Statistical Derivation of Demand Curves," *Economic Journal*, Vol. XL, pp. 384–400, turned his attention to the possibility of determining elasticities from price and quantity data and while his contribution to method was characteristically weighty and important, neither he nor his followers have, with all their great abilities, really added to our inductive knowledge of actual elasticities. In a somewhat similar fashion, the Cambridge mathematicians of the middle of the nineteenth century were at best indifferent to the possibility of the development of mathematical physics. Cf. Campbell and Garnett, *Life of James Clerk Maxwell*, and Sylvanus P. Thompson, *The Life of William Thomson, Baron Kelvin of Largs*, 2 vols.

The theory of distribution and the theory of wages need a similar development. The marginal productivity of the various factors at any one time is, of course, dependent upon: (1) the rate of diminishing productivity when additional units of each factor are added and (2) the relative quantity of each factor which has already been supplied.

Just as the Austrian theory of value did not answer the question as to why the supply of a given commodity happened to be what it was nor whether it would remain constant, or would increase or decrease, so does the productivity theory by itself give no explanation as to how labor, capital, and business ability came to be supplied in the quantities that they are, nor does it enable us to judge whether these quantities are likely to change in the future. Why, for example, is there not double the amount of capital that now exists, and why are there not 24,000,000 members of the normal labor supply in the United States instead of the 49,000,000 which there approximately are? If these were the respective quantities of labor and capital which were supplied, then the marginal productivity of capital would be much less than what it now is, while the marginal productivity of labor would be much greater. What then has prevented this situation or a myriad of others from coming about, rather than the one which we now have? The theory of marginal productivity can no more answer such queries by itself than could the Austrians explain why nine horses should be brought into the market instead of ninety. And yet it is just such questions as these that must be answered if we are to secure any real insight into the problems of distribution. In treating the supplies of labor and capital as fixed, the productivity theory has tended to neglect the possibility that the supply of these factors may be forced to increase or decrease in the near future with a consequent change in the equilibrium.

In other words, the followers of Professor Clark have tended to ignore the fact that the factors of production, with the possible exception of "bare" land, were brought into being at a money cost. If a given unit is to be produced, then, in the long run, the price which it obtains for its services must be at least sufficient to meet the costs entailed in producing it. If, on the contrary, each factor receives more than is needed to meet the expense attached to the marginal units, then the existence of this surplus will encourage more units to be produced provided, of course, that the factor is produced on economic principles.[16] The permanent equilibrium will, therefore, be one at which the return per unit of a factor will tend to be just sufficient to meet the expense occasioned by bringing to the market that unit which was employed whose cost was greatest.[17]

The supply function is, therefore, a force in determining the return to the factors as well as a force in determining the value of particular commodities. Together with the rate of diminishing productivity for each factor and the curve of total productivity, it determines the amount of a given factor which will ultimately be forthcoming and hence its marginal productivity. The fundamental features of the neo-classical theory apply, therefore, to the field of distribution as well as to that of value.

In the mutual relationship between the productivity and supply curves will be found the explanation as to why the factors have been combined in the porportions in which they have been and also the clue as to whether the existing rates of return represent a permanent equilibrium or not. This was pointed out by Marshall and by Carver[18] in the 1890's. Thus interpreted, the productivity theory falls into place as one of the columns of the arch of distribution rather than as its sole explanation.

But while the neo-classical analysis of the mutually interacting effects of productivity and cost of supply is as essentially sound for the theory of distribution as for that of value,[18a] it too

---

[16] The query then presents itself, is labor so produced; or capital?

[17] Strictly speaking, it is probable that the point of permanent equilibrium for commodities is not precisely at the intersection of the cost and productivity curves but at a slight distance beyond it. Recent cost studies have shown this to be true of particular commodities. There seem always to be some firms who are producing at a loss and who when forced out of business are replaced by other relatively inefficient concerns. The trend of thought since the war has emphasized "bulk-line costs" rather than marginal costs as the point at which price will tend to be fixed. By this is meant that price which will meet the expense of somewhere from 85 to 90 per cent of the product turned out. While the production of the factors is not precisely parallel to that of specific commodities, it is nevertheless probable that some of the same tendencies apply. It is not necessary, therefore, in practice that every unit should receive an amount at least equal to that entailed in its cost of production. But certainly the vast majority must if it is produced according to commercial principles, and if that supply is to be forthcoming in the future.

[18] T. N. Carver, "The Place of Abstinence in the Theory of Interest," *Quarterly Journal of Economics*, Vol. VIII (1893), pp. 40–61; "The Theory of Wages adjusted to Recent Theories of Value," *ibid.*, pp. 377–402. For an elaboration of these points ten years later, see his *The Distribution of Wealth* (1904).

[18a] In a previous footnote I have lamented the fact that the great talents of the Cambridge School have not been devoted to the determination of concrete

is empty and barren by itself. It is indeed correct to say that
the return for each unit of a factor of production, such as labor,
depends on the intersection of the productivity and supply
curves for the factor in question, but this by itself tells us but
little unless we can at least estimate appromixately the probable
nature of the slopes of these curves. If the productivity curve
slopes slowly· downwards while the supply curve slopes slowly
upward as is shown in the diagram [19] below, a large quantity of
the factor will be supplied at a relatively low marginal productivity. If the productivity curve were to slope downwards more
sharply, a smaller quantity of the factor would be supplied and
the return per unit would consequently be still lower. If the
supply curve were, moreover, to rise more abruptly, the quantity
supplied would be less and the return per unit more.

If the theory of distribution is then to be given definiteness,
it is necessary to ascertain for each of the various factors what
is the probable nature and what are the elasticities of these two
curves and what are the consequences which flow from them.
Previous writers have not determined the rate at which the
productivity imputed to each factor decreased as more units of
supply were added. Nor do we know the relative payments
needed to induce added units of each to be supplied.

What is needed then is an attempt to do for the factors of
production what American scholars have recently done for so
many individual commodities, namely to determine inductively
what are the relative slopes of the curves of production and
supply for each of the given factors. These points we shall
attempt in the following chapters to determine as precisely as
possible.

2. The Ends to Be Sought in Inductive Studies of Produc- tion and Distribution

But how can this inductive analysis be carried out so as to
determine what the probable elasticities of the imputed produc-

---

elasticities. Nowhere, however, has greater ingenuity been shown in working out
the theoretical implications of various sets of supply and demand schedules.
Marshall, Pigou, Robertson, Shove, Sraffa and the Robinsons have placed all
economics in their debt.

[19] Thus:

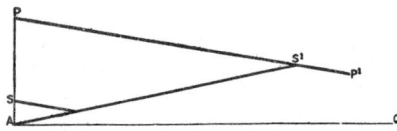

tivity and of the supply curves of the factors capital, labor, and natural resources actually are? In the succeeding sections I shall try to grapple with these problems, but a brief description of the precise ends which are sought and of the main methods employed may make the discussion which follows far more intelligible.

At first thought it might seem impossible to measure marginal productivity statistically, but the progressive refinement during recent years in the measurement of the volume of physical production [20] suggests the possibility that this can be done if we also are able to obtain fairly accurate measures of the changes in the quantities of labor and of capital which have taken place during the period. From an examination of these three series representing labor, capital and product it is possible to throw some fairly definite light upon a number of such problems as:

(1) Can we determine within limits whether the increase in production which has quite generally occurred in recent years was due to purely fortuitous causes, whether it was due to improvements in industrial technique, or whether it responded in any degree to changes in the quantities of labor and of capital?

(2) If a relationship between changes in labor and in capital is found, may it be possible to determine, again within limits, what has been the relative influence upon product of changes in the quantity of labor as compared with changes in the quantity of capital? If labor increases by one per cent, in other

---

[20] For indexes of production in the United States see E. E. Day and W. M. Persons, "An Index of the Physical Volume of Production," *Review of Economic Statistics*, II (1920), pp. 309–37, 361–7, and the subsequent issues of the *Review* in which the index has been revised and kept up to date. See also Woodlief Thomas and E. E. Day, *The Growth of Manufactures in the United States* (Census Monograph) and the index of the Federal Reserve Board as published in the Federal Reserve Bulletin. For England, see an article by N. A. Tolles and myself, "A Measurement of British Industrial Production," *Journal of Political Economy* (February, 1930) Vol. XXXVIII, pp. 1–28, and the index of the London-Cambridge Economic Service as published currently in their bulletins. See also an article by Colin G. Clark "Statistical Studies of the Present Economic Position of England," *Economic Journal*, Vol. XLI (1931), pp. 343–69; and his *The National Income 1924–1931*, especially pp. 100–118. For Canada, H. Michell, "An Index of Physical Volume of Production in Canada," Supplement to *Journal of the American Statistical Association*, March, 1929, Vol. XXIV, pp. 167–70 is valuable as are his articles in the *Review of Economic Statistics*, and the work of Babson's statistical organization. Arthur F. Burns in his article "The Measurement of the Physical Volume of Production" *Quarterly Journal of Economics*, February, 1930, Vol. XLIV, pp. 242–62 adopts a skeptical attitude towards all such measurements for a summary of all the indexes. See also the *Memorandum on Production and Trade, 1923 to 1929–30*, published by the League of Nations, (1931).

words, by how much will product normally increase, and similarly what will be the relative effect upon product of a change of one per cent in the quantity of capital?

(3) If these relationships can be discovered, may it then be possible to arrive at the curves of imputed marginal productivity for both of the factors? The chief means of determining these would be to find out what the average productivities of labor and of capital were in various years as the proportion between labor and capital varied.

(4) Such questions as have been discussed inevitably raise the question as to whether any results which we obtain from such historical data are, as some assert, applicable only to the particular place and period covered or whether they have a more general and universal application. Manifestly we shall be helped in answering this query by studying the movements of labor, capital, and product in as many countries and for as many different periods of time as is possible, and this we shall attempt to do.

(5) Finally, can any light be thrown upon the question whether the actual course of the distribution of the product of industry between capital and labor approximates what we might expect from our analysis of production? Thus, for example, we can compare the relative shares of the product which actually go to labor and capital respectively with the proportions which would be imputed to them by the derived equations of production. We can, moreover, compare the movement of the average "value productivity" of labor [21] through a period of time with the actual movement of real wages and determine the degree to which the latter follows the former. In a similar fashion we can compare the actual movement of the rate of interest with the theoretical movement of the value productivity of capital.

Such then are the main lines of inquiry which we shall pursue in the second part of this book. But all this, as we have indicated, is but half of the story. It is almost equally necessary to analyze the factors operating from the side of supply, and here again we find a series of questions to which ultimately some answers must be found.

(1) Are both the size of the labor supply and the rate of

---

[21] By "average value productivity" is meant the average physical productivity in a given line of industry multiplied by the ratio of the price relatives for those commodities to the general price index.

saving determined solely by non-economic causes, or are they in some sense functions of the rates of wages and of interest respectively? Many believe that the number of laborers is determined almost solely by the passion between the sexes and by the relative practice of birth control on the one hand and of medical science on the other. These forces, it is argued, are not economic and operate independently of the rate of wages. Similarly, it is frequently stated that saving is automatic and proceeds from an instinctive desire for security or for status and that it would be what it is irrespective of the rate of interest.

If these claims are true then it follows that it is virtually impossible to arrive at the supply curves of the factors. The relative quantities of the factors will be determined in a somewhat blind fashion, and while the rate of wages and of interest will largely be shaped by the quantities of these factors which actually appear on the market, these rates of return will, however, have no influence in return upon the quantities.

Whether this surmise is in fact true can, of course, only be determined by investigation. But while this approach is obvious, it has been neglected. Should inductive studies show that the rate of wages does affect the supply of labor or that the rate of interest does influence the volume of saving then three further problems would inevitably demand attention, namely:

(2) What effects do differences in the elasticities of supply of the factors have upon the amounts per unit and the share of the total product which labor and capital receive in the event of either an increase or a decrease in the effectiveness of industry? To what degree and how would shifts in the supply curve of one factor affect not only the return to that factor but to the other as well? And finally, to what degree would such results be modified by the proportion which wages and interest originally formed of the national income and the degree to which the wage-earners and the recipients of interest expended their income on commodities in which proportionately much or little labor was embodied? These problems must at present be approached primarily by a theoretical method of analysis. Since the importance of the part which relative elasticities of supply play in the processes of distribution has been relatively neglected by economists, such an analysis may shed much needed light on the whole problem and sharpen our appreciation of the points which are at issue.

(3) Just what is the nature and elasticity of the supply curve of labor? To what degree, if at all, and in what direction would the supply of labor change with a given change in wages? Here we shall find it necessary, as we shall see, to distinguish between the short-run and the long-run effects of changes in wages and to study in some detail the different streams which go to make up each.

(4) What is the nature and elasticity of the supply curve of capital? Here we are confronted not only with the difficulties of measuring the changes in the *real* rate of interest and the *real* volume of saving but also of trying to see what relationship exists between them. The problems here are both tangled and intricate, and it is not pretended that a completely satisfactory conclusion can be drawn.

From all of these diverse studies of both the productivity and the supply curves of labor and capital, some general conclusions may be drawn which will help to explain the actual course in the past of both the rate of interest and the rate of wages, and may be of some aid at least in forecasting what their probable movements will be in the future.

3. Have Statistical Results Theoretical Meaning?

Any inductive study dealing with the problems of distribution or of value is almost invariably either brushed aside or attacked by the devotees of "pure" theory on the ground that since statistical analysis is necessarily based on comparisons between time or space its units can never be identical with those timeless concepts which characterize "pure" theory. For the high priests of "pure" theory are never tired of pointing out that they are dealing only with static conditions—as of one moment of time for one community. When statistical series dealing with time sequences or even relative distributions in space are brought forward, the armchair theorists brush these aside on the ground that they may include either shiftings of the curves or different curves. These series are then dismissed as being merely historical or empirical.

Now it is of course true that one of the aims of statistical economics, although not its exclusive obligation, should be to approximate as far as possible the static concepts and to give concrete meaning and definite values to them. But if this cannot be completely carried out and if the barriers of time and space prevent a complete identity from being established, what then should be done? Should we abandon all efforts at the inductive determination of economic theory and remain in the ivory tower of "pure" theory. If this is what is done, we may as well abandon all hope of further developing the science of economics and content ourselves with merely the elaboration of hypothetical assumptions which will be of little aid in solving problems since we will not know the values. Or shall we try to make economics a progressive science? The path of progress seems to me to lie in the latter direction although the inclinations of many economists seem to tend toward the former. Nor does it seem to me nefarious, but rather inevitable, that in this process the new concepts which are developed will be somewhat different from those of static theory. Those concepts, while of great aid in furnishing hypotheses and methods of analysis, may prove nonoperational so far as solving problems is concerned. If this is so, science should move out beyond them and not confine itself to the ivory tower which otherwise would be indeed a prison-house. It is therefore with no apologies that we embark upon the inductive and historical analysis of the succeeding chapters.

NOTE

SOME ATTEMPTS TO TEST THE THEORY OF MARGINAL PRODUCTIVITY

The most notable attempt of this kind has perhaps been that of Professor H. L. Moore in his brilliant *Laws of Wages*. In this work, Professor Moore utilized statistics, collected by Professor François Simiand, of wages, output, and horse-power employed in the French coal mines from 1845 to 1902,[1] to determine what degree of relationship existed between changes in the rate of wages and changes in the value of the product. The first test of the productivity theory which Moore made was then to determine whether [2] "in an industry in which labor plays the leading rôle in production, the fluctuation in the daily rate of general wages varies directly with the fluctuation in the value of the daily product of the laborer." The value in francs of the average daily output in each of the years was found, as was the average daily wage. Then after the trends had been obtained for the average value of the daily product per laborer and for the average daily wages, the relative deviations of each from its trend were calculated, and the correlation between the two computed.[3] The coefficient of correlation was found to be $+ .84$, indicating a high degree of association between the two factors. An increase or

---

[1] François Simiand, *Le Salaire des Ouvriers des Mines de Charbon en France*.

[2] Moore, *Laws of Wages*, pp. 46–7.

[3] *Ibid.*, pp. 46–53.

decrease in the average daily productivity of labor tended, therefore, to be accompanied by a very close approximation to a movement in the same direction in wages.[4]

A further interesting test of the validity of the productivity theory can be made from a comparison of (1) the relative amount of power utilized per person in the various industrial countries with (2) the relative level of real wages in the respective nations. Statistics of the water power utilized in the chief countries of the world are contained in the proceedings of the first World Power Conference while those for oil and coal are given both in the proceedings of this conference[5] and in the annual reports of the United States Geological Survey on *The Mineral Resources of the United States.*[6] These have all been converted by the use of standard conversion units into kilowatt hours. Both the total K.W.H. amounts per capita are shown for 1921 in Table 2.

The same table also shows the relative purchasing power in 1924 of a common unit of work for city workers in these same countries. These indexes are secured by the International Labor Office by the method of comparing the relative money wages in the cities of the various countries with the cost of a composite family budget in these cities.[7] In preparing this budget the various constituent items were cross-weighted by their relative importance in the various countries

---

[4] Professor Moore's second statement that "the most essential proposition in the productivity theory of wages is that fluctuation in the laborer's *relative* share in the value of the product varies directly with the fluctuation in the amount of machine power per laborer employed in the industry," (*Ibid,* p. 55) seems, however, to have been a misunderstanding of the productivity theory. Moore determined the relative proportions of the value of a day's work which were paid to the miners in the various years and the amounts of machine power per laborer which was taken as a measurement of capital. After obtaining the respective trends of each, and computing the relative deviations from these trends, he found a coefficient of correlation between them of $+ .599$, and he concluded (p. 61) that "the fluctuation in the laborers' relative share of the product of industry varies directly with the fluctuation in the relative amount of capital employed." While the productivity theory does, of course, hold that the amount of product which is specifically imputed to each unit of capital will, if all other factors remain constant, decrease as the amount of capital increases, it does not necessarily follow that this decrease in absolute yield must be at such a rate that the relative share of the total product which goes to capital will be less than it was before. The increase in the number of units of capital which are supplied may be such as to offset the decline in marginal productivity. All that is essential to the marginal productivity theory is, therefore, that the absolute return for each unit of a given factor will decrease if the quantity of that factor increases relatively more rapidly than that of the other factors. It is not essential either that the total amount of product going to a given factor shall be less or that the share of that factor in the total output of industry shall be less than it was before. Whether or not these results will happen, will depend upon the relative elasticity of the curves of incremental productivity, the proportions in which the product was previously divided and whether production in general is a simple homogeneous function of the first degree. If it is, the proportions will be unchanged.

[5] See article by S. Balakshin, *Transactions, First World Power Conference,* Vol. I, pp. 1298–1307.

[6] See article by General P. A. M. Nash, *Ibid.,* Vol. IV, pp. 1306–22 and one by Sir Richard Rechmayne, *World's Coal Resources, Ibid.,* Vol. I., pp. 420–48.

[7] See *International Labour Review,* Vol. X (October 1924), p. 652.

according to the method suggested by Professor Irving Fisher.[8] This system of cross-weighting can, therefore, be used for different units in space as well as in time and hence can largely eliminate the discrepancy which a difference in nationality budgets would otherwise cause. Where statistics of real wages are given for two cities in any one country, as is the case in Italy, for Rome and Milan, the indexes of real earnings were weighted by the relative population in each city to secure the index for the country as a whole. These indexes are shown in column two of Table 2, with the relative real wages in London serving as 100.

TABLE 2

A COMPARISON OF THE AVERAGE RELATIVE POWER IN NINE COUNTRIES AND THE RELATIVE LEVEL OF AVERAGE REAL WAGES

Country	Average Power in 1000 K.W.H. per Capita (1924)	Average Relative Real Wage (London = 100)	Rank with Respect to Real Wages
United States...........	3.13	213	1
Germany................	2.71	55	8
Great Britain...........	2.52	100	3
Canada.................	2.31	155	2
France.................	1.32	65	6
Sweden.................	0.66	79	4
Norway.................	0.52	72	5
Spain..................	0.26	57	7
Italy..................	0.22	49	9

Using the Spearman formula of computing the rank correlation of $\rho = 1 - \dfrac{6\Sigma d^2}{N(N^2-1)}$ we secure a coefficient of correlation of $+$ .58 with a standard error of $\pm$ .149. Since the coefficient of correlation is quite high and is four times the standard error, a considerable degree of correlation appears between the amount of power per worker and the level of real wages.

Had conditions been more normal in Germany, the correlation would have been much higher. Germany ranked second as regards power, but only eighth as regards relative wages. Germany indeed contributed thirty-six of the fifty points that comprised the sum of the squares of the deviations in ranking. But this very low level of wages was due primarily to the aftermath of the war with its indemnities, to the extraordinary inflation of prices which she was just passing through, and to the occupation of the Ruhr by the French with its shutting off of coal, iron, and steel. The pre-war studies of the British Board of Trade together with recent indexes by the International Labor Office seem to indicate that Germany would normally not rank below fifth as regards per capita real wages. Were this to be the case, the sum of the squares of the deviations would amount to only 22 and the coefficient of correlation would be $+$ .82. This would be, of course, a relatively high correlation, and it is probably a closer approximation to the normal situation than the coefficient secured from the data in Table 2.

[8] Fisher, *The Making of Index Numbers.*

PART II

An Approach to the Imputed Productivity Curves of Labor and Capital

CHAPTER V

THE INFLUENCE OF LABOR AND CAPITAL UPON PRODUCTION IN THE UNITED STATES, 1899–1922, AND AN APPROACH TO THE CURVES OF DIMINISHING MARGINAL PRODUCTIVITY [1]

This chapter and those which follow attempt to deal with the questions outlined in Chapter IV and to throw some light upon them. But before this is done, it is, of course, necessary to construct indexes of the relative amounts of labor and capital which have been used, and it is this which is dealt with in the two succeeding sections, leaving the later sections for the treatment of the interrelationships which may be discovered.

1. The Growth of Fixed Capital in Manufacturing in The United States, 1899–1922

The census of manufactures has periodically included a question on the amount of capital invested in the various manufacturing enterprises and has tabulated the returns. This, however, includes in addition to fixed capital in the form of machinery and buildings, working capital including raw materials, goods in process of manufacture, and finished goods in warehouses. It also includes land. Since we are attempting to measure the capital which aids in the production of goods, we should exclude working capital, for this is the result and not a cause for the process of manufacture.[2] We should also exclude land values since these are largely composed of the unearned increment. We shall, therefore, attempt to measure the changes in the physical quantity of (1) machinery, tools, and equipment and (2) factory buildings.

Unfortunately, while statistics of total capital are given virtually every census year, they were only segregated for these specific groups in 1889, 1899, and 1904.[3] The Census Bureau

---

[1] This chapter is adapted from an article by Professor Charles W. Cobb and the present author in the supplement to the *American Economic Review*, March, 1928, pp. 139–65.

[2] Working capital of course normally "produces" value for its owner, but we are here not concerned with value but with physical production.

[3] See *13th Census* (1900), VI, p. xcvii, and the *Census of Manufactures*, 1904, Part I, pp. lxiv–lxv.

in its 1922 report on *Wealth, Public Debt and Taxation* estimated that manufacturing machinery, tools, and equipment formed 30 per cent of the total amount of manufacturing capital.[4] Since it set the latter at 52,610 millions, this would give a figure for machinery, etc., of 15,783 millions.

TABLE 3

FIXED CAPITAL IN MANUFACTURING IN CERTAIN CENSUS YEARS

Year	Value of Factory Buildings (in millions of dollars)	Percentage of Manufacturing Capital	Value of Machinery, Implements and Equipment (in millions of dollars)	Percentage of Total Manufacturing Capital
1889	879	13.4	1,584	24.3
1899	1,450	14.8	2,543	25.9
1904	1,996	15.8	3,490	27.5
1922			15,783	30.0[5]

The amounts which have thus been ascribed to each of these forms of capital and the percentages which they formed of total capital for the given years were as shown in Table 3.

These statistics furnish a basis for estimating the probable value of these forms of manufacturing capital in those years when no such segregation of items was carried out. Not only was the total amount of capital increasing, but fixed capital was coming to form a larger percentage of this greater sum.

It seems undeniable that buildings and machinery did not increase as rapidly in comparison with working capital during the eighties as they did during the fifteen years which followed 1889 when buildings advanced from 13.4 to 15.8 per cent, or an increase of 2.4 points, and machinery, etc., from 24.3 to 27.5, or a gain of 3.2 points. This was an advance of .16 and .21 points a year, respectively. We have assumed that the growth in the proportions which buildings formed of the total was at approximately only one-quarter of the rate of speed of the nineties and for machinery at only one-fifth. This would give 13.0 per cent as the probable figure for buildings in 1879 and 24.0 per cent as that for machinery, tools, and equipment.

If we accept the census estimate of 30 per cent as the proportion which machinery formed of the total in the terminal year of 1922, we may then distribute the 2.5 per cent increase

[4] Bureau of the Census, *Estimated National Wealth* (1925), pp. 9–10.
[5] Estimate of the Census Bureau.

from 27.5 per cent in 1904, according to a fairly even ratio. The rate of growth from 1914 on was, however, undoubtedly somewhat more rapid than during the previous decade, and allowance should be made for this fact.

The growth in the relative importance of buildings since 1904 is more problematical since we have no end value on which to build. While the absolute increases have been enormous, it has not seemed to us that the relative importance of buildings in comparison with other forms of capital has advanced at the same rate as during the years, 1889–1904. Because of this and the results of a Missouri investigation, we have estimated the percentage at 16.5 for 1922 and have distributed this over the preceding years but providing for a more rapid growth after 1914 than before. Table 4 gives the estimated percentage of each of these forms of manufacturing capital in the various years and the amounts in terms of dollars.

There is some evidence to indicate that the estimated total for buildings and machinery at 46.5 per cent is not far from correct. Thus the Missouri State Bureau of Labor Statistics shows that in 1923, 334.7 millions were invested in that state in manufacturing buildings, machinery, etc., and 58.7 millions in "grounds." [6] The amount of the working capital is not given, but this was set for the country as a whole by the Federal Trade Commission at 45.7 per cent of the total capital. [7] Since this is based upon the returns of 54,862 corporations with a total capital of 33.65 billions, it may be accepted as the best nation-wide estimate which we have. If we apply this ratio to Missouri, we would get 331.1 millions or a total with other items of 724.6 millions. Now buildings, machinery, and equipment were, as stated, evaluated independently by the Missouri study at 334.7 millions and this would be 46.2 per cent of the total. This is in almost exact agreement with the estimate of 46.5 per cent which we have made for these forms of capital in 1922. Since the types of manufacturing in Missouri are not unrepresentative [8] of conditions in the country as a whole, our estimate can be considered to be buttressed and until better statistics are collected to be probably the best which can be made.

[6] *Forty-fourth Annual Report Missouri Bureau of Labor* (1923), p. 155.
[7] Federal Trade Commission, *National Wealth and Income*, p. 135. (Senate Doc. 126, 69th Congress, 1st Session.)
[8] Thus while Missouri does not have any textile industries and but a small clothing industry, it does have a considerable amount of capital invested in printing, foundries, automobile manufacture, meat packing, smelting, and brick and lime works. There is also a fast growing shoe industry.

TABLE 4

ESTIMATED VALUES OF MANUFACTURING BUILDINGS AND MACHINERY, TOOLS AND
EQUIPMENT AND PERCENTAGES WHICH THEY FORMED OF TOTAL
MANUFACTURING CAPITAL, 1879–1922

Year	Percentage of Total Manufacturing Capital		Value in Millions of Dollars		
	Buildings	Machinery and Equipment	Buildings	Machinery and Equipment	Total
1879	13.0	24.0	363	670	1,033
1889	13.4	24.3	879	1,584	2,463
1899	14.8	25.9	1,450	2,543	3,993
1904	15.8	27.5	1,996	3,490	5,486
1909	16.0	28.1	2,948	5,178	8,126
1914	16.2	28.7	3,692	6,541	10,233
1919	16.4	29.5	7,293	13,118	20,411
1922	16.5	30.0	8,681	15,783	24,464

There remains, however, the natural query as to what these census returns mean and how much the original data are worth. In recent years, the Census Bureau has instructed its agents to see that these statistics be taken "at the amounts carried on the books." Does this book value then mean the original cost of the buildings, machinery, etc., or the cost of reproduction? Mr. La Verne Beals, the chief statistician for manufactures, who is probably the ablest expert in this general field, has stated [9] that the "manufacturers have as a rule reported capital on the basis of original cost rather than cost of reproduction."

These estimates of fixed capital, when they were first made by the author in 1927, were greeted with some skepticism by many economists. These critics have naturally pointed to the fact that the Census Bureau itself repeatedly issued cautions against the implicit acceptance of its statistics on the total of manufacturing capital and has omitted such a question from its schedules for the manufacturing censuses of 1921, 1923, and 1925. The doubting Thomases have not fully realized, however, that this reluctance on the part of the census to utilize the data on capital has been in large part due to the realization by that body of the difficulties introduced by changing price levels and to their realization that equal monetary additions to capital in different years might mean very unequal slices of additional "real" capital. If a way is found for deflating these increments by indexes of the probable relative cost of installing fixed capi-

---

[9] Letter to author, October 23, 1925.

tal, as is later done, this difficulty would be largely removed and the corrected index of "real" fixed capital would deserve much fuller credence.

Happily, however, there is far more direct evidence to indicate that our estimate of the money cost of manufacturing plant and equipment is not far from correct. This comes from the studies by the Bureau of Internal Revenue of the Treasury Department and by my colleague, Professor S. H. Nerlove,[10] into the real capital values of American corporations. Thus in 1922, the returns derived from the corporate income tax showed that the corporations reporting in manufacturing had total investments in buildings, real estate and equipment of 18.3 billions of dollars.[11] These figures did not, however, include those corporations which either had net deficits or whose net profits amounted to less than $3,000. Professor Nerlove in his study[12] found that in 1928 such corporations had 33 per cent of the fixed assets and 25 per cent of all the capital assets of those which did have net profits of more than $3,000. Since 1922 was distinctly a worse business year than 1928, it seems most safe to increase the fixed capital figures of 18.3 billions by 33 per cent to take account of these corporations in this year. This would give a total of 24.3 billions. This strikingly enough is virtually identical with my original estimate of 24.5 billions. It differs from my figure, however, in that it includes real estate but does not include the fixed capital owned by partnerships and individuals. In order to make these two sets of figures precisely comparable therefore it is necessary to add to the total of the Bureau of Internal Revenue an allowance for the capital of unincorporated businesses and to subtract an allowance for land. These largely serve to offset each other. Thus in 1919 the non-corporate enterprises in manufacturing added to the value of the product 15 per cent as much as the corporate enterprises.[13] While their proportionate capital equipment was undoubtedly somewhat less, it is probably safe to set it as approximately 12 per cent or at about 3.0 billions of dollars. This would raise the total to 27.3 billions of dollars. As we

[10] S. H. Nerlove, *A Decade of Corporate Incomes 1920 to 1929*. 76 pp. Studies in Business Administration of the School of Commerce and Administration of the University of Chicago (1932).
[11] *Statistics of Income*, 1922, p. 40.
[12] S. H. Nerlove, *op. cit.*, p. 70.
[13] See *Abstract of 14th Census of the United States*, 1920, p. 1031.

have seen from the Missouri study,[14] the value of land tends
there to equal 15 per cent of the total value of land, buildings
and equipment. Applying this percentage to the figures of fixed
capital would give a total of 4.1 billions of dollars. Subtracting
this amount from 27.3 billions would give a total of 23.2 billions
which is only approximately 1.3 billion dollars, or five per cent
less than the amount of my original estimate. Substantial
agreement between the totals seems therefore to have been
established.[15]

The differences between my estimate and that of Professor
Nerlove[16] are largely explained in a footnote.[17] We may, therefore, in all probability accept the computed capital statistics as
a fairly accurate approximation of the actual quantities.

It should, moreover, be realized that we are not using
these statistics of capital to obtain a measurement of the *absolute* amounts of fixed capital but rather of the *relative* changes
in quantity and that the series, when the difficulties caused by
the changing price levels of capital goods are eliminated, is likely
to be appreciably more accurate in measuring the relative
changes than it is in indicating the absolute amounts invested.

---

[14] See Forty-Fourth Annual Report Missouri Bureau of Labor, p. 155.

[15] When two different estimates of such a large total agree within the range
of 5 per cent, substantial verification can be claimed.

[16] It may be asked how my estimate of 24.5 billions can be reconciled with
Mr. Nerlove's estimate of 35.2 billions of "invested capital in corporations" for
1920 and 35.9 billions for 1922. (Nerlove, *op. cit.*, p. 37 and pp. 69–76.) The inclusion of unincorporated business in Mr. Nerlove's total would of course increase this difference. Mr. Nerlove's figure includes: (1) actual cash paid in for
capital stock + (2) actual cash value of property together with a certain allowance for intangibles, which was paid in for capital stock + (3) paid in or earned
surplus, including undivided profits. It does not include bonded indebtedness
which from the stockholder's point of view is of course a liability.

There are therefore three sources of assets in Mr. Nerlove's estimates which
are not included in our figures and which go far to explain the difference between
the two totals: (a) real estate. This as we have seen, probably accounts for
not far from 3.7 billions and hence reduces the difference to around 7.7 billions
plus the capital of unincorporated concerns (b) "Water" existing in the capitalization of the companies in 1920. In view of the common practise of issuing
stock which did not represent physical assets but merely expected or claimed
future earning power, this almost certainly accounted for several billions of dollars at the very least. In this connection one has only to remember the history
of the United States Steel Corporation and the methods of such promoters as
John W. Gates, etc. Mr. Nerlove was largely successful in excluding such
"write-ups" after 1920, but he had to accept the 1920 figures as they stood.
(c) To the degree to which working capital was financed by stock issues in excess
of the amount of bond issues and mortgages (which in turn amounted to 2.9
billions) there was a third source of difference.

The Nerlove estimate does not therefore seem to be greatly out of harmony
with mine if all of these factors are taken into account.

[17] For stock-watering practises see the Reports of the U. S. Commissioner of
Corporations and Lewis Corey, *The House of Morgan.*

To a consideration of the problems which are involved (1) in deflating the series to allow for the changes in the price level and (2) in estimating the investment in intercensal years, we now turn. We shall begin with this second problem.

Since the statistics are based upon original cost, the first problem consists in finding the probable annual increments of capital in terms of the prices of that year and of adding these to the values of the preceding year. The method followed was, in brief: (1) To ascertain the quantities of the following commodities produced in each year from 1899–1922: pig iron, rolled and forged steel, lumber, coke, cement, bricks, and copper.[18] It will be noted that these commodities are the most important of those which are used in the construction of machinery and of buildings. In those few cases where it was impossible to secure actual figures of production for a given year, these were estimated from other years on the basis of the relative change in Professor Day's index of physical production for that group of manufactured products in which the commodity in question was included.[19] For the period 1880–1889, the quantities of pig iron, steel, cement, copper, and coke were used. (2) The quantity produced of each commodity in each year was multiplied by its current price per unit of product.[20] The prices for the period from 1890–1922 were those collected and published by the United States Bureau of Labor Statistics,[21] while those used for the decade from 1880–1890 were those published in the reports of the Aldrich Committee.[22] In some cases it was possible directly to derive the value of the total product without multiplying the physical product by the price per unit, and wherever this was the case the directly quoted total was used. (3) The values of each commodity produced in a given year were then added together to obtain the total values of these producers' goods turned out in each year. (4) The values of these capital goods which were produced between two census years were then totaled (e.g.,

---

[18] The raw data were secured from the United States Statistical Abstract for the various years. Also *Mineral Resources of the United States* 1921, Part I, pp. 235–82, 565–98; Part II, pp. 371–440.

[19] E. E. Day, "An Index of the Physical Volume of Production," *Review of Economic Statistics,* Vol. II (1920), pp. 328–29; "The Physical Volume of Production in the United States for 1923," *Ibid.,* Vol. VI (1924), p. 201.

[20] The average of the prices of spruce and maple was used for lumber.

[21] Bulletin 335 of the United States Bureau of Labor Statistics, *Wholesale Prices,* 1890–1922, pp. 126–56.

[22] *Report of Senate Committee on Wholesale Prices and Wages,* Appendix A. The criticisms of the index of prices do not apply here since the absolute prices quoted were used without the many varieties of jackknives.

1880 to 1889 inclusive) and the value for each year was divided by the total for the period in order to get the percentage which it formed of the total value produced during the period as a whole. These percentages were then applied to the total increase in the value of buildings and machinery over the same period, and estimated yearly increases in the value of these items were thus obtained.

This process may be illustrated by the following example. The increase in the value of buildings and machinery between 1879 and 1889 was 1430 millions. The total money values in each of the years of these capital goods and the per cent which each of these yearly totals formed of the total for the period were as follows:

TABLE 5

ILLUSTRATION OF METHOD OF FINDING ADDITIONS
TO CAPITAL IN INTERCENSAL YEARS, 1880–1889

Year	Value of Specified Capital Goods (in millions of dollars)	Per Cent of Total Value for Decade
1880	200	9.6
1881	210	10.0
1882	216	10.3
1883	184	8.8
1884	148	7.1
1885	141	6.7
1886	211	10.0
1887	282	13.5
1888	241	11.5
1889	263	12.5
Total	2,096	100.0

The increase in the value of buildings and machinery during the decade, 1430 millions, was then multiplied by each of these percentages and the probable amounts of the yearly increases in value were obtained. These amounts when totaled and added to the total for 1879 would of necessity equal the 1889 value. The basic assumption is of course that the capital values in terms of original cost grew from year to year as the money value of the capital goods produced.

But since these estimated additions to capital are reckoned in terms of the dollars of the given years, if we are to secure an index of relative real capital, it is necessary to eliminate the effect of changing price levels. A capital cost index was accordingly computed which was based on three sets of relative prices:

(1) the wholesale prices of metals and metal products, (2) the wholesale prices of building materials and (3) money wages. The Aldrich Committee report was used to obtain prices for the first two groups of products from 1880 to 1889 [23] while the indexes of the Bureau of Labor Statistics were used for the years 1890 to 1922.[24] For wages, the index previously computed by the author was used for the period from 1890 on,[25] while the average wages computed by Dr. R. P. Falkner for the Aldrich report were taken to show the movement during the eighties. These three series were then reduced to relatives with 1880 serving as 100 and were combined into a weighted average.

TABLE 6

ESTIMATED ANNUAL ADDITIONS TO FIXED CAPITAL IN MANUFACTURING TOGETHER WITH CUMULATIVE TOTAL CAPITAL AS EXPRESSED IN TERMS OF COST AND 1880 PRICES (Millions of dollars), 1899–1922

Year	Annual Increase in Terms of Cost Price (1)	Cost Index (1880 = 100) (2)	Annual Increase in Terms of 1880 dollars (3)	Total Fixed Capital in 1880 dollars (4)	Relative Total Capital (1899 = 100) (5)
1899	339	88	387	4449	100
1900	264	89	297	4746	107
1901	277	88	315	5061	114
1902	342	89	383	5444	122
1903	328	91	362	5806	131
1904	282	87	326	6132	138
1905	457	92	494	6626	149
1906	612	100	611	7237	163
1907	629	106	595	7832	176
1908	373	94	397	8229	185
1909	569	96	591	8820	198
1910	422	100	420	9240	208
1911	379	99	384	9624	216
1912	457	103	443	10067	226
1913	497	110	453	10520	236
1914	356	101	353	10873	244
1915	1017	105	967	11840	266
1916	1899	135	1402	13242	298
1917	2891	173	1673	14915	335
1918	2473	183	1350	16265	366
1919	1898	196	969	17234	387
1920	2096	237	884	18118	407
1921	780	184	424	18542	417
1922	1177	181	650	19192	431

[23] *Report of Senate Committee on Wholesale Prices*, etc., pp. 92–99. The celebrated twenty-five varieties of jackknives were subtracted from the metal index before using it.

[24] Bulletin 335, *Wholesale Prices*, 1890–1922, pp. 8–9.

[25] Paul H. Douglas, "The Recent Movement of Real Wages and Its Economic Significance." Supplement, *American Economic Review*, March, 1926, p. 30.

The weights used were metals and metal products, 4; building materials, 2; and wages, 3.

Each yearly increase in the value of manufacturing buildings and machinery was then divided by the relative cost index for that year (as shown in Column 2 of Table 6) and a series of "deflated" increases were thus obtained, or rather a series of increases which were expressed in terms of the 1880 price level for capital goods. These are shown in Column 3 of Table 6. The next and final step was to add these deflated yearly increases to the estimated total for buildings and machinery for 1879 and thereafter to the total for each preceding year. Since our other data only extend from 1899–1922, the years prior to 1899 are omitted from this table.

The index is defective in that it does not allow for the replacement of original capital at differing price levels. The census statistics of book value undoubtedly include replacements made at different and generally higher prices than those which prevailed when the original capital was invested. Consequently, the advance from year to year is not solely the result of the saving of additional increments of capital, but includes in part the replacement at other price levels of the old capital as it wore out. The consequence is that our index is throughout most of its course somewhat higher than it should be. I hope to publish a revision of this index in the not distant future in which this error will be eliminated. In the meantime this is offered as a first approximation.

The index does not, of course, measure the short-time fluctuations in the amount of capital used. Thus, no allowance is made for the capital which is allowed to be idle during periods of business depression or for the greater than normal intensity of use in the form of second shifts, etc., which characterizes the periods of prosperity.

The validity of this index of growth is somewhat strengthened, however, when we compare the increase in terms of book value which we have estimated for the United States [26] during the years 1910–1920 with the growth of total capital in Massachusetts when computed upon a similar basis.[27] Using 1910 as a base, the relative increases were as shown in Table 7.

The coincidence between these two indexes is very striking,

---

[26] This column was omitted from Table 6 because of lack of space.
[27] See Annual Reports of the Massachusetts Bureau of Statistics, *Statistics of Manufactures, 1910–1920.*

and this becomes even more the case when we remember that most of the greater increase shown for the United States as a whole was due to the fact that the fixed capital was increasing at a more rapid rate than was the supply of total capital in manufacturing.

It may be remarked that this index shows a truly unprecedented growth in the volume of fixed capital. Thus the amount virtually doubled during the decade from 1899–1909.

TABLE 7

COMPARISON OF TOTAL CAPITAL IN MASSACHUSETTS WITH
ESTIMATES FOR THE UNITED STATES, 1911–1920

Year	Massachusetts (Total Capital)	Estimated for United States (Fixed Capital)
1911	105	104
1912	110	110
1913	113	116
1914	130	120
1915	130	132
1916	150	154
1917	188	188
1918	210	217
1919	248	239
1920	250	263

This was a compounded average yearly rate of increase of 7 per cent. This same rate of increase was virtually maintained during the succeeding decade. From 1919 on the rate of growth slackened during the three succeeding years, but while we have not computed the growth since 1922 it has beyond question increased greatly since then. Taken as a whole this period showed an approximate doubling in the quantity during every decade, which would probably be scaled down to about 6 per cent per year compounded if deductions were made for the increased cost of replacing the old capital. This is a rate of growth which it is believed has not been matched by any other country.[28] It will be remembered that Cassel estimates the rate of growth of capital in western Europe at 3 per cent a year. If this is true, the rate of industrial capital growth in the United States has been twice as great, while if the growth be reckoned on a per capita basis, the disparity is even greater.

---

[28] My index shows that manufacturing capital more than doubled during the eighties and increased approximately 90 per cent during the nineties.

2. The Growth in The Labor Supply, 1899–1922

The various censuses of manufactures give the average number of wage-earners employed in each of the census years.[29] Using these as the bases, we can find the probable numbers employed in the intercensus years by using an index of relative employment. This index was constructed for the years 1899–1904 by combining statistics of the relative number employed from year to year in Massachusetts[30] and Pennsylvania.[31] From 1904 to 1914, figures for New Jersey[32] were substituted for those of Pennsylvania. In both periods, the relative index for each state was then weighted by the number shown by the census to be employed in that state at the beginning of the period, and a combined index was thus secured. The assumption was then made that the volume of employment of the country as a whole followed a similar course to that in these two states. When the rate of change in these two states differed over a census period from the country-wide figures, then it was assumed that this greater or less degree of change had been distributed evenly over the intervening years, and the percentage changes for the two states were scaled down or up to conform to this standard.[33] Thus the increase in the number employed in 1909 over 1904 was as shown by the Census 1,147,000, or 21 per cent. If the increase shown for Massachusetts and New Jersey was 24 per cent, then it was assumed that the differences between the rate of growth for the country and for the two states increased annually at the rate of one-fifth of 3 per cent or .6 per cent. Then if the increase shown in Massachusetts and New Jersey for 1905 over 1904 was 8.6 per cent, this was scaled down to 8.0 per cent. Similar methods were used for the subsequent years.

From 1914 to 1919 the index was secured by combining that of the Bureau of Labor Statistics[34] for a number of industries with that for New York. In doing this, the Bureau's index was given a weight of 3 and that of New York a weight of 1.[35] From 1919 on, the index of the Federal Reserve Board was used, which in turn was largely based upon the index of the Bureau of Labor

[29] Namely 1899, 1904, 1909, 1914, 1919, and 1921.
[30] See Annual reports *Statistics of Manufactures, Massachusetts,* 1900–1905.
[31] See Reports Pennsylvania State Department of Internal Affairs.
[32] Annual volumes of New Jersey Bureau of Labor and Industries, *Statistics of Manufactures* (1904–1914).
[33] This is the identical method which I have followed in interpolating average annual earnings in the intercensal years from the statistics of earnings of the various states.
[34] See files of *Monthly Labor Review.*
[35] See New York *Labor Market Bulletin.*

Statistics. A substantially similar method was used to find the probable number employed in each of the intercensal years up to and including 1922. Table 3 gives these estimated numbers from 1899 on and also expresses them in terms of relatives.

TABLE 8

THE PROBABLE AVERAGE NUMBER OF WAGE-EARNERS EMPLOYED IN
MANUFACTURING FOR THE UNITED STATES, 1899–1922

Year	Average Number Employed (in thousands)	Relative Number (1899 = 100)	Year	Average Number Employed (in thousands)	Relative Number (1899 = 100)
1899	4713	100	1911	6855	145
1900	4968	105	1912	7167	152
1901	5184	110	1913	7277	154
1902	5554	118	1914	7026	149
1903	5784	123	1915	7269	154
1904	5468	116	1916	8601	182
1905	5906	125	1917	9218	196
1906	6251	133	1918	9446	200
1907	6483	138	1919	9096	193
1908	5714	121	1920	9110	193
1909	6615	140	1921	6947	147
1910	6807	144	1922	7602	161

This index is defective in certain respects as a perfect measure of the amount of labor. (1) It does not include clerical employees who have been increasing in number at approximately double the rate of the wage-earners. (2) It is based on man-years rather than "standard" man hours. The average number of hours constituting the standard week's work has declined during this period.[36] (3) It does not measure deviations from this standard week whether they take the form of short-time periods of depression or overtime in the years of prosperity.

Any such index, of course, makes no allowance for possible changes in the quality of the laborers or in the intensity of their work. These factors may be of considerable importance, but at present they certainly cannot be measured quantitatively and until they can be, it is better for any statistical study to ignore them than to make necessarily fantastic estimates as to their importance. When they can be measured, they then should be included.

The first two points mentioned above have been met by a

---

[36] In the opinion of J. M. Clark, however, man-years should be used to measure labor rather than man-hours, on the ground that the use of the latter mixes other variables with the proportion of the factors. See J. M. Clark, "Inductive Evidence on Marginal Productivity," *American Economic Review*, Vol. XVIII, pp. 453–4.

revision which has been carried through with the assistance of Mrs. Vivian Ratcliffe McPherson. The number of clerical and salaried workers were interpolated for the intercensal years according to the relative changes in their numbers from year to year in the states of Ohio and Pennsylvania which have been the only two states with continuous data. The average length of the standard working week in each of the years had already been computed by the author in his *Real Wages in the United States*,[37] and these figures were used to multiply the relatives of the number of employees to obtain the relative standard hours for all employees in each of the years during the period. All of this material is given in Table 9.

TABLE 9

RELATIVE MAN-HOURS OF WAGE-EARNERS AND CLERICAL WORKERS IN MANUFACTURING INDUSTRIES IN THE UNITED STATES, 1899–1922

Year	Relative Number of Clerical and Wage Workers (1)	Average Weekly Hours (2)	Relative Total Man-Hours of Clerical Workers and Wage-Earners (3) = (1) × (2)	Relative Total Man-Hours of Clerical Workers and Wage-Earners (1899 = 100) (4)
1899	100.0	59.1	5910.0	100.0
1900	105.0	59.0	6195.0	104.8
1901	110.7	58.7	6499.1	110.0
1902	118.8	58.3	6926.0	117.2
1903	124.4	57.9	7202.8	121.9
1904	118.4	57.7	6831.7	115.6
1905	128.0	57.7	7385.6	125.0
1906	138.4	57.3	7930.3	134.2
1907	144.3	57.3	8268.4	139.9
1908	128.2	56.8	7281.8	123.2
1909	148.5	56.8	8434.8	142.7
1910	153.5	56.6	8688.1	147.0
1911	155.2	56.4	8753.3	148.1
1912	163.6	56.0	9161.6	155.0
1913	166.3	55.5	9229.7	156.2
1914	162.9	55.2	8992.1	152.2
1915	167.4	55.0	9207.0	155.8
1916	197.0	54.9	10815.3	183.0
1917	213.8	54.6	11673.5	197.5
1918	221.7	53.6	11883.1	201.1
1919	221.4	52.3	11579.2	195.9
1920	225.3	51.0	11490.3	194.4
1921	170.6	50.7	8649.4	146.4
1922	185.3	51.2	9487.4	160.5

It will be seen that the decrease in the number of hours served to offset the greater increase in the number of salaried

[37] Douglas, Paul H., *Real Wages in the United States, 1890–1926*, pp. 112–8.

workers so that the new series of relative standard man-hours for all employees is almost identical with the former series of the relative man-years of the employed workers alone. The extraordinary closeness of agreement between the two series is indicated by the following table which shows the differences between the two in terms of points and percentages for each of the years.

TABLE 10

DIFFERENCES BETWEEN INDEX OF RELATIVE "STANDARD" MAN-HOURS OF ALL EMPLOYEES IN MANUFACTURING AND MAN-YEARS OF MANUAL WORKERS ALONE, 1899–1922 (1899 = 100)

Year (1)	Relation of Man-Hours Index to Man-Years Index		Year (1)	Relation of Man-Hours Index to Man-Years Index	
	In Points (2)	In Per Cent (3)		In Points (2)	In Per Cent (3)
1900	0	0	1912	+3	+2
1901	0	0	1913	+2	+1
1902	−1	−1	1914	+3	+2
1903	−1	−1	1915	+2	+1
1904	0	0	1916	+1	+1
1905	0	0	1917	+1	+1
1906	+1	+1	1918	+1	+.5
1907	+2	+1	1919	+3	+2
1908	+2	+2	1920	+1	+.5
1909	+3	+2	1921	−1	−1
1910	+3	+2	1922	0	0
1911	+3	+2			

In five of the twenty-three years, therefore, the indexes were identical, while in eleven more the differences amounted to only

TABLE 11

INDEX OF PHYSICAL VOLUME OF MANUFACTURES IN THE UNITED STATES, 1899–1922

Year	Index of Manufactures	Year	Index of Manufactures
1899	100	1911	153
1900	101	1912	177
1901	112	1913	184
1902	122	1914	169
1903	124	1915	189
1904	122	1916	225
1905	143	1917	227
1906	152	1918	223
1907	151	1919	218
1908	126	1920	231
1909	155	1921	179
1910	159	1922	240

1 per cent or less. In none of the remaining years did they exceed 2 per cent. Either index can, therefore, be used to measure the change in the labor force. Deviations of the hours actually worked from the standard hours cannot, however, be ascertained at present, and this defect must of necessity remain.

3. The Growth of Physical Production, 1899–1922

For this, we have used E. E. Day's well-known index of the physical volume of production for the years 1899–1922, since at the time we were carrying through our studies the later index given by Dr. Thomas was not available.[37a]

4. The Relation of Labor, Capital and Production

Chart 9 shows on a logarithmic scale the relative growth in manufacturing during this period of fixed capital, of the labor

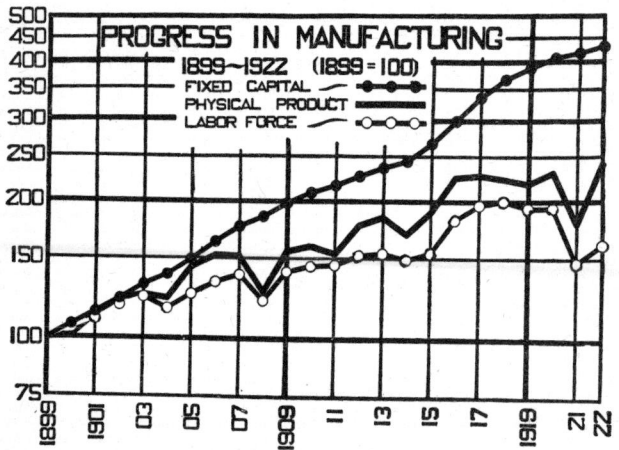

Chart 9. The Relative Changes in the Quantities of Fixed Capital, Labor, and Physical Product in Manufacturing in the United States, 1899–1922.

force, and of the physical product. It will be noticed that the product curve lies between the curves of labor and of fixed capital and that it is appreciably closer to the former than to the latter. By making rough measurements on the logarithmic scale, the curve of relative product appears normally throughout its course to be approximately one-fourth of the distance between the index of labor and the index of capital. By the end-year of

---

[37a] For a description of the methods and sources used in computing the index of production for manufactures, see E. E. Day and W. M. Persons, "An Index of the Physical Volume of Production." *Review of Economic Statistics*, II (1920), pp. 309–37; pp. 361–7. See also Ada M. Mathews, "The Physical Volume of Production in the United States in 1924," *Ibid.*, VII (1925), p. 215.

1922, product was 140 per cent more than in 1899 while the employed working force was 61 per cent more and the index of fixed capital 331 per cent more than in that base year.

5. The Ratios of the Relative Quantities of Labor and Capital to Each Other and Historical Changes in the Coefficients of Production

The data which we have thus far computed can now be combined into two forms which will express some of the changing relations in which labor, capital, and product were combined in the years subsequent to 1899 as compared with the relationship existing in that year. These are (1) the relative ratios in which labor and capital were combined in relation with each other and (2) the relative amounts of labor embodied in a unit of product in manufacturing as compared with 1899 and the relative quantity of capital per unit of product.

The first of these relationships is of primary interest for the determination of the relative effect of labor and capital upon production and can be expressed by dividing the relatives of labor by those of capital and vice versa, i.e. $\frac{L}{C}$ and $\frac{C}{L}$. The second is nothing more or less than historical coefficients of production similar to those discussed for any given period of time by Walras, Pareto, Cassel, and Schultz. These relationships can be expressed by the ratios $\frac{L}{P}$ and $\frac{C}{P}$.

TABLE 12

RELATIVE QUANTITIES OF LABOR AND CAPITAL IN RELATION TO EACH OTHER, 1899–1922, IN COMPARISON WITH QUANTITIES IN 1899

Year	Relation of Labor to Capital $\frac{L}{C}$	Relation of Capital to Labor $\frac{C}{L}$	Year	Relation of Labor to Capital $\frac{L}{C}$	Relation of Capital to Labor $\frac{C}{L}$
1899	1.00	1.00	1911	.67	1.50
1900	.98	1.02	1912	.67	1.50
1901	.96	1.04	1913	.65	1.54
1902	.97	1.03	1914	.61	1.64
1903	.94	1.06	1915	.58	1.72
1904	.84	1.19	1916	.61	1.64
1905	.84	1.19	1917	.59	1.70
1906	.72	1.39	1918	.55	1.82
1907	.78	1.28	1919	.50	2.00
1908	.65	1.54	1920	.47	2.13
1909	.71	1.43	1921	.35	2.86
1910	.69	1.45	1922	.37	2.70

This shows what is evident from Chart 9, that a decreasing amount of labor was combined with each unit of capital and reciprocally that an increasing quantity of capital was united with each unit of labor. This process continued throughout the period save for some cyclical changes, until in 1922 only 37 per cent as much labor was combined with each unit of capital as in 1899, and reciprocally 270 per cent as much capital was combined with a unit of labor as then.

The historical coefficients of production follow with 1899 taken as 100:

TABLE 13

HISTORICAL COEFFICIENTS OF PRODUCTION IN MANUFACTURING IN THE
UNITED STATES, 1899–1922 (1899 = 100)

Year	Coefficients of Production		Year	Coefficients of Production	
	$\frac{L}{P}$	$\frac{C}{P}$		$\frac{L}{P}$	$\frac{C}{P}$
1899	100	100			
1900	104	106	1912	86	128
1901	98	102	1913	84	128
1902	97	100	1914	88	144
1903	99	106	1915	81	141
1904	95	113	1916	81	132
1905	87	104	1917	86	148
1906	88	107	1918	90	164
1907	91	117	1919	89	178
1908	96	147	1920	84	176
1909	90	128	1921	82	233
1910	91	131	1922	67	180
1911	95	141			

The changes in these coefficients of production are especially interesting in view of the way in which the mathematical school has treated the question as to whether or not they must be fixed. Thus in the mathematical equations of Cassel [38] the factors and coefficients of production are treated as fixed, and this same assumption tends to be made in the work of his follower, Valk.[39]

---

[38] Cassel, *The Theory of Social Economy*, Chapter IV. Later Cassel admits the variability of the factors but fails to include them in his discussion.

[39] W. L. Valk. *The Principles of Wages*, pp. 119–29. This analysis is more guarded, however, than that of Cassel, for it recognizes not only that the technical coefficients determine the prices of the means (factors) of production but that the prices of the means (factors) of production determine the technical coefficients. Dr. Valk's reconciliation of these interacting considerations is that the combination of the factors which is made will be one which will give "the highest possible result under the given circumstances." (p. 129.)

Despite the contentions of J. R. Hicks,[40] however, the Lausanne school did not fall into such a rigid error.[41] Walras treated production in terms of stages with the coefficients of production varying from stage to stage, but was not apparently wholly clear as to whether they might be varied within any one stage. Pareto, however, recognized the fact that the coefficients might vary not only between stages but within any one stage and worked in terms of these assumptions as well as in terms of fixed factors and coefficients. It is clear, however, that in fact they certainly are not fixed over a period of time. In general, the drift during the period was decidedly in the direction of less labor and more capital being united in each unit of product so that by 1920 only 84 per cent as much labor was embodied in each unit of product as in 1899, whereas 176 per cent as much capital was so contained. In 1922 the corresponding percentages were respectively 67 and 180.

The caution should perhaps be added, in connection with the technical coefficients of production with respect to capital, that the index of capital represents the relative amounts of capital available rather than the relative amounts actually used. Since in depression periods a considerable percentage of this capital would lie idle, the relative quantities of capital actually used would then be less; conversely, in years in which the business cycle was on the up-swing, and machinery and plant was more fully utilized, the quantities of capital in each unit of product would then be greater.

6. The Relative Influence of Labor and Capital upon Product, 1899–1922, and the Equation of Production

Once given such data as have been cited in the preceding sections, the task remained of finding the probable quantitative influence of labor and capital upon production. To do this we need (1) to devise a formula which will disclose the type of relationship which existed between labor and capital on the one hand and product on the other, (2) to find the values for the constants which are used in this equation, (3) to compare the statistics of relative production obtained by the use of the theoretical formula with the actual course of production and

---

[40] Hicks, J. R. "Marginal Productivity and the Principle of Variation," *Economica*, February, 1932, pp. 79–88.
[41] See the reply of my colleague, Henry Schultz, to some of Mr. Hicks' statements about the Lausanne school. "Marginal Productivity and the Lausanne School," *Economica*, August, 1932, pp. 285–96.

determine the degree to which the theoretical product approximated the actual product.

Not being a mathematician, the author in the spring of 1927 called in the aid of his friend, Professor Charles W. Cobb, of Amherst College. It has been Professor Cobb who devised the formula used, who found the constants, and who has carried through the work of mathematical analysis. Any credit for this part of the work, therefore, belongs to him and not to me.

We realized that in trying to deduce the relationship between the indexes of labor, capital, and product (L, C, and P) we were building our system upon the following conscious assumptions.

(1) Changes in production are the resultants of changes in the quantities of labor and capital alone. We intentionally omitted land from consideration both because its quantity probably did not vary greatly during this period and because it was virtually impossible for us to measure such changes as did occur.

(2) That the volume of production due to manufacturing is proportional to the physical volume of manufactured products. Changes in the relative amount of fabrication were, in other words, ignored.

(3) That the productive power of an average laborer was presumed to be constant from year to year.

(4) That the productive power of a unit of capital (dollar of constant purchasing power of capital goods) was also presumed to be constant from year to year.

(5) No overtime or part-time work performed by either labor or capital was taken into consideration, but it was instead assumed that each factor would have a constant degree of intensity of use from year to year.

In practice, of course, all of these assumptions are to some degree false. Technique is changing, the skill of the workers is being altered from year to year, and the business cycle causes a more intensive use of both labor and capital during periods of prosperity and a less intensive use during the depression or recession phase of the cycle.

Such complicating forces might seem to prevent us from arriving at any law. But if a more or less constant relationship between labor, capital, and product is discovered, this makes the mathematical relationship all the more remarkable.

(6) The final assumption which was made was that if we increased both labor and capital by a factor m, we increase the product by the same proportion.

$$P' = f(L,C)$$
$$mP' = f(mL,mC)$$

This is simply equivalent to assuming that the function $P(L,C)$ is by definition a homogeneous linear function of the first order.

In order to determine whether this function would meet the requirement for a norm and to secure an equation which would describe the relationships, Professor Cobb tried and discarded various functions, and finally hit upon a function of the form.

$$P'(L,C) = bL^kC^{1-k}$$

This satisfies the assumption that the production function is a homogeneous one of the first order and that when either L or C is zero, the product (P) must be zero. Professor Cobb then set himself to find the "best" values of the constants b and k. For this purpose he used, of course, the index numbers of fixed capital (C) and of labor (L) and Day's index of production (P) and by a modification of the method of least squares, relative to these twenty-four sets of values of P, L, and C, found the best values of the constants b and k to be

$$b = 1.01 \qquad k = .75$$

This gives the following production function:

$$P' = 1.01 \, L^{\frac{3}{4}} \, C^{\frac{1}{4}}$$

It is possible then to subject this equation to the crucial test of computing what the theoretical index of production (P') would be from year to year according to this formula and to compare it with the actual index of production (P) during the period. The theoretical indexes of production were then obtained by (1) taking the fourth root of the third power of L and the fourth root of C and (2) multiplying these two together, and then in turn multiplying this product by the constant 1.01. This last figure is seen to be relatively unimportant, merely serving to raise the entire curve by 1 per cent. On Table 14 and Chart 10 a comparison is made between the index of the computed product (P') and the index of actual production. The agreement between the two series, as is evidenced by Chart 10, is striking. The fact that the plus and minus deviations virtually cancel each other is here not really a proof of this consilience, since the values of the constants were adjusted so as to make this happen. But what is significant is that the sum of the plus and minus deviations taken together without regard to sign was only a total of 102 per cent for the twenty-four years or an average of only 4.3 per cent per year. This shows how closely in general the computed curve follows the curve of actual product. The coefficient of correlation between the two indexes is no less than .97.

TABLE 14

The Relative Correspondence between the Actual Index of Production (P) and the Computed Index (P'), 1899–1922, United States $(P' = 1.01 \ L^{3/4} \ C^{1/4})$

Year	(1) Day's Index of Production (P) (1899 = 100)	(2) Index Computed by Formula (P')	(3) Deviation of Computed Index (P') from P $(P'-P)$	(4) Percentage Deviation of Computed Index P' from P $\dfrac{(P'-P)}{(P)}$
1899	100	101	+1	+1
1900	101	107	+6	+6
1901	112	112	0	0
1902	122	121	−1	−0.8
1903	124	126	+2	+1.6
1904	122	123	+1	+0.8
1905	143	133	−10	−7
1906	152	141	−11	−7
1907	151	148	−3	−2
1908	126	137	+11	+9
1909	155	155	0	0
1910	159	160	+1	+0.6
1911	153	163	+10	+6.5
1912	177	170	−7	−4
1913	184	174	−10	−5.4
1914	169	171	+2	+1.1
1915	189	179	−10	−5
1916	225	209	−16	−7.1
1917	227	227	0	0
1918	223	236	+13	+6
1919	218	233	+15	+7
1920	231	236	+5	+2.2
1921	179	194	+15	+8.4
1922	240	209	−31	−13

(1) Total deviations without regard to sign = 102 percentage points.

(2) Average deviation $= \dfrac{102}{24} = 4.3$ percentage points.

(3) Total deviation with regard to sign = $-51.3 + 50.2 = -1.1$

(4) Average deviation with regard to sign = 0.04

Let us now try to see whether an explanation can be offered for such differences between P' and P as do occur. From Chart 10, it is seen that these differences tend to be of a cyclical nature in which P' alternately moves up from and then down below P in that wave-like manner which characterizes cyclical change in its fluctuation from the trend. This immediately raises the query whether the differences may not in part be accounted for by the failure of our data to measure some of these cyclical fluctuations. It will be remembered that our index of capital measures the relative quantity available rather than the relative quantity used. If we assume that the relative proportion of used to available capacity remains relatively constant through time, then this index probably gives a fairly correct approximation to the "normal" capital. But it does fail to measure the cyclical swings in its use. In periods of depression a large percentage of fixed capital falls into disuse, and our index consequently exaggerates the relative amounts then actually used.

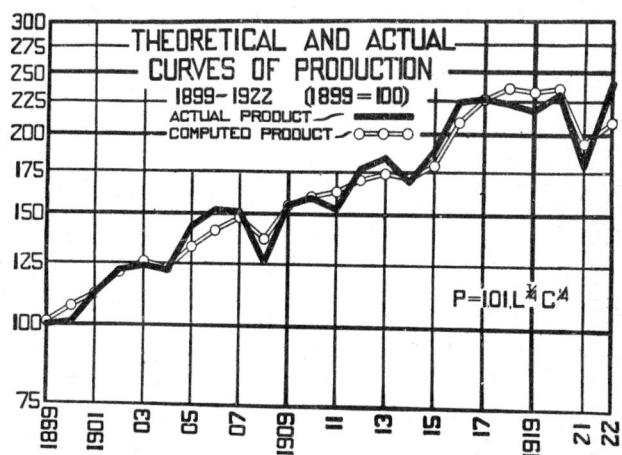

Chart 10. A Comparison between the Actual Index of Production (*P*) and the Computed Index (*P'*), 1899–1922. (*P'* = 1.01 *L*¾ *C*¼)

Conversely, in periods of prosperity the use of overtime and of additional shifts results in a more intensive use, with the result that our index minimizes the change which has occurred between the years of depression and of revival.

Similarly, in the case of labor, the use of short-time in the downward phase of the cycle and of overtime during the upswing prevents an index of even "normal" man-hours from measuring with complete accuracy the changes in actual working-time. The divergence is not, however, as great as in the case of the capital index. Our indexes of labor and capital are, therefore, higher in the depression years and are lower in the prosperity phase of the cycle than they should be. We should expect, therefore, the computed index of production (*P'*), which is built up from values of *C* and *L*, to be higher than the actual product *P* during periods of depression and to be lower than *P* during periods of prosperity. If this should prove in fact to be the case, the differences between P and P' could then be largely explained, and the validity of the equation $P' = 1.01 \ L^{3/4} \ C^{1/4}$ as an explanation of the "normal" relationship between labor, capital, and product would be still further strengthened. Let us see! In column 4 of Table 14 and in Chart 10A there is shown the degree to which P' varied from P during each of the years of this period.

In the depression years of 1908, 1911, 1914, and 1921, the computed index P' rose above the actual product by 9, 7, 1, and 8 per cent respectively, while in the years characterized by a

PERCENTAGE DEVIATIONS
OF COMPUTED FROM ACTUAL PRODUCT
1899 – 1922

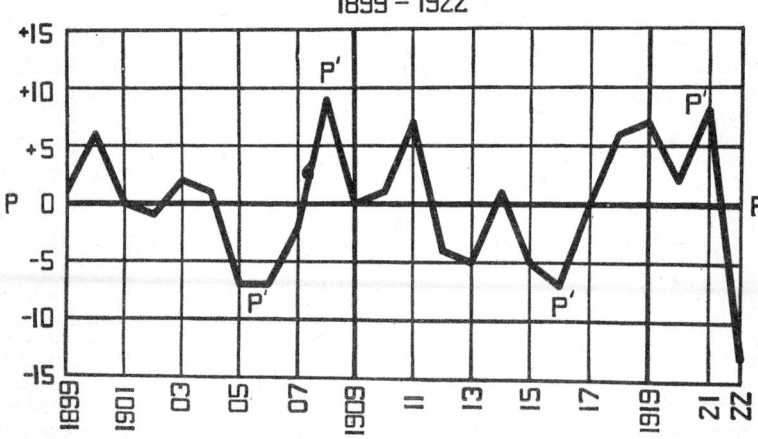

Chart 10A. The Percentage Deviations of the Computed Product from the Actual Product in U. S. Manufacturing, 1899–1922.

recession, or a slight depression, such as 1900,[42] 1903, 1904, and 1910, P' exceeded P by 6, 2, 1, and 1 per cent respectively. This is, as I have pointed out, precisely what we would expect on *a priori* grounds from the nature of the data.

In the years of revival and prosperity such as 1902, 1905, 1906, 1907, 1912, 1913, 1916, and 1922 on the other hand P', as might be expected, was less than P. In 1902 the deficiency was 1 per cent, while in 1905 and 1906, which were years of great expansion, the gap in each year was 7 per cent. In 1907, which was a year of prosperity until the last quarter, we find that P' was 2 per cent under P, while in 1912 and 1913 the percentages

[42] The recession in 1900 was only brief.

were 4 and 5 respectively. In 1916 the difference was 7 per cent and in 1922 no less than 13 per cent.[43] These results are again what we would expect from the failure of L and C fully to measure the increase in their use which occurred during the years of prosperity.

In sixteen of the twenty-three years, therefore, the divergences conform to what might be expected, and in three more, namely 1901, 1909, and 1917, there is a precise agreement between the two P's. There remain only the four years, 1915, 1918, 1919, and 1920 to be explained. If we accept Willard Thorp's classification of 1915 as a year of revival and prosperity,[44] then this year with P' 5 per cent below P fits precisely into the pattern and confirms our explanation. An index of unemployment which L. D. Stinebower and I have computed, however, shows that while there was a distinct improvement in the latter part of the year, the first part was characterized by so much unemployment as to make the average for the year only slightly less than 1914. If this is a more correct characterization of the year, then the actual difference is the opposite of what we might expect on *a priori* grounds.

The war and post-war years of 1918, 1919, and 1920 were also cases in which the actual differences were apparently the opposite of what would be anticipated. Save for the last quarter of 1920, these are years which are commonly thought of as being characterized by prosperity. Unemployment was low, prices were steadily rising until June 1920, and monetary profits were large. We would, therefore, believe at first thought that in these years P' would fall below P. But in reality, the opposite happened. P' was 6 per cent higher than P in 1918, 7 per cent higher in 1919, and 2 per cent higher in 1920. This apparent contradiction of the theory may, however, be at least partially explained by two factors: The dilution of labor in 1918 and 1919 which resulted in a lowering of the quality of the workers, and the immediate post-war reaction which lessened the will to work in 1919 and 1920. During these years there was probably a qualitative deterioration in the units of labor, and this may account for the apparent paradox.

A second cause of the discrepancy was the fact that our index of capital growth undoubtedly overestimates the actual

---

[43] It is probable that P exceeded P' by so much in 1922 more because of the great improvement in factory technique which began then rather than because of the understatement of labor and capital in my index.

[44] Thorp, W. L., *Business Annals*, p. 142.

amounts added to manufacturing equipment in the war years and, in particular, in 1918. It will be remembered that the growth in total fixed capital was interpolated for the years between 1914 and 1919 (as within all census periods) according to the relative quantity of capital goods produced in the respective years. Now the years 1917 and, particularly, 1918 were years when the quantity of lumber, iron, steel, copper, etc., produced was great and when necessarily there was a curtailment in the quantity of consumers goods which were produced. But a large fraction of these producers goods went not into machinery and plant, but into rifles, cannon, shells, cantonments, tanks, steel ships, and other military purposes. While the war industries did greatly expand their plant and equipment, other industries on the other hand such as shoes, textiles, clothing, furniture, pulp and paper, etc., scarcely expanded at all. It is, therefore, more than dubious whether the fixed capital in manufacturing was 12 per cent more in 1917 than it had been in 1916 and whether a further gain of 9 per cent was made in 1918. It is highly improbable that within these two years the fixed capital should have increased by no less than 23 per cent. This exaggeration of the quantity of capital available would naturally raise the computed product to a point higher than it should have been in reality, and hence may account in part at least for the fact that P' is so appreciably above P in 1918.

A comparison of P' with P by years reinforces then the conclusion which is gained from Table 14 and Chart 10, that given an accurate measurement of L and C, P could be computed with a close approximation to reality by the equation $1.01\ L^{3/4}\ C^{1/4}$.

By putting the two curves upon the basis of three-year moving averages (which as Drs. Thorp and Mitchell have shown [45] was close to the most common duration of a minor business cycle in the United States prior to 1927) we can eliminate a large portion of these cyclical disturbances and thus obtain a closer measure of the relative consilience of the computed and the actual curves of production. This is done in Table 15 and shown graphically in Chart 11. The sum of the deviations of the trend of P' from the trend of P without regard to sign is 58 per cent for the twenty-two years, or 2.6 per cent per year. This is only six-tenths of the average of the year to year fluctuations.

---

[45] Thorp, *Business Annals,* p. 43. The average length was more precisely about 40 months.

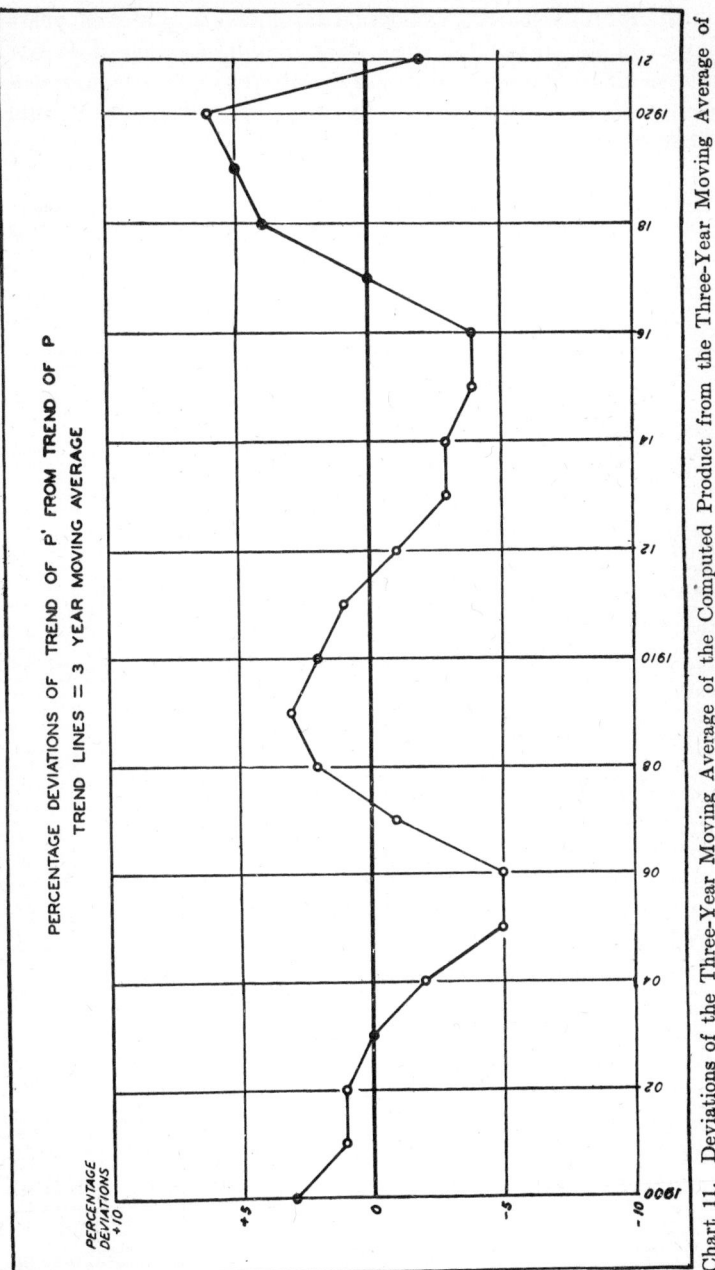

Chart 11. Deviations of the Three-Year Moving Average of the Computed Product from the Three-Year Moving Average of the Actual Product.

Since the major cycles [46] tend to be from seven to eleven years in duration, the use of the three year moving average does not eliminate all of the cyclical disturbances, and there would still be reason for the deviation of the computed from the actual product.

TABLE 15

THE RELATIVE CORRESPONDENCE BETWEEN THE TRENDS OF THE ACTUAL INDEX OF PRODUCTION (P) AND THE COMPUTED INDEX (P'), UNITED STATES, 1899–1922

Year	Trend of P (3 year moving average)	Trend of P' (3 year moving average)	Deviation of Trend of P' from Trend of P in Points ($P'-P$)	Percentage Deviation of Trend of P' from Trend of P $\frac{(P'-P)}{(P)}$
1900	104	107	+3	+3
1901	112	113	+1	+1
1902	119	120	+1	+1
1903	123	123	0	0
1904	130	127	−3	−2
1905	139	132	−7	−5
1906	149	141	−8	−5
1907	143	142	−1	−1
1908	144	147	+3	+2
1909	146	151	+5	+3
1910	156	159	+3	+2
1911	163	164	+1	+1
1912	171	169	−2	−1
1913	177	172	−5	−3
1914	181	175	−6	−3
1915	194	186	−8	−4
1916	214	205	−9	−4
1917	225	224	−1	0
1918	223	232	+9	+4
1919	224	235	+11	+5
1920	209	221	+12	+6
1921	217	213	−4	−2

(1) Total deviation without regard to sign = 58 percentage points.

(2) Average deviation = $\frac{58}{22}$ = 2.6 percentage points.

(3) Total deviation with regard to sign = $(-30) + (+28)$ = 2 per cent.

(4) Average deviation with regard to sign = $\frac{2}{22}$ = .09 per cent.

7. The Elimination of The Trends and Further Light upon The Relationship between P and P'

It has been contended by some that the close relationship during this period between the equation 1.01 $L^{3/4} C^{1/4}$ and the index of actual product was purely fortuitous, resulting from the fact that the trends of L, C, and P all happened to be

[46] See Hansen, A. H., *Economic Stabilization in an Unbalanced World*, pp. 92–3.

upward.   These critics have alleged that equally good results could be obtained by comparing the relative movement of hogs in Iowa, hens in Wisconsin, and product in manufacturing.   Such critics have, to be sure, not submitted the data to justify this contention, but their implication has been that the correlation found to exist between P' and P was nonsensical.

Several comments may be made with propriety upon this criticism.

(1) There is a logical connection between the quantities of labor and capital on the one hand and of product on the other which is not present in the attempted *reductio ad absurdum*. If economic science has any meaning, there certainly is a functional relationship between the variables of product, capital, and labor.

(2) From the standpoint of economic history alone it is worth while to see what this relationship was during the approximate quarter of a century which was covered.

(3) Statisticians in their zeal to establish causal relationships seem to have gone too far in eliminating secular trends completely from consideration and in only correlating the deviations from these trends.   This procedure was necessary in order to isolate the phenomena of the business cycle, and it was originally adopted for this very purpose.   But to insist that in any study of causal economic relationships, the trends must first be eliminated is, in effect, to throw the baby out with the bath. From the long-run point of view, the relative slopes of the various trends are indeed more important than the relative deviations from these slopes.   Moreover, these various trends are not entirely independent of each other, and one of the tasks of economic science is to discover what the nature of this relationship is.   Nor should the economist be deterred from studying it by the cry that he is indulging in nonsense correlations, when it is patent that the interrelations are not nonsensical. We can, therefore, accept the data as they stand as furnishing valuable evidence upon the actual relationship between L, C, and P during the period studied.

As a supplement to these studies, however, it is also desirable to try to eliminate the secular trend as much as possible and determine what the short-time relationships were.   The first method of measuring this was to compute the deviations in each year of P and P' from their respective three year moving averages and to see the degree to which these deviations corresponded with each other. This is shown in Table 16 and Chart 12.

TABLE 16

DEVIATIONS OF P AND P' FROM THEIR RESPECTIVE THREE YEAR MOVING AVERAGES IN UNITED STATES

Year	Deviation of P from Trend of P	Deviation of P' from Trend of P'	Year	Deviation of P from Trend of P	Deviation of P' from Trend of P'
1900	−3	0	1911	−10	−1
1901	0	−1	1912	6	1
1902	3	1	1913	7	2
1903	1	3	1914	−12	−4
1904	−8	−4	1915	−5	−7
1905	4	1	1916	11	4
1906	3	0	1917	2	3
1907	8	6	1918	0	4
1908	−18	−10	1919	−6	−2
1909	7	4	1920	22	15
1910	3	1	1921	−38	−19

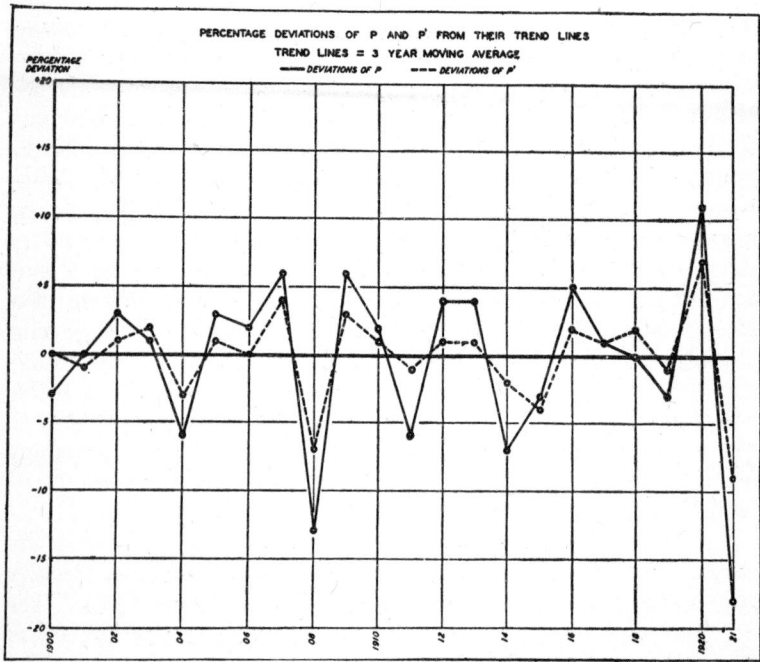

Chart 12. Deviations of P and P' from Their Respective Three Year Moving Averages.

There was, therefore, a truly striking agreement between the fluctuations of P' from its moving average with those of P from its corresponding average. In only three years, 1901, 1908 and 1915, did these deviations, as a matter of fact, move in opposite directions. In the remaining years the two moved together, although P, for reasons which have been fully explained, had a much greater amplitude of fluctuation both above and below its moving average than did P'.

The coefficient of correlation between these deviations of P and P' from their moving averages is .94. A fairly good measure of the degree of interrelationship between the correlated factors is the square of the coefficient of correlation (r^2), and this measure would be .884. This is certainly high enough to indicate a very high degree of causal relationship between 1.01 $L^{3/4} C^{1/4}$ and the actual product even when the time element has been largely eliminated. It is interesting also to note in this connection that P in its unadjusted form lies nearer to P' than it does to its own three year moving average, the corresponding standard deviations being 8.7 and 11.7 respectively.

Two former students of mine, Messrs. Maynard Krueger and Stanley Ross, have carried through a study of the relationship between the trend ratios of L, C, and P which also meets the objection that the time factor has not been eliminated. This study involved the three following main steps: (1) the determination of the trends of the labor, capital, and product series respectively, (2) the computation of the ratios of the actual indexes for each series in each year to the trends, (3) the determination of the relationship between the trend ratios of L and C and that of P. The three sets of trends were found by the method of least squares. For the capital series, a straight line was fitted to the logs of the data. In the case of labor and product, the best trends were found to be straight lines fitted to the original data.

The following equations were found for the various trends:

$$\text{Capital} \quad \log y = 1.97490 + 0.02810 \log x$$
$$\text{Labor} \quad y = 99.99 + 3.660\, x$$
$$\text{Product} \quad y = 93.57 + 5.7878\, x$$

These equations gave the trend values which are shown in the first three columns of Table 17. The ratios of the actual indexes to the trends were then found by dividing for identical years the former by the latter. These trend ratios are given in the last three columns of Table 17.

TABLE 17

TREND VALUES AND TREND RATIOS OF LABOR, CAPITAL, AND PRODUCT SERIES
FOR THE UNITED STATES MANUFACTURING INDUSTRIES, 1899–1922

Year	Trend Values			Trend Ratios		
	Capital	Labor	Product	Capital	Labor	Product
1899	100.7	103.6	99.4	99.3	96.5	100.6
1900	107.4	107.3	105.1	99.6	97.8	96.1
1901	114.6	111.0	110.9	99.5	99.1	101.0
1902	122.3	114.6	116.7	99.8	102.9	104.5
1903	130.4	118.3	122.5	100.5	104.0	101.2
1904	139.2	122.0	128.3	99.1	95.1	95.1
1905	148.5	125.6	134.1	100.3	99.5	106.6
1906	158.4	129.3	139.9	102.9	102.9	108.7
1907	169.0	133.0	145.7	104.1	103.8	103.7
1908	180.3	136.6	151.4	102.6	88.6	83.2
1909	192.3	140.3	157.2	103.0	99.8	98.6
1910	205.2	144.0	163.0	101.4	100.0	97.5
1911	218.9	147.6	168.8	98.7	98.2	90.6
1912	233.6	151.2	174.6	96.8	100.5	101.4
1913	249.2	155.0	180.4	94.7	99.4	102.0
1914	265.9	158.6	186.2	91.8	93.9	90.8
1915	283.7	162.2	192.0	93.8	94.9	98.4
1916	302.6	165.9	197.8	98.5	109.7	113.8
1917	322.9	169.5	203.5	103.8	115.6	111.5
1918	344.4	173.2	209.3	106.3	115.4	106.5
1919	367.5	176.9	215.1	105.3	109.0	101.3
1920	392.0	180.6	221.0	103.8	106.9	104.6
1921	418.2	184.3	226.7	99.7	79.8	79.0
1922	446.2	187.8	232.5	96.6	85.7	103.2

The same general formula was used for the trend ratios as
that which had been applied to the original series, namely,
$P' = bL^kC^{1-k}$, and the values of the constants b and k were
determined by the method of least squares. The generalized
normal equations necessary to the equation above are as follows:

(1) $\Sigma (\log P - \log C) = n \log b + k \Sigma (\log L - \log C)$

(2) $\Sigma [(\log P - \log C) (\log L - \log C)] = \log b \Sigma (\log L - \log C)$
$+ k \Sigma (\log L - \log C)^2$

The solution of these two equations gives b a value of .9998
and K a value of .84. For all practical purposes, therefore, b
may be disregarded because of its virtual identity with 1.0 and
the equation for the trend ratios can be treated as $P' = L^{.84}C^{.16}$.

This value of K is only 9 points or 12 per cent more than
the value of .75 as computed from the original data.

It will be noticed, however, from an examination of columns
4 to 6, inclusive, of Table 17 that in specific years the trend
ratios of P tend much more frequently to lie either above or
below the trend ratios of L and C than to lie between them, as

might be inferred from the nature of the exponents. In this it differs from the situation in respect to the original series, where P lay between L and C. The value of the formula in the case of the trend ratios is, therefore, much less for any individual year than in the case of the original data, and the results in individual years will not be approximated as closely by its use. It rather represents a generalized average picture of the period as a whole, in which years when the trend ratios of P fell below those of both L and C were balanced by the years when they ran above both.

8. An Approach to The Quantitative Determination of The Law of The Diminishing Increment

Light upon the relative marginal productivities during these years of labor and of capital can be secured if we assume that the law which seems to apply for the period as a whole is also true of the individual years as well, namely, that labor "contributes" three-fourths and capital "contributes" one-fourth of the total product. By the term "contributes" we mean the amount added to the product by the last unit of a factor multiplied by the number of units of that factor. By assuming that these proportions, i.e., three-fourths and one-fourth, are not altered during the period, it is possible to compute the relative productivities of the last units of the two factors for each of the successive years. The formula used for this was $\frac{3}{4}\cdot\frac{P'}{L}$ in the case of labor and $\frac{1}{4}\cdot\frac{P'}{C}$ in the case of capital.[46a] Since the

---

[46a] This follows from differentiating the function $P = bL^{3/4}C^{1/4}$ with respect to L and C. For the benefit of the students not trained in calculus, the steps are carried out in detail.

(1) $\dfrac{\partial P}{\partial L} = bL^{3/4}\dfrac{\partial C^{1/4}}{\partial L} + bC^{1/4}\dfrac{\partial L^{3/4}}{\partial L} + L^{3/4}C^{1/4}\dfrac{\partial b}{\partial L}$

Since the derivative of a constant is zero, this causes the first and third terms to drop out and we then have

$\dfrac{\partial P}{\partial L} = bC^{1/4}\dfrac{\partial L^{3/4}}{\partial L}$

$= bC^{1/4}\dfrac{3}{4}L^{-1/4}$

Since from the original function $\dfrac{P}{L^{3/4}} = bC^{1/4}$, we can substitute this and therefore

$\dfrac{\partial P}{\partial L} = \dfrac{3}{4}\dfrac{P}{L}.$

(2) Similarly

$\dfrac{\partial P}{\partial C} = bL^{3/4}\dfrac{\partial C^{1/4}}{\partial C} + bC^{1/4}\dfrac{\partial L^{3/4}}{\partial C} + L^{3/4}C^{1/4}\dfrac{\partial b}{\partial C}.$

fractions $\frac{3}{4}$ and $\frac{1}{4}$ are constant, the same results in terms of relatives of 1899 are obtained if we omit them and use only $\frac{P'}{L}$ and $\frac{P'}{C}$.

Substituting for P' the observed values we obtain the relative "marginal productivities" or "final productivity" which are given in Table 18. It should also be realized that in this and the following sections, the terms "marginal productivity" and "final productivity" are treated as interchangeable and identical terms. In short, Table 18 shows the results when the indexes of product (P) in each of the years are divided by the respective indexes of labor (L) and capital (C).

TABLE 18

RELATIVE PRODUCTIVITY OF FINAL UNIT OF LABOR AND CAPITAL IN
SUCCESSIVE YEARS FROM 1899 TO 1922 IN UNITED STATES (1899 = 100)

Year	Relative Final Productivity Per Unit Labor	Relative Final Productivity Per Unit Capital	Year	Relative Final Productivity Per Unit Labor	Relative Final Productivity Per Unit Capital
1899	100	100	1911	105	71
1900	96	95	1912	116	78
1901	102	98	1913	119	78
1902	103	99	1914	113	69
1903	101	95	1915	123	71
1904	105	88	1916	123	75
1905	114	96	1917	116	68
1906	115	93	1918	111	61
1907	110	86	1919	113	56
1908	104	68	1920	119	57
1909	110	78	1921	121	43
1910	110	76	1922	149	56

This table shows that the marginal productivities of labor rose quite steadily during the period, being 49 per cent higher in 1922 than in 1899. During the previous seven years, the average was 18 per cent above the 1899 base. This rise was, of course, attributable to the fact that the index of production was in-

---

Since the derivative of a constant is zero this causes the second and third terms to drop out and we have

$$\frac{\partial P}{\partial C} = bL^{\frac{3}{4}} \frac{1}{4} C^{-\frac{3}{4}}$$

Since from the original function $\frac{P}{C^{\frac{1}{4}}} = bL^{\frac{3}{4}}$ we can substitute this and therefore

$$\frac{\partial P}{\partial C} = \frac{1}{4} \frac{P}{C}$$

These are stated as formulae II and III in the mathematical note to this chapter.

creasing faster than the labor supply. It should be noted, however, that during the depression years, most notably 1908, 1911, and generally 1914, the index of production falls off by more than our index of labor supply, with the result that the relative marginal productivity of labor is lowered.

The relative marginal productivity of capital, on the other hand, was lowered during the period, reaching a point in 1922 which was 44 per cent lower than the 1899 base. This, of course, was the direct result of the fact that the index of capital was rising at a more rapid rate than the index of production. Since our capital index does not take account of idle plant and machinery in years of depression, but does record the fresh investments which are then made, the resultant fall in unit productivity is relatively greater than is true for labor in the corresponding years.[47] It is possible to represent graphically the curve of the diminishing increment. To do this we shall construct two charts 13 and 14, the former representing the curve of the diminishing increment of labor and the latter, that of capital. On the abscissa (horizontal axis) of 13, the ratios of labor to capital $\left(\frac{L}{C}\right)$, have been plotted while on the abscissa of 14 the ratios of capital to labor $\left(\frac{C}{L}\right)$ are represented, which of course are the reciprocals of the former. These have already been given in Table 12. The ordinates (vertical axis) represent in each case the relative marginal productivities. These may be expressed in two ways:

(1) The marginal productivity of labor $\quad \dfrac{(\partial P)}{(\partial L)} = \dfrac{3}{4} \cdot \dfrac{P}{L}$

The marginal productivity of capital $\quad \dfrac{(\partial P)}{(\partial C)} = \dfrac{1}{4} \cdot \dfrac{P}{C}$

or

(2) $\dfrac{\partial P}{\partial L} = 1.01 \times \dfrac{3}{4}\left(\dfrac{L}{C}\right)^{-\frac{1}{4}}$

$\dfrac{\partial P}{\partial L} = 1.01 \times \dfrac{1}{4}\left(\dfrac{L}{C}\right)^{\frac{3}{4}}$

The second equation was that which was used in expressing the theoretical productivities.

[47] In Table 18 we have treated both the marginal productivities of labor and of capital in 1899 as being equivalent to 100. For the purposes of clarity we have shifted the base to 99. This lowers the indexes of marginal productivity in subsequent years by 1 per cent, but of course in no way changes their relative position to 1899.

Thus in 1910 the ratio of labor to capital was 69 while the relative final productivity of labor according to Table 18 was 110. The point for that year on Chart 13 would then be at the intersection of perpendiculars from 69 on the abscissa and 110 on the ordinate. That point describes the relationship be-

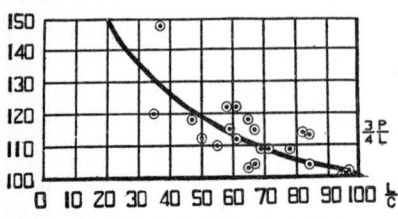

Chart 13. Relative Marginal Productivity of Labor in Terms of Different Ratios of Labor to Capital in American Manufacturing, 1899–1922.

tween the relative quantity of labor and its relative final productivity. Similarily in 1915 the relative ratio of labor to capital was 58 while the relative final productivity of labor was 123. Here again the point for that year would be at the intersection of perpendiculars from 58 on the

abscissa and 123 on the ordinate. In such a manner the points for each and every year were found and are shown in Chart 13.

A similar procedure was followed in the case of capital and is shown in Chart 14. Since the ratio of capital to labor was

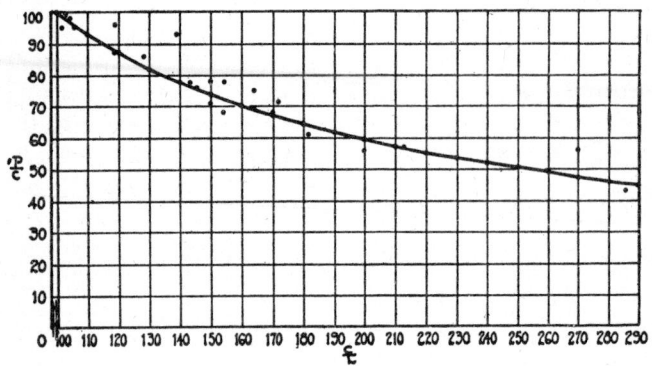

Chart 14. Relative Marginal Productivity of Capital in Terms of Different Ratios of Capital to Labor in American Manufacturing, 1899–1922.

increasing through the period, 100 was taken as the approximate point of origin. The higher ratios are shown to the right of this. In the case of both capital and labor, a movement from left to right on the abscissa indicates an increase in the quantity of the factor under consideration in relation to the other factor.

The query may very properly be raised as to what allowance

is made in these charts for the element of time. Time as such does not explicitly appear, since what is charted is the relationship of relative quantity and final productivity. There is, nevertheless, a general time-drift in both charts. Since the quantities of labor relative to capital were decreasing with the years and consequently those of capital to labor were increasing, the general time-drift on the chart representing labor is from right to left and that for capital from left to right. This is in consonance with the rise through time in the marginal productivities of labor and with the fall through time in the marginal productivities of capital.

But while the general time-drift is in the directions indicated there are some exceptions. Since the index for the quantity of labor is more responsive to the business cycle than that for capital, the ratio of the labor index to capital decreases more in the depression years than it does in the years of prosperity. This causes the ratio of capital to labor to increase at a faster rate in the depression years than it does in the prosperity phase of the cycle. Thus whereas the ratio of labor to capital was 78 in 1907 and 71 in 1909, it was 65 in 1908. The point representing labor in 1908 would, therefore, lie to the left of that representing 1909, thus running against the general time-drift. Similarly, while the index for the relative quantity of capital was 128 in 1907 and 143 in 1909, it was 154 in 1908. The point representing capital in 1908 is, therefore, to the right of that representing 1909, and thus also constitutes an exception to the general time-flow. Similarly, in 1914 and in 1921 the relative indexes of the ratios of labor to capital are lower than those of the succeeding years and hence are exceptions to the general rule. The same is true of the relative indexes for the ratio of capital to labor. There are, moreover, two pairs of years, namely, 1904 and 1905, and 1911 and 1912 for which the ratios are identical. But although the locations on the abscissas are identical for these pairs of years, their locations on the ordinates are not.

Now, from the formula $P' = 1.01 \ L^{\frac{3}{4}} C^{\frac{1}{4}}$ we can obtain theoretical curves which will measure what the marginal productivities of labor and capital would have been theoretically in the various years according to the terms of our equations. The productivity of the final units of labor would have been proportional to $\left(\frac{L}{C}\right)^{-\frac{1}{4}}$ and for the final units of capital to $\left(\frac{L}{C}\right)^{\frac{3}{4}}$. The values obtained in this manner and curves have been drawn in both charts to represent what the theoretical productivities would have been in the various years with given proportions of labor and capital.

These curves seem to describe so accurately the average relationship between the final productivities and the relative quantities of the factors and to be the line of "best fit" to the observations that it may be thought by many that they were in fact fitted to the data either by the method of least squares or by some modified form. Such is not, however, the case. The curves have been drawn from the formula itself, and the close resemblance which they bear to the line of "best fit" is further proof of the degree to which the formula expresses the "normal" effect of labor and capital upon production during the period.

The flexibilities of the marginal productivity curves, or the rates at which the marginal productivities of labor and capital change with given changes in the respective quantities of labor and capital, can be found directly from equations XI and XII in the mathematical note appended to this chapter and the steps followed are described in a footnote.[48] In brief it will be

---

[48] This can be shown from the following:

Let ϕ_L and ϕ_C = the ratio of the change in the marginal productivities of labor $\left(\dfrac{\partial P}{\partial L}\right)$ and capital $\left(\dfrac{\partial P}{\partial C}\right)$ to the changes in the quantities of labor (L) and capital (C). Then

(1) $\phi_L = \dfrac{\partial}{\partial L}\left[\dfrac{\partial P}{\partial L}\right] \cdot \dfrac{L}{\dfrac{\partial P}{\partial L}}$

From equation XI in the mathematical note to this chapter it will be seen that $\dfrac{\partial}{\partial L}\left[\dfrac{\partial P}{\partial L}\right] = K(K-1)\dfrac{P}{L^2}$ while from equation I, as already developed in footnote 46[a], $\dfrac{\partial P}{\partial L} = \dfrac{3}{4}\dfrac{P}{L} = K\dfrac{P}{L}$.

Therefore $\phi_L = K(K-1)\dfrac{P}{L^2} \cdot \dfrac{L}{\dfrac{KP}{L}} = \dfrac{K(K-1)P}{L^2} \cdot \dfrac{L^2}{KP}$.

Cancelling the L^2s, the P's and the K's we have
$\phi_L = K-1$. Given $K = \frac{3}{4}$. $\phi_L = -\frac{1}{4}$ or $-.25$.

(2) Similarly

$$\phi_C = \dfrac{\partial}{\partial C}\left[\dfrac{\partial P}{\partial C}\right] \quad \dfrac{C}{\dfrac{\partial P}{\partial C}}$$

From equation XII in the mathematical note to this chapter,
$$\dfrac{\partial}{\partial C}\left[\dfrac{\partial P}{\partial C}\right] = K(K-1)\dfrac{P}{C^2}.$$

seen that the flexibility of the marginal productivity curve of a factor is equal to the sum of the exponents of the other factors. Since we are dealing with only two factors, labor and capital, the flexibility of the marginal productivity curve of labor is the exponent for capital, namely—$\frac{1}{4}$, while the flexibility of the marginal productivity curve of capital is the exponent for labor, namely — $\frac{3}{4}$. This means that an increase of 1 per cent in the quantity of labor with capital constant would not merely cause the total product to be increased by $\frac{3}{4}$ of one per cent but would also lower the previous marginal productivity of labor by $\frac{1}{4}$ of one per cent. A decrease of 1 per cent in the quantity of labor would have a similar effect in the opposite direction. An increase of 1 per cent in the quantity of capital, with labor constant, would not merely normally increase total production by $\frac{1}{4}$ of one per cent but would lower its previous marginal productivity by $\frac{3}{4}$ of one per cent. A decrease in the quantity of capital would have a similar effect in an opposite direction.

Since the demand curves for labor and capital tend to approximate and to conform to the respective marginal productivity curves, it follows that an increase of 1 per cent in the quantity of labor would, other things being equal, normally tend to be followed by a decrease of $\frac{1}{4}$ of one per cent in the rate of wages. Similarly an increase of one per cent in the quantity of capital would, were other things equal, normally

---

And from equation II, as developed also in footnote 46a,

$$\frac{\partial P}{\partial C} = \frac{1}{4} \frac{P}{C} \text{ or } (1-K) \frac{P}{C}.$$

Therefore

$$\phi_c = K(K-1) \frac{P}{C^2} \cdot \frac{C}{\dfrac{(1-K)\,P}{C}}$$

$$= \frac{K(K-1)\,P}{C^2} \cdot \frac{C^2}{(1-K)\,P}$$

Cancelling the C^2's and the P's, we have

$$\phi_c = \frac{K(K-1)}{1-K} = \frac{-K(1-K)}{1-K} = -K = -\tfrac{3}{4} \text{ or } -.75$$

(3) It follows, therefore, from this proof that the flexibility of the marginal productivity curve of a factor is equal to the sum of the exponents of the other factors, or when we deal with any two factors, to the exponent of the other factor. The coefficients of the elasticities of the marginal productivity curves (i.e. the ratio of changes in the quantities of a factor to the changes in its marginal productivity) are the reciprocals of these or the reciprocals of the sum of the exponents of the other factors or factor. In the case of both the flexibilities and elasticities the signs are, of course, negative.

tend to lead to a relative decrease of ¾ of one per cent in the rate of interest.[49] The flexibility of the demand curve for and the marginal productivity curve of labor, which we have designated as ϕ_L, is therefore—.25, while the corresponding flexibility for capital (ϕ_C) is —.75.

This same relationship can be expressed in terms of the elasticities of the demand and productivity curves instead of their flexibilities. In terms of marginal productivities these would measure the relative changes in the quantities of labor and capital which would accompany a change of 1 per cent in their respective marginal productivities. It is clear that these are nothing but the reciprocals of the flexibilities and that they would therefore be —4.0 for labor and —1.33 for capital. Assuming that the demand curve for labor and for capital follows the marginal productivity curves, the elasticity of demand for labor would therefore be —4.0 as given above and that for capital would be —1.33. This would mean that an increase of 1 per cent in wages would, if everything else were equal, result in a decrease of 4 per cent in the quantity of labor demanded, and an increase of 1 per cent in the rate of interest would, under the same conditions, result in a decrease of 1.33 per cent in the quantity of capital demanded while decreases of 1 per cent in the respective rates of return would result in corresponding increases of 4.0 and 1.33 per cents in the quantities of labor and capital demanded.[50]

It follows that since the elasticities and flexibilities of productivity for labor and capital are what they are the aggregate returns to labor and capital will increase with an increase in their respective quantities and decrease with a decrease in quantity. For the relative fall in marginal productivity is in the case of labor only one-fourth as great as the relative increase in quantity ($\phi_L = -.25$), so that the new marginal productivity multiplied by the new quantity will be greater than the former marginal productivity multiplied by

---

[49] This is a relative and not an absolute decrease, i.e., from 4.0 to 3.97 per cent instead of from 4.0 to 3.25 per cent.

[50] All this coincides with the conclusion which Pigou and Hugh Dalton have reached by a different line of approach, namely, that the elasticity of demand for one factor will equal, under conditions of a constant share in the total product, the reciprocal of the sum of the exponents of the other factors. See Pigou, *The Economics of Welfare* (2nd edition), p. 623 (footnote), and Dalton, *Some Aspects of the Inequality of Incomes*, pp. 186–7. Both Dalton and Pigou deal with distribution formulae rather than productivity formulae.

the former quantity. Similarly, since the fall in the marginal productivity of capital will be less than the relative increase in capital ($\phi_c = -.75$), then an increase of 1 per cent in the quantity of capital will bring an increase in the aggregate return to capital. This increase resulting from an increase of 1 per cent in the quantity of capital will of course be only one-third as great as the increase which would accrue to labor as the result of a 1 per cent increase in the quantity of either labor or capital.

The elasticities of labor and capital must as a matter of fact be —4.0 and —1.33 and their respective flexibilities —.25 and —.75 if to labor is to be attributed three-fourths and to capital one-fourth of the total product. For only these values will yield constant shares. If, for example, the quantity of labor alone increases by 1 per cent, then the total product will increase by ¾ of one per cent. It will be necessary for the marginal productivity of labor to fall by ¼ of one per cent in order that labor may receive or have imputed to it three-fourths of this increase of ¾ of one per cent. Similarly, it is necessary that the flexibility of capital should be —.75 if capital is to receive one-fourth of the increase of ¼ of one per cent in total product which would attend an increase of 1 per cent in capital alone.

This point can be clearly seen from a simple arithmetical example. (1) Thus let us assume that we have 10,000 units of Labor (L) and 10,000 units of Capital (C) and 10,000 units of Product (P). Then the marginal productivity of labor $\left(\frac{\partial P}{\partial L}\right)$ will be .75, and the aggregate return of labor $\left(\frac{\partial P}{\partial L}\right)$. L will be 7500. The aggregate return to capital $\left(\frac{\partial P}{\partial C}\right)$. C will be 2500. The relative shares of labor and capital will then be three-fourths and one-fourth as outlined.

(2) Let us now increase the quantity of labor (L) by 1 per cent to 10,100. Product will increase by .75 per cent to 10,075, or an absolute increase of 75 units. The marginal productivity of labor will then fall by .25 per cent ($\phi_L = -.25$) to .748125. The aggregate return of labor $\left(\frac{\partial P}{\partial L} \cdot L\right)$ will then be .748125 × 10,100 = 7556.1, or an increase of 56.1 units. This is

almost precisely three-fourths of the increased product and it would be exactly three-fourths if we had used logarithms.[51] It follows, therefore, that the flexibility of the productivity curve of and the demand curve for labor (ϕ_L) must be $-.25$ if labor is to receive three-fourths of the product. It must be equal to the sum of the exponents of the other factors or, in this case, the exponent of capital. The absolute return to capital will increase by 18.9 units or approximately one-fourth of the total which again would be the precise fraction if we had used logarithms.

(3) Similarly if the quantity of capital (C) is increased by 1 per cent to 10,100, then product will increase by .25 per cent to a total of 10,025 or an absolute increase of 25 units. The marginal productivity of capital will fall by .75 per cent $(\phi_c = -.75)$ or from .250 to .248125. The aggregate return to capital $\left(\dfrac{\partial P}{\partial C} \cdot C\right)$ will then be .248125 $\times$ 10,100 $=$ 2506.1. This will be an absolute increase of 6.1 units or almost precisely one-fourth of the total absolute increase which occurred and will preserve capital's share of one-fourth of the total product. The return to labor will increase by 18.9 units or approximately three-fourths of the increase. Had we used logarithms and used equal proportionate as well as equal absolute changes in the marginal productivities and the quantities of capital there would have been a precise coincidence. It indeed follows that the flexibility of the productivity curve of capital (ϕ_c) must be precisely equal to $-.75$ or the exponent of labor, if capital is to receive the constant share of one-fourth of the total product.

If however the flexibilities of the marginal productivity curves of labor and capital $(\phi_L$ and $\phi_c)$ were not to be the same for further points on the curves, then the *proportions* of the total product received by the respective factors would not be the same but would necessarily change. Thus if the flexibility of marginal product with respect to labor should for subsequent units be less than $-.25$, then not only would the aggregate returns to labor increase but so would its proportionate share as well. In this case, if the production function was still homogeneous and of the first degree the flexibility of the

---

[51] An increase of 1 per cent is slightly less proportionately than a decrease of 1 per cent.

marginal productivity curve of capital would be increased and its share would fall. If, however, the flexibility of the marginal productivity curve for subsequent units of labor were to rise above —.25, then the relative share of labor would fall. Assuming that the production equation was still of the first degree and that the sum of the exponents was still equal to 1.0, or unity, this would mean a corresponding fall in the flexibilities of the marginal productivity curve of capital below —.75 and a consequent rise in the share of the product which it received.

Mathematical Note to Chapter V [1]

Mathematical Analysis—Given the function
$$P' = bL^k C^{1-k}$$
where b is independent of L and C and (to fix the ideas) k is supposed to be constant and equal to $\frac{3}{4}$. Then it follows that:

I. The marginal productivity of labor is $\frac{3}{4} \dfrac{P}{L}$.

$$(1) \qquad \frac{\partial P}{\partial L} = \frac{3}{4} \frac{P}{L}$$

II. The marginal productivity of capital is $\frac{1}{4} \dfrac{P}{C}$.

$$(2) \qquad \frac{\partial P}{\partial C} = \frac{1}{4} \frac{P}{C}$$

III. The productivity of total labor is $\frac{3}{4} P$.

$$(3) \qquad L \frac{\partial P}{\partial L} = \frac{3}{4} P$$

IV. The productivity of total capital is $\frac{1}{4} P$.

$$(4) \qquad C \frac{\partial P}{\partial C} = \frac{1}{4} P$$

V. The elasticity of the product with respect to small changes in labor alone is $\frac{3}{4}$.

$$(5) \qquad \frac{\partial(\log P)}{\partial(\log L)} = \frac{3}{4}$$

VI. The elasticity of the product with respect to small changes in capital alone is $\frac{1}{4}$.

$$(6) \qquad \frac{\partial(\log P)}{\partial(\log C)} = \frac{1}{4}$$

VII. If b is taken equal to 1.01 say, then the marginal productivity of labor is:

$$(7) \qquad \frac{\partial P}{\partial L} = 1.01 \times \frac{3}{4} \times \left(\frac{L}{C}\right)^{-1/4};$$

---

[1] The preparation of this note is the work of Professor Charles W. Cobb and Mr. Aaron Director to whom I am greatly indebted.

VIII. Similarly the marginal productivity of capital is:

$$(8) \quad \frac{\partial P}{\partial C} = 1.01 \times \frac{1}{4} \times \left(\frac{L}{C}\right)^{3/4} \; ; \quad b = 1.01$$

From (7) and (8) it follows that just as production has a norm which it approximates, so the marginal productivities of labor and capital have norms which they approximate; namely, the curves $y = 1.01 \, (L/C)^{-\frac{1}{4}}$ and $y = 1.01 \, (L/C)^{\frac{3}{4}}$ respectively.

The three norms and the corresponding quantities are so related that if one quantity, say production, rises above its norm by 5 per cent then each of the other two quantities rises above its norm by 5 per cent. This is due to the algebraic identity

$$\frac{P}{L} : \left(\frac{L}{C}\right)^{-1/4} = \frac{P}{C} : \left(\frac{L}{C}\right)^{3/4} = P : L^{3/4}C^{1/4} = b : 1.$$

We may now find the rates of change of the marginal productivities and total productivities by taking derivatives of equations (1) to (4), replacing the constant $\frac{3}{4}$ by the indefinite k, and remembering that k is to be constant, positive, and less than 1.

IX. The productivity of unit labor increases per unit increase in capital alone.

$$(9) \qquad \frac{\partial}{\partial C}\left[\frac{\partial P}{\partial L}\right] = k(1-k)\frac{P}{LC}$$

X. The productivity of unit capital increases per unit increase in labor alone.

$$(10) \qquad \frac{\partial}{\partial L}\left[\frac{\partial P}{\partial C}\right] = k(1-k)\frac{P}{LC}$$

These rates of increase (which are equal for fixed values of L and C) are given by the expression on the right hand side of equations (9) and (10).

XI. The productivity of unit labor *decreases* per unit increase in labor alone (since $k-1$ is negative) at a rate given by the right hand side of equation (11).

$$(11) \quad \frac{\partial}{\partial L}\left[\frac{\partial P}{\partial L}\right] = k(k-1)\frac{P}{L^2} \text{ and hence diminishing returns}$$

XII. The productivity of unit capital *decreases* per unit increase in capital alone at a rate given by the right hand side of equation (12).

$$(12) \quad \frac{\partial}{\partial C}\left[\frac{\partial P}{\partial C}\right] = k(k-1)\frac{P}{C^2} \text{ and hence diminishing returns}$$

XIII. The productivity of total labor *increases* per unit increase in labor alone, at a rate given by the right hand side of equation (13).

$$(13) \qquad \frac{\partial}{\partial L}\left[L\frac{\partial P}{\partial L}\right] = k^2\frac{P}{L}$$

XIV. The productivity of total capital *increases* per unit increase in capital alone at a rate given by the right hand side of equation (14).

$$(14) \qquad \frac{\partial}{\partial C}\left[C\frac{\partial P}{\partial C} \right] = (1-k)^2 \frac{P}{C}$$

XV. The productivity of total capital *increases* per unit increase in labor alone at a rate given by the right hand side of equation (15).

$$(15) \qquad \frac{\partial}{\partial L}\left[C\frac{\partial P}{\partial C} \right] = k(1-k) \frac{P}{L}$$

XVI. The productivity of total labor *increases* per unit increase in capital alone at a rate given by the right hand side of equation (16).

$$(16) \qquad \frac{\partial}{\partial C}\left[L\frac{\partial P}{\partial L} \right] = k(1-k) \frac{P}{C}$$

Finally, if k is supposed to vary then P' becomes a function of three variables, and we have a new set of theorems for example: "If k increases while L and C remain fixed then P' increases if L/C is greater than 1, and P' decreases if L/C is less than 1." It should be borne in mind, however, that our results have been given exact numerical values for the sake of fixing the ideas. But the numbers themselves are fixed tentatively, relative to a certain period and to certain indexes. When the indexes are refined or the period is changed it may be that the constant ¾ will appear as a constant .7 or .6 or perhaps as a variable. Even the *form* of the function P' may have to be changed.

Thus if we choose a smaller k than ¾ (say ⅔ for the whole period) the P' curve thus computed will lie above

TABLE 18A

RELATION BETWEEN P AND P' WHEN $P' = 1.01 \, L^{\frac{3}{4}} \, C^{\frac{1}{4}}$

Year	P	P'	$\dfrac{P-P'}{P} \times 100$	Year	P	P'	$\dfrac{P-P'}{P} \times 100$
1899	100	101	−1	1911	153	166	−8
1900	101	106	−5	1912	177	173	+2
1901	112	111	+1	1913	184	178	+3
1902	122	119	+3	1914	169	176	−4
1903	124	125	−1	1915	189	185	+2
1904	122	123	−1	1916	225	214	+5
1905	143	133	+7	1917	227	234	−3
1906	152	142	+7	1918	223	244	−9
1907	151	149	+1	1919	218	243	−11
1908	126	139	−10	1920	231	247	−7
1909	155	157	−1	1921	179	208	−16
1910	159	163	−3	1922	240	223	+7

the P' curve computed with $k = \frac{3}{4}$ whenever L/C is less than 1, that is over most of the period. The relation between P and the new $P' = 1.01L^{2/3}C^{1/3}$ is given in Table 18A.

It is the purpose of this chapter, then, not so much to state as to illustrate a method of attack. In choosing a definite norm for production as a first approximation it is not at all certain that we have arrived immediately at the best possible. The advantage in choosing a norm at all seems to be that it involves us in logical consequences which may be compared with the facts as we get the facts. It enables us to talk rightly or wrongly with more precision and to draw conclusions which become hypotheses.

CHAPTER VI

THE THEORY OF PRODUCTION AS TESTED BY MASSACHUSETTS DATA, 1890–1926

1. Production, Labor and Capital in Massachusetts Manufacturing

Because of the fact that Massachusetts has an annual *Census of Manufactures* it is possible to get a continuous record of the movement of labor, capital, and product which is impossible for the United States as a whole. It is consequently not necessary to resort to interpolation for the years within a census period, and the margin of error is in consequence appreciably reduced. Professor Cobb has carried through an analysis of these data for the years 1890–1926,[1] and it is due to his generous courtesy that I am permitted to publish it.

The index of labor consisted of the average number of laborers employed in the Massachusetts factories which reported in a given year. The index of capital was based on fixed and a portion of working capital[2] instead of on the former alone as was the case with the United States data. It was deflated by a price index of Massachusetts products. The index of product was computed by deflating the total value product manufacturing in each of the years by the price index which has just been referred to. This was obtained by weighting the wholesale indexes of various groups in the following manner according to their relative importance in Massachusetts;[3] food, 1; cloth, 5; metals, 2; and miscellaneous, 2. This latter group was in turn made up of the leather, paper, rope, rubber, and tobacco industries with relative weights of 4, 4, 1, 2, and 1 respectively.

---

[1] *Annual Reports on the Statistics of Manufactures of Massachusetts,* 1890–1926.

[2] The Massachusetts definition of capital devoted to production includes the following (Massachusetts, *Statistics of Manufacture,* 1895, p. 178): "value of land, if owned; value of buildings and fixtures, if owned; value of machinery and motive power, if owned; value of implements and tools; value of patent rights, patterns, etc.; value at cost of raw materials and articles to be used in the industry on hand Dec. 31 or at close of last fiscal year including also goods in process of manufacture and the amount of cash in hand or in bank at the same date." Finished goods on hand are not included.

[3] See Bulletin 390 of the United States Bureau of Labor Statistics.

While this index is not particularly well adapted for deflating fixed capital, it would be much better for working capital. The data for these three series with 1899 serving as 100 are given in Table 19 and Chart 15.

TABLE 19

The Movement of Labor, Capital, and Product in Massachusetts Manufacturing, 1890–1926

1899 = 100

Year	P	L	C
1890	72	78	95
1891	78	81	96
1892	84	85	99
1893	73	77	96
1894	72	72	93
1895	83	84	86
1896	81	81	82
1897	93	89	92
1898	96	91	92
1899	100	100	100
1900	105	105	104
1901	118	108	106
1902	129	118	116
1903	130	122	122
1904	130	117	127
1905	142	130	137
1906	150	139	144
1907	152	147	153
1908	146	131	157
1909	160	143	205
1910	169	158	251
1911	181	159	263
1912	193	166	274
1913	195	168	282
1914	201	165	324
1915	200	162	324
1916	209	186	361
1917	196	193	410
1918	220	196	436
1919	212	195	477
1920	216	190	475
1921	208	158	454
1922	224	167	454
1923	256	182	458
1924	234	160	458
1925	245	161	458
1926	258	164	454

It will be seen from Table 19 that P is again found to be in between L and C with a distinct tendency to lie much closer to L than to C. It will also be noticed that the general movement of the three indexes was also very similar to that shown in the preceding chapter for the country as a whole. The co-efficients of production and of the relative ratios of labor and capital can readily be computed from these series, but for reasons of space are omitted.[4]

The problem then remains of finding the values for b and k so that the squares of the deviations of the computed P' from P would approach a minimum. These values were found to be 1.007 for b and .743 for k. The production equation for Massachusetts data, therefore, is $P' = 1.007\ L^{.743}\ C^{.257}$. The exponents for L and C are, therefore, almost identical with those computed for the United States for the years 1899–1922. If the last six years from 1921 to 1926 inclusive are, however, omitted

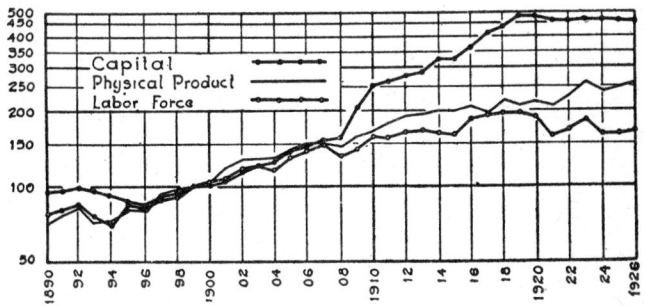

Chart 15. Relative Increase in Capital, Labor, and Physical Product in Manufacturing Industries of Massachusetts, 1889–1926.

and k is fitted for the thirty-one years from 1890 to 1920, then its numerical value is raised appreciably to .882 while the exponent for capital is reduced to .118.[5] For the longer period, however, the values of .743 and .257 applied.

The relationship between the computed P' and the actual P for this period of 1890–1926 is shown in Table 20 and Chart 16.

The average deviation of P' from P amounts to 6.5 per cent as compared with the average deviation of 4.3 per cent for the United States. The Massachusetts study, however, covers 37 years, while that for the United States covers but 24 years or only two-thirds as long a period.

If the three-year moving averages of the computed and the actual products are compared, the average deviation (disregard-

---

[4] Taking 1899 as 100, the technical coefficient with respect to labor was 110 in 1890 and 64 in 1926, while the coefficient with respect to capital in 1890 was 111 and in 1926, 175. The ratio of labor to capital in 1926 was but 36 per cent of what it had been in 1899, and the ratio of capital to labor was accordingly 278 per cent of what it then had been.

[5] If the trends of the three series for the years 1890–1920 are analyzed the exponents would be $L^{.916}\ C^{.084}$.

ing signs) is reduced to one of 5.8 per cent and for the five year moving averages to one of 4.7 per cent.

It is also interesting and indeed significant to note that there is a fairly high degree of correlation between the short-time deviations of P' from its moving average and of the actual product, or P from its similar moving average. The coefficient of correlation (r) between these deviations is + .6723 with a standard error of .0926. With r well over seven times the

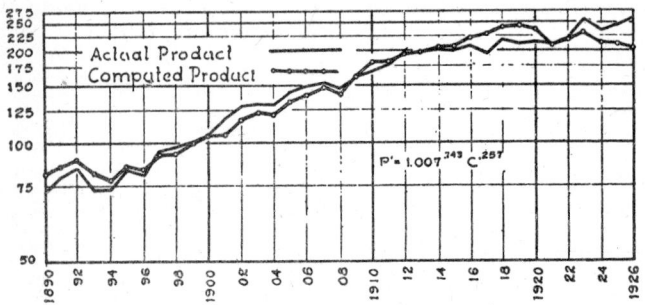

Chart 16. Theoretical and Actual Curves of Production, Massachusetts, 1889–1926.

P = Actual Product
P' = Computed Product

standard error, this value is clearly significant. The coefficient of correlation between the deviations of P and P' from their five-year moving average is in turn a little higher, amounting to + .714 with a standard error of .0853, thus making the former over eight times the latter.

2. The Possibility of Alternating Waves of Progress and Regression

In Chart 17 we have plotted the relative deviations of the computed product (P') from the actual product (P). If this is compared with the similar Chart 10A in the preceding chapter, it will be seen that there are essential differences between the movement of the two sets of deviations. In the case of the United States, we have seen that the course of the deviations roughly follows the business cycle and that they seem to be primarily caused by the fact that our indexes of labor and even more of capital are relatively overstated during periods of depressions and relatively understated during periods of prosperity. The deviations in Massachusetts, on the other hand, do not seem to conform to the business cycle and instead follow a long-time wavelike movement which is largely independent of

TABLE 20

THE RELATIONSHIP BETWEEN P' ($1.007\ L^{.743}\ C^{.257}$) AND P IN
MASSACHUSETTS, 1890–1926

Year	P'	P	Percentage Difference Between P' and P $\left(\dfrac{P'-P}{P}\right)$
1890	81	72	+13
1891	85	78	+9
1892	88	84	+5
1893	81	73	+11
1894	77	73	+4
1895	85	83	+2
1896	83	81	+2
1897	90	93	−3
1898	91	96	−5
1899	100	100	0
1900	105	105	0
1901	106	118	−10
1902	117	129	−9
1903	122	130	−6
1904	120	130	−8
1905	131	142	−8
1906	139	150	−7
1907	149	152	−2
1908	137	146	−6
1909	160	160	0
1910	179	169	+6
1911	183	181	+1
1912	191	193	−1
1913	195	195	0
1914	203	201	+1
1915	204	200	+2
1916	222	209	+6
1917	229	196	+17
1918	240	220	+9
1919	242	212	+14
1920	238	216	+10
1921	208	208	0
1922	217	224	−3
1923	230	256	−10
1924	211	234	−10
1925	208	245	−15
1926	204	258	−21

The sum of the percentage deviations without regard to sign = 241.

Average percentage deviation = $\dfrac{241}{37}$ = 6.5 per cent.

cyclical influences. Thus we find the index of actual product
falling below the computed product or the "norm" during the
first five years from 1890 to 1894 inclusive. During the years
from 1895 to 1900 the actual product closely approximated the
norm of the computed product. During the next eight years
(1901–1908) it rose above the computed product, and then dur-

ing the seven years from 1909–1915 remained close to this "norm" of the computed product. Then from 1916 to 1920 the index of actual product or P once more fell below the computed product, and after striking a precise equality with it in 1921 rose above it once more during the years from 1922 to 1926 inclusive. The disparity between P and P' in the case of Massachusetts seems, therefore, to be explainable in terms of wavelike periods in which P alternately falls below P', comes

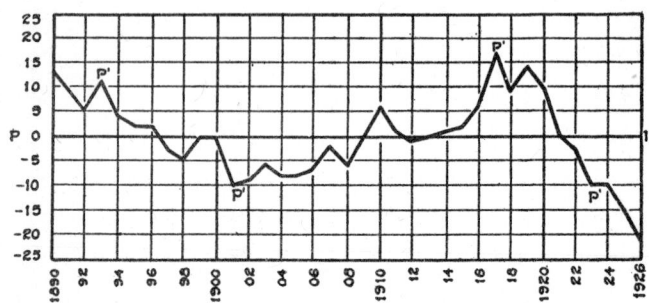

Chart 17. The Percentage Deviations of the Computed Product (P') from the Actual Product (P) in Massachusetts Manufacturing, 1890–1926.

to an approximate equality with it, and then rises above it only to drop back to the norm, and finally to rise above it again.

There is, therefore, the possibility that there were alternating cycles of technical progress and regress during this period which help to account for this disparity between P and P'. But it will be queried, What is "progress" and how can either it or its opposite be measured? If product, for example, increases relatively more rapidly than both the labor and the capital applied, it is, I take it, evident that something has happened to increase output other than the mere mechanical addition of more units of labor and of capital. If, on the contrary, product does not increase as rapidly as either labor or capital, it is also apparent that each unit of labor and capital is being applied with less average effectiveness than before. If the ratio of product to either labor or capital $\left(\dfrac{P}{L} \text{ and } \dfrac{P}{C} \right)$ were to increase while the ratio for the other factor remained constant, then that also could be classed as progress, while an opposite result would be regress. The ratios of product to labor and capital are shown in Table 21. From this it can be seen: (1) that during the period, 1890–1902, the ratios of product to labor $\frac{P}{L}$ and product to capital were both increasing. The former rose from 91 in 1890 to 110 in 1902 or an increase of 21 per cent, while the latter increased from 75 to 112 or an advance of no less than 49 per cent. (2) During the period, 1902–1919, the ratio of product to labor did not show a permanent increase and was 109 at the end while the relative average productivity of capital $\frac{P}{C}$ fell distinctly from 112 to 49 or a decrease of 56 per cent. It seems

TABLE 21

RATIOS OF PRODUCT TO LABOR AND CAPITAL, IN MASSACHUSETTS, 1890–1926

Year	$\frac{P}{L}$ (1899 = 100)	$\frac{P}{C}$ (1899 = 100)
1890	91	75
1891	96	81
1892	99	85
1893	95	76
1894	101	78
1895	100	97
1896	99	98
1897	105	102
1898	106	105
1899	100	100
1900	100	101
1901	110	112
1902	110	112
1903	106	107
1904	111	102
1905	110	104
1906	108	104
1907	104	100
1908	112	93
1909	112	78
1910	107	67
1911	114	69
1912	116	70
1913	116	69
1914	122	62
1915	123	62
1916	112	58
1917	102	48
1918	112	50
1919	109	44
1920	114	46
1921	132	46
1922	134	49
1923	141	56
1924	149	51
1925	152	54
1926	157	57

apparent, therefore, that there was on the whole a decrease in the effectiveness of Massachusetts industries during this period. (3) From 1919 on through 1926, however, the pendulum began to swing in the forward direction. The average productivity of both labor and capital came, in fact, to increase appreciably. The average for labor $\frac{P}{L}$ rose, for example, from 109 in 1919 to 157 in 1926, while that for capital rose from 44 to 57. Whether this period of progress will continue or whether it, in turn, will be succeeded by another wave of regression is, of course, unpredictable.

About all that can be said is that over the nearly forty years which have been covered in the Massachusetts study there has been a distinct tendency for production to be *on the average* a simple homogeneous function of the first degree of the quantities of labor and capital. But this tendency has not been uniform, and there have been apparent alternating periods of industrial progress and regress.

3. The Flexibilities of The Marginal Productivity Curves of Labor And Capital

From the foregoing material, it will be seen that as a norm the flexibility of marginal productivity of labor is −.26 and of capital −.74. This means that an increase of one per cent in the quantity of labor would cause, other things being equal, a reduction of twenty-six hundredths of one per cent in its marginal productivity, and a similar increase in the quantity of capital would cause a decrease of seventy-four hundredths of one per cent in its marginal productivity. The respective elasticities or the reciprocals of these, are, −3.85 and −1.35. This means that an increase of 1 per cent in the rate of wages, if unaccompanied by a rise in the marginal productivity of labor or other changes, would tend to cause a decrease of 3.85 per cent in the quantity of labor demanded. A similar increase in the rate of interest would tend to cause a decrease of 1.35 per cent in the quantity of capital demanded.

CHAPTER VII

THE THEORY OF PRODUCTION AS EXEMPLIFIED BY NEW SOUTH WALES DATA

1. Industrial Data for New South Wales

New South Wales and Victoria have very complete annual data on the numbers of workers employed in manufacturing establishments, the output in various industries, and capital values in money terms. My former associate, Mr. Aaron Director, has worked over this material and has constructed indexes of labor, capital and product for the years, 1901 to 1927, inclusive.[1]

The index of the average annual number of employees includes working proprietors and the salaried force, and has been corrected for changes in the proportion of female to male workers and for the average number of months worked during the year.

The index of production is a weighted arithmetic mean of the relatives for the various commodities in which the weights are based on the relative proportions of the value added by manufacturing[2] in the base year of 1911.

The index of capital is composed of two main forms of capital, namely (1) plant and machinery, and (2) buildings and fixtures. The gross monetary additions were estimated for each year for plant and machinery by subtracting the capital value for the preceding from that of the current year. A cost index was then constructed for each of these two elements of capital. For plant and machinery, this cost index is a weighted arithmetic mean of the Australian wholesale price indexes of metals and coal and the Australian index of wages in the engineering trades. The cost index for buildings and fixtures is a weighted arithmetic mean of the Australian wholesale price index of building

---

[1] For the sources for New South Wales see the *Official Yearbooks of New South Wales, 1901–27.*

[2] The formula used was $\dfrac{\Sigma Q_1 W_0}{\Sigma Q_0 W_0}$. Mr. Director has given a full description of this and other indexes of production in a monograph which I hope will soon appear.

materials and the Australian index of wages in the building trades. For both of these indexes, as indeed for all used, the year 1911 was treated as the base or 100.

The gross monetary additions in each year to plant and machinery and to buildings and fixtures were then deflated as in the studies for the United States and for Massachusetts by these indexes of cost.

Unlike these studies, however, an allowance was made for the replacement of depreciated capital at differing price levels. It was assumed that physical depreciation took place for buildings and fixtures on the basis of a twenty-five year cycle and for plant and machinery on one of sixteen years. It was also assumed that the values of the first year (1886) were composed of equal additions made previous to this year. The resulting net increments were then cumulated, thus giving the estimated value

TABLE 22

INDEXES OF LABOR, CAPITAL, AND PRODUCTION IN NEW SOUTH WALES MANUFACTURING INDUSTRIES, 1901–1927, (BASE 1911)

Year	Labor (1)	Capital		Production (4)
		Depreciated (2)	Undepreciated (3)	
1901	63	57	56	62
1902	62	64	62	61
1903	61	66	64	62
1904	63	69	67	67
1905	66	70	69	71
1906	72	72	71	76
1907	79	75	74	78
1908	82	79	79	80
1909	84	83	83	85
1910	92	92	92	96
1911	100	100	100	100
1912	107	110	109	108
1913	113	115	116	119
1915*	108	124	126	122
1916	107	127	131	111
1917	109	128	137	115
1918	110	127	142	118
1919	118	125	146	124
1920	133	127	153	138
1921	135	135	165	134
1922	137	145	177	140
1923	140	152	186	144
1924	149	164	199	154
1925	155	175	210	165
1926	163	184	220	176
1927	172	195	230	189

*Beginning with 1915 the year ends 30th June. Because of this change in the census year, data for the first half of 1914 are not available.

of each element of capital in use during the period. The two elements were then added and the resulting values reduced to relatives with 1911 as 100.[3]

Table 22 gives these indexes of L, P, and C.

Capital is given in two forms, the first with an allowance for depreciation and the second without such an allowance.

In Chart 18 this material is given in graphic form. It will be noticed that the growth of capital even on the undepreciated basis was slightly less than in the United States, the index for 1924 being 3.55 times what it had been in 1901, whereas in the United States the index for 1922 was 4.44 times what it had been twenty-three years before. It will also be noted that in some years, namely, in 1905, 1910, 1913 and 1920, the index of product rises above both the curve for L and for that of depreciated C. It is this depreciated C which we shall primarily use.[4]

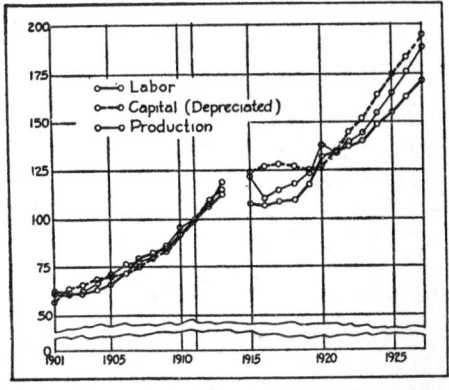

Chart 18.   Relative Growth of Capital (Depreciated), Labor, and Product in Manufacturing in New South Wales, 1901, 1926–1927.

2. The Equation of Production for New South Wales

Using the same formula of $P^1 = b\,L^K C^{1-K}$, we find that the best value of b is 1.0179 and of K .6504. This makes the equation $P^1 = 1.0179\,L^{.6504}\,C^{.3496}$. The computed product which is obtained by the use of this formula and how it compares with the actual product is shown in Table 23 and Chart 20.

The resemblance between the index of computed product (P^1) and that of the actual product (P) is quite striking. The average deviation of P^1 from P is only 2.2 per cent, while the maximum deviation is 5.7 per cent. In only three years was the deviation greater than 4 per cent, while in four years there was a complete identity between the two. The similarity between

---

[3] Mr. Director will, I hope, give a more complete discussion of this index of capital and the methods of allowing for depreciation in a forthcoming monograph *Studies in Marginal Productivity with Especial Reference to Australia.*

[4] Chart 19 shows the curve of undepreciated as well as depreciated capital in comparison with labor and product.

the two indexes, as indicated by Chart 20, is indeed appreciably
closer than that between the corresponding indexes for the
United States and for Massachusetts. The sum of the deviations without regard to sign is 64 and the average 2.5. In terms

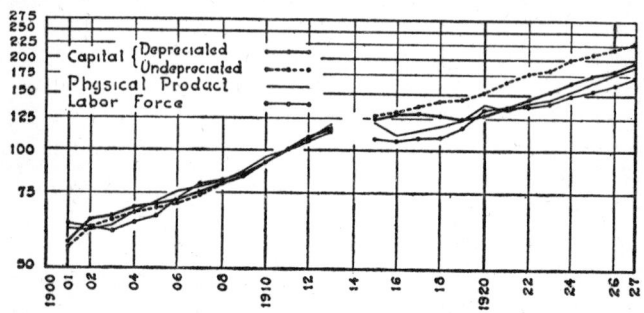

Chart. 19. Relative Growth of Both Depreciated and Undepreciated Capital in Comparison with Labor and Product in New
South Wales, 1901–1927.

of percentages, the average deviation was 2.2 per cent. This is
approximately one-half of what the average deviations are in
the United States series and one-third of the average for the
Massachusetts series.[5] The deviations between the moving averages of P and P^l are, of
course, still less than
those for the unadjusted
series.

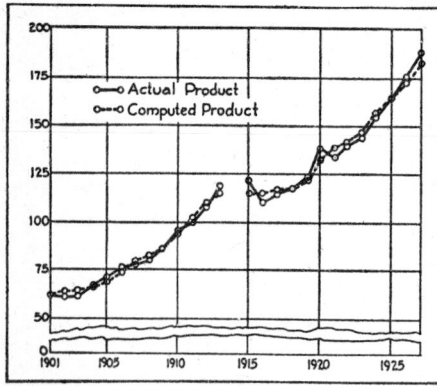

Chart 20. Comparison of Actual and Computed Product in Manufacturing in New South
Wales, 1901–1927.

In view of the com-
paratively close agree-
ment between the two
series themselves, the
question whether the re-
spective deviations from
trend of P and P^l follow
similar courses is not
very important.

The coefficient of cor-
relation between the re-
spective deviations of P

---

[5] The deviations do not seem to be explainable on such cyclical grounds as
is the case with the United States. (For an analysis of business conditions in
Australia see Thorp, *Business Annals,* pp. 322–9.) This may be caused by the
fact that the index of labor makes an allowance for part-time which is not true
for the United States labor index.

TABLE 23

OBSERVED AND COMPUTED INDEXES OF PRODUCTION* IN NEW SOUTH WALES
MANUFACTURING INDUSTRIES, 1901–1927

Year	Actual Product P	Computed Product P'	$d = P' - P$	$d' = \dfrac{P' - P}{P}$
1901	62	62	0	0.0
1902	61	64	3	4.9
1903	62	64	2	3.2
1904	67	66	−1	−1.5
1905	71	69	−2	−2.8
1906	76	73	−3	−3.9
1907	78	79	1	1.3
1908	80	82	2	2.5
1909	85	85	0	0.0
1910	96	94	−2	−2.1
1911	100	102	2	2.0
1912	108	110	2	1.9
1913	119	116	−3	−2.5
1915	122	115	−7	−5.7
1916	111	116	5	4.5
1917	115	117	2	1.7
1918	118	118	0	0.0
1919	124	123	−1	−.8
1920	138	133	−5	−3.6
1921	134	138	4	3.0
1922	140	142	2	1.4
1923	144	147	3	2.1
1924	154	157	3	1.9
1925	165	165	0	0.0
1926	176	173	−3	−1.7
1927	189	183	−6	−3.2

$\Sigma d = 64$ $\dfrac{\Sigma d}{N} = 2.5$ $\Sigma d' = 58.1$ $\dfrac{\Sigma d'}{N} = 2.2$

*The computed index was calculated from the formula: $P' = 1.0179 \; L^{.5504} \; C^{.3496}$.

and P^1 from their three year moving averages is $+ .514$. This is between two and three times its standard error of .1667.

3. Elasticities and Flexibilities of Labor and Capital in New South Wales

From the above material it is seen that as a norm an increase of one per cent in the quantity of labor would [6] cause a decrease in its marginal productivity of thirty-five hundredths of one per cent and that an increase of one per cent in the quantity of capital would by itself cause a decrease of approximately sixty-five hundredths of one per cent. The respective flexibilities of the marginal productivity curves are therefore —.35 for labor and —.65 for capital, while the elasticities are the reciprocals

---

[6] Other things being equal.

of this or — 2.86 and — 1.54. This means that if wage rates should be increased by one per cent, with all other things equal, the quantity of labor demanded would tend to decrease by 2.86

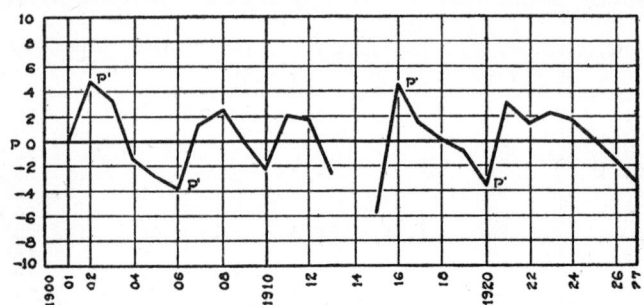

Chart 21. Percentage Deviations of Computed Product (*P'*) from Actual Product (*P*) in New South Wales Manufacturing Industries, 1901–1927.

per cent and that a similar increase in the rate of interest would tend to be accompanied by a decrease of 1.54 per cent in the quantity of capital demanded.

CHAPTER VIII

ARE THE APPARENT LAWS OF PRODUCTION REFLECTED IN THE ACTUAL PROCESSES OF DISTRIBUTION?

The theory and the facts of production which have been developed in the preceding chapters indicate certain approximate influences which labor and capital respectively seem to have had upon the product of manufactures. It is important to inquire whether the distribution of this product between labor and capital has approximated the mathematical relations which have thus far been revealed and whether the actual course of wages and of interest has been what we might expect. If there has been a fairly close approximation between the relationships in distribution and those in production, then their relative agreement still further confirms the productive effects of labor and capital which we have measured and carries with it the further implication that the processes of distribution at least follow those of marginal productivity in practise as well as in theory.

1. Does The Distribution of The Manufacturing Product in The United States Conform to The Productive Shares Attributed to Capital And Labor?

It will be remembered that when we attributed 75 per cent of the manufacturing product in the United States to labor, we obtained a close approximation to the actual normal course of production. With this should be compared the fact that when the National Bureau of Economic Research made its investigation into the proportion of the manufacturing product (net value added by manufactures) which went to labor during the decade, 1909–1918, they found wages and salaries formed on the average 74 per cent of the total value added by manufacture during these years.[1] This is certainly as close an agreement as could be expected and indicates that in practise labor tended to receive during this period approximately that share which our equation of production attributed to them. The results for the

---

[1] National Bureau of Economic Research, *Income in the United States,* Vol. 2, p. 98. The percentages by years were as follows:

| 1909 | 72.2 | 1911 | 76.4 | 1913 | 74.5 | 1915 | 75.4 | 1917 | 71.0 |
| 1910 | 71.6 | 1912 | 74.5 | 1914 | 77.8 | 1916 | 68.7 | 1918 | 78.1 |

period, 1923–1929, when the share of capital increased greatly would probably have been different from this.

2. Has The Movement of Real Wages in American Manufacturing Followed The Course of Average Value Productivity? [2]

A second test which should be imposed is whether the movement of real wages over the years has been substantially similar to the movement of average productivity. The record in manufacturing for the years 1900–1926 affords an excellent field for such a test, and this can be carried through not only for all manufacturing as a whole, but for nine main groups of manufacturing industries as well. What we are fundamentally seeking to do is: (1) to measure the average value productivity of the workers in manufacturing during this period; (2) to measure the relative movement of the real wages which these workers have received; and (3) to compare and correlate the relative movement of these two series with each other.

Since the measurement of the average value productivity is based both upon the relative physical production of manufactured goods and the exchange ratios at which these goods are sold, we shall begin, as our first step, with the relative changes in the actual physical quantities of production.

(1) The Index of Physical Production.

The main features of the index of physical production have already been explained in Chapter V, and the present index is substantially similar to that described there. There are, however, certain changes which were made for the sake of completeness from data which were not available when the earlier index was used.

In the first place, the indexes computed by Day and Thomas [3] for Census years for the nine specific groups of industries were used as being correct for those years. These groups were: (1) food, (2) textiles, (3) leather, (4) iron and steel, (5) nonferrous metals, (6) lumber, (7) stone, clay and glass, (8) paper and pulp, (9) chemicals. The indexes of production for these groups were then interpolated for the years within each census period. The data used for this were the yearly indexes of production computed for each group by E. E. Day and his as-

---

[2] I am indebted to my assistants, Mrs. Erika Schoenberg and Mr. Stanley Posner, for the laborious statistical computations upon which this chapter is based.

[3] Day and Thomas: *The Growth of Manufactures,* Census Monograph viii, 205 pp.

sociates.[4] The method adopted was that devised by my former associate Harold Weber and used in my *Real Wages in the United States* and which is now followed by the Division of Research of the Federal Reserve Board. This is to assume that any difference between the rates of change of the census data and those used for interpolation over a census period will be distributed evenly over the years within the period covered.

Since the Day-Thomas index did not give data for leather or for paper and pulp for the years from 1899 to 1914, separate indexes were computed for each of these for the years in question.[5]

These group indexes of physical quantities were then combined into an index for all manufacturing by weighting each by the relative value added to it by manufacturing in the year 1923.[6]

The resultant index for all manufacturing is given in the following table, while those for the nine constituent groups are given in Table I of the Appendix.

(2). The Change in Value Productivity.

It is, however, a mistake to believe that an index of physical production measures in itself the ability of an industry or a group of industries to pay either wages or interest. For if an increase in the output of an industry is accompanied by a fall in the price of each unit of its product, then provided that the prices of other commodities remain constant, the ability of the industry to pay wages or interest will not increase commen-

---

[4] For this material see the articles by Day and his associates: (1) *Journal American Statistical Association*, March, 1921 (Vol. 17), pp. 552–59; (2) *Review of Economic Statistics*, 1920, supplement to Vol. II., pp. 309 ff.; (3) *Ibid*. 1923, pp. 198 ff.; (4) *Ibid*. 1926, pp. 149 ff.

[5] In the case of leather this index was constructed by giving equal weights to (a) the relative cattle and calf receipts by years at nine markets, (b) the relative sheep receipts at nine markets, (c) the net imports of hides and skins. The annual *Agricultural Yearbooks* give the data for the first two of these, while the *Monthly Summary of Foreign and Domestic Commerce* contains the movement of the third. No data are given for 1899, and the relatives for that year were found by applying the relative change at the Chicago market between 1899 and 1900 of the receipts of cattle, calves, and sheep. (See Reports of the Chicago Board of Trade.)

An index of pulp wood consumption was used for the paper and pulp series (see *Statistical Abstract of the United States*, 1922, p. 484). Since no data existed for the years 1900 to 1903 inclusive, a straight line interpolation was used for the years between 1899 and 1904.

[6] These weights were as follows:

Group	Weight	Group	Weight
1. Food	169	6. Lumber	99
2. Textiles	197	7. Stone, Clay and Glass	66
3. Leather	68	8. Paper and Pulp	36
4. Iron and Steel	138	9. Chemicals	189
5. Non-Ferrous Metals	38		

surately with the advance in its output. Thus if product should double and the price per unit should fall to one-half of its former figure,[7] it would actually have no more money to pay out than before. If prices should fall by 25 per cent to 75, then the doubled product would yield 50 per cent more money income.

TABLE 24

The Revised Index of Physical Production for All Manufacturing in the United States, 1899–1926

Year	Index	Year	Index
1899	100	1913	180
1900	100	1914	171
1901	112	1915	187
1902	121	1916	218
1903	123	1917	219
1904	123	1918	237
1905	142	1919	210
1906	151	1920	224
1907	150	1921	181
1908	133	1922	229
1909	160	1923	260
1910	157	1924	247
1911	156	1925	274
1912	175	1926	285

It is, therefore, necessary to measure the exchange value of a product as well as its physical productivity. If the general price level is constant, this can be done by merely measuring the changes in the price of the commodity in question. But if general prices are also changing, then the variation in the exchange value of the product can be found by taking the ratio of the relative change in the price of the commodity in question to that of the relative change for all commodities. Thus if the price of article X falls from 100 to 75, while the prices of all commodities fall to 90, then a unit of X in exchanging for other commodities will command not 75 per cent as much as before, but 75/90 as much, or 83.3 per cent as much.

It is, therefore, necessary to measure the relative movements during this period of the prices of commodities in each of the nine manufacturing groups together with their combined average, and then find the ratio which the changes in these prices formed to the changes in the general price level itself. There will be found in this way the change in the exchange value of a unit of manufactured goods of these various types. The price indexes for these various groups and their combined average

---

[7] *i.e.,* if the elasticity of demand for the product is equal to unity.

were computed by the methods described in the footnote.[8] The combined average for the nine groups is given in the first column of Table 25, while those for the separate groups are found in Table II of the Appendix.

With these must, of course, go an index of the general price level to serve as a deflator. The two best measures of this are (1) the all-commodity wholesale price index of the United States Bureau of Labor Statistics, and (2) the index of Carl Snyder, of the New York Federal Reserve Bank.[9] The latter differs from the former primarily in the fact that it includes not only commodities at wholesale but also living costs, rents, and wages, and thus makes allowance for price changes of housing and of services. The Snyder index is superior to the Bureau's for many purposes, but it does not seem to be for ours. For what we are seeking to compare is the movement of wages with the movement of value productivity, and one element in the latter is the relative movement of prices. To give wage movements a prominent part in this price index would, therefore, be an act of circular reasoning, since they would then appear on both sides of the equation. It seems better, therefore, to use the Bureau of

---

[8] The Bureau of Labor Statistics has computed combined price indexes for each of these groups for the years from 1913 on. These were obtained by multiplying the absolute prices of the various commodities in each of the years by the physical quantities marketed in 1926. These absolutes were then reduced to relatives. (See *Bulletin 543,* U. S. Bureau of Labor Statistics, Wholesale Prices.)

For the period, 1899–1913, the Bureau of Labor Statistics has computed wholesale price indexes for four groups, namely, food, leather, textiles, and chemicals. The method used here was identical with that for the subsequent years, but the weights were the actual physical quantities marketed in 1919 instead of 1926. (See *Bulletin 415,* U. S. Bureau of Labor Statistics, Wholesale Prices, 1890–1925.)

We have computed new group indexes for the years, 1899–1913, for the five additional groups of, lumber, stone, clay and glass, paper and pulp, iron and steel, and non-ferrous metals. In each case the absolute prices in each year of the various commodities within each group were weighted (multiplied) by the actual physical quantities marketed in 1919. The method was thus made uniform with that of the Bureau of Labor Statistics. The commodities which were used within each group were as follows:

1. Lumber: hemlock, maple, oak, white pine, yellow pine, spruce, and shingles.

2. Stone, Clay and Glass: bricks, cement, lime, glass (3 varieties).

3. Paper and Pulp: newsprint and wrapping paper.

4. Iron and Steel: pig iron, bar iron, wire nails, steel billets (Bessemer), rails (Bessemer), sheets, tin plates, and wire fence.

5. Non-Ferrous Metals: copper ingots, copper wire, pig lead, pig tin, zinc slab, and silver bars.

Weighted averages for the nine groups as a whole were computed by multiplying the price relatives for each of the groups by the proportionate value added by manufacturing by each group in 1923.

[9] Carl Snyder: *Business Cycles and Business Measurement,* pp. 286–7.

Labor Statistics all-commodity index [10] as the measure for prices as a whole. And this is given in column 2 of Table 25.

TABLE 25

RELATIVE PRICE MOVEMENTS AND EXCHANGE VALUE OF A COMPOSITE UNIT OF MANUFACTURED GOODS (9 GROUPS) DURING THE YEARS, 1899–1926*
(1899 = 100)

Year	Relative Price Manufactured Goods (9 Groups) (1)	Bureau of Labor Statistics All Commodities Wholesale Price Index (2)	Relative Exchange Value of Unit of Manufactured Goods (9 Groups) (3) = ((1) ÷ (2))
1899	100	100	100
1900	106	108	98
1901	102	106	96
1902	105	113	93
1903	105	114	92
1904	103	114	90
1905	106	115	92
1906	110	118	93
1907	116	125	92
1908	109	121	90
1909	111	130	86
1910	113	135	84
1911	110	124	88
1912	114	132	86
1913	115	134	86
1914	112	131	85
1915	121	133	91
1916	161	164	98
1917	207	225	92
1918	231	252	92
1919	242	266	91
1920	285	296	96
1921	179	187	96
1922	176	185	95
1923	191	193	99
1924	183	188	97
1925	187	198	94
1926	180	192	94

*All indexes are given to the nearest integer, but the process of division is carried out from indexes computed to the nearest tenth of a per cent.

By dividing the price indexes for the various groups and for their combined average by the all-commodity index we obtain the ratios of changes in the prices of the former to those of the latter. These are given in column 3 of Table 25 for the nine groups as a whole and in Table III of the Appendix for each of them individually. 1899 is used as the base or 100, and the series is thus made parallel to that for physical production which

[10] This is also a summation of (1) the absolute prices in different years weighted by (2) the physical quantities marketed in a given year, and (3) reduced to relatives.

also uses 1899 as the base. Chart 22 shows the relative movement of the price indexes for manufactured goods and all commodities, and Chart 23 shows the ratio between them.

It will be seen from these indexes and the accompanying charts that the prices of manufactured goods and of all commodi-

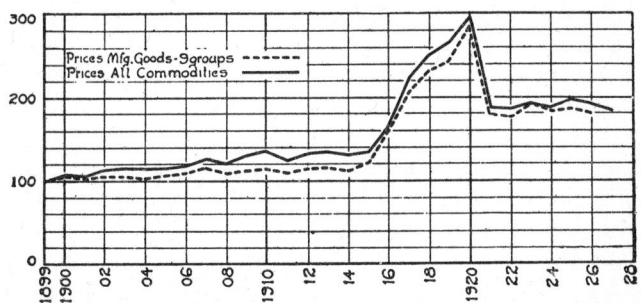

Chart 22. Relative Movement of Wholesale Prices of Nine Groups of Manufactured Goods as Compared with Movement of All-Commodity Index of Wholesale Prices in the United States, 1899–1926.

ties followed a substantially similar course, but that the former did not rise as rapidly as the latter during the years 1899–1914. By 1914, indeed, the index for manufactured goods had increased by 12 per cent, while the all-commodity index had risen by 31 per cent. The purchasing power of a unit of manu-

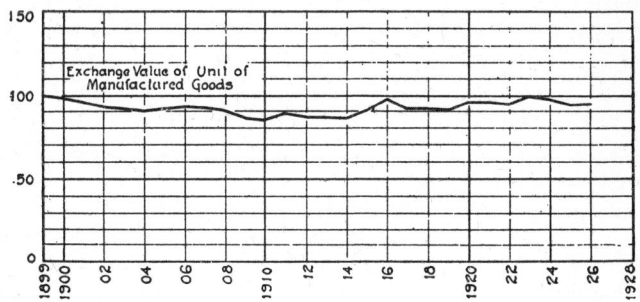

Chart 23. Relative Exchange Value of a Composite Unit of Manufactured Goods in the United States, 1899–1926.

factured goods was approximately 15 per cent less than it had been fifteen years earlier. During the war the prices of manufactured goods rose somewhat more rapidly than did those for all commodities but not sufficiently to make up for the earlier failure to keep pace, so that by 1920 the exchange value of a unit of manufactured goods was still 4 per cent below the average for 1899. By 1923 the exchange ratio was up to 99, but it declined during the following two years and ended the period at 94.

On the whole, therefore, the purchasing power of a unit of manufactured products was lower throughout the period than it was at the beginning. Although this decline was greater during the first fifteen years, the rise in the subsequent years was insufficient completely to restore the original ratio.

(3) Total Value Productivity and Average Value Productivity Per Employee.

We now have both an index of the relative total quantity of physical product produced in manufacturing and one of the relative exchange values of each unit. By multiplying these two together we obtain an index of the total value product of manufacturing. This is shown for all manufacturing in Table 26, and for each of the nine separate manufacturing groups in Table IV of the Appendix. Because of the lessened exchange value of a unit during the period as compared with the beginning, the index of value productivity was below that for physical productivity, being 259 in 1926 as compared with 285 for the index of production.

We wish, however, to reduce these indexes of total value productivity to a per capita basis in order to compare them with the movement of average real earnings, and in order to do so it is necessary to divide them by the relative changes in the number of workers employed. We constructed, therefore, indexes of the number employed in each of the nine groups from 1899 to 1926 [11] as is shown in Table V in the Appendix. From them a combined index for manufacturing as a whole was computed which is shown in Table 27.

---

[11] The methods used were to take the total number employed in each Census year both of wage-earners and salaried employees in all of the industries comprised under each of the nine groups. (See Censuses of Manufactures, 1899, 1904, 1909, 1914, 1919, 1921 1923, 1925.) These figures for Census years were then interpolated for the intercensal years within each period by constructing an index of employment from state sources for each of the nine groups. For the period prior to 1919 the annual statistics of manufactures for the following states were used:

Massachusetts, 1899–1919, Annual Statistics of Manufactures, Massachusetts.
New Jersey, 1899–1914, Annual Reports, Bureau of Statistics of New Jersey.
Pennsylvania, 1899–1919, Annual Reports, Secretary of Internal Affairs.
New York, 1914–1919, New York Labor Bulletin.

These data were compiled for as many industries within each of the nine groups as possible and covered the following: (1) Textiles: silk, cotton, woolen and worsted goods, dyeing and finishing textiles, hosiery and knit goods, men's and women's clothing. (2) Food: food products including canning and preserving,

TABLE 26

RELATIVE TOTAL VALUE PRODUCT OF ALL MANUFACTURING (9 GROUPS) BY
YEARS, 1899–1926 (1899 = 100)

Year	Relative Total Value Product	Year	Relative Total Value Product
1899	100	1913	152
1900	99	1914	141
1901	106	1915	165
1902	111	1916	209
1903	111	1917	193
1904	108	1918	201
1905	128	1919	184
1906	138	1920	210
1907	138	1921	159
1908	114	1922	209
1909	136	1923	252
1910	132	1924	228
1911	133	1925	246
1912	145	1926	259

TABLE 27

RELATIVE NUMBERS EMPLOYED IN MANUFACTURING, 1899–1927
(WAGE-EARNERS AND SALARIED WORKERS) 1899 = 100

Year	Relative Numbers Employed	Year	Relative Numbers Employed
1899	100	1914	148
1900	103	1915	149
1901	105	1916	167
1902	116	1917	174
1903	120	1918	171
1904	114	1919	174
1905	126	1920	174
1906	134	1921	144
1907	138	1922	159
1908	126	1923	176
1909	141	1924	167
1910	147	1925	171
1911	146	1926	174
1912	152	1927	173
1913	154		

slaughtering, bakery products, and confectionery. (3) Leather: boots and shoes, leather, leather goods. (4) Iron and Steel: pig iron, foundry iron, castings, rolling mill products, machinery. (5) Non-Ferrous Metals: brass and copper, silver goods, smelting and refining, silver and plated ware, jewelry. (6) Lumber: furniture, wooden boxes, saw and planing mill products, (7) Stone, Clay and Glass: brick and terra cotta, lime and cement, pottery, glass. (8) Paper and Pulp: paper and pulp, paper boxes, paper goods, printing and bookbinding. (9) Chemicals: high explosives, soap and tallow, soap, oils, chemicals, drugs and chemicals.

When data for the same industry were obtained from more than one state the absolute figures were added and then reduced to relatives. These relatives

TABLE 28

RELATIVE VALUE PRODUCT PER EMPLOYEE IN ALL MANUFACTURING (9 GROUPS),
1899–1926 (1899 = 100)

Year	Relative Average Value Product per Employee	Year	Relative Average Value Product per Employee
1899	100	1913	99
1900	96	1914	96
1901	100	1915	111
1902	96	1916	125
1903	93	1917	111
1904	95	1918	117
1905	101	1919	106
1906	103	1920	120
1907	100	1921	110
1908	91	1922	131
1909	96	1923	143
1910	90	1924	136
1911	91	1925	144
1912	95	1926	149

TABLE 28A

RELATIVE REAL WAGES IN MANUFACTURING, 1899–1926

1899	100	1913	108
1900	101	1914	106
1901	101	1915	107
1902	103	1916	107
1903	100	1917	102
1904	101	1918	105
1905	103	1919	110
1906	105	1920	114
1907	102	1921	116
1908	104	1922	121
1909	108	1923	129
1910	101	1924	128
1911	100	1925	127
1912	104	1926	129

By dividing the relative total value product of these various industries by the relative numbers employed we obtained the relative value productivity per employee. This is given for all manufacturing as a whole in Table 28, while the detailed

were then weighted by the average number of workers employed in the respective industries in the census years, and group indexes were thus obtained. These were then used for interpolation *within* but not between given census periods by the method which I have described in my *Real Wages in the United States, 1890–1926*. This in brief was based on the assumption that the numbers employed in the country as a whole would have varied from year to year within the census period as did the state samples, and that any difference in the rates of change for the sample for the period as a whole as compared with the Census totals was evenly distributed over the period as a whole.

indexes for each of the nine groups are contained in Table VI of
the Appendix. It will be noticed that so far as manufacturing
as a whole is concerned, that there was no net increase during
the fifteen years from 1899 to 1914, but that on the contrary,
except for four years, the average value productivity was below that for 1899. During the seven years which followed 1907,
the index was indeed on the average from 5 to 6 per cent below
the level in the base year.

The big increase came in the years, 1915 and 1916. In the
former year, the index of average value productivity rose by 16
per cent from 96 to 111, and in the following year by 14 points
and 13 per cent to 125. It fell back to 111 in 1917, rose to 117
in 1918, declined again to 106 in 1919, and went forward to 121
in 1920. This was still, however, 4 points below the relative
for 1916, and the depression of 1921 reduced it to 110, or one
point below the level of 1915 and 1917. In 1922 and 1923 it
surged forward again in a manner comparable to 1915 and 1916
and increased to 131 and 143 respectively, or a gain of 33 points
or 30 per cent in two years. The recession of 1924 brought the
index down to 136, but it again went forward to 144 in 1925 and
149 in 1926, which was a gain of 53 points or 55 per cent in
twelve years.

(4) Relative Average Real Earnings in Manufacturing in
Comparison with the Relative Value Productivity.

The relative real earnings of both the wage-earners and the
salaried workers in manufacturing were found for all of those
employed in the nine groups covered. The average annual
money earnings for all of the workers in the constituent industries within each group were first found for the census years,[12]
and then the probable earnings in the intercensal years of each
period were ascertained by the process of interpolation by using
the average earnings for those smaller number of industries
which the author had previously worked out in his book on *Real
Wages in the United States, 1890–1926*.[13] These average annual
money earnings were then reduced to relatives with 1899 as

---

[12] By dividing the total paid out in wages and salaries in each of these years
by the total average number employed in *all* of the industries classified within
each group.

[13] The final group indexes differ from those computed in that book in that
they (1) include salaried as well as wage employees and (2) are based upon
all of the industries within each group, whereas the earlier indexes merely used
those industries for which there were continuous records throughout the period
and not merely for census years. The earlier indexes were, however, used for
interpolating the probable group-earnings for the years within each census period.

a base and divided by the index of living costs.[14] This gave indexes of relative real earnings for all manufacturing which are found in Table 28A. To facilitate comparison with the relative movement of average value productivity the two indexes are represented graphically in Chart 24. The indexes of real wages for each of the nine groups are given in Table VIII of the Ap-

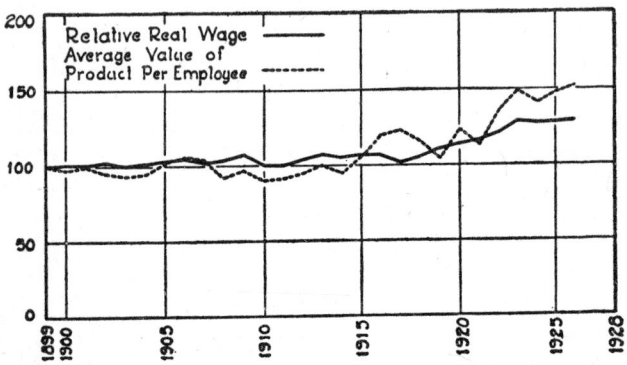

Chart 24. Comparative Movement of Relative Real Wages and Relative Value Product Per Employee in American Manufacturing, 1899–1926.

pendix, but are represented graphically in conjunction with their respective average value productivities in nine charts from 24A to 24I.

In terms of points, the index of the relative value productivity per employee in all manufacturing in the years when it fell below that of relative real wages accumulated a total of 108 minus points, while in the years in which it exceeded the relatives of real wages, it accumulated a total of 113 plus points or 5 more than the total of minus signs. If the twenty-seven year period be taken as a whole, therefore, the two sets of deviations approximately balanced each other.

It should be noted, however, that until 1916 the index of real wages was always invariably above that of average value productivity, but from then on it was almost invariably below that of value productivity. Although there was, therefore, comparative agreement between the two series if all the years are lumped together as a whole, there was an appreciable disparity between them in the two periods into which the span of years seems to divide itself. The failure of wages to increase com-

---

[14] See my *Real Wages in the United States, 1890–1926*, pp. 19–69, especially pp. 60–1.

mensurately with average value productivity during the years
following 1922, which is shown by the data which I have assembled, is confirmed by other studies. Thus Professor F. C.
Mills has shown that during the years 1922–1929 the volume of
physical production (excluding construction) increased by 34
per cent, or 3.4 per cent a year compounded. If construction

Charts 24 A to 24 I. Comparative Movement of Relative Real
Earnings with Relative Value Product Per Employee in Nine
Separate Groups of American Manufacturing, 1899–1926.

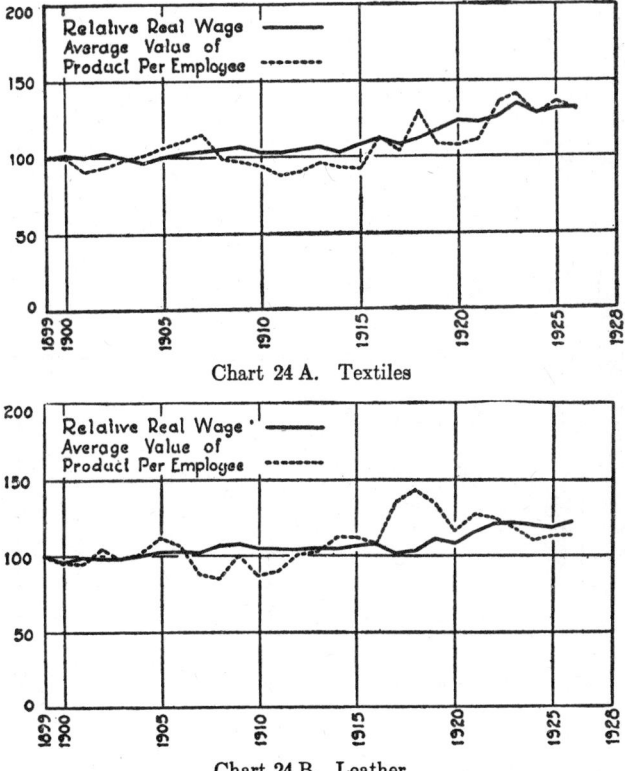

Chart 24 A.   Textiles

Chart 24 B.   Leather

were included the increase would have been approximately 38
per cent and the annual growth rate about 3.8 per cent.[15]   The
real wages of all the workers increased, however, by only approximately 22 per cent or 2.3 per cent a year.[16]   All profits,
however, increased by 83 per cent, or 7.3 per cent a year com-

[15] F. C. Mills, *Economic Tendencies in the United States,* pp. 243–46.
[16] *Ibid.,* pp. 476–481.

pounded, while financial profits increased by no less than 143 per cent, or 16 per cent a year.[17]

The Census of Manufactures also shows this tendency. Whereas wages formed 41 per cent of the total value added by manufacturing in 1914, 42 per cent in 1919, and 45 per cent in 1921, this percentage fell to 43 per cent in 1923, 40 per cent in 1925, 39 per cent in 1927, and 36.4 per cent in 1929.[18]   The

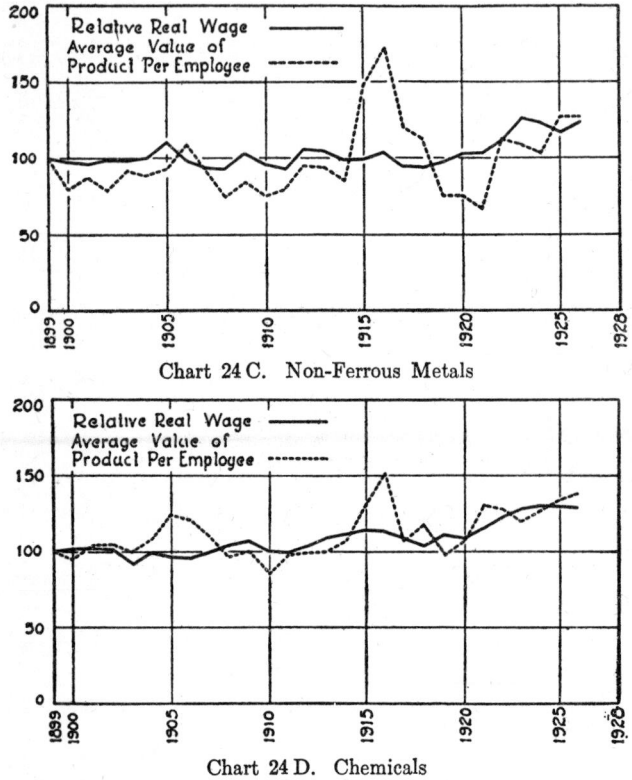

Chart 24 C.   Non-Ferrous Metals

Chart 24 D.   Chemicals

value product added by manufacturing rose indeed by approximately 6 billions of dollars between 1923 and 1929 (i.e., from 25.8 to 31.7 billions of dollars), while wages rose by only approximately 600 million dollars (i.e., from 11.0 to 11.6 billions), or only about one-tenth of the increase in the value of the product.

[17] *Ibid.*, p. 482.
[18] See *Census of Manufactures*, 1929, p. 15.

Even if we include salaries, a large portion of the increases in which went to the "insiders" at the top and which did not represent any real increase in purchasing by the main groups of low-salaried workers, the total distributed in wages and salaries fell from 54 per cent in 1914 and 53.5 per cent in 1923, to a little under 48 per cent in 1929.

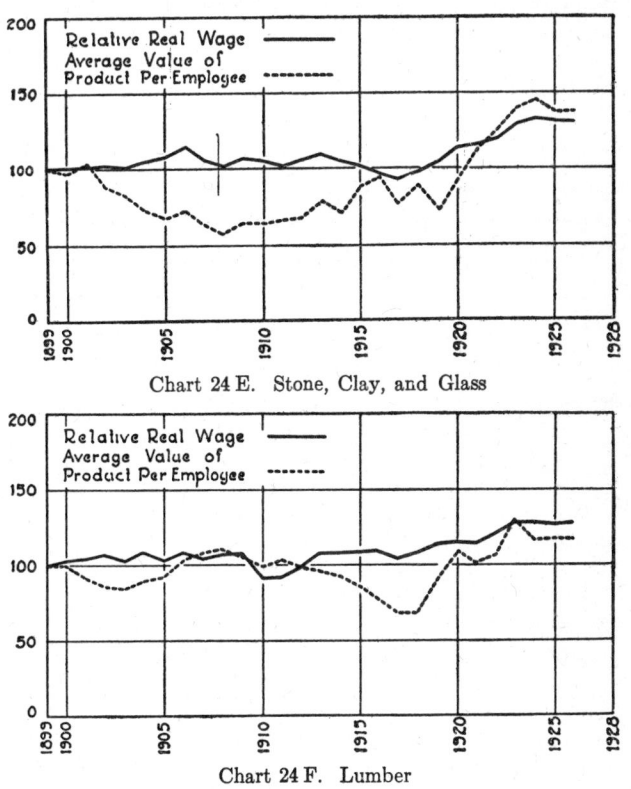

Chart 24 E. Stone, Clay, and Glass

Chart 24 F. Lumber

It is probable indeed that the far more rapid increase of value productivity than of real wages during the years, 1922–1926, and the at least partial maintenance of this disparity during the years from 1926 to 1929, was at least one of the causes for the great depression which began in the fall of the latter year. The failure of wages to expand during these years commensurately with the value of production led to vastly increased profits. These, in turn, at once stimulated the great speculative fever of the later years of this period, and since a large portion of the profits were reinvested, there was a great expansion in plant and equipment. When the increased flow of consumers' goods turned out by these factories came upon the market, the purchasing power available in the hands of the workers to buy them seems to have been insufficient to do so without a very appreciable slash in the prices of these goods.

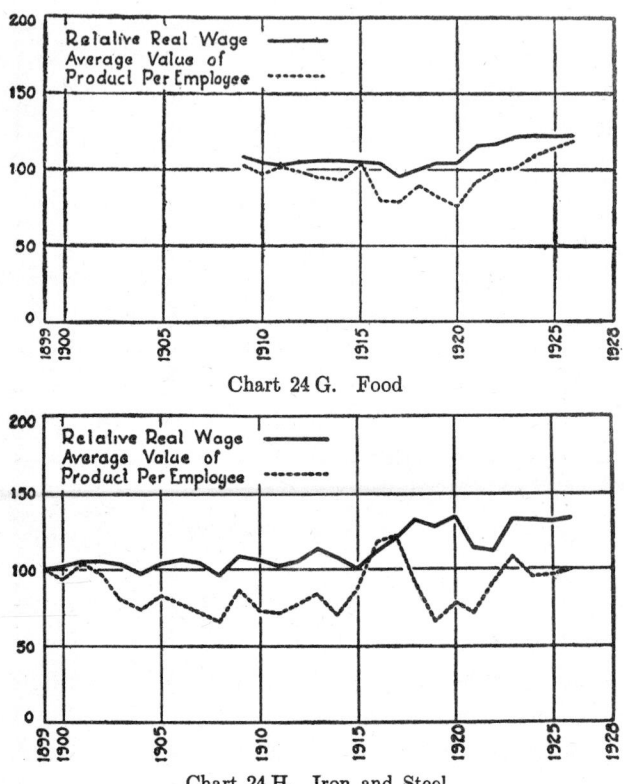

Chart 24 G.   Food

Chart 24 H.   Iron and Steel

There were, in fact, more goods produced than could be sold at the existing price level. Prices had to fall, and this fall in prices, instead of being a matter of indifference, set into motion cumulative forces of breakdown which deepened and intensified the depression. But while this disparity during the twenties helped to create the great depression in which we are now floundering, the degree of relative coincidence for the period as a whole should also be noted as a factor which is surely of some significance.

An even closer degree of conformity between the two series is, moreover, evidenced if we compare moving averages of the two series. Thus a three-year moving average for both the real wages in and the average value productivity of all manufacturing gives a total of minus deviations of 87.0 and of plus deviations of 98.9. A five-year moving average produces a still closer degree of correspondence between the two series with total minus deviations of 65.8 and plus deviations of 88.9.

From the charts for the various groups of industries, therefore, a number of points will be noticed. (1) It is evident that the fluctuations of real wages have been far less marked

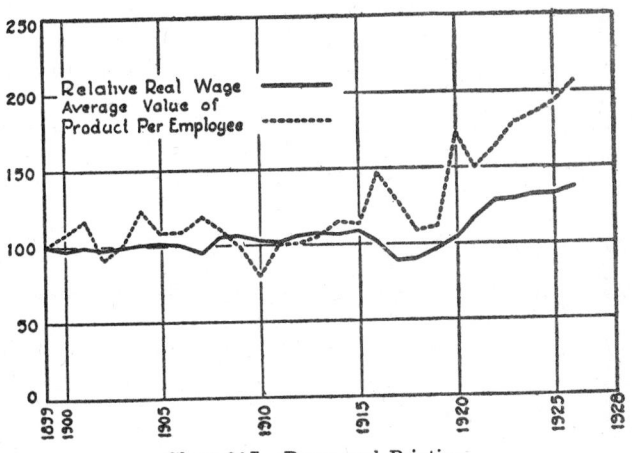

Chart 24 I. Paper and Printing

than those of average value productivity. If we take all manufacturing, textiles, leather, non-ferrous metals, chemicals, and stone, clay and glass, we find that the curve of real wages cuts in general through the peaks of average value productivity which characterize most of the years of prosperity and in turn is above the troughs of value productivity which commonly attend the depressions.

(2) For the industries named above and for the food industries as well, there was during the period in question a very pronounced tendency for the long run movement of these two variables to approximate each other. Thus, if we compare 1926 relatives only we find a gap of 20 points and 13 per cent between the relatives of real wages and of average value productivity for all manufacturing. This discrepancy amounts to only 10 points in the case of chemicals, 7 points for stone, clay

and glass, 4 points for food, 3 points for non-ferrous metals, and an almost exact coincidence in the case of textiles.

The use of a three-year moving average in order largely to remove cyclical fluctuations would in turn generally very appreciably reduce such differences as are shown above by the unadjusted yearly relatives. Thus in the case of all manufacturing the difference for the end year would be reduced from 20 to 15 points, for chemicals from 10 to 5 points, and for non-ferrous metals from 3 to 2 points. In the case of textiles the approximation between the two indexes is about the same, while the difference is slightly raised for food and stone, clay and glass. The correspondence between the two indexes is, however, made appreciably closer throughout the course of the period by the use of this three-year moving average and still more so by the use of a five-year moving average.

(3) The discrepancy between the relatives of real wages and of average value productivity is, however, distinctly more marked in the case of iron and steel, lumber, and paper and printing. In the first of these industries we have the spectacle of a falling average exchange value up to the outbreak of the world war. This was probably caused by the policy of the United States Steel Corporation of maintaining a pegged money price for steel which was followed by the independents. Since the general price level was advancing during this time, this maintenance of a relatively fixed money price meant in reality that the exchange value of a ton of steel was falling. So far indeed had this gone that in 1914 a ton of iron and steel products could only purchase 56 per cent as much of all commodities as it had been able to do fifteen years before. Even with the increase in physical output per worker, the average value productivity per employee was in 1914 still only 69 per cent of what it had been in 1899. The wartime demand of the belligerents together with technical improvements greatly raised the average exchange value in the three subsequent years to 88 in 1915, to 118 in 1916, and to 122 in 1917. The fixation of maximum prices by the War Industries Board, however, sent the exchange value of iron and steel down in 1918 by slightly over 25 per cent, and there was a still further drop in 1919. While the exchange value of a unit of iron and steel did not rise appreciably during the ensuing seven years, there was such an increase in the average physical productivity that the average value productivity rose very appreciably and by 1926 was only one per cent be-

low 1899. The real earnings of the workers had, however, increased during the previous twelve years so that they were in 1926, 33 per cent above those of 1899. There was thus a very great disparity between the movement of these two indexes.

The question which then naturally presents itself is how the rise in real wages as compared with what was on the whole an appreciably lowered average value productivity can be reconciled with the large profits which the United States Steel Corporation and most of the independents were able to make during this period. The answer is, however, relatively simple. The profits were made because there was a progressive substitution of technically improved capital instruments for labor, so that the share of the total product paid out in wages appreciably decreased. This made it possible to at once pay higher real wages, even though the average exchange value of a ton of steel was lower than before, and at the same time to net very large profits. As a matter of fact the percentage which wages formed of the total value of the product fell for blast furnaces from 42 in 1919 and 50 in 1921 to 33 in 1923, 31 in 1925, 34 in 1927, and 26 in 1929.[19] For steel works and rolling mills, the percentage changed from 56 per cent in 1929 and 68 per cent in 1921 to 57 per cent in 1923, 54 in 1925, 55 in 1927, and 47 per cent in 1929.[20]

Paper and printing apparently presents a somewhat different case in that the increase in real wages there was very much less than the apparent rise in average value productivity. Indeed, at the end of the period the index of real wages was 137 as compared to 206 for the apparent average value productivity. This discrepancy is, however, probably more apparent than real. The only statistics on production and prices which we could obtain were for the raw materials of pulp and paper. But the wages which were computed include also those employed in book and job printing and in newspaper printing as well. It is highly improbable that the exchange value of such printing work rose to the same degree as that for the raw material, and it is indeed even possible that it actually declined. Had it been possible to take this factor into account, it is believed that the discrepancy between the movement of real earnings and of the actual average value productivity would have been markedly

---

[19] *Census of Manufactures*, 1929, Vol. I, p. 66.
[20] Bulletin 567, U. S. Bureau of Labor Statistics, p. 19.

less. This would also operate to bring the two indexes for the
nine groups as a whole more closely together.

Lumber presents a more mixed relationship. During the
years from 1899 to 1905 inclusive real wages rose in these industries, while the average value product fell. The two series, however, drew somewhat more closely together during the ensuing
seven years but then separated widely as real wages rose and
the average value product declined. The gap was narrowed by
1920 to one of six points, and in 1923 the relative for average
value productivity was actually two points above that for real
wages. It sank thereafter, however, and in 1926 was 11 points
below the real wage index.

(5) The Degree of Correlation between the Indexes of Real
Wages and of Average Value Productivity.

It is apparent from a study of the charts that there is some
degree of relationship between the movements of the average
value productivity and of real wages. We can obtain a more
definite measurement of the degree of this interrelationship by
computing coefficients of correlation both for all manufacturing
and for each of the nine main groups. This has first been done
by taking the indexes as they stand and computing the coefficients from them without any correction for differences in
secular trends. This method gives the following coefficients:

Industry	*Coefficient of Correlation* (r)
All Manufacturing [21] (9) groups	.904
Textiles	.822
Paper and Printing	.802
Stone, Clay and Glass	.746
Food	.688
Chemicals	.609
Lumber	.499
Leather	.392
Non-Ferrous Metals	.332
Iron and Steel	.310

It will be seen that the degree of correlation for all manufacturing as a whole was very high, namely, .90. If we take the

---

[21] This is where the relative value product of the various groups were
weighted according to the relative value product added by manufacturing. The
coefficient when the weights used were the relative number of employees was
almost identical, i.e. + .901.

square of this (r^2) as the best measure of the interrelationship [22] this would give + .81. Five of the constituent groups (i.e. textiles, paper, stone, clay and glass, food and chemicals) show quite high coefficients ranging from + .61 to + .82. Lumber shows a moderately high coefficient of approximately .50, while three of the groups had relatively low coefficients of between .31 and .39. Since the changes in average value productivity would be expected to affect the long-time changes in real wages more than the short-time changes, we have correlated the five-year moving averages of the two series for the groups and find them to be as follows:

Industry	Coefficient of Correlation (r)
All Manufacturing	.940
Textiles	.907
Paper and Printing	.816
Stone, Clay and Glass	.779
Food	.672
Chemicals	.741
Lumber	.401
Leather	.556
Non-Ferrous Metals	.541
Iron and Steel	.523

It will be seen that in the majority of instances the use of the five-year moving averages appreciably raised the coefficient. That for all manufacturing was raised by nearly 4 points; iron and steel and non-ferrous metals were raised by nearly 21 points from low to moderately high coefficients. The coefficient for chemicals was raised by 13 points and that for textiles by approximately 8 points. The coefficient for stone, clay, and glass was increased by a little over two points. Only lumber suffered a real decrease from .5 to .4, while the coefficients for paper and printing and for the food trades remained approximately as they were.

Coefficients of correlation were also computed by eliminating the trends of the series and merely measuring the deviations from these respective trends. This somewhat lowered the coefficients (except in the case of foods, and iron and steel) which were as follows:

[22] See Mordecai Ezekiel: "Meaning and Significance of Correlation Coefficients," *American Economic Review*, Vol. XIX (1929), pp. 246–50.

Industry	Coefficient of Correlation (r)
All Manufacturing [23]	.702
Food	.802
Textiles	.629
Paper and Printing	.541
Stone, Clay and Glass	.505
Lumber	.394
Iron and Steel	.343
Chemicals	.268
Non-Ferrous Metals	.173
Leather	— .375

It will be seen from this that the correlation coefficient for all manufacturing of + .70 is still quite high, since the degree of interrelation indicated by r^2 is + .49. The other coefficients are, also, in general lower than they were. Food and textiles, it is true, still have quite high coefficients of + .802 and .629, and paper and printing and stone, clay and glass have moderately high coefficients of .541 and .505. Lumber, iron and steel, chemicals, and non-ferrous metals, however, have very low positive coefficients, and leather actually a negative one.

It should, however, be emphasized that deviations from the trend give what are primarily cyclical and short-run fluctuations. We know that the real wage per worker during such periods fluctuate much less widely than does the average value product. During the first part of a depression period the real earnings of the workers who continue to be employed tend to go up because of the fall in the cost of living, while the average value product, because of the decline in production, almost inevitably falls. As prosperity returns, the average value product leaps upward, while real wages are far more sluggish and in some cases, due to the rise in the cost of living, actually decline. Moreover, the war years produced great price fluctuations which greatly disturbed any normal relationship between value product and wages. The prices of non-ferrous metals, and iron and steel, for example, soared after the outbreak of the great war, but were pegged during the period of our participation. Their wage scales were, however, largely determined by general forces and hence went up far more slowly than the average value product in 1915 and 1916 and continued to rise as the values of these

---

[23] With numbers employed used as weights, r was + .705.

metals fell with the advance of prices during 1918 and 1919. We are more interested in the long time relationships and the year to year fluctuations.

3. The Relative Movement of Average Value Productivity And of Real Wages in Coal Mining

The American coal industry furnishes a further opportunity to test the degree of coincidence between movements of the average value productivity per worker and the actual movement of real wages. We have worked out indexes of the relative total exchange value of coal produced in various years by multiplying the relative physical output by the ratio between relatives of coal prices [24] and of the all-commodity index. By dividing this product by the number of workers employed $\frac{P}{L}$, we obtain, therefore, an index shown in Table 29 of average value productivity per worker for the bituminous industry alone for the years, 1890–1924, and for the bituminous and anthracite industries combined for the years, 1902–1924. The index of the relative real annual earnings of the coal miners in these groups is given in another column of the same table.

TABLE 29

RELATIVE REAL WAGES AND RELATIVE VALUE PRODUCT PER EMPLOYEE IN THE COAL INDUSTRY *Bituminous Coal* (1890–99 = 100)

Year	Relative Real Earnings	Relative Value Product per Employee	Percentage Deviation of Real Earnings from Value Product	Year	Relative Real Earnings	Relative Value Product per Employee	Percentage Deviation of Real Earnings from Value Product
1890	115	98	+17	1897	79	99	−20
1891	109	98	+11	1898	92	103	−11
1892	114	109	+ 5	1899	109	114	− 4
1893	112	96	+17	1900	116	124	− 6
1894	88	89	− 1	1901	124	121	+ 2
1895	93	95	− 2	1902	130	128	+ 2
1896	83	97	−14				

[24] See my book on *Real Wages in the United States, 1890–1926*, pp. 534–7. The excellent studies of W. E. Fisher and Miss Anne Bezanson promise to add much to our knowledge of rates and earnings in the coal industry. Unfortunately only their first volume on *Wage Rates and Working-Time in the Bituminous Coal Industry, 1912–1922* has appeared and that too late for inclusion in the present work. Their study on earnings which would be valuable to compare with my index is yet to be published.

Bituminous, and Bituminous and Anthracite

	Bituminous (1890–99 = 100)				Bituminous and Anthracite (1902 = 100)		
Year	Relative Real Earnings	Relative Value Product per Employee	Percentage Deviation of Real Earnings from Value Product	Year	Relative Real Earnings	Relative Value Product per Employee	Percentage Deviation of Real Earnings from Value Product
1903	132	136	− 3	1903	116	125	− 7
1904	120	113	+ 6	1904	113	105	+ 8
1905	128	116	+10	1905	115	105	+10
1906	132	124	+ 6	1906	115	108	+ 6
1907	135	129	+ 5	1907	120	115	+ 4
1908*	118	110	+ 7	1908*	106	103	+ 3
1910	128	115	+11	1910	113	103	+10
1911	123	121	+ 2	1911	110	111	− 1
1912	135	131	+ 3	1912	118	115	+ 3
1913	135	136	− 1	1913	118	121	− 2
1914	115	119	− 3	1914	103	109	− 6
1915	127	122	+ 4	1915	113	111	+ 2
1916	148	128	+16	1916	138	112	+23
1917	160	161	− 1	1917	141	137	+ 3
1918	163	172	− 5	1918	147	148	− 1
1919	130	124	+ 5	1919	121	113	+ 7
1920	142	201	−29	1920	131	172	−24
1921	121	170	−29	1921	120	164	−27
1922	122	170	−28	1922	110	146	−25
1923	156	192	−19	1923	149	181	−18
1924	140	158	−11	1924	139	156	−11

* There are no statistics of output for 1909.

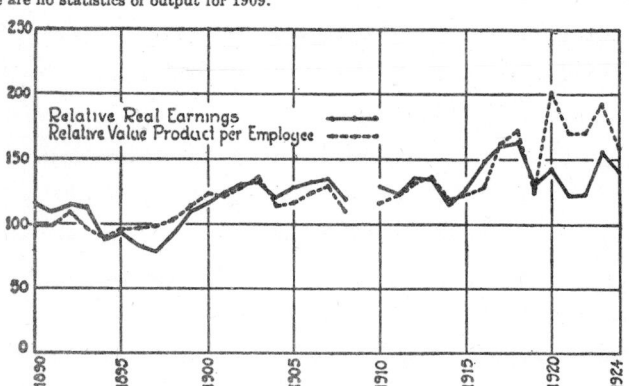

Chart 25. Relative Movement of Average Real Earnings of Workers in Bituminous Coal Mining and of Average Value Product Per Employee in the United States, 1890–1924.

These relationships are shown graphically in Charts 25 and 26. Chart 25 shows the movement of real wages and of average value productivity in the bituminous mines for the years, 1890–

1924, while Chart 26 shows the combined index for bituminous and anthracite mining for the years, 1903–1914. The very close correspondence between real wages and average value productivity up to and including 1919 is especially marked. In the succeeding year of 1920, however, the average value productivity rose much more rapidly than the index of real earnings. During the four ensuing years, the year to year movements of the two series were substantially similar, and there was, in ad-

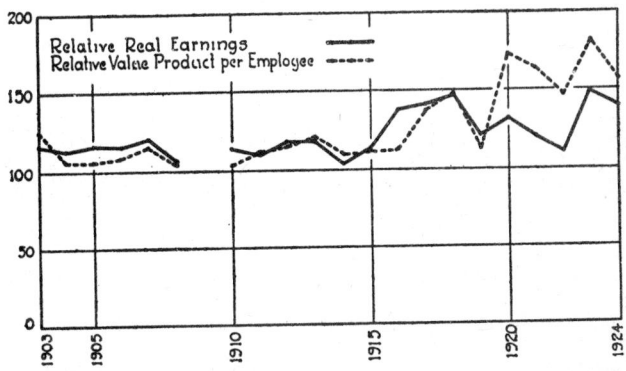

Chart 26. Relative Movement of Average Real Earnings of Workers in Bituminous and Anthracite Coal Mining and of Average Value Product Per Employee in the United States, 1903–1924.

dition, a distinct tendency for the index of average value productivity to fall sufficiently more rapidly as to bring the two series in the end years much more closely in agreement.

The use of a three-year moving average for both real wages and of average value productivity brings the two series together somewhat more closely, and this is still more so when a five-year moving average is used.

Coefficients of correlation were also computed between these series for identical years and also between the three-year moving average of the series with the following results:

Branch of Coal Industry	Years	Coefficients of Correlation	
		Between Indexes as They Stand	Between Three-Year Moving Averages
Bituminous	1890–1924	+.69	+.82
Bituminous and Anthracite	1902–1924	+.68	+.75

The coefficients between these two series are, therefore, significantly high, being over .67 for both series when the original relatives are used and .75 and .82 respectively when three-year moving averages are employed.[25] If we use r^2 as the measure of the degree of interrelationship existing between the phenomena, then it would appear that even for the year to year changes the interrelations of the two account for nearly one-half of these short-time influences and that when the three-year moving averages are used, these mutually interacting influences would seem to include from 55 to 67 per cent of the total forces. The more extended indeed is the moving average, the higher the correlation will be.

Since the movements of average value productivity are beyond doubt the causative factors, this relationship furnishes further statistical corroboration that the principles of imputed marginal productivity do help appreciably to determine what the movement of real wages will be.

4. The Degree of Correspondence Between The Productivity Attributable to Labor in New South Wales Manufactures And Real Wages in Those Industries

A third set of evidence which indicates how the processes of distribution tend to conform to the law of production is that from New South Wales. It is possible to find for the years since 1901 the proportions which wages and salaries have formed of the total value added by manufacturing. This last figure has been adjusted so as to take account of the depreciation of plant and equipment and buildings which have been depreciated at $6\frac{1}{4}$ per cent and 4 per cent respectively of their cost prices. The following table shows this material.

The average share of labor for the twenty-six years as a whole was 56.4 per cent. This is not greatly at variance with the exponent .65 which we found was the best exponent for labor when the index for depreciated capital was used, since with such an exponent as that we would expect according to the formula that labor would receive 65 per cent of the value product of manufacturing.[26] The movement of the real wages of the workers in the manufacturing industries of New South Wales can

---

[25] I am indebted to Miss Margaret Gibbon, a Commonwealth Fund Fellow, and to Erika Schoenberg for working out these coefficients.

[26] It should be noted, however, that there was a general drift upward in the share of the value product which went to labor. The average was approximately 53 per cent for the first seven years (1901–1907) and approximately 59 per cent for the last seven (1921–27).

TABLE 30

PROPORTION WHICH WAGES AND SALARIES FORMED OF TOTAL VALUE ADDED BY
MANUFACTURING IN NEW SOUTH WALES, 1901–1927

Year	Total Value Added by Manufacturing (in 1000 £)	Total Wages and Salaries (in 1000 £)	Percentage Wages and Salaries Formed of the Total
1901	9,321	4,945	53.1
1902	9,150	4,892	53.5
1903	8,949	4,940	54.1
1904	9,250	5,013	54.1
1905	9,874	5,192	52.6
1906	11,056	5,592	50.6
1907	12,549	6,651	53.0
1908	12,601	7,219	57.3
1909	13,447	7,665	57.0
1910	15,773	8,687	55.1
1911	17,990	10,048	55.9
1912	21,092	11,592	55.0
1913	22,023	12,683	57.6
1915*	22,443	12,668	56.4
1916	23,126	13,414	58.0
1917	24,840	14,381	57.9
1918	26,975	14,701	54.5
1919	30,097	16,958	56.3
1920	36,446	21,681	59.5
1921	39,946	25,619	64.1
1922	43,034	26,783	62.2
1923	47,404	27,136	57.2
1924	51,129	29,773	58.2
1925	54,051	31,521	58.3
1926	59,436	33,567	56.5
1927	64,068	37,092	57.9

* From 1915 on, the statistics are for fiscal and not for calendar years.

also be compared with the changes in the imputed marginal value
productivity per worker to determine what degree of correlation,
if any, existed between them. The method followed here was
almost precisely that which was followed in the case of the
United States. The index of real wages was found by (1) computing the average annual money earnings of the employed
workers. In obtaining this average due allowance was made for
the changes in the proportions of the sexes who were employed.[27]
(2) Reducing these to relatives in terms of the average for 1911
as 100. (3) Dividing this index of money earnings in turn by
the index of the cost of living as computed by the Commonwealth Bureau of Statistics for Sydney.[28]

[27] By treating women as forming the same productive ratio to a man as the
average of their earnings to those of men.
[28] From the fiscal year, 1914–15, on, the yearly average is computed from
the four quarterly averages. The index does not include clothing since statistics
for these items were only gathered by the Basic Wage Commission for the years

The index of imputed value productivity per worker was in turn computed by multiplying: (1) the index of physical production for manufacturing by (2) the ratio of the prices of manufactured goods to the all-commodity index and then (3) dividing these products by the relative number of workers employed in each of the years. Since under our formula an increase of 1 per cent in labor was found to increase product on the average by .65 per cent, labor's share of the total product $\left(\dfrac{\text{marginal productivity} \times \text{number of workers}}{\text{total product}}\right)$ was assumed as being 65 per cent throughout the period. Since this was a constant, it could for all practical purposes be neglected, and the total value product in each of the years could be divided by the relative numbers employed.[29]

The first part of Table 31 gives these indexes of real wages and of imputed marginal value productivity per worker for the years from 1900 to 1927, while the second part expresses each of these in terms of five year moving averages.

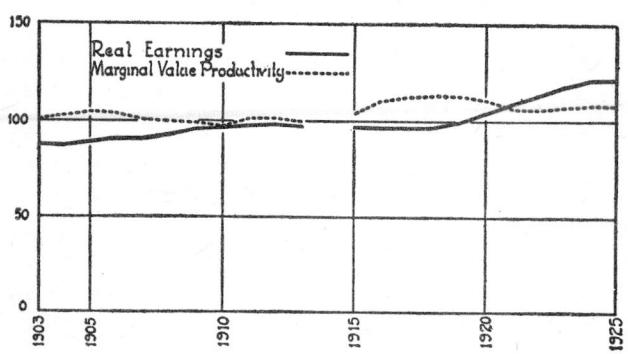

Chart 27. Relative Movement of Five-Year Moving Averages of Real Wages and Average Value Productivity in Manufacturing Industries of New South Wales, 1903–1925.

When the indexes as they stand for each year are correlated, the coefficient is found to be relatively low, being .33. This low degree of correlation, however, is not to be wondered at since we found from the study of corresponding American series that the year to year movements of real wages did not follow with any necessary closeness those of marginal value productivity. We

1914–20 and have not been included in the general index which is computed by the Commonwealth Bureau.

[29] For the sources used see the *Yearbooks of New South Wales,* 1900–1928 and the *Yearbooks of the Commonwealth of Australia,* 1900–1928.

might indeed expect that the lack of agreement would be even more marked in New South Wales, where the basic wage is set by state agencies and where money rates from year to year tend to be rather inflexible.

A better test is, therefore, to compare a moving average of relative real wages and of marginal value productivity since we would here be comparing the "normal" movements of the two. When this is done, as in the latter half of Table 31 and in Chart

TABLE 31

RELATIVE REAL ANNUAL EARNINGS OF EMPLOYED WORKERS IN MANUFACTURING INDUSTRIES OF NEW SOUTH WALES AND THE RELATIVE IMPUTED MARGINAL VALUE PRODUCTIVITY, 1900–1927

Year	Indexes of Each Year (1911 = 100)		Five-Year Moving Averages	
	Real Earnings	Marginal Value Productivity	Real Earnings	Marginal Value Productivity
1901	90.0	99.8		
1902	84.2	90.2		
1903	84.1	94.1	87.3	101.1
1904	93.3	114.3	86.4	102.5
1905	85.0	107.3	88.2	104.7
1906	85.5	106.8	89.9	103.6
1907	93.0	100.9	90.0	100.5
1908	92.5	88.5	92.5	100.1
1909	94.1	99.2	95.4	98.7
1910	97.5	105.1	96.3	97.0
1911	100.0	100.0	97.6	100.4
1912	97.4	92.4	98.4	100.9
1913	98.9	105.3	97.1	99.9
1915*	98.1	101.9	96.7	103.6
1916	91.0	100.0	96.4	110.3
1917	98.0	118.4	96.6	112.5
1918	96.2	126.1	96.6	113.2
1919	99.5	116.0	99.5	113.5
1920	98.4	105.6	104.7	111.0
1921	105.3	101.3	109.5	107.1
1922	124.0	106.1	113.7	106.1
1923	120.5	106.6	118.6	107.7
1924	120.3	110.9	121.2	108.6
1925	123.0	113.4	121.5	108.7
1926	118.3	106.1		
1927	125.2	106.5		

* From 1915 on, the statistics are for fiscal and not for calendar years.

27, where a five-year moving average is used, the coefficient of correlation is much higher. The coefficient of correlation for these series of moving averages is indeed no less than .974 with a probable error of ± .011. This is an almost perfect correlation and can only cause one to believe that there is a remarkably close relationship between changes in the "normal" amount of value which is imputed to each worker and changes in the "normal" movement of real wages. And it is only logical to presume that in this relationship it is value productivity which is the independent and relative real wages which is the dependent variable.

5. Do These Statistics Furnish An Ethical Justification for The Present Economic Order?

It should not, however, be concluded that because there seems to be this close correspondence between the imputed final productivity of labor and the wages of the workers that the present system of distribution is thereby ethically justified. This does not follow. In the first place, even though there should be a precise coincidence between the final imputed productivities and the rates of wages and of interest, some might still attack the whole process of imputation from an ethical point of view. Why, it will be queried, should the wages of a given set of workers be reduced when they are working just as hard and just as skillfully as before merely because more workers have been added to the force? Why also, it will be asked by others, should the wages of the workers increase because the volume of savings has risen more rapidly than the numbers of the working population? These are queries which present interesting ethical problems, but for the present we shall have to neglect them, in order to see more clearly the mechanics of the present productive order. For the moment, it is enough to realize that these results *do* tend to follow, but we should never allow ourselves to assume that by explaining the processes and the results that we have, therefore, necessarily justified them. Nor, moreover, does the tendency towards correspondence between marginal value productivity and the processes of distribution throw any real light upon the question as to the degree to which capital should be privately owned. For while capital is "productive" it does not follow that the capitalist always is. Capital would still be productive even though its ownership were changed. Nor does it follow that the uses to which capitalists put the income which they receive are on the whole socially the best. One may, therefore, be a supporter of either socialism, communism, or individualism and still square one's social philosophy with the theory of production which has been developed. Our whole system of social philosophy would be further advanced if men could everywhere realize that the mechanical operations of economic forces in a competitive and capitalistic society do not of themselves tell us whether such is the society under which it is best for mankind to live.

CHAPTER IX

FURTHER FEATURES OF THE THEORY OF PRODUCTION

1. The Equation of Production Need Not Be The Same For All Periods And Economies

We should not conclude because of the substantial uniformity of the production equation in the United States, Massachusetts, and New South Wales, that it will be the same for all times and countries. It necessarily varies from industry to industry; capital, for example, playing a more important part in some industries, such as iron and steel, than it does in others like cigar-making. A difference between countries in the types of industries which they include will necessarily cause, therefore, a difference between the two countries in the production exponents for labor and capital. Similarly a shift in the relative importance of the various industries over a period of time would also cause a change in the exponents. Differences or changes in the state of the industrial arts will also probably affect the exponents.

One of the most interesting lines of investigation would indeed be to work out the relative amounts of capital combined with labor in the various countries and the relative effect of each upon production. This could either be studied in a cross-section fashion for any one year,[1] or the historical data in each of the countries might be analyzed over a span of years to determine the relative exponents of labor and capital.

Similarly, if new inventions and appliances are being rapidly introduced, then a change in the exponents and perhaps also in the form of the equation will necessarily result. Thus, between 1919 and 1929 there was a great increase in the total output of

---

[1] It is only by some such method as this that the problem of the comparative efficiency of labor in the various countries can be solved. It is plainly wrong to divide the total product in each of the countries by the amount of labor expended in the particular industry. Capital goods also make a contribution to production, and the high average productivity of labor in the capitalistic countries is at least in part due to their abundance. The problem is to apportion the relative amount due to labor and to capital. Hitherto, this problem has been regarded as virtually insoluble, but it is suggested that the method outlined in the present study points the way.

manufacturing industry in the United States which amounted to approximately 28 per cent. This was accompanied, however, by an actual decrease in the size of the wage-working force. It is evident, therefore, that labor did not exercise anywhere near the same influence upon production in this decade that it had during the last two decades which preceded it. A different set of exponents at the very least would, therefore, be necessary to describe the relationships between labor, capital, and product during the years subsequent to our study.[2]

2. J. M. Clark's Modification of The Cobb Formula

We have pointed out how our equation, while describing the "normal" relationship between labor, capital, and product gives a computed product which is too high during years of depression and too low during years of prosperity. As Professor J. M. Clark has pointed out,[3] during the six cycles of recession and recovery which occurred between 1903 and 1922, an average increase in labor of 13.2 per cent during the periods of recoveries and of 12.8 per cent in capital was accompanied by an average increase in product of 23.4 per cent. In the periods of recovery, therefore, the gain in production was greater than the relative increases in either labor or capital. During the six periods of recession on the other hand, labor decreased on the average by 8.4 per cent, capital *increased* by 7.2 per cent, and product diminished by 10.2 per cent. Here again the change in product fell outside of the change in either of the two factors, one of which, capital, showed an apparent increase while product and labor were both decreasing.

These discrepancies were mainly due, as I have pointed out, to changes in the degree to which the available total plant capacity was utilized. The percentage of utilization was, of course, below the "normal" proportion during the recession years and above "normal" during the years of recovery and prosperity. As Professor Clark says, the degree of utilization of plant may also be described as "the ratio of labor employed to the labor the plants are adapted to work with."

From his knowledge of the behaviour of overhead costs, Professor Clark points out that because "part of the labor is 'indirect' and relatively constant with reference to such short-time

---

[2] The methods of Professor Copeland and Mr. Wilcox, which are later described, point the way to such attacks.

[3] J. M. Clark, "Inductive Evidence on Marginal Productivity," *American Economic Review*, September, 1928, Vol. XVIII, p. 459.

fluctuations one should naturally expect that fluctuation of product would be greater than those of labor." This latter inference is borne out by the facts.

Professor Clark then devised a modification of the Cobb formula so that it might better take account of these changes in plant utilization. He first computed seven year moving averages of labor and capital and found the ratios between the values of each of these trend lines in each of the years. These ratios were then assumed to represent [4] the "the changing 'normal' ratio of the labor to capital in terms of the changing technique of the times." By multiplying the indexes of actual available capital for each year by this ratio, he obtained a series which represented "the labor employed when existing plants are working at normal per cent of capacity." To this variable he gave the symbol L_n. The ratio of actual labor to this "normal" labor was then $\dfrac{L}{L_n}$, which he took as a rough measure of the degree of plant utilization. A compound formula was then constructed combining two factors: (1) the first was an equation which Professor Cobb had devised, namely $P' = bL^kC^{1-k}$, representing the effect of "capital and 'normal' labor for that amount of capital." (2) The second was the ratio of actual labor to "normal," or the degree of plant utilization, and this was represented by the factor $\left(\dfrac{L}{L_n}\right)^e$. The combined formula was, therefore, $P' = bL^kC^{1-k}\left(\dfrac{L}{L_n}\right)^e$. By eliminating the somewhat abnormal war and post-war years Professor Cobb found the exponent .67 for k was slightly more accurate than .75. Professor Clark in turn found the best value of e (by the method of least squares) to be .65 and that the method of computing L_n introduced an upward trend of approximately 1 per cent, thus eliminating the necessity for b in the equation.[5] The

---

[4] *Ibid.*, p. 459.

[5] This process may be made somewhat clearer if we carry through the computations for the depression year of 1908. The index of available capital (C) in that year was 185. The seven year moving average for capital was *184* and for labor *135*. The "normal ratio" of labor to capital was, therefore, taken as 135 ÷ 184 or .734. Applying this ratio to the figure of 185 for actual available capital we would have 135.8 as the relative quantity of labor which would have been employed had the existing plant worked at a "normal" per cent of capacity. This in Clark's formula was L_n. But the actual quantity of labor

final modified formula for the years 1902–1916 was therefore

$$P' = L^{2/3} C^{1/3} \left(\frac{L}{L_n} \right)^{.65}$$

This formula gave a computed product as shown in Table 32 and Chart 28 which was somewhat more sensitive to the fluctuations of the business cycle than was the original. The sum of the squares of the deviations of the computed product from the actual were according to this formula 581 as compared with 774 under the original formula. The greatest improvement of the new formula as compared with the old was the greater sensitivity to actual conditions in 1908. For whereas the original formula had given a product of 141 which was a full 15 ponts above the index of actual product of 126, the introduction of Clark's modification brought the computed product down to 130, or to within only 4 points of the actual product.

TABLE 32

PRODUCTION INDEXES COMPUTED FROM THE COBB AND CLARK FORMULAS AND THEIR RELATION TO THE OBSERVED PRODUCTION INDEX FOR THE UNITED STATES, 1902–1916

Year	P	$P' = 1.01L^{3/4}C^{1/4}$			$P' = L^{3/4}C^{1/4} \left(\frac{L}{L_n} \right)^{.65}$		
		P'	Dev. from P	d^2	P'	Dev. from P	d^2
1902	122	121	−1	1	122.7	+0.7	.5
1903	124	127	+3	9	129.0	+5.0	25.0
1904	122	124	+2	4	120.6	−1.4	2.0
1905	143	134	−9	81	134.3	−8.7	75.7
1906	152	144	−8	64	145.9	−6.1	37.2
1907	151	151	0	0	153.6	+2.6	6.8
1908	126	141	+15	225	130.0	+4.0	16.0
1909	153	159	+6	36	157.2	+4.2	17.6
1910	159	164	+5	25	163.3	+4.3	18.5
1911	153	167	+14	196	166.7	+13.7	187.0
1912	177	175	−2	4	177.4	+.4	.2
1913	184	179	−5	25	180.5	−3.5	12.2
1914	169	177	+8	64	174.0	+5.0	25.0
1915	189	187	−2	4	180.1	−8.9	79.2
1916	225	219	−6	36	225.6	+.6	.4
Sum of deviations.			86	774		69.1	580.7
Average			5.7	51.6		4.6	38.8

employed was only 121. So the degree of plant utilization or $\frac{L}{L_n}$ was $\frac{121}{135}$ or .89. This was then raised to the exponent .65 and used to modify the Cobb equation.

For the years subsequent to 1916, however, the Clark modification gives an appreciably poorer approximation to the actual course of production than does the original formula.

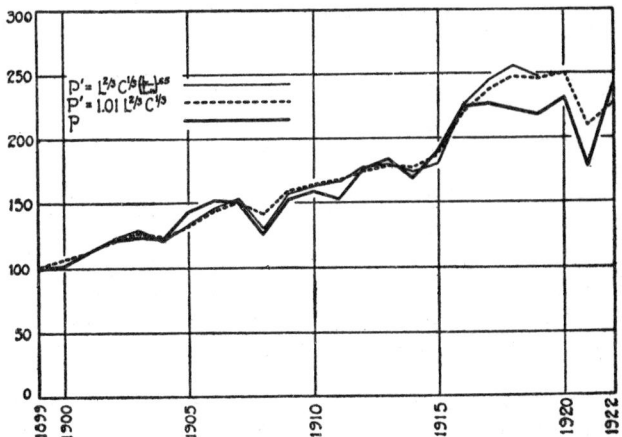

Chart 28. Comparison of the Actual Production Index with the Values Computed from the Clark and Cobb Formulas, United States, 1899–1922.

3. The Role of Working Capital

It will have been noted that with the exception of the Massachusetts study, the indexes of capital which have been computed have omitted working capital and have included only fixed capital. Yet working capital, in the form of raw materials and goods in the process of manufacture, is as necessary for a business as is plant and equipment. This working capital may play a passive role in the production of goods but it certainly shares in the creation of exchange values. For as raw materials pass through the various stages of production before they finally ripen as consumers' goods and are purchased by the buying public, they increase gradually in value from the accretion of interest which in our society must be paid for the use of capital through time.[6]

---

[6] It is just this fact which vitiates the Ricardian theory that commodities exchanged *in proportion* to the amounts of labor expended upon them and the Marxian theory that the value of commodities *consisted* of the quantities of labor expended upon them. Ricardo gave up the problem of reconciling his theory with the fact that capital in differing industries had unequal durations and that, therefore, equal advances of wages to labor have unequal accumulations of interest, although his conscience gave him at times twinges of uneasiness. See *Ricardo's Letters to McCulloch* (Hollander, editor), p. 71. Marx tried to grapple with the problem in the third volume of *Das Kapital* but

It has been a defect in the marginal productivity theory that it has dealt entirely with the additions which the use of fixed capital makes to product. It has explained, therefore, the forces which would govern the payment of interest on fixed capital were that the only form of capital; but it has not explained why interest is paid for working capital, nor where the amounts thus paid are derived, nor has it indicated what determined their amount.[7]

One method of treating this problem has been suggested by J. M. Clark. It is to regard working capital as being jointly productive with fixed capital and to compute the imputed share for the two as combined. Clark tentatively assumed that as product increased, goods in process, or working capital, increased in precisely the same ratio.[8] As Clark points out, working capital would then have no marginal productivity in the ordinary sense of the term since if working capital increased at a faster rate than product, this excess would have no effect on product and hence would be absolutely useless. If working capital decreased, then it would follow that product, since it constitutes the end result of goods in process and of the factors working upon them, would necessarily also diminish by an equal proportion, and thus a portion of each of the other factors of production would be rendered completely useless.

But the inclusion of working capital would change the form of the productivity curves for the composite factor "capital." Instead of its being compelled, as in the United States, to increase as the ratio $\left(\dfrac{P}{L^{3/4}}\right)^4$, this would be modified by the addition of another element which must only increase as the first power of the product. In order to increase production by a given proportion, therefore, total capital would not have to increase by as large a percentage as would be necessary for fixed capital alone. Another way of stating the same thing is that a percentage increase in total capital would be accompanied by a larger relative increase in fixed capital alone. The

---

wound up by abandoning his doctrine that the ratio of exchange of commodities was caused by the relative number of labor crystals of value embodied in a commodity.

[7] Or as J. M. Clark has put the matter in a note to the author, the marginal productivity theory has assumed that diminishing returns to fixed capital result in diminishing returns to total capital. This is probably not an unfair assumption.

[8] J. M. Clark, *Ibid.*, pp. 457-8.

logical consequence of this is that since the curve of total capital would lie closer to that of product than would the curve for fixed capital alone, the marginal productivity of capital would be greater than that indicated by Cobb's formula for fixed capital alone.

Nor is that all: The percentage of the total product imputed to capital would not be a constant as was apparently true for fixed capital but would instead vary as the proportions between capital and product (or this coefficient of production) varied with time. The proportion by which the imputed share of total capital exceeded that of fixed capital would be greatest when capital was scarcest, and this excess would diminish as the ratio of capital to product (the coefficient of production with respect to capital) increased. For when capital was most scarce then the proportion which goods in process, or working capital, formed of the total capital would be greatest. This would intensify the scarcity of fixed capital and therefore raise its marginal productivity.

Professor Clark has indeed computed, on the basis of the assumption that working capital is equal to product, that the imputed share in the total product of capital as a whole would vary from about 46 per cent in 1899 to approximately 38 per cent in 1922.[9] But as Professor Clark recognizes, this assumption tends to exaggerate the amount of the modification which is entailed by the inclusion of working capital. For it is probable that working capital increases more rapidly than product because of the gradual lengthening of the time-period of production which increases the ratio of goods in process to the end products of consumers goods. It is probable, therefore, that the rate of increase of working capital is some function of the increase in final product on the one hand and of the supply of fixed capital on the other.

4. Progress and The Equation of Production

One of the disconcerting features of the analyses of production which have been made in the preceding chapters is that it seems to eliminate "progress" or dynamic improvements in the quality of capital, labor, and the industrial arts from the industrial history of the periods studied. What constitutes

---

[9] Professor Clark describes his method as one of treating "product arbitrarily as the independent variable, calculating the total capital necessary to various values of P, graphing the results and measuring the slope of the curve." He adds that this method gives only a first approximation.

"progress" is not always clearly conceived. Some persons still regard an increase in total production as a measurement of progress. But this is a patently incomplete interpretation. If population increases as rapidly as production there has been from the standpoint of consumption no advance in average well-being. Nor, if the working force has increased at an equal ratio, has there been any increase in output per worker and hence in industrial progress. But while the standard of output per capita or per worker still tends to be the measure of progress most commonly used by economists, it in turn is inadequate. For the increase in output per worker may have been attributable not to better technique and efficiency but solely to an increase in the quantity of capital with which the laborers worked.

It is indeed dangerous to assume that differences between countries in the output per worker reflect corresponding differences in technical efficiency since the excess of product per worker in country A over country B may be simply caused by the greater amount of capital per worker in country A as compared with that in country B. Due to the necessity of paying more for the larger amount of capital, the money costs of production per piece may be as great as and the technical efficiency of industry as a whole no greater in country A than in country B.[10] Comparative efficiencies between countries need indeed to include a consideration of the relative amounts of capital used in relation to output as well as of the relative amounts of labor employed. Similarly, in making comparisons of technical efficiency or progress over a period of time, we need to take into consideration the movement of the relative quantity of capital.

Now, when this is done, it will be seen from our formula that if we take each of the periods studied as a whole that we account for the total product by the accumulation of capital and the increase in labor. By giving to each the exponent which was empirically derived, the curve of computed product was brought into a very close approximation to the actual product. Mere quantitative changes in the amounts of labor and of capital rather than qualitative changes in the nature of the factors seem, therefore, to have caused the increase in total output. But this is really not progress in any dynamic sense. It is a

---

[10] Here I assume that the rates of interest and of wages would be the same between the two countries, so that the equalization of money costs would not be caused by any such differences.

mere accumulation of greater quantities of the factors rather than a greater effectiveness of each unit.

Such a conclusion as this must, however, seem to be incredible both to the common sense and to the buoyant optimism of most Americans. Although Americans may be prone to reckon progress predominantly in terms of aggregates, yet they are also an inventive people and the last forty years have certainly witnessed a great increase in mechanical inventions and in the general state of industrial technique. The conveyor system has spread out from the Chicago stock yards over a wide area of American industry. The setting of production standards has become far more common and consequently average productivity would seem to have been appreciably raised. Loading machines have transformed many branches of work. Machines run at greater speed throughout nearly all industry. New processes have revolutionized the chemical, the rubber, and the pulp and paper industries. The linotype, monotype, and the even more complex presses have made the printing industry more productive. Better looms and spindles have come into the textile industries, and power-driven machinery into that of men's clothing. Machine design has so improved that the modern machine tools are seemingly far more effective than those of one or more decades back. The gradual change, moreover, from line-shafting with belts and pulleys as means of conveying steam or water power to electrical power with individual motors for each machine has also enhanced the productiveness of industry.

Such changes as these and a myriad of others would seem to be too substantial to be blandly exorcised away by a formula which takes no account of them.

Where then does the illusion lie? Is it in our formula or is qualitative progress after all only a delusion? Or can the apparent paradox perhaps be dissolved in a reconciliation which will still permit the reality of qualitative "progress" and the validity of the formula? Without pretending to find the full answer to the dilemma, the following suggestions may at least partially help to reassure the reader that progress has not entirely evaporated.

(1) The formula with its given exponents necessarily describes the situation only for each period when taken as a whole. Somewhat different conditions prevail for specific groups of years within the periods and apparently also for years outside

the periods covered. Thus for certain sub-periods, product either increased faster than either labor or capital, or different exponents would have to be ascribed to labor and capital than for the years as a whole. Progress might, therefore, exist in these years. Furthermore, in the United States, the years 1921–1926 seem very definitely to have been permeated by progress, for total output rose by about 28 per cent while the number of workers, as has been stated, actually fell. Even though the increase in capital was great during this period, it is virtually impossible to account for the advance [11] through the mere aggregation of larger quantities of the factors.

(2) It is also possible to say that "progress" is at once concealed in and has made possible the reduction in the hours of the manual workers and the expansion in the number of clerical workers. The average hours per week during this period were reduced by approximately 14 per cent. If the labor of the remaining hours was not proportionately increased in intensity,[12] then this would amount to a decrease in "labor" which is not reflected in the index of the man-years of manual labor. If only the manual laborers be considered, this factor is an element due to "progress" which is not evidenced in the formulas as such. The number of clerical and salaried workers, as I have pointed out in Chapter V, increased during this period so as almost completely to compensate for the decline in the standard hours of work.

(3) The improvement in the quality of the capital instruments may well have been accompanied by an almost corresponding improvement in the quality of the workers. These qualitative changes may then have had an equal cumulative effect and may have given the appearance that only the quantitative changes in the two had influenced the result.

There has been a common impression that the coming of machine technology has reduced the amount of skill which a worker needs, and thus it has tended to level nearly all of the workers to a rough equality with unskilled labor.[13] But this seems to be a very appreciable misapprehension. Less physical

---

[11] For these years at least.

[12] The fact that the average calorific content of the American dietary had been reduced during the period from 1900 to 1929 (*Recent Economic Changes*, Vol. I, pp. 27–9) is at least a straw to indicate that this intensification did not take place so far as the expenditure of physical energy was concerned.

[13] For a graphic description of this point of view see Arthur Pound's brilliant, *The Iron Man*. Something of the same import appears in my *American Apprenticeship and Industrial Education*, pp. 85–175.

exertion is required and in general less manual dexterity but on the other hand greater alertness and general intelligence. Costly machines can scarcely be trusted to stupid and cheap men. As the machines get more complicated they may well tend to require tenders of a different and of a higher order of intelligence.

If this be the case, then the improvement in the quality of the workers has served to balance the qualitative improvement of the capital instruments with the result that while "progress" would have affected the joint product through each of the factors it will not be reflected in the formula.

(4) The product apparently attributable to added capital alone is also in a sense attributable as well to progress. This has been very subtly pointed out by J. M. Clark, and one cannot do better on this point than to quote him directly: [14]

To find productive uses for such a vast increase in capital, it must be put in new forms. Were all these forms and their productive possibilities known in 1899? Of course not. There was then, and is now, a frontier zone of known devices just below the margin of economical use and capable of absorbing a considerable amount of capital if relative costs should become more favorable. But to find uses for a fourfold increase in equipment or $2\frac{2}{3}$ times the original amount per worker, this frontier zone has had to be pushed forward rapidly and continuously. At no time do definitely known and developed devices include more than a small part of those which would be found profitable if a shift in relative costs should give manufacturers a substantial incentive to further search. . . . It is typical of present day methods of management to set a research department to work definitely on the problem created by changing cost conditions. The result is that any such change will call forth a crop of new devices or cause others to be quickly developed which would otherwise have been very slow in getting past the experimental stage. . . . In a sense, the technical improvements may be said to have brought a deal of the new capital into being. They have enlarged the field of profitable investment. The prospective gains have caused manufacturers to go into the investment market to raise added capital, while the realized gains have furnished a painless source whence much of the necessary savings could come. . . . Industry has had to evolve not merely increasingly automatic machinery but also new commodities into which to put the increasing productive power without wasting it in a redundancy of familiar goods. What difference, for example, would it have made if the pleasure automobile had never been invented?

(5) On this whole tangled subject of technical progress, I have profited greatly from the writings of my friend and col-

[14] J. M. Clark, *op. cit.*, pp. 464–5.

league, Professor William F. Ogburn, and his associate, Mr. S. C. Gilfillan, and from many conversations with them. Mr. Gilfillan points out that, contrary to the common impression, not all inventions save labor. Some merely develop new types of consumers' goods such as the phonograph, the radio, and the development of rayon. Others save capital such as multiplex telegraphy, while others such as the skyscrapers and most agricultural improvements save land. Mr. Gilfillan has taken the 120 inventions which are commonly agreed upon as having been the most important of the last generation, and after discarding 11 as being too difficult to classify has tentatively classified the remainder into the four groups in the following proportions:

Types of Inventions	*Percentage of Inventions*
Labor Saving	33
Capital Saving	14
Land Saving	8
Development of Consumers' Goods	45

It will be seen that 45 per cent or nearly one-half of all these inventions were in the field of consumer's goods or some other form of qualitative rather than quantitative change. These inventions may have had great social significance and have produced changes in the types of machines used, etc. They did not, however, primarily or in themselves disturb the quantitative relationship between labor and capital.

If the inventions which have saved land are added to those which have saved capital we have a ratio of the two groups combined to those which have saved labor of 1 to 1.5. This may be compared with the approximate relative influence of 1 to 3, or 1 to 2, which we have found capital to exercise upon production. As Mr. Gilfillan observes, in a memorandum which he has furnished me, "the labor-saving inventions, since they both undermine labor and usually (though not always) call for large amounts of new capital, tend strongly to increase the capital/labor ratio. On the other hand, the capital-saving inventions, while having the reverse effect, have it not so strongly, since they usually call for the investment of new capital in some degree, and the reduced capital equipment (or land) almost always takes less men to operate it." By taking these influences into account the effect of inventions in increasing the importance of capital relative to labor may, therefore, be greater than the 1.5 to 1 relationship indicated by the mere number of inventions.

As Mr. Gilfillan, however, wisely points out, "In any case, invention seems to play on both sides in a manner not likely to be disturbing to the capital/labor ratio." This neutralizing influence which the capital and land-saving inventions have upon those which save labor and increase the importance of capital may, therefore, help to explain why our production equation accounts for the product in terms of the growth of labor and capital without necessitating any recourses to the course of mechanical progress and invention.

Professor Morris A. Copeland has, however, recently advanced [15] certain weighty criticisms of the theory and of the significance of our results which should be recognized. Troubled by the fact that the theory made allowance only for those technical changes which were conditional upon the relative prices of labor and capital, he set out to assume on the contrary that the most efficient proportion of labor and capital was instead determined by the existing state of the industrial arts. He then tried to see whether he could predict product as a function of labor and time rather than of labor and capital. For time he used a single trend of a straight line fitted roughly to the logarithm of $\frac{P}{L}$. By this method he obtained a computed product which apparently approximated the actual product almost as closely as our method. The correlation of the computed product with the actual was .97 which was the same as that obtained by our formula, while the correlation of the percentage deviations of the computed P from its three year moving average and the corresponding deviations of the actual product was .93 as compared with our .94.

Professor Copeland, therefore, suggests that the statistics may indicate a contrary hypothesis from that which I have suggested, namely, that it may have been technical change rather than the relatively greater increase in the quantity of capital which was responsible for the increase in the productivity and hence in the earnings of labor.

It is probable indeed that this whole question needs to be gone into much more thoroughly. Part of the difficulty seems to have been caused by the fact that capital has increased at an approximately even rate. This permits similar results to

---

[15] In an unpublished memorandum which he has courteously permitted me to see.

be obtained by the use of another straight line function with the same slope.

5. Graphic Representations of The Theory of Production

The theory of production which has been outlined in the preceding chapters may perhaps be grasped more effectively by the use of graphic forms and devices. Two of these have recently been devised by my former associates, Mr. Sidney W. Wilcox and Professor Charles W. Cobb.

Mr. Wilcox's device is a three-dimensional model represented in Chart 29. Here the relative quantities of labor and capital are represented by the two sides adjacent to the right angle at the back of the model. The quantity of each increases as one moves out from this angle. Every combination of labor and capital can then be represented by a point, as in a figure of two dimensions. A movement to the left from the angle indicates an increase in the quantity of labor used, while a movement to the right indicates an increase in capital.

Product is represented by the third dimension, height; the fan-shaped series of rods which come out from the cylinder which fits into the angle at the base represents what the relative quantity of product would be with given differing combinations of labor and capital. As one moves directly out from the point of origin with the quantities of labor and capital each increasing, the height of the production surface rises by an equal ratio and, therefore, conforms to Euler's law. If, however, an attempt were made to combine a given quantity of labor with absolutely no capital, there would be no product at all because both factors are needed for production. The model was so constructed that the ratio by which product increases on the vertical scale with changes in labor and capital respectively are very nearly those which Professor Cobb and I found to be "normal" for the United States during the years 1899–1922, namely, a change of one per cent in labor brought .75 of one per cent change in product and a change of one per cent in the amount of capital brought a change of .25 per cent in the product.[16] The values for the model were computed by Mr. Wilcox on

---

[16] Actually, as the model is constructed, the share of the total product imputed to labor varies from 72 per cent in 1899 to 77 per cent in 1922, as compared with our 75 per cent throughout the period. The share imputed to capital is 28 per cent in 1899 and 23 per cent in 1922. These values are comparable to our 25 per cent for each year. It will be noted that for either formula the sum of the shares imputed to the factors in a given year comes to 100 per cent. Both of the equations are of the first degree, from which it results that all of the product is imputed to both factors.

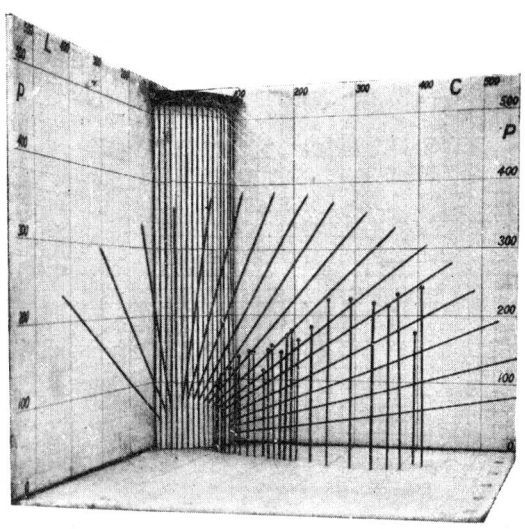

Chart 29. Three-Dimensional Model Devised by S. W.
Wilcox to Demonstrate the Theory of Production.

the basis of a more generalized formula discussed at the end of this chapter,[17] but to the unaided eye the appearance is the same as that which would have resulted from the use of the formula which has already been presented. The fan-shaped production surface can, therefore, be likened to the dome of a cathedral with the exception that it consists wholly of straight lines and that it falls away more sharply on one side, representing capital, than on the other, representing labor.

This production surface, in which the projecting rods serve as the ribs of the fan, represents with close approximation what the "normal" product would be according to our formula that $P' = bL^{.75}C^{.25}$. The heights of the pins shown in the model represent what the actual products were in the given years for the actual combinations of labor and capital indicated by the locations of the pins. The difference in height between the pins and the height of the production surface for the same quantities of capital and labor represents the amount by which the actual product differed from that computed.

The Wilcox model is a very effective device which seems to make it much easier to grasp the principles of the marginal productivity theory and to be almost unexcelled for pedagogical purposes.

Professor Cobb has used a two-dimensional system of contour lines to illustrate the relationship between the three variables of labor, capital, and product.[18] The plane LC in Chart 30 represents this relationship between production and the relative quantities of labor and capital.

Labor is shown on the ordinate, or vertical axis; capital on the abscissa, or horizontal axis. Product, as determined by the formula $P = L^{2/3} C^{1/3}$ (which Professor Cobb also used as well as $P = L^{3/4} C^{1/4}$), is shown by the series of curves. Each curve is a constant representing a given amount of "product," and the locus of each is determined by the amount by which labor and capital must vary in order to produce a constant product. Thus in the chart the curves drawn represent a pro-

---

[17] See Section 7.
[18] See C. W. Cobb, "Contour Lines in Economics", *Journal of Political Economy,* April, 1929, Vol. XXXVII, pp. 225–9. Professor Cobb developed the use of these contour lines independently as some years before he had independently proved that under Euler's theorem the marginal productivity theory led to the distribution of the whole product. It seems however that he was anticipated in this use of contour lines by Edgeworth, see Pareto, *Cours D'Économique Politique,* Vol. I, pp. 34–6. The use of contour lines by geographers and in cartography is of course well known.

duction of 80, 100, 120, 140, 160, 180, 200, 220, 240, and 260 respectively. A combination of 100 units of capital and 100 units of labor will give a product of 100. This is seen by the fact that the curve of 100 for product runs through the point describing the combination 100 C and 100 L. By reading off the values on the 100 product curve, we find the relative proportions of L and C which would have to be combined to give 100 P. Thus 140 L and 51 C would give 100 P as would 440 C and 48 L.

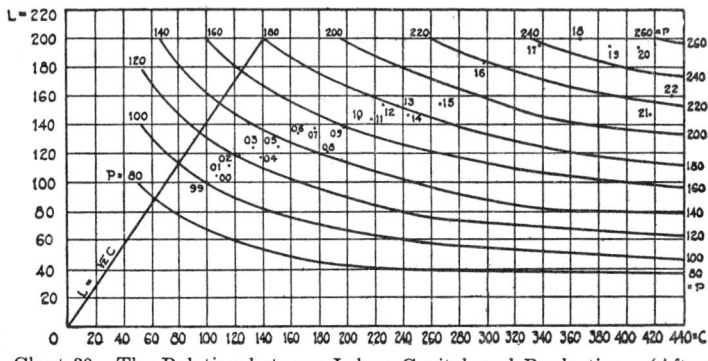

Chart 30. The Relation between Labor, Capital, and Production. (After C. W. Cobb)

The value of P increases as one moves along a straight line away from the point of origin. The change in P which results from a change in L with C constant is shown by the number of P lines which are crossed as one moves vertically a given distance along the L-axis. This rate is greater at the right hand side of the scale than at the left hand side, or where capital is more abundant in relation to labor than when it is less abundant. Where the starting point is $L = 100$, $C = 400$, product increases more rapidly with an increase of, say, 20 per cent in the quantity of labor, than it does when $L = 100$, $C = 300$; and this in turn more rapidly than with 100 L and 200 C, etc. This expresses the truth that the marginal productivity of labor increases as capital increases and decreases as labor increases.

Similarly, the change in P which results from a given change in C with L constant is shown by the number of P lines which are crossed as one moves horizontally a given distance along the C axis. This rate is greater at the left than at the right of the scale or where labor is more abundant in respect to capital than where it is less abundant. Where the starting point is

$C = 50$; $L = 100$, a change of 50 per cent of capital (on the basis of 100) would produce a greater relative change in product than a change of 50 per cent when C was 200 and $L = 100$, etc. This is nothing but a graphic representation of the fact that the marginal productivity of capital decreases as capital increases, and increases as labor increases.

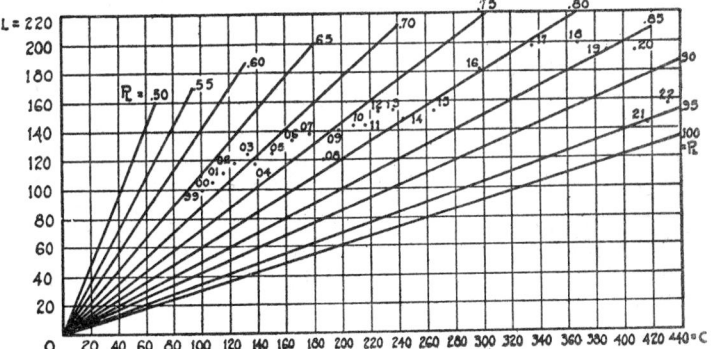

Chart 31. The Changing Marginal Productivity of Labor with Changes in Labor Relative to Fixed Quantities of Capital. (After C. W. Cobb)

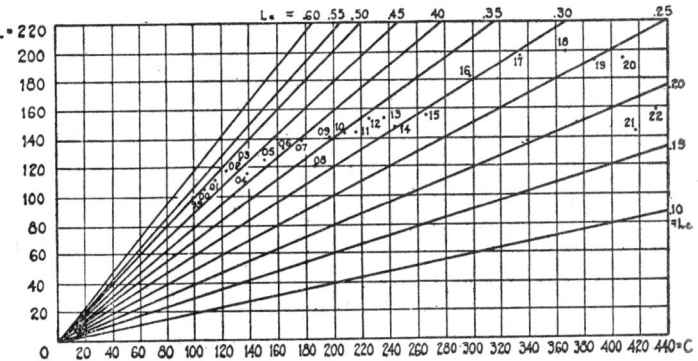

Chart 32. The Changing Marginal Productivity of Capital with Changes in Capital Relative to Fixed Quantities of Labor. (After C. W. Cobb)

Charts 31 and 32 also express in graphic form the effect upon production of holding one factor constant and increasing the other. Chart 31 measures the rate of change in product per unit change in labor. This is the partial derivative of product with respect to labor or the marginal productivity of labor. It will be seen from this set of contour lines the rate at which the marginal productivity of labor will decrease with given increases in the relative quantity of labor. In a similar fashion, moving from the top to the bottom of the vertical axis, it shows the rate at which the marginal productivity of labor increases with each decrease in its relative quantity.

Chart 32 does the same thing for capital and shows the change in the marginal productivity of capital with changes in the relative quantity of capital. As the quantity of capital increases along the horizontal axis, then with any given amount of labor on the ordinate, one moves progressively to the right from one contour line to another with lower marginal productiveness. While if one reverses the directions, as the quantity of capital mixed with a given amount of labor diminishes, one moves across contour lines to the left with higher marginal productivities.

The actual relative combinations of labor, capital, and computed product which existed in the various years of the period under analysis in the United States (1899–1922) are indicated by points in each of these three charts.

Two facts of some significance appear from a comparison of these points with the theoretical contour lines: (1) that in practise the actual productivities did not depart greatly from the theoretical values which the formula gave. (2) That the experience of the whole period covered only a relatively small range of all the possible combinations of labor and capital which might be made and that we do not have values for the large majority of potential combinations which lie outside the range covered.

6. Would Other Observations Yield Different Results?

The last point suggests immediately certain qualifications which should be made to the theory. If a wider range of observations were available, it might not only be found that different exponents should be given to labor and to capital, but that a different type of equation would be necessary to describe the relationship between the three variables.

But this qualification is not unique to the study of production. It is equally applicable to the study of the elasticities of demand for commodities and of elasticities of supply. There are available for such studies only a limited number of observations, and it is by no means certain that the relationships which exist between these points also characterize the relationship between quantity and price at other and very different points. Thus the elasticity of demand for wheat may be .5 as between

(1) a price of \$1.20 a bushel and a consumption of 700 million bushels, and yet be very different at a price of \$2.40 or at 60 cents. All we can say in such cases is that between observed points in a given period of time within a given geographic setting, the "normal" relationship is as described. This is not everything but it is something, and it at least tells us more than we knew before.

7. Are The Shares of The Product Going to Labor And Capital Constant?

If the factors of production are given exponents whose sum is equal to 1.0 and which are constant throughout a period of time, then the proportion of the total product which is imputed to each factor

$$\frac{\text{(i.e. Marginal product} \times \text{number of units of factor)}}{\text{Total product}}$$

$$\left(\frac{\partial P}{\partial L}.L\right)\frac{1}{P} \text{ and } \left(\frac{\partial P}{\partial C}.C\right)\frac{1}{P}$$

will also be constant and will be equal to the exponent of the factor in question.

This can easily be seen from the following simple relationships: When $k = .75$ or $\frac{3}{4}$, then

$$\frac{\partial P}{\partial L} = \frac{3}{4}\frac{P}{L}$$

$$\frac{\partial P}{\partial L} \cdot L = \frac{3}{4}\frac{P}{L}L$$

Simplifying:

$$\frac{\partial P}{\partial L} \cdot L = \frac{3}{4}P$$

It is not pretended that this constancy of the relative size of the share would apply for each and every year. If the exponents tend, however, to be constant over a period of time and if the processes of distribution follow approximately the imputed yields under the principle of diminishing marginal productivity, then we would expect the relative shares actually received by the various factors of production to be also approximately the same over the normal course of the years.

The most thorough studies in this respect have been those made by Bowley into the national income of Great Britain. Bowley found by a comparison of 1880 and 1913 that in each year 62½ per cent of the national income was distributed for services and work and 37½ per cent for the use of property.[19] There was thus apparently no change whatever in the relative shares obtained by each set of factors over the third of a century which was covered.

The study of Bowley and Stamp on the post-war distribution of the national income indicates that the relative shares in 1924 were approximately the same as in 1911. Thus 44 per cent was estimated as the proportion of the social income which in 1924 was expended in the form of wages, while the corresponding percentage for 1911 was 43.[20] The workers, of course, did make additional gains from social insurance and public services contributed either in whole or in part by the employers or by the state. The relative gains which they made in obtaining a larger slice of the national income seem to have come, therefore, from legislation and taxation rather than from the processes of distribution themselves.[21]

In Germany, however, there seems to have been wide changes in the distribution of the national income. The German Central Statistical Office has made the following estimates of the distribution between economic classes in that country in 1913, 1926, and 1928.[22]

From these data it would appear that although the share of labor diminished during the war and after a post-war increase declined again during the period of hyper-inflation, that on the

---

[19] A. L. Bowley, *The Change in the Distribution of the National Income, 1880–1913* (1920), pp. 24–5. The absolute figures were as follows:

Payments for	1880	In Millions of £ 1913
1. Property	420	810
2. Services and labor	705	1335
Total	1125	2145

The income from property, however, included income from overseas investment which C. K. Hobson has estimated at 50 million pounds in 1880, and Bowley at 200 million in 1913. By excluding these sums, we would find that the percentage of the national income produced inside the British Isles which went to Labor rose from 65.6 per cent to 69 per cent.
For another study of the pre-war situation as regards the distribution of income, see Bowley, *The Division of the Product of Industry* (1919).
[20] Bowley and Stamp, *The National Income, 1924*, p. 50. The classification here is not identical with that for *The Change in the Distribution of the National Income*, where salaries, etc., were included as well.
[21] This of course is an indication that labor can gain more from political action than many leaders of the labor movement in this country are accustomed to admit.
[22] See C. Bresciani-Turroni, "On Some Changes in the Distribution of Income and Property in Germany after 1913," *Revue Al Qanoun Wal Iqtisad,* Cairo (1931), p. 137–60, esp. p. 159.

eve of the depression it was very appreciably above the pre-war proportions.

	Distribution of the Total Income in Per Cent		
	1913	1926	1928
Agriculture.............	12–14	6	5
Commerce and Industry..	23–25	21	20
Capital.................	11–14	3	4
Wages and Salaries.......	46–49	65	66
Other Sources...........	3	5	5

So far as the United States is concerned, it is not yet quite clear what the actual tendencies have been. Dr. W. I. King's analysis seems to show an increase in the combined share of wage-earners and salaried workers from 51 per cent in 1909 to 57 per cent in 1928.[23] When this increase is analyzed, however, it is found to consist almost wholly in an increase in the amounts paid to salaried workers, while the share of the manual workers has, with some fluctuations, remained relatively constant. Thus the percentage credited to the wage-earners in all industries in 1909 was 35.6, while in 1928 the percentage was 36.0. The average for the twenty years was slightly over 36.2 per cent. This would indicate a distinct tendency towards a constancy of share so far as the manual workers are concerned. The share of the salaried workers, however, increased from 14.6 per cent in 1909 to 19.9 per cent in 1928. This increase of 5.3 per cent was nearly nine-tenths of the total increase which King attributed to services. Part of this increase, as Dr. King has noted, has resulted from the diminution in the number of independent entrepreneurs and the consequent transfer of income from the entrepreneurial to the salaried class.[24] Not all of it can, however, be so explained, and it seems probable that a portion of it is due to the increase of lower-grade clerical work. In this sense, therefore, it can be said that so far as Dr. King's results go, the relative share received by the American working-classes, including the soft-handed as well as the hard-handed elements, showed a general tendency to increase if the two decades which preceded the great depression are taken as a whole.

At the same time, despite Dr. King's figures, from such data as are available for manufacturing, public utilities, etc., there

[23] W. I. King, *The National Income*, p. 80.
[24] *Ibid.*, p. 82.

would seem to have been a very real decrease in labor's share of the total product, during the years from 1923 to 1929 inclusive. Whether or not this was merely enough to bring labor's share down to what it had been around 1900 or whether this was carried still lower is even now, despite Dr. King's excellent work, something of an unsolved question.

It is probable, therefore, that for certain periods of time we should be prepared to devise formulæ which will permit of greater flexibility in the relative shares attributed to labor and capital. Mr. Sidney W. Wilcox,[25] now of the New York State Department of Labor, who was formerly associated with me has worked out such a formula. It is:

$$P' = b\, R^{\,1-k-h}\; L^k\; C^h \quad where\; R = \sqrt{L^2 + C^2}$$

It will be noted that the sum of k and h need not be unity. By finding the values of b, k and h from the series given in Chapter V, the equation was found to be:

$$P' = 1.063\, R^{-0.146}\; L^{.788}\; C^{.358}$$

This formula gives approximately the same results as those obtained by our more simple equation.

Mr. Wilcox has explained the characteristics and advantages of his formula in an interesting letter to the author,[26] which I cannot do better than to quote at some length in a footnote.

---

[25] Mr. Wilcox first devised this formula in the summer of 1926 when we were primarily working on problems of elasticity of supply. It therefore really antedates the Cobb formula of 1927 but was laid aside because of Mr. Wilcox's subsequent absorption in administrative duties during the following two or three years. Mr. Wilcox has been exploring the theoretical and practical implications of his formula in a most interesting fashion and I hope that he will shortly publish the results of his work.

[26] Letter of S. W. Wilcox to the author:

The significance of my formula consists primarily in the fact that it permits the data to speak for themselves concerning the fixity or flexibility of the relative contributions of labor and capital to the product. If the values of k and h as found by a least square solution had turned out to be such that their sum came to unity the exponent of R would have been zero and the exponent of C would have been the particular value h = 1 — k and the equation would have resolved itself into, $P' = b\, L^k\, C^{1-k}$ which is the Cobb formula. The implication of this special case, when the sum of k and h equals unity, is that there is no change in the relative share of the product imputed to labor with any changes in the proportion of capital and labor. When, as in the actual solution, the sum of k and h exceeds unity (0.788 + 0.358 = 1.146) the implication is that the relative share imputed to labor becomes greater with any increase in the ratio of capital to labor. If the solution had yielded values of k and h whose sum fell short of equalling unity the implication would have been that with enrichment of the ratio of capital to labor the marginal productivity of labor did not keep pace with the absolute increase in capital in such fashion as to keep labor's imputed share unimpaired, but rather the relative contribution of capital increased while that of labor decreased.

These relationships become clearer with an examination of the algebraic expression for the relative share of labor.

$$\left(\frac{\partial P'}{\partial L}.L\right)\frac{1}{P'} = k + (1-k-h)\frac{L^2}{L^2+C^2}$$

$$= k + (1-k-h)\frac{1}{1+C^2/L^2}$$

$$= 0.788 - 0.146\frac{1}{1+C^2/L^2}$$

If the condition is imposed in advance that h = 1 − k, or in other words, that k + h = 1 then the term whose coefficient is (1 − k − h) drops out and labor's relative share is simply k, with a numerical value of 0.75 however, and not 0.788, which is the value found when the data determine whether k + h = 1. For the values of k and h actually found it may be noted that as the ratio of C to L increases the denominator increases, the fraction decreases, the deduction from k decreases, and because k has less subtracted from it the relative share of labor appears as an increase with the inflowing of capital. This may be paraphrased by saying that the new capital does a better job of increasing the marginal productivity of labor than of increasing the product itself, so much so that labor's imputed share shows a relative increase as compared with that of capital, though the change is very small even for somewhat large changes in the ratio C/L.

If the data were required to hand down a verdict as to the degree of the equation and as to the presence or absence of "dynamic" changes the equation might be thrown into the following form, though admittedly constituting rather a heavy superstructure for the foundation.

Generalized Production Formula, three factors, time as a variable, any degree:

$$P' = b\ R^d \left(\frac{L}{R}\right)^{K+kt} \left(\frac{C}{R}\right)^{H+ht} \left(\frac{E}{R}\right)^{J+jt}$$

$$= b\ R^d \left(\cos\lambda\right)^{K+kt} \left(\cos\gamma\right)^{H+ht} \left(\cos\epsilon\right)^{J+j}$$

Where L = Labor
C = Capital
E = Energy
R = $\sqrt{L^2 + C^2 + E^2}$ = radius vector
P' = Computed product
$\cos\lambda$ = L/R
$\cos\gamma$ = C/R
$\cos\epsilon$ = E/R
d = degree or dimension of the equation
t = time
$K+kt$ = weighting of the factor L.

PART III

The Probable Supply Curves of Labor, Capital, and Natural Resources

A. GENERAL CONSIDERATIONS

CHAPTER X

THE THEORETICAL IMPLICATIONS OF RELATIVE ELASTICITIES OF SUPPLY[1]

1. The Conscious or Unconscious Use of Supply Schedules in Economic Theory

It is the purpose of this chapter to develop some of the theoretical consequences in the process of distribution which result from differing sets of elasticities of supply of the factors of production and to indicate some of the lines of inductive investigation which should be followed if we are to determine them quantitatively. Before proceeding to this analysis, however, it may be worth while to point out that in practice virtually every theory of distribution which has aimed to explain the long-run tendencies has, in fact, rested its case upon some assumptions of the probable behavior of the supply of the factors consequent upon changes in their rate of remuneration.

Thus, most of the mercantilists believed that the real wages of the workers should be lowered and not increased. This followed from their belief that an increase in wages would cause a corresponding decrease in the number of hours the laborers would work since the latter would now be able to secure the same standard of living with fewer hours of work. A decrease in real wages would, therefore, cause the workers to put in more hours of work in order to maintain their former position.[2] Thus the public policy advocated by this group proceeded from their belief that the supply curve of labor was negatively inclined and that its elasticity was equal to unity.

The long-time theory of distribution which was held by the classical school from Ricardo on was also fundamentally based on a concept of supply curves. Thus if wages rose above the minimum, which furnished at any one time the basis of subsistence or the standard of living but which was for long periods

---

[1] This chapter is adapted from a chapter of the author's which appeared in *Economic Essays in Honor of John Bates Clark* (edited by Jacob H. Hollander).
[2] For a review of mercantilistic doctrine on this point, see E. S. Furniss, *The Position of the Laborer in a System of Nationalism*, and an article by T. E. Gregory in Volume I, *Economica*.

constant, then this would call into being the forces of Malthusianism. Births would increase, deaths would decrease, population and ultimately the number of workers would expand, and this would cause wages to fall back to their former level. This tendency was supposed to be reinforced by the change in the supply of capital. If without any change in the total product, wages increased at the expense of the rate of interest, this would cause a decrease in the rate and would lead to a curtailment in saving. This fear was particularly marked in the orthodox followers of Ricardo who felt that the rate of profits was already within a hand's breadth of *the* minimum, and that if it were to fall much lower, virtually all of the capital would cease to be saved. This great decrease in the supply of capital would, of course, mean an equal contraction in the fund from which wages were paid and consequently would cause the rate of wages to fall greatly. Thus behind the writings of Senior, Mill, and Cairnes there is the belief in the almost infinite elasticity of the supply of labor, and of at least an equal shrinkability in the supply of capital.

Similarly, those who like Sidney and Beatrice Webb believe that it is relative bargaining strength alone, or force and craft, which determines what each factor shall receive, tend either explicitly or implicitly to assume that the supplies of the factors are almost completely inelastic and will be the same irrespective of the price which they receive. Thus the Webbs reason that if through trade-union organization wages should increase and the rate of interest fall, the supply of capital would not decrease. To support this contention, they accept for certain classes the doctrine advanced by Sargent [3] that a fall in the rate of interest would cause an increase in the amount saved. Sargent had argued that the lower the rate the more men must save in order to secure the same annuity, and the Webbs declared that this would offset the tendency of other classes, such as the wealthy, to save less. But the Webbs held that not only would there probably be no diminution in the amount of capital but that there would also be little or no increase in the *supply of labor*. The increased wage would lead to a higher standard of living and hence to a decrease in the birth rate. This being so, the workers could improve their position at the expense of the capitalists and relative bargaining strength alone determine the amounts which each would secure. Other bargain theorists, such

---

[3] W. L. Sargent, *Recent Political Economy.*

as Davidson,[4] Ira Steward, George Gunton,[5] and others, either made similar assumptions or blithely took for granted that the supplies would not be altered. The modern residual theories of distribution, notably those of Taussig and Kleene, postulate almost infinitely elastic supply curves of one factor, but tend to regard the supply of the other as unconnected with the return to it. Thus to Taussig[6] the joint product of labor and of capital has deducted from it *the* rate of interest, with the result that the residual goes to labor. This rate of interest Taussig imagines has been historically steady through time, and this to him seems to be proof that there is a "broad margin of savings." If the rate of interest rises through technical progress or from some other cause, there will be such an outpouring of savings as will bring the rate back to the point where the broad margin is located. If the rate of interest should fall, then the supply of capital would fall off so greatly that its relative scarcity would cause its price to rise again and ultimately find its way back to its original figure. There is thus an "effective rate of accumulation," and the joint product is discounted at an approximately constant rate, with the residue going to labor in the form of wages.

Kleene[7] has a somewhat similar theory, although with him the rate of wages is the constant and not the rate of interest. He rejects the broad margin of savings but postulates a broad margin of population growth in the non-capitalistic areas of the world where he believes the principle of Malthusianism still holds. Through migration within and emigration from these countries, this rate of procreation establishes the wages of unskilled labor in capitalistic countries and upon these in turn, with appropriate differentials, the rates for skilled labor are based. An increase in wages will stimulate a further flow of such labor, and this lessened pressure upon natural resources in the backward areas will give rise to a further increase in population and hence to a filling of the reservoirs upon which the industrialized sections may draw.

There are several extraordinary features in such theories as those advanced by Taussig and Kleene. Not the least is the

[4] John Davidson, *The Bargain Theory of Wages.*

[5] Gunton, *Wealth and Progress.*

[6] F. W. Taussig, "Outlines of a Theory of Wages," *Publications of the American Economic Association,* 3rd series (1910), Vol. II, pp. 136–56; *Principles of Economics,* Vol. II.

[7] G. A. Kleene, *Profits and Wages.*

fact that Taussig, who has been such an unsparing critic of the residual theory of wages of General Francis A. Walker, should nevertheless have constructed a very similar explanation as his own. Furthermore, the tendency of both to regard the supply of the other factor, in Taussig's case labor and in Kleene's case capital, as not being related to the price it receives is crucially defective. Finally, the belief of both that the supply curve of a factor does not have any influence on the processes of distribution unless it is virtually parallel to the base (*i.e.*, of almost infinite elasticity) and that if there is no such supply curve bargaining strength alone determines what the final result will be, is a misapprehension of the economic process.[8] The economic process is, in fact, one in which equilibrium is attained through the interactions of various forces—of supply curves as well as of total and marginal products. As we shall see, supply curves of whatever description affect the result and do not by any means need to be of infinite elasticity.

2. Various Types of Supply Curves and The Meaning of Elasticity of Supply

We shall secure a clearer concept of the influence of the forces of supply if we first examine the various types of supply

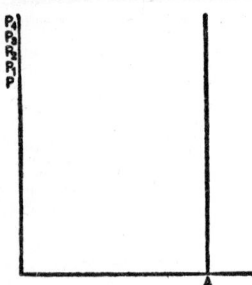

curves that may conceivably operate, and explore the meaning of relative elasticity. An absolutely inelastic supply, which tends to be that postulated by the bargain theorists is represented in Chart 33; namely, a straight line perpendicular to the base and parallel to the price axis. Here the supply will be the same, irrespective of whether the price is P, P_1, P_2, etc.

Chart 33. Case 1. Absolutely Inelastic Supply of the Factors.

Chart 34 represents a supply curve of infinite elasticity which was postulated by the Malthusians for labor and by the later members of the classical school for capital. This, with some modifications,[9] represents Taussig's concept of the

---

[8] For the discussion by Taussig and Kleene on this point, see F. W. Taussig, "Kleene's Profits and Wages," *Quarterly Journal of Economics*, Vol. XXXI (1917), pp. 705–10; G. A. Kleene, "The Supply Price of Labor," *Ibid.*, Vol. XXXII, pp. 402–4.

[9] Taussig's assumed curve permits of a fraction of the total supply being saved at less than the broad margin.

supply curve for capital. A virtually unlimited number of the units of a given factor will be produced at the return P. It is thus identical with production under constant cost. If the rate of return rises above P, the supply will expand almost indefinitely until the increase of that factor may bring the return to this factor back to its original point P. Similarly, if the return should fall below P, then the supply would dwindle away to almost nothing, being checked only by the fact that so rapid a decrease would cause its unit return to rise and when it had reached P, the contraction would cease.

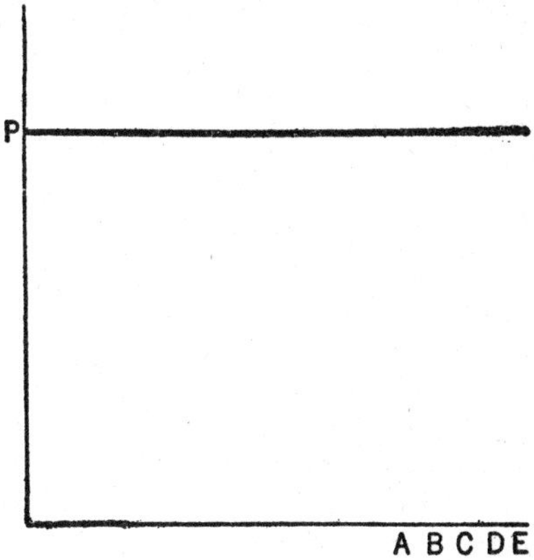

We should also note the

Chart 34. Case 2. Infinitely Elastic Supply of the Factors.

difference between positive and negative supply curves which are shown in Chart 35. With a positive supply curve an increase in price is accompanied by an increase in the quantity supplied, and a reduction in price is accompanied by a decrease in the quantity supplied. The negative supply curve, PP_1, on the other hand, represents a supply schedule where the higher the price the less is supplied and where with a reduction in price more is offered.

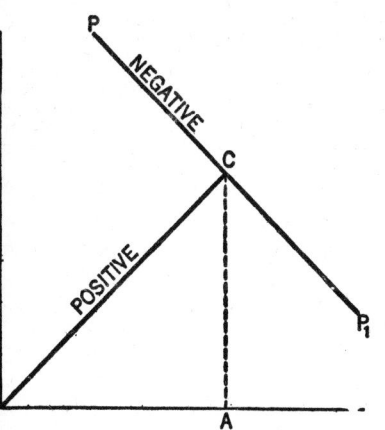

Chart 35. Case 3. Positive and Negative Sloping Supply Curves.

Elasticity of supply is the *relative* change in quantity supplied which accompanies a *relative* change in price. Virtually the same formula which Marshall[10] used to measure the elasticity of de-

[10] Marshall, *Principles of Economics* (6th Edit.), p. 839. Marshall's formula for the elasticity of a demand curve has a negative sign.

mand can be applied to measure the elasticity of supply. We
may then write this formula:

$$E = \frac{\dfrac{dX}{X}}{\dfrac{dP}{P}}$$

Where E = elasticity of supply

X = quantity of factor (or commodity) offered

P = price per unit

d = the symbol to designate a derivative, in this case an
infinitesimal difference in X or P. While both dX
and dP approach zero as a limit, the ratio $\dfrac{dX}{dP}$ is in
general not equal to zero. In the example im-
mediately following it has been assumed that a
change of one per cent may be considered to represent an infinitesimal change with sufficient accuracy
for the purpose in hand.

Let us assume then that in a given economy the price of
labor increases from 50.0 to 50.5 units per hour and the number
of man-hours offered from 1000 to 1010, then

$$\frac{\dfrac{1010-1000}{1000}}{\dfrac{50.5-50.0}{50.0}} = \frac{\dfrac{10}{1000}}{\dfrac{.5}{50.0}} = \frac{\dfrac{1}{100}}{\dfrac{1}{100}} = 1.$$

This then is unit elasticity where a change of one per cent in
price is accompanied by a change of one per cent in quantity
offered. If the quantity decreased by one per cent as the price
increased by one per cent, it would be unit negative elasticity.

If, however, the number of man-hours were only to increase
to 1005, then the elasticity would be

$$\frac{\dfrac{5}{1000}}{\dfrac{.5}{50.0}} = \frac{\dfrac{.5}{100.0}}{\dfrac{1}{100}} = .5$$

while if the supply of labor increased to 1020, then

$$\frac{\dfrac{20}{1000}}{\dfrac{.5}{50.0}} = \frac{\dfrac{2}{100}}{\dfrac{1}{100}} = 2.$$

There is, indeed, but one important difference between the measurement of supply schedules and those of demand. By far the major portion of all demand schedules are negatively inclined.[11] Unit elasticity here is identical with a constant outlay, the change in price being commensurate with an opposite change in quantity demanded so that the total area of gross returns (PX) is constant. In the case of elasticities greater than unity, an increase in price causes a lesser area of gross returns (PX) while a decreased price leads to a greater outlay. The reverse situation holds when the elasticities are less than unity. These relations hold in the case of negative supply schedules, but in the case of positive supply curves an increase in price will always mean a greater, and a decreased price a lesser total outlay upon the commodity or factor in question. Thus, in the case of an increase, not only will each of the units formerly supplied receive more than before, but the new units which have presented themselves will each receive the old price plus the increase which has occurred.

It should be realized, however, that the formula given above is only adapted for measuring the elasticity of demand where the changes in quantities are infinitesimal. It does not meet the situation where finite changes occur. Thus if an increase in price from 50 cents to $1.00 per hour causes an increase in the quantity of labor offered of from 1000 to 1600 hours, then the coefficient of elasticity would seem to be

$$\frac{\frac{600}{1000}}{\frac{50}{50}} = \frac{600 \times 50}{1000 \times 50} = \frac{30,000}{50,000} = .6$$

But if we reckon the elasticity from $1.00 backwards, then

$$\frac{\frac{-600}{1600}}{\frac{-50}{100}} = \frac{600 \times 100}{1600 \times 50} = \frac{60,000}{80,000} = .75$$

We secure then two differing coefficients depending upon whether we compute in terms of increases or decreases, although the absolute changes are, of course, the same. Our formula in other words does not meet the reversal test. The Marshallian formula, therefore, does measure elasticity at a given point, but

---

[11] Most economists reason as though all demand curves must be negatively inclined, but this is not necessarily so.

as Dalton has pointed out,[12] it does not measure in itself arc elasticity, or the elasticity between two points.

By using the midpoint as the point of reference we can secure an approximation that meets the reversal test though at the cost of not necessarily having our point of reference lie on the curve, thus:

$$\frac{\dfrac{X_2-X_1}{\frac{1}{2}(X_2+X_1)}}{\dfrac{P_2-P_1}{\frac{1}{2}(P_2+P_1)}} = \frac{\dfrac{\triangle X}{\overline{X}}}{\dfrac{\triangle P}{\overline{P}}} = \frac{\overline{P}\triangle X}{\overline{X}\triangle P}$$

A still better way of measuring elasticities when we are dealing with finite differences is to divide the differences between the logarithms of the various quantities supplied by the difference between the logarithms of the prices paid per unit of the factors.

This would be $\dfrac{d \log X}{d \log P}$. When the variables are plotted on a double logarithmic scale where equal distances show equal proportions, a straight line has constant elasticity throughout its course. In the charts which are drawn for this chapter we are assuming such a double logarithmic scale for both X and P or for both quantities and rate of return per unit. In Chart 36, there are shown on a double logarithmic scale three supply curves of .5, 1.0, and 2.0 elasticities respectively. All assume constant elasticity throughout, and on the logarithmic scale all are straight lines. Starting all the curves at a common point of intersection which we may take as 1, the curve of unit elasticity bisects the angle at the base at 45°, while where the elasticities are .5 and 2.0, the angle is cut at 67½° and 22½° respectively.

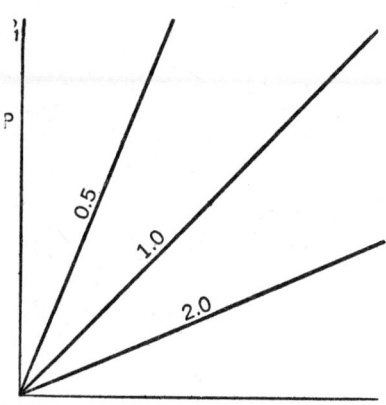

Chart 36. Case 4. Supply Curves with Different Elasticities.

It is of course true that virtually all supply as well as demand curves are not characterized by uniform elasticity

[12] Hugh Dalton, *The Inequality of Incomes*, pp. 192–7.

throughout but exhibit varying degrees of elasticity during their course. The supply of a factor may, for example, be relatively elastic for a considerable period and may then take a sharper pitch and become relatively inelastic. To simplify the discussion of the relative effects of differing elasticities of supply, however, we shall assume in the following discussion that the given elasticities apply throughout the supply schedules of any one factor. What is found to apply to the curve as a whole will, of course, apply to the movement around any one point where the elasticity is the same.

One other final distinction should be made clear. The supply of a factor will depend not only on its elasticity but on its position. Chart 37 shows two supply curves each of which has unit elasticity, but where different quantities are supplied at the same price because of the fact that their intercepts are different.

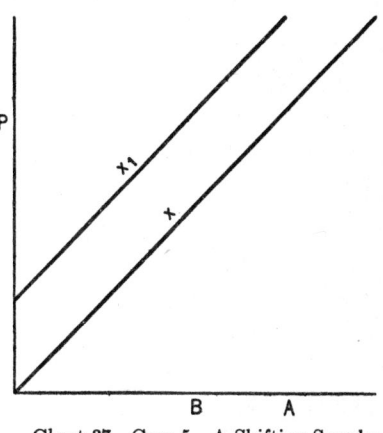

Chart 37. Case 5. A Shifting Supply Curve.

We may now proceed to come to closer grips with the problem. Assuming that we are dealing only with one commodity and with two factors, we shall try to determine what the effects of various elasticities of supply of the factors will be under the three following sets of changes:

1. An increase in the effectiveness of industry. This might be caused by an improvement of technical processes, by inventions, or by a gain in the exchange rate of the commodity produced in this community as compared with those produced in other communities.

2. A decrease in the effectiveness of industry. This in turn might result from a war, from a loss in social vitality, or from a decrease in the exchange ratio between this and other communities.

3. A change in the bargaining powers of the factors. A fuller discussion as to what constitutes bargaining power will be given in a later section, but here it is enough to define such

a change as occurring when one factor improves its relative strength in this regard over its former status.

3. Elasticities of Supply in Relation to Increases in The Effectiveness of Industry

Let us assume that without any initial change in the quantities of the factors the effectiveness of industry increases by let us say, one-third. What then is the effect which this has, under varying elasticities, upon (1) quantities of factors offered, (2) the return per unit of each factor, and (3) the proportion of the total product received?

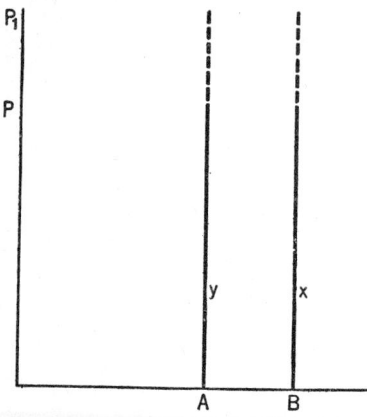

We may begin with a situation where the supplies of both factors are absolutely inelastic, as in Chart 38. The increase in output will, of course, cause the return to each to rise from P to P_1, but this will not lead to any change in supply, since the same amount will be offered whatever may chance to be the price. There will, therefore, not be any readjustment in marginal productivities and the situation will remain as it was immediately after the increase in output took place and the return to each factor increased by PP_1.

Chart 38. Case 6. Increase in Remuneration with Two Absolutely Inelastic Factors.

Let us assume for a second illustration that Taussig is correct with regard to capital and Kleene with regard to labor, and that the supply curves of both factors are infinitely elastic as is represented in Chart 39. Then an increase in total output and in return to both factors X and Y would cause a great expansion of each along its respective supply curve. It might seem as though there would be an unlimited expansion of the quantities of X and Y since their respective rates of remuneration would be higher than the amounts P_1 and P at which almost infinite amounts of the factors would be produced and offered. But in real life there would be obstacles which would prevent this from happening. In the first place, the third factor, land, would not tend to increase in any such ratio, and if its supply remained constant, then the product jointly attributable to labor and capital would decrease. Within this joint product, the relative productivity of these two factors would be the same but their absolute shares would shrink and this would bring the unit return for each down toward the P_1 and P points which originally prevailed.

Secondly, it is of course virtually inconceivable that the supply curves of two factors or even of one would be thus infinitely elastic. The natural forces of resistance to labor and to saving would tend to cause them to turn upward after a time, and when this happened the approach to an equilibrium would be hastened. Irrespective of changes in marginal productivity, the upward movement of the supply curves would at some time intercept the new returns. This would be hastened, of course, by the failure of a third factor to expand commensurately and would be complicated, as we shall see, if the upward tilt of the supply curve of either X or Y began earlier or sloped more sharply than that of the other factor.

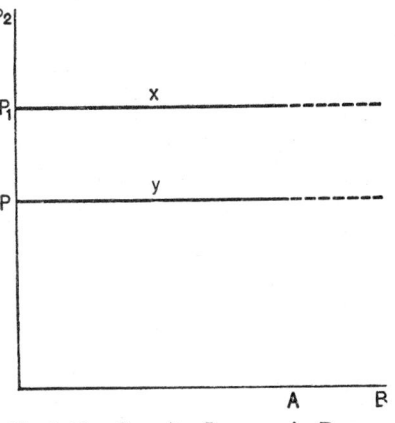

Chart 39. Case 7. Increase in Remuneration with Two Infinitely Elastic Factors.

A third illustration which may be chosen is that where both elasticities are positive and equal to unity. In Chart 40, both X and Y are given unit positive elasticity and are given a common point of origin. They are both therefore represented by the curve of S in which the quantity A is offered for the return P.

A word should be added here concerning the scale on which quantities of two differing factors are drawn, since it may well be asked how it is possible to represent hours of labor and physical units of capital upon the same scale. The author makes no effort to prove, as Cairnes sought to do, that both factors can be reduced to common and commensurate units of disutility, for each of which the same money price is paid. For each factor there can be chosen arbitrary units which will bring it on the scale. The scales represent the relative rates of increase in the supplies of the two factors. A given distance represents equal rates of change in their respective supplies or equal rates of change in that which is paid. It is, therefore, a double logarithmic scale which we are using.

Returning to the situation illustrated in Chart 40, it is apparent that an increase in the effectiveness of industry and the rise in the payment to both X and Y from P to P_1 would cause a proportional increase in the quantity of each. But since both factors would increase at the same rate, the proportions between X and Y would tend to be unaltered. When the elasticities of supply are equal, the two factors tend to share equally, in terms of both unit and proportional returns, in the gains resulting from an increased effectiveness of industry.

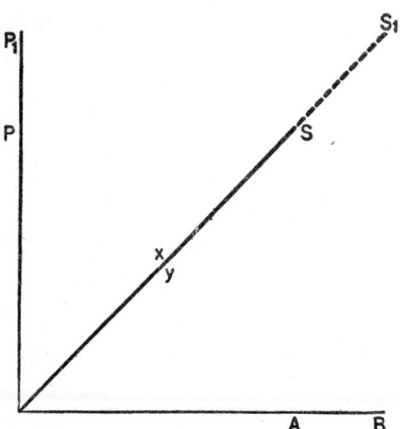

Chart 40. Case 8. Increase in Remuneration with Two Factors Having Positive Unit Elasticity.

We turn now to a slightly more complicated and more interesting case, namely, that where the supply of the factor X is completely inelastic and that where the supply of the other factor Y has positive elasticity. This may be represented by Chart 41 where the line AS represents the inelastic factor X, and that of SS_1 the factor Y with an elasticity of 1.0. The supplies of both when in an original state of equilibrium are represented by A, and the price paid to each by P. The initial increase in the rate of remuneration to each from P to P_1 will create a difference in the relative supplies of the factors. That of X will not increase at all since it is by hypothesis absolutely inelastic, but that of Y will tend to expand at a ratio equal to the relative increase in return per unit. If no obstacles intervened it would increase by the proportion AB, which in this case of unit elasticity would bear the same relation to A as PP_1 to P. But since the supply of Y had increased and that of X had remained constant, the marginal productivity of X would certainly be greater in terms of Y than it would have been had their elasticities been equal. The unit return to X would, therefore, rise *above* P_1 to, let us say, P_2. The marginal productivity of factor Y, on the other hand, would have fallen since there would be relatively more of it mixed with each unit of X than before. Its return per unit would, therefore, *fall* below P_1 to, let us say, P_3. But this very decrease in the marginal productivity of Y would in turn dampen off the amount produced and would lessen the rate of increase in the unit return to X and bring it down below P_2.

But how far would this process of readjustment go? It would not be sufficient to bring the return to X back to P_1 or of Y to P_1, since Y would certainly show some increase in its total quantity and *any* increase in unit return over OP would call forth a proportionate increase in the quantity of Y supplied, while the supply of X would not increase. There would, therefore, be a permanent increase in the quantity of Y offered over the supply A and hence an increase in the relative marginal productivity of X relative to that of Y. The return per unit of X would rise above P_1 while

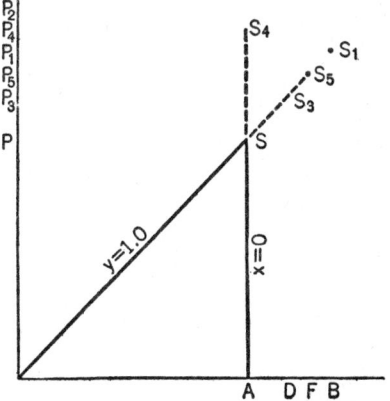

Chart 41. Case 9. Increase in Remuneration with One Factor Completely Inelastic and the Other Factor Having Positive Unit Elasticity.

that of Y would fall below P_1. X would not rise to P_2, however, because of the dampening off of Y's rate of growth, and would settle, let us say, at P_4. The return to Y in turn would not be equal to P_1 but would, instead, be something less than this amount but more than P_3 and would be fixed at P_5. The ultimate result will, therefore, be that X will secure a greater proportionate return per unit than the increase in the total effectiveness of industry, while Y will secure a lesser unit increase.

It is not conclusively demonstrable by graphic methods alone whether X as a whole will secure a larger share of the total product than before, or whether the greater number of units of Y which have been supplied will be more than sufficient to offset the lesser increase per unit.

We may now proceed to a slightly more complicated case, namely, that where both factors have positive but differing elasticities, which we may represent in Chart 42 as X with .5 and

Y with 1.0. In this chart, as in all others in this chapter, the double logarithmic scale is used so that equal distances represent equal proportions. We have represented them in the original state of equilibrium as having the supply A and the price P. The increase in the total effectiveness of industry which raises the initial payment to each to P_1, calls forth an increase in the supply of both, but Y will expand at twice the rate of X, and in consequence the marginal productivity of X will rise above and that of Y will fall below P_1, but not by as much as when the elasticity of X was 0. But this further rise in the return to X will cause its supply to expand beyond B,

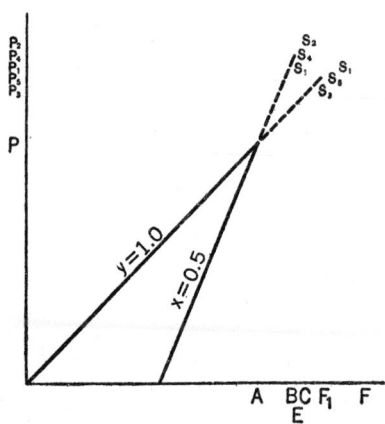

Chart 42. Case 10. Increase in Remuneration with One Factor Having an Elasticity of $+0.5$ and the Other of $+1.0$.

and the fall in the return to Y will cause its supply to contract from C. There will thus be a double force operating to lower the marginal productivity of X down towards P_1 and to raise that of Y up again towards P_1. It will be stronger than in the case previously chosen, since the quantity of X will now be expanding as well as that of Y shrinking. The final equilibrium will, therefore, be nearer P_1. For it should be remembered that both would certainly receive more than P and that every per cent increase in price above this point will cause the supply of Y to expand twice as rapidly as that of X, and hence will increase the marginal productivity of X above the point which it would otherwise have reached, and will cause a diminution in the marginal productivity of Y. Since the total expansion of the productive powers of industry are such as could cause an increase in output to F_1, were both elasticities equal to unity, and yet would permit both to enjoy the increase of P P_1 in return per unit. When the elasticity of X is less than unity, then its unit rate of return tends to be somewhat above P_1 and that of Y will be somewhat below. X will still have gained but not as much as when its elasticity was O and that of Y was still 1.0.

If we follow out other illustrations of varying elasticities it will be seen that X's gain at zero elasticity will be greater if Y has an elasticity of 2.0 than if it has 1.0, for Y in the former case will increase twice as rapidly as in the latter, and hence the original proportions between X and Y will be more disturbed and the marginal productivity of X still further enhanced. Similarly, although X will gain less when its elasticity is .5 rather than 0, while that of Y is 1.0, it will plainly gain more if Y's elasticity is 4.0, than if it is 1.0.

The problems which arise out of negatively sloping supply curves are, however, still more fascinating. Thus, let us assume a situation where we have one positive and one negative supply curve, but where the elasticities themselves are equal as is represented in Chart 43, where unit elasticity characterizes both X and Y. The relative supply of both X and Y in the original equilibrium is represented by A and the relative price paid to each by P. Then an increase in the effectiveness of industry would initially raise the return to each above P to, let us say, P_1. But this, in the sequence now familiar, would cause the supply of X (since it is negatively elastic) to con-

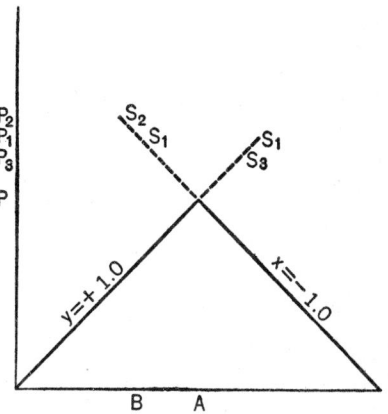

Chart 43. Case 11. Increase in Remuneration with One Factor Having Positive Unit Elasticity and the Other Negative Unit Elasticity.

tract to B, while that of Y would increase by an equal amount. Since the supplies of the two factors would thus move in opposite directions, the marginal productivity of X would rise greatly above the amount P_1 while that of Y would fall. But while this rise in the marginal productivity of X to, let us say, P_2 would cause a still further contraction in the supply of X, the fall in the productivity of Y would cause an equal decrease in its quantity. The differences in marginal productivity would not, therefore, be further accentuated from what they were as the result of the initial change in quantities arising from the expansion of production. An equilibrium would result in which the return to X would be greater than P_1 and that of Y would be less; and the amount of the differences of the return of X and Y from P_1

would be greater than in Chart 41, where we assumed elasticities of 0 and 1.0 respectively.

What would happen, however, were the negative elasticity of X to be greater than the positive elasticity, namely —1.0 as compared with + .5 as is illustrated in Chart 44. Then the initial increase in effectiveness and in unit return to each would cause the supply of X to decrease twice as fast relatively as that of Y increased. Its marginal productivity would consequently

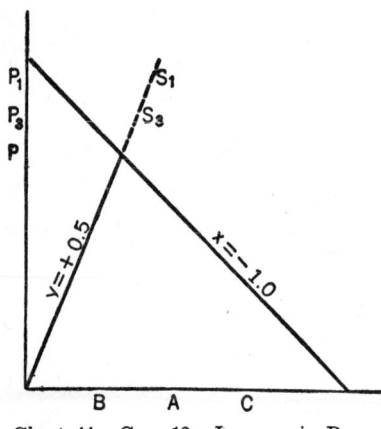

rise and that of Y would fall, but this would lead to twice as great a relative decrease in the quantity of X as it would in that of Y, so that its marginal productivity would rise still further and that of Y would decline yet more. This in turn would stimulate X to decrease at twice the rate of Y and would lead to another increase in X's marginal productivity. There would thus be a cumulative process.

Chart 44. Case 12. Increase in Remuneration with One Factor Having an Elasticity of — 1.0 and the Other of + 0.5.

Here, as in all these cases, the point of equilibrium would depend on the type of productivity equation which prevails. Its partial derivatives furnish the demand curves for the factors which must be thought of as equations to be solved simultaneously with the supply curves under discussion.

When, however, the negative elasticities are less than the positive elasticities, as in Chart 45 with X as —.5 and Y as + 1.0, then though the initial increase to both would cause the supply of X to contract and that of Y to expand, there would not be the same after-effect. In the first place, there would not be the same relative differences in the supplies of the factors created as would have been the case had X's elasticity been —1.0 rather than —.5. Secondly, the supply of Y would now decrease from the amount B at twice the rate at which that of X would increase from C. Hence, there would be something of a readjustment of marginal productivities, with Y rising from the lowly station to which the movement in opposite directions had consigned it, while that of X would be lowered from its high estate. The final equilibrium (*i.e.*, P_3 for Y and P_4 for X) then would be one which would be distinctly more favorable to Y than when the elasticities were plus and minus 1.0 respectively.

Finally, what is the situation when both supply curves are negative? If they are equal, then an advance in the return paid to each unit will cause equal proportionate reductions in the quantity offered and hence will not throw the relative marginal productivities of the two factors out of line with each other. If, however, they are of different elasticities, namely, of —.5 and —1.0, as in Chart 46, then the initial advance in the return per unit will of course cause a greater relative contraction in the supply of X than in that of Y. The marginal productivity of X will, therefore, rise relatively to

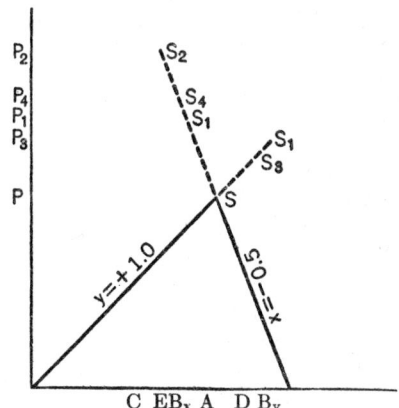

Chart 45. Case 13. Increase in Remuneration with One Factor Having an Elasticity of $+1.0$ and the Other of -0.5.

Y, but this rise in X will lead to a still further contraction in the quantity of X to amounts less than B_x. The decrease in the marginal productivity of Y from P_1 will cause an expansion of the number of units beyond C. This, however, will be a movement in opposite directions, with the result that the marginal productivities of X will be still further enhanced and those of Y still further depressed. But this will cause still less X to present itself and still more Y to be supplied, so that the process would almost seem to go on cumulatively with every indication of unstable equilibrium.

Since this description in terms of successive processes has been for purely pedagogical purposes, while in actuality all of the forces would be operating simultaneously, the increase in the net effectiveness of industry would be a force serving to offset the diminished marginal productivity and hence preventing the supply of Y from expanding continuously with the cumulative break-down of equilibrium which has been sketched above. But there would seem to be no assurance that such would be the case.

In conclusion, we may then say that if an advance in the technical or exchange efficiency of a society occurs,

1. The factor which increases least will secure the greater benefits per unit. The factor whose elasticity of supply is negative will, provided that of the other factor is positive, gain more than if it were also positive.

2. The greater the *difference* between the elasticities of the factors, the greater the unit gain secured by the more inelastic. It is, in other words, to the advantage of a factor that it should not expand but rather contract under prosperity and that its rival should increase in quantity as much as possible.

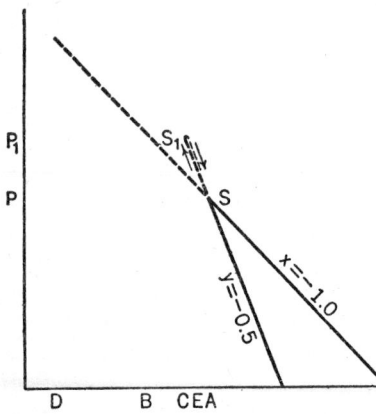

Chart 46. Case 14. Increase in Remuneration with One Factor Having an Elasticity of —0.5 and the Other of —1.0.

3. Although the compass of this chapter is altogether too short to develop this point, it can be said that such mathematical computations as have been made according to the Wilcox formula indicate that these two conclusions apply also as regards the relative shares of the total product as well as the return per unit. This is not true, however, if the formula $P = L^k C^{1-k}$ is strictly followed. For this formula calls for a constancy in the share of the total product which is received by each factor.

There is indeed grim irony in the fact that the principles of distribution run so counter to the heart of the Christian ethic with its faith that "whosoever will lose his life shall find it," and with its injunction to go the second mile. Within the world of purely economic values and motives, however, that factor which gives of itself most sparingly reaps the greater reward per unit and reaps the more, the more the other factors expand and give of themselves.

4. Where one factor has a negative elasticity of supply which is greater than the positive elasticity of the other, there is a cumulative process tending to enhance the return to the negatively elastic factor. The same may also be true when both factors have negative supply curves but of differing magnitudes.

4. Elasticity of Supply in Relation to Decreases in The Net Effectiveness of Industry

Precisely the reverse set of results would occur were the efficiency or exchange powers of a society to decrease without any prior change in the quantities of the factors themselves.

If the supplies of both were completely inelastic, then for a symmetrical productivity surface each would suffer an equal proportionate loss without, of course, causing any diminution in the quantity of either. Were they both of infinite elasticity, then there would be a great contraction in the supply which would only be checked by (1) the lessened strain put upon some third factor such as land, and hence the higher joint product credited to the two factors in question, (2) the probability that some of the supply of the factors would be offered for a somewhat lower price rather than not at all. If both of the elasticities were positive but equal, then the initial decrease in return to each would cause an equal proportionate shrinkage in quantity, but would not throw out of balance their relative marginal productivities if these slopes are the same.

If, however, we were to deal with differing elasticities, one let us say being 0 and the other $+ 1.0$, then the supply of the former or X would not contract while that of Y would, and this would raise the marginal productivity of Y above and depress that of X below the point to which they had originally fallen as a result of the decrease in the effectiveness of industry. Were the elasticity of X to be .5 instead of zero, then X's loss would be less because its supply would also shrink as a result of the decline in efficiency, although not by as much as that of Y. The situation would be still further mitigated by the fact that the further decline in X's productivity as compared with Y would be partially arrested by shrinkage in its quantity, while that of Y would advance somewhat as a result of the change in proportions. But X would still bear more of the brunt of the burden than Y.

When we are dealing with a combination of a negative with a positive supply curve, then the fall in unit return will cause the quantity of the former to expand and that of the latter to decrease. This will greatly increase the marginal productivity of the latter and diminish that of the former, especially if the negative elasticity is greater than the positive.

When both supply curves are negative, the one with the greater negative elasticity will suffer most, since a fall in the rate of return will cause a greater expansion of its supply and hence will lower its marginal productivity. With each fall in return more of X would be supplied, while the rise in the marginal productivity of Y would cause less of this factor to be offered so that the disparity between the two would be accentuated.

The conclusion is obvious, therefore, that when there has been a decline in the net effectiveness of industry, the factor which is more elastic and which withdraws itself by a greater proportionate amount—loses less than the other factor, and such units of the factor as remain are able to throw a larger part of the burden off upon the shoulders of the other factor. The best protection, so far as return per unit is concerned, is to contract the supply greatly.

For a factor, therefore, to secure the maximum advantage in periods of industrial advance and to suffer the least losses in periods of industrial depression, it should have (1) a highly inelastic supply curve above the point of present return and (2) a highly elastic supply curve below this point.

The above conclusions may throw some light upon why the owners of land derive great advantages from an advance in industrial effectiveness, in which their factor does not increase, and also why they suffer most during periods of industrial retrogression when their supply cannot contract.

5. Elasticities of Supply in Relation to Changes in Bargaining Power

Let us turn now to what the results would be if the relative bargaining power of any one factor were to be increased without any change in the effectiveness of industry as a whole.[12a]

A. What is an Improvement in Bargaining Power?

This forces us to a consideration of what is meant by bar-

[12a] The literature on the influence of bargaining power and economic and political strength falls into two groups, the Anglo-American and the Austro-German. Of the former, John Davidson, *The Bargain Theory of Wages*, S. & B. Webb, *Industrial Democracy* emphasize the influence of bargaining strength, while W. H. Hutt, in his *The Theory of Collective Bargaining*, is very skeptical. See also, J. R. Hicks, "The Indeterminateness Of Wages," *Economic Journal*, June, 1930 (Vol. XL), pp. 215–31; Maurice Dobb, "A Skeptical View of the Theory of Wages," *Economic Journal*, December, 1929 (Vol. XXXIX), pp. 506–19. For the Austro-German controversy see Böhm-Bawerk, "Macht oder Oekonomisches Gesetz," *Zeitschrift für Volkswirtschaft, Sozialpolitik und Verwaltung*, Vol. XXIII, pp. 205–71, 1914, translated and published by John R. Mez, Eugene, Oregon, 1931; Zwiedineck-Suedenhorst, *Lohn Theorien* (1901); Richard Strigl, *Angewandte Lohntheorie*, Wien, 1926, especially pp. 1–80; J. Marschak, *Die Lohndiskussion* (1930); Alfred Ammon, *Das Lohnproblem* (1930).

gaining power and what constitutes an improvement in it. There are three possible forms which this improvement may take, of which the last two are by far the most important: (1) An improvement in the technique of negotiations, such as greater knowledge of the situation and personal adroitness and shrewdness in driving a bargain. (2) A shifting of the supply schedule in some measure to the left so that at the same price a smaller quantity will be offered than before. (3) The introduction of at least a partial monopoly of supply so that a large number of units will have to be accepted or rejected as a block instead of the atomistic competition usually posited.

In so far as greater knowledge of the economic situation is a factor, this enables the final adjustment to be more closely in harmony with the equilibrium which the economic forces would tend to bring about than would otherwise be the case. Greater technical skill in driving a bargain would undoubtedly help many individuals, but it certainly would not alter the five fundamental conditions outlined in the concluding paragraph of Section 2. It would assist the weaker factor in securing more nearly what pure economic forces would tend to secure for them, but it would not seem that craft and bargaining ability could by themselves alter permanently in all circumstances the amounts which each would receive. Men who think that this can be done forget that there is a great deal of competition between capitalists for labor and between laborers for employment. Such an increase in the bargaining ability of individuals in either group would, under conditions of purely individual contracts, be in part turned against the advantage of other members of that group. Where the work contract is, however, regulated by collective agreements or by legislative enactments, there are certain conditions where such an improvement in bargaining technique may result in permanent changes.

The change in the supply schedules, whereby less will be offered at identical prices than before, may be expressed (a) by shifting the whole supply curve (on a double logarithmic chart) to the left but retaining the same elasticity (slope) as before, or (b) thru keeping the same curve for a portion of the supply but making it become more inelastic for other stretches. Since prices are seldom determined in the lower ranges of the curve, the difference between the two is difficult to distinguish in the price making regions of the curve and may for all practical purposes be disregarded. Whether the curve has shifted its position to the left but kept its same elasticity, or reduced its elasticity after starting from the same position, the result is that less will be offered at the same price than before.

The cause for this, in the case of the factor labor, may be the organization of the men into a trade-union which will distinctly lessen the fears of the workers as to what will happen if the employers refuse to pay the wage demanded. An individual may well be reluctant to hold out for a given wage if he is acting all alone, lest he be not employed. With scanty funds to maintain him and with many workmen, who he believes are ready to step into his shoes, he will tend to lower the price at which he will sell his labor. But in a trade-union he has the consciousness that his fellows are pledged not to undercut the union rate for which they, like himself, are striving. This reassurance gives him and others more strength to hold out. Similarly, the fact that the members of the union in various regions of the country have subscribed to a common fund which is used for strike benefits, allows the group to contemplate more philosophically their possible failure to be hired. It is no longer a possible choice between employment at the terms of the employers and no employment at all in that trade, but between the wage the employer offers and the benefits paid by the union. Loss of work loses, in consequence, much of its terrors. There are still, to be sure, many fears which are left; such as the fear that the strike benefits may give out, the fear that the employers' resources may be stronger, the fear that either non-union workmen may be brought in from outside or that the work may be sent out to non-union shops, the fear that in the event that the strike should prove unsuccessful the strikers may be blacklisted from employment or discriminated against as regards promotion. But these fears are less than they otherwise would be, and at the same price less labor is offered than would otherwise be the case. The greater is the number who are thus organized, the more the supply curve will approach something of a plateau when the level of the union rate for which the unionists are striving is reached. The nature of the change effected by trade-union organization may be illustrated in Chart 47. Curve AA_3 is assumed to represent the supply schedule of labor before and Curve BB_3 after a sturdy organization has been built up. The laborers from A to B are common to both situations, namely, those who would work for little and who do not wish to join the union lest it impair their ability to secure work. Their bids, therefore, are still low in the hope that they will be employed. The group from B to B_1 represents those who do not join the union but who will ask for more than they otherwise would, because they know that the large group in the union will demand a still higher wage. The group from B_1 to B_2 are the union members who are sticking out for the wage of height P. This may well be somewhat less than the minimum which they are ostensibly demanding of the employers. The units of labor offered from B_2 to B_3 may be regarded as the number of overtime hours which would be furnished by the workers at given prices. It will be noticed that it will take a larger price than formerly to induce an equal quantity to offer itself. This is because the basic wage is itself higher and because the practice of demanding bonuses for overtime work becomes

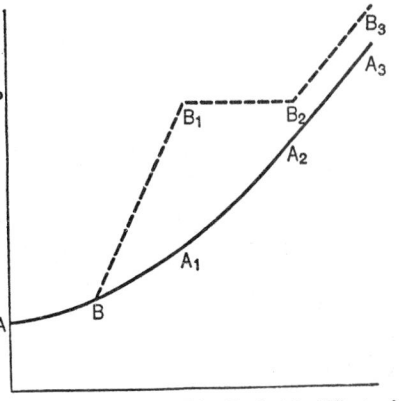

Chart 47. Case 15. The Probable Effect of Trade Union Organization upon the Shape of the Supply Curve of Labor.

more and more firmly established as the unions increase in power.

There are two qualifications which should be thoroughly appreciated. The first is that if the strike should prove difficult to win the union members might well lower their rate below the level B_1. This would cause those from B_1 to B_2 to lower their section of the curve and would lead to a lowering in absolute units of the curve between B_2 and B_3 with or without change in the elasticity for these points. Second, such a supply curve as has been predicated would tend to be much more of a short-time than a long-time curve. The long-time supply would be greatly modified by the rate of population growth which any change in wages would induce. If the relative strength of organization persisted without a corresponding increase in that of the rival factors, such an alteration in the supply curve as has been suggested would still persist although in a somewhat mitigated form.

The effects on the supply curves of the factors of properly enforced legislation dealing with wages, hours, and interest

rates are even more apparent and these may assume considerable importance under the National Recovery Act.

When through state action a minimum wage ruling is passed
forbidding employers to hire labor for less than a given sum,
say 40 cents an hour, the supply curve of labor is immediately
given a point of origin which is above and to the left of the
former supply curve. Even though those who would originally
have offered themselves for only 40 cents an hour do not increase
their sticking-points, still the new supply curve will be higher
than the old for a portion at
least of the supply. The
quantity of labor which
would previously have been
forthcoming at less than 40
cents an hour will not now be
supplied unless this amount
is paid. If, because of the
higher curve in the lower
reaches of the labor supply,
those in the upper reaches
were also to ask for more, the
supply curve here would shift
to the left also. Such a situation can be shown by Chart
48 when AA_2 represents the

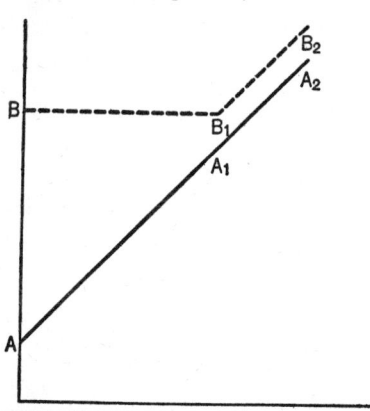

Chart 48. Case 16. The Change in the
Supply Curve Due to Minimum Wage
Legislation.

original supply curve and BB_1B_2 the curve resulting from minimum wage fixation by the state.

The effect of shortening the hours of work, were it not accompanied by a corresponding increase in the intensity of labor,
would, of course, be tantamount to a decrease in the supply of
labor and this seems indeed to have been one of the results
of the codes promulgated under the National Recovery Act.

For purposes of analysis we can then represent an improvement in bargaining power whether secured through voluntary
or state action, as a leftward movement of the supply curve of
the factor. It would probably not be characterized by a uniform elasticity throughout its course, but for the purpose of
simplifying our analysis we shall assume that there is such a
uniformity. This, however, is not nearly so important relatively
as the fact that the elasticity is on the whole less than before.
And this is the point which should be stressed and the effects
of which will be traced.

B. The Effects of Changes in Bargaining Power

We may now proceed to examine what would be the effects of increase in bargaining power under different sets of elasticities of supply, and we may use for the first case, that of complete inelasticity of supply of both factors. We may represent in Chart 49 the line AS as characterizing the original supply curves for both X and Y. But with the improvement in the bargaining power of X, the supply "curve" of that factor, while continuing to be inelastic, moves to the left to the point B. At various prices equal amounts of X will be offered but they will in each instance be less than what was offered before. The ratio of X to Y will now be B to A, and in consequence the marginal productivity of X will rise to, let us say, P_1 and that of Y will fall to P_2. But this will create no further change in the quantities of either, so that as long as these quantities are unchanged, X can continue to enjoy the greater return which will come from its higher marginal productivity. Except for the limitations in the productivity curve there is no limit

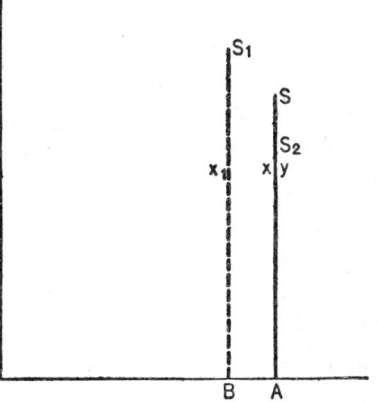

Chart 49. Case 17. Change in the Supply Curve Due to Changes in Bargaining Power, Both Factors Being Completely Inelastic.

to the increased per unit gains which a factor can enjoy if by limiting its supply it can increase its bargaining power. Where both factors have therefore absolutely inelastic supplies, the arguments of the so-called bargain theorists, that the result will depend on the relative bargaining strength of the two factors, is approximately true if we take as our test of bargaining power, the relative changes in position and slope of the supply curves.

But this interpretation of bargaining power is one that has been little understood by the bargain theorists themselves. The ultimate unit return of X may, therefore, be represented by P_1 instead of by P as was originally the case, while the ultimate return to Y may be shown as P_2 instead of P as at first.

Let us assume, however, another case in which X is completely inelastic and Y has unit positive elasticity. (Chart 50.) Then if we indicate an increase in the effectiveness of X's bargaining power by shifting it to the left to B and designating its supply curve by BS_2, we have the ratio of the quantity of X to Y as one of B to A instead of A to A as before. The unit return to X will in consequence rise to let us say P_1 and that to Y will fall to P_2 in consequence of the forces which have been so often mentioned in this chapter. But while the increase in payment to X will not lead to any increase in its supply, the diminished return to Y will cause the supply of this factor to diminish from A *towards* B. But the supply will not fall to B because as it moves towards this point, marginal productivity will rise and this will break the force of the fall. It cannot return to A, however, because of the initial change in quantities which the moving of the supply curve of X to the left effected. The new equilibrium will, therefore, be reached at the point where B quantities of X and approximately C quantities of Y will be supplied, and with a unit return to Y of P_3 and to X of P_4. The factor X would, therefore, have enhanced its former return per unit while Y would lose, but the losses and the gains would not be as great as when Y as well as X was completely inelastic.

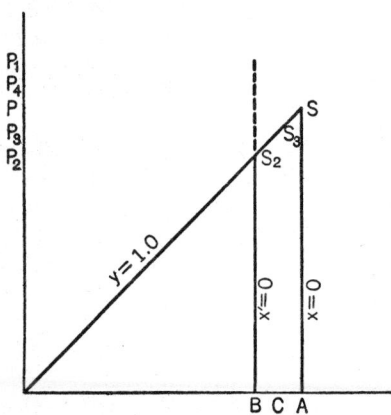

Chart 50. Case 18. Effect of Changes in Bargaining Power with One Factor Completely Inelastic and the Other Having an Elasticity of $+ 1.0$.

Let us now assume (Chart 51) that the initial elasticities of the supply curves of both X and Y are 1.0 and that they are both represented by the curve S, and that the supply of the two factors originally offered was that represented by A with the rate of payment P or AS. X now secures added bargaining strength, which we shall represent here by a decrease in its elasticity from 1.0 to .9 instead of by a parallel shift of its supply curve, the new supply curve being represented by X_1 so that at the price P, only B instead of A units as before are offered. This sets into motion the familiar train of consequences. But as a result of the marginal productivity of X rising to P_1 the supply of X will expand while that of Y will contract. There will thus be a double force at work to restore the original equilibrium. The combined movement will restore the ultimate marginal productivities of each factor nearer the original equilibrium than was the case when we were dealing with 1.0 and zero elasticities. But it will not completely restore it since the fact that the elasticity of X was .9 will mean that the supply of this factor will not increase as rapidly as a result of its increase in remuneration as that of Y will decrease. The effect of the initial change in elasticities will, therefore, not be completely removed. There will be some change in the ultimate amounts paid for units of each factors, that of X rising above P but appreciably below P_1, while that of Y will fall below P but will still be appreciably above P_2. The ultimate points of equilibrium may then be designated as P_3 and P_4, and at these prices AE fewer units of X and AD fewer units of Y will be forthcoming.

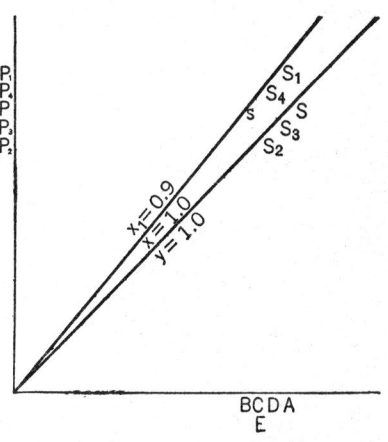

Chart 51. Case 19. Effect of Changes in Bargaining Power upon the Supply Curves with Both Factors Having an Initial Elasticity of $+1.0$.

Had the elasticity of Y been 2.0 instead of 1.0, then the ultimate unit gain secured by X would have been still less; for as the marginal productivity of Y fell because of the fact that less X was combined with it, the supply of Y would contract twice as rapidly as before and hence the forces working for the reëstablishment of the equilibrium would be strengthened. But while the unit returns to X and Y would ultimately approach nearer to P, than P_3 or P_4, they would not quite reach it. X would, therefore, retain some gain, and Y would suffer some loss.

The conclusion is, therefore, that (1) the more inelastic a factor becomes the more it will gain from an increase in bargain-power, while (2)—and this is less appreciated—the more inelastic is the supply of the rival factor, the better it is for the factor whose bargaining power has improved. The units of a factor which remain in the market will desire, therefore, that their numbers should neither expand under prosperity nor that those of its rival should decrease under adversity.

Still more interesting results of the same general character are secured when we deal with one or more negative supply curves. Let us suppose (Chart 52) that X has originally a positive elasticity of 1.0 and Y an equal negative elasticity. We shall designate the supply offered of each by A and the unit price paid as P (AS). Let us now decrease the elasticity of X to $+.9$. This will cause only B units of X to be offered for P, and in consequence its marginal productivity would rise and that of Y would fall. This increase in return would cause the quantity of X to expand while the fall in the price of Y would, since its supply curve is negative, cause the quantity of Y to expand also. But since Y's negative elasticity is unity while X's positive elasticity is now .9, this would mean that the quantity of Y would tend to increase more rapidly than that of X, and hence its marginal productivity would continue to fall and that of X would continue to rise, so that the supply of Y would be continuously increasing faster than X and there would tend to be a cumulative increase in the remuneration of X and a corresponding fall in that of Y. Under these elasticities it might be thought that there would not be stable equilibrium. But the final outcome depends on the type of productivity equation which is assumed, for its partial derivatives furnish the demand curves for the factors whose intersections with the supply curves determine the point of equilibrium.

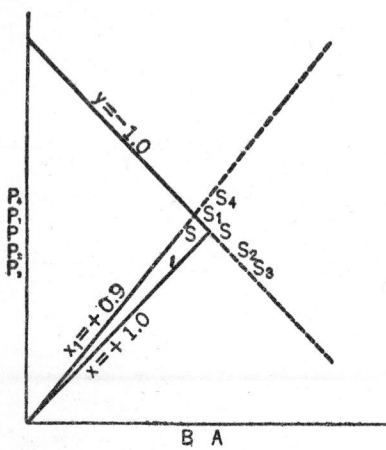

Chart 52. Case 20. Effect of Changes in Bargaining Power upon the Supply Curves When One Factor Has an Initial Elasticity of $+1.0$ and the Other of -1.0.

If, however, the negative elasticity of the one were equal to the ultimate positive elasticity of the other, after the initial alteration in productivities developed, there would be no further alteration of the equilibrium since the increase in quantity would be the same for both.

If the final positive elasticity were to be higher than the negative elasticity, then there would be a counteracting force tending to bring the relative returns nearer even to the original level than that which would result from equal elasticities.

Where both supply curves are negatively inclined (Chart 53) there are further possibilities of unstable equilibrium. Thus, if the supply curve of one factor X is to shift to the left, so that less will be offered at the same price as before, then the increase in payment to X will cause its supply to contract while that of Y will expand. This will in turn mean a still greater increase in the marginal productivity of X and a further decrease in Y, and this in turn will unleash added quantities of Y and will cause the supply of X to shrink still more. Though mathematically a new point of equilibrium may be found, its economic significance, if any, is not certain.

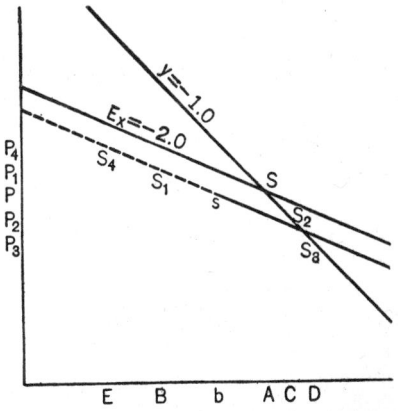

If only those units of a factor which continue to be supplied were to be consulted, they would wish not only that their number should remain stationary under prosperity, but that they should actually decrease. The surviving units would be still further aided if the rival factor actually poured forth more of itself whenever the remuneration per unit of this second factor is decreased.

Chart 53. Case 21. The Effect of Changes in Bargaining Power upon the Supply Curve When Both Curves Are Negatively Inclined.

With two factors having negative supply curves, an increase in the effective bargaining power of one results in a cumulative showering of advantages upon the factor which improves its position and a cumulative degradation of the factor which does not. It would be a continued process of giving to him that hath and of taking away from him that hath not. This would indeed be unstable equilibrium. The same forces would be set at work although to a lesser degree, if the factor which improved its position were, while of positive elasticity, to have a lower coefficient of elasticity than that of the factor with the negatively inclined supply curve.

Whether or not there would be changes in the shares of the

total product received by the two factors, as well as changes in the return per unit, would depend again upon the nature of the equation of production. If it were one where the exponents were fixed, which is what we have developed in Part Two of this book, then the relatively greater gain per unit of one factor would just be offset by the relative decrease in the number of units, so that the proportionate shares received by it and by the other factor would be the same as before. If, however, it conformed to the equation which Mr. Wilcox has developed and applied to the American data, then the factor which obtained a gain per unit as a result of improved bargaining power would also secure an increased share of the total product.

6. The Influence of The Relative Proportion of The Total Product Received by The Factors

It is not pretended that the influences upon distribution of the respective supply curves which have been sketched above are the sole forces determining the unit and proportional returns received by each of the factors of production. That they do affect in an important manner the amounts and shares received has, I hope, been demonstrated by the necessarily summary discussion which has been given. But there are other factors to be considered and other problems which must be solved before we can arrive at a correct theoretical explanation of the forces governing the processes of distribution.

It will be noted from the discussion in the three preceding sections that we have tacitly assumed that the shares of the total product which the factors originally secured were equal, and that where only a change in bargaining power had occurred, an increase of one per cent in the return to one factor meant a corresponding decrease of one per cent in the return per unit of the other factor. But neither of these assumptions need be true. What modifications would changes in these assumptions necessitate in our theory? Let us suppose that labor originally received two-thirds and capital but one-third of the total product. Then if, without any change in the net effectiveness of industry, labor were to increase its return per unit by 5 per cent, its share of the total product would then rise to 70 per cent; but the share of capital would fall to 30 per cent, and if we assume that the total product would be unaltered, this would mean a fall of 10 per cent in the payment for each unit of capital. Thus, what would be a 5 per cent increase in the return for each unit of labor would be a decrease of 10 per cent for each unit of capital. This would, of course, cause different movements of the supplies of these factors even though their elasticities were to be the same. Thus if each of their elasticities were positive and equal to unity, there would be an increase of 5 per cent in the quantity of labor and a decrease of 10 per cent in the quantity of capital. This would be a stronger force towards restoring the original equilibrium than if the supply of capital had only contracted in the same proportion by which the supply of labor had expanded.

If the supply of labor were completely inelastic, while that of capital had positive unit elasticity, then an improvement in labor's bargaining power would have similar results. For while the supply of labor would not increase, the supply of capital would decrease at twice the rate which it would have done, had the total product of industry been originally divided equally between the two. In consequence, the final gain of labor would be less than it would be were a one per cent gain for labor to cause a loss of only one per cent to capital.

The same results can be traced for all sets of positive elasticities. The larger is the share of the total product which is received by the factor which improves its bargaining position, the less will be its ultimate gains. For a gain of a given percentage in the unit return to this factor will cause a loss of more than this percentage in the unit return of the other. This in turn will cause the supply of the factor which has experienced the loss to contract more rapidly than it would have done had the relationship between the shares been one of equality. This greater contraction in the supply will, of course, tend towards establishing the ultimate equilibrium nearer the original situation. But it will not restore the original equilibrium since the initial shift in bargaining powers and in the quantity of the one factor must be remembered.

Conversely, the smaller the share of the total product received by a factor, the more per unit it can secure (other things being equal) from an increase in bargaining power. This is so because the smaller its share, the less is the decrease in the price per unit of the other factor, and the less consequently is the diminution in the quantity of this second factor.

When the supply curve of one factor is negatively and that of the other factor positively inclined, then if the former has the smaller share of the total product and if the positive factor, or that with the larger share, improves its bargaining position, the latter will gain more than if the shares were originally equal. For a 5 per cent unit increase to the positive factor would mean a 10 per cent decrease to the negative factor. If both their elasticities were originally equal to unity, then the supply of the negative factor would increase by 10 instead of by 5 per cent, while that of the positive factor would grow by only 5 per cent. The resultant increased marginal productivity of the positive factor and the decrease of the negative factor would alter the situation still more in favor of the former.

If, however, the original elasticity of the negatively inclined factor had been but .5, then after the initial change in bargaining power, there would be no further changes since the quantities of each would now expand in the same ratio. But this, it should be noted, would give a result more advantageous to the positive factor than that which would have obtained had the shares been equal. For then the supply of the positive factor would have increased more rapidly than that of the negative factor, so that the final equilibrium would give a unit return to the former which would be *below* the point which the change in bargaining powers had immediately effected.

Conversely, if the smaller and negatively inclined factor were to improve its position by becoming more negatively elastic or by shifting its whole supply curve to the left, then the attendant percentage gain per unit which it secured would be greater than the loss per unit suffered by the rival and positive factor. Its supply would, therefore, tend to contract more rapidly as compared with the positive factor than would be the case were the factors to receive equal shares, for then the positive factor would decrease with equal rapidity. Consequently, the ultimate unit return to the negative factor would be greater than it would have been under the condition of equal shares. When the negative factor therefore takes the aggressive and is able to force up its unit return, it is aided if the positive factor originally received a larger share of the total product, so that it will not contract as rapidly as it would otherwise do.

Where the positive factor received a smaller share than the negative, then if the former raises its bargaining strength, the decrease in remuneration per unit of the negative factor will now be less than the increase in the return per unit for the positive factor. This will cause the quantity of the negative factor to increase less rapidly than under the assumption of equal shares and hence will decrease the amount of the gain per unit, which the positive factor will be able ultimately to secure.

If the negative and larger factor, on the other hand, improves its bargaining position, it causes a greater percentage fall in the return per unit to the positive and smaller factor than the increase per unit which it is able to secure for itself. This means that the supply of the positive factor will be curtailed by a given advance in the bargaining power of the negative factor more than would be the case under the condition of equal shares. The negative factor would, therefore, as a result of its possessing a greater share of the total product, gain less than it would under equal sharing.

When both factors are negative, then an increase in the bargaining power of the one with the greater initial share will cause the unit return of the other factor to fall more rapidly than would otherwise be the case, and consequently would cause the supply of this other factor to be produced more abundantly. This in turn would raise the marginal productivity of the larger [13] factor more than under the condition of equal sharing in the product. Where, however, the smaller factor successfully takes the aggressive, the unit loss to the larger factor is of a smaller relative magnitude than its own gain, and consequently the quantity of the other and larger factor will expand less than would be the case where equal sharing prevailed, and a one per cent increase to one factor was accompanied by a one per cent loss to the other. Hence the ultimate marginal productivity of the smaller factor will be less than it otherwise would be and it would profit less from an increase in the effectiveness of its bargaining power.

The matter may indeed be summed up by saying that it is to the advantage of the factor which improves its bargaining power to expand as little as possible in quantity, and indeed to decrease as rapidly as possible, while the less the other factor decreases and indeed the more it increases, the greater will be the permanent gain secured by the factor which has advanced its bargaining power. But such movements in the relative quantities of the factors are not only caused by (a) the relative elasticities of the supply of the factors as analyzed in the sections five, six and seven, but also (b) the relative proportions of the total product obtained originally by the two factors.

(1) When both factors have positively inclined supply

---

[13] By the larger factor is meant the factor enjoying the greater share of the product.

curves, the smaller the share enjoyed by the factor which improves its position, the more it can gain, and the larger its share the less it can gain. (2) When both factors have negative supply curves, the larger the share of the factor which improves its position the more it can gain, and the smaller its share the smaller will be its ultimate increased return per unit. (3) When one factor is negative and the other is positive, both will gain more if, when they improve their bargaining strength, the positive factor has the larger share, while both would lose more than they would otherwise do if the negative factor were to have the larger share.

With regard to the quantity of a factor supplied, the combined effect of (1) its relative elasticity of supply and (2) its share of the total product can be obtained by multiplying the former by the ratio of the share of the other to the one in question. Thus, if the elasticity of X were .5, and if it received one-third and Y two-thirds of the total product, then the relative change in the quantity of X, which an increase in the return to each unit of Y would occasion, would be the same as that caused by an elasticity of supply of 1.0 for X $\left(i.e., .5 \times \dfrac{\frac{2}{3}}{\frac{1}{3}} = .5 \times 2 = 1.0\right)$.

If X received but one-fourth of the total product, it would be identical with an elasticity of 1.5 $i.e., .5 \times \dfrac{\frac{3}{4}}{\frac{1}{4}} = .5 \times 3 = 1.5.$

Where, however, there is an increase or decrease in the net effectiveness of industry, both factors will tend initially to be affected to the same relative degree whatever may have been the share of the total product which each originally received. For a decline of 5 per cent in the total product would virtually tend to be distributed over the factors in the same proportion which each originally secured, let us say in the ratio of two-thirds and one-third, and this would mean that the remuneration per unit would decline by 5 per cent for each factor. An increase in the net effectiveness of industry of a given percentage would also tend to be initially reflected for both factors in equal percentage increases in reward per unit.

In these cases, therefore, the relative proportion of the product secured by the factors does not affect the final result. The relative elasticity of supply will determine the nature and degree of the alterations in the supply which a given change in effectiveness will create and consequently will shape the ultimate equilibrium which will be established.

7. Other Factors

But there are still other forces which must be plumbed and whose influences upon distribution must be analyzed. The most important of these are: (1) the complications introduced by considering more than two factors of production, (2) the complications introduced by considering more than one commodity, (3) the influence which is exercised by the relative amounts of labor, capital, and land rent embodied in the commodities and services which are consumed by the recipients of interest, wages, and rent, (4) the influence of the relative elasticity of demand for these commodities and services. Each of these forces will now be briefly considered and their influence evaluated.

1. The complications introduced by considering more than two factors of production. We have hitherto been considering in a very simplified manner only two factors which we have at times labelled labor and capital. But there is, of course, land and natural resources which is a third factor. Most modern theorists following Francis A. Walker also set up a fourth factor, namely management. It is difficult to recognize this, however, as a distinct economic category or to regard its payment, profits, as any unified return. The management of an enterprise would seem to fall under the category of labor and the wages of management to be indeed but a species of wages. The work of management undoubtedly calls for talents of a high order. Such talents may be so rare that there is intense competitive bidding for them, which makes the returns received partake of the nature of what is commonly regarded as rent, in the sense that a surplus is paid over the cost of furnishing the service. Management also bears the risk, but this can more and more be treated on an actuarial basis. It is, moreover, doubtful whether taking business as a whole, the payments for risk bearing are greater than the losses incurred.[14] There remain residual profits and these have been resorted to by economists as a catchall to take account of returns which cannot be attributed to land, capital and labor, as well as

---

[14] On this point, see Knight, *Risk, Uncertainty and Profit;* Hardy, *Risk and Risk-bearing.*

a reward for a separate type of service. They result from dynamic changes in production which are not immediately distributed to the factors and from changes in the demand schedules of commodities, which for a space give great rewards to some. They arise from the failure of the factors to move with the speed and intelligence which are ordinarily ascribed to them by economists. Residual profits, therefore, accrue because of friction, and time lags rather than as a reward for a positive contribution by a fourth factor of production.

But natural resources, at least, are a third factor and the question naturally arises how they may be fitted into the analysis? A method which naturally suggests itself is to compare labor with a combination of land and capital. Since the supply of natural resources is on the whole quite inelastic, the combination of land with capital will (if the supply curve of the latter is positive) make the composite elasticity of the two less than that for capital alone. In securing the composite elasticity for these two factors, the elasticity of each factor should, of course, be weighted by the percentage of the national income originally enjoyed by each. The comparison of how labor fared as compared with the composite fortunes of the owners of land and capital would afford a basis for judging the effect of given changes upon service income as compared with property income, and hence would be valuable in itself.

The relative effects produced upon rent as compared with (1) wages and (2) interest, could then be studied in turn and their results isolated. Since labor and capital (and hence wages and interest) have previously been compared for the purpose of isolating the effects, labor and natural resources could also be merged together and compared with capital. It would be possible then to disentangle the approximate effects produced on each of the factors and to frame a general conclusion for each according to its relative coefficient of elasticity and the relative share which it originally received of the total product.

2. Real difficulties are encountered when we move to a consideration of several commodities. Hitherto we have been dealing with only one and consequently have taken into account only one general productivity surface, composed as it was of (a) the rate of increase of the total product with equal proportional changes in the factors, (b) the rate of slope of the product as the proportion of X to a constant quantity Y was altered, and

(c) the rate of slope of the product as the ratio of Y to a constant quantity of X was altered.

But as we deal with several commodities, we encounter diverging slopes of marginal productivity as measured in terms of physical units, and the question naturally arises how these divergent rates of change in the total product which follow an alteration in the physical quantity of the factors, may be so equated as to be reduced to a common function. How, in other words, can the production of potatoes, copper ore, loaves of bread, and neckties be reduced to common units in which we have different technical coefficients of production? This, however, can be effected by computing index numbers of production in which the quantities of each product, weighted by their values, are reduced to relatives. If the change is to be studied over a period of time, this general index of production, similar to those constructed by the Federal Reserve Board and the Harvard Committee on Economic Research, will measure sufficiently well what we desire. And if it be objected that the relative values will change from year to year and that consequently an index based on fixed weights will be wrong, it can be shown that Professor Irving Fisher has eliminated this difficulty in his "ideal" index number where he commends the use of the geometrical average of the index of a commodity in a given year weighted by its value in the base year multipled by the index for the given year weighted by the values of the given year.[15]

In this way a satisfactory physical index of general production can be secured to measure the physical effects of altered quantities of the factors. Within these physical outputs, of course, productivity will be measured in terms of value, but for the society as a whole we can measure fairly accurately the productivity as a whole. Even here, however, there will be difficulties in taking into account (1) the relative degree of fabrication in manufacturing at different intervals, and (2) the relative amount of services supplied at differing periods.

3. The relative amount of labor, capital, and imputed services of natural resources which are contained in the commodities upon which laborers expend their wages as compared with the

---

[15] See Fisher, *The Making of Index Numbers* (1st edition), p. 482. The formula is:

$$\sqrt{\frac{\Sigma q_1 p_0}{\Sigma q_0 p_0} \times \frac{\Sigma q_1 p_1}{\Sigma q_0 p_1}}$$

relative quantities of these factors which are consumed by the recipients of interest and of rent, also affect the final apportionment of the product to the factors of production. It is important, therefore, to trace the effects of consumption as well as of production upon distribution. While personal distribution is, of course, not identical with functional distribution, since one man, such as a farmer, may receive an income from land, labor, and capital, nevertheless for the great masses of men the economic classes tend to conform to the categories. Thus the wage-earners receive but a small fraction of their income from the interest on their capital holdings, while the possessors of large fortunes derive most of their income from returns on their property. A change in the ratios received by factors will then alter the relative income of individuals.

If a factor then increases its share of the national income, the question is important as to whether it will spend this increased percentage upon goods in which there is much labor but little capital, or for articles or services in which there is relatively little labor and much capital.[16] Thus, let us suppose that labor were to receive a larger proportion of the total product than before, if it were to expend its gains upon articles in which an extraordinarily large amount of waiting had gone, then the demand for capital and consequently its marginal productivity would go up by far more than would be the case were labor to buy articles and services in which only a small quantity of capital was embodied. Conversely, if it were to buy articles in which much labor was embodied, it, as a class, would profit still further from the increased demand and increased marginal product which would result. Hence the more labor purchases personal services, the more laborers will profit from the *existing national income,* while the more capitalists buy products in which a large amount of capital is contained, the more capital will profit.

The suggestion presents itself from this that since the recipients of large amounts of interest spend a much larger fraction of their income upon personal services in the form of servants, entertainers, etc., and buy goods upon which a great deal of hand work has been lavished, therefore, an increase in return to the capitalists would be partially offset by the increased demand for labor which would result. The rise in de-

---

[16] Professor Jacob Viner has made this suggestion to me.

mand for chauffeurs, butlers, custom tailors, and violinists would increase the wages for teamsters, bakers, cutters, and general labor. Conversely since the wage and salaried workers primarily spend their income upon mass production goods in which a relatively large quantity of capital is mixed, when they spend their gains, a part of the increase goes back to the capitalists.

4. If the goods in which relatively much labor is contained have on the whole elasticities of demand different from those which characterize the commodities in which relatively little labor is embodied, the processes of distribution will be affected.

Let us suppose that the demand for the goods in which much labor is mixed (A goods) is much more elastic than that for commodities (B goods) in which there is relatively little labor. Then if the net effectiveness of industry increases with the same number as before of labor units and capital units, the values of the B goods will fall relatively to the A goods. The marginal productivity of labor will therefore rise as will its reward. There will, of course, be a movement of labor from the B to the A industries which will reduce the gains somewhat, but they will nevertheless still be considerable. If the B industries were, however, to be characterized by the more elastic demand, labor would not make such gains, for the values of B in terms of A would rise and with this the demand for and the marginal productivity of capital.

Should a diminution in the effectiveness of industry occur, the prices of the B goods would rise much more rapidly than those of the A category and hence their relative values would increase. This would increase the demand for and the marginal productivity of capital above the point which it would, in the absence of such differences in elasticity of demand, attain. The marginal productivity of labor would, on the other hand, be lowered. This assumes A's elasticity greater than B's.

If the supply of labor should shift to the left and if the elasticity of demand were greater for the A than for the B commodities, then the curtailment in production which the reduction in the number of labor units would occasion, would cause the prices of the B goods to rise more rapidly than those of class A. There would, consequently, be a movement of labor out of A into B with an attendant probable reduction in the price of labor below what it would otherwise have been had the opposite condition obtained as to elasticities.

8. Some Next Steps in Research

What is clearly needed is inductive research to determine (1) the actual elasticities of supply of the factors of production, (2) the changes in physical output effected by varying the quantities of the factors. A beginning along these lines has been made in Part Two of this book. (3) The degree to which the actual course of wages, interest rates, and the proportions of the total product received by the factors have conformed to what would be expected from our analysis once the elasticities, etc., are known. (4) The relationship between the actual flexibilities of the marginal productivity curves of the factors and their supply curves.[17]

Some of these tasks are attempted in the chapters which follow.

---

[17] In taking account of the changes in bargaining strength, the effect of a shortening of hours by governmental mandate, as under the NRA, with a consequent rise in the wage per hour should also be considered. This would be merely another illustration of the same set of principles which have been developed.

B. The Short-Run Supply of ·Labor

CHAPTER XI

THE SHORT-RUN SUPPLY CURVE OF LABOR

The Proportion Gainfully Employed

1. Economic thinking of the classical type has not in general clearly conceived the precise meaning of the term "supply of labor." The economists of the orthodox tradition have tended to regard this as synonymous with the total population. Any changes in this supply of labor would, therefore, be slow and would operate through the birth and death rates or through immigration and emigration. When the economists spoke, therefore, of those changes in the labor supply which would be occasioned by changes in the rate of remuneration, they were thinking only of long-run and not of short-run changes. At any one time, the supply of labor was fixed since there were just so many people and no more.

But because two countries have equal populations it does not follow that they have equal supplies of labor. One, as is the case with Ireland, may have an abnormal proportion in the advanced age groups of those who are incapacitated for hard work. Another, like the United States, may have an abnormal proportion in the age groups of those from 25 to 50 years who form the bulk of the active workers. Out of every hundred persons, therefore, the second country will, of course, have an appreciably larger number who will be eligible for industry and for gainful employment. But this is not all. The supply of labor may differ very appreciably between two countries which have equal populations and identical age distributions. (1) Within the same age-groups the proportion gainfully employed may vary because of differences in social tradition and in wages. (2) The number of hours worked per day may differ and (3) the number of days which the worker absents himself from labor may differ. The supply of labor is not, therefore, as most classical economists have conceived it, identical with the *stock* of labor available but may vary quite widely as between two otherwise identical populations. It follows, therefore, that changes in the rate of remuneration may affect the quantity of labor which offers itself at any one time,[1] since each of the three variables enumerated above may fluctuate with variations in the rate of wages. This was pointed out by Longe in 1866 in his attempted refutation of the wage-fund theory when he declared,[1a] "A supply of labour is a supply of potential work and every practical man knows that the quantity of work to be got from labourers is no more determined by their numbers, than the quantity of apples to be got from an orchard by the number of trees in it."

Practical economists who have been outside the classical tradition have recognized this tendency of the short-run supply of labor to bear some functional relationship to the rate of wages. The majority of the English mercantilists of the seventeenth and eighteenth centuries for example believed that the supply curve of labor was negatively inclined, and that an increase in wages caused a decrease in the amount of work done and that a decrease in wages would cause them to work more hours.[2] Thus Thomas Manly declared that the results of an increase in wages were that [3] "the men have just so much the more to spend in tipple and remain now poorer than when their wages were less. . . . They work so much the fewer days by how much more they exact in their wages." While Josiah Child wrote [4] of the laboring poor "that in a cheap year they will not work above two days in a week, their humor being such that they will not provide for a hard time but just work so much and no more as may maintain them in that mean condition to which they have become accustomed." Similar views were advanced by many others including Daniel Defoe,[5] John Houghton [6] and Arthur Young.[7]

---

[1] Irving Fisher has seen this in his *Elementary Principles of Economics,* pp. v, 436 ff., and so has Jacob Viner in his mimeographed material on *Value and Distribution.*

[1a] F. D. Longe, *A Refutation of the Wage-Fund Theory* (reprinted under the editorship of J. H. Hollander), pp. 55–56.

[2] See also Lionel Robbins, "The Economic Effects of Variations of the Hours of Labor," *Economic Journal,* Vol. XXXIX (1929), pp. 25–40; and D. H. Robertson, "Economic Incentives," *Economica,* Vol. I (1921); F. H. Knight, *Risk, Uncertainty, and Profit,* p. 117; Ragnar Frisch, *New Methods of Measuring Marginal Utility,* pp. 83–113.

[3] Manly, *Usury at Six Per Cent* (1669), p. 19.

[4] Josiah Child, *A New Discourse of Trade* (6th Edition), p. 12.

[5] Daniel Defoe, *Tours,* II, p. 40.

[6] John Houghton, *Collection of Letters,* p. 177.

[7] Arthur Young, "Everyone but an idiot knows that the lower classes must be kept poor or they will never be industrious . . . they must be (like all mankind) in poverty or they will not work." *Eastern Tour,* Vol. IV, p. 361.

These writers not only believed, therefore, that the supply curve of labor was negatively inclined but that its elasticity was equal to unity. Not only would the amount of labor offered decrease as wages increased, but it would decrease in precisely the same proportion as wages advanced, so that the total yearly earnings of a laborer tended to remain constant. This belief was, of course, based on the assumption that the standard of living of working-class families was virtually stationary. An increase in wages would, therefore, not be utilized to buy more commodities but rather to work correspondingly fewer hours.

In modern days the chief proponents of this theory have been the imperialists, who are the spiritual descendants of the mercantilists and who have applied to the inhabitants of the tropics the same theory which their mercantilistic forbears promulgated two centuries before concerning the laboring poor of England.

The utility theorists have been another group who have emphasized the variability of the short-run supply of labor. Richard Jennings [8] pointed out that discomfort increased with successive hours of work. His implication that the working day would cease when the disutility of work for the last unit of time just equaled the utility obtained from the commodities produced by or purchased with this last unit was made explicit by Jevons [9] who represented diagramatically the equivalence of pain and pleasure at the marginal hour.[10] Jevons and his son have, however, both pointed out that an increase in wages need not lead to an increase in hours worked, because the decrease in the utility of each dollar might more than offset the increase in the number of dollars received for the last hours of work.[11] Patten has stressed the fact that if a worker is paid more money, he will want more time in which to spend it, and, consequently, the worker [12] "ceases to work before the pain of the last increment of production equals the utility of the last increment of consumption."

For similar references see *Ibid.,* Vol. II, p. 75; *Northern Tour,* I, p. 192; III, p. 248; *Southern Tour,* p. 331.

[8] Jennings, *Natural Elements of Political Economy,* 1855, pp. 98-9, 118-20.

[9] W. S. Jevons, *The Theory of Political Economy.*

[10] This has also been taken over amongst others by A. T. Hadley, *Economics,* pp. 320-8; S. N. Patten, *The Theory of Dynamic Economics,* pp. 69-75; H. R. Seager, *Principles of Economics,* p. 180.

[11] W. S. Jevons, *The Theory of Political Economy,* p. 180, and H. Stanley Jevons, *Essays on Economics,* pp. 144-97, especially pp. 186-8.

[12] Patten, *The Theory of Dynamic Economics,* p. 71.

The reasoning of Knight and Robbins on these points is discussed in the next chapter.

But all such speculations have been little better than surmises, and it is highly desirable to determine inductively what has been the precise influence which changes in wages have exercised upon the quantity of labor offered. We shall, therefore, try to trace the relationship between changes in wages and (1) changes in the proportion of the working population which habitually offers itself for employment and (2) changes in the standard hours of work per week. We shall consider the first of these inter-relationships in this chapter and take up the question of hours in the chapter which follows:

2. The Relationship Between Real Wages and The Proportion Gainfully Employed in The United States And Great Britain

A comparison of the occupational statistics of Great Britain and the United States furnishes strong inferential evidence that so far as the proportion of persons employed is concerned the supply curve of labor is indeed negatively inclined. The comparative studies which the British Board of Trade made in 1907–1909 of wages and the cost of living in the United States, Great Britain, Belgium, and Germany show that an American worker could on the average with his week's wage buy from 25 to 30 per cent more goods and services than the British wage-earner. Real wages were, therefore, to this extent higher in the United States than in England. It is most significant to note that in 1911, 83.8 per cent of all the males of 10 years of age and over in England and Wales [13] were gainfully employed while in the United States a somewhat smaller proportion of this same group, namely 81.3 per cent were so employed. [14] This smaller percentage in the United States was all the more striking in view of the fact that the population of the United States contained, because of the large volume of immigrants, an abnormally large proportion of persons in the active age groups from 25 to 45 years and a smaller proportion of those over 65 years than would have been the case in a standard population. The percentage of males in the United States of over 10 years who were gainfully employed, might, therefore, have been expected to be greater than the percentage so employed in Great Britain. But as a matter of fact it was 2.5 per cent less.

The difference between the two countries in the proportion of females over 10 years who were gainfully employed was even greater. The percentage in England and Wales was 32.5,[13] while in the United States it was but 23.4.[14] The average for the United States was indeed somewhat padded because the Census included many farmers' wives. Out of a hundred females over 10 years in each of the countries, there would, therefore, have been at least 9 fewer gainfully employed workers here than in Great Britain. This was despite the fact that the greater household facilities in this country might have been expected, had other things been equal, to release more women for gainful employment than in Great Britain.

The natural query, which is raised by such statistics as these, is whether these differences were not caused by more stringent child-labor laws in the United States rather than by a negative elasticity of the supply-curve for labor. There are two answers to this suggestion. The first is that the American child labor laws in 1910 were not very strict. The second is that as a matter of fact there was a slightly larger proportion of the juveniles under 16 years employed in the United States than there were of those under 15 years in Great Britain. The percentages were:

Great Britain (10–14 years) Males 22.7 per cent and
    females 10.4 per cent.[15]

United States (10–15 years) Males 24.7 per cent and
    females 11.9 per cent.[16]

The real differences came in the next group, namely, those from 15 to 19 years in Great Britain and from 16 to 20 in the United States. In Great Britain 91.7 per cent of the males of these ages were gainfully employed, whereas only 79.2 per cent were so employed in the United States. The percentage of the young women in this group who were employed in Great Britain was no less than 68.8, while the percentage in the United States was but 39.8 or only slightly over one-half as many. The higher earnings of the American workers were, therefore, in part expended in keeping their children longer in school than the British parents felt themselves able.

While there was no appreciable difference between the relative proportions of the men between the ages of 21 and 45 who were employed in each country, there was a real gap

---

[13] *Census of England and Wales,* 1911, Vol. X. Cd. 7018.
[14] *Thirteenth Census of the United States* (1910), Vol. IV, pp. 71–3.
[15] *Census of England and Wales,* 1911, Vol. X, p. 13.
[16] *Thirteenth Census of United States,* Vol. IV, pp. 71–3.

between the percentages for the women of those ages. This was 36.8 in Great Britain as contrasted with only 26.3 in the United States. The explanation of this difference undoubtedly lies in the fact that since the American working-class families were not as hard pressed economically as the British, there were not the same economic forces to push adult women into industry in the United States as there were in Great Britain.

3. The Relation Between Wages And The Proportion Gainfully Employed in The United States

It is possible, however, to measure much more precisely the relationship between wages and the proportions gainfully employed.

The Census of Manufacture for 1920 [17] enables us to compute the average earnings of the wage-earners in manufacturing during the preceding year in all the cities of the country which had a population of over 100,000. The Census of Occupations [18] in the same year also enables us to compute the proportion of each of the some eighteen age and sex groups in these same cities who were gainfully employed. These two sets of figures are shown in Tables X and XI of the appendix.[19] It is also possible to reduce the various cities to a standard age and sex distribution, and to show the proportions in each which would be employed were the composition of these populations to be in these respects identical.

We thus have for the same set of cities at the same time wages as one variable and the proportions gainfully employed as another. The question is whether there is any inter-relationship between these two series. We can begin to find out by computing simple coefficients of correlation and by fitting regression lines to the various series.[20]

Table 33 shows the various coefficients of correlation which exist between the average annual money earnings in manufacturing in 41 cities in 1919 and the proportions in each age and sex group who were gainfully employed in those cities.

---

[17] *Fourteenth Census*, 1920, Vol. VIII (Manufactures), pp. 222–38.

[18] *Ibid.*, (1920), Vol. IV (Occupations), pp. 452–4. The number listed as gainfully employed are not precisely those who actually have a job at the time the census is taken. They are instead those who are actually in the labor market seeking work.

[19] We have used only those cities for which there are statistics on retail food prices, so that the study of the relationship between (1) the proportions employed and (2) the relative money wages might cover the same area as that between the former and relative real wages.

[20] I am greatly indebted to Erika Schoenberg for the statistical computations on the points which follow.

TABLE 33

Coefficients of Correlation Between Average Money Earnings in Manufacturing in 41 Cities in 1919 and Proportions Gainfully Employed

Age Group	Male	Female
14 years	—.55	—.49
15	—.58	—.45
16	—.46	—.28
17	—.37	—.14
18–19	—.33	—.11
20–24	—.26	—.26
25–44	—.13	—.37
45–64	—.20	—.35
65 and over	—.37	—.44

On the whole, therefore, there seems to have been a decided negative relationship between the relative money earnings and the proportion who sought employment which was particularly marked in the case of (1) the young (2) women of the central age group and (3) the older groups. We would expect that when incomes were higher that proportionately fewer children would go to work and that more would be in school. Such a relationship is shown in fact to exist. The coefficients of correlation for the 14 year and the 15 year groups are moderately high, ranging between —.55 and —.58 for the boys and —.49 and —.45 for the girls. It is most interesting to note that the coefficient is also appreciably higher for the boys of 16, 17, and even 18 and 19 years than for the girls of those ages. This is probably due to the fact that since the boys have higher earning power than their sisters, they tend to go to work in larger proportions in the poorer families. An increase in earnings will, therefore, result in a larger percentage staying in school, who otherwise would be in industry, than is the case among girls of the same economic class.

It will be noticed that the degree of negative correlation between earnings and the proportions employed decreases for the males as the ages increase up to the 45 year mark, and that thereafter the correlation increases again. The coefficient is so low (—.13) as to be negligible for the great group of male workers in the 25 to 44 year class. These workers would tend to be employed in approximately the same proportions were their earnings to vary within any such normal range as is indicated by the 1919 averages.

It will also be observed that the inter-relationship between earnings and employment is relatively slight for young women from 17 to 20 years of age (i.e. —.14 and —.11). They apparently would tend to distribute themselves between industry, school, and the home, in much the same proportions even with such changes in wages as were covered by our figures.

The coefficient rises, however, to —.37 for women from 25 to 44 years and remains at virtually this level (—.35) for those between 45 and 64 years. This also is what would be expected since whether wives are gainfully employed depends in a very large measure upon the earnings of their husbands. Where wages are low they will be driven into the labor market in much greater numbers in order to eke out the family income than where the earnings of their husbands are higher.

The appreciable negative relationship which is disclosed between the ratios of those seeking employment in the group of 65 years and over and the level of wages is interesting and is susceptible of at least two interpretations: (1) that the high wage cities are also cities of a high degree of industrialization and that because of the latter factor, the aged find the pace too severe and are forced into retirement, and (2) that the higher wage levels in cities enable working class families to support old people more readily and permit the latter to leave work at an earlier age. This suggests that the historical decrease in the proportion over 65 who are gainfully employed may be due in part at least to the increase in real wages which occurred between 1890 and 1930.

The statistical purist may, however, very properly object to the apparent conclusiveness of these coefficients by pointing out that there is at least the possibility of circular reasoning and spurious correlation. The average annual earnings were found by dividing the total amounts paid out to the wage-earners by the average number employed. This latter figure, therefore, included women and children as well as men. It might, therefore, be argued that average earnings in some cities might have been lower than the average, because a larger than average proportion of women and children were employed in manufacturing, rather than that the larger proportion of women and children were so employed because the average earnings were low. If this were the case then, of course, any correlations as to the negative effect of changes in wages upon the proportions gainfully employed would be unwarranted.

Happily it is, however, possible to determine whether or not such spurious correlation is of any importance. This can be done by reducing the average earnings to an "equivalent male" basis so that differences in the proportion of women and children in the working force will not affect the average wage itself. This reduction of average earnings to an average "male equivalent" can in brief be carried through by finding out how many women are needed to equal a man in earning power and then dividing the total number of gainfully employed women by this figure to obtain the number of "equivalent males" whom in terms of earnings they equal. This number would then be added to the actual males and the combined total used as the divisor would then be applied to the total wage payments to find the average earnings per equivalent male. It should perhaps be added that while the earnings of children under 16 years are below the average for adult females their relative numbers in manufacturing are so slight that little error is caused by treating them as women.

The method followed may then be described as follows:

1. Estimating the probable ratio of women's earnings to men in each of the various cities

2. Multiplying the average number of women and children employed in each city by this ratio in order to obtain

3. The number of "equivalent males" which the women and children equalled.

This last figure when added to the actual males in each group gave the total "equivalent males," and with this, average earnings per "equivalent male" were, of course, easy to compute. The same method may be shown somewhat differently by the following formula.

$$\text{Earnings per "equivalent male"} = \frac{\text{Average earnings per worker}}{\frac{\text{Number male workers}}{\text{Total workers}} + \left(\frac{\text{Female workers}}{\text{Total workers}} \times \frac{\text{Average Female Earnings}}{\text{Average Male Earnings}}\right)}$$

But this refinement necessarily rests upon the ability to determine the ratio of women's wages to men in each of the cities, and it may well be asked how this can possibly be done in view of the fact that the census of manufactures does not differentiate between the sums which are paid to men and those paid to women. Happily, however, the United States Bureau of Labor Statistics in 1919 conducted an industrial survey of wages in different industries and different parts of the country which showed the ratio of women's daily earnings to those of men in the various states.[21] We took, therefore, these various state ratios as applying to the cities which were located within the respective states.

An excellent check upon the validity of this method is afforded in the case of New York State where there are studies both for wages of women and of men. The ratio of women's wages (hourly earnings × the standard number of hours per day) to those of men was given by the survey of the Bureau of Labor Statistics as .545. In Special Bulletin 143 of the New York State Bureau of Labor Statistics the ratio between the wages of women and men is given as .55, or a virtually identical proportion to that shown by the study of the Federal Bureau. The ratio in New York City is shown by the state study to have been .59 while that for "Upstate" was .50. In industries which are present in both New York City and Upstate, the greatest difference between the two ratios is .17, so that we may conclude that the maximum error of the state average from the local averages is probably not over .10. This would result in an error in the average wage per "male" in manufacturing of not over 3 per cent.

By thus eliminating the influence of women's wages from the general average and correlating the average earnings per "equivalent male," with the proportions of each age and sex group who were gainfully employed, we obtain the coefficients of correlation which are shown in Table 34. The detailed statistical material both for the average earnings in manufacturing per adult male and the proportions of each age and sex groups who were gainfully employed is given in the appendix in Tables X to XIV.

It will thus be seen that this correction instead of reducing the coefficients of correlation has in general increased them. This is particularly the case in the groups of women above the age of 25. The coefficients for these three groups, 25–44 years, 45–64 years, and over 65 years, are as a matter of fact raised by .10, .13, and .11 respectively. The coefficients for men in the 45–64 year group is also raised from —.20 to —.25 and for those of 65 and over from —.37 to —.43. The apparent negative relationship between the level of earnings and the proportion of the population employed may, therefore, be said to have survived the first wave of criticism.

---

[21] See *Bulletin 265 of the United States Bureau of Labor Statistics*, "Industrial Survey of Selected Industries in the United States, 1919."

TABLE 34

COEFFICIENTS OF CORRELATION BETWEEN AVERAGE MONEY EARNINGS PER
"EQUIVALENT MALE" IN 41 CITIES IN MANUFACTURING IN 1919 AND
PROPORTIONS OF AGE AND SEX GROUPS GAINFULLY EMPLOYED

Age Group	Male	Female
14	−.60	−.46
15	−.56	−.36
16	−.35	−.13
17	−.24	+.04
18–19	−.22	+.07
20–24	−.18	−.20
25–44	−.08	−.47
45–64	−.25	−.48
65 and over	−.43	−.55

4. The Relationship Between Differences in Real Wages And Differences in The Proportions Gainfully Employed

But a second wave of criticism follows closely. How can we assume, it will be queried, that differences in *money wages* between cities represent differences in *real wages?* If we were to reduce the differences in money wages to differences in effective purchasing power might not this apparent relationship disappear? Let us see.

In order to transpose relative differences in money wages as between cities into differences in real wages, it is, of course, necessary to compute an index of the relative cost of living as between these cities. Cost of living studies in their concentration upon differences in time have tended to ignore differences in space.[22] There has been no index thus far computed in this country which would measure these comparative differences and so it was necessary to construct one for this purpose. The methods used in obtaining this geographical index for 1919 were as follows:

First, the average budget of commodities consumed in 1918–1919 by the 12,000 families who were sampled by the Bureau of Labor Statistics [23] was taken as the standard for each of the cities and this is given in Table XV of the appendix. Then the average quantities of the various food items which were consumed in the country as a whole were multiplied by the aver-

---

[22] Yet see the study by the International Labor Office: *An International Inquiry into Costs of Living* (1931).

[23] Bulletin 354 of the U. S. Bureau of Labor Statistics, *Cost of Living in the United States.*

age prices of each item in each of the cities during this time.[24]
These products were then summed, and the total cost of an
identical food budget was thus obtained for 41 cities. The
costs for each city were then reduced to relatives by dividing
the respective totals by the average for the cities as a whole.
The average yearly earnings per equivalent adult male in manufacturing for each of the cities were then divided by the index
of food costs to obtain averages of relative real annual earnings
in terms of dollars which, so far as food were concerned, had a
constant purchasing power.

I have thus far spoken of one index of comparative living
costs, namely, that of food items, and consequently of only one
index of real earnings. In reality, three such indexes were constructed. The second index added to food the following items:
heat, light, and dry goods. The third consisted of the commodities used in the second index, plus rent. The cost of the rent
items was computed by multiplying the average number of
rooms used per family in the United States (i.e., 4.5 for apart-
ments and 5.0 for houses) by the cost in each city of a "room"
as reckoned on both a house and an apartment basis.

It is now possible to compute the degree of relationship
between differences in the real wages between cities and the
proportions gainfully employed. Table 35 shows this in terms
of the average wages of the "males" as corrected for differences
in food costs alone.

TABLE 35

COEFFICIENTS OF CORRELATION BETWEEN AVERAGE REAL WAGES PER
EQUIVALENT MALE IN 41 CITIES AS CORRECTED FOR DIFFERENCES
IN FOOD COSTS AND THE PROPORTIONS OF VARIOUS AGE AND SEX
GROUPS WHO ARE GAINFULLY EMPLOYED

Age Group	Male	Female
14	−.66	−.53
15	−.65	−.45
16	−.50	−.20
17	−.32	−.01
18–19	−.31	+.02
20–24	−.28	−.23
25–44	−.16	−.52
45–64	−.28	−.56
65 and over	−.48	−.63

It will be seen that by thus refining our figures the coefficients
are raised appreciably. The increase in the coefficients over

[24] *Ibid.*

those obtained for "equivalent adult" money wages in 41 cities
are as follows for each of the groups.

TABLE 36

NUMBER OF POINTS BY WHICH COEFFICIENT OF CORRELATION WAS RAISED BY
USE OF INDEX OF REAL INSTEAD OF MONEY WAGES

Age Group	Male	Female
14	+.06	+.07
15	+.09	+.09
16	+.15	+.07
17	+.08	....[1]
18–19	+.09	....[2]
20–24	+.10	+.03
25–44	+.08	+.05
45–64	+.03	+.08
65 and over	+.05	+.08

[1] Changed from +.04 to —.01
[2] Changed from +.07 to +.02

Some of the correlation coefficients were in fact raised to a
very appreciable height. Those for the boys of 14 and 15 years
were raised to —.66 and —.65 respectively, while those for the
girls of these ages were increased to —.53 and —.45 respectively.
The coefficients for the women over 25 years became also materially higher to values of —.52 for those between the ages of
25 and 45, —.56 for those in the next twenty-year group from
45 to 65 years and to no less than —.63 for those over 65.

The use of the second index of living costs (which included
heat, light, and dry goods, in addition to food) gave indexes of
comparative real wages which in turn resulted in slightly lower
coefficients of correlation with proportions gainfully employed.
The difference between the first two sets of correlations were,
however, slight, and the second index still gives somewhat higher
coefficients than the use of relative money earnings. Experiments were also made with the third index of living costs, but
it was finally discarded because the housing accommodations
which were sampled in the various cities were quite small and
inadequate and because there was no surety that the unit used,
namely a "room" was uniform as between the different cities.

5. The Reduction of The Cities to A Common Sex And
     Age Composition And The Determination of A Short
     Time Supply Curve of Labor in so far as The Propor-
     tion Gainfully Employed Is Concerned

The statistical work developed thus far has left us with
18 different population groups for which coefficients of correla-

tion have been found. There are two further problems which confront us, and with them the third and fourth waves bear down upon us. These are, first to consolidate these separate measures into one set of relationships for each city as a whole, and second to derive that portion of the supply curve of labor which is based on the relative numbers employed in relation to various amounts of wages. To these tasks we now turn.

Since the various cities differ in their relative age and sex distribution, one cannot correctly compare the proportions of their total populations which are gainfully employed unless we take account of these differences.

The following table shows the composition of the populations of Chicago and Detroit in 1920.[25]

TABLE 37

The Age and Sex Distribution in Chicago and Detroit in 1920
(Number of Persons per 1000 of Total Population Who
Belonged to the Respective Age and Sex Groups)

Years	Chicago		Detroit	
	Male	Female	Male	Female
14	7.6	7.5	6.3	6.2
15	6.9	7.2	5.7	5.8
16	7.5	7.9	6.4	6.8
17	7.2	7.5	6.7	6.7
18–19	14.4	16.1	16.8	15.6
20–24	42.3	49.0	59.4	50.7
25–44	187.2	172.3	229.5	164.7
45–64	85.7	76.5	70.6	58.0
65 and over	15.6	17.7	11.6	13.3

Thus far we have only found the coefficients of correlation between earnings and the proportions gainfully employed for each of the eighteen separate age and sex groups. We have not found the relationship between these phenomena for the combined population in each of the forty-one cities.

Cities like Detroit may have an apparently high proportion of the population gainfully employed because they have an abnormally large proportion of men in the active years from 25 to 45, while cities like Los Angeles and Miami may have a low proportion of their total number who will be so employed simply because they have so many in the super-annuated groups over 65 years. Some of the differences between these crude

---

[25] This is derived from Volume II of the Fourteenth (1920) Census, Table 15.

proportions would, therefore, be due to a differing composition of the population, and we could not be justified in ascribing these differences to differing levels of real wages.

It is, therefore, necessary to eliminate this source of error by reducing the population of each city to a standard age and sex distribution. We have indeed chosen a double standard for refining our figures and have used the relative age and sex composition in 1920 of both Chicago and Detroit as the standards to be applied to other cities. To the numbers in every 1000 of total population who would fall into each of the eighteen sub-groups in these two cities were applied the percentages of these groups which were gainfully employed in each of the forty-one cities. By summating the results for these groups, we therefore found for each city the number out of each thousand who would have been employed had the population conformed to the Chicago and Detroit standards.

These series as given in Table XVI in the appendix were then correlated with that of the comparative real earnings in the cities.[26] The coefficient of correlation was —.627 for the 41 cities when the population of Chicago was used as the standard and —.619 in the case of Detroit. These are relatively high correlations in themselves and approximately seven times the standard error which was .09 on the basis of the Chicago distribution. Since the square of the coefficient of correlation (r^2) is probably the best measure of the degree of inter-relationship we can say that the mutually interacting effects of variations in wages and in those seeking employment probably accounted for about two-fifths of the variations which occurred.

It is probable that a better measure would be obtained if we were to drop Washington, Salt Lake City, and Fall River. The first is a city inhabited mainly by Government employees, and although wages were only about average there, the proportion employed was abnormally high. In Salt Lake City on the other hand, although the earnings were about the same, the proportion employed was very low. In Fall River, with its large foreign mill population and its textile mills, wages were very low, and the proportions employed far more than would be expected. Reducing our series in this manner from 41 to 38 cities raises the coefficients to —.70 according to the Chicago distribution and to —.69 on that of Detroit. The standard error in the former

---

[26] As measured by average annual money earnings corrected for differences in food costs.

series was 0.082 or less than one-eighth the size of the coefficient.[27]

The question then inevitably arises why we should obtain such a high degree of correlation for the population as a whole, namely one which is as high as the best for the 18 individual groups.

It might indeed be expected at first thought that the lower coefficients of the other groups would naturally reduce that for

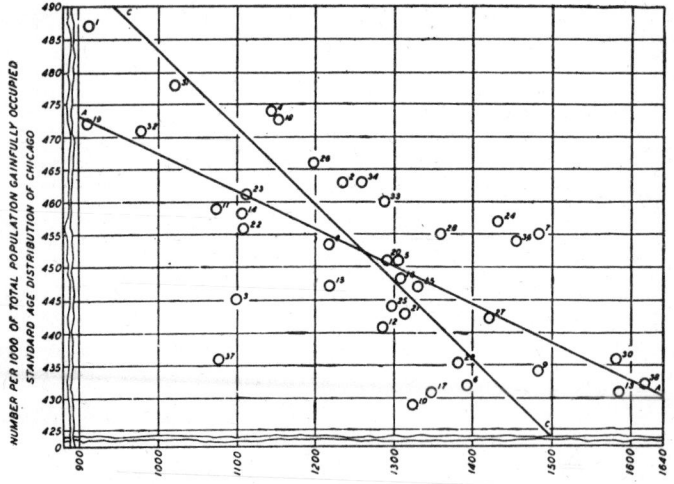

AVERAGE REAL EARNINGS PER MALE WORKER

Chart 54. The Short-Run Supply Curve of Labor in so far as the Proportions Employed Are Concerned. (Distribution on the Basis of Chicago Standard Population, 38 Cities.) The line AA is the regression of the number gainfully employed per 1000 standard population on the average real earnings per male worker; the line CC is the regression of earnings on the number employed. (The numbers refer to the cities in alphabetical order.)

the population as a whole. But such a line of reasoning mistakes the essential nature of correlation. Correlation takes into account not the absolute amounts of the differences from the mean, but merely the relative coincidence of the differences. By summating all the age and sex groups, those groups which were not correlated with the real wage series had no other effect than to add to the absolute value of the average and thus in themselves did not lessen the deviations from the averages

---

[27] The standard error of estimate in the case of the 41 cities was 15.6 persons per 1000 persons of standard (Chicago) distribution and $138.20. In the case of the 38 cities, the corresponding standard errors of estimate were lowered to 10.4 persons and $125.30.

which were then correlated. The high degree of correlation for the population as a whole does show, however, that the tendencies within the various groups do not conflict with but rather supplement each other.

Charts 54 and 55 are a graphic representation of the observed relation between the number gainfully employed per 1000 of total population (x) and the average real annual earnings per equivalent male worker (y). It is evident from these scatter diagrams that the relation between the variables is

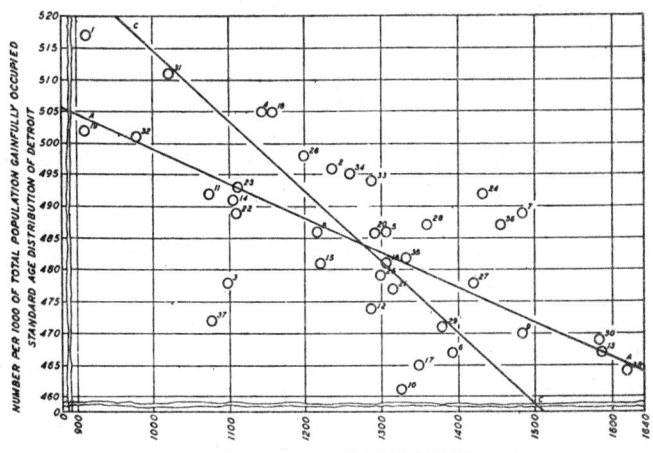

Chart 55. The Short-Run Supply Curve of Labor in so far as the Proportions Employed Are Concerned. (Distribution on the Basis of Detroit Standard Population, 38 Cities.) The line AA is the regression of the number gainfully employed per 1000 standard population on the average real earnings per male worker; the line CC is the regression of earnings on the number employed.

linear. The line A in chart 54 (the regression of x on y) which was fitted by the method of least squares gives the most probable change in the number employed corresponding to a given change in the real earnings. Since earnings are taken as the independent variable and the number employed as the dependent variable, the former is measured on the horizontal axis (abscissa) and the latter on the vertical axis (ordinate). This is the reverse of the procedure usually followed by English and American economists who tend to measure quantity on the horizontal and price on the vertical axis. This chart and those which follow may therefore seem at first unfamiliar, but the arrangement is more logical and those who find it somewhat strange can simply reverse the charts. The equation of line A in chart 54 is:

$$x = 528.68 - .0584 \, (\pm 0.010)y \qquad (1)$$

This means that, based upon the experience of 38 American cities in 1919 an increase of one dollar in the real annual earnings was on the average associated with a decrease of 0.06 persons per 1000 of total "standard" population. This is the equivalent of saying that for each increase of \$17.12 in the average real annual earnings there would be a decrease of one person

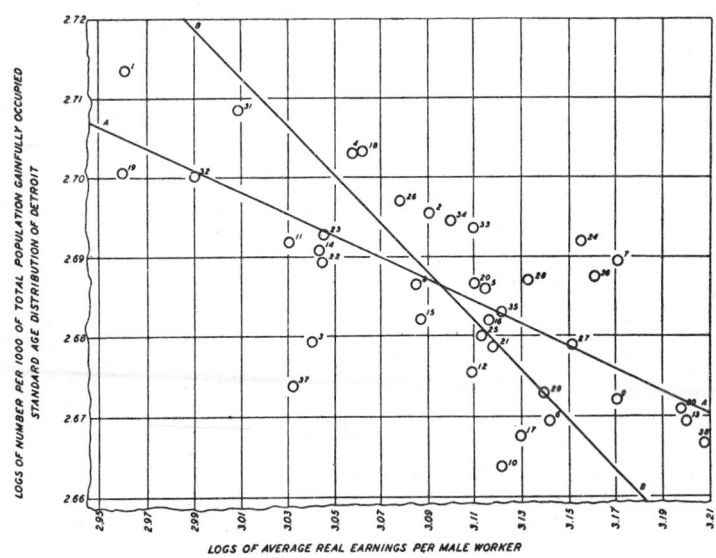

Chart 56. The Short-Run Supply Curve of Labor in so far as the Proportions Gainfully Employed Are Concerned Fitted to the Logarithms of the Observations. (Distribution on the Basis of Chicago Standard Population.) The line AA is the regression of the number employed on earnings; the line BB is the regression of earnings on the number employed.

employed per 1000 of total standard population. If we use the material for 41 cities equation (1) becomes:

$$x = 542.76 - .0707 \, (\pm 0.014)y \qquad (2)$$

Based upon the experience of 41 cities, an increase of one dollar in the real annual earnings was therefore on the average associated with a decrease of 0.07 persons employed per 1000 of total population, and an increase of \$14.14 in the average real annual earnings was accompanied by a decrease of one person employed in every 1000 of total standard population.

The corresponding equations on the basis of the Detroit age and sex distribution are as follows:

(for 38 cities) $x = 552.46 - .0532 (\pm 0.009)y$ (3)
(for 41 cities) $x = 568.20 - .0646 (\pm 0.013)y$ (4)

These are substantially the same results as those obtained on the Chicago basis.

Regression lines have also been fitted to the logarithms of the observations, and these are shown in charts 56 and 57 where again earnings as the independent variable are plotted on the abscissa and the number employed is plotted on the ordinate.

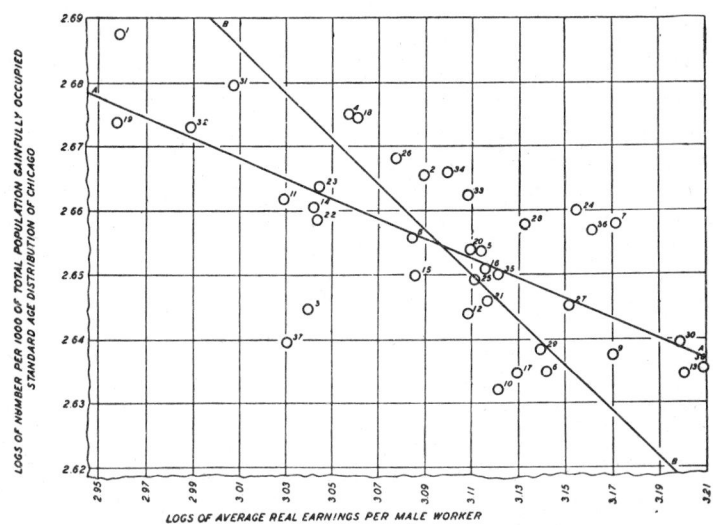

Chart 57. The Short-Run Supply Curve of Labor in so far as the Proportions Gainfully Employed Are Concerned Fitted to the Logarithms of the Observations. (Distribution on the Basis of Detroit Standard Population.)   The line AA is the regression of the number employed on earnings; the line BB is the regression of earnings on the number employed.

The equations to the lines A (the regression of x on y) are as follows:

Chicago basis, 38 cities:
$\log x = 3.13847 - 0.15614 (\pm 0.030) \log y$ (5)

Detroit basis, 38 cities:
$\log x = 3.09888 - 0.13336 (\pm 0.025) \log y$ (6)

The numbers in parentheses refer in all equations to the standard error of the regression coefficient. It will be noticed that these standard errors are relatively small ranging from one-fifth to one-seventh of the values of the parameters. The probability that the results were obtained purely by chance is therefore small.

The regression equations of earnings on the number employed (the regression of y on x) were also computed. The values are given in the footnote,[28] but the lines have been drawn in the respective charts. Thus the line C in chart 54 gives the most probable change in the real annual earnings corresponding to a given change in the number employed. It is, however, more logical to assume that the earnings in the various cities affected the number employed, and for that reason the regression of x on y is more significant than that of y on x, and it has accordingly been emphasized.

Having obtained the supply curve of labor in terms of the population gainfully employed we are now in a position to compute the coefficients of the elasticity of supply (e) which is defined as the ratio of the relative change in the number employed to the corresponding relative change in real annual earnings, when the relative changes are infinitesimal. In mathematical symbols, the coefficient of elasticity of supply is therefore:

$$e_{xy} = \frac{dx}{x} \left/ \frac{dy}{y} \right. = \frac{dx}{dy} \cdot \frac{y}{x}$$

In the case of a straight line fitted to the arithmetic data the coefficient of elasticity will vary from point to point. It will be higher for higher earnings and a small number employed than for low earnings and a large proportion employed. This follows from the fact that while the ratio $\dfrac{dx}{dy}$ is constant, the ratio $\dfrac{y}{x}$ varies. Its numerical value will obviously be greater the farther to the right one progresses.

At the means of both series the coefficients of elasticity are as follows:

Chicago basis: $e_{xy} = -0.16$
Detroit basis: $e_{xy} = -0.14$

This means that if the earnings are increased by 1 per cent, other things remaining the same, there will be a decrease of

[28] || Chicago basis: 38 cities.
$y = 5071.48 - 8.425 \, (\pm 1.427)x$
$\log y = 10.53405 - 2.80108 \, (\pm 0.530) \log x$
Detroit basis: 38 cities:
$y = 5589.23 - 8.912 \, (\pm 1.57) \, x$
$\log y = 11.90042 - 3.27755 \, (\pm 0.620) \log x$

0.16 per cent in the number employed per 1000 of total population standardized on the Chicago age and sex distribution.

This coefficient of elasticity was obtained in the following fashion. According to equation (1) $\frac{dx}{dy}$ is equal to — 0.0584. The average real annual earnings for the 38 cities (y) were $1264.84, while the average number employed per 1000 standard population (x) was 451.84. Substituting these values in the above formula, we obtain:

$$e_{xy} = -0.0584 \cdot \frac{1264.84}{451.84}$$
$$= -.163$$

If, on the other hand, the elasticity of demand is deduced from equation (5), or from the logarithms of the numbers, its value is constant for every point on the supply curve and equal to the slope of the supply curve. The numerical values of these constant coefficients are given below:

Chicago basis: $e_{log\,x\,log\,y} = -0.16$
Detroit basis: $e_{log\,x\,log\,y} = -0.13$

It will be seen that the results are almost identically the same and it is, therefore, apparently correct to conclude, so far as the 1919 data are concerned, that the elasticity of the number employed in respect to changes in real annual earnings lies somewhere between — 0.13 and — 0.16.

6. The Elasticities of Supply of The Numbers Employed for Specific Age And Sex Groups

We may now revert for a moment to the elasticities not for the population as a whole but for the separate age and sex groups. These have been found for the 38 cities on the basis of the Chicago standard distribution by an identical method to that just described. The following table shows the coefficients of elasticity for each of the eighteen groups.

This study shows some very interesting results:

(1) The elasticity of the supply of labor in the juvenile groups of 14 and 15 years is extremely high. Thus a change of 1 per cent in average annual earnings will produce a change in the opposite direction of 3.76 per cent of the fourteen year old girls seeking employment, about 3 per cent of the fourteen year old boys, and about 1.9 and 1.6 per cent in the case of the fifteen year girls and boys.

(2) The coefficient of elasticity then decreases rapidly as one moves into the higher age groups. For the males it falls to — .57

for the 16 year olds, to — .24 for those of 17 years, and to — .14 for those who are 18 and 19 years. It decreases to — .45 for the girls of 16. The effects of differences in earnings upon the proportion of young women of from 17 to 19 years who seek work seems to be negligible. The coefficient amounts to only — .01 for the 17 year olds and to + .02 for those of 18 and 19.

TABLE 38

ELASTICITIES OF SUPPLY OF PROPORTION OF WORKERS SEEKING EMPLOYMENT IN RELATION TO REAL AVERAGE EARNINGS (REGRESSION OF X ON Y) AS SHOWN BY STATISTICS FOR 38 CITIES IN 1919
Coefficients of Elasticity

Age Group	Males	Females
14	−2.98	−3.76
15	−1.56	−1.88
16	−0.57	−0.45
17	−0.24	−0.01
18–19	−0.14	+0.02
20–24	−0.06	−0.22
25–44	−0.01	−0.72
45–64	−0.03	−0.96
65 and over	−0.22	−1.55

(3) The effect of differences in real earnings is very slight upon the proportions of the male population who seek employment during the active years from 20 to 65. Thus the coefficient for the 20–24 year group is only — .06 while for those between 25 and 44 it is — .01 and for the 45–64 year class it is still but — .03.

(4) For the women between 20 and 65, however, differences in earnings seem appreciably to affect the proportion who seek work. Thus the coefficient rises to — .22 for those from 20 to 24 years of age, to — .72 for those from 25 to 44 years and to no less than .96 for those who are between 45 and 65 years.

(5) For those over 65 years the elasticity of supply is particularly high for women namely — 1.55 and higher than it was for men *i.e.* — .22.

We can therefore say that changes in earnings affect particularly the proportions of young children, of youths, of women from 20 years upward, and those over 65, particularly females. There seems to be little effect upon young girls from 17 to 19 or upon men in the active years.

It would seem, therefore, that if real wages should rise so that a much smaller proportion of children under 17 and old people over 65 who sought work would sharply decrease, then the subsequent negative elasticity of the labor supply would be less than that indicated in the preceding section of this chapter.

7. The Elimination of Possibly Extraneous Influences: The Partial Coefficient of Correlation and Partial Elasticities of Supply

One final objection may still be levelled at our method. The differences between the cities in the proportions gainfully employed may not have been caused primarily by differences in real average earnings at all but rather by differences in the nationality and racial stocks which composed the cities. Thus the presence of a large proportion of foreign-born with their assumed tradition that every one should work may have been the force rather than low earnings to send up the proportions employed in certain cities, while large groups of negroes may have exercised some influence in others.

Some way must, therefore, be found to eliminate the effects of these factors by holding them constant. This can be done through the method of partial correlation which enables us to find the net correlation between the number employed and real wages when the effect of the foreign-born and negroes is eliminated.[29] Let us first see how different the results will be when we use this method for the standardized populations as a whole and then for the separate age and sex groups. Instead of writing $x = a + by$, we wrote the equation as follows: $x = a + by + cz$, where z is the proportion of the population which was either foreign-born or negro. Account was also taken of the native-born of foreign parentage by adding them to the negroes and foreign-born to form a group labelled as v, so that still another equation was written, namely, $x = a + by + cv$. The partial coefficients of correlation for the 38 cities with their standard errors and as compared with the simple correlation coefficients which have already been given were as follows:

	Chicago basis	Detroit basis
r_{xy}	$-0.701 \ (\pm 0.082)$	$-0.688 \ (\pm 0.085)$
$r_{xy.z}$	$-0.677 \ (\pm 0.088)$	$-0.660 \ (\pm 0.092)$
$r_{xy.v}$	$-0.721 \ (\pm 0.078)$	$-0.689 \ (\pm 0.085)$

It will thus be seen that the influence of the foreign-born and negroes upon the number employed is negligible, and that approximately the same degree of relationship exists between the

---

[29] For a description of the method of partial correlation see F. C. Mills, *Statistical Methods*, pp. 500–14.

number employed and real wages, when the proportion of foreign-born and negroes are not allowed to influence the former.

The elasticity of the number employed in relation to real annual earnings was, it will be remembered, — 0.16 and — 0.14 for the Chicago and Detroit age distribution respectively. When the number employed is a function of the real earnings, and of the proportion foreign-born and negroes, we must make use of the concept of partial elasticity

$$e_{xy.z} = \frac{\partial x}{\partial y} \cdot \frac{y}{x}^{30}$$

The numerical values of these partial elasticities of supply for the populations as a whole were as follows:

	Chicago basis	Detroit basis
$e_{xy.z}$	−0.15	−0.13
$e_{xy.v}$	−0.17	−0.15

Turning now to the separate age and sex groups, we are compelled to re-classify these somewhat because of the form in

TABLE 38A

COMPARATIVE SIMPLE AND PARTIAL COEFFICIENTS OF CORRELATION BETWEEN PROPORTIONS GAINFULLY EMPLOYED AND REAL ANNUAL EARNINGS IN 1919

Age and Sex Groups	Simple Correlation		Partial Correlation			
	r_{xy}	S.E.	$r_{xy.z}$	S.E.	$r_{xy.v}$	S.E.
1. 10–14 yrs.						
Males.......	−.575	(±.11)	−.329	(±.14)	−.575	(±.11)
Females.....	−.642	(±.10)	−.589	(±.11)	−.693	(±.08)
2. 15–19 yrs.						
Males.......	−.409	(±.14)	−.260	(±.14)	−.472	(±.13)
Females.....	−.003	(±.16)	−.140	(±.16)	−.057	(±.16)
3. 20–24 yrs.						
Males.......	−.257	(±.15)	−.091	(±.16)	.....	......
Females.....	−.113	(±.16)	−.229	(±.15)	.....	......
4. 25–44 yrs.						
Males.......	−.073	(±.16)	−.114	(±.16)	.....	......
Females.....	−.604	(±.10)	−.616	(±.10)	.....	......
5. 45–64 yrs.						
Males.......	−.321	(±.15)	−.346	(±.14)	.....	......
Females.....	−.485	(±.12)	−.458	(±.13)	.....	......
6. 65 yrs. and over						
Males.......	−.501	(±.12)	−.532	(±.12)	.....	......
Females.....	−.707	(±.08)	−.659	(±.09)	.....	......

---

[30] H. L. Moore, *Synthetic Economics*, 1929, p. 55.

which the statistics concerning the foreign-born and negroes are given.

Let us first compare the partial coefficients of correlation with the simple for each of these groups as in Table 38A. It is thus apparent that taking account of the foreign-born, negroes and native-born children of foreign parentage produces no significant change in the correlation coefficients. It is true if we consider only the foreign-born and negroes that the partial coefficient ($r_{xy.z}$) is lower than the simple coefficient (r_x) for both sexes in the 10–14 year group and for the males in the 15–19 year group. If, however, we include the native-born children of foreign parentage, the partial coefficients for two of these groups ($r_{xy.v}$) are slightly higher than the simple coefficients, and in the third case an identical coefficient is obtained. This shows that the foreign-born have apparently an even greater

TABLE 38B

COMPARATIVE SIMPLE AND PARTIAL ELASTICITIES OF PROPORTIONS GAINFULLY EMPLOYED IN RELATION TO REAL ANNUAL EARNINGS OF VARIOUS AGE AND SEX GROUPS IN 1919

Age and Sex Groups	Simple Elasticity e_{xy}	Partial Elasticity (Foreign-Born and Negroes Constant) $e_{xy.z}$	Partial Elasticity (Foreign-Born, Negroes and Native Children of Foreign Parentage Constant) $e_{xy.v}$
1. 10–14 yrs.			
Males........	−2.205	−1.187	−2.120
Females.....	−2.849	−3.016	−2.938
2. 15–19 yrs.			
Males........	−.268	−.177	−.298
Females*.....	,......	....	....
3. 20–24 yrs.			
Males*.......	−.053	....	....
Females*.....	....	....	....
4. 25–44 yrs.			
Males*.......	−.003	....	....
Females.....	−.649	−.673	....
5. 45–64 yrs.			
Males*.......	−.031	−.034	....
Females*.....	−.780	−.715	....
6. 65 yrs. and over			
Males*.......	−.275	−.319	....
Females*.....	−1.728	−1.571	....

* No coefficients of elasticity are given where the results are not believed to have significance.

zeal for the education of their native-born children than have
the native Americans.

Passing now to the partial elasticities of supply for these
various groups the results are shown in Table 38B. Here again
it is seen that the results are not appreciably altered by taking
the foreign-born, the negroes, and the native-born children of
foreign parentage into account.

The fact that the supply curve of labor, in so far as the proportions employed are concerned, is negatively inclined is therefore almost conclusively reinforced and confirmed. We may
therefore take — .16 as the most probable value of the elasticity
in 1919, although it should be realized that this negative elasticity is almost entirely confined to children, youths, old people
and women over 25 years. In terms of productive effectiveness,
therefore, it is probable that the effect upon production is less
than if these numbers were drawn evenly from adult workers of
both sexes as well as from the classes indicated.

NOTE

THE CORRELATION BETWEEN DIFFERENCES IN REAL
EARNINGS AND SCHOOL ATTENDANCE

Dr. F. A. Ross[31] in his monograph on *School Attendance* has
worked out valuable inter-relationships between the proportions who
attended school in 1920 in various localities and other phenomena.
By correlating our data on real earnings with the census statistics on
school attendance, we obtain the following coefficients.

COEFFICIENTS OF CORRELATION (r) BETWEEN RELATIVE SCHOOL ATTENDANCE AND
RELATIVE REAL EARNINGS IN 41 AMERICAN CITIES, 1920

Age Group	Males	Females
14–15 years	+0.62	+0.52
16–17 years	+0.35	+0.23
18–19 years	+0.36	+0.24

This shows that when earnings were relatively high, that not only
did a smaller number not go to work but a larger number went to
school.

[31] F. A. Ross, *School Attendance in 1920*, Census Monograph V.

CHAPTER XII

THE SHORT-RUN SUPPLY CURVE OF LABOR

Hours of Work

The second main variable in the short-run supply of labor is that of the number of hours worked per week. The economists of the last half century have occasionally noted that there seemed to be a negative relationship between wages per hour and the number of hours worked. Thus Simiand, the celebrated French statistician and economist, in his classic study of wages in the French coal mines from 1847 to 1902 found that in the years when the tonnage rates were decreased the daily output increased, while in the years when the rates were appreciably advanced, the output per day either actually diminished or did not increase. Simiand concluded from this that[1] "if the amount of the wage be reduced the tendency of the workers to maintain the same daily wage is, under this form, sufficiently strong to call forth a greater intensity of effort."

In recent years Knight and Robbins have subjected the question of the effect of changes of income upon hours to a penetrating analysis. Thus Knight pointed out[2] that a worker would rationally only work to that point where the utility or satisfaction derived from the money received for the last unit of employed time was just equal to the disutility experienced as a result of that same unit of work. This disutility might of course either be an outright loss of satisfaction resulting from the work itself, or a sacrifice of alternative satisfaction which might have been derived from leisure, or a combination of both. There would however be equivalence between "utility" and "disutility" at this margin. If wages were increased, then because of the familiar principle of the diminishing utility of money, the added units of money would give fewer additional units of satisfaction than did the previous smaller payment for

---

[1] F. S. Simiand, *Le Salaire des Ouvriers des Mines de Charbon en France,* pp. 243 ff.

[2] Knight, *Risk, Uncertainty and Profit.* pp. 117–118. This was in fact an extension of the principle of equivalence at the margins which Wicksteed had so suggestively developed in his *The Commonsense of Political Economy.*

the last unit of time. There would therefore be a lack of balance at the last unit of employed time and the added disutility would now be greater than the added utility. The worker in order to redress this balance would therefore presumably decrease the length of his working day until there was once again an equivalence. Increases in wages caused, therefore, a decrease in the quantity of labor offered, while a decrease in wages had presumably the opposite effect. Knight therefore believed that the short-time supply curve of labor so far as hours were concerned was negatively inclined.[3] He did not however push the matter further to inquire what was the probable elasticity of this negative supply curve.

The conclusiveness of this line of reasoning has recently been challenged by Lionel Robbins [4] who has pointed out that were it invariably true then no one would work longer hours in return for a higher income. He reasoned with logic that whether or not one worked shorter hours with more pay and longer hours with less, depended on the elasticity of demand for income in terms of effort. To develop this point, Robbins used a diagrammatic method of analysis which was virtually identical with that employed to show relative elasticities of demand for commodities in terms of prices. Thus quantity of income was measured on the horizontal, or X axis (abscissa), while "units of effort per unit of income" were measured on the vertical, or Y axis (ordinate). Robbins did not define what he meant by "effort," and this ambiguity makes his argument seem more difficult than it really is. It is probable that he meant by this the units of labor-time expended per unit of income and that he did not mean to measure effort in terms of average or marginal psychic disutility per unit of income. In any event, since his analysis makes sense if time is made the equivalent of "effort," and is of very doubtful sense if disutility is used, we shall use time.

The number of hours which would be worked for a given income would be a function of these two variables, namely total income desired in terms of the time required to obtain each unit of income. If real wages per unit of time worked increased, causing the number of units of labor-time per unit of income to

---

[3] Pigou was apparently of the same opinion. See *Economics of Welfare,* 1st edition, p. 593, and *Public Finance,* pp. 83–84.

[4] Lionel Robbins. "On the Elasticity of Demand for Income in Terms of Effort." *Economica,* Vol. X (1930), pp. 123–129.

fall in a reciprocal fashion, the question as to whether more or less time would be expended would in practise depend on the elasticity of one's demand for income in terms of labor-time. The principles involved may be demonstrated both by a graphic illustration and by the working out of some hypothetical examples.

Thus in Chart 57A OE_2 represents the original number of units of labor-time which has to be expended for each unit of income and OI_2 the total units of income which the worker received. The total amount of time worked was therefore $OE_2 \times OI_2$ or $OI_2P_2E_2$. Now let us assume that the hourly rate of real wages is raised. This will mean that fewer units of labor-time will be required to obtain each unit of income. This new ratio is represented by OE_1 instead of OE_2 as before. Now let us suppose that under these new conditions, the worker wants OI_1 units of income or I_2I_1 more units than before. The total length of time worked would now be $OI_1P_1E_1$. Whether or not this would be greater than the previous

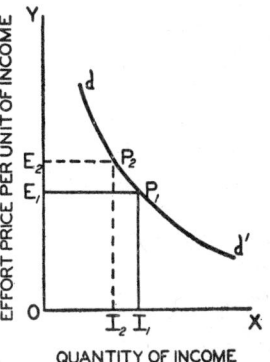

Chart 57. A. A Graphic Illustration of the Demand for Income in Terms of Effort, after Lionel Robbins.

time worked, $OI_2P_2E_2$, would depend upon whether or not the elasticity of demand for income was greater than unity. It it were, then the proportional increase in the total quantity of income demanded would be greater than the decrease in the amount of time required for each unit of income. Under these conditions, the worker would work more rather than fewer hours, and this of course would mean a positively inclined supply curve of labor. If, however, the elasticity of demand for income was less than unity, the increased total income desired would not be sufficient to balance the decline in the amount of working time required to obtain each unit of income, and the result would be that the total length of the working week or year would decrease. This would mean a negatively inclined supply curve.

The nature of the problem may be still more clearly illustrated if we work through certain numerical illustrations of the principles involved. Thus let us assume that at an hourly rate of pay of 30 cents, a worker chose to work 10 hours or 600 minutes a day. His total daily income (X) was therefore \$3.00

a day, and he had to work 2 minutes for each cent he received (Y). Now let us assume that his hourly rate is raised to 40 cents so that he now has to work only $1\frac{1}{2}$ minutes for each cent. If under these conditions he now chooses a $4.00 daily income this will mean that his elasticity of demand for income is equal to unity, and he will work precisely the same amount of time as before, namely for 10 hours.

Since the elasticity of demand is measured by the formula:

(1) $e = \dfrac{dx}{dy} \cdot \dfrac{y}{x}$ which can also be written

(2) $e = \dfrac{d \log x}{d \log y}$, we obtain

$$\frac{\log 400 - \log 300}{\log 1.5 - \log 2.0} = \frac{2.60206 - 2.47712}{.17609 - .30103} = \frac{.12494}{-.12494} = -1.0$$

It follows, therefore, that, when the elasticity of demand for income is equal to unity, the same amount of labor will be expended, whatever the income.

Robbins did not touch on the precise nature of the interrelations between the elasticity of demand for income and the elasticity of supply of labor except to determine whether the supply function would be negative or positive. And yet it is apparent that, under the conditions outlined above, the elasticity of supply of hours of work will be zero.

If the worker under the new condition should desire a daily income of $3.60 then the elasticity of demand for income would be:

$$\frac{\log 360 - \log 300}{\log 150 - \log 200} = \frac{2.55630 - 2.47712}{.17609 - .30103} = \frac{.07918}{-.12494} = -0.63$$

Thus when the elasticity of demand for income is less than unity, there would be less labor offered than before and the supply curve would be negatively inclined. In the illustration above, nine hours would be the new length of the working day, i.e. $3.60 ÷ $.40 = 9. Since an increase of $\frac{1}{3}$ in the hourly rate of wages was accompanied by a decrease of $\frac{1}{10}$ in the number of hours worked, then the approximate elasticity of supply would be — .37 i.e.

$$\frac{\log 600 - \log 540}{\log 30 - \log 40} = \frac{2.77815 - 2.73239}{1.47712 - 1.60206} = -0.37$$

If the workers were to be completely satisfied with an income of $3.00 and if their elasticity of demand for income were therefore, as both the earlier and the modern mercantilists assumed, equal to zero, then only 7½ hours of labor would be forth-coming. Since the number of hours would decrease in the same ratio as the return per hour increased, this negative elasticity of supply would be 1.0 or unity. Since the elasticity of demand for income cannot be less than zero, it follows that the negative elasticity of supply (in so far as this element is concerned) can never exceed 1.0.

Let us now turn to cases where the elasticity of demand for income is greater than unity. Under these circumstances the decrease in the number of minutes required to earn a unit of money would be accompanied by a more than proportionate in-crease in the amount of total income desired. If the income desired under the new conditions went up to $4.40, then the elasticity of demand for income would be:

$$\frac{\log 440 - \log 300}{\log 1.50 - \log 2.00} = \frac{2.64345 - 2.47712}{.17609 - .30103} = \frac{.16633}{-.12494} = -.133$$

The worker would now be employed for more than 10 hours or, to be precise, for 11 hours. This would be a positive elasticity of supply and in fact approximately equivalent to $+ .33$ *i.e.*

$$\frac{\log 600 - \log 660}{\log 30 - \log 40} = \frac{2.77815 - 2.81954}{1.47712 - 1.60206} = +0.33$$

We thus see (1) that not only do positive supply curves go with elasticities of demand for income which are greater than unity and negative supply curves with elasticities of demand for income which are less than unity, but also a further con-sequence follows which was not stated by Robbins, namely, (2) that the numerical values of these positive and negative co-efficients of the elasticity of supply depend upon the size of the coefficients of the elasticity of demand for income. When the latter is at 0, the former is at $-$ 1.0, and as the latter in-creases, the negative values of the former decrease until, as the coefficient of demand for income reaches unity, or $-$ 1.0, the coefficient of elasticity of supply is at 0. Thereafter as the elasticity of demand for income rises above $-$ 1.0, the positive elasticities of supply increase. The following table shows this mathematical relationship between these two sets of elasticities so that if we are given one, we can find the other. The elasticity of demand for income will be referred to as e_D and the elasticity of supply of labor (time) as e_S.

It will therefore be seen that the relationship between the elas-ticities of the supply of labor in terms of hours (e_S) and the

Coefficient of Elasticity of Demand for Income (e_d)	Coefficient of Elasticity of Supply of Labor (e_s)	Coefficient of Elasticity of Demand for Income (e_d)	Coefficient of Elasticity of Supply of Labor (e_s)
0	−1.0	−1.1	+0.1
−0.1	−0.9	−1.2	+0.2
−0.2	−0.8	−1.3	+0.3
−0.3	−0.7	−1.4	+0.4
−0.4	−0.6	−1.5	+0.5
−0.5	−0.5	−1.6	+0.6
−0.6	−0.4	−1.7	+0.7
−0.7	−0.3	−1.8	+0.8
−0.8	−0.2	−1.9	+0.9
−0.9	−0.1	−2.0	+1.0
−1.0	0		

elasticity of demand for income in terms of labor-time (e_D) is such that:

(1) Beginning when the elasticity of demand (e_D) is 0, and the elasticity of labor supply (e_S) is − 1.0, then with each numerical increase in the former coefficient there is a corresponding and equal numerical decrease in the latter until when e_D is − 1.0, e_S is 0. Then as the numerical values of the coefficient of the elasticity of demand for income increase, the numerical values of the coefficients of e_S (which are now positive) increase by equal numerical amounts.

(2) The sums of the two elasticities, e_D and e_S are always equal to − 1.0, or unity. Thus when e_D equals − .4, e_S equals − .6, and when e_D is − 1.3, then e_S is + .3, and so on. The fact that the sum of the two coefficients equals unity (i.e. $e_D = -1 - e_S$) is really only the mathematical equivalent of saying that the change, such as an increase in hourly income, is distributed between an increase in the total income and a change in the time worked, and its alternative leisure.

The same type of analysis may be applied where hourly wages are decreased and the number of units of labor-time required to obtain a unit of income are correspondingly increased.

It is, however, somewhat difficult to conceive of an elasticity of demand for income which under these conditions of a lowered hourly rate would be greater than unity. For this would mean that if people had worked 10 hours a day for a total daily income of $4.00, then if the hourly wage-rate was decreased from 40 to 30 cents, the workers would cut their hours of work to less than 10 a day, and hence would reduce their daily income below $3.00. Since the general effort of people is either to increase their income or to maintain it as much as possible, it would seem as though only in exceptional cases would they reduce their total income by more than the reduction in hourly rates. If they had plots of land or handicrafts to fall back upon they might withdraw a certain portion of their time from wage-labor and transfer it to independent production. The same course might also be followed by men with an appreciable surplus to whom leisure time pursuits and hobbies were extremely important. But not many of the wage-earning population would belong to these classes. These groups, if given a reduced hourly wage, would be far more likely to work longer hours in an effort to keep up their already scanty total income to as full a measure as possible. Under these conditions they would therefore have an elasticity of demand for income in terms of effort, which would be less than unity, with the result that the elasticity of the supply of labor would be negative in nature.

But one can only agree heartily with Professor Robbins when he declares that "any attempt to predict the effect of a change in the terms on which income is earned must proceed by inductive investigations of elasticities."[5] To that task we shall proceed in this chapter. Instead however of directly measuring elasticities of demand in terms of effort, as Professor Robbins seems to advocate, we shall directly measure the elasticities of supply as indicated by the responsiveness of hours of work to hourly earnings, and then from these proceed backwards to obtain the probable elasticities of the demand for income.

So far as is known, no attempt has hitherto been made to find the quantitative relationships between hourly earnings and the number of hours worked. It is that which is attempted in this chapter in no less than five different ways. These are to correlate and find coefficients of elasticity and flexibility for: (1) The relationship between average absolute earnings per hour in various industries at any one time and the average absolute hours per week in these industries, with each industry serving as an observation. (2) The relative movement of hourly earnings and of hours per week for a given year in various industries in terms of the averages for a previous year as a base. Here again the averages for each industry constitute an observation. (3) The time series of real hourly earnings and standard hours of work for individual industries and groups of industries both in terms of the data as they stand and link relatives, with each

[5] Robbins, *op. cit.* p. 129.

year serving as an observation. (4) The relationship *within* a given industry at any one time between the absolute earnings per hour and the absolute length of the working week for various geographical sections. Here each state is an observation. (5) The relationship between actual earnings per hour and the actual hours worked per day, using both industries and states as observations.

We shall now proceed to discuss the methods followed and the results obtained in each of these lines of investigation.

1. The Relationship between Hours of Work and Hourly Wages in Different Industries and in Different Years

In my book on *Real Wages in the United States*, I computed among other series, for some seventeen different industries for the thirty years from 1890 to 1926 inclusive, (1) the average hours which constituted the standard working week and (2) the absolute and relative earnings and rates per hour in terms both of money receipts and effective purchasing power.[6]

The average hourly earnings in cents were then taken for each of the industries for the three years 1890, 1914, and 1926, respectively and were correlated with the average number of hours constituting a full-time week's work in the respective industries in each of these three years. The coefficients of correlation between the average money earnings per hour in the various industries in each of these years and the length of the standard working week are as follows:

Year of Data	r.
1890	−.78
1914	−.80
1926	−.84

It is thus apparent that within a group of industries at any one time there is a high negative correlation between hourly earnings and hours of work. The industries with relatively high hourly earnings tend to be those with a relatively shorter week than the average, while the industries characterized by a relatively low hourly wage scale tend to be those with a longer than average working week. There seems also to have been a slight tendency for the strength of this negative relationship to increase with time since r rose from − .78 in 1890 to − .80 in 1914 and − .84 in 1926.

---

[6] Paul H. Douglas, *Real Wages in the United States 1890–1926*, pp. 73–204. The industries covered were cotton manufacturing, woolen manufacturing, boots and shoes, clothing, hosiery and knit goods, lumber, iron and steel, slaughtering and meat packing, foundries and machine shops, building trades, granite and stone, book and job printing, millwork, baking, coal mining, and unskilled labor.

The observations were then plotted with earnings per hour on the ordinate and full-time hours per week on the abscissa. Regression lines were then fitted to the seventeen observations by the method of least squares, and the elasticities of supply at the means were measured. These elasticities were as follows:

TABLE 39

COEFFICIENTS OF ELASTICITY AT THE MEANS
STANDARD HOURS AND HOURLY EARNINGS FOR
SEVENTEEN INDUSTRIES IN 1890, 1914, AND 1926

Year	Regression of Full-time Hours on Hourly Earnings[1]	Regression of Hourly Earnings on Full-time Hours
1890	−.16	−.26
1914	−.20	−.32
1926	−.17	−.24

[1] The regression equations are:

(1) 1890: $X = 67.14 - 0.040Y$
    The average hours per week = 58.13; average wages per hour = 22.5 cents.

(2) 1914: $X = 63.61 - 0.033Y$
    The average hours per week = 52.9; average wages per hour = 32.7 cents.

(3) 1926: $X = 57.01 - 0.011Y$
    The average hours per week = 48.7; average wages per hour = 75.9 cents.

It is indeed interesting to observe that the coefficients of elasticity tend to be relatively constant as between these years ranging from − .16 in 1890 to − .20 in 1914, and back again to − .17 in 1926.

2. The Relationship between Relative Changes in Hours and Hourly Earnings for a Group of Industries, 1914 and 1926, Compared with 1890

The preceding set of relationships did not show, except by inference, what would happen to the working hours of any one industry if its hourly earnings should change. What was shown was, instead, the functional relationship of these two variables between different groups at the same time. If each group were to respond to such *changes* as the various groups seemed to respond, then only would we be justified in regarding the preceding elasticities as conclusive.

But this would assume a uniformity of behavior which we are not thus far justified in making. We may, however, largely resolve this difficulty by measuring for each of the different industries the relative changes which occurred in each over a span of years in the standard hours per week and the wages per hour. We can then see whether in those cases where the gain in hourly wages was greater than the average there was a tendency for the hours per week to decrease more than the average and, if so, how strong it was. We have, therefore, taken the actual hourly earnings for each of the seventeen industries in 1914 and 1926 and reduced these to relatives in terms of the corresponding 1890 figures as a base.

We have then measured the relationship between the changes in hourly earnings and hours between 1890 and 1914 and also the changes between 1890 and 1926.

The coefficients of correlation between these relative changes were as follows:

$$r.$$
1914 relative to 1890...... $-.72$
1926 relative to 1890...... $-.67$

This indicates a relatively high negative correlation between changes in hourly wages and standard hours of work. When the gain in hourly wages was less than the average, there was a tendency for the hours to fall by less than the average, and when the gain in wages was greater than the average the tendency was for the fall in hours to be greater. A line fitted to these observations by the method of least squares would therefore slope downward from left to right. The coefficients of elasticity of these regression lines at the means were:

Group	Coefficient of Elasticity of Hours Upon Earnings[1]	Coefficient of Elasticity of Earnings Upon Hours
1914 relative to 1890	$-.28$	$-.53$
1926 relative to 1890	$-.17$	$-.38$

[1] The regression of X upon Y for the 1914 indexes is $X = 116.32 - 0.172Y$. The average of the X's was 90.96 and of the Y's 147.29. The corresponding regression for 1926 is $X = 98.14 - 0.041Y$. The average of the X's was 83.92 and of the Y's 346.57.

These coefficients are rather close to the cross section coefficients for any given year as a unit. Thus, in 1926 the coefficient of elasticity between industries was $-.17$ which was the precise figure for the relative changes as between 1890 and 1926. In 1914, however, it will be remembered that the cross section coefficient was $-.20$ as compared with the $-.28$ obtained by this method. The two sets of results so far, however, tend to corroborate each other and seem to indicate that an increase of one per cent in hourly earnings tended to be accompanied by a decrease of from one-fifth to one-sixth of one per cent in the standard hours per week.

3. The Elasticity of Working Hours as Shown by Time Series

A third way of measuring the effect of changes in hourly earnings upon the hours worked is to take the record of a number of industries and see how these variables fluctuated in relation to each other over a considerable period of time. Such data are available for a number of industries from 1890 to 1926 both for real hourly earnings and for the standard hours per week.[7]

As a first step to observe the actual historical relationships we have chosen to use the data as they stand without eliminating the historical trends and have computed the correlation coefficients and the coefficients of elasticity for the building trades and for fourteen manufacturing industries. For seven of these industries union rates were used, while for the remainder the averages are those shown by the pay-roll industries. Table 40 shows the correlation coefficients between these series for each of the fifteen industries.

TABLE 40

CORRELATION COEFFICIENTS BETWEEN REAL HOURLY WAGES AND STANDARD HOURS PER WEEK FOR FIFTEEN INDUSTRIES, 1890–1926

Industry	r.	Industry	r.
I. Union Group		II. Payroll Group	
1. Building..............	−.65	8. Cotton..............	−.94
2. Baking...............	−.82	9. Boots and Shoes......	−.81
3. Planing Mills..........	−.55	10. Men's Clothing........	−.95
4. Newspaper Printing.....	+.30	11. Hosiery and Knit Goods	−.89
5. Book and Job Printing..	−.61	12. Woolens..............	−.88
6. Granite and Stone......	−.08	13. Lumber..............	−.52
7. Metal Industries........	−.38	14. Iron and Steel.........	−.65
		15. Slaughtering..........	−.76

It will be seen that on the whole there was a very appreciable negative correlation, especially in the payroll industries. In twelve of the fifteen industries, the coefficient of correlation was over − .50. Indeed in four industries it was over − .88 while in two it was over − .80, making six industries where it was above the latter figure. In four more industries it was between − .60 and − .80, and in an additional two the coefficient was between − .50 and − .60.

In three industries the coefficient was either lower or negligible, namely, the metal trades with a coefficient of − .38, granite and stone with a coefficient of − .08 and newspaper printing with + .30.

[7] See my *Real Wages in the United States,* pp. 108–16.

For the fourteen manufacturing industries taken as a whole, the correlation between real hourly earnings and the standard hours per week was − .85, a relatively high figure, while for the six union manufacturing industries as a whole, the coefficient, as might be expected from the preceding table, was appreciably lower, amounting to − .38. For the payroll industries as a group, the coefficient was no less than − .97 or almost perfect correlation.

Regression lines were also fitted to these data and the coefficients of elasticity at the means were also computed. These are given in the succeeding table, 41.

TABLE 41

COEFFICIENTS OF ELASTICITY DERIVED FROM RECORD OF HOURS AND EARNINGS FOR FIFTEEN INDUSTRIES, 1890–1926
Coefficients of Elasticity at the Means

Industry	Hours Upon Earnings	Earnings Upon Hours
I. Union Group		
1. Building....................	−.26	−.61
2. Baking....................	−.33	−.49
3. Planing Mills...............	−.21	−.68
4. Newspaper Printing...........	+.12	+1.31
5. Book and Job Printing........	−.33	−.89
6. Granite and Stone............	−.02	−.42
7. Metal Industries.............	−.29	−1.96
II. Payroll Group		
8. Cotton.....................	−.32	−.35
9. Boots and Shoes..............	−.54	−.82
10. Men's Clothing...............	−.23	−.26
11. Hosiery and Knit Goods.......	−.31	−.39
12. Woolens....................	−.23	−.30
13. Lumber....................	−.54	−1.98
14. Iron and Steel................	−.37	−.87
15. Slaughtering.................	−.49	−.85

Since it is the effect of earnings upon hours in which we are interested, we may concentrate our attention upon the first column. This shows five industries with a coefficient of elasticity at the means of between − .20 and − .30 and five more between − .30 and − .37. There are two with coefficients of elasticity under − .2 and three with coefficients in excess of − .4. The arithmetic average of the fifteen coefficients is − .30.

If the series for the fourteen manufacturing industries are combined into a weighted average, the coefficient of elasticity is − .47, while for the six combined "union" manufacturing industries [7a] the corresponding coefficient is — .26 and for payroll industries — .40.

The difficulty however with all of the foregoing material is that it does not eliminate time. Part of the decrease in hours may not have been caused by the increase in hourly earnings but by a changed attitude towards leisure on the part of the workers. The waning of the Puritan and frontier spirit, the rise of sport and amusement, and the growth of city life with the increased time required to go to and from work and the necessity for relaxation from heat and noise, may all have played their part in making the workers more desirous for rest and hence more determined to reduce their hours of work. If we are to measure the purely economic effects of changes in earnings upon hours, we must find some way of eliminating these possible influences which in the preceding series, based as it was on the data as they stand, were inextricably intermingled in the results. It should however be realized that it would have been difficult to have obtained this increased leisure had it not been for increases in hourly earnings so that the changes in traditions and in circumstances would probably have been ineffectual by themselves.

There are at least two ways of largely disentangling these extraneous influences. One of these is by the method of link relatives whereby the earnings and hours of each year are expressed in terms of relatives of the preceding year. When this is done for all manufacturing as a whole we obtain a coefficient of correlation of only — .26 between these relatives for identical years, and an extremely low coefficient of elasticity at the means.

It is also possible to eliminate the effect of "time" by taking it into the equation itself so that the hours per week would be a function not of earnings alone but of "time" as well. This relationship was symbolized as follows:

$$x = a + by + ct + dt^2$$

and this, after finding the constants using 1908 as the point of origin, became

$$x = 100.1 - 0.045\ (\pm 0.01)y - 0.440\ (\pm 0.01)t - 0.01\ (\pm 0.003)t^2$$

This means that on the average during this period a change of one per cent in real hourly earnings would be accompanied by a change in the opposite direction of .045 or about one-twentieth of one per cent of the relative hours per week. But

---

[7a] Omitting the building trades.

this was an average relationship for the period 1890–1926 as a whole, whereas the supply curve in practise shifted to the left so that even at the same wage there would have been a tendency for fewer hours to be worked. The rate at which this decrease in hours has varied from year to year is measured by the terms involving t (time) in the preceding equation. By com-

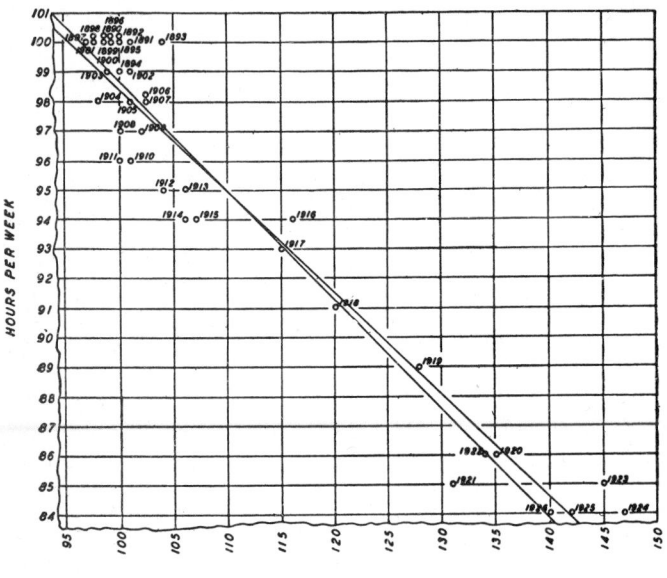

RELATIVE HOURS PER WEEK AND RELATIVE REAL HOURLY EARNINGS IN THE PAYROLL MANUFACTURING INDUSTRIES, 1890 – 1926

HOURLY EARNINGS

Chart 58. The Short-Run Supply Curve of Labor Derived from Hours Worked Per Week and Hourly Earnings in the Payroll Manufacturing Industries, 1890–1926. The line AA is the regression of relative hours worked per week on relative hourly earnings, the line CC is the regression of earnings on hours.

puting a multiple coefficient of correlation between not only hours and earnings directly but also time as well, we obtain a coefficient of 0.98, while the standard error of estimate is but 0.36 hours, which was only between two-thirds of one per cent of the average weekly hours of work during this period.

The coefficient of partial elasticity of supply for the year 1926 was − 0.07, with a standard error which had as its upper limit 0.015.[8]

_____
[8] This was computed according to the formula suggested by my colleague, Professor Henry Schultz: "The Standard Error of the Coefficient of Elasticity of Demand." *Journal American Statistical Association*, March, 1933, pp. 64–69.

This would mean that, so far as the year 1926 was concerned, an increase of one per cent in real hourly earnings would lead to a decrease of seven-hundredths of one per cent in the standard hours of work per week. It should be remembered, however, that there was a general drift of the supply curve to the left.

4. The Elasticity of Working Hours as Shown between Localities for Given Industries

The United States Bureau of Labor Statistics in its bulletins on hours and earnings in various industries gives averages of

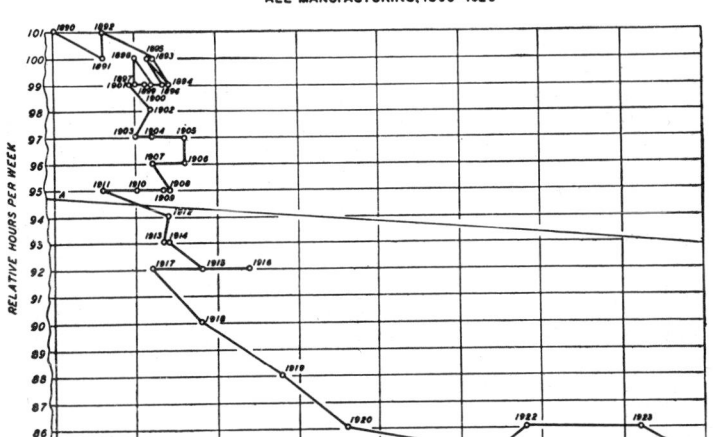

Chart 59. The Short-Run Supply Curve of Labor Derived from Hours Worked Per Week and Hourly Earnings in All Manufacturing Industries Combined, 1890–1926. The line AA is the net regression of relative hours worked per week on relative hourly earnings.

each of these variables by states. We have chosen two of these bulletins, namely, that on foundries and machine shops for 1925 [9] and on hosiery and knit goods for 1926 [10] as the sources to determine whether any relation exists between average hourly earnings and the standard working-week in the various localities of the country. The averages for each state served as an observation. The coefficients of correlation were found to be as follows for the seven main groups studied:

---

[9] "Hours and Earnings in Foundries and Machine Shops," *Bulletin 422 U. S. Bureau of Labor Statistics.*

[10] "Hours and Earnings in Hosiery and Knit Goods Industries 1926," *Bulletin 452 U. S. Bureau of Labor Statistics.*

Industrial Group	Coefficient of Correlation Between Hourly Earnings and Full-time Hours (r)
Foundries.................................	−.63
Machine Shops............................	−.79
Hosiery and Underwear (Male and Female).	−.73
Hosiery (Male)............................	−.63
Hosiery (Female)..........................	−.79
Underwear (Female).......................	−.93
Underwear (Male).........................	−.97

The coefficients are thus seen to be quite high, since in only two of the seven cases was r less than .7, while in two cases the coefficient was more than .9. The degree of inverse relation-

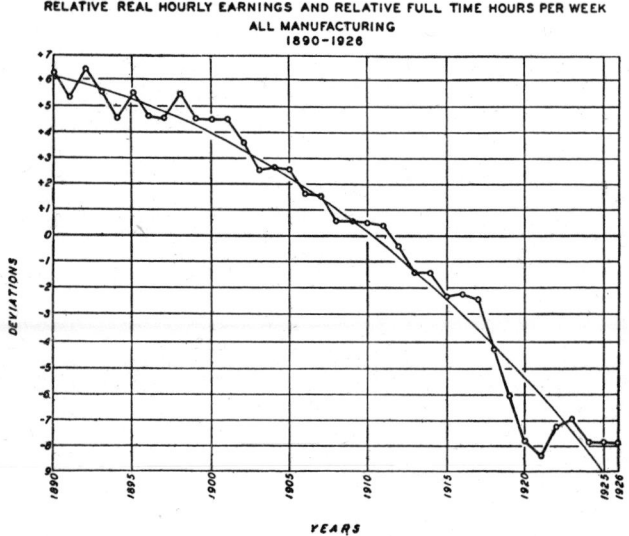

RELATIVE REAL HOURLY EARNINGS AND RELATIVE FULL TIME HOURS PER WEEK
ALL MANUFACTURING
1890–1926

Chart 60. Relative Hours Per Week Plotted as a Function of Time after Allowance Has Been Made for the Changes in Relative Hourly Earnings. The Parabola Represents the Net Regression of Hours Per Week on Time.

ship between the two is, therefore, once again demonstrated to be high.

The elasticities of supply were found by fitting regression lines to these observations and showed the following coefficients of elasticity at the point of averages given in Table 42.

We are primarily concerned with the first set of coefficients, namely, the elasticity of hours with respect to earnings. These all show negative coefficients ranging from − .07 to − .29, with an average of − .19.

TABLE 42

COEFFICIENTS OF ELASTICITY OF HOURS AND EARNINGS IN
VARIOUS INDUSTRIAL GROUPS, 1925 AND 1926

Industry	Coefficient of Elasticity Regression of Hours Upon Earnings	Regression of Earnings Upon Hours
Foundries........................	−.19	−.48
Machine Shops...................	−.29	−.46
Hosiery and Underwear (Males and Females)......................	−.10	−.19
Hosiery (Males).................	−.07	−.17
Hosiery (Females)...............	−.14	−.22
Underwear (Females).............	−.27	−.31
Underwear (Males)..............	−.27	−.29

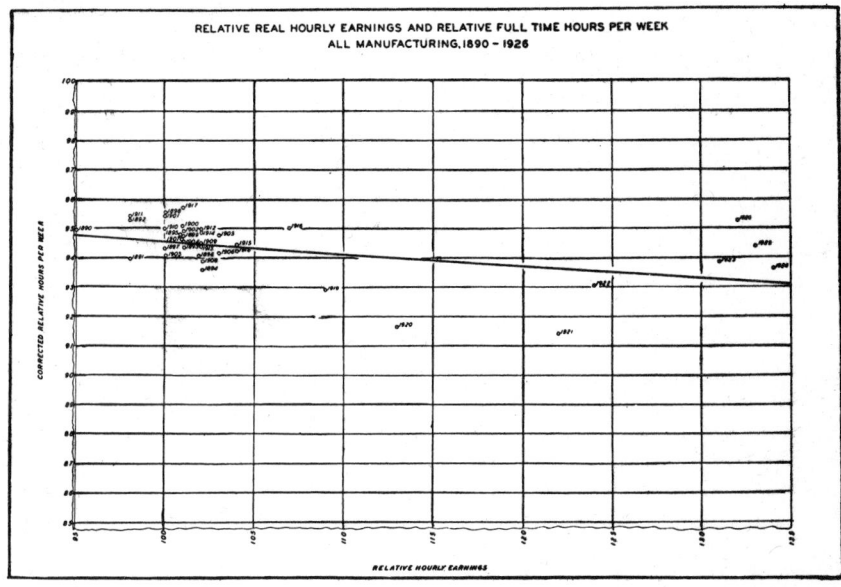

Chart 61. Relative Hours Per Week which Have Been Corrected for the Changes Due to Time Plotted Against Hourly Earnings. The Regression Line Is the Short Run Supply Curve of Labor.

Another study which furnishes us with additional material is the survey of hours worked per day and hourly earnings which the Bureau of Labor Statistics made of a large number of industries in 1919.[11] These results were classified in the form of averages both by industries and by states.

It is therefore possible to correlate this material from this

[11] *Bulletin 265 U. S. Bureau of Labor Statistics.*

double standpoint. The following coefficients of correlation were obtained.

Between Industries   *r.*
  Males (29 cases) .... −.31
  Females (21 cases) .... −.41
Between States
  Males (43 cases) .... −.55
  Females (33 cases) .... −.36

The coefficients of elasticity at the means obtained after the fitting of the regression lines were:

	Hours on Earnings	*Earnings on Hours*
Between Industries		
Males	−.13	−1.40
Females	−.16	−.94
Between States		
Males	−.30	−1.00
Females	−.20	−1.56

Here the coefficients of the degree to which hours changed with hourly earnings varied from −.13 to −.30 with an average of −.20.

5. Summary

If we review these various methods of measuring the elasticity of the supply of standard hours of work, we find coefficients which run from −.07 to −.30. The lowest is that obtained by eliminating the factor "time" from the historical series. Aside from this there is a distinct tendency for those computed on a cross-section basis at any one time or for relative movements as between given years to average somewhere around −.2. While much more work needs to be done it is probably safe to estimate that the elasticity of this factor of the labor supply is in all probability somewhere between −.1 and −.2 and that therefore an increase of 1 per cent in hourly earnings would tend (other things being equal) to cause a decrease of from one-tenth to two-tenths of one per cent in the hours normally worked.

If we accept the conclusion that the most probable elasticity of the proportions employed to changes in real annual earnings, is −.16, we may now combine these two coefficients into an estimate of the most probable elasticity of the short time supply of labor. This may be done in the following way:

(1) If the elasticity of hours in respect to hourly earnings is — .20 then

(2) An increase of 1 per cent in hourly earnings will result in an increase of .80 per cent in weekly earnings. (*i.e.* 1.0 — .20)

(3) Assuming that yearly and weekly earnings bear a constant ratio to each other then an increase of .8 per cent in weekly or yearly earnings would cause a decrease of .13 per cent in the numbers employed. (*i.e.* .80 × .16 = .128)

(4) The gain in real annual income resulting from a 1 per cent increase in hourly earnings would therefore be approximately 0.67 per cent. (*i.e.* .80 — .13)

(5) The decrease in the total quantity of labor offered would be approximately 0.33 per cent. On this basis the elasticity of the short-time supply of labor would be approximately — .33.

If we use — .1 as the most probable elasticity of standard hours in respect to hourly earnings, then the approximate elasticity of the short-time supply of labor is — .24, (*i.e.* — .10 + [(1.00 — .10) × .16] = — .24).

If we take our lowest coefficient of elasticity of the supply of hours of work namely — .07, which was obtained when "time" was eliminated, then the combined coefficient of elasticity would be — .22 (*i.e.* — .07 + [(1.00 — .07) × — .16]).

From such evidence as has been produced therefore it would seem as though an increase of one per cent in hourly wages would cause a decrease of from one-fourth to one-third of one per cent in the quantity of labor offered and that a decrease of one per cent in hourly wages would cause an increase of from one-quarter to one-third of one per cent in the quantity of labor supplied. Since we have seen from the earlier discussion in this chapter that the sum of the coefficients of the elasticity of demand for income in terms of effort (time) and that of the elasticity of supply of labor will be equal to unity, it follows (a) that if we only consider the hours worked by those employed, the elasticity of the demand for income in terms of effort (or time) will range between — .8 and — .9 (b) that if we include the proportions employed as well as the hours of work, the elasticity of demand for income will apparently range between — .75 and — .67. Knight therefore seems to have been correct in his general interpretation of what would happen if incomes were increased. We may express the result in another way by saying that on the basis of the evidence advanced, the workers in the United States tend to divide an increase in hourly wage rates into two parts. The first is a higher material standard of living while the second is increased leisure for themselves or their families. Approximately two-thirds to three-quarters of the gain is devoted to the first and approximately one-third to one-quarter to the second of these purposes. These results are of course only approximate but the accumulated evidence indicates that they are probably not far from the facts. That the supply curve of hours of work is negatively inclined with respect to earnings is also indicated by the experience in agriculture during the great depression which began in 1929. The real income of the farmers per unit of product and per hour of work has greatly declined. The farmers have attempted to counterbalance this shrinkage at least in part by working longer hours.[12]

If we could measure the effect of changes in earnings upon absenteeism and upon vacations, we would find that the negative coefficients of elasticity of labor would be somewhat raised although by how much is uncertain.[13] In all probability however an increase in hourly earnings increases absenteeism most in those cases where hours are not immediately decreased and when the general elasticity of hours is taken into account, the effects of absenteeism will not be so appreciable as might at first thought be concluded.

---

[12] That total output has not increased proportionately is largely due to the decrease of acreage under cultivation.

[13] For some of the war-time effects of wage increases upon absenteeism see my article, "Absenteeism in Labor," *Political Science Quarterly*, December, 1920.

CHAPTER XIII

THE LONG-RUN SUPPLY OF LABOR AS CONCEIVED BY ECONOMISTS AND STUDENTS OF THE POPULATION PROBLEM

The long-run supply of labor is determined not only by all the factors which influence the short-run supply of labor but, also in addition, by the rate and volume of population growth.

Since we have already considered the factors affecting the short-run supply of labor and have found them to lead to a negative supply curve with an elasticity of not far from — .24 or — .33 we shall turn our attention to the new factor, namely, the rate of growth of the population. If measured in absolute quantities, this of course depends upon both the previous size of the population and the rate of growth; but since we are primarily concerned only with relative changes, we shall in the main confine our attention to the latter and consider the former only in so far as it affects the rate of growth.

The birth rate is frequently considered as the measurement of population increase but people, of course, die as well. Raymond Pearl uses the ratio of births to deaths as the best vital index of population growth. This measures the relationship which births bear to deaths but not the relative rate of population growth. For this we would need to use the formula $\frac{\text{Births} - \text{Deaths}}{\text{Population}}$. Even with this formula one population may seem to be increasing more rapidly than another when the difference is in reality due to a different age composition with a larger percentage of the population grouped in the fertile years.

1. Malthus and the Curve of Labor Supply

Although the question of population had been frequently discussed before the appearance of the famous essay by Malthus,[1] the latter really marks the beginning of modern thought upon the problem. Malthus, as is well known, saw "a constant tend-

---

[1] For a review of this literature, see Stangeland, *Pre-Malthusian Doctrines of Population;* R. Gonnard, *Histoire des Doctrines de la Population,* pp. 11–256; Small, *The Cameralists.*

ency in all animated life to increase beyond the nourishment prepared for it . . . Through the animal and vegetable kingdoms, nature has scattered the seeds of life abroad with the most profuse and liberal hand; but has been comparatively sparing in the room and nourishment necessary to rear them."[2]

Human population was subject to the same tendency. Basing his estimate in the main upon the rate of increase which Franklin had observed for America, Malthus computed[3] that "population when unchecked goes on doubling itself every twenty-five years." This was, of course, a geometrical rate of increase. But the production of commodities to support this population did not increase as rapidly It was instead of a totally "different nature from the ratio of the increase of population."[4] "Man," Malthus continued, "is necessarily confined in room. When acre has been added to acre till all the fertile land is occupied the yearly increase of food must depend upon the amelioration of the land already in possession. This is a stream, which from the nature of all soils, instead of increasing, must be gradually diminishing."[5] Such a statement as this is a clear proof that Cannan is mistaken when he implies that Malthus was ignorant of the principle of diminishing returns. It is true that he does admit that a doubling of the population might also be accompanied by a doubling of the average produce, but he immediately adds that this is[6] "a greater increase than could with reason be expected." He moreover goes on to point out that a further doubling of population could not lead to a corresponding increase in the volume of agricultural products for[7] "in proportion as cultivation extended, the additions that could yearly be made to the former average produce must be gradually and regularly diminishing."

Population therefore, if unchecked, would tend to increase at a geometrical ratio, but the supply of food could not keep pace. Malthus estimated that the latter could not increase, even under the most favorable circumstances[8] "faster than in

---

[2] T. R. Malthus, *An Essay on the Principle of Population* (2nd Edition), 1803, p. 2.

[3] *Ibid.*, p. 5.

[4] T. R. Malthus, *An Essay on the Principle of Population* (2nd Edition), 1803, p. 5.

[5] *Ibid.*, p. 5.

[6] *Ibid.*, p. 7.

[7] *Ibid.*, p. 7.

[8] T. R. Malthus, *An Essay on the Principle of Population* (2nd Edition), 1803, p. 7.

an arithmetical ratio." When these two rates of increase were compared,[9] "the human species would increase as the numbers 1, 2, 4, 8, 16, 32, 64, 128, 256 and subsistence as 1, 2, 3, 4, 5, 6, 7, 8, 9. In two centuries the population would be to the means of subsistence as 256 to 9; in three centuries, as 4096 to 13, and in two thousand years the difference would be almost incalculable."

Such an increase in population as this would of course be impossible. So large a number of people could not be maintained upon such small resources. Even were the food supply to increase more rapidly than the arithmetical ratio, which Malthus chose for his illustration, it would be impossible for all the people whom he assumed as coming into existence to be fed and supported. As a matter of fact, it would seem that *if* the population were to increase at the rate he assumes, the food supply would also increase by more than by the ratio which he indicates. For if the population were to increase from 128 to 256 millions, it would seem on *a priori* grounds to be highly dubious that the food supply would only increase by one-seventh. But the essence of the Malthusian theory does not consist in the contrasted geometrical and arithmetical ratios. These were striking figures of speech which were used merely to illustrate the argument. What Malthus was really laboring to demonstrate was simply that the population tended to increase faster than the food supply.

But it could not in the long-run continue to do so. It was held in restraint by two forces, namely, the positive and the preventive checks. The first consisted of all those measures that destroyed life after birth, while the second included those lines of action which lessened the number of births themselves. In the first edition of the Essay, Malthus threw nearly all of his emphasis upon the positive checks and assigned but little importance to the preventive. Writing as he did to counteract the equalitarian views of Godwin and Condorcet, he stressed the argument that the pressure of population would render nugatory all temporary improvements in the economic condition of the workers. Should they become more prosperous through a re-distribution of property, the expansion of population would reduce the per capita product to where it was before. Increased material well-being would cause earlier marriages and conse-

[9] *Ibid.*, p. 8.

quently more births. It would also lessen the death rate. From these two causes, population would increase rapidly, and the ratio of produce to people would be lowered.

If population, on the other hand, increased so that the people were not able to secure even a physical minimum of subsistence, then they would be more subject to disease and the death rate would rise. The pressure of numbers would also drive nations to war in order to secure more territory for their people and this would decimate the population. Finally, there was famine. This was [10]

the last, the most dreadful resource of nature. The power of population is so superior to the power in the earth to produce subsistence for man that unless arrested by the preventive check, premature death must in some shape or other visit the human race. The vices of mankind are active and able ministers of depopulation. They are the precursors in the great army of destruction and often finish the dreadful work themselves. But should they fail in this war of extermination, sickly seasons, epidemics, pestilence and plague advance in terrific array and sweep off their thousands and ten thousands. Should success be still incomplete, gigantic inevitable famine stalks in the rear and with one mighty blow levels the population with the food of the world.

Vice, Pestilence, War and Famine were thus Nature's Four Horsemen who kept the population down.

Private property and the inequalities of wealth helped to preserve some islands of comfort and luxury in the sea of misery. Were economic equality to be introduced, the gracious life of the wealthy would be engulfed by the sheer multiplication of numbers. The workers would ultimately be no better off than before; there would merely be more of them. Even though the children of the poor suffer from want, it is inadvisable to take any resources from the wealthy to help support them for [11]

a man who is born into a world already possessed, if he cannot get subsistence from his parents, on whom he has a just demand, and if the society do not want his labor, has no claim of *right* to the smallest portion of food, and in fact, has no business to be where he is. At Nature's mighty feast there is no vacant cover for him. She tells him to be gone, and will quickly execute her own orders; if he do not work upon the compassion of some of her guests. If these guests get up and make room for him, other intruders immediately appear de-

---

[10] T. R. Malthus, *An Essay on the Principle of Population* (2nd Edition), 1803, p. 350.
[11] T. R. Malthus, *An Essay on the Principle of Population* (2nd Edition), 1803, pp. 531-2.

manding the same favor. The report of a provision for all that come, fills the hall with numerous claimants. The order and harmony of the feast is disturbed, the plenty that before reigned is changed into scarcity and the happiness of the guests is destroyed by the spectacle of misery and dependence in every part of the hall, and by the clamorous importunity of those who are justly enraged at not finding the provision they had been taught to expect. The guests learn too late their error in counteracting those strict orders to all intruders, issued by the great mistress of the feast, who, wishing that all her guests should have plenty, and knowing that she could not provide for unlimited numbers, humanely refused to admit fresh comers when the table was already full.

Dismissing the unfortunate poor who are doomed to be crushed out as those "who in the great lottery of life have drawn a blank," Malthus believed that the principle of population vindicated the maintenance of economic inequality.

In a similar fashion, gains for the mass of mankind everywhere tended to be only transient. Whatever the system of society, the pressure of population would tend ultimately to reduce the main mass of the population to a condition of only a physical subsistence. This pressure of population was a natural law which was not dependent upon the distributive system for its operation. It was at work in Tierra del Fuego and among the South Sea Islands, where the wage system was unknown, as well as in the industrialized countries. Malthus took great pains indeed to show how, over large areas of the earth's surface, men lived at the barest physical minimum.

But the greater prosperity of the population in Europe and America presented difficulties of explanation for which the theory in its simple form seemed inadequate; consequently, in the second and greatly expanded edition which was published in 1803, Malthus gave a somewhat greater emphasis to the preventive check than he had in his original essay. "I think it appears that in modern Europe," he wrote,[12] "the positive checks to population prevail less and the preventive checks more, than in past times and in the more uncivilized parts of the world." The chief preventive check which Malthus recognized and approved was postponement of marriage. Thus he defined the preventive check as implying in the general acceptance of the word, "An infrequency of the marriage union from fear of a family" and declared that "it might be considered in

---

[12] T. H. Malthus, *An Essay on the Principle of Population* (2nd Edition), 1803, p. 350.

this light as the most powerful of the checks which in modern Europe keep down the population to the level of the means of subsistence." Sexual restraint within the marriage relationship was seemingly not considered possible, while any suggestion of preventing conception would have aroused his strong opposition. Vice, which he thought would lessen fertility, was another type of the preventive check which he abhorred.

But it should be noted that Malthus primarily thought of the preventive check as merely serving to prevent famine and war from carrying away the population. It prevented population from increasing beyond "the level of the means of subsistence," but it did not help to maintain their standard of life on a much higher level.

While Malthus strongly recommended that moral restraint should be exercised, he did not, even in his second edition, place much reliance upon it. "Few of my readers," he wrote,[13] "can be less sanguine in their expectations of any great change in the general conduct of men on this subject than I am." Indeed, he openly confesses that he devoted as much space as he did to the possibility of moral restraint in order [14] "to remove any imputation on the goodness of the Deity by showing that the evils arising from the principle of population were exactly of the same nature as the generality of other evils which excite fewer complaints; that they were increased by human ignorance and indolence and diminished by human knowledge and virtue." A minister, as he was, of the established church, Malthus was more concerned in vindicating the goodness of God than in offering hope to man. Since the gloomy view advanced in the original essay had been attacked as an impeachment of the benevolence of the Creator in establishing a world in which such disharmony existed, Malthus took great pains to point out that it was not God and Nature which were at fault, but man himself. In this way he defended both God and his own orthodoxy. But he had little confidence that man would so restrain himself, and hence he still thought of the people as being condemned by the very laws of their own passions to virtually a physical minimum of life. Even in America where, at the moment, the rewards of labor were high, the pressure of numbers would in progress of the country cause the laborers to

---

[13] T. R. Malthus, *An Essay on the Principle of Population* (2nd Edition), 1803, p. 504.
[14] *Ibid.*, p. 504.

"be much less liberally rewarded." [15]   The whole trend of Malthus' writings in the first two editions of the essay was, then, that the laborers could hope for but little more than a physical minimum.   This was the norm about which the reward of labor, whether under the system of wages or independent production, tended to fluctuate.

In later editions, it is true, he laid increasing stress upon the preventive check.   "It is probable," he wrote in 1817 in an appendix to the fifth edition of his celebrated essay, "that having found the bow bent too much one way, I was induced to bend it too much the other in order to make it straight." Moral restraint, or postponement of marriage, was now thought possible for others beside members of the aristocracy.   This was indeed the force which enabled the poor of England to live upon a higher level than those of less civilized countries.

In his *Principles of Political Economy*, Malthus made still further qualifications.   While an increase in wages might only mean that there would be such an increase in the supply of labor as to bring the remuneration of labor back to its former point, there was also the possibility that it might lead to "a decided improvement in the modes of subsistence and the convenience and comforts enjoyed, without a proportionate acceleration in the rate of increase." [16]   Civil and political liberty plus education were the forces which he relied upon to make men unable to deprive "themselves and their children of the means of being respectable, virtuous and happy" [17] and hence to cause them to postpone marriage.   If we may translate this reasoning into our own terms, it was therefore thought possible, and in countries like England probable, that the long-run supply curve of labor, instead of running parallel to the base, sloped upward and to the right.   But it seems evident, nevertheless, that Malthus, even in his later years, did not expect the workers to secure great gains in this manner and that consequently the probable slope of the supply curve of labor which he envisaged was but gentle.

An interesting feature of Malthus' thought was his belief that real wages and population growth went through cycles of in-

---

[15] T. R. Malthus, *An Essay on the Principle of Population* (2nd Edition), 1803, p. 348.
[16] T. R. Malthus, *Principles of Political Economy* (2nd Edition), 1836, p. 226.
[17] *Ibid.*, p. 52.

crease and of decrease. Malthus indeed believed that he had in fact detected not only one but two such cycles.

One was that after a population was on the physical minimum, the further increase of numbers would cause such misery and would so unleash the positive checks that the population would be reduced to a much smaller number than it was originally. The ratio of natural resources to population would consequently be higher than it was before, and labor's reward would now be appreciably above the physical minimum. But this caused the population to expand once more, and not only would wages be reduced but the cycle which we have described would begin over again. Not only would the *return per worker* therefore oscillate about the physical minimum, but the *numbers of the population* would also swing back and forth from the same center. There would be no secular trend of population upward or downward.

The course of the second cycle, after an increase in population and decreased wages, was described by Malthus in the following terms: [18]

During this season of distress, the discouragements to marriage and the difficulty of rearing a family are so great, that population is nearly at a stand. In the meantime, the cheapness of labour, the plenty of labourers and the necessity of an increased industry among them, encourage cultivators to employ more labour upon their land; to turn up fresh soil, and to manure and improve more completely what is already in tillage; till ultimately the means of subsistence may become in the same proportion to the population, as at the period from which we set out. The situation of the labourers being then again tolerably comfortable, the restraints to population are in some degree loosened; and, after a short period, the same retrograde and progressive movements, with respect to happiness, are repeated.

Here an increase in population by lowering wages and increasing profits is thought to cause such an improvement in cultivation as to produce more food. Such an increase when combined with the slackening in the rate of population growth helped to restore the per capita balance, which had formerly existed, between food and people. Malthus seemed to think that this equilibrium was a "tolerably comfortable" state, although the main trend of his theory would lead one to suppose that it was only a physical minimum. At any event, while the former per capita return would have been restored, the num-

---

[18] T. R. Malthus, *An Essay on the Principle of Population* (2nd Edition), p. 12.

bers in the population, according to this explanation, would have risen because of the added food which would have been raised. The secular trend of population would thus be upward even though the standard of life was constant.

But by how much would population increase and how rapid would be its movement? Nowhere does Malthus give even a clear statement of this problem, and he made no attempt to solve it. The supposition that population would increase two hundred fifty-six times to food's nine is plainly ridiculous, and yet the added workers would at once increase the total supply of food and hence enable an ultimately larger population than the preceding one to survive. According to Malthus it would also so stimulate the resourcefulness of the land-owners that improved methods would be developed and the capacity of the soil to support an increased population would be enhanced. While it is quite certain that Malthus did not think this increase would be enough to maintain a geometrically expanding population, it is impossible to determine just how great an actual expansion of population he thought was possible. His treatment of the population problem was, therefore, primarily philosophical and general. He framed a law of population pressure but he did not frame a law of quantitative population growth.

Nor did Malthus devote much thought to the amount of the relative release of population which would result from independent improvements in production or from the discovery during the nineteenth century of newer and more fertile soils.

2. Ricardo's Interpretation of Malthus: The Constant Cost Curve of Supplying Labor

It was primarily Ricardo, however, who took over the Malthusian theory of population and applied it to the problem of the distribution of the social product among the factors of production. He did this without attaching the qualifications which Malthus later made. Ricardo thought that there was a "natural" price of labor to which wages in the long-run must correspond. This natural price was that which was [19] "necessary to enable the labourers, one with another to subsist and to perpetuate their race, without increase or diminution." Despite Ricardo's demand that it should [20] "not be understood that the natural price of labor, estimated even in food and necessaries, is absolutely fixed and constant," in practice he thought that

---

[19] Ricardo, *Works* (McCulloch edition), p. 50.
[20] *Ibid.*, p. 52.

this natural rate of wages was over long periods of time virtually constant and uniform. Not only was this rate of wages practically fixed, but it was, as a matter of fact, thought to be close to the point of physical subsistence.

Just as market values might differ temporarily from natural values, so might the market rates of wages differ from the natural rate. But these aberrations could only be temporary. Temporary disparities between the quantity of labor offered and the demand for labor, for example, might cause [21] "the market price of labour to exceed its natural price." But the fatal principle of population would prevent this gain from being made permanent, for Ricardo proceeds to observe, that "when by the encouragement which high wages give to the increase of population, the number of labourers is increased, wages again fall to their natural price."

Such a statement as this shows how relatively fixed in reality Ricardo thought this "natural" price to be. It did not shift upward as wages rose. It remained constant, and the temporary increase of wages through the separate or combined influences of a higher birth rate or a lower death rate merely released such an increase of population as to lower the margin of cultivation until wages were once more at their natural level.

Nor could market wages long remain below this "natural" standard for [22] "then poverty deprives them of those comforts which custom renders absolute necessaries. It is only after their privations have reduced their number, or the demand for labour has increased, that the market price of labour will rise to its natural price." Thus the reason why the natural price of labor would not be permanently lowered was, apparently, that this natural price was already so near the subsistence level that any appreciable impairment of it could only result in such a reduction of physical vitality as to appreciably decrease the size of the population. This in turn would raise the margin of cultivation and cause wages to return to this natural price.

If further evidence were needed of the constancy with which Ricardo's natural wage remained close to the subsistence point, one has but to turn to the mechanism of his theory of distribution. An increase in the population necessitates, of course, the cultivation of inferior soils, and by increasing the differentials between the output on the better soils and production at the

[21] Ricardo, *Works* (McCulloch edition), p. 51.
[22] Ricardo, *op. cit.*, p. 51.

new margin causes rents to rise. The joint return to labor and to capital is the amount produced on the no-rent margin, and this of course falls. None of this loss, according to Ricardo, is borne by labor in the form of reduced wages, and all of it is instead transferred to capital through a reduction in "profits." Were the "natural" rate of wages such that wages could be permanently impaired this result need not follow for labor could then bear a share of the loss. But that Ricardo regarded this natural rate of wages as so low that it could not be reduced is evidenced by his declaration that [23] "it is impossible to conceive that the money price of wages should fall or remain stationary with a gradually increasing price of necessaries; and therefore it may be taken for granted that, under ordinary circumstances, no permanent rise takes place in the price of necessaries, without occasioning or having been preceded by a rise in wages." The size of the population was, therefore, determined at any one time by the inroads which could be made upon the profits of capital and was limited by the irreducible amount which had to be paid to that factor.

Ricardo therefore fundamentally conceived of labor as being supplied under conditions of constant cost and with an almost infinite elasticity of supply. An improvement in production giving higher real wages for the time would merely call forth more population which would in turn reduce the rate to the former level when the increase in population would then cease. Not only did Ricardo thus assume a constancy in the amount of real wages per worker, but if his theory of distribution be analyzed it will also be found that the proportionate share of the total product of industry which labor as a whole received was to be constant as well.

3. The Early Attempts to Frame a Quantitative Law of Population Growth. Quetelet and Verhulst

The first attempt to form a more definite law of population growth was made by Quetelet. He pointed out that if there were no obstacles, population would tend to increase, as it had in the United States, in a geometric ratio; but that as it did increase, the mere size of the aggregate would cause the rate of increase to fall until the population would tend "more and more to become stationary." [24] Quetelet, however, made no attempt

---

[23] Ricardo, *op. cit.*, p. 65.
[24] Quetelet. *Sur L'Homme* (1835), Vol. I, p. 277. "*La population tend à croître selon une progression géométrique. La résistance, ou la somme des obstacles à son développement, est, toutes choses égales d'ailleurs, comme le*

to work out any mathematical formula to illustrate this vague theory.

Three years later, however, the Belgian mathematician, Verhulst, stimulated perhaps by Quetelet's hint, worked out a formula which has been singularly neglected until recent years.[25] Verhulst pointed out that there must be an upper limit to the population which could be supported on a given area. The relative rate of increase must consequently grow constantly less as the population itself expands. The percentage of growth must, therefore, be some function of the population itself which will decrease as the population increases.

Verhulst derived a theoretical curve of population growth which was evenly divided into two halves. The first half of the curve from the point of origin upward was convex to the base, with the absolute amount of the annual growth increasing with each year. After this half-way point or the point of inflection was reached, the amount of the absolute annual growth began to diminish steadily and at a constant figure. The upper half of the curve was consequently concave to the base. At the upper and lower extremes the curve, of course, merged approximately into a straight line which furnished the limits, or asymptotes, within which the curve operated. In a pure example of this type of curve, to which Verhulst gave the name of "logistic," the two halves are symmetrical. The curve falls away after the point of inflection has been passed at precisely the same rate and to the same degree by which it has risen during the period in which the annual increments of population increase. If only the increases in population were to be shown we would indeed have the familiar symmetrical bell-shaped curve.

---

carré de la vitesse avec laquelle la population tend à croître." (Italics author's)

Later, "Ainsi, quand une population peut se développer librement et sans obstacles, elle croît selon une progression géométrique; si le développement a lieu au milieu d'obstacles de toute espèce qui tendent à l'arrêter et qui agissent d'une manière uniforme, c'est-à-dire si *l'état social ne change point* la population n'augmente pas d'une manière indéfinie, mais elle tend de plus en plus à devenir *stationnaire.* p. 278.

[25] P. F. Verhulst, *Notice sur la loi que la population suit dans son accroissement.* Correspondance mathématique et physique publié par A. Quetelet, Tome X, 1838, pp. 113–21. For his two later papers see Recherches Mathématiques sur la loi d'accroissement de la population. *Nouveaux Mémoires de l'Académie Royale des Sciences et Belles-Lettres de Bruxelles,* Vol. XVIII, 1845, pp. 1–38 and, Deuxième Mémoire sur la loi d'accroissement de la population. *Ibid.,* Vol. XX, 1847, pp. 1–32. For a translation of the essential passages and an explanation of Verhulst's work, see G. U. Yule, *Journal Royal Statistical Society,* (1925), pp. 42–5.

There might of course be an almost infinite variety of such logistic curves with wide differences in their slopes. These would depend on the distance between the lower and upper limits and the length of the period before the population reached the saturation point. Verhulst pointed out that there was not sufficient statistical evidence to indicate the degree to which this theoretical formula actually measured the course of population growth, although the agreement between the results secured by his formula and the population of France from 1817 to 1831, of Belgium from 1815 to 1833, and the county of Essex in England from 1811 to 1831, were close.[26]

4. Raymond Pearl's Law of Population Growth

Verhulst's work was however relatively unnoticed and it was not until 1920 that the American biometricians, Pearl and Reed, of Johns Hopkins University, in trying to frame a law of population growth for the United States, arrived independently at precisely the same formula.[27] They then pointed out, however, that this was but a first approximation of the true law of population growth since it was highly improbable that the point of inflection would be precisely half-way in the cycle and that the two sections of the curve should be absolutely symmetrical with each other.[28] In the intervening years they have worked out mathematical modifications of the formula, which takes account of the actual movement of population in the past and is thus made much more flexible than it was when originally formulated. It may be expressed by the following equation.

$$y = \frac{k}{1 + me^{a_1 x + a_2 x^2 + a_3 x^3 + \dots + a_n x^n}}$$

Where y denotes the population in millions and x represents time.[29]

Pearl has also tested the actual course of population in no less than seventeen countries with the values secured from the formula with its appropriate constants,[30] while by an extensive program of research he has attempted to determine the probable

[26] Yule, *op. cit.*, p. 43.

[27] Raymond Pearl and L. J. Reed, "On the Rate of Growth of the Population of the United States since 1790, and Its Mathematical Representation." *Proceedings National Academy of Sciences*, Vol. 6 (1920), pp. 275–88.

[28] "A Further Note on the Mathematical Theory of Population Growth." *Ibid.*, Vol. 8 (1922), pp. 365–8; "On the Mathematical Theory of Population Growth." *Metron*, Vol. 3 (1923), pp. 6–19; Pearl, *Studies in Human Biology*, pp. 571–83.

[29] For a fuller description of this formula and its properties see Raymond Pearl, *Studies in Human Biology*, Chapter XXIV.

[30] See *Biology of Population Growth* (1925), pp. 11–24; 45–130.

causes which induce the course of population to follow the general type of the S-shaped curve.[31]

The coincidence between the curves of population growth for various countries which Pearl and Reed have worked out from their formulae and the actual census counts for the respective nations is striking. For some countries, however, the census returns exist for so short a space of time that it is difficult to determine whether the agreement between the two is due solely to the law of growth or whether the curve within the known points has not been formed by the observations themselves. Ordinarily, when figures are available for less than a century the observations form so small a portion of the entire curve that it is difficult to lay down a rule as to the degree to which the actual ratio of growth conforms to the general formulae of Pearl and Reed.

There are fairly adequate data, however, for five countries, namely, Sweden, the United States, France, England, and Algeria. Population censuses have been taken decennially in the first country since 1750, in the United States since 1790, and in France and England since 1800.

Accurate population counts have been made in Algeria only since 1886, but due to the rapidity with which that country had moved through its population cycle and to the fortunate taking of the census every five rather than every ten years, we have a fairly complete picture of an apparently almost completed epoch of population growth.

The degree of correspondence between the population curve for each of these countries as computed by the Pearl-Reed formulae and the actual census counts is shown graphically in the series of charts from 62 to 66 inclusive. The circles represent the population in the various census years, the solid lines in the curve the rate of population growth during this period which would be expected from the Pearl-Reed formulae, and the dotted lines at each extreme of the solid lines, the extrapolated curve of growth. The agreement between the actual rate of population growth and that secured by the Pearl-Reed formulae is remarkable. The exact degree of concurrence for Sweden, the United States, and England is shown in Table 43, and the percentages by which the populations calculated by Pearl for these countries differed from the actual count are

---

[31] Pearl, *The Biology of Population Growth*, pp. 25–44, 131–57.

given in Table 44.   Table 45 gives this same material together with the percentages of difference for both France and the native population of Algeria.

TABLE 43

A COMPARISON OF POPULATION GROWTH IN SWEDEN, THE UNITED STATES, AND
ENGLAND AND WALES UP TO 1920 AS CALCULATED FROM
PEARL-REED FORMULA AND AS OBSERVED

Population in Millions

Year	Sweden		United States		England-Wales[1]	
	Calculated	Observed	Calculated	Observed	Calculated	Observed
1750	1.800	1.763				
1760	1.864	1.893				
1770	1.944	2.030				
1780	2.041	2.118				
1790	2.160	2.158	3.929	3.929	9.084	8.893
1800	2.302	2.347	5.336	5.308	9.084	8.893
1810	2.471	2.378	7.228	7.240	10.364	10.164
1820	2.669	2.585	9.757	9.638	11.853	12.000
1830	2.900	2.888	13.109	12.866	13.570	13.897
1840	3.162	3.139	17.506	17.069	15.531	15.914
1850	3.455	3.483	23.192	23.192	17.746	17.928
1860	3.776	3.800	30.412	31.443	20.219	20.066
1870	4.119	4.168	39.372	38.558	22.942	22.712
1880	4.477	4.566	50.177	50.156	25.894	25.974
1890	4.841	4.785	62.769	62.948	29.046	29.003
1900	5.202	5.136	76.870	75.995	32.351	32.528
1910	5.549	5.522	91.972	91.972	35.755	36.070
1920	5.876	5.904	107.394	105.711	39.169	37.887

[1] The figures for England and Wales are in reality for 1801, 1811, 1821, etc. instead of for 1800, 1810, 1820, etc.   For purposes of rough comparability with Sweden and the United States, however, they have each been pushed back one year.

The degree of correspondence is on the whole impressive.   In only one case out of the last ten Swedish censuses has the deviation been more than 2 per cent, while out of the first thirteen censuses in the United States the difference amounted to over 2 per cent in but two cases, while in seven it was less than 1 per cent.   The record for England and Wales is even more striking. The deviation there had never up to 1921 exceeded 2.5 per cent and in six cases had been less than 1 per cent.   Most impressive of all, however, is the case of France.   Not only has the divergence never exceeded 1.7 per cent, but in no less than 10 cases it has been less than 1 per cent.

Pearl has been able to derive from his formula what he regards as the probable upper limit of the population in the various countries if conditions remain as they have been during

TABLE 44

PERCENTAGE DEVIATION OF POPULATIONS CALCULATED FROM THE PEARL-REED
FORMULA FROM THE ACTUAL NUMBERS IN SWEDEN, THE UNITED STATES, AND
ENGLAND AND WALES UP TO 1920

Year	Percentage Deviation in		
	Sweden	United States	England and Wales
1750	+2.1		
1760	−1.5		
1770	−4.2		
1780	−3.6		
1790	+0.1	0.0	
1800	−1.9	+0.5	+2.0
1810	+3.9	−0.2	+2.0
1820	+3.2	+1.2	−1.2
1830	+0.4	+1.9	−2.4
1840	+0.7	+2.6	−2.5
1850	−1.1	0.0	−1.0
1860	−0.6	−3.3	+0.7
1870	−1.2	+2.0	+1.0
1880	−1.9	0[1]	−0.3
1890	+1.2	−0.3	+0.1
1900	+1.3	+1.2	−0.5
1910	+4.9	0.0	−0.9
1920	−0.5	+1.7	+3.3

[1] Less than .1 of 1%.

the present industrial epoch or cycle. These he finds to be as
follows for the most important countries.

Country	Estimated Upper Limit of Population (in millions)	Country	Estimated Upper Limit of Population (in millions)
United States........	197.3	Hungary..........	39.0
Denmark............	13.4	Italy..............	49.1
England and Wales...	73.0	Norway............	3.8
France..............	42.6	Scotland...........	8.2
Germany............	116.5	Japan.............	86.6

While virtually all of the countries have not passed the point
of inflection, France and Sweden are found to be in the latter
stages of their population cycle. Germany presents a somewhat
different problem. Up to 1861 its increase was not particularly
rapid, but from then on its rate of development was much
greater. This would seem to refute Pearl's theory. He explains
this apparent discrepancy, however, on the ground that during
the earlier years Germany was in the latter part of a previous
population cycle, but that the great industrial changes which
occurred both before and after the war of 1871 launched it in
turn upon a new cycle of growth.

TABLE 45

A COMPARISON OF THE GROWTH OF THE POPULATION OF FRANCE AND OF THE
NATIVE POPULATION OF ALGERIA AS CALCULATED FROM THE
PEARL-REED FORMULA AND AS OBSERVED IN ACTUALITY

Population in Millions

Year	France			Algeria		
	Calculated	Observed	Percentage Deviation of Calculated from Observed	Calculated	Observed	Percentage Deviation of Calculated from Observed
1801	26.668	26.931	−1.0			
1821	30.059	29.871	+0.6			
1841	33.063	33.401	−1.0			
1861	35.563	35.845	−0.8			
1866	36.104	36.495	−1.1			
1872	36.709	36.103	+1.7			
1876	37.087	36.906	−0.5	2.753	2.463	+10.5
1881	37.531	37.672	−0.4	2.962	2.842	+4.0
1886	37.944	38.219	−0.7	3.224	3.287	−1.9
1891	38.328	38.343	0[1]	3.529	3.577	−1.3
1896	38.685	38.518	+0.4	3.859	3.781	+2.0
1901	39.015	38.962	+0.1	4.184	4.098	+2.1
1906	39.319	39.252	+0.2	4.478	4.478	0.0
1911	39.600	39.602	0[1]	4.723	4.741	−0.4
1921	40.051	39.200	+0.8	5.060	4.925	+2.7

[1] Less than .1 of 1%.

An interesting parallelism to the growth of human population is shown in Pearl's experiments with Drosophila, or fruit flies. They are found to increase in half-pint bottles, where the food supply is kept constant, according to a logistic curve. The same parallelism applies in the case of yeast which multiplies according to a closely similar curve. This suggests to Pearl that there may well be a common cause which operates upon both flies and men.

What, then, is the probable cause for this observed tendency of population aggregates to follow some form of an S-shaped curve, and for the relative and then the absolute rate of growth to decrease? Pearl tends to give an almost purely biological answer. Growth decreases because density lessens fertility. Three sets of data are advanced in support of this hypothesis. The first bit of proof is that of the experiment with poultry which Pearl made at the Maine Agricultural Experiment Station from 1904 to 1907. "The birds in the experiment," Pearl states,[32] "were handled in flocks of 50, 100 and 150 each. The

[32] Pearl, *The Biology of Population Growth*, p. 141.

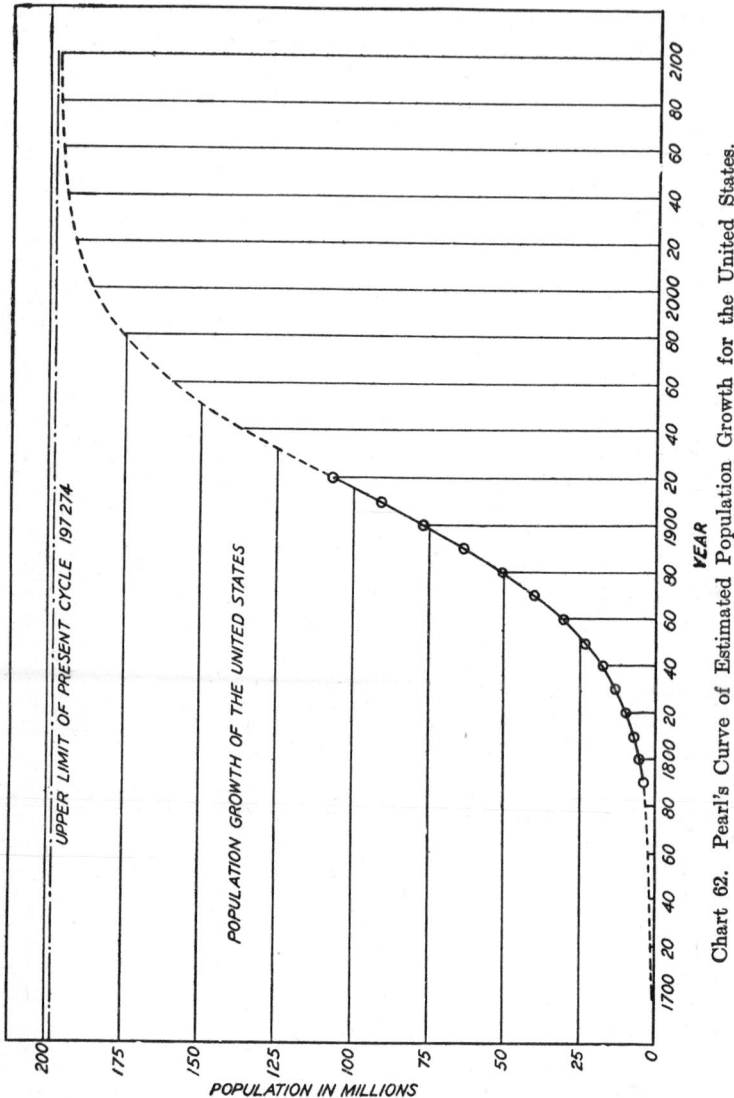

UPPER LIMIT OF PRESENT CYCLE 197.274

POPULATION GROWTH OF THE UNITED STATES

POPULATION IN MILLIONS

YEAR

Chart 62. Pearl's Curve of Estimated Population Growth for the United States.

pens in which they were kept were so constructed that in the flocks of 50 and 100 birds each there was an allotment of 4.8 square feet of floor space per bird, while in the flocks of 150 birds there was an allotment of 3.2 square feet of floor space per bird." Since the composition of each flock was made comparable

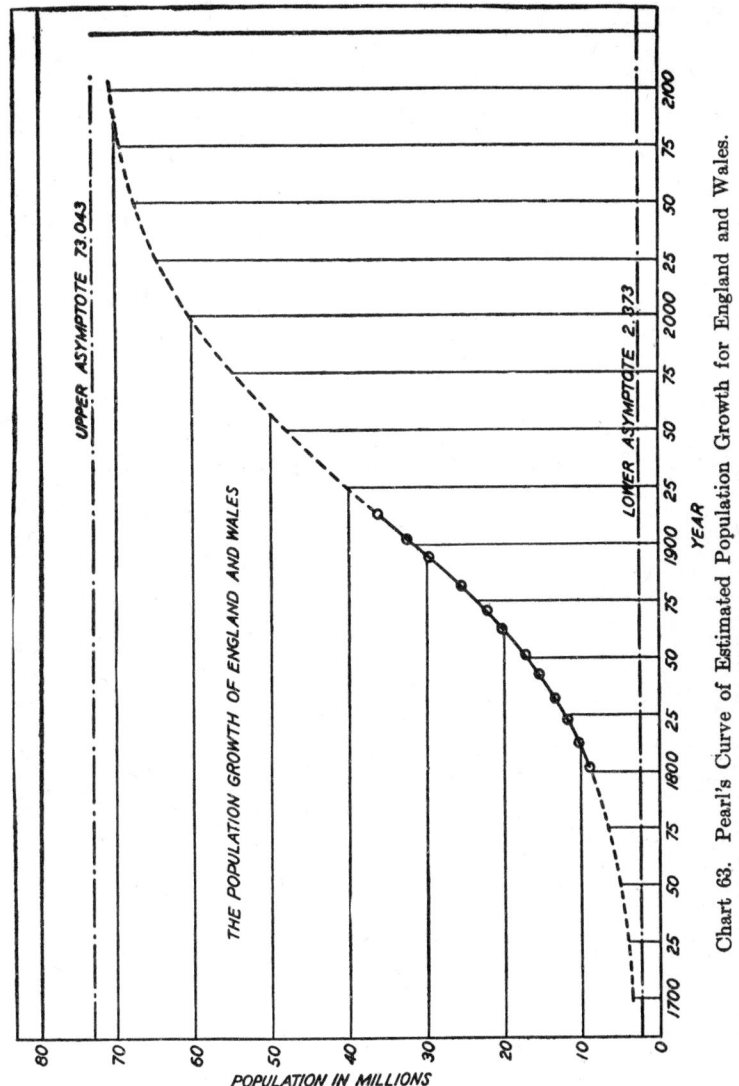

Chart 63. Pearl's Curve of Estimated Population Growth for England and Wales.

as regards strain, quality, etc., the results were said to indicate the effect upon the egg producing capacities of hens of: (1) the number of birds associated together. This is shown by comparing the 50 bird pen with the 100 bird pen in which the amount of floor space per hen was equal. The average annual production of eggs per bird during the three years in the 50 bird pen

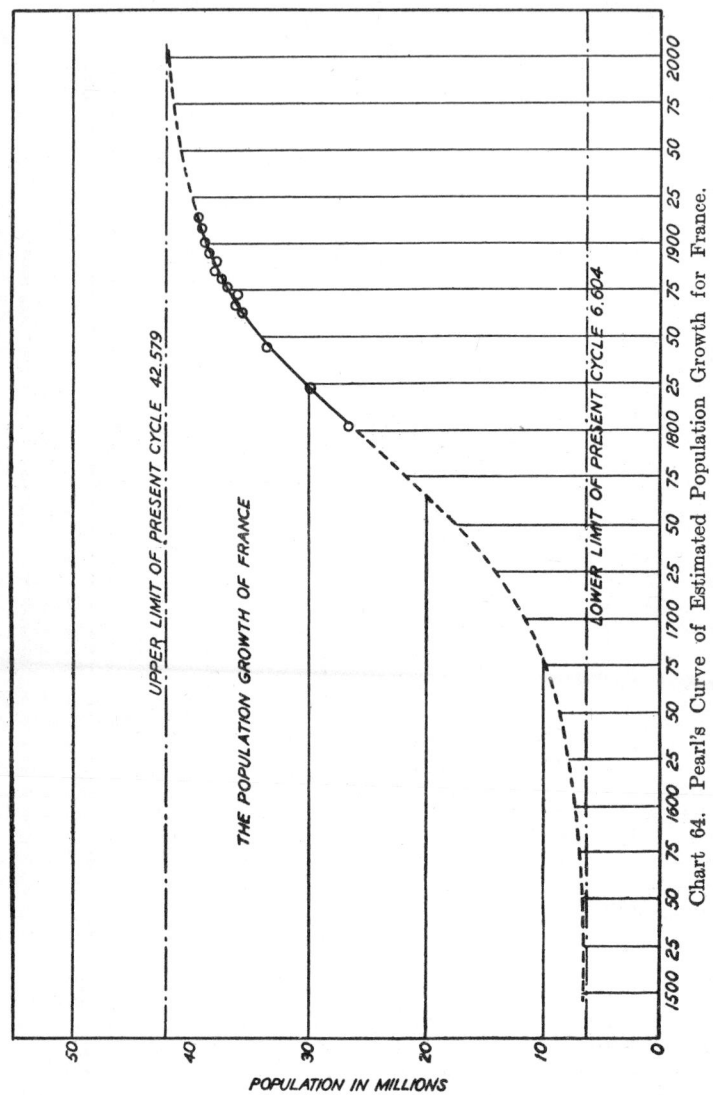

POPULATION IN MILLIONS

Chart 64. Pearl's Curve of Estimated Population Growth for France.

was 129.7 while it was but 123.2 in the 100 bird pen.[33] This indicated that the mere increase of contacts without any decrease in the space per bird lowered fertility. (2) Increased density. The fowls in the 150 bird pen produced an average of only **111.7**

[33] *Ibid.*, p. 143.

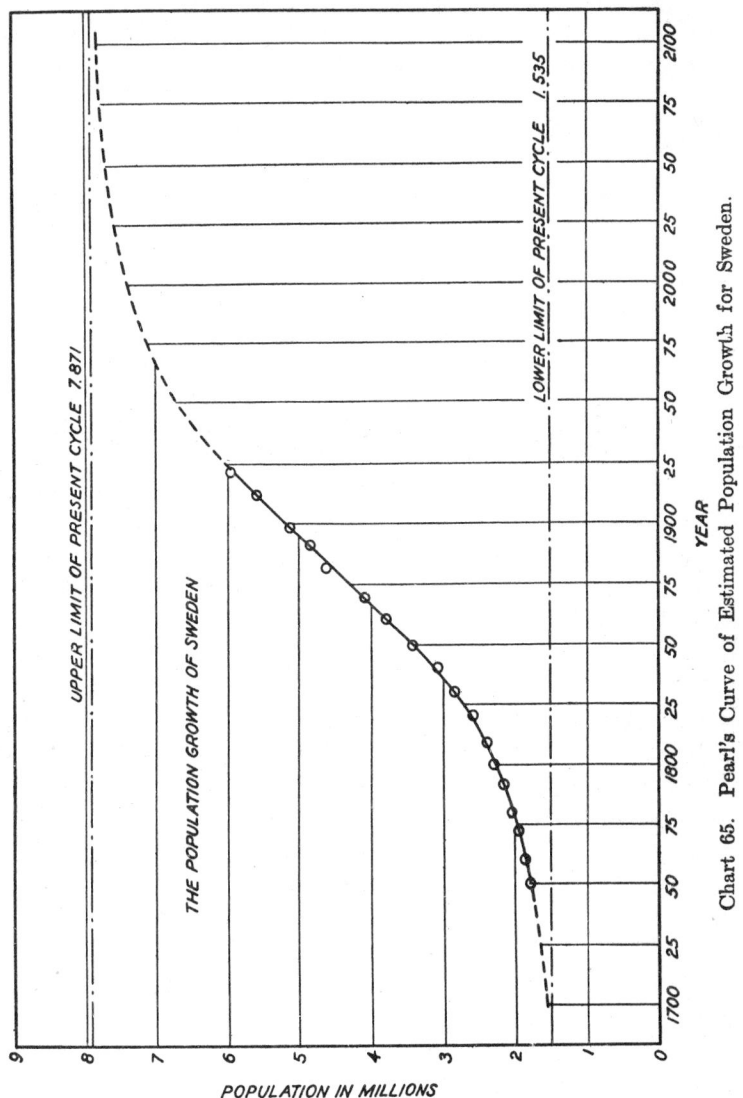

POPULATION IN MILLIONS

Chart 65.   Pearl's Curve of Estimated Population Growth for Sweden.

eggs annually. This was 11.5 eggs or approximately 10 per cent less than the average for the 100 bird pen, and 18 eggs or 14 per cent less than the 50 bird pen. It should be noted that Pearl cites this latter fact as proof that lessened space *per se* decreases fertility. But this was probably caused in part and possibly may have been entirely caused by the fact that there were more hens

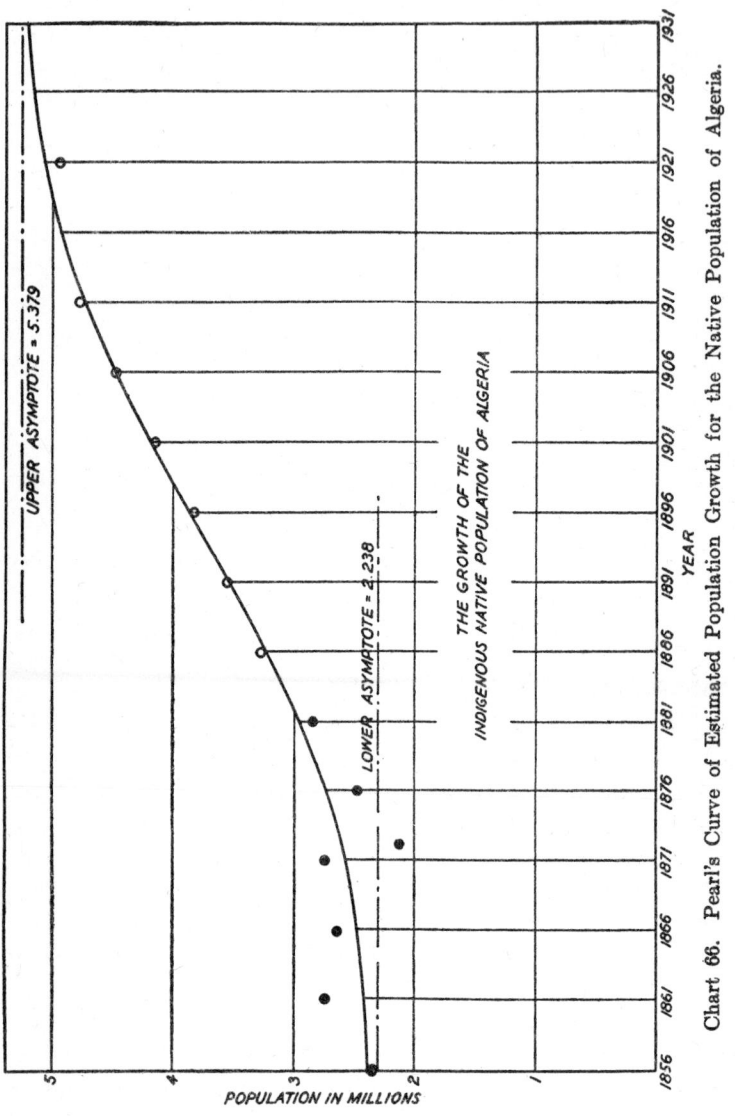

Chart 66. Pearl's Curve of Estimated Population Growth for the Native Population of Algeria.

in the pen.[34] The first factor discussed may, therefore, have influenced the second.

The second set of statistical data are those for Drosophila, or

---

[34] To isolate this possibility, the hens which were given 3.2 square feet of floor space should have been combined in flocks of 50 or 100 instead of one of 150.

fruit flies. A number of bottles with equal amounts of food were started with varying numbers of pairs of flies. The flies in the relatively uncrowded bottles were found to produce a much greater number of progeny [35] than the flies in those which were more densely populated.

In his third set of proof, Pearl has attempted to draw a similar conclusion for man. Correlating the statistics for a large number of American cities of (1) the average number of persons per dwelling and (2) the birth rate per 1000 married women in the child-bearing ages, he finds a negative coefficient of correlation of $-.175 \pm .057$. Since the net correlation was slightly more than three times its probable error, he concludes,[36] "that in these urban human populations, *the real net correlation between birth rate and density is of the same character fundamentally as that we have found in experimental populations of flies and hens.*" [37]

Such a conclusion as this seems to be somewhat forced when it is remembered that the degree of relationship is supposed to be indicated fairly accurately by the square of the coefficient of correlation. When $-.175$ is squared, density appears to be responsible at the most for only 3 per cent or one-thirty-third of the decline in the birth rate.

The validity of Pearl's generalization becomes still more dubious when it is remembered that he compared only the relative densities and birth rates as between cities. He did not try to determine the degree of relationship between those two factors within the cities. Had he done this, he would have found, as all other studies have shown, that the most densely populated sections have appreciably higher birth rates than the less crowded areas.[38] The most crowded residential sections of cities

[35] Pearl, *The Biology of Population Growth*, pp. 133–36.

[36] *Ibid.*, p. 155.

[37] Italics author's.

[38] Thus the standardized legitimate birth rates of the three most and the three least crowded boroughs of London in 1911 and 1921–1922 were as follows:

Borough	Rooms per Person	Birth Rate per 1000 Married Women of Child-bearing Age	
		1911	*1921*
Shoreditch	.65	242	228
Bethnal Green	.68	237	203
Stepney	.69	235	201
Westminster	1.23	141	120
Lewisham	1.24	175	157
Hampstead	1.41	147	138

See T. T. S. De Jastrzebski, "Changes in the Birth Rate and in Legitimate

are those populated by the less skilled workers. Their birth rate is the highest in the whole population while the birth rate of the wealthy who have infinitely more elbow room than any other group is the lowest of all. Pearl's attempt, therefore, to reduce Drosophila and man to a common basis as regards the causes of population growth is singularly inconclusive.

5. An Examination of Pearl's Theory.

This theory has such a boldness of conception and is apparently so corroborated by the actual course of events that many have concluded that Pearl has discovered the secret of population growth and hence of the most important factor in the long-run supply of labor. The theory does, however, have a number of very important qualifications and weaknesses which distinctly limit its significance.

(1) In the first place, Pearl's addition• of the several constants which were designed to make the point of inflection more flexible, and which in turn determine the relative slope of the two portions of the curve, tend to make the curve a generalized picture of what has happened rather than an inflexible law of growth to which populations must and will conform. It does not necessarily indicate that any biological forms of the kind Pearl mentions are at work.

Closely allied with this is the fact that by continually revising the curve in the light of the new data, Pearl succeeds in keeping it in rather close conformity to the facts. The question then presents itself as to how different the results secured would be were the end values to be omitted. Pearl has, to be sure, made just such tests in the case of the United States and Algeria and has found that the omission of these final observations and the use of the earlier data alone gave results which at the most did not vary by more than 2 per cent from those secured by utilizing the end values. But this test needs to be applied to many other populations before this criticism can be regarded as having been satisfactorily met.

(2) The value of the formula as a predictive device decreases the farther it is projected into the future. My colleague, Professor Henry Schultz,[39] has shown that the relative size of the probable error increases with the period of extrapolation. Thus

---

Fertility in London," *Journal Royal Statistical Society,* Vol. LXXXVI (1923), pp. 26–45.

[39] Henry Schultz, "The Standard Error of a Forecast from a Curve." *Journal American Statistical Association,* June, 1930, p. 173.

instead of the estimated upper limit of the population of the United States, which Pearl estimates as 197 millions in the year 2100, being subject to a standard error of ± 0.82 millions, Schultz shows that the real probable error is ± 10.5 millions, or over twelve times as much. Even if we grant all of Pearl's other assumptions, therefore, it would be difficult to predict population growth for very long in advance. The much greater decrease in the birth rate during the twenties than had been expected has, as a matter of fact, probably lowered the probable maximum population from Pearl's estimate of 197 millions to nearer 170 millions. This maximum is, moreover, likely to be reached by 1970 or 1980 instead of in 2100 as Pearl had forecast. Pearl's estimate for 1930 was however very close to the mark being 122.4 millions as compared with the actual count of 122.8 millions.

(3) Pearl's theory of what constitutes an industrial cycle or epoch seems, moreover, to be faulty. He thinks of the transition from one epoch to another as essentially spasmodic and discontinuous. Thus the agricultural stage replaces in a sudden burst the pastoral mode of life, while machine industry and the factory system are introduced with an almost cataclysmic abruptness. Once the new industrial epoch has been entered, the upper limit remains fixed and is not raised until a new cycle is in turn launched. His view of the way in which progress occurs can be illustrated diagrammatically as follows:

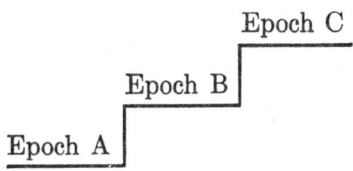

But progress in the organization of our productive mechanism is not as jerky and spasmodic as this. It is of course true that the successful development of steam power rapidly unleashed increased productive energy, but the transitions into other stages have been more gradual. More important still is the fact that the upper limit is not constant for long periods of time as Pearl assumes, but is, instead, in our modern dynamic age rising steadily. When the limiting force to population is the amount of product which can be turned out with a given body of technical knowledge,[40] it is then apparent that this technical knowledge is now being increased steadily and that it does not conform to the principle of discontinuous progress which Pearl postulates. Thus while the development of harvesting machinery came many years after the advent of the factory system, it too increased the productive capacities of society and thus raised the fixed limits above what they would otherwise have been. The development of more efficient methods of cultivation, of stock-raising, and of manufacture, serves in effect to do the same thing. In an age such as ours, when inventions and improvements are the order of the day, the limit is constantly being advanced. The upper ceiling of population growth is therefore not constant within a long time cycle but, instead, slopes upward. Since there are some periods in which impressive relative changes occur more rapidly than they do at other times, it seems probable that the upper limit of population growth moves upward at uneven rates of speed. The following diagram would, therefore, seem to represent the changes in upper asymptotes more accurately than that which has been used for Pearl's theory.

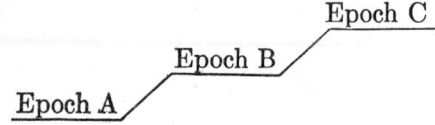

(4) Pearl's theory of cataclysmic changes in industrial processes seems, moreover, to be at war with his doctrine that the amount of population growth decreases at the end of one cycle by infinitesimal amounts and increases at the beginning of another epoch by infinitesimal amounts. While it is true that these amounts of growth are relative to different cycles, it would seem nevertheless that if his theory were true there would not be a great absolute difference between the increase in population at these times. Yet if the cataclysmic changes in production which Pearl postulates are true we could only expect a very quick response in the form of a big upward jump in population. Pearl's theories, therefore, seem to be inconsistent with themselves at this point.

(5) Still another unsatisfactory feature of Pearl's concept of a cycle is evidenced in the explanations which he offers for a number of countries. Thus he assumes that France has been

---

[40] That is assuming capital per capita to be constant.

in its present cycle ever since 1500, while Germany is assumed to have been in its present epoch only since 1870. Two questions immediately present themselves. First, is it credible that the industrial organization of France has not been improved in the last four hundred years, and that France has not shared in the general advance which all the rest of the western world has made? Second, how did it happen that Germany should have been over four and a half centuries behind France in entering into this new epoch? It may be replied to this that the cycle which Germany began in 1870 was not the one which France is now in, but a more advanced stage, which France even yet has not entered. But this in turn overlooks the fact that Pearl fixes the date for the inception of the previous German cycle as only slightly before 1700.[41] Even this date was approximately two hundred years after the beginning of the so-called "present" French epoch. In view of the cultural interdependence of the world, it can, I think, hardly be maintained that the Germans have had two new cycles since the French began theirs! It seems probable, therefore, that the timing of Pearl's assumed cycles does not fit the facts of the case.

There are a number of other instances in which Pearl's theory makes the new cycle arrive in various countries at somewhat widely diverging times. His theory offers no explanation for this lag in the geographical extension of what the anthropologists designate as material culture. Yet the relative speed of this diffusion is clearly one factor in determining the amount of increase in population and in the labor supply which one country can expect in any given period of time. The suspicion that Pearl's dating of the commencement of growth cycles is frequently incorrect is deepened when we consider the case of Japan. In order to construct his S-shaped curve, Pearl extrapolates his curve backwards and apparently finds the inception of the modern era at 1850.[42] Now despite the forcible opening of Japan in 1846 to western trade and commerce by Commodore Perry, no competent student of Japanese history would maintain that the new system of trade and industry had attained much strength before 1870. It seems probable, therefore, that if the real dates for the inception of what Pearl chooses to term cycles were actually determined, the curve of population growth would not exhibit the smoothed regularity which he assumes.

---

[41] See *The Biology of Death*, p. 21.
[42] *Studies in Human Biology*, p. 59.

(6) Another point which Pearl's theory fails to explain is what determines the length of the cycle and why some nations, according to his computations, pass through it much more rapidly than others. Thus the population cycle in Algeria is assumed to be either 60 or 85 years.[43] But the French cycle, which is assumed to have begun in 1500, is not to finish its course until the year 2000. This is from six to eight times as long as the cycle which Pearl computes for Algeria. What then is the reason for this great difference? Pearl would probably ascribe as the cause the great love of sexual pleasure which seems to be so characteristic of the Arab and which is fostered by his religion and culture.[44] Even such an explanation as this indicates that there are cultural and psychological factors which cause the rate of speed at which nations move from their lower to their upper asymptote to vary widely.

A comparison of the approximate length of the cycles, which Pearl computes for various countries, indicates some of these striking differences, although there is a general tendency for most of his present "cycles" to approximate 400 years.[45]

Country	Approximate Length of Present Cycle (in years)	Country	Approximate Length of Present Cycle (in years)
Scotland	500	Denmark	400
France	500	Hungary	400
Italy	500	Norway	400
England and Wales	400	Japan	325
Sweden	400	Java	300
United States	400	Serbia	250
Austria	400	Germany	180
Belgium	400		

The supply of labor available at different periods of an industrial epoch will, therefore, vary according to the degree that there is a difference in the rate of speed in which the cycle is traversed. Thus two countries might start from equal lower limits and ultimately arrive at the same upper limit but differ in the time required to complete their journey. During the first century or so of growth, one country would have a much

---

[43] *Ibid.*, p. 72.

[44] For a brief discussion of this, see Pearl, *The Biology of Population Growth*, pp. 105–20.

[45] Data from Pearl, *Studies in Human Biology*. I have regarded the cycle as existing between those points where the calculated population would be not more than approximately 2 per cent from the asymptotes.

larger laboring force than the other, and this would alter the results of the distributive process.

(7) Finally and perhaps most important of all is the fact that when the various nations arrive at their upper limits, there is no necessary equivalence in their per capita standard of living. Thus the upper asymptote for France is fixed at 42.6 millions and for the United States at 197.3. If all other elements remain constant, the ultimate population of the United States according to Pearl will therefore be 4.6 times that of France. Yet all students of the World's food, mineral, and energy resources know that the total resources of the United States are more than 4.6 times those of France. Even allowing for modifications produced by the relative exchange values of commodities in international trade, the conclusion seems obvious that there will be a higher standard of living for the American population at its maximum than for the French people at their upper limit.

Similarly, the upper asymptote for Italy is estimated as 49 millions or approximately one quarter the limit for the American people. Yet since Italy's total resources are much less than one-quarter of those which belong to the United States, this can only mean a lower standard of living for her people at her saturation point than the American people will enjoy at theirs. Pearl's formula does not, therefore, mean that the population pressure will ultimately be equalized at different portions of the earth's surface but, instead, that wide variations will probably still be existent when the present cycles have been completed. Purely biological factors would seem to be insufficient to explain the existence of these differences.

That there are cultural forces which help to determine the maximum point of population which a country may attain can easily be demonstrated. Had the Chinese, with their cultural traditions of large families and ancestor worship, discovered and settled America instead of the European races, is it not overwhelmingly probable that their upper limit would have been much more than 197 millions? There must, therefore, be another limiting factor to population besides national resources and industrial processes. This can only be the standard of living or the scale of life which people prefer to enjoy rather than to have more children. If, therefore, the people were to raise their standard of living, the upper limit would be lowered, while a permanent fall in the standard of life would lift the upper asymptote. Yet there is no mention in Pearl's theory of the standard of living as a causative force upon population. Pearl conceives instead of the standard of living as being only a derivative of man's tendency to expand and of the purely biological effect of density upon fertility. Yet although man cannot perhaps, by taking thought, add a cubit to his stature, it seems probable that he can help to determine the upper limits of the population of his society.

Upon closer analysis, therefore, the problem of population growth is seen to be much more indeterminate than Pearl believes. His curve of growth is probably fairly accurate in predicting the increases in population which will occur within the next ten or twenty years, but its predictive value beyond that period is much more dubious. It is of course probably true that the actual growth will tend to conform to some form of an S-shaped curve, but this will vary widely according to (a) the date of starting the movement of growth, (b) the length of the cycle, (c) the slope of the curve, (d) the possible difference between the upper and lower limits, (e) the degree of improvements in industrial processes, and (f) changes in the standard of living.

The hints which Quetelet, Verhulst, and Pearl have offered us, therefore, while suggestive, are not yet capable of being formulated into a precise mathematical law. They do, however, indicate in themselves that in all probability not only will the relative rate of growth per year in the population decrease in the future, but that the absolute quantity of growth will decrease in the case of most western European nations which seem indeed to be already past the point of inflections in their growth curves.

6. The Influence of Higher Standards of Living Made Possible by Wage Increases upon Population Growth

Increases in the standard of living, or the quantity of goods and services which people prefer to children, will slacken the rate of population growth. How then do these more expensive standards come to be adopted as their own by the wage-earners? Does an increase in wages merely leave the workers with the same fundamental set of material desires as before, or does it arouse them not only to claim but also to obtain the newer pleasures which for a time they have been enabled to enjoy? Does the existence of a considerable amount of economic inequality so stimulate with envy those in the lower economic ways of life that this group will make great sacrifices to obtain the comforts and luxuries which they see that the more well-to-do possess? Finally to what extent will a reduction in the number of hours worked release new wants which will lead in turn to a reduction in the birth rate? These issues have been widely discussed in the century that has elapsed since the final revision of Malthus' essay.[46]

The generation of economists which followed Malthus were divided on the question as to whether an increase in real earnings would set into play forces which would reduce the number of births. The elder Mill and McCulloch did not believe so. More Malthusian than Malthus himself, they held fast to the doctrines of the first edition of the *Essay on Population*. "The power of increase in the human species," declared McCulloch,[47] "must always, in the long run, prove an overmatch for the increase in the means of subsistence." Even if the real income of the workers were to be suddenly doubled "such a powerful stimulus would be given to the principle of increase, that in a very short period the population would be again on a level with the means of subsistence."[48] James Mill's analysis, as befitted the father of a large family, was even gloomier. Population tended to increase faster than the supply of capital, and since wages were determined by the ratio between these two factors, there was a "perpetual tendency" for them to fall. The poverty and misery in which the great body of the people lived in all countries was adduced as conclusive proof of this tendency, for such misery[49] "would have been impossible had capital increased faster than population."

This is an interesting adumbration of the point which was emphasized in Chapter XI, namely, that the return to the units of each factor depends upon their relative elasticities of supply and that the less elastic factor will always tend to gain at the expense of the more elastic one. Wages, moreover, according to Mill's view, actually tended to fall. This was very different from the teachings of Ricardo, McCulloch, and of Malthus in his younger days, that wages tended to remain constant. The difference was caused by the implicit assumption which Mill

---

[46] For a brilliantly suggestive appraisal of the Post-Malthusian literature see the paper by my former colleague, the late Professor James A. Field, "The Malthusian Controversy in England," in his posthumous *Essays on Population*, pp. 1–86.

[47] McCulloch's edition of Smith's *Wealth of Nations*, IV, p. 133.

[48] *Ibid.*, p. 1.

[49] James Mill, *Principles of Political Economy*, Chapter II.

made that the economic condition of the people had originally been superior to what it then was. Mill conceived of the pressure of population, therefore, as eating in upon the surplus which the workers had formerly enjoyed. Ricardo and McCulloch, on the other hand, assumed that the workers were normally living at the bare minimum of existence and that the expansion of population caused such a reduction in the number of people as to re-establish the old equilibrium or even temporarily to raise wages above the minimum.

This view of Mill's was challenged sharply by Senior who pointed out that primitive man, as well as workers in retarded industrial communities, lived on even a much lower level than the mass of the English workers of that day and that hence the real income of the workers had risen. Instead, therefore, of population tending to increase more rapidly than capital, the opposite was true. Labor was really more inelastic than capital, and savings were said to be generated more rapidly than children were born. But how could such a doctrine be reconciled with Malthusianism? Because "the habits of prudence in contracting marriage and of considerable superfluous expenditure afford the only permanent protection against a population pressing so closely on the means of subsistence as to be continually incurring the misery of the positive checks." [50] But since such habits of prudence existed only in a "civilized" society, and a strong desire for luxuries and decencies only in an opulent one, it followed that, "as a nation advances in civilization and opulence, the positive checks are likely to be superseded by the preventive." [51] The danger that the population will suffer from a lack of the necessaries of life will steadily decrease with time. "As wealth increases, what were the luxuries of one generation become the decencies of their successors." The birth rate therefore falls with the increase of earnings.

Senior did not, however, hazard a guess as to the rate of decrease which would be occasioned by a given increase in the level of real wages. Nor did he mention the relative influence of the death rate. The improvement of the economic conditions of the workers would undoubtedly lower the mortality rate, and this might very well be more than sufficient to compensate for the decline in the birth rate. If so, it would cause population

[50] Senior, *Principles of Political Economy*, p. 42.
[51] *Ibid.*, p. 42.

to increase at a more rapid rate than before, and would bring
wages down to their former level unless prevented by one or
both of two causes. The first would be the possibility of fresh
improvements in production which would once more raise the
level of real wages, while the second would be the still further
reduction in the birth rate which might well result if the gains
which had been made were to be eaten into. This would help
to restore the balance disturbed by the reduction in the death
rate and might lead to a re-establishment upon a higher level
of the old equilibrium with a population which neither increased
nor decreased.

While Senior had not carefully thought out his position, his
theory is very clearly based upon the belief that the increase
in the population which resulted from an increase in wages
would not be sufficient to reduce wages to their old level. The
long-time supply curve of labor would, therefore, slope upward
and to the right, but at what rate of slope is uncertain.

J. S. Mill somewhat wistfully recognized that an increase in
wages might be made permanent if "the standard of comfort
regarded as indispensable by the class, is permanently raised." [52]
Somewhat disheartened, however, because of the failure of his
early efforts to spread the knowledge of birth-control, he felt
that such an increase in the workers' wants seldom occurred. "It
is but rarely," he wrote, "that improvements in the condition
of the labouring classes do anything more than give a temporary
margin, speedily filled up by an increase of their numbers." [53]
Such an increase in the size of population would result from a
fall in the death rate of children, from "earlier and more numerous marriages, or by an increased number of births to a
marriage."

Such a change in what is regarded as the indispensable standard of living as will reduce the number of births or marriages
cannot come from improvements which make the laborers only
a little better off. Events which affected the workers only a
very little, in his opinion, made no permanent impression upon
their habits and requirements, and they would soon slide back
into their former state. To produce a permanent advantage, the
temporary increase of real wages "must be sufficient to make a
great change in their condition—a change such as will be felt
for many years, notwithstanding any stimulus which it may

---

[52] J. S. Mill, *Principles of Political Economy* (Ashley edition), p. 348.
[53] J. S. Mill, *Principles of Political Economy*, p. 161.

give during one generation to the increase of peoples." [54]   Since such increases occurred but rarely, Mill's doctrine was in the main that of Ricardo, and he fundamentally assumed that the supply of labor followed in the main the conditions of constant cost.

Several writers have strongly maintained that higher standards of living tend powerfully to reduce rather than to increase the birth rate. Some of them, notably Doubleday and Herbert Spencer, have ascribed such a diminution to physiological causes, while others, such as Dumont, have imputed it to social and to psychological causes.

Doubleday in his *True Law of Population* advanced the theory that fertility varied in inverse relation to nutrition. [55]   In support of this theory Doubleday cited the decay in numbers of the hereditary nobility of England and the failure of birthright members of the Society of Friends to increase, together with the rapid rates of increase shown by people such as the Scottish Highlanders, who were economically hard pressed. Doubleday's theory, therefore, that a plethora of food would cause the population to decline was tantamount to a belief that the long-run supply schedule of labor was negatively inclined and that it varied in some inverse ratio with the height of real wages.

Spencer's well-known theory of the conflict between individuation and genesis was based upon the belief that the increasing expenditure of energy upon intellectual and emotional things decreased fertility. [56]   Spencer consequently looked forward to a decline in the birth rate as individuals and societies improved their economic position. These interesting hypotheses have not received any adequate corroboration from the biological and genetic studies that have been made, although Dr. Brownlee [57] and Professor Gini [58] apparently believe that modern life has led

---

[54] *Ibid.*, pp. 348–9.

[55] Thomas Doubleday, *The True Law of Population* (1846), especially pp. 5–6.

[56] Spencer, *The Principles of Biology* (paragraphs 319–77), Vol. II, pp. 397–508. Also, *A Theory of Population deduced from the General Law of Animal Fertility* (1852).

[57] Brownlee, "Germinal Vitality", *Proceedings Royal Philosophical Society*, 1908; "Present Tendencies of Population in Great Britain with respect to Quantity and Quality." *Eugenics Review*, July, 1925.

[58] Corrado Gini, "Decline in the Birth-rate and the Fecundability of Woman," *Eugenics Review*, January, 1926 (Vol. XVII), pp. 259–74. Nitti in his *Population and the Social System*, in opposing birth-control through the prevention of conception, also relies upon this assumed physiological tendency for the capacity to produce children to decrease as well-being advances.

to physiological changes which have decreased the fecundability of men and women.

In his striking *Dépopulation et Civilisation,*[59] based primarily upon his observation of French life, Dumont also defended the thesis that an improvement in economic station led to a decline in the rate of population growth. Unlike Doubleday and Spencer, however, he attributed the decrease to social rather than to physiological causes. As he points out, the decay of feudalism and the rise of individualistic democracy caused the system of fixed and hereditary castes largely to disappear. Careers were opened to the talents. In their desire to attain superiority, men competed with each other for political position, for intellectual and aesthetic attainment, and most important of all for economic power. Few could fail to join the race, for if one did not compete, he soon found that he had lost ground. In this struggle to get ahead in the world, children were on the whole an embarrassment. The fewer one's children, the more energy and money could be devoted to those pursuits whereby a man secured prestige. Thus what Dumont happily termed "social capillarity" caused individuation to be indeed at war with genesis.[60]

The sunken poor who had little hope of improving their station would naturally breed more rapidly than those who had the prospect of "getting on." An improvement in their material condition would, however, tend to shake them out of this attitude of mind and by giving them a taste of the good things of life would awaken in them the desire for still more and would cause them to compete with their fellows for social and economic advancement.

Thus a democratic and industrial society converts an increase in real wages into a force which reduces the rate of population growth. This was the tendency which Dumont believed was everywhere·at work in western civilization.

Brentano [61] and Mombert [62] have perhaps made the most thorough advocacy of the theory that an increase in real wages will cause a decline in the birth rate. They have pointed out

---

[59] Arsène Dumont, *Dépopulation et Civilisation,* 1890.

[60] or as Kipling phrased it:
> "From the utmost tropics up to the Pole,
> He travels the fastest, who travels alone."

[61] See Brentano, "The Doctrine of Malthus and the Increase of Population During the Last Decades," *Economic Journal* (1910), Vol. XX, pp. 371–93.

[62] Paul Mombert, *Studien zur Bevölkerungsbewegung in Deutschland* (1907).

that the more prosperous countries of Europe have appreciably lower birth and marriage rates than the less prosperous countries, and moreover that within each country, the births are relatively fewer and the average age of marriage higher among the more well-to-do classes than among those who are lower in the economic scale. They furthermore have shown with a wealth of statistical data that the birth rate for the wage-earning classes of Europe has been falling during the last half century while their real wages have increased. This was not primarily caused by fewer people marrying or by a later average age at marriage. The latter factor was, it is true, at work in England, but in Germany the improved economic status which the agricultural workers who moved into the towns secured, led to an actual reduction in the average marriage age. By far the major part of the decrease has come, therefore, from the lessened number of births per marriage.

This decrease was in turn caused by the increase in material prosperity which led both husbands and wives to value other pleasures more highly in comparison with children than they formerly had. In homes of abject poverty, sexual pleasures, declared Brentano, are the predominant joy. Since the very poor are debarred by the lack of economic means from most other satisfactions, they turn with the more readiness to sex, and this tendency is also accentuated by the dinginess and dirt which characterize so much of their working lives. This is perhaps one of the reasons why the birth rate of the miners is in virtually every country higher [63] than that of other workmen with occupations requiring equal skill.

An increase in real wages makes it possible for the family to enjoy more pleasures and this produces in the woman [64] "a distaste for the spending of her entire existence in pregnancy and child-bed; this distaste becomes more pronounced in proportion to the increased variety and tempting character of the pleasures which must be foregone."

Similarly, the husband also comes to desire fewer children not merely in consideration of the health of his wife but also because if [65] "he were to call a great number of children into existence, the increased demand thus made upon his resources would cut him off from other possessions." Once having enjoyed

---

[63] See Zola's *Germinal* for a psychological study of this point.
[64] Brentano, *Economic Journal*, Vol. XX, p. 385.
[65] *Ibid.*, p. 387.

these new pleasures, he will not give them up for a new increase in the size of his family, but he will instead decrease the number of his children. The workers can participate in the new pleasures only if they can command the requisite means, and this, says Brentano,[66] "has popularized the state of affairs which at first was found only among the upper classes."

The greater feeling of affection towards children operates in the same direction. "Parents become more and more conscious of their responsibility both for the character and number of the human beings whom they bring into the world." They "strive to ensure to the children a good education and a larger patrimony, so as to equip them better for the modern struggle of life."

Such arguments as these, based upon a wide statistical record of birth and marriage rates throughout Europe, command respect. There is one important omission, however, in Brentano's treatment and that is his slurring over the death rate. Malthusianism is not completely refuted merely by showing a reduction in the birth rate as real wages rise. The long-run supply of workmen is affected not only by the birth rate, but also by the death rate. As a matter of fact, at the time Brentano first wrote, the latter had fallen even more rapidly than the former. There had therefore been a great expansion of population and of the labor supply. From Brentano's reasoning, it might sometimes be inferred that the long-run supply of labor was negatively inclined and that a higher price yielded a smaller supply. This might be true if births alone were considered, but it has not yet been shown to be the case if the total population and its rate of growth are to be considered. To this question we turn in the chapter which follows.

---

[66] Brentano, *Economic Journal,* Vol. XX, p. 387.

CHAPTER XIV

THE LONG-TIME MOVEMENT OF POPULATION IN DIFFERENT COUNTRIES

We can test, in part, the doctrine of the classical economists, that the long-run supply of labor is very elastic and the consequent belief that an increase in real wages will cause a very appreciable increase in the rate of population growth by examining what the actual tendencies in this rate of growth have been in a number of countries during the last century.

This has been a period in which the material income of the people in all western countries has risen markedly. What then have been the changes, if any, in the natural rates of growth of the populations of the various nations? The rate of natural change in the size of the population is of course the difference between the birth rate per 1000 and the death rate per 1000 [1] At the opening of the nineteenth century both the birth and the death rates were high and in most countries the difference between them, or the rate of natural increase, though larger than it had been one or two centuries before, was still not great. During the latter part of the nineteenth century, however, there was a decided fall in the birth rate in most countries. Had the death rate remained constant, the rate of population growth would of course have decreased. But in most countries, due to the improvement of medicine and of public health, the death rate fell even more rapidly than did births; with the result that the *rate* of population growth increased. The death rate as a matter of fact began in most cases to decrease before the birth rate. This tendency did not appear in all countries simultaneously, and different nations went through this phase at different times. But it was this great reduction in deaths, even in the face of a falling birth rate, which led to the extraordinary expansion of the population of Europe during the nineteenth century.

In more recent years, however, the birth rate has been falling

---

[1] That is, assuming that the age and sex composition of the population remains constant.

very much more rapidly than the death rate, with the result that the difference between the two has very appreciably narrowed and the rate at which the population has been growing has in consequence been reduced. This raises the definite query as to whether we need fear a great future increase in the population were wages to be increased. If the devil of Malthus has been chained and the feared expansion of the working force is not occurring, then the workers may face the future with some confidence that the increase in the supply of capital and the improvement of technical knowledge will, barring continued depressions and extensive wars, result in raising their marginal productivity.

We cannot, however, pass with any confidence on this possibility until we examine the population history of a number of nations for as long a period as records are available. From this material we may be able to form some fairly approximate conclusions as to where the drift of the times is leading us.

We shall begin with the Scandinavian countries whose vital statistics cover a longer span of time than those of other countries and then review the movements in the other main European countries.

1. Sweden

The Swedish statistics of births and deaths go back as far as 1750, and we have, therefore, a record of one hundred and eighty years which we can trace.[2] As is shown by Chart 67, and by Table XXV in the Appendix, the birth rate during the years from 1750 to 1755 was approximately 37 to the thousand, and the death rate about 27, leaving an average annual net fertility rate of approximately 11 per thousand or 1.1 per cent. During the succeeding forty years the birth rate tended to average somewhere around 3 to 4 points lower or at approximately 33 to 34 a thousand. There was, however, no marked tendency for the death rate to be reduced,[3] so that the rate of natural increase declined.

There was little tendency for the birth rate to decline still further during the succeeding seventy years, save for a dip of 2 to 3 points during the twenty years from 1835 to 1855. The period indeed closed with the average annual birth rate for the seven years 1860 to 1866, amounting to approximately 33.5, or

---

[2] The data used are drawn from the *Statistisk Arsbok*, 1931, pp. 35 ff.

[3] There were epidemics which swept away large numbers in 1772 and 1773 and to a somewhat lesser degree in 1789 and 1790.

virtually the same average as that which had prevailed during
the decade of the 1790's. During this long period, however,
there was on the whole a decline in the death rate. Except for
the high mortality during the Napoleonic wars, there was a distinct tendency for the relative number of deaths to fall, particularly from 1830 on, until for the first seven years of the decade
of the sixties, the average rate was approximately 19.5 to the
thousand, making the net annual rate of population increase
to approximately 13.9 to the thousand.

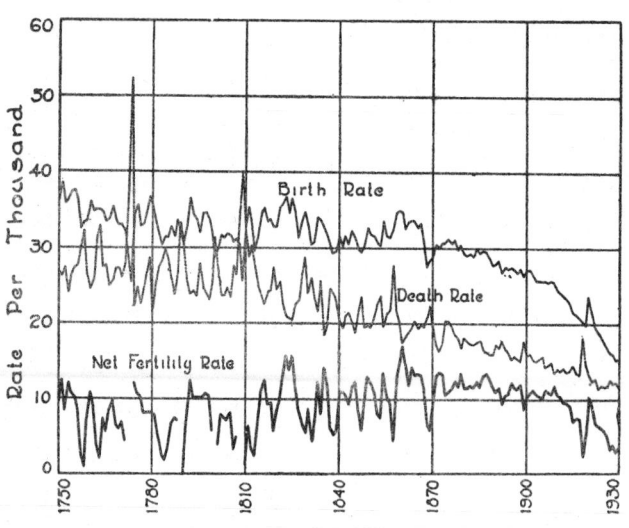

Chart 67. Birth, Death and Net Fertility Rates in Sweden,
1750–1930.

During the latter part of the sixties there was a rise in the
death rate and a fall in the birth rate, which very appreciably
reduced the net fertility rate. But after these rates had readjusted themselves there was a striking uniformity in the next
forty years in the relative decline of both births and deaths.
The result was that the difference between the two, or the
natural rate of population growth, remained fairly constant
throughout the period up to 1910 at the rate of 11 to the thousand, or 1.1 per cent. This strikingly enough was the same
relative rate of growth which Sweden had apparently experienced over a century before, during the years which immediately
followed 1750. From 1910 on, however, the birth rate fell much

more rapidly than the death rate, with the corresponding result that the net fertility rate declined. Thus the birth rate fell from 25.6 in 1909 to 21.6 in 1915 and, as in other countries, continued to fall still further during the war years until it reached 19.8 in 1919. After the sharp rise in births during 1920, the decline kept on until, in 1929 and 1930, it was only slightly over 15. The birth rate thus decreased over 10 to the thousand or approximately 40 per cent in twenty years. Deaths, on the other hand, diminished far more slowly, from about 14 in 1909 and 1910 to 12.2 in 1929, and 11.7 in 1930.

The result was, of course, a startling decrease in the surplus of births over deaths. Instead of the net fertility rate of approximately 11 which had prevailed during the closing years of the first decade, the third decade closed with a growth rate of somewhere between 3 and 4 to the thousand. This was only about 30 per cent of the most typical rate which had prevailed up to 1910. In 1931 when the birth rate was 14.8 and the death rate 12.5 the actual growth rate was only 2.3.

The real wages of the Swedish workers increased very appreciably during these years. In 1927 the daily earnings of male workers were 122 per cent higher than in 1913,[4] while the cost of living was approximately 72 per cent higher.[5] This was equivalent to an increase of 29 per cent in real daily earnings. Professor Bagge in his recent study shows that real annual earnings in 1930 were 27 per cent higher than they had been in 1913 and 1920.[5a]

During the very period, therefore, when real wages were rising rapidly the net fertility rate was falling sharply.

2. Norway

The data on Norwegian births and deaths[6] which are given in Chart 68 and in Table XXVI of the Appendix date from 1801. At this time, the birth rate, if the statistics are accurate, was not as high as in Sweden, and during the period of the Napoleonic wars ranged between 24 and 29 and averaged approximately 27.2. During these years the death rate was approximately 25 to the thousand which was also very much less than the corresponding rate in Sweden. The net fertility rate, therefore, averaged around 2.2 per thousand.

---

[4] *International Labour Review*, July, 1929 (Vol. XX), p. 123.
[5] *Ibid.*, October-November, 1928 (Vol. XVIII), p. 648.
[5a] Bagge, *Wages in Sweden*, p. 261.
[6] *Norges Officielle Statistik*, 1890, pp. 126 ff; *Ibid.*, 1886–1900, p. 74; *Ibid.*, 1901–1910, p. 74; *Statistisk Arbok*, 1929, p. 16; *Ibid.*, 1930, p. 16.

Beginning with 1815, the recorded birth rate showed a very appreciable increase.[7] In 1816 it was no less than 35 and with the exception of a dip in the late thirties and early forties,[8] it ranged between 30 and 35 during the next half century. The death rate during the early part of this period was not far from 19 and during the latter part declined still more.

The result of these changes was a very large apparent increase from 1815 in the rate of population growth, which save for the sag during the late 30's and early 40's was not far from 14 to the thousand, or 1.4 per cent a year.

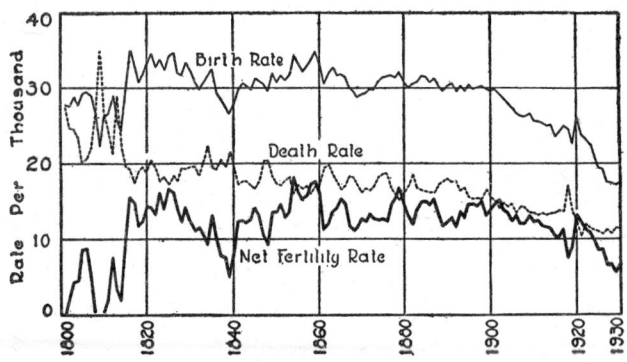

Chart 68.   Birth, Death, and Net Fertility Rates in Norway, 1800–1930.

From 1865 to 1902 the birth rate ranged between 29 and 31, while the death rate sank slowly until by the latter part of the nineties it was between 15 and 16 to the thousand. The net fertility rate, therefore, remained high throughout the remainder of the century, averaging about 13 in the seventies, 14 in the eighties, and between 13 and 14 in the nineties.

Although the birth rate fell from its average of between 29 and 30 at the turn of the century to 25 in 1913 and 1914, the death rate also declined almost as much, so that the net fertility rate was still between 12 and 13 in 1910–11.

Due to the constancy of the death rate during the rest of the decade at somewhere between 13 and 14, and the continued fall in the birth rate, the rate of population growth was between 11 and 12 during most of these years. After 1922, however, the birth rate fell sharply, declining from 23.1 in that year

---

[7] This may have been due to an improved registration of births.

[8] During the six years, 1836 to 1841 inclusive, the average was approximately 28.

to 17.3 in 1929 and to approximately that figure in 1930, or a decrease in seven years of approximately 25 per cent. There was far less slack which could be absorbed by a reduction in deaths. These it is true decreased to around 11, and indeed in 1930 to as low a figure as 10.4, but the result was a very great shrinkage in the rate of growth. This amounted to only 6.5 for the last four years (1927–1930), or only about 60 per cent of what they had been a decade earlier. In 1931 when the birth rate was 16.7 and the death rate 10.7, the growth rate was 6.0 or a still lower figure.

This decline was, moreover, in the face of an increase in real wages—although this increase seems to have been less in Norway than in Sweden.

3. Denmark

The Danish statistics which we use begin with 1800.[9] During the opening decade of the nineteenth century, the birth rate in that country varied between 29 and 33 per thousand and

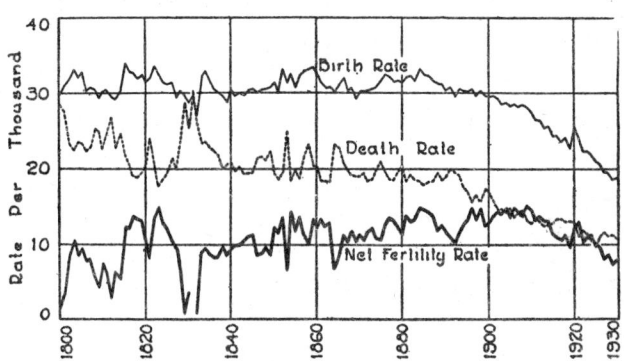

Chart 69. Birth, Death, and Net Fertility Rates in Denmark, 1800–1930

averaged about 31.5. The death rate for the first two years was around 28, but thereafter sank to about 23, rising to 25 for 1808 and 1809, and leaving a net rate of growth of approximately 8 to the thousand for the years 1802–1809. During the remainder of the period of the Napoleonic Wars, the rate of natural increase was relatively low, amounting on the average to only about 5.4 a year. After the conclusion of the wars, the birth rate jumped up rapidly and, though sinking slightly afterward, still remained on a higher level. The death rate, on the

[9] *Statistisk Aarbog*, 1917, p. 17; *Ibid.*, 1931, p. 20.

other hand, fell so that the net rate of population growth rose sharply to an average of 13 for the remaining years of the decade. In the twenties the net rate of fertility slackened somewhat both because of a slight rise in the death rate and a fall in the birth rate, so that the net growth was only about 10 per thousand. During the next decade this movement on the whole continued so that the net fertility rate did not average above 7 for the decade, although this was primarily due to high death rates in the early years.[10] In the forties the birth rate remained relatively constant at 30, while the death rate ranged between 19.3 and 22.4 with an average net fertility rate of approximately 9.7.

Beginning with 1850, however, the rate of population growth became distinctly higher. The death rate fell slowly. The birth rate, however, actually advanced during the fifties and did not fall below 29 until the turn of the century when the death rate was down to 17. The net fertility rate was, therefore, something over 11 in the fifties and sixties and seventies and rose to 13 in the eighties. It was about 12.5 in the nineties, and during the first decade of the twentieth century, while the birth rate fell slowly, to a little over 28, the death rate dropped to a little over 14. This caused the rate of net growth to rise to approximately 14. During the next twelve years the birth rate did decline somewhat more rapidly than the deaths, falling by nearly 5 points as compared with a 1 to 2 point decline in deaths. The average rate of growth for the years up to the war was a little over 13 and while this declined during the war period to somewhat under 11, it too had risen by 1921 back to 13. This was approximately the average rate during the preceding forty years.

From 1921 on, however, the birth rate as in other countries fell swiftly. From 24 in that year it declined to between 18.6 in 1929 and 18.7 in 1930. The death rate, however, fell by only about 1 point during this period which caused the rate of net growth to shrink to 7.3 in 1929 and 7.9 in 1930, or an average of 7.6. This was a decrease in eight years of 5.4 points or about 40 per cent. In 1931 when the birth rate had dropped to 18.0, the death rate was 11.4, leaving the net growth rate at only 6.6 or the lowest figure of all.

But real wages during this period had advanced very ap-

---

[10] The death rates were particularly high in 1829, 1830, 1831, and 1832, but thereafter declined.

preciably. In 1928 the general average hourly earnings were 159 per cent above 1914.[11] The cost of living in that year was, however, only 72 per cent higher than it had been in 1914[12] so that the purchasing power of an hour's work was no less than 50 per cent more than it had been in the prewar period. The decrease in the length of the normal working week caused the increase in full-time weekly earnings to be somewhat less, but even this figure was very greatly in excess of what it had been at the outbreak of the war.[13] As in the preceding countries which have been studied, the great rise in material prosperity, therefore, did not check the rapid downward movement in net fertility.

4. Great Britain (England and Wales)

The British statistics[14] as given in Chart 70 and Table XXVIII of the Appendix show that between 1850 and 1910 the net fertility rate never fell below 10. During the 50's when the birth rate averaged about 34 and the death rate approximately 22, the average rate of population growth was in consequence 12 to the thousand. In the next decade, the birth rate rose by one point to approximately 35, while the death rate remained constant at about 22. This sent the net fertility rate up slightly to 13. In the seventies the birth rate averaged 35.5 while the death rate sank slightly, particularly after 1875. The result was an increase in the net growth rate to approximately 14. During the eighties, however, the birth rate began to fall and by the end of the decade was only a little over 31. The death rate, however, declined during this period from 20.6 to 18.2, so that the net fertility rate only fell on the average for the decade as a whole to somewhere between 13.0 and 13.5. In the last decade of the century, however, the birth rate fell by about two points while the death rate declined by only a little over one point. This caused the net fertility to decline to slightly under 12 to the thousand. During the first ten years of the present century births and deaths fell almost equally, namely, from 29.1 to 25.8 and from 18.2 to 14.6, so that the net fertility rate was still between 11.5 and 12.0.

[11] *International Labour Review*, July, 1929 (Vol. XX), p. 121. This is the average for both skilled and unskilled men and for women.

[12] *Ibid.*, December, 1929 (Vol. XX), p. 872.

[13] *i.e.*, (259/172) × 100 = 150 +.

[14] For the data given see *Statistical Abstract for the United Kingdom*, 1912, Vol. 60, pp. 407-8; Vol. 47, pp. 250-1; Vol. 35, pp. 205-6; Vol. 21, pp. 119-20; Vol. 12, p. 108; Vol. 11, p. 84; Vol. 66, pp. 387-8; Vol. 74 (1929), p. 467. The data given for the war years refer to the civil population only.

During the years preceding the outbreak of the war, the birth rate continued to decline and reached 23.8 in 1914. The death rate, however, went down below 14, so that the rate of net growth averaged 10.0 for the years 1913 and 1914. If we disregard the war years with their great fall in births and the great jump in 1920, we find the birth rate sinking back to 22.4 in 1921, and from then on falling very rapidly, so that in 1929 and 1930 it amounted to only 16.3 or 27 per cent below 1921, and 43 per cent below what it had been in 1900. The death rate

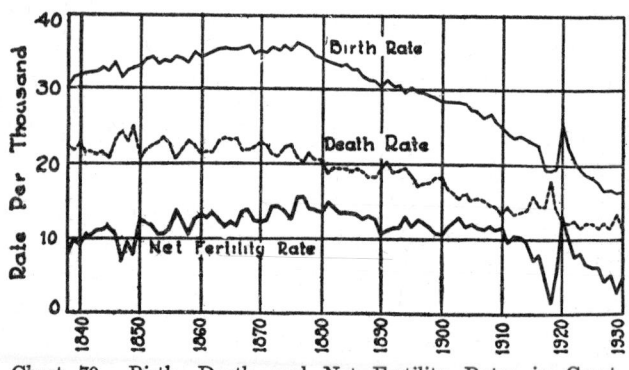

Chart 70. Birth, Death, and Net Fertility Rates in Great Britain, 1838–1930.

could not, of course, decrease by the same number of points and declined from 12.8 in 1922 to 11.7 in 1928, and after a rise to 13.4 in 1929 fell back to 11.4 in 1930. This meant of course that the excess of births over deaths shrank very appreciably and averaged for the last four years (1927–1930) only 4.3 per thousand or .43 of one per cent a year. This was only a little over one-third the rate of growth during the years 1902–1905, and only a little over two-fifths of the rate for 1913. During 1931 and 1932 the net growth rate fell still lower being only 3.5 in 1931 and 3.3 in 1932.

As in the Scandinavian countries, the period of the twenties has been one of distinct wage advance for the workers. According to Professor Bowley,[15] the average real wages for a standard

---

[15] A. L. Bowley: *A New Index-Number of Wages*, London and Cambridge Economic Service (1929), p. 7. The average percentage of unemployment during the pre-war years was 4.6 and during the decade of the 1920's 11.8. (Douglas and Director, *The Problem of Unemployment*, pp. 36–7.) This loss of 7 per cent would leave a net gain of approximately 9 per cent plus the gains from increased social services provided by the community. These last have been considerable.

week increased approximately 8 per cent between July 1914 and December 1924 and approximately 8 per cent more during the ensuing four years. While some of this gain should be deducted for such unemployment and short-time as the workers suffered which was not compensated for, there was still left a comfortable balance for the working class as a whole.

The great decline in the effective fertility rate has, therefore, occurred during a period in which the material condition of the workers was being very appreciably improved.

5. France

The population statistics for France[16] can be traced back to 1801 and are shown in Chart 71 and Table XXIX in the Appendix. During the first thirty years of the century the birth rate fell slowly from 33 to 30 per thousand and the death rate from approximately 28 to approximately 25. The result was that the rate of national increase was on the average somewhere between 5 and 6 per thousand. During the next twenty years, the birth rate declined by a little over 2 points to something under 28.[17] The death rate fell slowly to 23.2 in 1841 where with some deviation it tended to remain during that decade. The rate of net fertility, however, remained at around 5 except for a few years in which the mortality was especially severe, and this rough average rate of net growth tended to prevail until 1845. During the last four years of the forties, it was, however, distinctly lower than this and indeed averaged only a little over 2.

What seems startling in reviewing the history of the population movement during the half century from 1850 to 1900 is the fact that the death rate remained virtually constant during this period and showed virtually no signs of decreasing. It was indeed 21.4 in 1850 and fifty years later in 1900, it was 21.9. This failure to reduce the death rate was probably due to the relatively retarded state of public hygiene and public health work. Although France produced a number of great medical pathfinders during the nineteenth century, notably Pasteur[18] and Claude Bernard, the newer knowledge was not organized for popular dissemination as in Germany, the Scandi-

---

[16] For the French vital statistics see *Statistique Annuelle*, 1919–1920, pp. 11–2; and for subsequent years the annual *Statistiques Générales de la France*.

[17] In 1847 the birth rate fell as low as 25.4.

[18] See Vallery-Radot, *Pasteur;* and Duclaux, *Pasteur, the History of a Mind.*

navian countries, England, and the United States. The death rate in consequence failed to decline.

During the last half of the nineteenth century, however, although the death rate was approximately constant, the birth rate continued to decline. From a figure of 26.8 in 1850, it sank to one of 21.8 in 1899 or a fall of 5 points and nearly 20 per cent. This caused the net fertility rate to fall at a greatly accelerated rate. In 1850 the surplus of births over deaths was at the rate of 5.4 per 1000 population, but in 1899 the rate of

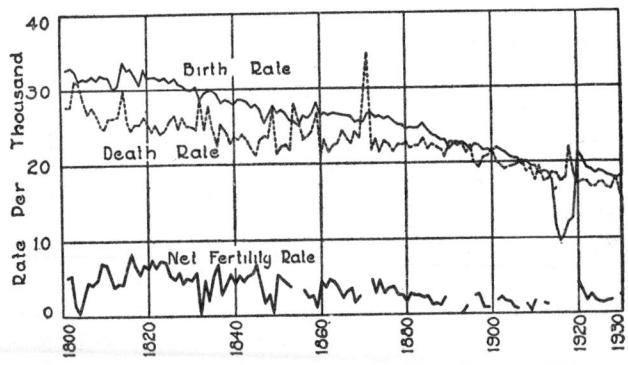

Chart 71. Birth, Death, and Net Fertility Rates in France, 1801–1930.

growth was only 0.8 per 1000, or only eight-hundredths of one per cent. For the fifties as a whole the average rate of growth was 2.3 per year, and if we omit two years in which the death rate was abnormally high, the average was approximately 3.3. In the sixties the average net fertility was approximately 3.5, and if we omit the years of the Franco-Prussian war in 1870 and 1871, this remained the average for the residue of the seventies. During the eighties it fell to about 2.1 and during the nineties averaged only 0.6.

With the turn of the century the death rate did begin to fall and from 21.0 in 1899 reached 19.1 in 1909. The birth rate, however, fell almost as rapidly so that the rate of net fertility rose to only 0.9. The average for the four years (1910–1913) which preceded the outbreak of the war witnessed a still lower growth of less than 1 per thousand.

If we exclude the war years and the immediate post-war period, we find a slightly higher rate of increase during the twenties. The death rate fell from 17.7 in 1921 which had also been the 1913 figure, to 15.7 in 1930, while births ranged around 18 during the latter years of the period. The average rate of growth for the ten years from 1921 to 1930 inclusive was approximately 1.8. This was a higher average rate than had existed since the eighties, but it was still very appreciably below that of other European countries. This was due not to the low birth rate which at 18.1 in 1930 was nearly 2 points higher than that of England, 1 point above Switzerland and Norway, and nearly 1 point above Germany. The lower rate of growth was therefore due to the relatively high death rate, which at the 1931 figure of 16.3 was still from 3 to 5 points above those of northern European countries which in that year had the following death rates:

Switzerland	12.1	Germany	11.2
Sweden	12.5	Denmark	11.4
England and Wales	12.3	Norway	10.7

It is probable that not all of this excess can be charged to the age composition of the French population, and it would seem that at least a portion is attributable to the relatively retarded state of French public health measures. If the new social insurance law serves to provide better health care for the masses, it is quite possible that we shall see a decline in the death rate and an attendant rise in the net fertility rate.

On the whole, however, it is apparent that France reached much earlier, though on a higher level, that relatively close balance between births and deaths towards which, if the experience of the last decade is any guide, the rest of the nations of northwestern Europe seem rapidly to be tending.

It is not at present possible for us to measure the long-time movement of real wages in France in order to compare them with the decrease in net fertility. For while Professor Simiand's learned and exhaustive treatise on wages [19] covers the course of money wages in great detail from 1790 to the present, he has not as yet constructed an index of living costs by which the money wages may be deflated.

From statistics which have been compiled by the French Statistical Department, however, it would seem that there has been little increase in real wages as compared with the pre-war level. In October 1928 the average day wages in Paris were

---

[19] François Simiand: *Le Salaire, Evolution Sociale et la Monnaie*, 3 vols. Felix Alcan, Paris, 1931–1932.

425 per cent higher than in 1911,[20] while living costs in that month were also approximately 425 per cent above their pre-war figure.[21] The study by Professors Ogburn and Jaffe on the post-war development of France seems to prove that during the period of inflation, money wages did not advance nearly as rapidly as wholesale prices and probably not as rapidly as retail prices.[22]

6. Germany and Prussia

The German statistics [23] since the unification of that country in 1871 are given in Chart 72 and Table XXX of the Appendix. They show a birth rate which was initially extremely high, ranging around 40 during the seventies and not falling below 35 until 1903. During this period the death rate fell from 29 to 19.4 so that the rate of net fertility increase was extremely rapid. During the eight years from 1872 to 1879, it averaged a little under 13. In the eighties this rate diminished to approximately 11.5, but in the nineties it leaped up again to an average of 13.6.

In the first ten years of the present century, the birth rate declined by more than during the preceding 30 years, and indeed fell from 35.8 in 1899 to 31.0 in 1909. But the death rate not only fell just as rapidly for the decade as a whole, but during the first few years the death rate fell at an even greater rate, so that the average net fertility for the decade was a little over 14 per thousand population, or 1.4 per cent a year. The birth rate decreased still more rapidly during the next four years and was down to 27.5 by 1913, while deaths were reduced by 2 points to 15. The result was a slight reduction in the rate of population growth to an average of 12.5 during the years 1910 to 1913 inclusive.

[20] *International Labour Review,* July, 1929 (Vol. XX), p. 122.

[21] *International Labour Review,* May, 1929 (Vol. XIX), p. 721. The index for September was 519 and for November, 531. Assuming an even rate of change this would give an index of 525 for October.

[22] Ogburn and Jaffe, *The Economic Development of Post-War France,* pp. 160–5.

[23] See *Statistiches Jahrbuch,* 1929, p. 7 and p. 30; *Ibid.,* 1931, p. 70. We have carried the statistics for Prussia back to 1816. During the next seven years, the average birth rate was over 44 with a death rate of near 30 which then decreased to a little over 27. The average net growth was about 16. During the sixties the average birth rate was a little over 40 and the death rate (including the war year of 1866) about 28. The net growth was then 12. By 1927, the birth rate was 18.4, the death rate 11.9, and the rate of population growth, therefore, 6.5. These were approximately the same rates as prevailed in Germany as a whole in that year. See *Statistisches Jahrbuch für den Preussischen Staat, 1904,* pp. 2 and 25, and *Statistisches Jahrbuch für den Freistaat Preussen,* 25 Band., 1929, p. 50.

After the rapid rise in births to 25.9 and 25.0 in 1920 and 1921, the birth rate began to decline rapidly during the next nine years. It continued to do so even after the mark had been stabilized and inflation stopped, until in 1930 it was only 17.5 or 10 points, and 37 per cent less than it had been in 1913. The death rate was also falling during this period but by a smaller proportion. Instead of 15.0 as in 1913, it touched 11.5 in 1928, and after rising to 12.6 in 1929, it sank to 11.1 in 1930. The net rate of fertility was, in consequence, sharply reduced, and for the nine years from 1922 to 1930 inclusive it averaged only a little over 7, and for the last four years only 6.2.

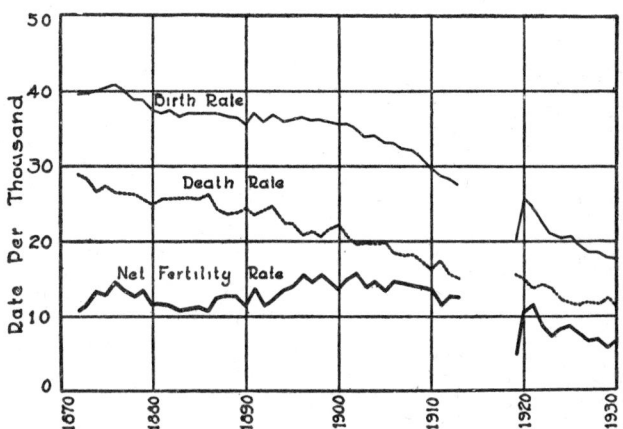

Chart 72. Birth, Death, and Net Fertility Rates in Germany, 1870–1930.

So far as the movement of real wages [24] is concerned, they, as Bresciani-Turroni has shown, greatly decreased during the inflation period from 1920 to the spring of 1924.[25] During this period the rate of net fertility was diminishing appreciably. From 1924 on, however, the workers improved their position until by March 1929 the index of money wages stood at 160 [26] as compared with the pre-war base, while the cost of living index was 157.[27] The previous losses had, therefore, been recov-

[24] For an able discussion of the movement of real wages in the post-war period see the article by Professor Bresciani-Turroni, *Journal Royal Statistical Society*, Vol. 92, pp. 374–414. For sources see *Wirtschaft und Statistik* and the *Reichsarbeitsblatt*.

[25] For wage data during the early part of this period see *Lohn und Gehaltserhebung vom Februar 1920*. Statistik des Deutschen Reichs, Band 293, 438 pp.

[26] *International Labour Review*, July, 1929 (Vol. XX), p. 120.

[27] *Ibid.*, May, 1929 (Vol. XIX), p. 721.

ered. And yet during the five years in which the conditions of the German workingmen had been improved, the birth rate continued to fall more rapidly than the death rate, and the net fertility declined from 8.1 in 1924 to 5.1 in 1929, and 6.4 in 1930.

7. Switzerland

The comparable statistics for Switzerland as shown in Chart 73 and Table XXXI of the Appendix indicate an average birth rate in the seventies of a little under 31 and a death rate (ignoring 1871) of approximately 23 with a consequent net fertility of slightly less than 8. The birth rate had reached its high water mark in 1876 with a figure of 32.8, but it fell thereafter

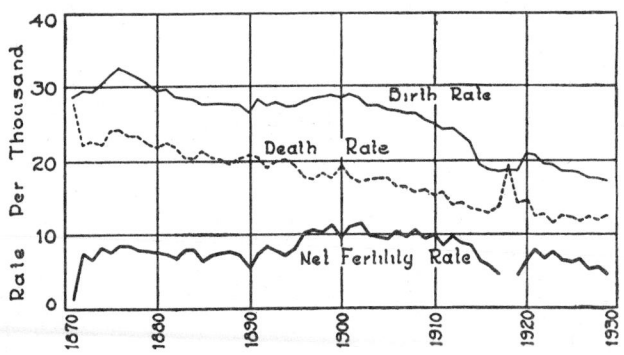

Chart 73. Birth, Death, and Net Fertility Rates in Switzerland, 1870–1929.

until by 1889 it was about 27.6. During this period, however, the death rate was also falling from 24.0 in 1876 to 20.3 in 1889, so that the net fertility only declined to an average of 7.5 for the eighties as a whole.

During the nineties the birth rate not only remained constant but actually increased towards the end of the decade to 29.0. The death rate, however, fell still more swiftly than it had and particularly so after 1894, reaching 17.7 in 1899. Net fertility, therefore, rose appreciably to an average of 8.6 for the ten years as a whole and 10.5 for the last four years. The decade which opened the present century witnessed a decline in the birth rate which brought it down to 25.5 in 1909 while the death rate fell to 16.1. The average net fertility for the decade was 10. This was maintained to a relatively even degree through the period.

The fall in the birth rate in the years preceding the war, namely, from 25.5 in 1909 to 22.4 in 1914, was more precipitous than the decline in deaths from 16.1 to 13.8, and the net growth rate was correspondingly reduced to a little over 9. When the wartime difficulties were terminated in 1921, the birth rate was down to 20.8 and the death rate to 12.7, leaving 8.1 as the net fertility rate. This was reduced in subsequent years since the death rate remained at approximately the same figure, whilᵥ births went down to 17.0 in 1929.[28] Net fertility was, therefore, only 4.6 for 1929 and an average of 6.0 for the eight years, 1922 to 1929. In 1931 and 1932 the net growth rate averaged 5.1.

Switzerland was, moreover, a country where the workers had enjoyed during this period a very appreciable increase in real wages. In 1928 the indexes of money wages in terms of the pre-war averages were as follows: (1) skilled and semi-skilled men, 201; (2) unskilled men, 202; (3) women, 197.[29] Since the index of the living costs in terms of its pre-war base averaged approximately 161 for that year,[30] this gave an index of real wages for men of 125 and for women of 122.

Here again, therefore, the rise in real wages failed to arrest the rapid downward movement in the net fertility.

8. Italy

Due to the fact that Italy was not unified until the latter half of the nineteenth century, we cannot carry our study of vital statistics back of 1862. From then on the data are shown in Chart 74 and Table XXXII of the Appendix.[31] From 1862 until 1890 we find a high birth rate of over 35 per thousand which during the eighties was not far from 38. The death rate was, however, also high, ranging around 30 in 1880, and for the next decade at about 28. The result was that despite the high rate of births, the net fertility rate during the sixties was only about 7 and at only slightly above this figure during the seventies. In the eighties the fall in the death rate, accompanied by the maintenance of the birth rate at its former level, sent the net growth rate up to an average of nearly 10. In the nineties the more rapid fall of deaths than births raised the net fertility to approximately 10.5.

This rate of growth was maintained during the opening decade of the present century. During the next five years the reduction in the death rate from 22 to around 18 more than

---

[28] *Statistisches Jahrbuch der Schweiz*, 1929, pp. 50–52.
[29] *International Labour Review*, July, 1929, vol. XX, p. 124.
[30] *Ibid.*, May, 1929, p. 721.
[31] See *Annuario Statistico Italiano* II. serie. Vol. 1 (1911), p. 17: III. serie, Vol. V (1931), p. 588.

counter-balanced the fall in the birth rate, so that net fertility advanced to an average of 12.7. After the wartime dip the net fertility advanced to 13.2 in 1920 and 13.0 in 1921.

During the eight years from 1922 to 1929 the birth rate, despite the injunctions of Mussolini, declined still further, though not as sharply as in other countries. From 30.6 in 1921 it fell to 25.1 in 1929, a decrease of 18 per cent. Since deaths only fell during this period from 17.6 to 16.0, there was a consequent de-

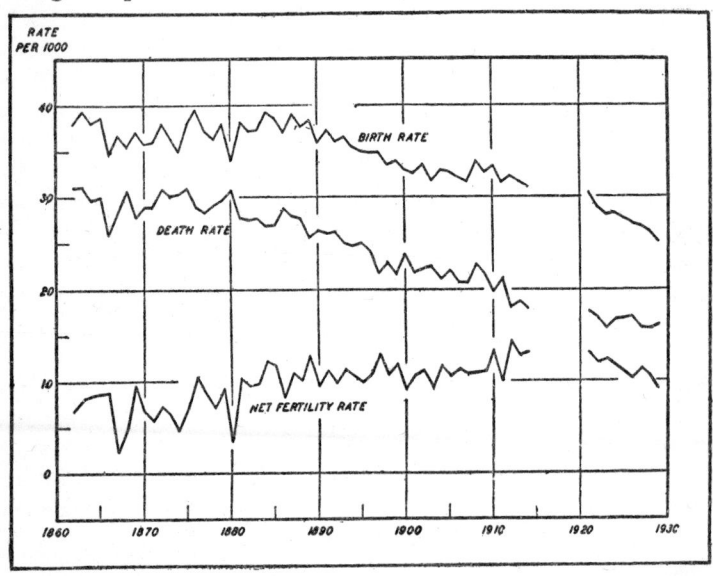

Chart 74. Birth, Death, and Net Fertility Rates in Italy, 1862–1929.

crease in the net fertility rate from 13.0 to 9.1, or a fall of 30 per cent. The decline in the death rate since 1929 has slightly more than counter-balanced the fall in births so that the net growth rate has not declined since then.

Although, therefore, both the Italian birth and net fertility rates are still higher than those of the other European countries we have examined, Italy has not been immune from the downward drift of births and the even more accentuated decline in net fertility. In some sections of Italy indeed, notably those in the industrial regions of Piedmont and of North Italy, the birth rate is even now as low as 17 or 18 and the net fertility rate not more than 7. It is in the main the more industrially backward regions of South Italy which keep the birth rate at as high a figure as it is.

It is somewhat difficult to tell what has been the course of real wages during this period. From all the material available, however, it seems that any increases which may have occurred are at best but slight and the most probable conclusion is that they have not risen.[32]

9. Canada

Quebec is the only province for which thorough-going vital statistics exist prior to 1920 when the National Registration area was established. The records of the Catholic population of Quebec, however, go back to 1665 and show what was probably the highest birth rate that any known population has maintained in modern times for so long a period. For up until 1850 the birth rate was over 50 per thousand and during part of this time exceeded 60.[33] While the birth rate amongst this French Canadian group fell slightly during the next seventy years, it was 40 at the beginning of the twentieth century and averaged 37 during the five years of 1921 to 1925 inclusive. More recently it has declined still further. The birth and death rates for the province as a whole, of which the Catholic population forms approximately 85 per cent of the total, has been as follows since 1920.

TABLE 46

POPULATION GROWTH IN QUEBEC, 1920–1931[1]

PER 1,000

Year	Birth Rate	Death Rate	Net Fertility Rate
1920	37.2	17.5	19.7
1921	37.6	14.1	23.5
1922	35.1	13.3	21.8
1923	32.2	13.6	18.6
1924	33.3	12.4	20.9
1925	33.1	12.2	20.9
1926	31.6	14.3	17.3
1927	31.3	13.6	17.7
1928	30.8	13.5	17.3
1929	29.4	13.4	16.0
1930	29.6	12.7	16.9
1931	29.1	12.0	17.1

[1] *Canada Year Book,* 1931, p. xxv and p. 137.

[32] A thorough study of real wages in Italy during the last thirty, and particularly during the last ten, years would be an extremely interesting and much needed venture. For some of the sources which might be used see, (1) Instituto Centrale di Statistica del Regno d'Italia, *Bollettino dei Prezzi,* Anno I–VI. (2) *Indici del Movimento Economico Italiano,* Vols. I–IV, (3) *La Vita Economica Italiana,* I–VI, (4) *L'Economia Italiana, 1919–1929.*

[33] For an analysis of these figures see Kuczynski, *Birth Registration and Birth Statistics in Canada,* p. 199, and pp. 30–68. There were apparent rates of 49 and 45 during the period 1680–1688.

The net fertility rate, therefore, while lower than it has been, is still extraordinarily high.

Elsewhere in the Dominion, the birth rate has been falling and is on a much lower level as is indicated by the rates in the registration area since 1920.

TABLE 47

POPULATION GROWTH IN CANADA (EXCLUSIVE OF QUEBEC) 1920–1929[1]

PER 1,000

Year	Birth Rate	Death Rate	Net Fertility Rate
1920	26.6	12.4	14.2
1921	26.4	10.6	15.8
1922	25.1	10.5	14.6
1923	23.7	10.6	13.1
1924	23.7	9.9	13.8
1925	23.0	9.9	13.1
1926	22.1	10.3	11.8
1927	21.9	10.0	11.9
1928	21.9	10.3	11.6
1929	21.6	10.7	10.9
1930	21.7	10.0	11.7
1931			

[1] *Canada Year Book*, 1925, p. 147; 1931, p. 137; 1932, pp. 110–117.

This rate of net fertility which in 1929 was nearly 11 to the thousand was one which, after all correction for an abnormal number of women in the child bearing ages, still yielded an appreciable rate of reproductive increase. This growth was, however, primarily caused by the high fertility in the three prairie provinces of Manitoba, Alberta, and Saskatchewan. In Ontario and in the four Maritime provinces,[34] where the British stock greatly predominate, the real fertility rate [35] "approached the present low level of western and northern Europe." In the three prairie provinces and in Quebec the rate of net reproduction is, however, still high.

10. The United States

As is well-known, American vital statistics have in the past been lamentable. Since the Federal Registration Area was inaugurated in 1915 conditions have improved greatly, but prior to that time Massachusetts had about the only system of birth registration which went back appreciably into the past. Chart

[34] Prince Edward Island, Nova Scotia, New Brunswick, and British Columbia.

[35] Kuczynski, *Birth Registration and Birth Statistics in Canada*, p. 214.

75 and Table 48 show the movement of births and deaths, and net fertility in Massachusetts since 1889.[36]

It will be seen that there was an apparent rise in the birth rate during the first part of the nineties, from around 26 to 28, and that not until 1900 did it fall to between 25 and 26. The death rate was, however, high during this period and did not fall below 19 until 1897, so that the net rate of population growth was only between 7 and 8 per thousand.

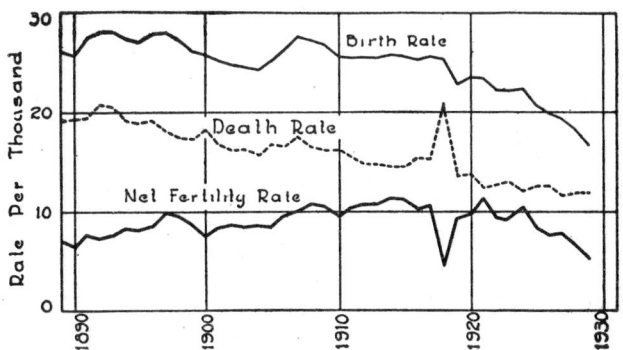

Chart 75. Birth, Death, and Net Fertility Rates in Massachusetts, 1889–1931.

From 1900 to 1918 the birth rate remained relatively constant at somewhere between 25 and 26.[37] During these years, however, the death rate fell from 18.2 in 1900 to 15.2 in 1917, so that the net fertility rose to an average of approximately 10.5 during the eleven years from 1907 to 1917 inclusive. After the war in 1920, the birth rate at 23.6 was on a lower level than it had been in 1917 and 1918. During the next four years it declined slowly to 22.3 in 1924. But during the years which followed it went down with startling rapidity. In 1925, alone, the birth rate fell from 22.3 to 20.8 and by 1929, it was only 16.9. This was a decline of 34 per cent from the rate of 12 years before. Up until 1924 the death rate did decline about as rapidly as the birth rate, falling from 15.2 in 1917 to 12.0 in 1924, so that the net fertility rate was not appreciably reduced, and indeed in the latter year, it amounted to 10.3. From 1924 to 1929, however, there were no appreciable reductions in the

---

[36] See the annual volumes on *Massachusetts Mortality Statistics*, 1923–1927; U. S. Department of Commerce, *Birth Statistics*, 1928.

[37] From 1902 to 1904 inclusive it was between 24 and 25 and from 1906 to 1909 inclusive it was between 26 and 27.

TABLE 48

BIRTH, DEATH, AND NET FERTILITY RATES IN MASSACHUSETTS, 1889–1931
PER 1,000

Year	Birth Rate	Death Rate	Net Fertility Rate
1889	26.2	19.2	7.0
1890	25.8	19.4	6.4
1891	27.5	19.7	7.8
1892	28.1	20.8	7.3
1893	28.1	20.5	7.6
1894	27.4	19.1	8.3
1895	27.0	19.0	8.0
1896	27.9	19.3	8.6
1897	28.0	18.1	9.9
1898	27.1	17.5	9.6
1899	26.2	17.4	8.8
1900	25.8	18.2	7.6
1901	25.1	16.8	8.3
1902	24.8	16.2	8.6
1903	24.7	16.3	8.4
1904	24.3	15.8	8.5
1905	25.2	16.8	8.4
1906	26.3	16.6	9.7
1907	27.6	17.6	10.0
1908	27.4	16.6	10.8
1909	26.8	16.2	10.6
1910	25.7	16.2	9.5
1911	25.6	15.4	10.2
1912	25.6	14.9	10.7
1913	25.5	14.8	10.7
1914	25.9	14.7	11.2
1915	25.7	14.6	11.1
1916	25.4	15.3	10.1
1917	25.7	15.2	10.5
1918	25.3	20.9	4.4
1919	22.9	13.6	9.3
1920	23.6	13.8	9.8
1921	23.5	12.2	11.3
1922	22.1	12.8	9.3
1923	22.1	13.0	9.1
1924	22.3	12.0	10.3
1925	20.8	12.5	8.3
1926	19.9	12.5	7.4
1927	19.4	11.6	7.8
1928	18.3	11.9	6.4
1929	16.9	11.9	5.0
1930	17.3	11.6	5.7
1931	16.2	11.4	4.8

death rate, so that the net fertility declined by almost the amount of the reduction in the rate of births. Within five years the rate of population growth had been reduced from 10.3 to 5.0, or a fall of slightly over 50 per cent. In 1930 the birth rate rose slightly to 17.3, while the death rate declined from 11.9 to 11.6 sending the net fertility rate up to 5.7. In the following year, however, the birth rate declined by more than a full point to an all-time low for that state of 16.2. While the death rate also fell to 11.4 this was of course insufficient to offset the decrease in the birth rate so that net fertility fell to 4.8, which was also the low water mark. This was only 47 per cent of the net growth rate for 1924.

During the years from 1917 on, there was a great increase in the real wages of the Massachusetts workers. The average annual earnings of workers in Massachusetts factories could, for example, have purchased 27 per cent in 1923 more than in 1917.[38]

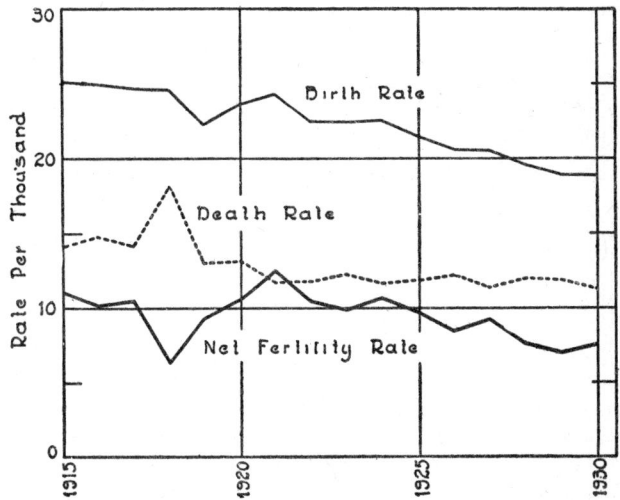

Chart 76. Birth, Death, and Net Fertility Rates in the Registration Area of the United States, 1915–1930.

In 1915 the United States established a birth registration area which initially included only ten states, but which has now come to include all but four. The statistics of birth and death rates which are given below are therefore for a widening group of states, but comparisons of the original with the extending area indicate that the averages in a given year for the registration area were in all probability very close to that which prevailed for the country as a whole. Chart 76 and Table 49 show

[38] The average annual money earnings were computed from the annual *Massachusetts Reports on Statistics of Manufactures*, and were $1196 in 1923 as compared with $758 in 1917. This was an increase of 58 per cent. The statistics of relative living costs are taken from those compiled by the *Massachusetts Special Commission on the Necessaries of Life*, and which showed an average in 1923 for the state which was between 22 and 23 per cent higher than in 1917.

what the movement of birth, death, and net fertility rates have been in the last sixteen years.[39]

TABLE 49

BIRTH, DEATH, AND NET FERTILITY RATES IN THE
REGISTRATION AREA OF THE UNITED STATES
PER 1,000

Year	Birth Rate	Death Rate	Net Fertility Rate
1915	25.1	14.1	11.0
1916	25.0	14.8	10.2
1917	24.7	14.2	10.5
1918	24.6	18.3	6.3
1919	22.3	13.0	9.3
1920	23.7	13.1	10.6
1921	24.3	11.7	12.5
1922	22.5	11.8	10.5
1923	22.4	12.3	9.9
1924	22.6	11.7	10.7
1925	21.4	11.8	9.7
1926	20.6	12.2	8.5
1927	20.6	11.4	9.2
1928	19.7	12.0	7.7
1929	18.9	11.9	7.0
1930	18.9	11.3	7.6
1931	17.8	11.1	6.7
1932	17.3	10.9	6.4

It is thus apparent that during the years immediately prior to our entrance into the war, with a birth rate of approximately 25 and a death rate between 14 and 15, our net fertility rate was between 10 and 11 to the thousand. The birth rate fell but slightly in the years which followed and in 1921 was 24.3. The death rate, aside from the rise caused by the influenza epidemic in 1918, fell, however, during these years and was as low as 11.7 in 1921. In that year, therefore, the net rate of population growth rose to 12.5.

This was the high water mark, for beginning with the next year the birth rate moved downward with considerable rapidity, reaching an average of 18.9 in 1930. This was a fall of 5.4 points since 1921 or of about 22 per cent. In 1931, the birth rate fell by 1.1 points to 17.8 or a decrease of nearly 27 per cent in ten years and in 1932 it fell still further to 17.3. During this decade, moreover, the death rate virtually ceased to fall, so that almost the full decline in the births was transferred to an almost equal absolute but a greater relative decrease in the net fertility

---

[39] *Birth Statistics*, U. S. Department of Commerce, 1928, p. 5; *Statistical Abstract*, 1931, p. 84; *World Almanac*, 1932, p. 443. *Provisional Figures for Live Births*, 1931, Bureau of the Census, p. 1.

rate. This fell from 12.5 in 1921 to 7.0 in 1929, 7.6 in 1930 and 6.7 in 1931, or decreases of 46, 41 and 47 per cent respectively.

11. The Apparent Rate of Net Fertility Largely Due to the Abnormal Proportion of Women in the Child-Bearing Ages

The apparent rates of population growth indicate on their face that although the population of the western European nations is increasing much less rapidly than before the war, it is nevertheless still growing. This would seem to be conclusively demonstrated by the fact that births still exceed deaths.

This apparent rate of increase is, however, caused by the fact that there are now a much larger number of women in the child-bearing ages of from 15 to 45, and particularly in the fertile 20 to 35 year old group, than there would be in a stationary population. This unduly large proportion is primarily the result both of the high birth rates of the past and of their recent reduction. This has meant that the large number of female children in the pre-war period are now the women in the child-bearing ages, while the recent decline in the birth rate has resulted in there being an actually smaller number of females in northwestern Europe who are under 15 years than there are from 15 to 30 years.[40]

In consequence of this hump in the age distribution, there are proportionately more children born than will be the case later when the percentage of total population in these groups will diminish as a result of the reduced birth rate. The present birth rate and net fertility rate are, therefore, unduly raised by this factor. Even though the women in the various groups within the child-bearing ages (15 to 45) should continue to bear children with the same frequency as at present, the birth rate will inevitably fall since there will be proportionately fewer of them in the population.

Sound and ingenious methods for eliminating this disturbing factor and of arriving at what is termed the "net reproduction rate," or the "true rate of natural increase," have been proposed independently by Dr. R. R. Kuczynski[41] and Messrs. Dublin and

---

[40] In 1921 there were 23.7 million females under 15 years and 25.8 million between 15 and 30 years. Kuczynski, *The Balance of Births and Deaths*, Vol. 1, p. 60.

[41] See his "Balance of Births and Deaths," Vol. I; *Fertility and Reproduction*. This method, according to Dr. Kuczynski's statement, was first worked out by Richard Boeckh, the Berlin statistician in 1886.

Lotka.[42] This consists in determining how many children, and more particularly girls, will at existing birth rates be born in the future to every 1000 girls who begin life together. If 1000 girls are born, then it is apparent that the human race is just replenishing itself without diminution or increase. If more than 1000 girls are born there is a net increase, and if less, a decrease. The ratio of girl births to the original thousand furnishes indeed a coefficient of net reproduction. The same principle may also be applied to determine the total number of both girls and boys which will be born at existing birth and death rates to 1000 girls and 1000 boys who are just starting life.[43]

The method which is used to determine how many girls will be born in the future on the basis of existing birth rates by every 1000 girl babies who are themselves just starting life is as follows:

(1) From the standard life table for each county there is found the average number of females out of every thousand born who survive to the various ages. This gives therefore the number who will come to be 15, and the numbers who will pass on to the other ages within the child-bearing period until this terminates at the very outside at 50. We thus obtain the number of females out of a thousand who will be "exposed" to each of these years of age. Thus in England in 1920–1922, 870.67 out of every 1000 female children born tended to reach 15 years and 742.45 reached the age of 50.

(2) The birth rate for women at each of these years within the child-bearing period is, if possible, then found. Wherever it is not possible to get these rates by single years, five-year periods are used. Thus in England in 1921, out of every 1000 women between the ages of 20 and 25, there were 107.96 confinements and there were 156.09 for every thousand between 25 and 30.

(3) These relative birth rates for the various age groups were then applied to the number of females who would come to be of that age. Thus if in England there were on the average 854 females who came to be on the average 20 to 24 years of age, these would be multiplied by the average birth rate of

[42] Dublin and Lotka, "On the True Rate of Natural Increase," *Journal American Statistical Association*, 1925 (Vol. 20), pp. 305–39, and "The True Rate of Natural Increase of the Population of the United States," *Metron* (Vol. VIII), 1930, pp. 107–19.

[43] For this refinement on Kuczynski's earlier method see his *Fertility and Reproduction*, pp. 35–8.

107.96 which in this case would yield 92.04 as the real average number of births for each of the years, or 460.2 for the group as a whole. A similar procedure would be carried through for each age group, and products would then be totalled. This would give the total number of births which at present rates would result from 1000 girls. Thus in England in 1921 the total number of live births per 1000 girls in a stationary population was 2229.9.

(4) This figure total of births was then transformed into a figure representing female births by multiplying the former by the ratio which female births bore to total births. Since this ratio in England was approximately one of 100 : 204, this gave a total of 1087 girl babies which would have been born at 1921 birth rates to every 1000 girls. This indicated a net reproduction rate of approximately 9 per cent during the course of a generation.

Kuczynski then calculated what the net reproduction rate would be in 1926 for all of the combined nations of northern and western Europe which in that year had a total population of 189 millions.[44] He found this to be only .93 or a rate which was 7 per cent less than the amount required to maintain a stationary population. Kuczynski indeed concluded[45] "with the fertility of 1926, the population is bound to die out unless the mortality of potential mothers decreases beyond reasonable expectations." The net reproduction rates were of course still lower in some of the northern and western European nations. Thus in England and Wales where the rate had been 1.087 in 1921, it was only .88 in 1926, while in Germany it was about .89.

Since 1926, the continued rapid fall in the birth rate has of course still further reduced the net reproduction rate. Indeed by 1927 this rate had fallen to .91 in France, .83 in Germany, and .82 in England and Wales.[46] Since these three countries together comprise approximately four-fifths of the total population of northern and western Europe, this meant a very appreciable reduction in the general average below the rate of the preceding year. Since then the decline has, as we have seen, continued. It is, therefore, safe to conclude that were it not for the abnormal number of women in the child-bearing ages, the

[44] i.e. Sweden, Norway, Denmark, Finland, Germany, France, England, Ireland, Holland, Belgium, and Switzerland.
[45] Kuczynski, *The Balance of Births and Deaths*, Vol. I.
[46] Kuczynski, *The Balance of Births and Deaths*, Vol. I, p. 53.

population in these countries would, instead of increasing, be actually declining at an appreciable rate.

In a subsequent volume, Dr. Kuczynski applied the same method to the countries of eastern, central and southwestern Europe.[47] He found that the net reproduction rate in Austria and the Baltic countries was appreciably below that required to keep the population constant. In Austria the rate in 1928 was only .78, in Esthonia approximately .80, and in Latvia it was about .90.[48] Only in Russia and the agricultural sections of southern, southeastern, and southwestern Europe was there a real surplus.[49]

In Russia this net rate of reproduction was approximately as high as it had been 30 years ago, but in most of the other countries it had appreciably declined.

A somewhat similar method to that of Kuczynski which attempted to measure what the true rate of natural increase was in 1920[50] in the United States was employed by Dublin and Lotka in a paper published in 1924. Dublin and Lotka pointed out that the apparent birth rate in the United States was raised by the fact that the immigration and the high birth rates of the past had resulted in a disproportionately large proportion of women being in the child-bearing ages and that this could not be expected to continue in the future. They found, indeed, by the method which has previously been outlined, that the real rate of natural increase in 1920 was not approximately between 10 and 11 as indicated by the surplus of births over deaths, but was instead only 5.5 per thousand,[51] or 50 per cent less than that shown by the annual surplus of births over deaths. In a later study,[52] Dublin and Lotka found that the "true rate of natural increase" in 1928 was not the apparent 7.8 per thousand indicated by the birth and death figures themselves, but instead only 1.7. In two additional papers[53] Dr. Dublin has estimated that in view of the continued decline in net fertility in 1929 and 1930, the true rate of natural increase

---

[47] Kuczynski, *The Balance of Births and Deaths,* Vol. II.

[48] *Ibid.,* pp. 55–6.

[49] *Ibid.,* pp. 60–4.

[50] Louis I. Dublin and A. J. Lotka, "On the True Rate of Natural Increase," *Journal American Statistical Association,* Vol. 20 (1925), pp. 304–39.

[51] *Ibid.,* p. 328.

[52] Louis I. Dublin and A. J. Lotka, "The True Rate of Natural Increase of the Population of the United States," *Metron,* Vol. VIII (1930), pp. 107–19.

[53] Dublin: "Our Ageing Population," reprinted by the author from the *New York Times,* January 4, 1931, p. 5. *Statistical Bulletin, Metropolitan Life Insurance Co.,* September, 1932 (Vol. XIII), pp. 4–5.

in 1930 was a slightly minus quantity. If the 1931 figures were to be worked over on this basis, they would beyond question show a still greater true loss. Were it not for the abnormal proportion of women and men in the active and fecund age groups we should, therefore, have even at present a constant and perhaps even a slightly declining population. When in the course of time the present excess in these age groups disappears, we shall have in fact at least a stationary and more probably a diminishing population. Some evidence that the latter possibility may actually be realized is afforded by the fact that the last few years have witnessed a decline in the total number of children in the elementary grades of the public schools of the country. Barring sudden reverses of recent trends, we need not, therefore, expect any marked expansion of the population after 1960 or at the most 1970 when a total of around 160 millions may be reached. If moreover the birth rate continues to fall in the future, the maximum may be reached both earlier and at a lower figure. Thereafter the decline in population may be appreciable.

12. A Summary of Historical Changes

Judging by the historical experience of the countries which we have studied, the interrelationship between the long run rates of real wages and of population growth has been somewhat as follows: (1) Real wages increase both because the quantity of capital grows more rapidly than the supply of labor and hence raises the marginal productivity of the latter and because of improvements in technique. (2) As real wages rise the standard of living of the workers also rises. Since the standard of living fundamentally consists of the commodities and services which people prefer to having children, the result is that the birth rate through the practise of birth control adjusts itself at a lower point from that which it would be were the previous and cheaper standard of living to persist in the presence of the higher wage. (3) As wages continue to increase, the same process tends to be repeated. So far as the European and American experience of the past decades is concerned this process tends to continue until the true rate of natural increase either falls to nothing or actually becomes a minus quantity.

We may indeed diagram the past historical tendencies somewhat as is done in Chart 77.

The chart shows that as the marginal productivity of labor rises, the standard of living rises but not as much as it would have risen if the population were stationary. Thus the lines *A, B, C,* and *D* represent a shifting productivity curve of labor. When the quantity of labor is *OX*, the marginal productivity is *XP* and the standard of living is equal to *OS*. The situation here is one of equilibrium. Now let the productivity curve of labor shift from *A* to *B* because of a greater increase in capital or improvements in the state of the arts. The marginal

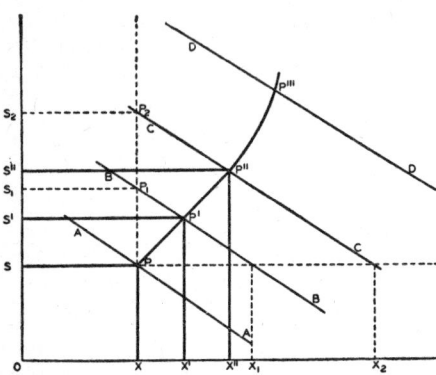

Chart 77. The Way in Which An Increase in Productivity Tends to Lead to Rising Living Standards and Hence to An Upward Slope in the Long-Time Supply Curve of Labor.

productivity of labor rises therefore to XP_1. In a numerically stationary state the standard of living would rise to S_1, but in the case of an expanding population (expanding at a rate which is however slackened by the increased standard of living) the increase in the labor supply will result in a standard of living equal to *OS'*. If McCulloch's contention were true that the increase in real wages would give such a powerful stimulus to the principle of increase that the standard of living would be reduced to its former level, population would have to increase to X_1.

A fresh shifting of the productivity curve to *C* sets into play a similar set of forces with the result that population will expand to *X''* and the standard of living will be *OS''*. If we connect the points *P, P', P''*, we obtain an approximation to the historical long-run supply curve of labor which slopes upward and to the right, even though at any one time it may be described as a straight line parallel to the base.[53a]

Since the real wages of the workers have tended historically to move upward fairly gradually rather than in sharp discontinuous movements, this has meant that in practise the rise in living standards has proceeded with almost equal gradualness. The historical long-run supply curve of labor has, therefore, moved

---

[53a] The above illustration is of course greatly simplified. At any one time there is not one standard of living but rather many different standards of living for different classes in the population.

upward and to the right. Such a curve, however, clearly embodies time as one of the variables, and it is not a short-run curve of the *ceteris paribus* type with which the neo-classical economists are accustomed to deal. Its upward slope would not be true at any one time but would have rather resulted from the increase over the course of the years in living standards. This has served to join together, as points on the same apparent supply curve, different points in time, such as S' and S'', each of which may have been on a "other things being equal" supply curve which was parallel or approximately parallel to the base. But the historical validity of such an upward sloping curve may none the less be important.

The skeptic about historical tendencies will, however, object to all this, that there is no surety that such a movement will continue in the future, and will assert that there is no presumption that the future will repeat the past. This seems, however, to be too cavalier a dismissal of the implications of past tendencies. For the motives and drives of men are not greatly different from country to country or from period to period.[54] Differences of course there are, but these seem to be less than the similarities. There is a strong presumption, therefore, that as other societies find that their level of per capita real income increases, their accepted standard of life will also advance. With this will tend to go a birth rate which will be lower than it otherwise would have been had the lower standard continued in the midst of the new prosperity.

Similarly, it is very doubtful whether fresh increases of prosperity in European and American society would lead in the future to any great unleashing of births and hence to an abrupt reversal of the trends which have characterized the more recent past. It is, however, possible and indeed probable, as we shall see from the next chapter, that an increase in real wages would cause many families, acquainted with the practise of birth-control not to cut their families to as low a point as they otherwise would and to raise the level of the no-child or one child family to a two or three child basis. But this would not cause any great increase in population. It would probably at the most serve to offset a decrease.

13. A Projection for The Future

There is every evidence that largely through the practise of birth-control, the devil of Malthus is being laid in the countries

---

[54] Or as the Latin proverb puts it, *Natura non facit saltum.*

of northern and western European stock.[55] Real increases in population are still occurring in southern and eastern Europe but with the exception of Russia, the rate of this increase seems to be distinctly slackening. The possibility of these surplus populations spilling over into those of other nations has moreover been greatly reduced by the restrictive immigration laws and practises which are increasingly being imposed by industrial nations.

Outside of Europe lie Africa and Asia. Here the introduction of modern medicine and sanitation together with an improvement in industrial technique may and probably will reduce the death rate before the spread of birth-control can operate effectively on the birth rate. We shall, therefore, probably have increases of population in these continents which may force out the white imperialisms which have developed there in the last century and a quarter. But a mass movement from the east to the west will certainly not occur for an extraordinarily long period of time and during this time the practise of birth-control will probably spread in those areas much as it has in ours and in time relieve the population pressure there. This rapid downward drift in the rate of population growth to a point where in the United States and most northern European countries, the actual balance of births over deaths is apparent rather than real has been an affair in the main of the last decade.[56] It has been accompanied at least up until 1929 by a general advance in the real wages of the workers in most industrial countries. The experience of this period has, therefore, sharply contradicted the gloomy Malthusianism of the Georgian and Victorian era that an increase in real wages would be followed inevitably by a sharp expansion of population. Unless there is a sharp change in social attitudes towards the proper size of a family, we shall therefore find in the not distant future that the populations of the stocks of northern and western Europe after increasing at a greatly decreased rate will have reached their maximum and may indeed begin to recede. When that happens the long-time supply of labor will either be almost completely inelastic or an actually decreasing magnitude.

It is true of course that this projection of historical trends

---

[55] Except in Quebec.

[56] The population writers of only ten to fifteen years ago were frightened by what seemed to be the devouring ogre of population increase. See E. M. East, *Mankind at the Cross-Road*, E. A. Ross, *Standing Room Only* and G. H. Knibbs, *The Mathematical Theory of Population*.

into the future may be subject to a wide margin of error. It is quite possible that the children now growing up in one and two child families may desire in the main to have three children of their own and thus not only prevent the threatened decline in population from occurring but actually provide for a moderate rate of population growth. It may even be that the great growth of Fascistic nationalism all over the world with its strong emphasis upon relegating women to the home and upon breeding children for the service of the state may reverse the stream of recent history and cause births to move appreciably upward and populations to show once more a real rate of true increase. But while this may happen, it is most appropriate to note that a decade of Fascism in Italy has not produced any such tendency since the birth rate has continued to fall. On the whole therefore it seems probable that the period of great expansion in the population of the European nations is in all probability over. The chief economic effect of this will be that increases in the supply of capital and in the total volume of production can and will go into the form of raising both the average and the marginal productivity of labor and with this the level of real wages.[57]

---

[57] If national and class wars, however, rage during this period, this result may very well not happen and the coming half century will be very much more gloomy.

CHAPTER XV

AN APPROACH TO THE QUANTITATIVE DETERMINA-TION OF THE LONG-RUN SUPPLY CURVE OF LABOR

It is fortunate that we need not be confined exclusively to purely deductive and historical reasoning concerning the probable effect which changes in wages have upon the long-run supply of labor. We now have statistics not only of the birth and death rates in England and Massachusetts for long periods of time, but also indexes of the relative movement of real wages. It is possible, therefore, to compare the movements of real wages with those of (1) the birth rate and (2) the effective fertility rate (*i.e.* the birth rate minus the death rate) and determine what has been the relationship between them.

1. **The Interrelationship between Real Wages, Birth Rates, and Population Growth in England and Wales, 1861–1912**

The Reports of the Registrar-General give annual statistics of the number of births and the probable total population of England and Wales.[1] By dividing the first of these series for the years 1860–1912 by the second, we obtain the crude birth rates for this period, and these have in turn been standardized to obtain a uniform sex and age distribution in order to eliminate any effects caused by alterations in the sex and age composition of the population.[2]

---

[1] See the *Annual Reports of the Registrar-General of England and Wales*, especially those for 1876 (39th) and for 1915 (78th).

[2] The standardized birth rates were based upon those worked out by Sir Arthur Newsholme and T. H. C. Stevenson for 1861, 1871, 1881, 1891, and 1901 in their paper, "The Decline of Human Fertility in the United Kingdom as Shown by Corrected Birth-rates," *Journal Royal Statistical Society*, Vol. LXIX (1906), pp. 34–87. See also Newsholme, *The F˙ ˙ments of Vital Statistics*, p. 87, for the corrected rate for 1911. The rates we   standardized for the intervening years by the following method: (1) The corrected or standardized birth rate for each of these years was divided by the crude birth rates for the given years. This gave correction factors to apply to the crude birth rates in each of these years. (2) It was assumed that where two correction factors at the beginning and end of a decennial period differed, the change occurred evenly during the years. Correction factors were thus obtained for all of the intervening years. It was assumed that the correction factors were the same for 1912, 1913, 1914, and 1915 as for 1911. (3) These correction factors were then applied to the crude birth rates in each year, and thus standardized birth rates were obtained.

384

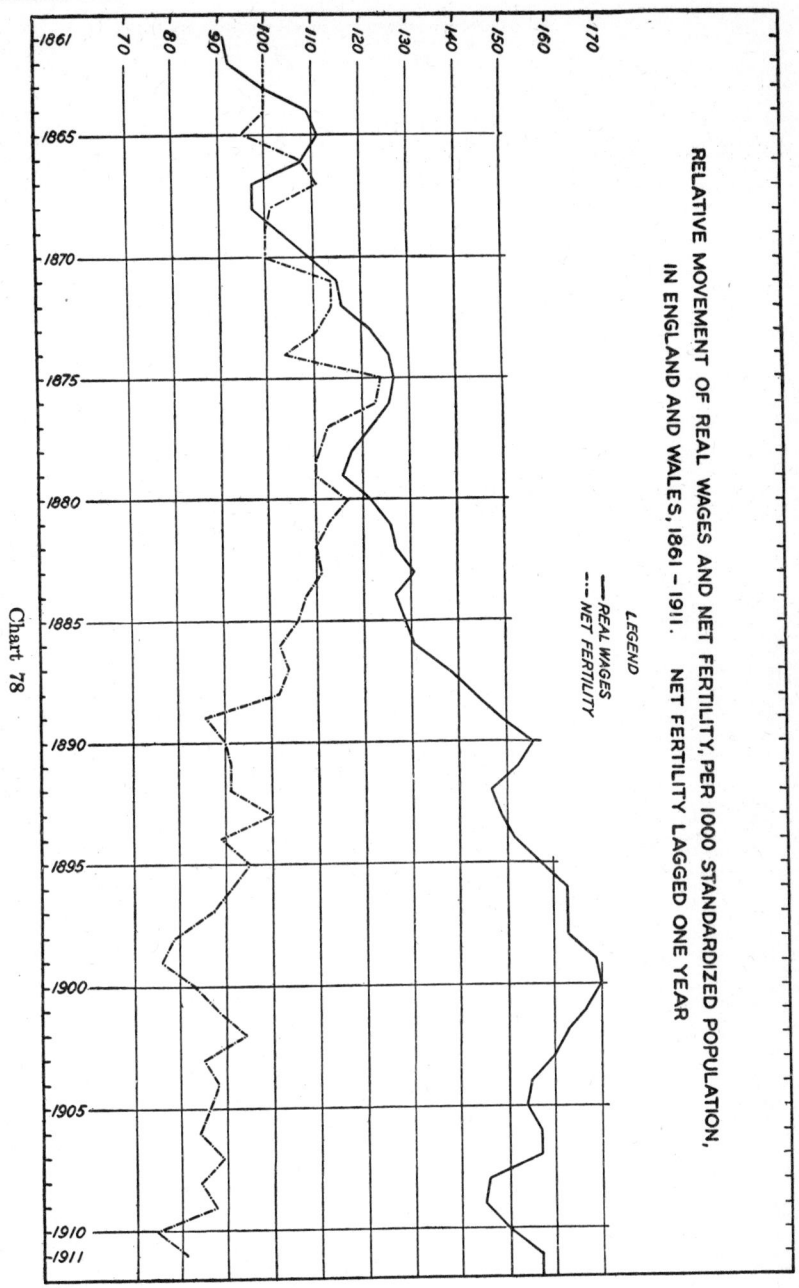

RELATIVE MOVEMENT OF REAL WAGES AND NET FERTILITY, PER 1000 STANDARDIZED POPULATION, IN ENGLAND AND WALES, 1861 - 1911. NET FERTILITY LAGGED ONE YEAR

LEGEND
——— REAL WAGES
—·—· NET FERTILITY

Chart 78

385

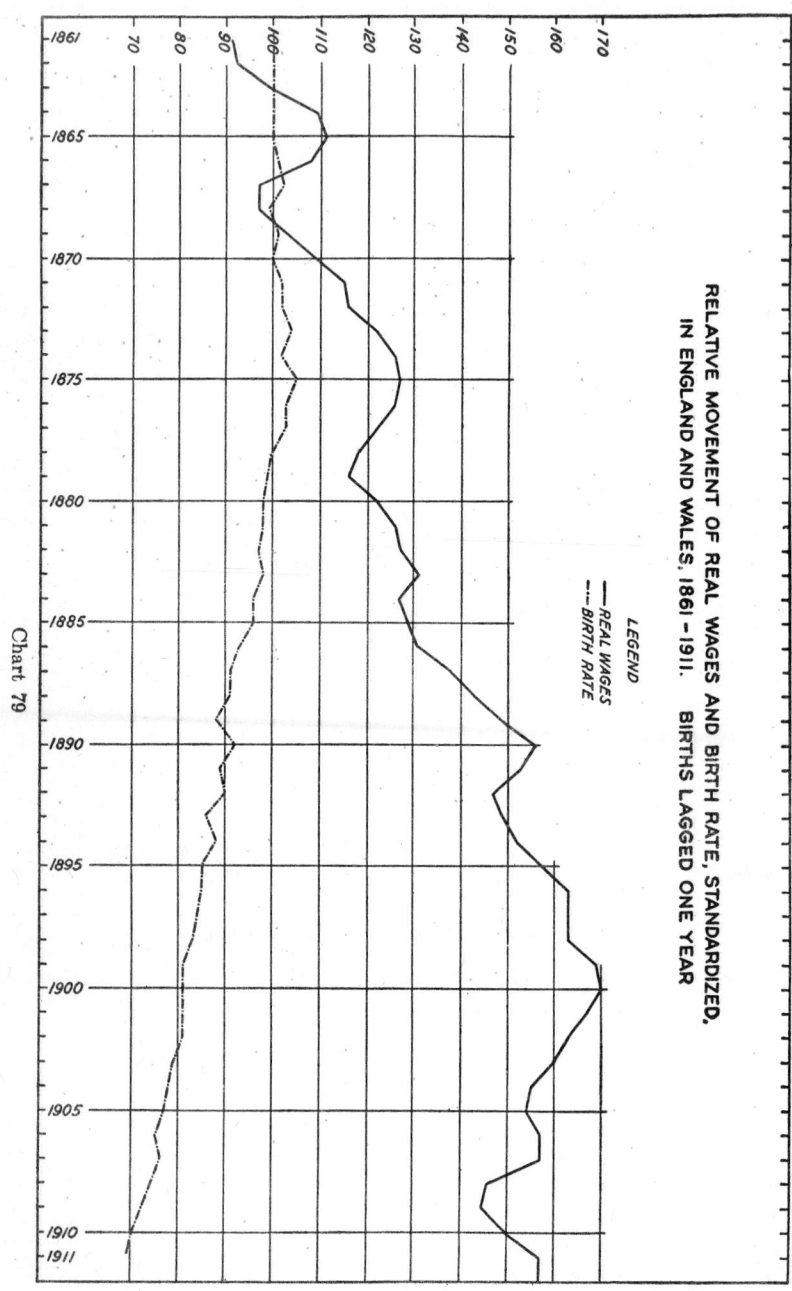

RELATIVE MOVEMENT OF REAL WAGES AND BIRTH RATE, STANDARDIZED,
IN ENGLAND AND WALES, 1861-1911. BIRTHS LAGGED ONE YEAR

LEGEND
——— REAL WAGES
——·—— BIRTH RATE

Chart 79

TABLE 50

RELATIVE REAL WAGES, STANDARDIZED BIRTH RATES, AND NET FERTILITY
RATES FOR ENGLAND AND WALES, 1861–1912

(RELATIVES ON BASE 1861–65 = 100)

Year	Real Wages Relatives	Birth Rates Relatives	Net Growth Rates Relatives
1861	91	98	102
1862	92	99	105
1863	99	100	98
1864	109	101	96
1865	111	101	99
1866	108	101	96
1867	97	101	109
1868	97	102	111
1869	103	99	101
1870	109	101	100
1871	115	100	100
1872	116	102	113
1873	112	101	114
1874	126	103	110
1875	127	101	102
1876	126	104	121
1877	122	103	123
1878	118	103	113
1879	116	100	111
1880	122	99	110
1881	126	98	118
1882	127	98	113
1883	131	97	109
1884	127	97	111
1885	129	96	109
1886	131	95	106
1887	138	93	102
1888	143	91	104
1889	149	91	102
1890	156	88	86
1891	153	92	90
1892	147	89	91
1893	149	90	91
1894	152	86	100
1895	157	88	89
1896	163	85	95
1897	163	85	91
1898	163	84	88
1899	169	83	79
1900	170	81	76
1901	167	80	82
1902	163	81	89
1903	160	81	94
1904	155	79	85
1905	154	78	88

TABLE 50—CONTINUED

RELATIVE REAL WAGES, STANDARDIZED BIRTH RATES, AND NET FERTILITY
RATES FOR ENGLAND AND WALES, 1861–1912

(RELATIVES ON BASE 1861–65 = 100)

Year	Real Wages	Birth Rates	Net Growth Rates
	Relatives	Relatives	Relatives
1906	157	77	86
1907	157	75	84
1908	146	76	89
1909	145	74	84
1910	150	72	88
1911	157	70	75
1912	157	69	81

The net growth rate for these years was then found by subtracting the standardized death rates from these standardized
birth rates. Both the standardized birth rates and net fertility
rates are given in Table XXVIII of the Appendix.

The index of real wages was constructed by splicing that
computed by George H. Wood for the years from 1853 to 1902 [3]
to the index of Frances Wood for London for the years from
1900 to 1912.[4] It includes an allowance for unemployment.

All three of these series for the years 1860–1912 were then
reduced to relatives in terms of the average for the five years
1861–1865 as 100. These are given in Table 50 and are shown
graphically in charts 78 and 79.

It will be noticed that on the whole real wages rose from
1861 to a point in 1875, 27 per cent above the base, while the
corrected birth rate had also risen slightly so that by the years
1874–78 it was from 3 to 4 per cent more than it had been
fifteen years before. Because of the decline in the death rate,
the increase in the net fertility rate was even more marked
than was the case with the birth rate. By 1877 it was indeed
no less than 23 per cent higher than it had been a decade and
a half before.

Real wages fell somewhat during the depression years of
the late seventies but increased very appreciably during the
twenty years from 1880 to 1900. In the latter years they were

[3] George H. Wood, "Wages and the Standard of Comfort since 1850,"
Journal Royal Statistical Society, Vol. LXXII, pp. 91–103.
[4] Frances Wood, "The Course of Real Wages in London," *Journal Royal
Statistical Society*, Vol. LXXVII, pp. 1–55.

indeed 70 per cent above their 1861–1865 average and 39 per cent above that of 1880. There was, however, apparently a decline during the years which followed.

During this later period from 1877 on however, both the birth rate and the net fertility rates fell very appreciably. Thus the birth rate in 1900 was only 81 per cent of what it had been during the first half of the sixties, and by 1912 it was only 69 per cent of what it had been during this base period. The net fertility rate in turn fell very rapidly up to 1900 when it was only 76 per cent of its rate in 1861 and but 64 per cent of the rate during the years 1876–1878. The great reduction in the death rate during the first twelve years of the present century kept pace with the decrease in the birth rate so that the rate of net growth did not continue to fall during these years.

It will be seen, therefore, that this half century is really divided into two periods, namely the years from 1861 to 1877 inclusive, when both the birth and net growth rates were increasing, and the succeeding years, when they were on the whole falling. It is only proper, therefore, that we should study the relationship between the movement of real wages on the one hand and the birth and net fertility rates on the other for each of these periods separately instead of trying to lump the dissimilar periods together. If we correlate these original series, using the year to year quotations, we find the coefficients of correlation to be as follows:

COEFFICIENTS OF CORRELATION BETWEEN RELATIVES OF REAL WAGES AND OF STANDARDIZED BIRTH RATES (ENGLAND AND WALES)

Period	No Lag	Births Lagged One Year
1861–1877	+.70 (±0.12)	+.74 (±0.11)
1878–1912	−.75 (±0.07)	−.73 (±0.08)

We thus find a high positive correlation in the first period and an equally high negative correlation in the second. The coefficients are approximately the same when we lag births by one year and correlate them with the index of real wages for the preceding rather than for the same year.

The relationship between the movement of real wages and the net growth rate is, however, more important than that for the birth rate alone. These coefficients of correlation are given on the following page.

Period	No Lag	Net Growth Rate Lagged One Year
1861–1877	+.43 (±0.20)	+.58 (±0.16)
1878–1912	−.88 (±0.04)	−.86 (±0.04)

Here the coefficient of correlation is somewhat lower than when birth rates were compared, though still positive for the years 1861–77; being + .43 instead of + .70 for identical years, and + .58 instead of + .74 when the growth rates are lagged by a year.

The coefficients for the succeeding thirty-five years are, however, not only negative, but are appreciably higher than was the case when birth rates were used. The coefficient for identical years was − .88 instead of − .75 and when a one year lag is introduced, − .86 instead of − .73.

It will, however, be argued that it is illegitimate to make such comparisons since the connection between these phenomena may have been accidental rather than causal. Thus the spread of the birth control movement from 1877 on was probably the chief cause for the decline in the birth rate during the succeeding years and for the fall in the effective fertility rate down to the close of the century. It will be argued that this movement was caused by the diffusion of new methods of contraception aided by the effective efforts of the Neo-Malthusian movement as led by Charles Bradlaugh and Annie Besant. These developments, it will be urged, were really independent of the movement of real wages and should not be confused with it.

Let us therefore attempt to meet this criticism by eliminating these long-time movements (although in doing so we are frequently throwing out the baby with the bath). This can, of course, be done by computing the trends for each of these series in the two periods and then correlating the relative deviations of the real wage series from its trends, with the relative deviations of the birth and net growth series from theirs. It is first necessary to fit trends to these series.

A single trend was fitted to the real wage series with the following equation:

$$x = 141.265 + 1.005\,t - 0.0066\,t^2 - 0.0002\,t^3 \text{ (origin at 1887)}$$

Two trends were fitted to the birth rate series, namely,

1861–1877: $y = 101.0 + 0.223\,t$ (origin at 1869)
1878–1912: $y = 86.31 - 0.902\,t$ (origin at 1895)

In a similar fashion two trends were fitted to the net growth series with the following equations:

1861–1877: $y' = 105.88 + 1.112\,t$ (origin at 1889)
1878–1912: $y' = 95.54 - 1.011\,t$ (origin at 1895)

By dividing the relatives for the various years by their respective trend values, we obtain the trend-ratios. These are given in Table XXXIII of the Appendix. By correlating the trend-ratios of real wages with those of the standardized birth-rates, we obtain the following coefficients:

COEFFICIENTS OF CORRELATION BETWEEN TREND RATIOS OF RELATIVE REAL WAGES AND OF BIRTH RATES (ENGLAND AND WALES)

Period	No Lag (1)	Births Lagged One Year (2)	Births Lagged Two Years (3)
1861–1877	+.23 (±0.23)	+.28 (±0.23)	+.22 (±0.25)
1878–1912	−.38 (±0.17)	+.05 (±0.25)	+.36 (±0.15)

The coefficients for the first seventeen years, though small, are still positive, ranging from + .22 to + .28. The highest of the three coefficients is that obtained when births are lagged one year and the lowest is that resulting from a two years' lag. The standard errors are however so large in comparison with the coefficients as to make the latter of relatively little significance. The coefficients for the second period, on the other hand, give no clear clue to the relationship between real wages and the birth rate. While the comparison of identical years gives a negative coefficient of − .38, there is an almost complete lack of correlation if births are lagged one year ($r = + .05$), while if a two years' lag is used the coefficient is raised to + .36.

But, as we have pointed out, the net growth rates, rather than the birth rates, are the important factors in the change of the labor supply, and it is to a consideration of the relationship between their trend-ratios and those of real wages to which we now turn. Here the coefficients were:

COEFFICIENTS OF CORRELATION BETWEEN TREND RATIOS OF RELATIVE REAL WAGES AND NET GROWTH RATES (ENGLAND AND WALES)

Period	Identical Years	Growth Rates Lagged One Year	Growth Rates Lagged Two Years
1861–1877	−.49 (±0.18)	−.05 (±0.25)	+.51 (±0.19)
1878–1912	−.58 (±0.11)	−.51 (±0.13)	−.46 (±0.14)

The coefficients for the first period are both puzzling and unsatisfactory. While r is fairly high for identical years (— .49), it is negligible when the growth rates are lagged one year, and while it again becomes fairly high when a two year lag is used (+ .51) it is with an opposite sign from the coefficient for identical years, being positive instead of negative. It is virtually impossible, therefore, to draw any clear conclusion from these data for the first period, namely, that from 1861 to 1877, as to the interrelationship between changes in the trend-values of real wages and of the net growth rates of the population.

The inter-connection between these two variables is, however, much more evident during the succeeding thirty-five years. The coefficient is fairly high for the comparison of identical years, being — .58, and while it decreases to — .51 and — .46 it is always appreciable and is always several times the standard error. It will be noticed, of course, that the relationship between changes in real wages and changes in rates of population growth is not positive, as Malthus and his followers taught, but instead negative. In general, during these thirty-five years of British history when real wages rose above their trend, there was a tendency for the rate of population growth to fall below its trend and vice versa. Since the square of the coefficient of correlation (r^2) is probably the best measure of the degree of interrelationship between phenomena, it is probable that at least one-quarter of the totality of influence is attributable to this inter-connection. Which then of these factors is primarily the causative force? Did the changes in real wages cause the net growth rate to move in the opposite direction or did the changes in the rate of population cause the index of real wages to fluctuate in an opposite manner? This question, of course, cannot be settled by the coefficient itself which merely measures correlation and not cause in its usual sense. The probabilities, however, are all in favor of the assumption that it is the changes in real wages which caused the opposite changes in the rates of population growth; for the possible downward effect of an increase in the rate of population growth upon wages could not be fully manifest until a number of years had passed,[5] while the effect of a change

[5] Save for the fact that a decreased death rate might increase immediately the rate at which the number of adult workers was increasing. The burden of deaths falls, however, in the main upon children and old people who are at the time outside the labor supply.

in the rate of real wages upon the birth and death rates would be far more immediate.

The experience of England during this third of a century, therefore, goes far to disprove the practical validity of the Malthusian theory in an age of birth-control and instead to suggest that the consequences of a change in real wages are indeed the opposite of what Malthus had assumed. While the natural forces of fecundity together with the progress of medical science were leading to an expansion of the total population of Great Britain, the increase in real wages was exercising on the whole a considerable influence towards a *decrease in the rate of growth*. The coefficients of elasticity of the regression of the birth rate and net growth rate upon relative real earnings have been computed for no less than twenty combinations of these series. These coefficients were insignificant in the case of unadjusted series (*i.e.* the actual data) of real wages and the birth rate during the years 1861–1878 and also in the case of the trend-ratios of real wages and the birth rate for both this earlier period and the later one from 1878 to 1912 and this was true not only when identical years were compared but when lags were introduced. In the case of the period 1861–1867 contradictory results were obtained, as has been indicated, for the relationship between the trend ratios of real wages and the trend ratios of the net growth rates. For identical years the elasticity of the trend ratios of the net growth rate as a function of the changes in the trend-ratios of real wages was — 0.44.[6] When births were lagged by one year the elasticity was close to zero, and when they were lagged by two years the coefficient of elasticity became + .43.

For four sets of data however relatively high elasticities were found. (1) In the case of the unadjusted data for the birth rate (y) and the relative real wages (x) for identical years during the period 1878–1912, the equation was $y = 153.47 - 0.45 (\pm 0.07)\ x$ and the coefficient of elasticity at the means was — 0.78. When births were lagged by one year the coefficient of elasticity was — 0.73. It will however be remembered that the comparison of the trend ratios of these data yielded very low coefficients of correlation so too much reliance should not be placed on these unadjusted elasticities.

(2) In the case of the unadjusted data for the net growth

---

[6] That is at the means.

rate and the rate of real wages, for the period 1861–1877, the equation for identical years was $y' = 73.55 + 0.29 \,(\pm\, 0.16)\, x$ and the coefficient of elasticity at the means $+ 0.31$. When births were lagged one year the coefficient of elasticity was $+ 0.43$. This suggests the possibility of a causal positive connection during this early period between increases in real wages and a subsequent increase in the birth rate, and with the latter changing at approximately three-sevenths of the gain in real wages. But this possibility is however greatly weakened by the fact that when we compare the trend ratios of these data, we obtain, as we have stated, very conflicting results depending upon whether or not a lag is introduced and if so whether it is for one or two years.

(3) The unadjusted series of the net growth and real wage rates during the period from 1878 to 1912 show significant coefficients of elasticity. For identical years, the equation was $y' = 195.26 - 0.68 \,(\pm\, 0.06)\, x$, and the coefficient of elasticity at the means was $- 1.07$. When births were lagged by one year the coefficient of elasticity of the net growth rate as a function of relative real wages was $- 1.01$. This meant that an increase of one per cent in real wages tended to be accompanied by a decrease of slightly more than one per cent in the rate of population growth.

(4) The inference that there was a negative relationship between real earnings and the net growth rate during the thirty-five years from 1878 to 1912 is reinforced when we consider the trend ratios of these series. Treating Y' (the trend ratios of net growth) as a function of X (the trend ratios of the real wage indexes), we have the following equations:

(a) For identical years, 1878–1912
$$Y' = 190.10 - 0.91 \,(\pm\, 0.22)\, X$$

(b) Net growth rate lagged one year, 1878–1912
$$Y' = 181.76 - 0.83 \,(\pm\, 0.25)\, X$$

(c) Net growth rate lagged two years, 1878–1912
$$Y' = 175.09 - 0.76 \,(\pm\, 0.26)\, X$$

The coefficients of elasticity at the means were as follows:

Identical years: $e = - 0.90$

Net growth lagged one year: $e = - 0.82$

Net growth lagged two years: $e = - 0.75$.

Here it will be seen that an increase of 1 per cent in the trend ratios of real wages tended in practice to be accompanied by a decrease of from three-fourths to nine-tenths of one per cent in the trend ratio of the net growth rate.

The evidence seems therefore to indicate a distinctly negative relationship during the years 1878–1912 between real wages and the rate of net growth of the population which applies not only when we consider the data as they stand but also when they are adjusted for trend. This indeed emerges as the most significant result which we have obtained from a study of British data. Further studies are needed before we can consider the point definitely established for this period, but the present results furnish a certain presumption in this direction. It seems however safe to conclude at the very least that the Malthusian predictions were not borne out during this period. Certainly no one can contend that an increase in real wages during these years caused an increase in the net growth rate.

As we have intimated, moreover, the recent tendency to disregard the comparative trends of statistical time series and to consider only the deviations from these trends has been pushed too far. The relationship between these trends is also important. For although these trends may have been affected by differing historical forces, it is also possible that one trend may have influenced another. This cannot perhaps be definitely established, but the possibility should at least be noted. During the first period from 1861–1877, all three trends moved upwards. During the later period from 1878 to 1918 the trends of both the birth and net growth rates were downwards, while that for real wages sloped upward during the first part of the period. It might be argued that the improvement in material conditions during these years encouraged the spread of birth-control amongst the upper ranks of the working class.

2. The Movement of Real Wages, Birth Rates and Net Growth Rates in Massachusetts, 1889–1929

Massachusetts is the only state in this country with accurate vital statistics covering any long span of years. It is also the state with the best statistics of earnings and of the cost of living. Because of the fact that it is difficult to construct an index of the cost of living and hence of real wages back of 1889, and because it probably took some time after the 1880 law requiring the registration of births before such reporting became universal, we have begun our study with the year 1889 and have continued it to 1929.[7] It has not, however, been possible to standardize the birth and net fertility rates by reducing the population to the same age and sex composition. These series are all given in Table 51.

It will be seen that the period divides itself logically into two sub-divisions. The first covers the years 1889–1915 when real wages were falling slightly and when though the birth rate was also decreasing, the death rate was decreasing by so much more that the net growth rate was rising appreciably. The second period covers the years 1915–1929 when real wages were rising and when the sharp decline in the birth rate was not offset by the reduction in the death rate, so that the net growth rate was also appreciably falling.

If we take the original series as they stand, we find that the coefficients of correlation for the period 1889–1915 between the relatives of real wages and those of the birth rates were + .68, both for identical years and for a lagging of births by one year. In the case of the net growth rates, however, the coefficients were — .55 and — .56 respectively.

The trend of real wages was found by the method of least squares with an equation of $x = 95.88 - .347\ t$ when 1902 was the point of origin. The equation of the trend of the birth rate was found to be $y = 96.5 - .233\ t$ and that of the net growth rate to be $y' = 110.03 + 1.81\ t$. These trend values and the trend ratios (observed values ÷ trend values) are given in Table 52. It will be observed that the trends of real wages and of the birth rate were both slightly downward during this period. The former decreased at the rate of approximately one-third of one per cent per year and the latter at the rate of approximately one-quarter of one per cent. Due to the fact that the fall in the death rate was greater up to 1915 than was the decrease in the birth rate, the trend of the net growth rate was upwards. This was in the opposite direction from the trend of real wages.

When these trend ratios are correlated with each other, we

[7] The Annual Reports of the Massachusetts Board of Health and the Annual Reports of the United States Census on Birth Statistics and Mortality Statistics give data on births and deaths from which rates may be computed. The average annual money earnings of the employed wage-earners in manufacturing can be obtained from the annual Statistics of Manufactures, while the cost of living index back to 1910 is given in the *Report of the Massachusetts Special Commission on the Necessaries of Life (1926)*. This can be carried back to 1889 by using my country-wide index for the years 1889–1910; see Douglas, *Real Wages in the United States, 1890–1926*, pp. 19–42.

TABLE 51

MASSACHUSETTS BIRTH, DEATH, AND NET FERTILITY RATES (PER 1000) AND
RELATIVE REAL WAGES IN MANUFACTURING INDUSTRIES OF THAT STATE,
1889–1929 (AVERAGE 1890 TO 1899 = 100)

Year	Birth Rate (1)	Death Rate (2)	Net Fertility (3 = 1 − 2)	Relative Birth Rate (27.3 = 100) (4)	Relative Net Fertility Rate (8.2 = 100) (5)	Relative Real Wages (6)
1889	26.2	19.2	7.0	96.0	85.4	97
1890	25.8	19.4	6.4	94.5	78.0	98
1891	27.5	19.7	7.8	100.7	95.1	102
1892	28.1	20.8	7.3	102.9	89.0	103
1893	28.1	20.5	7.6	102.9	92.7	101
1894	27.4	19.1	8.3	100.4	101.2	99
1895	27.0	19.0	8.0	98.9	97.6	101
1896	27.9	19.3	8.6	102.2	104.9	100
1897	28.0	18.1	9.9	102.6	120.7	98
1898	27.1	17.5	9.6	99.3	117.1	98
1899	26.2	17.4	8.8	96.0	107.3	97
1900	25.8	18.2	7.6	94.5	92.7	96
1901	25.1	16.8	8.3	91.9	101.2	95
1902	24.8	16.2	8.6	90.8	104.9	94
1903	24.7	16.3	8.4	90.5	102.4	91
1904	24.3	15.8	8.5	89.0	103.7	92
1905	25.2	16.8	8.4	92.3	102.4	94
1906	26.3	16.6	9.7	96.3	118.3	93
1907	27.6	17.6	10.0	101.1	122.0	92
1908	27.4	16.6	10.8	100.4	131.7	94
1909	26.8	16.2	10.6	98.2	129.3	95
1910	25.7	16.2	9.5	94.1	115.9	91
1911	25.6	15.4	10.2	93.8	124.4	93
1912	25.6	14.9	10.7	93.8	130.5	91
1913	25.5	14.8	10.7	93.4	130.5	96
1914	25.9	14.7	11.2	94.9	136.6	92
1915	25.7	14.6	11.1	94.1	135.4	95
1916	25.4	15.3	10.1	93.0	123.2	99
1917	25.7	15.2	10.5	94.1	128.0	98
1918	25.3	20.9	4.4	92.7	53.7	102
1919	22.9	13.6	9.3	83.9	113.4	103
1920	23.6	13.8	9.8	86.4	119.5	110
1921	23.5	12.2	11.3	86.1	137.8	113
1922	22.1	12.8	9.3	81.0	113.4	119
1923	22.1	13.0	9.1	81.0	111.0	125
1924	22.3	12.0	10.3	81.7	125.6	126
1925	20.8	12.5	8.3	76.2	101.2	123
1926	19.9	12.5	7.4	72.9	90.2	125
1927	19.4	11.6	7.8	71.1	95.1	128
1928	18.3	11.9	6.4	67.0	78.0	129
1929	16.9	11.9	5.0	61.9	61.0	127

have coefficients of correlation of + .58 for identical years and + .55 when births are lagged by one year. The corresponding coefficients for the trend-ratios of real wages and of net growth were + .37 and + .43. The negative relationship which prevailed in England during this period between the trend-ratios of real wages and of net growth rates did not, therefore, exist.

TABLE 52
TREND VALUES AND TREND RATIOS OF REAL WAGES, BIRTH RATES AND
NET GROWTH RATES IN MASSACHUSETTS, 1889-1929

Year	Trend of Real Wages	Trend of Birth Rate	Trend of Net Growth Rates	Trend Ratios of Real Wages	Trend Ratios of Birth Rates	Trend Ratios of Net Growth Rates
1889	100.4	99.5	86.5	96.6	96.5	98.7
1890	100.0	99.3	88.3	98.0	95.2	88.3
1891	99.7	99.1	90.1	102.3	101.6	105.5
1892	99.3	98.8	91.9	103.7	104.1	96.8
1893	99.0	98.6	93.7	102.1	104.4	98.9
1894	98.6	98.4	95.6	100.4	102.0	105.9
1895	98.3	98.1	97.4	102.7	100.8	100.2
1896	97.9	97.9	99.2	102.1	104.4	105.7
1897	97.6	97.7	100.0	100.4	105.0	119.5
1898	97.2	97.4	102.8	100.8	102.0	113.9
1899	96.9	97.2	104.6	100.1	98.8	102.6
1900	96.5	97.0	106.4	99.5	97.4	87.1
1901	96.2	96.7	108.2	98.8	95.0	93.5
1902	95.9	96.5	110.0	98.0	94.1	95.3
1903	95.5	96.3	111.8	95.3	94.0	91.6
1904	95.2	96.0	113.7	96.6	92.7	91.2
1905	94.8	95.8	115.5	99.2	96.3	88.7
1906	94.5	95.6	117.3	98.5	100.7	100.9
1907	94.1	95.3	119.1	97.8	106.1	102.4
1908	93.8	95.1	120.9	100.2	105.6	108.9
1909	93.4	94.9	122.7	101.7	103.5	105.4
1910	93.1	94.6	124.5	97.7	99.5	93.1
1911	92.7	94.4	126.3	100.3	99.4	98.5
1912	92.4	94.2	128.1	98.5	99.7	101.9
1913	92.0	93.9	129.9	104.3	99.5	100.5
1914	91.7	93.7	131.8	100.3	101.3	103.7
1915	91.3	93.5	133.6	104.1	100.6	101.4
1916	99.6	95.1	136.9	99.4	97.8	90.0
1917	102.2	92.9	132.6	96.8	101.3	96.6
1918	. . . .	. . . .	. . . .	. . . .	. . . .	. . . .
1919	107.3	88.4	124.0	96.0	94.9	91.5
1920	109.9	86.2	119.7	100.1	101.3	99.8
1921	112.5	83.9	115.4	100.4	102.6	119.4
1922	115.1	81.7	111.1	103.4	99.2	102.1
1923	117.7	79.4	106.8	106.2	102.0	103.9
1924	120.3	77.2	102.5	104.7	105.8	122.5
1925	122.9	75.0	98.3	101.1	101.8	103.0
1926	125.5	72.7	94.0	99.6	100.2	96.0
1927	128.1	70.5	89.7	100.0	100.9	106.1
1928	130.7	68.2	85.4	98.7	98.2	91.4
1929	132.9	65.9	81.1	95.3	93.8	75.2

Turning now to the regression of birth rates and of net growth rates upon real wages, we find that if we compare the trend ratio of the birth rate with that of real wages, the elasticity of the former in terms of the latter was for identical years + .9414. This meant that a decrease of one per cent in the trend ratios of real wages was normally accompanied by a decrease of nine-tenths of one per cent in the trend ratios of the birth rate.

Let us now turn to the relationship between these variables during the years 1916–1929. If we take the original series as they stand and correlate the changes in relative real wages with changes for identical years in the birth rate and net growth rates, we find the coefficients of correlation to be — .85 for real wages and birth rates and — .64 for real wages and net growth rates. If we lag the birth and growth rates by one year, the corresponding coefficients are — .8379 and — .544.

If we eliminate the trends (which have a great deal of meaning in themselves) we find the coefficients of correlation between the trend ratios for identical years of real wages and birth rates to be + .70 and real wages and net growth + .69. When the trend ratios of the birth and net growth rates are lagged by one year, the coefficients are reduced to + .2725 and + .1784 respectively.

It is not easy to interpret these results. On the one hand, the rise of real wages was accompanied by an actual fall in both the birth and net growth rates. The trends were, therefore, in the opposite direction. On the other hand, the trend ratios of real wages and of birth and net growth rates were fairly similar for identical years, with no distinct tendency one way or the other if the birth and net fertility rates were lagged.

3. Summary

It is distinctly difficult to draw sharply defined conclusions about the effect of changes in real wages upon the rate of population growth from the data which have been presented in this chapter. On the whole, however, the following conclusions seem to be sound.

1. In a period during which birth control is little practised by the working classes, such as the years 1860–1877 in England and 1890–1915 in Massachusetts, the birth rate does not fall appreciably even though real wages advance and may indeed even increase as was the case in England. A rise in real wages by improving the health of the population and by releasing energy for the public health movement tends to help in the reduction of the death rate so that the rate of population growth tends to increase along with, although of course not necessarily in the same ratio to, the advance in real wages.

On the other hand, even though real wages fall to some degree and the public health movement nevertheless develops, the consequent reduction in the death rate will tend to increase the rate of population growth even with an opposite movement of real wages.

2. In a period during which birth-control is spreading through the working class, the birth rate will fall, even though real wages are advancing. Such was indeed the situation in Great Britain during the period 1877–1912 and in Massachusetts during the years 1915–1929. As birth-control reaches the major sections of the working class, births fall more rapidly than deaths, so that the net fertility rate after a time declines even as real wages advance.

3. If we try to eliminate historical trends in order to measure the pure effects of wages on births and net growth unaffected by the trend of the birth-control and of public health movements, we come upon much more shadowy ground. The experience of Great Britain from 1878 to 1912 suggests, however, that there is a tendency for an increase in real wages greater than the average, to be accompanied by a fall in the net growth rate by more than the average. It will be remembered that the coefficients of correlation between the trend ratios of relative real wages and relative net growth rates ranged between — .45 and — .57 depending on the amount of lag and that the coefficients of the elasticity of population growth in respect to wages ranged between — .75 and — .90. These were by far the most definite results which we obtained, since the Massachusetts figures for the years 1915–1929 are not as yet susceptible of a very clear interpretation.

CHAPTER XVI

THE LONG-RUN SUPPLY CURVE OF LABOR IN THE LIGHT OF DIFFERENCES IN THE BIRTH AND NET GROWTH RATES OF VARIOUS ECONOMIC STRATA OF THE POPULATION

Inferential evidence on the effect of changes in real wages and upon the labor supply can be obtained from a study of differences in the birth rates and in the net fertility rates of different economic and social classes of the population. As we study different economic classes we shall find that, except in the larger cities of Continental Europe, the higher is the income of the class the progressively lower in general tends to be the birth rate. This furnishes a basis for contending that if the earnings of the lower paid groups were increased, their birth rate would in turn decrease. A similar contention may also be advanced from the fact that at any one time the net fertility rates of the various economic classes on the whole decrease as one moves from lower to higher income classes.

Such reasoning is prevented from being absolutely convincing by the lurking possibility that the differences in both earnings and in fertility may in turn be at least partially functions of some third factor, such as general intelligence. The unskilled may have both low earnings and large families, for example, because they have on the average low intelligence, and the upper business groups high earnings and small families because of high average intelligence. It may be argued, therefore, that since an increase in the real wages of the unskilled would not increase their intelligence and innate capacity, it hence might not reduce either their birth rate or their net fertility rate.

But while the evidence on the differences of fecundity and net fertility between economic and social classes is at best inferential rather than conclusive evidence of a relationship between changes in the real income of a class and its rate of growth, it is worth while to canvass the problem and to see what the facts are. While the general tendencies are fairly well known, the detailed statistical evidence is worthy of more detailed examination.

1. The Comparative Birth Rates of Different Economic Classes

A pioneer study on this subject was that made by Bertillon of the comparative refined birth rates (per 1000 women of child-bearing age) during the eighties and early nineties in the chief capitals of Europe, namely, Paris, London, Berlin, and Vienna.[1] The various sections of each of these cities were classified into six sets of districts according to the average degree of economic well-being, and separate birth rates were computed for each. These are shown in Table 53.

TABLE 53

RELATIVE BIRTH RATE PER 1000 FERTILE WOMEN IN PARIS, LONDON, BERLIN, AND VIENNA (1886–1894) ACCORDING TO RELATIVE ECONOMIC CONDITION OF DISTRICT IN WHICH THEY LIVED

Class	Birth Rate per 1000 Fertile Women			
	Paris 1889–93	London 1881–90	Berlin 1886–94	Vienna 1890
Very poor...................	108	147	157	200
Poor......................	95	140	129	164
Comfortable................	72	107	114	155
Very Comfortable...........	65	107	96	153
Wealthy...................	53	87	63	107
Exceptionally wealthy.......	34	63	47	71
Average...................	79	109	102	153

These figures show a uniform tendency for the birth rates of given sections to vary in an opposite direction from that of their average incomes. The relative difference between the birth rates of the very poor and of the upper groups is shown by the following ratios:

City	Ratio of Birth Rate of Very Poor to That of Other Classes				
	Ratio to Poor	Ratio to Comfortable	Ratio to Very Comfortable	Ratio to Wealthy	Ratio to Very Wealthy
Paris............	1.14	1.50	1.66	2.04	3.18
London..........	1.05	1.37	1.37	1.69	2.33
Berlin...........	1.22	1.38	1.64	2.49	3.34
Vienna..........	1.22	1.29	1.31	1.87	2.82

Thus the birth rate of the very poor was from 5 to 22 per cent above that of the poor, from 29 to 50 per cent more than that

[1] Jacques Bertillon, "La Natalité selon le degré d'aisance," *Bulletin de l'Institut International de Statistique*, Vol. XI, pp. 163–76.

of the comfortable, and from 31 to 66 per cent higher than that of the very poor. The excess of the birth rate of the very poor over that of the two wealthy groups was still greater, being from 70 to 150 per cent more than that of "the wealthy" and from two and a third to three and a third times that of "the exceptionally wealthy."

This early study by Bertillon stimulated other investigations. One of the first of these was that conducted by Verrijn-Stuart[2]

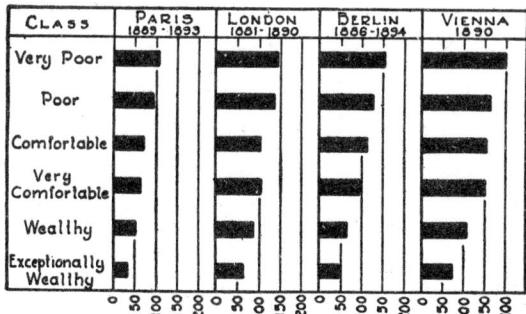

Chart 80. Relative Birth Rates Per 1000 Fertile Women in European Capitals (1881–1894) According to Relative Economic Condition of the District in Which They Lived. (Based on Statistics of Bertillon)

into the birth rates of similar sections of Amsterdam, Rotterdam, and Utrecht. The differences between the various classes were found to be far less marked than in Bertillon's study, the rates for Amsterdam being as follows:

District	Birth Rate per 100 Women of Child-bearing Age	Comparative Birth Rate of Other Classes to Very Wealthy
Very poor.....................	170	1.19
Poor.........................	175	1.22
Comfortable..................	160	1.12
Very comfortable.............	145	1.01
Wealthy......................	168	1.17
Very Wealthy................	143	1.00
Average..............	163	

[2] C. A. Verrijn-Stuart, "Natalité, mortinatalité et mortalité enfantine selon le degré d'aisance dans quelques villes et un nombre de communes rurales dans les Pays-Bas," *Bulletin de l'Institut International de Statistique*, Vol. XIII (1903), pp. 357–68. The birth-control movement had at this time made more headway in Holland than in the other countries. This may have accounted for the smaller differences in the birth rate between the classes.

Thus not only was the birth rate of the very poor but 19 per cent above that of the "very wealthy" but it was only one per cent above that of the "wealthy" and actually three per cent less than the group immediately above them.

A parallel study by Verrijn-Stuart [3] of approximately 4800 urban families who had been married from sixteen to twenty years and who were classified into four economic groups by the amount of their house tax, gave more pronounced differences in the average number of births per household.

Class	Average Number of Births	Relative Number of Births (Class IV = 100)
I	5.61	134
II	5.21	125
III	4.35	104
IV	4.18	100
Average	5.30	

The birth rate in Class I was therefore approximately 34 per cent higher than in Class IV, while an inverse relationship existed throughout between economic comfort and fertility.

A third original investigation was made by Professor Harald Westergaard and M. Rubin [4] from Danish church records of the birth and vital statistics of 34,000 families. These families were classified into the following five groups:

Class	Number of Families
1. Public officials, doctors, liberal professions, manufacturers, merchants, bankers, and other men of large business	3700
2. Small independent handicraftsmen, small traders, etc.	8816
3. Teachers, musicians, subordinate officials, etc.	1919
4. Clerks, waiters, servants, etc.	3568
5. Manual workers	16,072

If we take the families in each of the groups who had been married over fifteen years, the average number of births was as given in Table 54.

It will be seen from this that the two classes with the lowest birth rates were (1) the poorly paid professional and lower official class who were compelled to keep up appearances on small incomes and (2) the group of clerks and domestic servants, to some of whom children would be an incumbrance in securing

---

[3] *Ibid.*, p. 361.
[4] Rubin and Westergaard, *Statistik der Ehen auf Grund der Sozialen Gliederung der Bevölkerung* (Jena), 1890.

TABLE 54

AVERAGE NUMBER OF BIRTHS PER MARRIAGE IN DENMARK BY ECONOMIC CLASSES

Class	15–24 Years	Relative (Class 3 = 100)	25 Years and Over	Relative (Class 3 = 100)
3	3.77	100	4.35	100
4	4.13	110	4.70	108
1	4.24	113	4.80	110
2	4.32	112	4.91	113
5	4.79	127	5.26	121

employment. The second of these classes also tended to imitate the standards of living of the well-to-do on altogether insufficient earnings. Next after these two classes came that of the most well-to-do, and following these was the group of small handicraftsmen. The group with the largest birth rate was that of the manual workers with a rate between 21 and 27 per cent more than that of the lower class professions.

Rubin and Westergaard also standardized the marriages in each group by reducing them all to a common duration and found approximately the same results as those for the marriages of over fifteen years' duration, except for the fact that the birth rate of the well-to-do class was now placed above the small handicraftsmen and was indeed only three per cent less than the fertility of the wage-earners.

Another very interesting investigation, which was also modelled upon the pioneer work of Bertillon, was that made by Mombert for seven German cities.[5] The sections of each city were classified according to their economic position, and birth rates were computed for each. The birth rates in the various sections of Hamburg, Leipzig, Dresden, and Frankfurt in 1900–1901 are given in Table 55.

Thus the poorest section of Hamburg had a birth rate which was nearly three times that of the most affluent, while in Leipzig, it was nearly four times as great. In Frankfurt, the rate of the poorest sections was indeed between five and six times that of the wealthiest districts. The results for Munich, Berlin, and Magdeburg were essentially similar, although the sequence was not always as regular as in the case of the four cities mentioned.

Another admirable continental study which gives additional

---

[5] Paul Mombert, *Studien zur Bevölkerungsbewegung in Deutschland* (1907), pp. 150–60.

TABLE 55

The Birth Rate per 1000 Women of Child-bearing Ages in Various Social Districts of Hamburg, Leipzig, Dresden, and Frankfurt, 1900–1901

Section of City (arranged in order of affluence)	Hamburg	Leipzig	Dresden	Frankfurt
1–3	59	68	69	40
4–6	85	88	117	89
7–9	111	113	147	112
10–12	124	155		135
13–15	126	166		170
16–18	153	175		223
19–21	151	192		
22–24		209		
25–26		241		

data on the tendency of births to decrease among the more prosperous economic classes was conducted by the Danish statistician, Kiaer, who produced still further evidence on this point,[6]

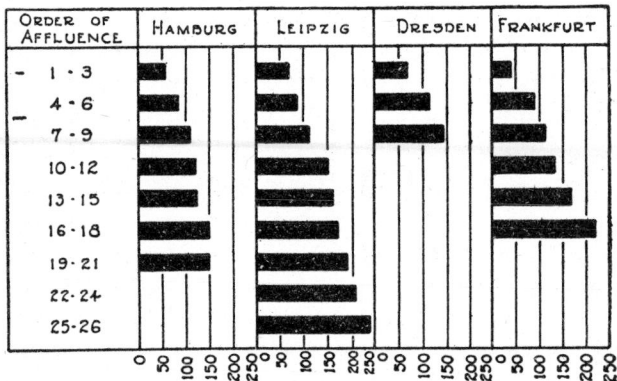

Chart 81. Relative Birth Rates Per 1,000 Fertile Women in 1900–1901 in Various Sections of Four German Cities Classified According to Economic Status. (From Statistics of Mombert)

while other incidental studies have given similar results.[7]

The report of the British census on fertility is, however, the

---

[6] A. N. Kiaer, *Statistische Beiträge zur Beleuchtung der Ehelichen Fruchtbarkeit*, 2 vols, 164 and 225, pp. Christiania (1903–1905).

[7] Thus see the study of the family· statistics of 76,000 Bavarian state officials in 1916, which showed that among the lower officials there were 2.7 children on the average, in the middle group 1.7, and among the highest 1.5. *Beiträge zur Statistik Bayerns* Heft 88, München, 1918, quoted by A. Grotjahn, *Proceedings World Population Conference*, 1927, pp. 152–3. See also the material presented by Professors Gini and Boldrini at the conference, *Ibid.*, pp. 161–2; 194–5. Thus in Trieste the birth rate in the wealthiest part of the city was 17.4, while in the poorest part it was 32.1.

most extensive and thorough-going study which has ever been made.[8] The census gathered data in 1911 from approximately 1.6 million couples who had been married for varying periods of time and obtained a fairly large sized sample of marriages which had taken place as early as 1851.

These families were then divided into the following five main classes, according to the occupation of the father and upon the basis of the relative remuneration and social status attached to them.

Class I. Capitalists, enterprisers, scientists, artists, professional workers, etc.

Class II. Small shopkeepers, artisans whose work contained some elements of the creative, and lower ranks of the professional, scientific, and artistic group, and farmers, that is, agricultural employers.

Class III. Skilled labor. Transport service, metal trades, building trades, furnishing, leather, paper trades, etc., domestic servants.

Class IV. Semi-skilled labor where skill required was slight and muscular strength was essential.

Class V. Unskilled labor.

The average number of children born to wives in the various classes who were 45 years and over and hence had finished their

TABLE 56

RELATIVE NUMBER OF CHILDREN BORN TO MARRIED COUPLES IN DIFFERENT ECONOMIC CLASSES IN GREAT BRITAIN

Class	Children Born per 100 Couples	Relation to Average for Country as a Whole
I	389	80
II	451	93
III	489	100
IV	492	101
V	528	108
Average for all classes	487	100

[8] *Census of England and Wales 1911*, vol. XIII. *Fertility of Marriage*, Part 1., 477 pp. Cd. 8678 (1917); Part II, pp. CLXX and 260 (1923). For other discussions of this material see T. H. C. Stevenson, "The Fertility of the Various Social Classes in England and Wales from the Middle of the Nineteenth Century to 1911." *Journal Royal Statistical Society*, vol. LXXXIII (1920), pp. 401–32 and R. M. MacIver, *Civilization and Population* read before the British Association at its Toronto meeting, 1924. Some parts of this paper are included in the symposium edited by Dr. Louis I. Dublin, *Population Problems*, pp. 287–310.

period of fertility, and the relation which these averages bore
to the general average for the country as a whole are given
in Table 56.[9] Differences in ages have been standardized and
the groups reduced to a comparable basis.

The birth rate for the period as a whole was, therefore, 35 per
cent higher among the unskilled than among the highest social
and economic class, and 8 per cent higher than among the skilled
workers. These average differences between the birth rates of

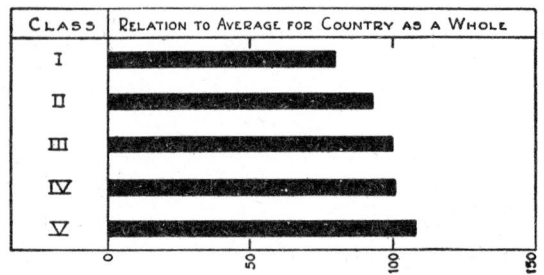

Chart 82. Relative Number of Children Born to Married Couples in Different Economic Strata in Great
Britain, 1851–1911.

the various economic and social classes were not, however, constant through time but instead varied according to the dates of
marriage. In the following table the families in the various
classes are listed according to the period of their marriage and
the differences between classes shown for marriages of various
durations.

TABLE 56-A

RELATIVE FERTILITY OF VARIOUS SOCIAL CLASSES IN ENGLAND AND WALES BY
DATE OF MARRIAGE, 1851–1911. ("CENSUS OF ENGLAND AND WALES,"
·Report on Fertility, VOL. XIII, PART II, p. xciii)

Date of Marriage	Relative Fertility of Classes (Average = 100)				
	I	II	III	IV	V
1851–61	89	99	101	99	103
1861–71	88	96	101	100	104
1871–81	81	93	101	101	107
1881–86	76	89	100	101	110
1886–91	74	87	100	101	112
1891–96	74	88	99	101	113
1896–1901	76	89	98	101	113
1901–1906	79	91	98	101	112
1906–1911	80	92	98	102	114

[9] British Census of 1911, Vol. XIII, Report on Fertility, Part II, p. xcviii.

It will be seen from this:

(1) That for marriages contracted during the 1850's, while the birth rate for the unskilled was higher than that of any other class, it was only 2 per cent more than for the skilled worker, 4 per cent more than for the semi-skilled and lower professional and bourgeois classes, and 16 per cent more than that of the highest economic and social class. The differences in the birth rate between the various social classes were not therefore striking.

(2) These differences steadily increased during the succeeding thirty-five years so that in the case of marriages contracted during the years from 1891 to 1896, the birth rate of the unskilled was 12 per cent more than that of the semi-skilled, 14 per cent more than the skilled, 28 per cent more than the lower professional and lower bourgeoisie, and a full 53 per cent above the birth rate of the highest class. The probable reason for this increasing disparity was the increasing adoption of birth-control by the upper classes and the relative slowness of this information either to be made available to the unskilled or to be adopted by them.

(3) During the succeeding fifteen years, as the general birth rate continued to fall, these discrepancies between the unskilled and classes I and II on the whole narrowed. For those married between 1906 and 1911, the birth rate of the unskilled was to be sure still 12 per cent higher than that for the semi-skilled and indeed 16 rather than 14 per cent higher than the birth rate of the skilled. But it was at the same time 42 per cent rather than 53 per cent above the birth rate of the highest group. The rate at which birth-control was spreading through the lower economic classes was now more rapid than its continued progress in the upper groups, although, of course, it was still more prevalent in the two upper economic classes than in the three manual classes.

The births in 1921 in England and Wales have also been classified by the Registrar-General according to the occupational status of the heads of the family and were as follows: [10]

---

[10] A. M. Carr-Saunders, "Differential Fertility" in *Proceedings World Population Conference 1927*, p. 138.

Class	Number of Births in 1921 per 1,000 Married Men Under 55	Relative Birth Rate
1. Upper and middle..........	98	100
2. Intermediate...............	105	107
3. Skilled Workmen...........	134	137
4. Intermediate...............	153	156
5. Unskilled Workmen........	178	182

This shows a very distinct reduction in the birth rate for each and every class from that which prevailed in 1911, and it also indicates that the differences between the various social classes were still pronounced. The birth rate among the unskilled was, for example, approximately one-third higher than among the skilled and over 80 per cent above that for the upper and middle economic classes.

There are very clear indications that the decline in the birth rate of the unskilled is steadily progressing and that the differences in fecundity between the social extremes are appreciably narrowing. Thus De Jastrzebski's analysis [11] of the comparative birth rates of various London boroughs in 1911 and 1921–1922 showed that the decline in boroughs where there were more than 1.25 persons on the average to a room was approximately as great as that for London as a whole. The decrease in these poorer boroughs was indeed appreciably greater than that in well-to-do districts. In 1911 the standardized legitimate fertilities in Bethnal Green, Shoreditch, and Stepney (where there were approximately 1.5 persons to a room) was 40 per cent greater than in Chelsea, Kensington, and Hampstead (where there was on the average approximately .8 of a person to a room). But by 1921 this difference had been reduced to one of approximately 33 per cent. As De Jastrzebski remarks, "this approach is brought about, not by any increase in fertility in the more advantageously placed classes, but by the more rapid decline among those of an inferior economic and social position."

During this period the economic position of the unskilled workers seems beyond doubt to have been improved. Bowley and Hogg in their 1924 [12] study of five provincial towns esti-

[11] T. T. S. De Jastrzebski, "Changes in the Birth-rate and in Legitimate Fertility in London, 1911–1921," *Journal Royal Statistical Society*, Vol. LXXXVI (1923), pp. 26–45.
[12] Bowley and Hogg, *Has Poverty Diminished*, p. 21. See also Bowley, "A New Index Number of Wages," *Memorandum No. 12* of the London and Cambridge Economic Service (1929).

mated that the weekly money wages of the unskilled were approximately double what they had been ten years before, whereas the cost of living, according to their estimates, had increased by only 70 per cent. In addition to the gain in real wages, should, of course, be reckoned the increased free income in the form of social insurance and other social services provided by the government. The birth rate of the unskilled was, therefore, falling during a period in which they were making decided material progress. If a further analysis were made comparing 1921 with 1931, the difference would apparently have been decreased still further.

A comparatively recent study for Bremen, Germany, of the relative birth rates in 1925 as compared with 1901 brings this tendency out quite clearly. The city was divided into four rather clearly defined zones and the following birth rates were found to prevail.[13]

Type of District	Number of Births per 100 Population	
	1901	1925
1. Wealthy..................	1.27	1.47
2. Middle-class..............	2.89	1.42
3. Artizan..................	4.37	1.95
4. Mainly laboring...........	4.62	1.89

Thus while the birth rate of the laboring classes in 1925 was 30 per cent higher than that of the wealthy, the differences between the classes had been greatly diminished. The birth rate among the wealthy actually increased during this period by approximately one-sixth while that of the other three classes decreased to an extraordinary degree. Thus the rate for the second class fell by 50 per cent, that for the third class by 55 and that for the fourth by 60 per cent. Instead of the birth rate among the wealthy, therefore, being only four-ninths of that among the middle class as in 1901, it had come by 1925 to be actually 3 per cent more. Whereas at the turn of the century, the birth rate of the artisan was 244 per cent more than that of the wealthy and that of the laborers 264 per cent more, these differences had shrunk to 37 and 29 per cent respectively. The rate for the laborers was indeed slightly below that for the artisans.

[13] See Röhmert, "100 Jahre Geburtsstatistik in Bremen," quoted by A. Grotjahn, *Proceedings World Population Conference, 1927*, p. 153.

An excellent study on the differential birth rate in this country has been made by Professor W. F. Ogburn and Clark Tibbits.[14] They have worked over reports by the Census Bureau on the birth rates in 1925 for women whose husbands belonged to some 139 separate occupational classes and obtained the following results:

TABLE 57

FERTILITY OF SOCIAL CLASSES IN FAMILIES OF REGISTRATION AREA IN THE
UNITED STATES WHERE MOTHERS IN 1925 WERE FROM 40–44 YEARS OF AGE

Social Classes[1]	Average Number of Children Ever Born to Mothers of 1925, 40–44 Years of Age
Miners	8.9
Agricultural Laborers	8.6
Farmers	8.0
Non-Agricultural Laborers	8.3
Semi-Skilled	7.9
Declining Old Skilled	7.1
Foremen	6.9
Skilled	6.8
White Collar Laborers	6.6
Servants	6.3
Bourgeoisie	6.2
Petty Bourgeoisie	5.3
Managers	5.3
Professions	4.9
Capitalists	4.5

[1] For the sub-groups in these classes see Ogburn and Tibbits, *op. cit.*, p. 6.

This shows substantially similar results. Mining is again the occupation with the highest birth rate, followed by agriculture, and with the urban industries following. Agricultural laborers, however, had a higher birth rate than land-owning farmers. The unskilled industrial workers had relatively more births than the semi-skilled, and these in turn more than the skilled. Below the latter were the white collar laborers,[15] the servants, and the bourgeoisie. Those with the lowest rates were the petty bourgeoisie,[16] the managers, the professional workers, and lowest of all the capitalists.

If we take the number of children born to mothers from 40 to 44 in this last class of capitalists as 100, we find the rate for the mining group to be virtually twice as great, for the agri-

[14] W. F. Ogburn and Clark Tibbits, Birth Rates and Social Classes, *Social Forces*, Vol. VIII (1929), pp. 1–10.
[15] These were manual workers such as tailors, mail carriers, policemen, barbers, etc.
[16] These included stenographers and clerks.

cultural laborers to be 90 per cent more, and for the farmers to be a little under 80 per cent more. The unskilled laborers in the towns and cities had had about 85 per cent more children, the semi-skilled a little less than 80 per cent while the skilled manual workers have had a little over 50 per cent more.

All this tends to be corroborated by the recent report of the President's Committee on *Recent Social Trends*. They found the average size of family in 1930 for the various occupational groups to be: [17]

Professional	3.01	Semi-Skilled	3.47
Clerical	3.04	Unskilled	3.91
Proprietory	3.25	Farm Owners and Renters	4.48
Skilled	3.51	Farm Laborers	4.32

In cities of around 100,000 "the sizes of the family for the different rental classes beginning with the $15–$20 class were 4.60, 4.33, 3.96, 3.68 and 3.50." . . . In the metropolises of the country the size of the family declined as the rents increased up to the $100 a month level. Thereafter the size of the family increased as rents rose. [18]

2. The Net Growth Rates of Various Social Classes

The differences between the birth rates of the various social classes are not of course identical with the differences in the rates of increase. For if they were, it would be necessary for the death rates of the several classes to be equal, and it is well known that they are not. The death rate is higher among the less skilled and more poorly paid, and this serves, at least in part, to offset their higher birth rates. The question is the degree to which the differences in the death rates counteract those in the birth rates.

Rubin and Westergaard's study for Denmark indicated that when the deaths were taken into consideration, there were actually 9 per cent more children to a marriage who survived in the upper class than in the lowest class. [19] But the differences in the death rates were not sufficient completely to offset the varying birth rates in the other classes, so that the net growth rate of the lowest class (Class V) was still 3 per cent higher than that of Class II, 6 per cent more than Class IV, and 10 per cent more than Class III.

Verrijn-Stuart's study also showed that despite the higher

---

[17] *Recent Social Trends*, Vol. I, pp. 685–6.
[18] *Ibid.*, p. 687.
[19] Rubin and Westergaard, *op. cit.*, p. 122.

death rate, the net fertility of the lowest class was still appreciably higher than that of the other classes.[20] The number of children per marriage surviving at five years was 3.92 for the lowest group, 3.22 for the next lowest group, 3.72 for the second highest class, and 3.48 for the families in the upper class.

The net growth rates for the various social classes in England, after allowance for deaths, were found by the British Census to be as follows: [21]

TABLE 58

THE NUMBER OF SURVIVING CHILDREN PER 100 MARRIED COUPLES IN VARIOUS SOCIAL STRATA IN GREAT BRITAIN, 1851–1911

Class	Number of Children Surviving per 100 Couples	Relative Number of Children Surviving in Class V as Compared with other Classes
I	311	1.24
II	352	1.10
III	371	1.04
IV	374	1.03
V	386	

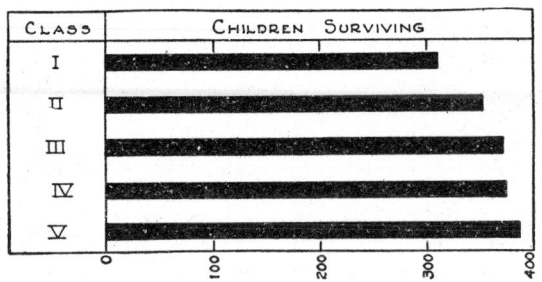

Chart 83. Relative Number of Survivors per Married Couple in Various Social Strata in Great Britain, 1851–1911.

The differences between the classes, though less than in the case of births, were therefore still appreciable. The relative number of surviving children were 24 per cent greater in the lowest than in the highest group, as compared with the 35 per cent difference in births. The surviving children per family of the unskilled were moreover 10 per cent more than among the lower middle-class, and 4 and 3 per cent more than among the skilled and semi-skilled respectively.

---

[20] Verrijn-Stuart, *op. cit.*, p. 361.
[21] "Census of England and Wales" (1911), Vol. XIII, *Report on Fertility*, Part II, p. xcviii.

A detailed study of the differential class fertility in the Liverpool region has recently been made by D. C. Jones as the result of the Merseyside Survey.[22] The following statistics show the number of children born and surviving in the various social classes: [23]

TABLE 59

DIFFERENTIAL FERTILITY IN LIVERPOOL REGION, 1930

Class	Distinguishing Characteristics	Average Number of Children per Family		
		Born	Dead	Surviving
A	*Lowest Class*—frequently one room tenement—receiving public assistance....................	3.90	.90	3.00
B	*Very Poor*—family income less than 34 s. per week............	4.24	.91	3.33
CD	*The Poor*—casual workers—family income from 34–40 s. or receiving unemployment benefit...	4.06	.56	3.50
E	*Ordinary Labor*—above poverty line—family income 2£–3£ per week......................	3.14	.36	2.78
F	*Higher Class Labor*—income 3£–5£ per week.....................	2.55	.26	2.29
GH	*Lower and Upper Middle Class*—5£ a week and upwards..........	2.09	.15	1.94

This shows a birth rate which, though lower for the poorest group than for the very poor, steadily declined thereafter as one moved into higher economic classes. The birth rate for the very poor was over twice that of the middle classes and for the poor nearly twice. Ordinary labor had a rate which was 50 per cent higher than the middle class, and higher class labor between 20 and 25 per cent higher. The higher death rate somewhat reduced the difference in living children between the lower and the higher groups, but even here the differences were appreciable. The poor to be sure had more surviving children than the two groups below them, although they had averaged fewer births than the class immediately beneath them.

The average number of surviving children for ordinary labor was, however, over 25 per cent less than for the poor, 7 per cent below that for the lowest class, and 20 per cent below the very poor. Higher labor had a rate 35 per cent below the poor, and

[22] D. Caradog Jones, "Differential Class Fertility," *The Eugenics Review*, Vol. XXIV; Oct. 1932, pp. 175–90.
[23] *Ibid.*, p. 181.

the surviving children in the middle-class averaged **44** per cent below the average of the poor.[24]

A report by the United States Census covering a much smaller sample throws further light on the differences between occupations in the average number of living children.[25] The following table gives the average number of living children of fathers from 45 to 49 years in various occupations as disclosed by a study in 1923 of birth registration certificates in a number of states. Since these families cannot in all classes be regarded as necessarily completed, the relative number of children in the professional groups may be slightly understated.

TABLE 60

NUMBER OF LIVING CHILDREN IN FAMILIES OF REGISTRATION AREA IN UNITED STATES WHERE FATHERS ARE FROM 45–49 YEARS, CLASSIFIED BY OCCUPATION OF FATHER

Craft	Average Number of Living Children	Craft	Average Number of Living Children
Furnace men	6.8	Machinists	5.0
Coal-miners	6.6	Plumbers	5.0
Farm Laborers	6.0	Electricians	4.9
Laborers (Building and general)	5.8	Glass-blowers	4.6
		Locomotive engineers	4.5
Blacksmiths	5.5	Electrotypers	4.3
Carpenters	5.4	Compositors	4.0
Bakers	5.3	Architects	3.0
Tailors	5.1	All occupations	5.5
Cabinet-makers	5.0		

It is thus seen that the average number of living children in the families of unskilled laborers tended to be six or more, for

---

[24] Very similar, although less distinct, differences are shown by classifying 5200 families upon an occupational basis (*Ibid.*, p. 181):

Grade of Occupation	Average Number of Children per Family		
	Born	Dead	Surviving
1, 2, 3 (higher)	2.49	.33	2.16
4, 5 (clerks, shop assistants)	2.41	.36	2.05
6 (skilled manual)	3.28	.56	2.72
7 (semi-skilled)	3.51	.68	2.83
8 (unskilled)	4.16	1.06	3.10

[25] Mimeographed Report of the United States Census Bureau, issued December 29, 1924.

the skilled workers between four and six, and for a representative professional group, approximately three.[26]

3. May the Tide be Moving in the Other Direction?

The fact that in those countries where birth-control has been practised for a considerable period of time, such as England and Germany, the birth rate has recently been falling more rapidly among the poor than among the well-to-do and that the differences in fecundity between the various economic classes have in consequence been very appreciably narrowing, raises the question as to whether this tendency is likely to continue until the manual workers have an actually lower birth rate than the more affluent strata of society. While they learned of the methods of birth-control later than the more prosperous they might, nevertheless, because of their poverty, carry this practise further and restrict births more rigidly once the general popularization of these methods had occurred and a pervasive control over the birth rate had been effected.

Indications that this is in fact occurring, are afforded by the statistics of the birth rate in a number of European cities. One of the earliest of these studies was that made for Stockholm by Dr. Karl Edin.[27] Stockholm is a city where the birth-control movement early became wide-spread. The crude birth rate in 1916 was as low as 16.6, and by 1922 it had fallen to the extraordinarily low figure of 13.8 or a rate per 1000 fertile women of only 45. Dr. Edin found that those families in 1920 where the husband received less than 6000 crowns annually had 114 children per 1000 years of marriage, while those with over 6000 crowns had 130 children, or 14 per cent more than the former. Dr. Edin also discovered that the fertility of those with more than 10,000 crowns a year was 45 per cent while that for the class receiving from 6000 to 10,000 crowns was 17 per cent higher than that of the industrial workers. The non-manual workers who received under 6000 crowns a year, however, had a birth rate which was only 3 per cent above that of the industrial workers.

Since the infant mortality rate was appreciably higher among the low than the higher income groups,[28] this meant that the

---

[26] The average size of the families in a number of other professions was less than three, but in the case of ministers the average was slightly over four.

[27] Karl Arvid Edin, "The Birth Rate Changes," *Eugenics Review*, Vol. 20, pp. 258–66.

[28] Dr. Edin states that the infantile death rate was approximately 26 per cent higher among the industrial workers than among the upper economic classes. *Proceedings World Population Conference 1927*, p. 206.

relative number of children who survived would be still greater among the upper economic classes as compared with the industrial workers than would be indicated by the statistics of births alone.

This general tendency is confirmed by recent studies for certain cities in Germany, France, and Switzerland. F. Burgdörfer, on the basis of the German income tax returns for 1925, has classified the size of German families according to income and obtained the following very interesting results: [29]

TABLE 61

AVERAGE NUMBER OF CHILDREN IN VARIOUS ECONOMIC CLASSES ACCORDING TO GERMAN INCOME TAX STATISTICS IN 1925

Income Group	Number of Children per 100 Families					
	In Germany as a Whole	In Large Cities	Berlin	Munich	Middle Sized Cities	Remaining Communities
Under 1500 marks......	160	96	75	98	129	176
1500–3,000 marks......	174	110	87	110	147	199
3,000–5,000 marks......	164	116	91	107	145	189
5,000–8,000 marks......	152	119	94	107	150	176
8,000–12,000 marks.....	144	125	109	108	148	166
12,000–16,000 marks....	142	124	106	115	145	162
16,000–25,000 marks....	141	129	110	120	150	160
25,000–50,000 marks....	142	131	120	114	154	160
Over 50,000 marks.....	148	140	130	121	157	164

This table shows that in the larger cities where the size of families is already extremely low, the number of children in a family steadily increases as the incomes of the families increase. For the larger cities as a whole, the number of children in families with incomes of over 50,000 marks is approximately 45 per cent more than in families with less than 1500 marks of income per year. This difference is particularly marked in Berlin, which is both the largest city and the one with about the lowest birth rate. Here the average number of children in the wealthiest group is 73 per cent more than in the poorest. In Munich, which is a strong Catholic city, the differences, though less, are still appreciable. Here the topmost group has a birth rate 23 per cent above that of the lowest and 10 per cent more than in the group with annual incomes of from 1500 to 3000 marks.

It is also interesting to note that in the non-urban communities the birth rate is higher than in the cities and that in

[29] Friedrich Burgdörfer, *Volk Ohne Jugend*, Berlin, 1932, p. 59.

general the number of children decreases as income increases. It is true that the number increases from 176 to 199 as one moves from the group with less than 1500 marks annually, to that with from 1500 to 3000 marks. But thereafter the size of the family decreases, although more slowly than before, as one moves up in the income scale. There is, however, a slight rise upward from 160 to 164 for the over 50,000 mark group as compared with those of the 16,000 to 50,000 mark group.

Even as far back as 1920, the birth rates in the Swiss city of Zurich were tending to be higher in the lower than in the higher classes [30] while a similar movement has recently been discovered to exist for Paris.[31]

Since in these metropolitan centers the number of children are now tending to be greater in more prosperous than in less prosperous families, can it then be concluded that an increase in real earnings would raise the birth rate and lead after all, as Malthus feared, to a great expansion of population?

To our mind, this conclusion does not follow. In the first place, this condition has been reached in only the large urban centers of northern continental Europe. It is still not characteristic of southern Europe, Great Britain, America, or of the smaller cities and towns of northern Europe itself. In all of these areas, as the birth-control movement spreads through the working classes, we may expect a fall in their birth rate even though their economic status should improve. During this period, therefore, an increase in real wages would not offset the decline in the birth rate which would be caused by the diffusion of birth-control.

[30] R. Schmid, *Der Geburtenrückgang in der Schweiz*, Zurich, 1925. Schmid classifies the families with various numbers of children as follows (*Ibid.*, p. 119):

Number of Children in Family	Capitalists and Professionals	Middle-Class	White-Collared	Skilled Labor	Unskilled Labor
No children...........	25.8	28.2	32.0	28.7	29.6
1 child...............	24.4	26.8	29.8	28.0	26.5
2 children............	27.4	22.7	22.6	21.9	21.1
3 children............	14.3	12.6	9.7	11.7	11.3
4 children............	5.6	5.4	3.7	5.4	6.1
5 or more children.....	2.5	4.3	2.3	4.3	5.4

This shows that in the topmost class a smaller per cent had one and no-child families than the skilled or unskilled laborers, and a larger per cent had two or three child families. A smaller percentage, however, had five children or more.

[31] See Barnouw, p. 81. *Birth Control Review* (vol. xvi), March 1932.

Second, it is apparently only when the birth rate is relatively low that the more prosperous families begin to have more children than the less prosperous. Thus in the German figures which have just been cited, the average number of children per 100 families was only 88 in Berlin, 105 in Munich, and 109 in all the large cities.[32] Even though most of these families were not "completed" and hence would have some more children, it is apparent that this rate was grossly insufficient to maintain even a stationary population. It is in such a situation as this, where childless marriages are common and where one and two child families are predominant that the birth rate amongst the more well-to-do will either not fall as far as the general average or will rise above it. For married couples in general want some children and if they can afford them they will not willingly be childless. Similarly couples are more and more aware of the psychological difficulties from which an only child is likely to suffer and tend to prefer a two- to a one-child family if it can be managed without too severe an impairment of family standards of living. Many will also want to have three children, but it is more than doubtful whether there will be many who will desire to have four or more. The relative desire of husbands and wives for additional children will, therefore, tend to decline as the number of children in the family increases. It would seem that this newer tendency, which we have noted, will therefore help more to offset the decrease in population than to provide for an appreciable net growth in the population. For we should never forget that an *average* of nearly three children is needed from each fertile family in order merely to keep the population constant. Two children are needed to replace the immediate parents while there is need for a surplus to provide for those who die in childhood and youth, for those who remain bachelors or spinsters, and for sterile marriages.

There is little reason, therefore, to fear that this reverse movement of the differential birth rate points the way, were real wages to increase, to a rapidly expanding population. On the contrary, we would probably tend more to have a constant or at the most a slightly increasing labor supply. The long-run supply of labor would still be extremely inelastic.

---

[32] Burgdörfer, *op. cit.*, p. 59.

CHAPTER XVII

THE PROBABLE SUPPLY CURVE OF CAPITAL AS CONCEIVED BY ECONOMISTS

There is perhaps no subject in all of modern economics upon which there has been more unsatisfactory and contradictory reasoning than upon the probable nature of the supply curve of capital. There has, in the first place, been a general failure to perceive that the supply of capital must of necessity grow relatively slowly through the addition of annual increments and that the rate of interest at most exercises its effects upon these increments rather than upon the preceding total itself. In addition, one may find in the theories of the economists almost every conceivable type of supply curve which one can imagine, and nearly all of these, if taken separately, are mutually inconsistent with the others. It is worth while, therefore, to consider some of these fundamental issues and then to make some attempt at least at a synthesis.

1. **Since the Supply of Capital Is Fed from Annual Increments, Its Supply in the Short-Run Is Relatively Fixed**

The supply of capital is similar in nature to the supply of gold or to the supply of water in a lake. It is at any moment a fund built up from past accumulations, but it is being fed by a stream of fresh additions and depleted by another stream of depreciation and obsolescence. The quantity of gold in the world during the sixty years from 1850 to 1910 was on the average about thirty-six times the amount annually mined. A halving of the rate of growth in any one year, therefore, did not mean that the total quantity of gold had diminished in any such ratio but merely that it was 1.4 per cent less than it would otherwise have been. Great changes in the increments would, therefore, be accompanied by but slight changes in the totals.

The situation with respect to the supply of capital is very similar. Factory buildings, offices, barns, tools, machinery, power-stations, transmission lines, railways, steamboats, docks, live-stock, trucks, and such like, constitute the supply of capital at any one time. In all, save the most primitive, societies, the quantity of this capital is many multiples of the amounts which are annually added to it. Cassel has estimated that in northern and western Europe the amount of capital during the latter part of the nineteenth and the first part of the twentieth centuries was approximately thirty-three times the annual volume of net savings. From my own studies of capital growth it seems that in Great Britain, the total quantity of capital from 1850 to 1910 averaged nearly forty times the annual increment,[1] while in the United States from 1880 to 1920 with our more rapid rate of capital saving, the total was on the average approximately twenty-two times the annual amounts saved.

The supply of capital is, therefore, at any one time relatively fixed. Relatively large changes in the amounts which are saved annually will have but a slight immediate effect upon the total quantity of capital which is available. In the long run, to be sure, the changes in these increments will have a multiplied effect, but in the short run the supply of capital is relatively fixed.[2]

In so far, therefore, as the rate of interest does affect the quantity of capital, it does so primarily through the annual increments. Its effect upon the total supply of capital available at a given time is comparatively negligible. If it falls too low, it may, to be sure, lead business men and investors not to replace depreciated and obsolete equipment and to use the funds, instead, for current consumption. It may thus speed up the rate of decay as well as retard the rate of growth. But while it is untrue that capital once created perpetuates itself automatically and painlessly, as J. B. Clark presumed, it is also true that a change in the rate of interest would probably not affect the amounts actually spent to make up for depreciation and obsolescence as much as it would affect the volume of fresh savings.

There is perhaps a further point to be noted. In modern times, at least, the quantity of capital has been an almost con-

---

[1] See my "Growth of Capital in Great Britain, 1850–1908," *Journal of Economic and Business History*, Vol. II, pp. 659–84.

[2] I developed this point in some detail in the original manuscript which I submitted for this competition in 1926. Since then my colleague, Professor Frank H. Knight, has developed this idea in complete independence as will be seen from his articles, "Interest and Interest Theories," *Journal of Political Economy*, Vol. XXXIX, No. 2, 1931, and "Interest," *Encyclopedia of the Social Sciences*, Vol. VIII.

stantly increasing magnitude. Assuming that depreciation and obsolescence would, therefore, have been provided for, this means that a change in the rate of interest which would have caused a reduction in the rate of saving would not have resulted in an absolutely smaller quantity of capital. The result would have been merely a quantity, which though smaller than it would otherwise have been, would still have been larger than it was originally.

2. **The Doctrine That the Supply of Capital Is Saved Under Conditions of Constant Cost and That the Supply Curve Is Parallel to the Base**

As the classical school came to explain interest in terms of the pain cost of saving, it developed the doctrine that saving was carried on at a constant and uniform cost. Had the classical economists been in the habit of drawing diagrams to illustrate their thought, they would therefore have pictured the supply of capital as being described by a straight line parallel to the base and at right angles to the ordinate upon which the rate of interest was measured. This doctrine was first developed by Senior and, with the amplifications introduced by that original genius John Rae, was taken over by J. S. Mill and then by Cairnes, until it now finds its modern expression in the theories of Taussig.

Ricardo's explanation of interest, or "profits," was vague and shadowy. Its share of the national dividend was to be sure decreasing because of the constancy of wages in the face of increasing rent. But long before "profits" fell to zero all accumulation would stop. Precisely why it would stop, Ricardo, with his rather unquestioning acceptance of capitalistic society, never explained.

This task of explanation was first assumed by Senior. He declared that interest was paid because, if capital were to be accumulated, abstinence on the part of the saver was necessary. Abstinence was indeed, along with labour and natural resources, one of the three main agencies of production, and was said by Senior to stand "in the same relation to profit as labour does to wages." [3] The sacrifices required in the accumulation of capital were so great that a considerable amount of interest was needed as compensation. "For to abstain from the enjoyment which is in power," said Senior, "or to seek distant rather

---

[3] N. W. Senior, *Political Economy* (6th edition), p. 59.

than immediate results form among the most painful exertions of the human will." [4]

Senior drew no distinction between the relative amounts of abstinence which were involved in the savings of different persons and of different classes of society. This failure to distinguish between the sacrifice required in the case of the savings of an artisan and in that of a millionaire enabled Lassalle to utter his classic gibe about the "abstinence" of a Rothschild. Thus, to Senior, the cost of production of capital was identical for all persons and apparently for all units as well. Savings might, therefore, be said to be carried on under conditions of constant cost.

Although John Stuart Mill elaborated the interest theories of Ricardo and of Senior, he made no notable contribution to them. "The profits of the capitalist," he declared, "are properly, according to Mr. Senior's well-chosen expression, the remuneration of abstinence. They are what he gains by forbearing to consume his capital for his own uses. For this forbearance he requires a recompense." [5] In addition to this basic rate of interest, extra allowances must be made for the degree of risk involved in the investment and for the amount of waiting required. The amount, however, which will have to be paid for the pure interest will depend [6] (and this is an interesting adumbration of Böhm-Bawerk) "on the comparative value placed in the given society, upon the present and the future: on the strength of the effective desire of accumulation."

This minimum rate will vary from society to society and from time to time according to the degree to which people prefer the present to the future. But, according to Mill, it cannot fall to zero because while there would still be some savings at such a point to provide for possible future misfortunes, they would not have "much tendency to increase the amount of capital permanently in existence." [7] What would be saved at one period to provide for illness, old age, or unemployment, would be withdrawn at another, so that the total stock would not increase by "much."

According to Mill, "the savings by which an addition is made to the national capital usually emanate from the desire

---

[4] *Ibid.*, p. 57.
[5] J. S. Mill, *Principles of Political Economy* (Ashley edition), p. 405.
[6] *Ibid.*, p. 407.
[7] J. S. Mill, *op. cit.*, p. 729.

of persons to improve what is termed their conditions in life, or to make a provision for children or others, independent of their exertions. Now to the strength of these inclinations, it makes a very material difference how much of the desired object can be effected by a given amount and duration of self denial, which again depends on the rate of profit." [8] This is the rate of profit "below which persons in general will not find sufficient motive to save." [9] This is further defined as the "rate which an *average* [10] person will deem to be equivalent for abstinence." [11]

That Mill had a partial comprehension that the necessary rate to induce saving varies as between different individuals is shown by his remark that "there are always some persons in whom the effective desire for accumulation is above the average." [12] But in the confused way in which economists wrote before the days of the marginal school, he believed that these merely offset others whose preferences for the present were greater than those of the average. As he said "these merely step into the place of others whose taste for expense and indulgence is beyond the average and who, instead of saving, perhaps even dissipate what they have received. [13]

Cairnes, who followed Mill, was as anxious to preserve his master's doctrine as was McCulloch to protect the teachings of Ricardo. They were indeed more royalist than the king, and Cairnes thought that he knew the mind of Mill better than Mill himself. Writing as he did to defend the classical doctrine of cost of production [14] as the regulator of value against the new marginal [15] utility analysis of Jevons, he attacked the idea that the utility of the marginal or "final" unit was that at which the price was determined. Value was said by him to be determined by cost, and, following Senior, cost was made to consist of the pain involved in labor and the sacrifice of abstaining from the consumption of capital. Here Cairnes recognized even more distinctly than Mill that the cost of abstinence was different for various persons. "Abstinence may be for the rich," he admitted, "with whom its exercise rarely implies any sensible en-

---

[8] *Ibid.,* p. 729.
[9] J. S. Mill, *op. cit.,* p. 729.
[10] Italics mine.
[11] *Ibid.,* p. 729.
[12] J. S. Mill, *op. cit.,* p. 729.
[13] *Ibid.,* p. 729.
[14] Modified, to be sure, by the theory of non-competing groups.
[15] Or in Jevons' terms "final utility."

croachment on customary comforts and luxuries, and still
less on necessaries, but a trifling sacrifice." [16]   On the other
hand he declared that for the "great class of dealers and producers, from the ranks of unskilled labor upward, whose aggregate savings form the main support of the capital of civilized
states, abstinence, far from being a slight, is always a severe,
and often a very severe, sacrifice." [17]   This might be expected
to prepare the way for a marginal cost analysis, but Cairnes
explicitly rejects this concept in favor of the arithmetic average.
"Another possible ambiguity it may be well to clear up," he
writes.[18] "As was intimated just now, the sacrifice involved in
a given act of abstinence is very different in the case of different
persons. . . . And it is similar with labor. . . . This being so,
the question arises—How are such differences to be dealt with in
computing the cost of production? Are we to take account of
what is personal and peculiar to the actual producers, and regard
the cost of the commodity as higher or lower according as it has
been produced by a weak or a strong workman, or by capital
the result of painful or of painless saving?

*The answer must be in the negative. The sacrifices to be
taken account of, and which govern exchange value, are, not
those undergone by A, B, or C, but the average sacrifices undergone by the class of laborers or capitalists to which the producers
of the commodity belong."* [19]

Thus the average amount of abstinence involved in saving a
unit of capital determined the rate of interest, and the average
sacrifice, the rate of wages, because they determine the ratio
at which commodities exchange for each other. There will be
equal proportions of low cost and high cost savers in the various
industries which will lead to an exchange of goods upon the
basis of their average cost.

The confusion which results from making the average rate
of abstinence the determinant of the rate of interest has already
been mentioned. The propounders of this theory never seriously
considered the question as to why anyone who was more im-
patient than the average and to whom the sacrifice was, therefore, great would be willing to save for a rate of interest which
was not enough to compensate him for the sacrifice he had

---

[16] Cairnes, *Some Leading Principles of Political Economy, Newly Expounded,* p. 82.

[17] *Ibid.,* p. 82.

[18] Cairnes, *op. cit.,* pp. 84–5.

[19] Italics mine.

undergone. The answer, that he would save because someone else, who would have saved for less than the average rate of interest, enjoyed a psychic surplus which was exactly equal to his deficit and that, therefore, in the large all these aberrances from the average even themselves out, completely misses the point. The decision to save is not arrived at in a cosmic conference, but by the judgment of individuals. If they sacrifice more than they gain, then they will in all probability not save.

It is noteworthy that both Mill and Cairnes believed the actual rate of profits, or "interest," was in practise close to the theoretical minimum and was always tending to approach it. This naturally followed from their acceptance of the Ricardian theory of progress. The secular increase in population would result in increased pressure upon the land and would in consequence raise rents. Wages would tend to remain at the same level as before. The expanding percentage which rent secured of the national income would, therefore, lower the rate of interest. This tendency would continue until profits reached their minimum, and all further accumulation would cease.[20] But when capital did not increase, then the wage fund must remain stationary. Wages consequently would not thereafter rise, and hence population would remain constant. The margin of cultivation would as a result remain unaltered, and society would be in the "stationary state" adumbrated by Ricardo.[21]

Society was "always on the verge" of this stationary state and was only prevented from attaining it because of three forces which swept away the surplus capital. The first of these was the waste of a great deal of capital in unproductive ventures. The lowering of the rate of interest "inclines persons to give a ready ear to any projects which hold out, though at the risk of loss, the hope of a higher rate of profit, and speculations ensue which, with the subsequent revulsions, destroy or transfer to foreigners a considerable amount of capital, produce a temporary rise of interest and profit, make room for fresh accumulations, and the same round is recommenced."[22] The second factor was that of improvements in production. "All inventions which cheapen any of the things consumed by the labourers, unless their requirements are raised in an equivalent degree, in time

---

[20] *Principles of Political Economy*, p. 733.
[21] See Mill, *Principles of Political Economy*, Chapters IV, V and VI, Book IV.
[22] *Ibid.* (Ashley edition), p. 734.

lower money wages and, by doing so, enable a greater quantity of capital to be supplied.

In modern times, Professor Taussig has developed a theory about the supply curve of capital which also makes the rate at which the "effective" supply is furnished parallel to the base for the final part of its course and hence subject to constant costs. Professor Taussig recognized that there were some who would save even though there were no interest and others who would save for a low rate. He was, however, impressed with the fact that the rate of interest on long-time loans had in the last two centuries only varied between a minimum of three and a maximum of six per cent, and he believed that it had been remarkably steady for the period as a whole. Since accumulations had been extremely rapid during this period he came to the conclusion that two forces had been at work. The first was a continuous improvement in technique which was constantly shifting the demand curve for capital to the right. But since this did not permanently raise the rate of interest, which after a time tended to fall again to about its former level, Taussig believed that there must be an extremely large quantity of savings which would be induced at this rate. He, therefore, concluded that there was a very broad margin of savings at this point which seemed to keep the interest rate relatively steady. Professor Taussig, therefore, envisaged the supply curve of capital as rising for a time and then moving parallel to the base as is shown by the following chart in his "Principles of Economics."[23]

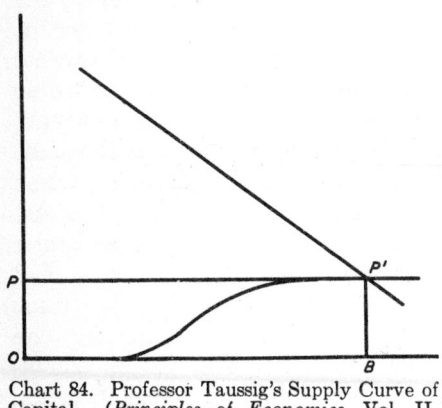

Chart 84. Professor Taussig's Supply Curve of Capital. (*Principles of Economics,* Vol. II, p. 29)

---

[23] For the statement of this theory see F. W. Taussig, *Principles of Economics* (1915 Edition), Vol. II, pp. 24–8. See also *Quarterly Journal of Economics,* Vol. XXII, pp. 353–65. Professor Taussig pointed out, however, that the increase in the numbers and wealth of the well-to-do with the greater ease of savings which would result might cause this broad margin of accumulation to fall to some such rate as two per cent.

3. The Doctrine That the Supply Curve of Capital Is Negatively Inclined

In a suggestive little book, Sargent, in 1867,[24] argued that the supply curve of savings was negatively inclined and that a lower rate of interest would cause more savings to be made. He reasoned that people saved in order to provide a given yearly income for their own old age or for their dependents, and that the amount which was saved would tend to vary inversely with the rate of interest. "A clerk calculates," he wrote,[25] "that when his family have married away from his house he shall be able to live on £80 a year. If interest were as low as in Holland formerly (2 per cent) it would require £4000 to supply his moderate income; at 5 per cent, £1600 would suffice; at 10 per cent, £800. As interest rises the necessary savings diminish."[26] Sargent then concluded that where a person was saving to provide for sickness, old age, or the maintenance of his family after death, the object was "to secure a certain future income." In this situation Sargent declared that a low rate of interest "directly increases the principal saved," and that "in order to furnish a certain income hereafter, I must accumulate a sum all the larger as the rate of interest is less." Not only, therefore, did Sargent believe that the supply curve of saving had a negative slope, but he believed that its elasticity was approximately equal to unity. For the assumption that men saved in order to enjoy a constant income necessarily involved this implicit conclusion about the supply of capital as the assumption of the mercantilists and their followers, that labor worked for a fixed standard of living necessitated a similar belief in the negative unit elasticity of the short-run supply of labor.

This view of Sargent's for a time influenced Alfred Marshall,[27] and it formed, as we shall see, an important part of the interest theory which Sidney and Beatrice Webb advanced in their discussion of the economic effects of trade-unionism.

The German economist, Schmoller, also supported the theory that the amount of capital would increase if the rate of interest decreased.[28] By a comprehensive survey of the rates of interest

---

[24] W. L. Sargent, *Recent Political Economy*.
[25] Sargent, *op. cit.*, p. 76.
[26] *Ibid.*, p. 77.
[27] More especially in the *Economics of Industry* which he wrote in collaboration with Mrs. Marshall.
[28] Gustav Schmoller, *Grundriss der Allgemeinen Volkswirtschaftslehre*, Zweiter Teil, pp. 206–21.

paid at various times and places, he showed that there has been an apparent historical tendency for the rate of interest to fall. From 1820 to 1845, a slow fall of the interest rate from about 5 to 3½ per cent occurred throughout all of western Europe. During the next quarter of a century, the rate rose again because of the demand for capital to build and equip the fast developing railroads and factories. During the decade of the sixties many capitalists became accustomed to a rate of interest which ranged between 5 and 7 per cent.

From 1873 on, however, the rate of interest again fell to between 2½ and 3 per cent. From this historical review, Schmoller concluded that "it is not impossible that the rate of interest which sank to 3 per cent in the eighteenth century and to 2¾ and 2½ in the nineteenth, will decrease in the twentieth century to 2 and even to 1½ per cent."

Schmoller then declared that "the assertion which is often made by people interested in capital that a falling rate of interest lessens the amount of capital formation and that this fall in the rate is consequently undesirable and actually harmful to society, cannot stand a close examination into the facts." Not only has the historical fall in the interest rate been accompanied by a truly extraordinary increase in the volume of savings, but also the countries where the rate of interest is lowest tend to be those where the savings are the greatest. As Schmoller said "the countries and period in which the rates of interest are lowest are those in which the amounts of capital saved are the greatest." Schmoller did not however make adequate allowance for differences in risk between countries and periods.

He continued, "we shall scarcely find many persons who would prefer to consume and spend their resources because the rate of interest was reduced or who in such a circumstance would prefer to start a business of their own rather than loan out their capital. Careless spendthrifts will not be induced to lead luxurious lives because of the reduction in the rate of interest. Furthermore, the person who must decide the question as to whether he will live on his interest or start a business of his own will not be primarily influenced by the relative height of the rate of interest. The savings of capital would not cease even were the rate of interest to fall to 2 or 1½ per cent. One would even be justified in saying that the formation of capital would receive a new stimulus because it would be only through an increase in the amount of capital that the owner could be compensated for the loss of interest." [29]

4. The Doctrine That the Supply Curve of Capital Is Positively Inclined

Modern interest theory, as Professor Knight has remarked, begins with the work of Böhm-Bawerk.[30] As is well known three of his four celebrated reasons why people prefer the present to the future and which, to overcome, necessitate the payment of interest, were primarily subjective, namely, the inability to visualize the needs of the future as strongly as those of the present, defects of will, and the uncertainty of life. Böhm-Bawerk [31] was wise enough to see that these subjective difficulties were not the same for all persons, but that they manifested "themselves in extremely different degrees in different individuals." [32] Recognizing this fact, no member of the Austrian school could commit the blunder, which Mill and Cairnes had made, of averaging different degrees of time-preference into one figure which would represent the amount needed to induce savings. Böhm-Bawerk instead pointed out that these differences in time-preference on the part of potential lenders created a supply schedule in which high rates of interest would attract into the market additional lenders whose preference for the present in comparison with the future was greater than those who were willing to lend at lower rates of interest.

Böhm-Bawerk also built up a demand schedule for capital which was ostensibly based on the time-preference of borrowers. Those who very highly preferred the present to the future would be willing to pay high rates of interest for the use of capital, and those whose preference was less pronounced would pay a low rate, and so on. To explain the demand for capital solely in terms of time-preference would be merely taking account of loans for financing consumption and would ignore the so-called "productive" loans. Böhm-Bawerk, as is well known, attempted

---

[29] These passages are from Schmoller's, *Grundriss*, Zweiter Teil, pp. 209–10.

[30] See Böhm-Bawerk's, *The Positive Theory of Capital* and his history of interest theories, *Capital and Interest*, and *Recent Literature on Interest*.

[31] The first reason, namely, the increased productivity of roundabout processes is, as many critics have stated, not a subjective explanation at all, but an explanation from the productivity side. The reasons why persons prefer the present to the future were developed even more fully by John Rae in 1834. Rae in addition worked out the influences upon interest of relative productivity and of invention far more adequately than Böhm-Bawerk. See John Rae, *Sociological Theory of Capital*, pp. 151–204.

[32] Böhm-Bawerk, *Positive Theory of Capital* (translated by Wm. Smart), p. 257.

to extricate himself from this difficulty by introducing the productivity principle through the back door. The increased productivity of the "roundabout process" was adduced as one of the reasons why people preferred the present to the future, although why it should logically be brought under this psychological factor is difficult to understand.

Having thus constructed a positively sloping supply schedule and a negatively sloping demand schedule, both of which were subject to discontinuous changes and which were not smooth curves, Böhm-Bawerk then declared that the rate of interest would be fixed between the rates which the marginal borrower would pay and the marginal lender would demand. The failure to use a curve with continuous variations caused Böhm-Bawerk, therefore, to create in the determination of exchange value and of the rate of interest a slight zone of indeterminateness between the preferences of the marginal pair.

So far as the supply of capital is, however, concerned, Böhm-Bawerk believed that it was positively inclined and that it would increase or decrease as the rate of interest rose or fell. He, however, ascribed this to the different time preferences of different individuals and did not go into the question whether higher rates of interest would be needed to induce each person to save successively larger portions of his income. He dealt, in other words, with what in the classical theory of rent would be called the extensive margin and ignored the intensive margin.

The analysis of both of these sets of forces was carried much farther by Landry [33] and Irving Fisher [34] in their brilliant books on the theory of interest. Landry pointed out that in so far as men are swayed by rational motives they try to distribute their consumption through time so that the utilities of the last dollars expended in the various years shall be equal. Men will seek so to readjust their expenditures in the various years that they will secure no less satisfaction with the last dollar expended in one year than they can obtain from a similar dollar in any other year. Saving takes place because of these endeavors to transfer consumers' income from one time period to another. But the degree to which rational men will save and the amount of interest required to induce them to do so will depend

---

[33] Adolphe Landry, *L'Intérêt du Capital*, and also his, *Manuel d'Économique*, pp. 621–64.

[34] Irving Fisher, *The Rate of Interest* (1907), and his later, *The Theory of Interest* (1930), which lays more stress upon the influence of the productive use of capital than did the earlier book.

on three types of factors, namely, (1) changes in the needs of men, (2) changes in resources and (3) the relative degree to which saving by itself disturbs the equilibrium of consumption when needs and resources remain constant through time.

(1) *The needs of men change with the years.* Young married couples may in general look forward to years when their wants will be greater while in some cases men may anticipate a future when their desires will not be so imperious. When people feel that their needs will increase in the future, then there is an inducement for them to save even though no interest be paid, for a greater amount of satisfaction is secured by transferring dollars to the future, when the need for them will be more acute, than by consuming them in the present. If men's needs are to decrease, however, equal amounts of money have greater significance in the present than in the future. People will not save and further aggravate this already unbalanced condition unless they are more than compensated by the payment of such a rate of interest as will more than offset the greater utility attached to the dollars in the immediate present.

(2) *The relative resources of people vary from time to time.* If the income of a man is to decrease, as is normally the case during the years of his retirement, then he will tend to save dollars from the present when they are plentiful in order that they may be applied to the future when they will be much more scanty. This would be a sufficient inducement for some saving even though no interest were to be paid. But if one's resources are to be greater in the future, then it would be poor economy to transfer sums of value from the present, which is relatively understocked, to future years which offer every prospect of being more abundantly provided for. Nor would such savings be made unless such a rate of interest were offered, which would pay the saver such a sufficiently increased number of dollars, as to more than offset the decreased satisfaction which could be secured from each dollar.

(3) *Finally, interest would have to be paid to induce savings even though needs and resources were to remain the same through time.* To take dollars from the present and to consume this purchasing power in the future would be to satisfy less urgent desires. For if one's income in a given year is $5000 and is to remain at the same figure during the next year, then to save $1000 during the first year in order to consume $6000 during the second will give rise to a net psychic loss. For be-

cause of the tendency of man to spend his first dollars in satisfying his most vital wants and then to devote successive dollars for the gratification of less urgent desires, it follows that the fifth installment of a thousand dollars will purchase goods which give greater utility than will the sixth installment of a thousand dollars. Since each dollar will, therefore, give less satisfaction than before, it is not enough that the borrower should merely be repaid the same number of dollars which he previously had loaned, for then he would obtain less utility or have satisfied fewer desires than he had previously foregone. In order to compensate, therefore, for the diminished value of each dollar to him, it will be necessary to pay him more dollars. But these additional dollars will, of course, be interest.

What Landry, therefore, fundamentally demonstrates is the tendency of a person [35] to so distribute his income through time, that in relation to his needs, the last dollars of income in the various years will yield equal utility. Where, therefore, present income in relation to present needs is greater than prospective future income in relation to future needs, a man will save without the payment of interest in order to obtain more utility from these dollars in the future than he can secure in the present. He will carry these savings to the point where the marginal utilities of the expended incomes are equal. If he goes beyond this point of equilibrium, however, he would lose in total utility and would have to be compensated by the payment of more dollars in the future than he had saved in the past. He would, in short, demand the payment of interest.

Similarly in those cases where present income is less in relation to present needs than the prospective future income is to the needs of that period, any savings will have to be compensated for by the payment of interest. This, as we have seen, is also the case where needs and income are constant through time.

This tying up of the supply curve of capital with the theory of diminishing utility was brilliant and suggestive. Landry went on from this to point out that the psychic cost for any individual to save would increase with each additional increment of saving and therefore higher and higher rates of interest would be needed

---

[35] Landry, *op. cit.*, pp. 55-6. Landry also of course provides for the influence which the under-estimation of the future has upon the rate of interest. *Ibid.*, pp. 57-9.

to induce it.[36] For if a person saved two instead of one thousand dollars in a given year and cut his expenditures to three instead of four thousand and then received seven thousand in the succeeding year, the difference in psychic income between that given by the fourth and that by the seventh thousand would naturally be greater than between the fifth and sixth thousand. Since the loss in utility per dollar would be greater than in the case of the first thousand of savings, it would be necessary to pay more dollars to compensate for this difference. In order, therefore, to induce persons with prospectively constant incomes and needs to save more it will be necessary to pay a higher rate of interest. But this is simply equivalent to saying that the individual supply curve of savings, in such circumstances and in so far as it is swayed by rational considerations, is positively inclined and therefore slopes upward and to the right.

Although Landry does not develop this point, it would also seem that the individual supply curve would also be positively inclined even when present income exceeded the prospective future income or when future needs promised to be greater than those of the present. In those cases to be sure there would be an actual increase in utility from a transfer of a given amount of monetary income, and, if a person had no other means of saving, he would actually be willing to pay something for the surety that he would receive the remaining dollars at the time when each dollar meant more to him. Negative interest would, therefore, be possible were it not for the fact that people could save their income in the form of money itself and thus avoid paying interest for its being kept.[37] But as successive units of income were transferred from the present to the future, the relative gain from each transfer would diminish as one approached the equal apportionment of resources to need. As one went beyond this point, then, positive interest would have to be paid to induce further savings. In other words, even though in some circumstances the individual supply curve of capital were to begin at a negative rate of interest, it would still slope positively upward and to the right.

The original location of an individual's curve of savings is, according to Landry, determined not only by the relation of

---

[36] Adolphe Landry, *L'Intérêt du Capital*, pp. 320–2.

[37] Even here, however, there would be some costs in the form of rent for safety deposit boxes and hence a form of negative interest.

present to prospective future income and needs, but also to the amount of income which he receives. For as income increases the amount of desire which will be gratified by the last dollar diminishes, and less interest will be required to induce a man with 50,000 francs a year to save 5000 francs than would be needed to get someone with 10,000 francs a year to save that amount.[38] The richer man would forego less pleasure from such savings than would the poorer and hence would not need as much interest. On the absolute scale of savings, therefore, the well-to-do would make their initial savings at a lower rate than would the others and the wealthier they were, the farther their savings curves would lie to the right. This was succinctly summarized by Landry when he declared that the payment necessary to induce savings diminished as the income of the capitalist increased.[39] Landry went on to illustrate this by assuming that "those with an income of 5000 francs a year would save 1000 francs if the rate of interest were 5 per cent and 2000 francs if interest were 10 per cent, while those with a yearly income of 10,000 francs would save 1000 francs if the rate of interest were 3 per cent and would save 2000 francs if the interest were 4 per cent, and so on."[40]

But while this analysis does show how the savings curves of individuals if measured in terms of absolute quantities of savings differ according to the rise of their income, it does not, of itself, indicate that *proportionately* more would be saved by those with larger incomes within our present society or by a society in which there were still more marked inequalities of income. For it is but natural that a person with an income of $50,000 (or francs) would save more at any given rate of interest than would one with $5000. Most economists, including the justly celebrated J. M. Keynes,[41] have tended to reason as though inequality would promote a greater volume of savings. All too often, however, this reasoning has been based upon the observed fact that the average wealthy man saved a greater total quantity than the average man of moderate means. This is of course perfectly obvious. The real question, however, is whether he will save a larger *proportion* of his income and whether one man with $50,000 a year will save more than ten men with $5000

---

[38] Landry, *op. cit.*, pp. 323–7.
[39] *Ibid.*, p. 323.
[40] *Ibid.*, p. 326.
[41] J. M. Keynes, *The Economic Consequences of the Peace*, p. 298.

a piece.[42] We can in fact only compare the effect of changes in the relative distribution of wealth and income upon the social or market supply curve of capital by measuring the savings made with a fixed total income under varying conditions of relative distribution. To make our results comparable, in other words, it is essential that we should vary only the distribution of the income but not its total amount.

This is one of the most subtle questions in the whole field of economics. Its solution depends upon the rate at which the marginal utility of money decreases and whether (1) the utility which a rich man loses by saving one per cent of his income is greater than that which the poor man foregoes by saving one per cent and (2) whether this means the loss of a larger or smaller fraction of the previous total utility enjoyed respectively by the rich man and the poor man. These are not questions to which any easy answer can be made although there has been a tendency for economists to give off-hand conclusions without plumbing the depths of the issues involved. A promising beginning in furnishing the raw material for a solution has been made by Ragnar Frisch[43] who from budgetary and consumption studies in France and the United States has shown an apparent tendency for the marginal utility of money to decrease at a less rapid rate as income increases.[44] If and when these conclusions are corroborated and the precise values found, we shall be in a far better position to solve this problem.

Turning back to a general classification of interest theorists who believe the supply curve of capital to be positively inclined, we should include Irving Fisher in a prominent place. His *Rate of Interest*, which was published in 1907, and his later *Theory of Interest*, which was brought out in 1930, both emphasized the character of the income stream and also the way in which it was distributed through time. With many original features, the main tenor of the argument was very similar to that of Landry's and was couched in terms of the attempts of individuals to maximize utility. A salient quotation from

---

[42] My friend, Charles E. Persons, in an unpublished manuscript cogently contends that inequality results in a smaller proportionate amount being saved.

[43] Ragnar Frisch, *New Methods of Measuring Marginal Utility*, Tübingen, 1932.

[44] For a simple statement of Frisch's methods and a sensible appraisal of his results see Henry Schultz' "Frisch on the Measurement of Marginal Utility," *Journal of Political Economy*, Vol. XLI (February, 1933), pp. 95–116.

Fisher will show how, in practise, he seems to regard the supply curve as positively inclined.

"Suppose that at the outset the rate of interest is arbitrarily set very high, say 20 per cent. There will be relatively few borrowers and many would-be lenders, so that the total extent to which would-be lenders are willing to reduce their income streams for the present year for the sake of a much larger future income will be, say 100 million dollars; whereas, the extent to which would-be borrowers are willing to increase their income streams in the present at the high rate of 20 per cent will be only, say one million. Under such conditions the demand for loans is far short of the supply and the rate of interest will therefore go down. At an interest rate of 10 per cent the lenders may offer 50 millions, and the borrowers bid for 20 millions. There is still an excess of supply over demand and interest must needs fall still further. At 5 per cent we may suppose the market cleared, borrowers and lenders being willing to take or give respectively 30 millions. In like manner it can be shown that the ratio would not fall below this, as in that case it would result in an excess of demand over supply and cause the rate to rise again." [45]

5. Cassel's Theory That the Supply Curve of Capital Has High Positive Elasticity Up to 3 Per Cent and Is Thereafter Inelastic

One of the most stimulating of modern interest theories is that of Professor Gustav Cassel.[46] He sharply distinguishes between the quantities of capital which would be saved with interest rates of between 3 and 6 per cent and that which would be saved with a rate of less than 3 per cent. Cassel believes that above 3 per cent variations in the rate of interest would produce no appreciable change in the quantities of capital saved. Should the rate of interest, however, fall below 3 per cent, he believes there would be a sharp reduction in the quantity of savings. We shall, therefore, divide his theory into two parts, namely, that which applies to changes in savings when interest is above 3 per cent and when it is below three per cent. So far as the first issue is involved, Cassel believes that the total savings will be approximately the same whatever the rate of interest, as long as it does not go below 3 per cent. This conclusion is reached by an examination of the motives and resources of the three chief classes of individual savers in the country, namely, the skilled workers, capitalists, and the middle classes.

---

[45] Fisher, *The Theory of Interest*, pp. 120-1; *The Rate of Interest*, p. 131.
[46] *The Nature and Necessity of Interest*, *The Theory of Social Economy*, Chapter IV.

The first group, Cassel thinks, will save the same amount whatever may be the rate of interest since they accumulate capital only "as a kind of insurance fund against lack of employment, sickness and so on." [46a] In supporting this view he points out that deposits in savings banks have shown themselves not to alter appreciably when the interest rate changed. The savings of the capitalists and the middle classes would on the other hand move in opposite directions as the rate of interest changed and would mutually neutralize each other. The capitalists would save less as the rate of interest fell, while the middle class would save more. The capitalists would save less because they would have less with which to save. Since most of their income is derived from property, a reduction in the rate of interest would decrease their income and diminish the streams from which their savings were fed.

In the case of the middle class, however, Cassel, like Sargent, believes that a reduction in the rate of interest will stimulate a proportionately greater quantity of savings. Thus if the rate falls from 6 to 3 per cent, this class will save twice as much as before in order to receive the same yearly income from their capital. This increased saving would not result from people laying aside twice as much each year but rather from their saving approximately the same annual amount for twice as many years. Cassel points out that a man will not want to save more in a given year than the annual income which he is planning to obtain from his capital. Thus if an investor is planning to obtain a yearly income of $1000, he will not forego more than $1000 a year in the present. This will mean that the number of years needed to accumulate the requisite amount of capital will vary inversely with the rate of interest. If the rate of interest is six per cent, it would require twelve years with the interest compounded to accumulate the sum necessary to yield a yearly income equal to the annual amounts thus saved. With the rate of interest at 3 per cent, it would require twice as long as this, or twenty-four years. But this, Cassel believes, would not be too long a period since the active period of life when a man is close to the flood-tide of his powers is about equal to this. The middle class would, therefore, save over their lifetime proportionately more were the interest rate reduced. Cassel then jumps somewhat hastily to the conclusion that this would

---

[46a] *The Nature and Necessity of Interest*, p. 145.

precisely balance the reduction in the savings of the wealthy which would follow a fall in the rate of interest.[47]

Should the rate of interest fall below 3 per cent, however, the case would, according to Cassel, be far different. For then the period of years required to accumulate a stake which would yield an annual income equal to that which was foregone would lengthen rapidly. With a rate of 2 per cent it would require no less than 35 years to build up such a capital while if the rate of interest were to fall to 1½ and 1 per cent respectively, it would require 47 and 70 years. It should thus be apparent, according to Cassel, if the rate of interest were to fall as low as 1½ per cent, it would require such an extremely long period of time to save for such a sum that accumulation would be enormously discouraged. For very few men have an active period of life of 47 years during which they will save in order to accumulate for a future income equal to present annual savings. They would not be willing to save for as long a period as this and savings would consequently fall very greatly. If the rate of interest were to fall to 1 per cent, there would be almost no possibility for these men permanently to accumulate capital since it would require 70 years for their capital to yield an income equal to the amounts they had annually put by. In other words, the limited duration of life imposes a limit to the extent to which the rate of interest can fall and sharply decreases savings when it goes below 3 per cent.

The way in which the relative shortness of life operates to check savings when interest falls below 3 per cent is perhaps even more clearly demonstrated by another of Cassel's illustrations. If we assume that a man will not normally devote more than 25 years in accumulating his capital, then it is highly significant to note what the ratio will be between his annual savings and his later income from capital at various rates of interest. Thus if the rate of interest is 6 per cent, by the end of these 25 years the subsequent annual income ·will be 3⅓ times the previous annual savings. If the rate is 3 per cent, the subsequent income will be 1.1 times the previous rate of savings. At 2 per

---

[47] *The Nature and Necessity of Interest*, pp. 155–6. This would only follow if (1) the savings of the wealthy men equal in the aggregate those of the middle class and (2) if the rate at which the savings of the wealthy would change directly and positively with changes in the rate of interest were equal to the rates at which the savings of the middle class varied negatively, or (3) the degree to which variations in either one of these relationships were offset by opposite variations of the other.

cent, however, the annual income from capital will be only 63 per cent of the previous savings, while at 1½ per cent, it would only be 45 per cent. If the rate should fall as low as 1 per cent, then the future yearly income would be only 28 per cent of the past annual savings. Since, as Cassel points out, it is highly improbable that men of this group would save more in any year than the amount of income which they would receive from the capital sum they were accumulating, we can then see how great a decrease in saving would result if the interest rate went down to 2 per cent and how very little would be saved were the rate to fall to as low as 1 per cent.

But this is not all. For if the rate of interest falls to too low a figure, those who already possess capital will begin consuming it through the purchase of annuities, and the lower the rate of interest the greater will be the inducement to consume one's capital in this fashion. Thus let us assume that a capitalist believes that he has 30 years more in which to live and that he purchases an annuity, then the lower the rate of interest the greater would be his annual income from the annuity in comparison with the amounts he would receive if he maintained his capital and drew interest upon it. This is well illustrated by the following table:

Rate of Interest	Ratio of Annual Income from Annuity in Comparison with Interest	Rate of Interest	Ratio of Annual Income from Annuity in Comparison with Interest
10	1.06	1½	2.78
6	1.21	1	3.87
5	1.30	¾	4.98
4	1.45	½	7.20
3	1.70	¼	13.90
2	2.23		

It will be seen that if the rate of interest descends to 2 per cent, a man can more than double his income by purchasing an annuity with his capital and that at a rate of 1 per cent, he can nearly quadruple it. If rates should fall to ½ of 1 per cent, the yearly income from the annuity would be over 7 times as much as that from the interest on maintained capital and if ¼ of 1 per cent, virtually 14 times as much.

If the capitalist should wish also to provide for his children and to buy an annuity for 60 instead of for 30 years, he would not of course be able to increase his annual insurance by as much,[48] but at 2 per cent he would be able to get 1.44 times and at 1 per cent 2.22 times as much. The great stimulation which a lowering of interest will give to the individual consumption of capital in this fashion can also be shown by asking how long one's capital will last under the annuity system if one wishes to double or treble one's income, and this is shown in the following table: [48a]

TABLE 61-A

YEARS WHICH CAPITAL WOULD LAST UNDER ANNUITY PLAN PROVIDING FOR DOUBLE OR TREBLE THE ANNUAL INCOME FROM INTEREST ON UNIMPAIRED CAPITAL

Rate	Years Under	
	Double Income	Treble Income
10	7.3	4.3
6	11.9	7.0
5	14.2	8.3
4	17.7	10.3
3	23.4	13.7
2	35.0	20.5
1½	46.6	27.0
1	69.7	40.7
¾	92.8	54.3
½	139.0	84.3
¼	277.6	162.3

Thus if the rate of interest fell to 2 per cent one's capital would last for 35 years with a doubled income and for slightly over 20 years with a trebled income, while if it fell to 1 per cent it would last for 70 and 41 years respectively. If it were to be as low as ¼ of 1 per cent, it would last for no less than 277 and 162 years.

Cassel, therefore, points out that the rate of interest is largely a function of the expectancy of life and that there is a very

[48] If the capital were consumed in 60 years the ratio of annuity to interest income would be as follows:

Rate of Interest	Ratio of Annual Annuity Income to Income from Interest	Rate of Interest	Ratio of Annual Annuity Income to Income from Interest
10	1.003	2	1.44
6	1.03	1	2.22
5	1.06	¾	2.77
4	1.11	½	3.87
3	1.20	¼	7.19

[48a] This need not be and in fact generally would not be an outright destruction of capital. For those who paid the annuity would take over the ownership of the capital. The net result would not be so much a reduction in the total quantity of capital as (a) a decrease in the rate of growth of capital and possibly (b) some shifting of fixed capital into circulating capital.

good reason why it tends to hover at from 3 to 4 per cent. For this would mean that property will sell for from 33 to 25 years its annual net income. This it tends to do, declares Cassel, because that tends to be near the average life expectancy of men who are in the active period of life.

Cassel, therefore, postulates a highly elastic curve of savings up to 3 per cent and virtually a completely inelastic curve thereafter. Joined to this is a highly elastic demand curve for capital below 3 per cent, so that he believes that "there is no reason for assuming that the rate of interest will sink in the future below the lowest level which it has reached hitherto on any great market," . . . and "that the rate of interest will never sink below 1½ per cent." [49]

This highly stimulating theory of Cassel's and the ingenious way in which he shows how the expectancy of life helps to determine the rate of interest is worthy of all praise. There are at least two considerations, however, which need to be noted in connection with it. The first is the fact that with the prolongation of life, the years of activity have been somewhat lengthened. This permits the interest rate to fall to a lower level. Since the reductions in the death rate have, however, primarily been effected in infancy and childhood, this has not increased the expectancy of life of adults as much as might at first thought be expected. The second consideration is the increasing degree to which parents are considering the welfare of their children and are accumulating property to yield an income for the latter and not for themselves. This extends the period of time for which they are saving beyond their own expectancy of life, and hence also operates to lower the rate of interest. The interest in grandchildren is, however, much less than in children, particularly in view of the fact that these are generally nonexistent during the active period of life. It is, moreover, very rare that any personal interest at all extends beyond the grandchildren, and to the degree that it does it is associated with the pride of building up and maintaining a family line. Hence the interest rate under capitalism cannot fall to zero.

6. The Theory That the Supply of Capital Is Almost Absolutely Independent of the Rate of Interest, and Hence Is Almost Completely Inelastic

There are, however, two groups which maintain that savings are not appreciably affected by the rate of interest and that they

[49] *The Nature and Necessity of Interest*, p. 156.

would be what they are, no matter what the rate of interest might be. One of these groups takes account of economic factors which affect the supply of capital from various social classes but believes that they offset each other in such a fashion as to make the combined volume of savings independent of the rate of interest. The other group emphasizes more the non-economic factors which lead to savings and which, therefore, in their opinion would cause savings to be the same whatever the interest paid. These two groups are not always sharply distinct since there is commonly an admixture of the second line of argument in the contentions of the first group; but in the main these distinctions can be drawn.

The most prominent representatives of the first group are Beatrice and Sidney Webb. In their classic volume on *Industrial Democracy* they were naturally concerned with the contention that trade-union action by forcing up wages would decrease the rate of interest and lead to such a decrease in savings as would again reduce wages. This the Webbs denied. Savings, they pointed out, came from three classes, the poor, the middle, class, and the very rich. The poor saved but little, and since their savings were to protect themselves against the great catastrophes of illness, accidents, unemployment, and death, the Webbs concluded that their savings would continue unabated "whether profit or interest is reaped or not." The Webbs then adopted Sargent's reasoning concerning the savings of the middle classes and concluded with him that a reduction in interest would actually stimulate savings on their part. The rich, the Webbs believed, would, however, be somewhat affected in their savings by the relative rate of interest which they could obtain and would somewhat reduce their savings if the rate of interest were lessened. But since the main mass of the savings of this class were believed to be automatic, coming as they did from what was left over after certain customary habits of expenditure had been satisfied, the Webbs believed that alterations in the rate of interest would not greatly alter the total amounts which they saved. The Webbs concluded that the inverse response of the savings of the middle classes to the rate of interest would offset the positive response of the savings of the wealthy and that the supply of capital as a whole would, therefore, be independent of the rate of interest. The Webbs therefore apply the same reasoning to the entire supply curve of capital which Cassel employs for that portion above the point of 3 per cent.

F. H. Knight is perhaps the most prominent of the modern economists who believe that the supply of capital is almost completely inelastic at any moment of time.[50] In the first place, like the present author, he emphasizes the fact that the annual savings form but a very small fraction of the total quantity of capital which is in existence at any one time and that therefore changes in the rate of savings would produce in the short run but an infinitesimal change in the total quantity of capital. Furthermore, he doubts whether a change in the rate of interest would cause much, if any, alteration in the annual rate of savings. Knight puts this as follows: "No correspondence between the rate of saving and interest rate has been shown and the visible facts connect the amount of saving with many other considerations more intimately than with the return on investment. It is generally conceded that a considerable though unknown part of saving is probably inversely correlated with the return obtainable. It is surely safe to say that the elasticity of response is in the region of 'small if any.' "[51] In a footnote, he expresses his doubt whether people "prefer" the present to the future and discount the latter, and declares that "in general, there is perhaps more ground for the inverse allegation as against the modern European peoples and especially the Teutonic stock namely, that they 'look before and after and sigh for what is not' and neglect the present moment."[52]

Kleene is another writer who does not believe that changes in the rate of interest will produce much of an alteration in the willingness of savers to accumulate, although they will affect the amounts available for savings. He declares that the "abstinential marginal savings" of individuals are relatively unimportant and that far more important are (1) "the large accumulations of capital made without thought by recipients of large incomes, the unspent residua of income of careless, happy spenders, (2) the impersonal creation of capital made by managers accumulating surplus out of earnings without consulting the willingness of the stockholder to abstain from consumption, and (3) the 'rainy day' savings which would be made

---

[50] Frank H. Knight, "Professor Fisher's Interest Theory—A Case in Point," *Journal Political Economy,* Vol. XXXIX (1931), No. 2, pp. 176–212; see also his article on "Interest" in the *Encyclopedia of the Social Sciences,* Vol. VIII, pp. 131–44.

[51] Knight, "Professor Fisher's Interest Theory," *op. cit.,* p. 202.

[52] Knight, *op. cit.,* p. 203.

even if there were no such thing as interest or profit on capital." [53]

Doubting whether the effect of changes in the rate of interest have any determinative influence on the calculated savings of individuals, Kleene goes on to say: "Even if the painful calculations of some marginal savers pursue the course described by the exponents of the abstinence theory, are they of sufficient consequence to make any real difference? Are not their contributions to the current supply of capital so insignificant compared with those from other sources, that a general theory of the income to capital is warranted in disregarding them? The great factors determining the supply of capital we may call, for lack of a better term, objective in contrast with the subjective determinants set forth by the abstinence and time-preference theories. Set over against these objective forces, the calculated, abstinential savings appear to the full extent of their tenuous being, a mere epiphenomenon of our modern industrial system." [54]

7. Savings Made by Corporations Through the Re-Investment of Corporate Surpluses

As Kleene hinted, a very large proportion of savings in the United States, at least, are not made by individuals but by corporations which reinvest a large portion of their profits.

The National Bureau of Economic Research has made several studies of the amounts which have been saved in this manner. The earliest by Dr. O. W. Knauth [55] made certain estimates which were subsequently increased by later estimates which were made by Dr. W. I. King. [56] These estimates of King were as follows:

Year	Millions of Dollars Saved by Corporations	Year	Millions of Dollars Saved by Corporations
1910	1,185	1915	2,174
1911	719	1916	4,773
1912	1,281	1917	6,327
1913	1,443	1918	4,128
1914	624	1919	5,190

The total corporate savings for this period amounted, according to King, to 27.8 billions. And the percentages which they

[53] Kleene, *Profit and Wages*, p. 63, Class 3 is listed by Kleene as Class 4.
[54] Kleene, *op. cit.*, pp. 76–77.
[55] O. W. Knauth, "The Place of the Corporate Surplus in the National Income," *Journal American Statistical Association*, Vol. XVIII, pp. 157–66.
[56] W. I. King, *National Income*, p. 280.

formed of the total realized income of the nation [57] were as given in the following table:

Year	Per Cent Corporate Savings of Realized National Income	Year	Per Cent Corporate Savings of Realized National Income
1910	3.77	1915	5.84
1911	2.25	1916	11.03
1912	3.77	1917	12.32
1913	4.04	1918	6.83
1914	1.75	1919	7.87

For the ten years as a whole Dr. King's figures would indicate that corporate savings amounted to about 6.5 per cent of the realized national income. Since Dr. King in another study [58] showed that during the decade from 1909 to 1918, somewhere between 15 and 16 per cent of the national income was saved, we may estimate that corporate savings formed not far from 40 per cent of all savings.

F. C. Mills has made further estimates of the amounts saved by corporations during the boom years from 1922 and 1929 which run as follows: [59]

Year	Estimated Corporate Savings (in millions)	Year	Estimated Corporate Savings (in millions)
1922	1,747	1926	2,335
1923	2,528	1927	1,115
1924	1,575	1928	2,479
1925	2,957	1929	2,320

Taking the period as a whole, Mills estimated "that about 34 per cent of the new capital requirements of American corporations were met out of corporate savings." [60]

The proportion of the net profits of the corporations which is thus reinvested is in fact very high. Dr. King, on the basis of a study of a large number of concerns, comes to the following estimates: [61]

[57] For these figures see King, *op. cit.*, p. 222.

[58] W. I. King, "The Net Volume of Saving in the United States," *Journal American Statistical Association*, Vol. XVIII, pp. 455–470.

[59] F. C. Mills, *Economic Tendencies in the United States*, p. 429.

[60] Mills, *op. cit.*, p. 429.

[61] King, *The Nat. Income and Its Purchasing Power*, p. 285.

Year	Proportion of Net Income Saved by Corporations	Year	Proportion of Net Income Saved by Corporations
1910	39	1918	54
1911	28	1919	62
1912	39	1920	47
1913	40	1921	—
1914	23	1922	44
1915	51	1923	47
1916	59	1924	35
1917	63	1925	45
		1926	37

Certain organizations, of which the most notable example has been that of the Ford Motor Company, have indeed secured the funds for their expansion almost entirely from their own surplus earnings. Thus, when this company was organized in 1903, only $28,000 of capital was paid in. By reinvesting almost all of the profits of the company, plant and machinery have been built and raw materials purchased which now have a total value of approximately $300,000,000. Another familiar example is that of the United States Steel Corporation which has probably ploughed back into its plant and equipment at least a billion and a quarter of dollars. The question then arises whether corporations would continue to save as much were the rate of interest to fall and whether they are willing to save more at the same rate of interest than would individuals?[62]

It seems quite clear that at a given interest rate corporations will, on the whole, save a larger percentage of their net earnings than if the sums now withheld as the corporate surplus were distributed among the stockholders. In the case of the corporate surplus, it is only necessary for the few who form the majority of the board of directors to decide that half of the net gains, for example, are to be reinvested. If these were distributed among the stockholders, on the other hand, the individuals would be more likely to spend a larger proportion on present needs. Had all of the net profits of American business been distributed to the stockholders it is difficult for example to imagine that they would have saved 51 per cent of these sums as in 1915, or 37 per cent as in 1926.

Perhaps the most important cause of this stronger tendency to save results, however, from the lack of identity between the

[62] George Soule in his, *The Accumulation of Capital* (League for Industrial Democracy), 19 pp., raises these and other questions.

owners and managers of large corporations.[62a] The directors of the large modern corporations seldom own all of the stock and frequently own but a small fraction. This means that when they decide to plow part of their earnings back into the business, they have made a decision to save income most of which would otherwise go to other people. Such a decision is always less painful than a resolve to save one's own income. If we were all to decide how much others must save, more would be saved than if each of us were to decide how much we ourselves must save.[63] In a very similar fashion, therefore, the control over the receipts of stockholders which is given to the directors leads to a greater volume of savings than would otherwise be the case.

This tendency is accentuated by the natural desire of managers to be connected with and to administer an ever-growing enterprise. To the business man, the bigger the enterprise which he manages, the more is the glory and honor which accrues to him. The active administrators of an enterprise will, therefore, tend to be always pushing for an expansion of plant and for devoting a large share of the company's net earnings to this purpose. While the Board of Directors, because of their less active participation in the affairs of the company, will not feel this desire as strongly as will the active managers themselves, they will, nevertheless, share it in a large measure. Certainly they feel much more desirous of having the business grow than does the average stockholder who feels little loyalty to the enterprise as such and whose ego will not be fed or his position in the eyes of his fellows enhanced by the fact that the corporation in which he holds stock has come to own three steel mills instead of one.

Thus the pride of business men in their undertakings and the spirit of workmanship which permeates most of the directors of American business will cause more to be saved than if the decisions were to be made solely by investors who considered nothing but relative monetary advantages.[64]

[62a] See Berle and Means, *The Modern Corporation,* The Macmillan Company, 1933.

[63] Or as Artemas Ward put it, "I am in favor of war, even though I have to send all of my wife's relatives."

[64] This certainly tends to offset the tendency towards a reduction of savings which some have believed would follow the replacement of the individual enterprise, with the strong urge that it afforded the proprietor to save, by the impersonality of the corporate relationship and the lessened pride of the owner resulting from his holding of intangibles. For a statement of this supposedly

There are two other factors which lead to a reinvestment of the net earnings of a business. The first is the fact that this is virtually the only way in which an enterprise during the earlier period of its growth can expand. Banks are reluctant to loan appreciable sums to such a concern until it has firmly proved its worth. For a similar reason it is generally impossible for it to float an issue of securities in the investment market until it is fairly firmly established.

Conversely, in the period after a concern has failed and has been reorganized, it will also have to plow back its net earnings if it is to re-establish its credit and prestige. The practice of the Baltimore and Ohio, during the last twenty years, in its attempt to rehabilitate itself is an excellent example of what is under such circumstances an almost universal practice.[65]

There are, of course, limits to the proportion of the net profits which the directors may thus permanently withhold. The stockholders in a rapidly growing concern may acquiesce for a considerable period in the continual reinvestment of the net earnings, as will the owners of a concern which is struggling desperately to rehabilitate itself. But in the long run all of the net earnings cannot permanently be withheld. To do so would provoke a revolt on the part of the stockholders which would ultimately sweep from office any management that persisted in such a course. In practice, therefore, the stockholders must be placated by the distribution of a considerable proportion of the net earnings of the corporation. In general, the amounts paid out in dividends in prosperous enterprises cannot for long periods fall greatly below the average rate of pure interest, for to do so would be to court an insurrection upon the part of the stockholders. It is, however, possible to pay lower dividends for considerable periods of time and for the stockholders to acquiesce because of the continually enhanced value of their principal. Sooner or later, however, the stockholders must be admitted to a more generous share of the earnings.

From what has been said it will be inferred that the corporate surplus, at least in expanding concerns, accrues in firms where the profits amount to more than the average rate of return upon capital in industry as a whole. This is the case. It is because the business generally yields more than the average,

---

lessened incentive, see Alvin S. Johnson, "Influences Affecting the Development of Thrift," *Political Science Quart.*, Vol. XXII, pp. 228–9.

[65] For a discussion of these policies see A. S. Dewing, *The Financial Policy of Corporations*, Vol. IV, pp. 169–70.

or promises to yield more, that the earnings instead of being re-distributed are turned back into the enterprise. In such cir-cumstances business men will wish to enjoy the fruits of the enterprise and will not wish to share them with outside in-vestors. They will consequently try to keep the surplus gains for themselves as much as is possible and hence to finance them-selves as far as they can. High profits will, therefore, stimulate greater savings. Friday in stressing the importance of the capi-tal surplus emphasizes this point when he writes, "the volume of capital accumulation is affected first and foremost by the volume of productive output. Every increase in production leads quite directly to an increase in capital accumulation." [66] It was indeed only the extraordinary profits which were made by the Ford Company and by the United States Steel which led them to reinvest as large a proportion of their earnings as they did.

If corporate surplus, therefore, mainly accrues where the profits of individual concerns are higher than the average rate of interest, would the amounts so reinvested decrease appreci-ably, if at all, were this average rate of interest to be reduced? Since it is the *difference* between the net profits and the rate of interest which mainly determines the amount of the corporate surplus, it might well be argued that if this difference were maintained, the same amount would be saved even were the average rate of interest to fall. Thus if the profits of a business are 12 per cent whereas the average rate of interest is but 4 per cent, the probable amount to be reinvested will be the 8 per cent of surplus gains. If the rate of interest were to fall to 2 per cent and the net profits of this particular concern to 10 per cent, the difference would still be 8 per cent and there would still be as great an incentive for the reinvestment of this sum as before. There might well indeed be more, for while the business formerly earned three times the rate of interest it would now earn five times as much, and consequently it would be a still more choice opportunity for investment than it was previously.

From the foregoing discussion it seems (1) that at a given interest rate a larger supply of capital will be saved from the corporate surplus than if this were given to private individuals. This is equivalent to saying that the supply of corporate surplus

---

[66] See Friday, *Profits, Wages and Prices,* p. 97.

which will be saved has a lower position than that for individual savings in the investment market.[67]   (2) That since the difference between the profits of a given concern and the pre-

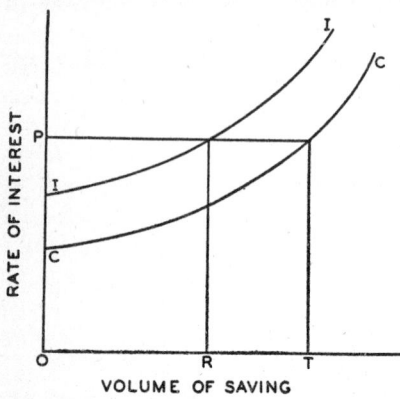

vailing rate of interest is one of the main incentives for the creation of such a surplus, the lowering of the rate of interest would not cause any reduction in the volume of such accumulations as long as this differential rate of profit were maintained. Thus the volume· of corporate savings would seem to depend more on the technical developments in specific industries or upon the relative advantageousness[68] of their position than upon the absolute rate of interest as such.

Chart 85.   Comparative Positions of the Supply Curve of Savings for Individuals and Corporations.

8. The Creation by Commercial Banks of Fixed Capital Through the Use of Bank Credit

Even today banks are not commonly regarded as actually creating credit which is used to expand capital facilities.   Savings banks are thought merely to stand between the individual savers and the lines of industry in which the savings are ultimately invested, while commercial banks are conceived of as merely creating short-term credit which is used to finance the flow of goods through our economic system until they reach or are paid for by the ultimate consumer.

In fact, however, commercial banks do far more than this. They actually furnish some of the monetary purchasing power which is used to create actual capital equipment.   This is seen most clearly in the way the commercial banks during a period of prosperity help to finance the issuance of stocks and bonds by corporations, which in turn is designed to furnish them with funds for expansion.   Many individuals subscribe for the se-

---

[67] Thus the supply curve of the reinvested corporate earnings would be represented by the line CC and of individual savings by II.   At the rate OP, therefore, OR units of individual savings would be made and OT units of corporate savings.

[68] Or, as the German economists say, on the "Konjunktur" of the particular enterprise.

curities who at the moment are unable to pay for them in full. They make a partial payment, and the banks, taking the stock as security, either loan the individuals directly or, as is more common, loan to them indirectly through brokers the funds necessary to complete the purchase. The creation of this credit goes into the treasuries of the corporations and is then available for their use. While these loans are in general later repaid out of the savings of individuals, they may in part come out of the subsequent earnings of the corporations themselves. Certainly, for a time at least, the creation of the fixed capital is financed by the bank loans.

The banks also make loans directly to concerns to build up fixed capital. Thus Moulton estimated that in 1916 one-fifth of the unsecured or non-collateral loans were used for this purpose, while a large portion of the collateral loans, for which bonds and stock were pledged as security, were also employed by business men for the creation of fixed capital. The fact that the original loans were apparently made for only short periods of time does not preclude bank credit being used for these purposes, since it is a common practise for the banks to renew these loans for a considerable period of time.[69] It was in fact the use of short-time funds by German banks, which had been loaned to them by American and British banking groups, for what were really long-time investments that has led to the "freezing" of German credit from 1931 to the present.

When we add to all this the direct purchase of stocks and bonds of banks, H. G. Moulton's estimate of some fifteen years ago that "in the neighborhood of two-thirds of all the credit extended by commercial banks goes for fixed rather than for working capital"[70] does not seem unreasonable. The truth of the matter seems to be, as Keynes[71] and Wicksell[72] have pointed out, that the operations of the banking system prevent savings by individuals from being exactly equal to investments in industry.

During most of the depression period the banks do not invest as much money in industry as is deposited with them. During

[69] See W. F. Mitchell, *The Uses of Bank Funds.*

[70] H. G. Moulton, "Commercial Banking and Capital Formation," *Journal of Political Economy,* Vol. XXVI, p. 658. See also his series of articles in the above *Journal* (Vol. XXVI), pp. 484–508, 638–63, 705–31, 849–81.

[71] J. M. Keynes, *A Treatise on Money,* Vol. I, pp. 171–325; Vol. II, pp. 95–208.

[72] Knut Wicksell, *Geldzins and Güterpreise* (1898).

periods of prosperity, however, they invest more. This is done by making loans the proceeds of which are credited to the borrower, and thus deposits are created. This creation of credit puts workers who would otherwise be unemployed to work and, after unemployment is absorbed, it furnishes business men with funds which they use to transfer men from the production of consumers goods to the production of capital goods, with the result that the prices of consumers goods are forced up. The real incomes of the mass of the population are diminished by this practice from what they would otherwise have been. The making of the loans may have been painless on the part of the banks, but they are not painless in their effect upon the consumers who in the long run pay for them.

Even if in the long run a larger net quantity of savings is stimulated by such loans of bank credit than would otherwise be made, the fact that the saving has been painless does not mean that the capital will be offered gratuitously. Banks, like manufacturing concerns, have expenses, and there are costs attached to the manufacturing of credit. There are, in the first place, the costs of bank salaries, housing, equipment, and supplies. Although few studies have been made, it seems fairly certain that these expenses do not increase commensurately as a bank increases its loans. A great deal more business can generally be handled with the same building space, the services of the banking staff can be utilized more fully, and even the costs of credit investigation and analysis will not rise in proportion to the expansion in loans made. It seems probable, therefore, that the administrative costs for each dollar of credit which is extended tend to shrink as the amount of credit increases.

The expense of maintaining the legal reserve for this credit may also be viewed as an overhead or constant cost which it is economical to utilize to the fullest capacity. If it is possible, for example, to create $9 worth of credit from $1 of gold reserve, then it is to the interest of the bank to create as much of this sum as is possible. As the relative amount of credit increases, therefore, the supply costs which are attached, because of this item, to each unit, will consequently decrease.

The supply curve of such capital as is "created" by the banks would seem, therefore, to be somewhat negatively inclined. If a great deal more capital were demanded at a lower rate the banks could afford to furnish at least some of it.

The fact that in practice a higher rate of interest tends to accompany an expansion in the volume of loans does not disprove the validity of this statement. The rise in the rate of interest does not result from the increased costs of banking, but from the increased demand for loan capital. In the revival period of the business cycle, business men foresee the possibility of great profits if they can but secure credit, and they are consequently willing to pay liberally for it. As the cycle approaches its climax, the demands for credit become ever more insistent. The incentive for borrowing is now the necessity of keeping one's head above water, and so a high rate of interest will be paid by business men rather than lose the loans which are so necessary for them. Were the extension of bank credit to be considered solely by itself, the reason for the rise in the interest rate as borrowing increases would be found in the conditions of demand rather than in the slope of the supply curve of bank credit. The rise in the interest rate at such times is also caused by the fact that the demand for investments is heavy in the country as a whole. This induces savings from individuals at a heightened supply cost and the rate of bank interest will rise sympathetically in consequence.

9. A Summary and Attempted Synthesis

We have thus seen that almost every type of supply curve of capital has been postulated by economists. The bewildering confusion in the various relationships which have been assumed by various economists between changes in the rate of interest and the volume of savings is shown in Chart 86 which attempts to picture in a graphic manner the various supply curves of savings (or sometimes of capital) which have been conceived. If there is a type of supply curve of capital which has not been postulated, it is indeed difficult to visualize it. The chart may indeed be of value not only in showing the extraordinary confusion which exists on this fundamental point but also in indicating the necessity for clearing this matter up and getting some definite measurements of the actual relationship. For until this is done economic theory will be at the best a maimed and stunted thing.

The real solution of this problem, as of others, will in all probability have to come from inductive studies, some of which are attempted in the following chapter. It is probable moreover that investigations into the curve of the diminishing utility of money, such as has been outlined by Professor Ragnar Frisch, will throw light upon this question as well as upon others. But even without such inductive studies it is still possible on the basis both of the reasoning and the evidence which we have examined to draw certain tentative and general conclusions.

There is undoubtedly a considerable volume of savings which would be made even though no interest were paid. Some would save without interest to provide against such future contingencies as accidents, illness, unemployment, old age, and death itself. Others would save without interest in order to acquire power, and power is most surely obtained through wealth. Still others would save in order to obtain social esteem, and in a capitalistic society esteem attaches itself most quickly and surely to money. Others would still save in order to found a family line. Finally, there are those who save because they have nothing else to do with their surplus. In all of these cases it would not be necessary to pay any interest at all to induce such savings.

It is moreover probable that some individuals seeking fixed annuities would, as Sargent argued, save more at a lower than at a higher rate of interest, and that banks would have lower average costs of creating capital as the volume of their loans increased.

In addition to all this, it may be admitted that there is a serious flaw in the ordinary way in which savings are explained. The time preference school of Böhm-Bawerk, Fisher, and Landry are accustomed to reason as though people, in saving, postponed the consumption of goods now in order to enjoy them in the future and that interest serves merely to bring this stream of income to yield an equality of utility at the various points in the flow of time. But if this were all, then there would, after a time, be no permanent growth in the quantity of capital. For each man would then exhaust in his old age what he had previously acquired and would leave the world no richer than he found it. It is true that as more people caught the habit of saving, the reservoir of capital would swell, but when this habit became generalized the withdrawals would equal the individual accretions. It is plain then that there must be other forces at work to account for individual accumulations. One is perhaps the tendency on the part of the middle and upper classes to overestimate the dangers which they are likely to face in their old age. The contingencies which they fear do not on the average occur and when they die their unspent accumulations pass on to the next generation. Affection for one's children and

a desire to see them protected and assured a status in the world
is responsible for further savings, while the chain of more im-
palpable motives such as those of power, love of esteem, and a
desire for permanence in the family line also account for some
of the permanent accretions to capital.   We may then grant
that sociological considerations are perhaps even more important than economic in
the passing on of indi-
vidual wealth from one
generation to another.

But despite all this it
is also true that when
the prospects for the
present as compared
with the future are
ironed out to an approxi-
mate equality, a fore-
going of consumption in
the present in favor of
consumption or accumu-
lation in the future will
ordinarily be attended
by a loss of utility which
will have to be balanced
by a payment of interest.
This loss and the interest
required to compensate
for it will of necessity increase as a larger and
larger fraction of one's

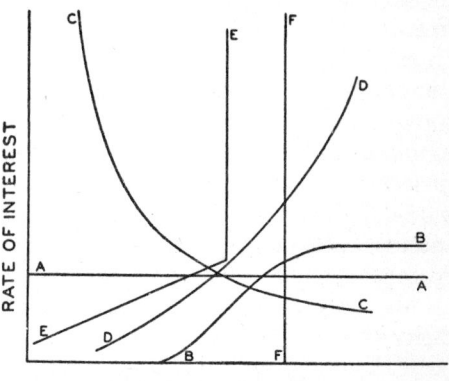

VOLUME OF SAVING

Chart 86.   The Supply Curves of Savings and
Capital as Conceived by Various Economists.

Line AA   The Classical   Line DD   Landry—
              School   Böhm-Bawerk
Line BB   Taussig   Line EE   Cassel
Line CC   Sargent   Line FF   Webb-Knight

Footnote: The arrangement of the supply
curves in relation to the base line is arbitrary
and does not purport to show the relative
amounts saved by one type of curve as compared with another. Each curve, however, when
taken by itself represents the approximate concept of supply by the given author.

income is saved.   Furthermore, an appreciable reduction in the
rate of interest would, as Cassel says, probably cause people to
save less because of the very much greater number of years
needed to produce a future annual income equal to current savings and would at the same time lead to a great dissipation of
current capital accumulations through the stimulation which
it would give to the purchase of annuities.   This class with their
positively inclined curve of savings would seem to play a more
important part in the capital market than those with a negatively sloped savings curve.   It is probable, therefore, that they
more than offset the latter class and give to the combined savings curve something of a positive slope.

The reinvested savings by corporations would, as we have seen, normally be made for a lower rate of return than that which private persons would require for similar investments. And yet they would not be made if no interest at all were paid, and not as much would be saved at a low as at a higher rate of return. The total supply curve would be lowered by their inclusion but the slope would still be upward and to the right. We should, moreover, realize that since most savings are made from income, which in turn for the wealthier groups has under our capitalistic systems been derived from interest and profits,[73] a reduction in the rate of interest would materially diminish the amounts available for saving by this class, and, under capitalism, probably by the community as a whole. Decreased savings would, therefore, be likely to follow in the wake of a fall in the interest rate, although the chain of causation would be different from that which is commonly stated.

We may perhaps summarize this analysis in the following fashion:

1. The supply of capital is at any one moment absolutely fixed, and the annual changes in its quantity are but relatively slight.

2. A considerable quantity of capital would be saved even without interest, both to provide against contingencies and for sociological reasons. Still more would be saved for low rates of interest.

3. Interest rates of less than 2 per cent would, however, so encourage the dissipation of present capital through the purchase of annuities that this would probably, at the very least, neutralize the increments of fresh savings which would be effected at such rates, leaving the total supply of capital no greater than before. The dissipation of capital might indeed proceed at such a rate as to more than offset the fresh savings and to cause an ultimate diminution in the total supply of capital.

4. The higher the rate of interest, the greater would be the fund from which the major portion of current savings by indi-

---

[73] Herein lies a suggestion as to how savings might be effected in a socialistic state. Interest on capital should be reckoned as a cost not only in order to appraise the relative effectiveness of various industries but also as a means of furnishing the socialized agencies with the funds for further investment. From this interest and from conjunctural profits adequate savings could probably be made. There would be no deductions for the luxury of a capitalistic class.

viduals are drawn. A great diminution in the rate of interest would appreciably diminish this fund and with it probably diminish the net volume of annual savings.

5. Probably more will be saved from equal incomes at a higher rate of interest than will be the case at a lower.

6. Corporations will save more at a given rate of interest than will individuals. The total supply curve of capital, therefore, lies to the right of the individual supply curve of calculating savers.

7. Whether inequality will promote a greater or smaller volume of total savings is still not definitely established.

8. On the whole, unless the rate of interest falls to, say, 2 per cent or less, existing capital will not be dissipated as rapidly as fresh capital will come into being through annual savings. The total supply of capital will, therefore, under these conditions continue to grow through time.

9. Although it is probable that the total supply curve of savings is positively inclined, it is not certain how much savings would be affected by a change in the rate of interest. Unless this rate were to fall greatly, such changes would merely affect the rate at which the total capital was increasing. It may perhaps be hazarded that the elasticity of the savings curve within the zone from 2 to 6 per cent is appreciably less than unity and that changes in the interest rate would consequently produce less than proportionate changes in the annual quantities saved. It is also probably true that if the reinvestment of corporate surpluses and the creation of purchasing power by the banks come to form a larger proportion of the annual flow of fresh investment, then the supply curve of investment will shift still further to the right and a larger quantity will be invested at the same rate of interest than would otherwise have been the case.

CHAPTER XVIII

AN ATTEMPT AT THE QUANTITATIVE DETERMINATION OF THE SUPPLY CURVE OF CAPITAL

1. Introduction

We can make an approach to the problem of determining the supply curve of capital by correlating the changes in the rate of interest with changes in the rate of capital growth. It is important to remember that the supply of capital (like the total population) is at any one time, as has been pointed out, a fund rather than a flow. It consists of the buildings, machinery, etc., which are being used for production purposes.[1] This fund is being fed by the fresh savings which are being made and which take the form of additional fixed and working capital. At the same time, the existing capital instruments are undergoing a continuous process of depreciation and some are being constantly retired from use because they either are worn out or are obsolete. In highly industrialized communities, moreover, the fund of existing capital goods is many times the amount of fresh capital which is annually added.

We should not expect, therefore, that changes in the rate of interest would produce immediate changes in the fund of pre-existing capital. Those instruments, the results of past savings, are already in existence and will continue to be utilized irrespective of the rate of interest, although it should be recognized that the rate of interest may help to determine how long machines will be kept in operation.

But the chief way in which the rate of interest can affect the supply of capital is through the flow of fresh capital into the fund. As this flow rises or falls, the total supply of capital will also rise or fall, although to an appreciably smaller degree. Ultimately if an increase in the flow is maintained, then when the pre-existing capital is retired, the new fund of capital will exceed the old fund in the proportion to which the new flow exceeds the old. We are dealing therefore with the relations between changes in the interest rate and changes in the flow of

---

[1] Together with the raw materials, etc., which are being processed by it.

fresh capital, just as we dealt with changes in real wages and changes in the rate at which a population grew.

There are, in fact, four methods by which we may measure the change in the flow of capital:

(1) We may measure *the absolute amount of the flow or of the annual increments*. If we consult Table 62, for example, we will find that in 1866 the total estimated increase in fixed capital owned by citizens of the United Kingdom was 86 million pounds, whereas in 1909 the increase amounted to 175 million pounds. The total saved in the latter year was, therefore, 103 per cent greater than it had been forty-four years before. But the population was 48 per cent greater than it was in the earlier year, and the national income per capita was in addition appreciably greater. We should, therefore, expect larger savings from both of these causes. For total savings would naturally increase if there were more people with the same incomes who saved, and each person would tend to save a larger absolute amount if his income increased. We cannot, therefore, legitimately compare for widely separated years the changes in interest rate with the changes in the absolute quantity of capital saved. When, however, we compare these changes for immediately adjoining years the errors are greatly minimized and are, in fact, reduced to relatively small proportions.

(2) A second possibility would be to measure *the proportion of the national income* which was annually saved. This would be a very desirable procedure, but, at the present stage of economic knowledge, we are unfortunately prevented from following it if for no other reason than because statistics on the annual income are very scanty for both Great Britain and the United States for the years prior to 1910.[2]

(3) What we are primarily interested in measuring, however, is the *rate of growth of the capital fund itself*. For our study of elasticities of supply is based upon the *relative* degree to which the supplies of capital and labor expand and contract with changes in their rates of return. We should then divide

---

[2] For Great Britain we have Bowley's estimate for 1880 in his *The Change in the Distribution of the National Income, 1880–1913* and Chiozza-Money's estimate for 1907 in his *Riches and Poverty*. Bowley's *Division of the Product of Industry* covers the year 1911. In the United States we have the studies of the National Bureau of Economic Research for the years subsequent to 1909, but before that date we have only King's estimates for decennial years in his *Wealth and Income of the People of the United States*, and the necessarily more fragmentary material of Spahr in his 1896 study on *The Present Distribution of Wealth in the United States*.

the increment of capital added in a given year by the total amount of the capital fund in the preceding year in order to obtain this percentage of growth. We may then compute link-relatives of these percentages for successive pairs of years.

(4) A final method of measurement would be to compute *the relative change in the relative rates of capital growth* for successive years. This method can be briefly illustrated. Let us assume that the rates of capital growth for three successive years are 2.5, 3.0, and 3.5 per cent. Then the link-relative for the second year in terms of the first would be 120,

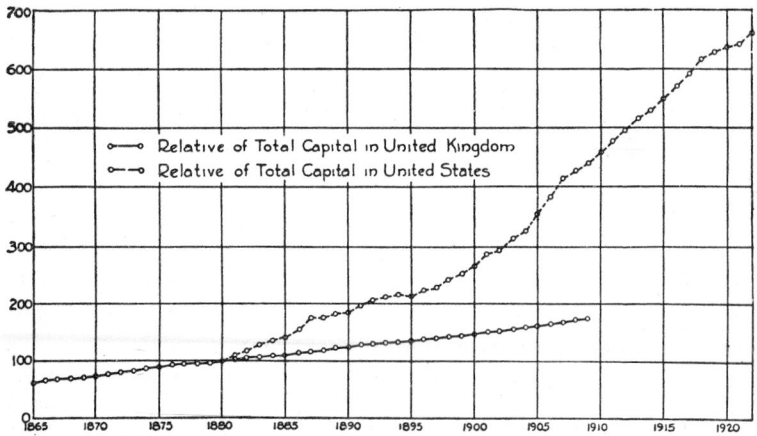

Chart 87. The Growth of Capital in the United Kingdom and in the United States. (U. K., 1865–1928; U. S., 1880–1922)

and for the third in terms of the second, 116.7 or 117. By dividing the latter link-relative by the former, or 117 by 120, we obtain the relative representing the change in the rate of change— a decrease of 3 per cent. If in the fourth year, the percentage of growth should fall to 2.0, the corresponding link-relative in terms of the rate of growth for the third year would be 57. The relative decrease in the rate of change would therefore be 51 per cent (*i.e.* $100 - \frac{57}{117} \times 100$).

In the sections which follow we shall present for both the United Kingdom and for the United States data on the growth of fixed capital and on the fluctuations in the rate of interest, and in a final section we shall attempt to discover what statistical interrelationship, if any, exists between these changes.

2. The Growth of Capital in Great Britain and the United States

An index of fixed capital in all branches of industry in the United Kingdom from 1865 to 1909 has been computed by the author from the previous studies of Giffen, the Economist, Harris, Mallet, Stamp, and Crammond, and from C. K. Hobson's estimates of the export of capital. These studies were coordinated and utilized for certain specific years, while values for the intervening years were found by interpolation according

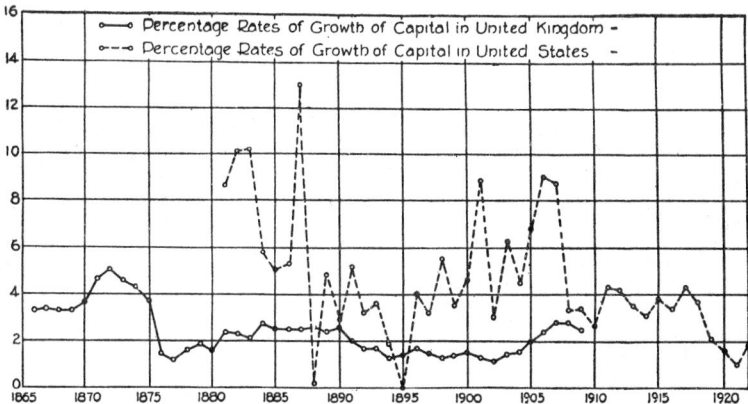

Chart 88. Percentage Rates of Growth of Capital by Years in United Kingdom and United States.

to the relative proportion of capital goods which were produced in them. Finally all annual investments in terms of dollars were deflated by an index of the cost of producing capital goods, and this was reduced to dollars of constant purchasing power.[3]

The final results giving for the various years from 1865 to 1909 (1) the annual increments of fresh capital, (2) the total fund of fixed capital and (3) the rate of increase in the supply of fixed capital are shown in Table 62. It will be noticed that the total supply of capital increased by approximately 180 per cent during these forty-four years. The rate of growth of course varied from period to period. Thus from 1865 to 1875, the rate of increase ranged between 3 and 5 per cent, while during the depression years of the late seventies the annual increase was

---

[3] For a detailed statement of the methods followed and sources used see my article, "The Growth of Capital in Great Britain, 1865–1909," *Journal of Economic and Business History*, August, 1930, pp. 559–84.

TABLE 62

ESTIMATED TOTAL BRITISH CAPITAL IN TERMS OF THE 1865 PRICE LEVEL
INVESTED INSIDE AND OUTSIDE THE UNITED KINGDOM BY YEARS FROM
1865 TO 1909, AND RATE OF GROWTH OF THIS CAPITAL

Year	Total Capital		Annual Amount Saved	
	In millions £ (1)	Relative Index 1865 = 100 (2)	In millions £ (3)	Percentage Increase[1] (4)
1865	2,585	100		
1866	2,671	103	86	3.3
1867	2,763	107	92	3.4
1868	2,855	110	92	3.3
1869	2,949	114	94	3.3
1870	3,058	118	109	3.7
1871	3,203	124	145	4.7
1872	3,362	130	159	5.0
1873	3,515	136	153	4.6
1874	3,666	142	151	4.3
1875	3,801	147	135	3.7
1876	3,857	149	56	1.5
1877	3,903	151	46	1.2
1878	3,964	153	61	1.6
1879	4,039	156	75	1.9
1880	4,105	159	66	1.6
1881	4,205	163	100	2.4
1882	4,300	166	95	2.3
1883	4,391	170	91	2.1
1884	4,508	174	117	2.7
1885	4,619	179	111	2.5
1886	4,734	183	115	2.5
1887	4,852	188	118	2.5
1888	4,979	193	127	2.6
1889	5,100	197	121	2.4
1890	5,233	202	133	2.6
1891	5,337	206	104	2.0
1892	5,427	210	90	1.7
1893	5,521	214	94	1.7
1894	5,595	216	74	1.3
1895	5,673	219	78	1.4
1896	5,772	223	99	1.7
1897	5,859	227	87	1.5
1898	5,937	230	78	1.3
1899	6,023	233	86	1.4
1900	6,111	236	88	1.5
1901	6,189	239	78	1.3
1902	6,264	242	75	1.2
1903	6,353	246	89	1.4
1904	6,446	249	93	1.5
1905	6,572	254	126	2.0
1906	6,729	260	157	2.4
1907	6,920	268	191	2.8
1908	7,113	275	193	2.8
1909	7,288	282	175	2.5

[1]Column 4 is obtained by dividing the annual increase by the total capital of the preceding year

TABLE 63

GROWTH OF CAPITAL IN THE UNITED STATES, 1880–1922

Year	Total Capital (in millions of 1880 dollars) (1)	Annual Increase (in millions of 1880 dollars) (2)	Percentage Rate of Growth[1] (3)
1880	9761		
1881	10602	841	8.6
1882	11676	1074	10.1
1883	12871	1195	10.2
1884	13616	745	5.8
1885	14295	679	5.0
1886	15055	760	5.3
1887	17018	1963	13.0
1888	17059	41	.2
1889	17879	820	4.8
1890	18401	522	2.9
1891	19363	962	5.2
1892	19985	622	3.2
1893	20698	713	3.6
1894	21091	393	1.9
1895	21065	−26	−.1
1896	21915	850	4.0
1897	22617	702	3.2
1898	23861	1244	5.5
1899	24708	847	3.5
1900	25942	1234	5.0
1901	28134	2192	8.4
1902	28977	843	3.0
1903	30796	1819	6.3
1904	32193	1397	4.5
1905	34384	2191	6.8
1906	37476	3092	9.0
1907	40745	3269	8.7
1908	42094	1349	3.3
1909	43505	1411	3.4
1910	44692	1187	2.7
1911	46635	1943	4.3
1912	48601	1966	4.2
1913	50315	1714	3.5
1914	51863	1548	3.1
1915	53853	1990	3.8
1916	55692	1839	3.4
1917	58087	2395	4.3
1918	60239	2152	3.7
1919	61486	1247	2.1
1920	62442	956	1.6
1921	63087	645	1.0
1922	64253	1166	1.8

[1] Column 3 is obtained by dividing the annual increase by the total capital of the preceding year.

somewhat less than 2 per cent. During the eighties, the annual rate of expansion rose above 2 per cent, only to fall back during the next fifteen years. The last five years, from 1905 to 1909, apparently witnessed a rise in the rate of saving to around an average of 2½ per cent. For the forty-four years as a whole the average rate of capital growth was approximately 2⅓ per cent which was somewhat below Cassel's rough estimate of a growth rate of 3 per cent.

A similar study has been made for the United States for the period 1880–1922. The growth of fixed capital was computed for virtually all of the chief American industries [4] and combined into a general index. This was in turn reduced to dollars of constant purchasing power by dividing the annual monetary increments by an index of the cost of capital goods, with 1880 as the base. The results are given in Table 63 and, along with the British figures, are given graphically in Charts 87 and 88, where the growth of total capital and the annual rates of increase are both shown.

It will be seen that the relative growth of fixed capital was very much more rapid in the United States than in Great Britain. British capital increased by 182 per cent in forty-four years, whereas American capital increased by approximately 550 per cent in forty-two years.[5] While British capital in per capita terms rose by 90 per cent, the ratio in America increased by approximately 200 per cent. The difference in these rates of growth from 1880 to 1909 was especially marked. During these years the total British fixed capital increased by approximately only 75 per cent whereas American capital more than quadrupled. The per capita increase in the United States, moreover, amounted to more than 140 per cent as compared with the British advance of but 37 per cent. This more rapid rate of growth in the amount of fixed capital is indeed probably one explanation for the greater relative material progress which the United States made during this period, and it was appreciably above the estimate of 3 per cent a year which Cassel made for western Europe.

That there is a considerable margin of error in all these estimates is, of course, evident. It could hardly be otherwise in view of the scanty and incomplete sources. It is believed, however, that the estimates are the best which can be made with

---

[4] *I.e.* manufacturing, steam railroads, street railways, telegraph, telephone, electric light and power, farm machinery, productive farm buildings, and livestock. In a later article I plan to give the details of the process which are too lengthy to be stated fully in this book.

[5] A part of the American increase was of course provided from capital saved by foreigners and invested in the United States. Since the British index includes capital invested overseas, there is indeed some double-counting. The foreign investments were not, however, sufficient to account for more than a small fraction of the greater rate of capital growth displayed by the United States.

TABLE 64

THE RATE OF INTEREST IN ENGLAND, 1853–1914[1]

Year	Average Yield of Consols[1]	Relatives		Year	Average Yield of Consols[1]	Relatives	
		1865 =100	1900 =100			1865 =100	1900 =100
1853	3.07	92	111	1884	2.97	89	108
1854	3.27	98	118	1885	3.02	90	109
1855	3.31	99	120	1886	2.98	89	108
1856	3.22	96	117	1887	2.95	88	107
1857	3.27	98	118	1888	2.72	81	99
1858	3.17	93	112	1889	2.81	84	102
1859	3.15	94	114	1890	2.85	85	103
1860	3.19	95	116	1891	2.87	86	104
1861	3.28	98	119	1892	2.84	85	103
1862	3.23	96	117	1893	2.79	83	101
1863	3.24	97	117	1894	2.72	81	99
1864	3.33	99	121	1895	2.59	77	94
1865	3.35	100	121	1896	2.48	74	90
1866	3.41	102	124	1897	2.45	73	89
1867	3.23	96	117	1898	2.48	74	90
1868	3.20	96	116	1899	2.57	77	93
1869	3.23	96	117	1900	2.76	82	100
1870	3.24	97	117	1901	2.92	87	106
1871	3.23	96	117	1902	2.91	87	105
1872	3.24	97	117	1903	2.75	82	100
1873	3.24	97	117	1904	2.83	84	103
1874	3.24	97	117	1905	2.78	83	101
1875	3.20	96	116	1906	2.83	84	103
1876	3.16	94	114	1907	2.97	89	108
1877	3.15	94	114	1908	2.90	87	105
1878	3.15	94	114	1909	2.98	89	108
1879	3.08	92	112	1910	3.08	92	112
1880	3.05	91	111	1911	3.15	94	114
1881	3.00	90	109	1912	3.28	98	119
1882	2.99	89	108	1913	3.39	101	123
1883	2.96	88	107	1914	3.34	100	121

[1] Computed from data given in William Page, *Commerce and Industry*, Constable, 1919, pp. 224–5. These yields are in virtual agreement with those used by Irving Fisher in his *The Theory of Interest*, p. 530 and taken in turn from A. H. Gibson's, "The Future Course of High Class Interest Values," *Bankers Insurance Managers and Agents Magazine*, January, 1923, pp. 15–34.

existent data and that the general outlines of the picture are approximately correct. Should more complete data become available, improved and more accurate estimates can then be made.

3. The Rate of Interest in Great Britain and the United States

In trying to obtain the real rate of interest we should measure the yield on securities to which as little risk as possible is attached. This test is admirably satisfied by British government bonds or consols, and the average yield upon this type of security is shown in Table 64 by years from 1853 to 1914.

It is more difficult to compute a similar index for the United States because of the fact that prior to the creation of the Federal Reserve System the note issue of the National banks was based upon government bonds. This fact helped to influence their price and gave them a value at variance with investments as a whole. Two very good indexes of bond yields have, however, been computed. The first is by Dr. F. R. Macaulay of the National Bureau of Economic Research who has studied the yields of railway bonds from 1859 to 1925 [6] and who has worked out an ingenious method for eliminating changes in the quality of the bonds and who, therefore, has been able to get very close to the pure rate of interest.

Another index is that computed by the Standard Statistics Company for the years since 1900, which includes 60 issues evenly divided among the four fields of industrial, railroad, public utility, and municipal bonds.[7] The general average yield for this composite group was somewhat higher than was the case with Macaulay's index, although this difference narrowed appreciably with the years. The yields on the Standard Statistics Company's selected group of municipal bonds, on the other hand, closely approximated Macaulay's index for the period 1900–1925.

Macaulay's index has, therefore, been chosen as the one to be used, with the exception of the year 1917, when it fell from 4.01 to 3.90. For this year there has been substituted the index 4.25, which bore the same relation to the yield of 4.01 in 1916 and 4.52 in 1918, as the 1917 yield on the Standard Statistics Company's group of municipal bonds bore to their average 1916 and 1918 yields. These rates of yield are given in Table 65 and are shown in comparison with the movement of the English rates of interest in Chart 89. The much greater fall in the American interest rate from 1873 to 1881 might seem to invalidate this comparison. Fortunately for our purposes, however, we shall need to use the index of American interest rates only for the years subsequent to 1880, which is the period when our index of capital begins, and since the currency had been put on a gold

---

[6] F. R. Macaulay, "The Construction of an Index Number of Bond Yields," *Journal American Statistical Association*, March 1926, pp. 27–39. The best of his various indexes seems to be Index D, which is given on the logarithmic chart on page 38 of his article. No table accompanies the chart and the precise rates are not given in the article itself. They have, however, been published in a bulletin of the National Bureau of Economic Research.

[7] See *Annual Statistical Bulletin*, 1926, Standard Statistics Co., pp. 10–11 and subsequent annual bulletins.

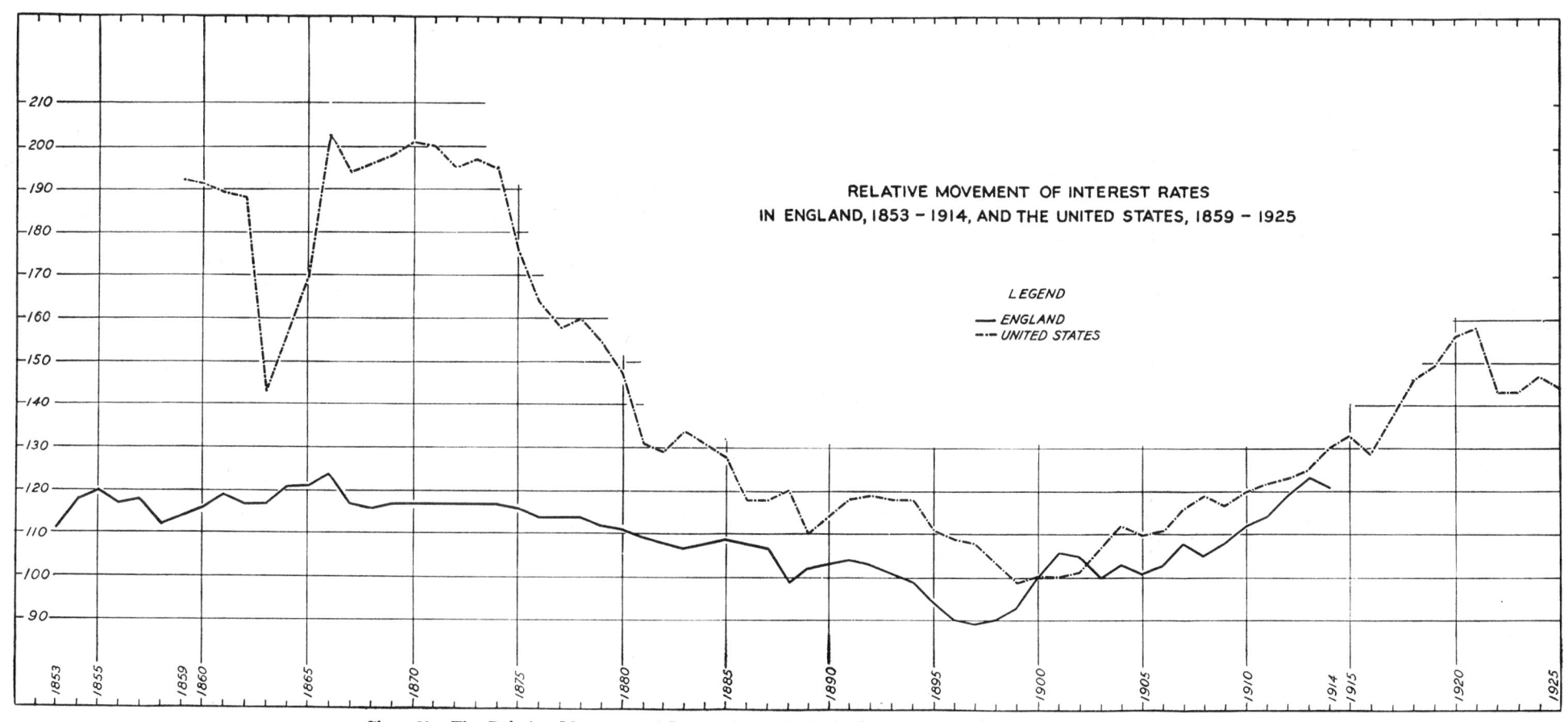

RELATIVE MOVEMENT OF INTEREST RATES
IN ENGLAND, 1853 – 1914, AND THE UNITED STATES, 1859 – 1925

LEGEND
—— ENGLAND
—·—· UNITED STATES

Chart 89. The Relative Movement of Interest Rates in England, 1853–1914, and in the United States, 1859–1925.

TABLE 65

THE AVERAGE INTEREST RATE IN THE UNITED STATES AS SHOWN BY
BOND YIELDS, 1859–1925 (ACCORDING TO F. R. MACAULAY)

Year	Average Bond Yield	Relative Bond Yield	
		1890–99 = 100	*1900 = 100*
Jan.			
1859	5.94	171	192
1860	5.92	171	191
1861	5.86	169	189
1862	5.82	168	188
1863	4.43	128	143
1864	4.91	142	158
1865	5.27	152	170
1866	6.28	181	203
1867	6.00	173	194
1868	6.09	176	196
1869	6.12	177	197
1870	6.24	180	201
1871	6.21	179	200
1872	6.03	174	195
1873	6.12	177	197
1874	6.04	174	195
1875	5.46	158	176
1876	5.09	147	164
1877	4.89	141	158
1878	4.96	143	160
1879	4.81	139	155
1880	4.56	132	147
1881	4.06	117	131
1882	3.99	115	129
1883	4.14	119	134
1884	4.06	117	131
1885	3.96	114	128
1886	3.67	106	118
1887	3.67	106	118
1888	3.71	107	120
1889	3.42	99	110
1890	3.53	102	114
1891	3.66	106	118
1892	3.70	107	119
1893	3.67	106	118
1894	3.65	105	118
1895	3.44	99	111
1896	3.39	98	109
1897	3.35	97	108
1898	3.18	92	103
1899	3.08	89	99
1900	3.10	89	100
1901	3.10	89	100
1902	3.12	90	101
1903	3.31	96	107
1904	3.46	100	112
1905	3.40	98	110
1906	3.44	99	111
1907	3.61	104	116
1908	3.68	106	119

TABLE 65—Continued

THE AVERAGE INTEREST RATE IN THE UNITED STATES AS SHOWN BY
BOND YIELDS, 1859–1925 (ACCORDING TO F. R. MACAULAY)

Year	Average Bond Yield	Relative Bond Yield	
		1890–99 = 100	1900 = 100
1909	3.63	105	117
1910	3.73	108	120
1911	3.79	109	122
1912	3.80	110	123
1913	3.88	112	125
1914	4.04	117	130
1915	4.11	119	133
1916	4.01	116	129
1917	4.25	113	137
1918	4.52	130	146
1919	4.62	133	149
1920	4.84	140	156
1921	4.90	141	158
1922	4.43	128	143
1923	4.42	128	143
1924	4.45	128	147
1925	4.47	129	144

basis by that time, we shall be spared any error resulting from the depreciation of our paper currency in terms of the world price level in terms of gold.

After 1880 the movements of the two sets of interest rates were approximately similar, although the relative fall of the American rate was somewhat greater. The English rate, moreover, began to turn up in 1898 and 1899, or from three to four years before the American rate showed any appreciable rise. The Boer war probably caused the very appreciable advance in the English rate in 1901 from which there was a decline in 1902 and 1903 when it again began to move upward.

There is, however, a complicating factor in the attempt to compute long-time changes in the interest rate. This is the tendency of the interest rate to move in such a fashion as partially to compensate for prospective changes in the price level and hence in the value of the principal.[8] In a period of rising prices a bond which runs for a given period of years will be retired by the payment of the principal which, however, will have less purchasing power than when the loan was floated. The value of the bond will, therefore, shrink during this period, and the borrowers will gain at the expense of the lenders. In such

[8] For a development of this point see Irving Fisher, *Appreciation and Interest,* and, *The Theory of Interest.*

a situation as this, lenders will after a time realize the situation and will tend to ask for a higher interest rate as at least partial insurance against the depreciation of their principal. What may seem to be a rise in the interest rate may therefore be an attempt of lenders to protect themselves against a risk caused by the upward movement of the general price level.

Conversely, when prices are falling, the repayment of the monetary face-value of a bond will be in dollars of increased purchasing power. The value of the bond will have increased, and the lenders will have gained at the expense of the borrowers. Borrowers in anticipation of a continued downward fall in prices will tend to adjust the interest rates which they will pay downward, to help protect themselves against the appreciation of the principal.

Since the downward slope of the interest rate from 1873 to 1897 coincided with a decline during this period in the general price level, and the upward movement of the rate from the turn of the century to 1920 was accompanied by a very appreciable rise in the price level, we find the actual course to have been somewhat in accord with what we might on theoretical grounds expect to occur.

These adjustments in the interest rate, however, are made incompletely and belatedly and are generally not sufficient to compensate for changes in the value of the principal. Professor Irving Fisher has attempted to compute what he terms the relative "real" interest rate by subtracting from the yield on securities which in a period of constant prices would be riskless the rate of annual change in the level of wholesale prices. Unfortunately, however, he has published his results only for periods as a whole and not for specific years. His results showing the "real" bank rate of interest in London and "real" prime commercial paper rates in New York were as given in Tables 66 and 67.[9]

We would obtain less violent fluctuations in what Fisher terms the "real" rates of interest if we were to subtract the changes in the level of some general price level such as that which Carl Snyder has computed and which includes the cost of living, wages, and rents in addition to wholesale prices.[10] But it would seem, nevertheless, that there is a great variation in the real rates of return. In periods of great increases in prices, as from

[9] Fisher, *The Theory of Interest*, p. 527.
[10] See his, *Business Cycles and Measurements*, pp. 286–7.

TABLE 66

RATES OF INTEREST IN RELATION TO ANNUAL RATES OF CHANGE IN THE
PRICE LEVEL, LONDON 1864–1927 (AFTER IRVING FISHER)

Period	Bank Rate (1)	Annual Rate of Change in Price Level (2)	Real Interest in Commodities (Bank) 3 = (1-2)
1864–1870	4.3	−1.6	+5.9
1870–1873	3.7	+4.8	−1.1
1873–1896	3.2	−2.6	+5.8
1896–1913	3.6	+1.9	+1.7
1914–1920	5.2	+14.5	−9.3
1920–1927	4.8	−10.9	+15.7

TABLE 67

RATES OF INTEREST IN RELATION TO ANNUAL RATES OF CHANGE IN THE
PRICE LEVEL, NEW YORK, 1860–1927 (AFTER IRVING FISHER)

Period	Rate of Interest on Prime Commercial Paper (60–90 days) (1)	Annual Rate of Change in the Price Level (2)	Real Rate of Interest in Commodities (Market) (3) = (1-2)
1860–1865	6.9	+14.3	−7.4
1865–1871	7.8	−8.1	+15.9
1871–1879	6.4	−4.3	+10.7
1879–1889	5.1	−0.2	+5.3
1889–1896	4.9	−3.1	+8.0
1896–1915	4.7	+2.1	+2.6
1915–1920	5.1	+14.9	−9.8
1920–1927	5.0	−6.3	+11.3

1914 to 1920, the rise in the price level, according to Fisher's
computations, was more than sufficient to wipe out the entire
interest rate and leave a negative rate with a consequent impairment of the principal. On the other hand, in periods of
falling prices, as in Great Britain from 1873 to 1896 and the
United States from 1865 to 1896, the annual rate of increase
in value of the principal was sufficient, when added to the interest rate, to raise the "real" rate greatly above its former or
subsequent level. Thus Fisher computes the "real" bank rate
in England from 1873 to 1896 to have been 5.8 per cent in
comparison with a negative interest rate of — 1.1 per cent for
the years 1870–1873 and the low positive rate of 1.7 per cent
for the years 1896–1913. In the United States the "real" commercial paper rate from 1871 to 1879 is estimated by him to
have been 10.7 per cent, while the rate during the Civil War

was — 7.4 per cent and from 1879 to 1889 was but 5.3 per cent.

It may well be queried, therefore, whether these results are not sufficiently startling to vitiate the possible use of nominal yields as a measure of the price paid for the use of capital and whether we should not turn instead to the construction of real interest rates for each by subtracting the annual percentage changes in the general price level from the ratios of yield?

In our opinion, this is not necessary. For what we are measuring are the amounts which the investor will save at what he regards as the rates of interest.[11] The nominal rate of interest or yield is what he believes the real rate of interest to be and while he is frequently mistaken, we should use as our variable what he thinks are the facts, rather than what actually are the facts. For this reason, therefore, we shall use the yield of these high-class securities as the measure of the interest rate as it affects investments. We recognize, however, that some of the apparent movements in the yields are not so much changes in the rate of interest itself as partially compensatory allowances for changes in the value of money. But this source of error is at least partially minimized by the method of link-relatives.

4. The Correlation of Changes in the Interest Rate and of Changes in the Rate of Growth of Capital

We can now correlate these changes in the interest rate and in the capital growth rate and determine what relationship, if any, can be discovered between them. As a first measure link-relatives were computed for interest rates and for the annual *absolute* increments of fixed capital.[12] The coefficients of correlation between these variables for identical years were as follows:

Country	Period	r
United Kingdom..........	1866–1909	−0.069 (±0.152)
United States............	1881–1922[1]	−0.380 (±0.136)

[1] Omitting 1895 and 1896 because of decrement in capital in 1895.

It will thus be seen that there was no correlation between the changes in these phenomena so far as England was concerned,

[11] I am of course well aware that, as Wicksell and Keynes have pointed out, the rate of investment in industry may, because of the operations of the banking system, not be equal to the rate of savings. I am however measuring the actual additions to capital and correlating changes in the interest rate with changes in the volume of investments.

[12] I am indebted to Miss Rose Director, Mr. Aaron Director, Mrs. Erika Schoenberg, and Mr. Stanley Posner for the computation of these coefficients.

and only a low degree of negative correlation in the United States. Since the square of the coefficient of correlation (r^2) can be taken as a fair measure of the degree of interconnection between two variables, this would indicate that this relationship comprised approximately one-seventh of the total forces which played upon the two sets of phenomena in the United States. It is also interesting that such relationship as existed was negative rather than positive.

A somewhat more refined measure of the relationships would be to correlate the link-relatives of the interest rates with the link-relatives of the *percentage increments* to the total supply of capital. This has also been carried out for identical years with the result that the coefficient of correlation for the United Kingdom was — 0.045 ($\pm$ 0.152) for the years 1867–1910, indicating no relationship between these variables. For the United States the coefficient of correlation for the years from 1880 to 1922, omitting those of 1895 and 1896, was —0.379 ($\pm$ 0.137). This would again indicate an influence of about one-seventh (r^2), but it should be noted that the relationship between changes in the rate of interest and the rate of investment is again negative. The coefficients obtained from using link-relatives of the percentage increments to capital are in fact virtually identical with those obtained by using link-relatives of the absolute increments.

It may be contended, however, that the correlation of changes in the interest rate with changes in the rate at which capital is growing may measure not the supply curve of investment but rather the demand curve for investment. Thus when the supply of fresh investments runs low, because it is not fed in the usual degree by corporate surpluses and bank loans, it may be argued that the rate of interest would naturally rise as a means of attracting fresh funds. There is a certain degree of plausibility in this contention and, if it were true, it might explain the negative correlation obtained for the United States, since the demand curve for capital or investment would naturally be thought to have a negative slope. The two real difficulties with this argument, however, are: (1) that it is in the years of depression when the increments to capital are greatly reduced that we find the interest rate to fall most markedly, while in the years of prosperity, when fresh sources of investment are available, that the interest rate again rises and (2), that if we conceive of the rate of interest being primarily determined by the marginal yield upon the total supply of capital, then a change in the rate of growth could scarcely tend to produce a very appreciable alteration in the rate of interest itself.

It is worth while, however, to correlate changes in the rate of interest for a given year with changes in the rate of capital growth for the succeeding year, and when this is done we have the following coefficients which, though negligible, are in both cases positive.

Country	Period	Coefficient of Correlation
United Kingdom..........	1866–1909	+0.0065 (±0.160)
United States............	1881–1922	+0.0373 (±0.131)

Thus, in Great Britain there seems to be no interrelation between changes in the rate of interest and the rate of savings whether we make our comparisons for identical or succeeding years, while in the United States the use of the succeeding year eliminates the negative relationship which was observed for identical years.

A still further method is, as has been suggested, to correlate the relative rates of change in the interest rates with link-relatives of the link-relatives of the absolute increments of capital. This, in turn, yields for identical years coefficients of -0.176 (± 0.149) for the United Kingdom. This, although still low, is higher than the coefficients obtained by the use of first differences. The coefficient of correlation for the United States was -0.319 (± 0.146) indicating a degree of influence (r^2) of about one-tenth.

As we have pointed out, the interest rate is also affected by changes in the price level. It tends to rise in periods of rising prices in order to compensate at least partially for the fall in the value of the principal of the fixed debts and to fall in periods of falling prices as a partial means of compensating for the appreciation of this principal. It is therefore advisable to take changes in the price level into account in trying to measure the relationship, if any, which may exist between changes in the interest rate and in the volume of savings. This has been done by computing partial coefficients of correlation where $y =$ link-relatives of the interest rate, $x =$ link-relatives of the absolute annual increments of fixed capital and $z =$ link-relatives of the general price level. We have taken Snyder's index as the best

measurement of the changes in the general price level.[13]   It
will be remembered that the simple correlation coefficient between x and y for the years 1881–1922 in the United States
was — 0.380.   The partial coefficient of correlation ($r_{xy.z}$) for
identical years was — 0.366 ($\pm$ 0.139) or a slightly lower figure.
When z' was however taken as the link-relative of the prices
in the previous year which presumably would affect the interest
rate in any given year more than the dimly perceived concomitant changes, then the partial coefficient $r_{xy.z'}$ was raised
to — 0.537 ($\pm$ 0.114).[14]   This is an appreciable coefficient and
indeed the highest which has been obtained.   It is however
puzzling that it should still be negative and that the allowance
for the changes in the price level should actually make the
coefficient more negative than it was.   This is very difficult to
explain on *a priori* grounds which point, as we have indicated,
to a positively sloping supply curve.   It is also difficult to explain in view of the cyclical influences which tend to have rising
prices, advancing interest rates, and a greater volume of investments all associated together in the upswing phase of the cycle
and to have the reverse movements associated together in the
downswings.   The moving of price changes backwards by a year
blurs this relationship and probably accounts for the increase in
the size of the negative relationship.   But that there should be a
negative relationship at all instead of a positive one is indeed
somewhat disconcerting.   But such seem to be the facts.

So far then as the facts which have been analyzed are concerned the complete lack of correlation between the British data
combined with the puzzling nature of the results for the United
States should make us chary about drawing any very definite
conclusion.   Certainly there is as yet no inductive evidence to
corroborate the assumption that the supply curve of capital is
positively inclined.

5. Changes in the Rate of Interest on Savings and in the Volume of Savings Deposits

A further way of testing the effect, if any, which changes in
the interest rate have upon the volume of savings is afforded
by data which are collected annually by the Comptroller of the
Currency.   That office gathers each year from the national banks
in some eighty cities which have separate savings departments

---

[13] See Carl Snyder, *Business Cycles and Measurements*, p. 288.
[14] The coefficient $r_{yz'}$ was + 0.613.

data on the total volume of savings deposits and the average rate of interest paid on such deposits.[15] It is possible therefore to observe for each city for successive pairs of years whether there was a change in the interest rate and the change in the total volume of savings. Six successive pairs of these years were selected during the decade of the twenties and after discarding the data for certain cities because of either too few banks reporting or of appreciable variation in the number of reporting banks, the following number of cities were taken where the data for changes were believed to be comparable:

Paired Years	Number of Cities Where the Number of Banks Was Comparable and Changes in the Interest Rate Occurred	Paired Years	Number of Cities Where the Number of Banks Was Comparable and Changes in the Interest Rate Occurred
1922–23	10	1925–26	15
1923–24	11	1926–27	8
1924–25	11	1927–28	17

The statistical basis while not as extensive as would be desired is therefore probably sufficient to permit the results to have some validity.

Let us now see what the coefficients of correlation were between the changes in x (the link-relatives of savings deposits) and y (the link-relatives of the interest rates). These were as follows:

Paired Years	Coefficient of Correlation r	Standard Error
1922–23	−0.058	±0.315
1923–24	+0.009	±0.301
1924–25	+0.134	±0.296
1925–26	+0.519	±0.189
1926–27	−0.123	±0.348
1927–28	+0.335	±0.215

It will thus be seen that in only one of the six pairs of years was the coefficient of appreciable size, namely, 1925–26 when it was + 0.519 or two and a half times the standard error of 0.208. In four of the five remaining cases the coefficients of correlation

---

[15] See Annual Reports U. S. Comptroller of the Currency, 1922–29. For the type of data gathered see the report for 1925, pp. 42–44.

George K. McCabe, "No Relation Between Time Deposit Rates and Total Savings in Banks," *The Annalist*, Vol. 31, p. 1101–2.

were so small in themselves (twice being negative) as to indicate virtually no interrelationship while their standard errors were from two to thirty times as great. In the remaining case of 1927–28, the coefficient was still small, namely, 0.335, indicating by itself an interconnection of about one-ninth (i.e. $r^2 = 0.112$) and it was only one and a half times its standard error of 0.215.

The results cannot therefore be said to demonstrate any real connection between changes in the rate of interest and changes in the total volume of savings. It is possible however that changes in the interest rate between 1925 and 1926 did have some effect upon the amount of savings and that in 1927–28 there may have been a somewhat similar though very much weaker connection.

In none of the other four years, however, was there any evidence at all of any such inter-connection.

It is therefore only worth while to compute coefficients of elasticity of savings in terms of interest rates for the years 1925–26 and 1927–28. In the former year the coefficient of elasticity was + 0.569 and in the latter + 0.907. These would by themselves tend to indicate that a relative change of one per cent in the link-relatives of the interest rate would tend to be associated in these years with a change in the same direction of from five-ninths to nine-tenths of one per cent in the link-relatives of savings. But the fact that the coefficient of correlation was distinctly low in the latter case and was not high in the former should not lead us to place too great reliance upon even these results.

The apparently high relative elasticity for these two years may moreover seem surprising in view of the fact that the total volume of savings is not far from twenty to twenty-five times the normal annual rate of savings. Under these circumstances, therefore, it could hardly be expected that a change in the interest rate could cause the total volume of savings to change at from five-ninths to nine-tenths as rapid a rate. To the degree that there was such an influence, it probably reflects however (1) the shifting of funds into and out of savings deposits hence a mere transferal in the type of deposits which were made rather than any such actual change in the quantity of capital itself and (2) what may be even more important, geographical shifts of savings from one city to another when the interest rate is altered.

These considerations would in themselves tend to give a high correlation and a high elasticity. It is, therefore, all the more surprising that the other years showed such a low correlation which in two of the cases was actually negative. This may in turn have been caused by the fact that if a change in the rate of interest on savings deposits is accompanied by a corresponding change in the rate of return upon capital in society as a whole, then the high flexibility caused by the transfer of capital from one type of investment to another would be removed and only the changes produced by the flow of savings would be considered. Even this would however leave negative results to be explained since such a relationship is on deductive grounds highly improbable. The coefficients of correlation in these cases are however so low as to give no substantive evidence of any such negative influence. Even if it did appear from these data, it might be caused by the fact that the interest rates on savings deposits fell by less than the general rate with the result that capital would be attracted to this type or place of investment or in the opposite circumstance that the rate of interest for this kind of deposits rose by less than the general rate so that capital was on the whole repelled.

Certainly it is fair to say that the evidence thus far analyzed gives no clear indication what the nature of the supply function of savings actually is. Statisticians and economists need to apply themselves with energy and ingenuity to see if they cannot shed light upon what is the actual relationship between these variables. For as long as this is not known one of the most fundamental forces in economic life will be unplumbed.

CHAPTER XIX

THE SUPPLY OF LAND AND NATURAL RESOURCES

The classical economists regarded the supply of land and natural resources as a fixed and unalterable quantity. There was just so much land in the sense that this consisted of the "original and indestructible powers of the soil" and man could no more add to it than by taking thought he could add a cubit to his stature. This being so, an increase in the variable factors of production, namely, labor and capital, could have no other effect than to force the cultivation of inferior soils and the more intensive cultivation of the better soils. This increased the differential yield of the better soils and the earlier "doses" of labor and capital as compared with the new marginal land and later doses. This increased differential went to the landlord as rent.

This treatment of land and natural resources as a fixed, and hence a completely inelastic, factor of production has been challenged by various writers. Thus Henry C. Carey,[1] living in America with its apparently boundless territories and its expanding frontier, pointed out that the quantity of used land was by no means fixed and that the actual movement of cultivation was not one in which the progress of cultivation invariably moved from better to poorer soils. No one who had watched the movement from the barren hillsides of New England to the fertile fields of the Mississippi Valley could ever have believed that. It is indeed probable that during the century and a quarter from 1800 to 1925 the quantity of land from which the people of western European stock drew their sustenance actually increased faster than the population of those races. For it was during this period that America, Canada, Australia, Siberia, Africa, Brazil and the Argentine were opened up and developed. From the historical standpoint, therefore, Carey was more nearly correct than Ricardo, who was not reasoning his-

---

[1] H. C. Carey, *Principles of Political Economy* and *Principles of Social Science*. Carey went, of course, too far in claiming that the progress of cultivation was always from the worse to the better land.

torically at all but from the standpoint of "other things being equal."

But the period of the frontier and of untapped continents is over. In the main there is relatively little unused land in the United States and Canada which is not already employed for agriculture, pasturage, forestry, building sites, or recreation. The margin is also slight in Australia and is rapidly diminishing in the Argentine and Brazil. Here territory may still be opened up but its quantity, from the world standpoint, will, comparatively speaking, not be great. The supply of natural resources is not completely fixed but it is rather highly inelastic.

A second group of critics, among whom may be mentioned Professor Fetter, have argued that man can and does create land as well as capital. Thus they point out that new land is created by drainage and the filling in of swamps while, by irrigation, dry and desert land which otherwise could not be cultivated is rendered extraordinarily fertile. This again is true; but it is proper to ask how important are the additions to the total land area which have been and are being made in this fashion. They may seem large in the aggregate; but they are surely a very small fraction of the total supply, and they render the quantity of land only slightly less inelastic.

But here a third group, led by Professor Knight, point out that much of the present powers of the soil are neither original nor indestructible. Human labor and capital have gone into clearing, draining, and fertilizing the land. This labor and this capital are inextricably and irretrievably mixed with the original properties. Some indeed go so far as to say that what is called "land" is composed more of past capital and labor than it is of those "original and indestructible" powers which Ricardo meant by that term.

Here again we may perhaps admit the indictment, but say that for the purposes of distribution this is largely water over the dam. The labor and capital which have been mixed with the land are a past matter. For the present they are there, and the quantity of "land" which is available is relatively fixed. It is true that the land may be allowed to run down and that we may have not a constant, but a wasting quantity. But in the short run, at least, the supply is virtually inelastic.

In the long-run, however, it is true that the quantity of what is commonly called "land" may vary. To the degree that this is so, the supply curve of land has a positive slope since it seems improbable that an addition to it would occur unless the return from it increased.[2]

But at least two qualifications need to be interposed here: (1) That even though this capital and labor when mixed with the soil is called "land," it is still nevertheless true that the rate at which the combined mixture will increase is very much less than the rate at which capital has increased in the past century and a half and in all probability much less than the rate at which it bids fair to increase in the future. For capital is fed by annual additions, while the supply of "land" is not increased in this fashion to any such degree. We should not forget the fact that much of so-called agriculture during the last century has in reality partaken of the nature of mining. Much of the original fertility of the soil in the Mississippi Valley, for example, has been depleted through the failure to rotate crops and to allow the land periodically to lie fallow. In addition the process of erosion, hastened by the cutting down of the forests and the failure to develop root grasses, has carried a large portion of the best soil into the creeks and the rivers and thence out to sea. Alongside the process of building up the supply of land has, therefore, also gone the process of depletion.

The rate of increase in "land" during the last century and a quarter has as a whole however probably been faster than the rate of growth of the population and its quantity may still continue to increase when the population becomes stationary.

(2) It is unlikely that a permanent addition of labor and capital in land will be made unless these factors obtain a return approximately equal to that which they would obtain in other fields. Part of what is nominally termed "rent," namely, the payment for the use of land and natural resources will, therefore, be in effect wages and interest. But this is not what we mean by "economic rent," which is after all what we are dealing with.

It is, therefore, safe to conclude that the supply of land, like that of capital, is at any one time fixed and inelastic. Changes in rent will not alter appreciably the relative quantities

---

[2] An exception might be made to this statement through the tendency of more capital to flow into land as the rate of interest fell because of the accumulation of capital. But this would be at least partially and possibly wholly offset by the increased wages of labor which would also have to be mixed with the land were the capital to be so applied. Wages, it will be remembered, increase as interest falls from the more rapid growth of capital than labor.

of land utilized, although they will produce a shift in the respective uses to which it is put.

In the long run there is a certain positive elasticity of supply although, in all probability, this is very much less than unity. For one can hardly conceive of a doubling of rent per acre resulting in anywhere near a doubling in the total quantity of "land" used. Even the long-time elasticity of land is, therefore, also relatively slight. This elasticity would seem to be very much less than that of capital. When our population becomes stationary or declining, however, labor will probably be the most inelastic of the factors.

PART IV

CHAPTER XX

SUMMARY AND CONCLUSIONS

We may now bring our results together and determine what they show about production and distribution and the degree to which they explain the rate of wages and the rate of interest. The author is as conscious as the most severe critic of the many inadequacies in the data which he has assembled and of how far they fall short of the evidence which ideally it would be desirable to obtain. But in economics one must for the present at least work with the material which is available. The author believes, moreover, that a more powerful and refined mathematical technique may well disclose new relationships which have not been revealed in the present study as well as make more precise those which have apparently been discovered. All that is claimed is that certain approximate results have been obtained and a method of analysis developed which may yield more definite results in the future. As the lines in the frontispiece say: "This is no door but only a little window that opens out upon a great world."

Subject therefore to these qualifications the following relationships would seem to be tentatively and approximately indicated.

1. During the period from 1890 to 1922 an increase of one per cent in the quantity of labor in manufacturing in the United States, with the quantity of capital constant, would normally lead to an increase of three-fourths of one per cent in physical product. During this same period an increase of one per cent in the quantity of capital in manufacturing, with labor constant, would normally lead to an increase of one-quarter of one per cent in physical product. These changes might also be approximately described by proportionate gains of two-thirds and one-third of a per cent respectively.

2. The statistics of production for Massachusetts manufacturing during the years from 1890 to 1926 indicate that an increase of one per cent in labor with capital constant tended normally to be accompanied by an increase of seventy-four-hundredths of one per cent in the quantity of physical product.

An increase of one per cent in capital with labor constant tended normally to be accompanied by an increase of twenty-six-hundredths of one per cent in physical product. These results are almost identical with those obtained for the country as a whole.

3. The statistics of manufacturing in New South Wales during the period 1901–1927 indicate that an increase of one per cent in labor, with capital constant, would normally result in an increase of approximately sixty-five-hundredths of one per cent in physical product. An increase of one per cent in capital, with labor constant, would normally result in an increase of thirty-five-hundredths of one per cent in physical product. These results are very similar to those obtained for the United States.

4. From the foregoing equations of production we would expect that, if production follows the form of a linear equation, then in the United States labor would receive seventy-five per cent of the net value product of manufacturing industry and in New South Wales sixty-five per cent. In practice, American statistics seem to indicate that during the years 1909–1918 labor received seventy-four per cent of the total net product and that in New South Wales, during the period 1901–1927, labor received between 56 and 57 per cent. These results indicate that the processes of production tend to be at least approximated in the field of distribution.

A study of the relative movement of real wages as compared with the relative social marginal productivity of labor in a number of industries showed a rather striking agreement between the two variables up until 1922. The failure of this correspondence to continue during the years which followed was striking and may have been responsible in part for the cumulative breakdown which began in 1929.

5. It was shown that the elasticity of the marginal productivity curve for a factor was the reciprocal of the sum of the coefficients of the other factors. This would make the elasticity of the marginal productivity curves of labor and capital equal to the following:

Manufacturing in	Period	Elasticity of Marginal Productivity Curve for	
		Labor	Capital
United States.............	1899–1922	4.00	1.33
Massachusetts............	1890–1926	3.85	1.34
New South Wales........	1901–1927	2.86	1.54

Since the demand for each unit of a factor would normally be governed by what the marginal unit or units would add to the total social product, these coefficients may also be taken to measure the elasticities of the demand for labor and capital respectively.

The elasticities of demand and of production, however, measure the degree to which the proportionate quantities of labor (and capital) change with proportionate changes in marginal productivity and hence presumably in the amounts which will be paid per unit of each.[1] But what is perhaps more important is the proportion in which the marginal productivity of labor and capital change with proportionate changes in their respective quantities. In other words, where x is used to denote the quantities and y the marginal productivity, this involves the relative changes of y in relation to proportionate changes in x instead of vice-versa as in the case when we are dealing with elasticities. This flexibility of the productivity curve is clearly the reciprocal of its elasticity.[2] Then the flexibilities, for so we may call them, of the marginal productivity curves of labor and capital are as follows:

		Labor	Capital
United States............	1899–1922	.25	.75
Massachusetts...........	1890–1926	.26	.74
New South Wales........	1901–1927	.35	.65

This means that an increase of one per cent in the quantity of labor in manufacturing in the United States (with capital constant) was normally accompanied by a decrease of one-quarter of one per cent in its marginal productivity, while such an increase in New South Wales was accompanied by a decrease of thirty-five-hundredths or about one-third of one per cent in its marginal productivity. For capital, on the other hand, an increase of one per cent with labor constant was normally accompanied in the United States by a decrease of three-fourths of one per cent in its marginal productivities and in New South Wales by sixty-five-hundredths or about two-thirds of

[1]This is according to the familiar equation $e = \dfrac{dx}{x} \Big/ \dfrac{dy}{y} = \dfrac{dx}{dy} \cdot \dfrac{y}{x}$ where x equals quantity of labor or capital and y equals marginal productivity or demand price.

[2]$F = \dfrac{dy}{y} \Big/ \dfrac{dx}{x} = \dfrac{dy}{dx} \cdot \dfrac{x}{y}$

one per cent. These changes in marginal productivities should, under normal conditions, also reflect the changes in the amounts which would be paid for the units of these respective factors. It follows indeed as a general rule that where the production function can be described by a homogeneous linear function that the flexibility of the productivity curve of one factor is equal to the sum of the exponents of the other factors.

6. The statistics on the probable distribution of the national income between labor and capital in various countries permit us to make possible approximations of the elasticities and flexibilities of the marginal productivity curves of labor and capital for industry as a whole in these countries. This, of course, assumes that the processes of distribution follow those of production. This assumption has found a good deal of statistical confirmation in the studies which we have made. If it is true of the following countries, not merely for manufacturing but for all society as a whole, we have a key to the probable slopes of the marginal productivity curves of the factors in these nations. But the results should most certainly be regarded as tentative until it is more fully proved that distribution accurately reflects production.

The following table shows estimates which have been made by competent authorities on the relative distribution of the national income of a number of nations between labor and capital:

| Country | Period | Author | Percentage Going to: | |
			Labor	Capital and Land
Great Britain.......	1880	Bowley[3]	62½	37½
Great Britain.......	1913	Bowley[3]	62½	37½
United States.......	Pre-war	Stamp–Dalton[4]	71	29
Canada............	Pre-war	Stamp–Dalton[4]	62½	37½
France............	Pre-war	Stamp–Dalton	61	39
Germany.........	Pre-war	Stamp–Dalton[4]	60	40
Germany.........	1928	Bresciani–Turroni[5]	66	34
Australia..........	Pre-war	Stamp–Dalton	70	30

[3] A. L. Bowley, *The Change in the Distribution of the National Income, 1880–1913.* If income from overseas were excluded, the shares of labor would have been 65.6 and 69 per cent respectively.

[4] J. C. Stamp in his, "The Wealth and Income of the Chief Powers," *Journal Royal Statistical Society,* July, 1919, gave estimates of the amounts of capital and the annual wage-payments as well as estimated national income. Hugh Dalton in his, *Some Aspects of the Inequality of Incomes,* p. 209, assumed that the rate of interest on capital was five per cent and, applying this percentage to Stamp's figures, made estimates on the relative amounts going to labor and capital.

[5] C. Bresciani–Turroni: *On Some Changes in the Distribution of Income and Property in Germany after 1913, Revue Al Quanoun Wal Iqtisad,* Cairo, 1931, p. 159.

It will be observed that there is a striking degree of uniformity between these estimates, the share of labor ranging between sixty and seventy-one per cent. Despite the fact that there is probably a considerable margin of error in the estimates, it is extremely doubtful whether the degree of coincidence between these proportions is purely accidental. The indications seem to point to some broadly similar influences which are at work in all countries.

Assuming then that these ratios indicate the respective "contributions" to the net social product which were made by labor and capital respectively and that production was linear, we would have the following coefficients of flexibility and of elasticity of the marginal productivity curves.

TABLE 68

Estimated Relative Coefficients of Flexibility and Elasticity of the Marginal Productivity Curves of Labor and Capital, as Derived from the Estimated Distribution of the National Incomes of Various Countries, on the Assumption That Production Follows a Linear Function Which Is Reflected in Distribution

Country	Period	Coefficients of Flexibility		Coefficients of Elasticity	
		Labor	Capital and Land	Labor	Capital and Land
Great Britain....	1880	−.375	−.625	−2.67	−1.60
Great Britain....	1913	−.375	−.625	−2.67	−1.60
United States....	Pre-war	−.29	−.71	−3.45	−1.40
Canada.........	Pre-war	−.375	−.625	−2.67	−1.60
France.........	Pre-war	−.39	−.61	−2.60	−1.64
Germany........	Pre-war	−.40	−.60	−2.50	−1.67
Germany........	1928	−.34	−.66	−2.94	−1.52
Australia........	Pre-war	−.30	−.70	−3.33	−1.43

To the degree to which these statistics can be relied upon they indicate that a change of one per cent in the quantity of labor would, if other things were equal, normally cause a change in the opposite direction of from three-tenths to four-tenths of one per cent in the marginal productivities of labor, that is, an increase of one per cent in the quantity of labor would cause the marginal productivity of labor to fall by from three-tenths to four-tenths of one per cent, while a decrease of one per cent in quantity would cause the marginal productivity to rise from three-tenths to four-tenths of one per cent.

Conversely, if capital increased by one per cent and all other things remained equal the marginal productivity of capital would fall from six-tenths to seven-tenths of one per cent, and, if the quantity of capital decreased by this amount, the marginal productivities would rise from six-tenths to seven-tenths of one per cent. These results should, however, be considered as only approximate.

7. The problem of total and marginal productivities can also be analyzed from a more flexible approach than that of constant shares of the product along the lines of the Wilcox formula. A very real tendency towards constancy is indicated by the British statistics on the distribution of the national income at different periods of time, but this should by no means be regarded as invariable and the way should be opened to explore other approaches and methods of analysis.

8. When we turn to the elasticities of supply of the factors of production, we find that in the short-run the supply of capital is fixed and almost completely inelastic. So is the supply of land. The supply of labor, on the other hand, has something of a negative elasticity. The American evidence indicates that the elasticity of hours in respect to hourly earnings is between — 0.1 and — 0.2, and the elasticity of the proportions employed to annual earnings is approximately — 0.16. The combined short-run elasticity of labor is probably between — .24 and — .33, that is, an increase of one per cent in the real earnings of labor would normally cause a decrease of from one-quarter to one-third of one per cent in the quantity of man-hours offered.

9. Since we have seen that the sum of the coefficients of the elasticity of the short-run supply of labor and of the demand for income in terms of effort will be equal to — 1.0, it follows that if the former is equal to — 0.24 or — 0.33, then the latter will be approximately equal to either — 0.76 or — 0.67. If we deal only with the supply of hours of work by those who continue to be employed and neglect the proportions employed, then the elasticity of demand for income in terms of hours of effort alone will approximate either — 0.8 or — 0.9.

10. It follows from all this that if, because of a sudden change in the industrial arts, the general efficiency of industry were to be raised by ten per cent, the quantity of land and capital would remain almost exactly the same, but the quantity of labor would normally diminish from 2½ to 3⅓ per cent. The marginal productivity of land and capital would indeed rise, but that of labor would rise more. The marginal productivity of labor would not merely rise by the ten per cent, but the added decrease in its quantity would cause a further increase of not

far from one per cent. This follows from the fact that if we assume the flexibility of the marginal productivity curve to be — .3, then a decrease of from 2.5 to 3.3 per cent in the quantity of labor would raise the marginal productivity from 0.75 to 1.0 per cent.

Similarly if the general efficiency of industry were to fall, then not only would the marginal productivities of land and capital fall but that of labor would fall more. For the decrease in wages would bring forth an increase in the total man-hours offered which would lower the marginal productivities in the ratio outlined above.

11. It also follows that if the workers were able by better bargaining and by a shifting of their supply curve to the left to exact higher wages at the expense of interest and rent, the quantities of land and capital would not diminish. This situation could, therefore, continue for some time at least. More-over, the higher wage to labor would cause a contraction in its supply which would send up its marginal productivity. Thus a gain from bargaining of ten per cent would lead to a reduction in the quantity of labor of from two and one-half to three and one-third per cent and a rise in the marginal productivity of from three-quarters of one per cent to one per cent.

On the other hand, if labor should lose in the bargaining struggle and its wages be forced down, with the result that the rate of interest and rent would rise, then the quantity of capital would not expand for some time. The lower rate of pay would, however, draw out a larger quantity of labor, so that its marginal productivity would fall and a further decrease in wages per unit of labor would occur. This would be at the rate of from ap-proximately one-tenth to one-thirteenth of the original fall in wages. For a ten per cent decrease in wages would call forth an increase of two and one-half to three and one-third per cent in man-hours which would cause a decrease of from 0.75 to 1.0 per cent in the marginal productivity. From these considera-tions it may be seen that, properly interpreted, the bargain theory still has a place in the theory of distribution.

12. The respective proportions of the social product which labor and capital obtain vitally affect both the bargaining and the distributive processes. In manufacturing, labor seems nor-mally to receive not far from three-quarters of the product, or three times as much as capital, while for society as a whole the ratio is perhaps nearer two-thirds and one-third. This means

494 THE THEORY OF WAGES

that a five per cent increase in wages will, other things being equal, cause a decrease in the rate of interest of from ten to fifteen per cent. Conversely, an increase in interest of fifteen per cent will cause a decrease of from five to seven and a half per cent in wages. This means that a gain of fifteen per cent in wages will cause a decline of from three and one-half to five per cent in the quantities of labor offered and in the face of constant quantities of capital a further rise in the marginal productivities of labor of from one to one and one-half per cent. A rise of fifteen per cent in the rate of interest will, by causing a five to seven and one-half per cent fall in wages, lead to an increase of from one and one-fourth to two and a half per cent in the quantity of labor and lead to a further reduction of from three-tenths to eight-tenths of one per cent in the rate of wages. It follows, therefore, that labor has more to gain from a given percentage addition through bargaining than it has to lose from an equal percentage gain by capital. This is not only true of the sums directly transferred from one factor to another but also of the subsequent changes in marginal productivity.

13. The inter-relationship of the supply curves of the factors with their respective marginal productivity curves present very interesting problems which are of both practical and theoretical importance.

Where the supply curve is positively inclined, as seems deductively to be the case with the annual volume of savings, and the marginal productivity curve is negatively inclined, as seems universally to be the case, an equilibrium at the point of intersection of the two curves is easily visualized,[6] as in Chart 35. For more would not be saved than the amount indicated at the point of intersection, since to do so would slightly lower the rate of interest which would be paid, while more than the rate at the point of intersection would be required to draw out the added units of saving. A similar condition exists in the case of natural resources.

Where, however, the supply curve as well as that of incremental productivity is negatively inclined, as is the case with the short-run supply of labor, we have a more complicated situation. There are two main possibilities as regards the respective position of these curves. These are: (1) where the

[6] It is of course true that the productivity curve represents all of capital, while the supply curve refers predominantly to annual savings. The principle outlined above is nevertheless with this modification substantially correct.

supply curve cuts the marginal productivity curve from above
and then continues below it. This is illustrated in Chart 90.
This is really the result of the supply curve being less elastic,
or more inelastic, than the curve of marginal productivity.
(2) Where the supply curve cuts the marginal productivity
curve from below and then continues above it. This is illustrated in Chart 91. This is the result of the supply curve being appreciably more elastic, or less inelastic, than the curve of
marginal productivity.

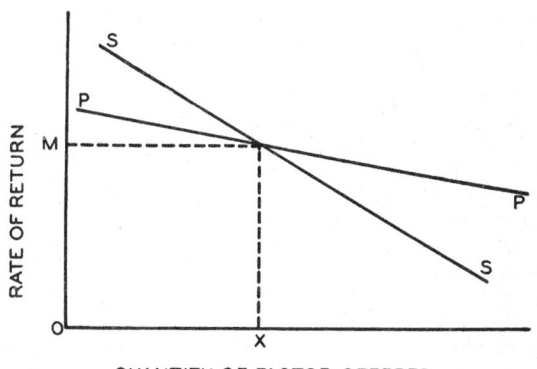

QUANTITY OF FACTOR OFFERED

Chart 90. Equilibrium when Negatively Sloping Supply
Curve Cuts Negatively Sloping Marginal Productivity
Curve from Above.

It is the first of these possibilities which seems to conform to
the real facts of economic life. For, as we have seen, the short-
run elasticity of labor seems to range from — 0.24 to — 0.33,
while the elasticity of the curve of marginal productivity of
labor seems to be not far from — 4.0. But while our results
are probably only applicable to the first of these cases, we shall
apply our analysis to both.

So far as is known, Cournot [7] was the first to deal with the
complications of negatively sloping demand and supply schedules in so far as they applied to the quantity of commodities
which would be produced and their prices. As students of the
mathematical school know, his conclusions were that there were
no determinate points of price fixation in either of these cases
and that disequilibrium characterized both. Where the supply
curve cut the demand curve from above, as in Chart 90, and

[7] Cournot, *The Mathematical Principles of the Theory of Wealth*, 1838, p. 91.

then proceeded below the latter, the situation to the right of the point of intersection was one where marginal and average costs were always below the marginal demand price. Business would, therefore, gain from always increasing production beyond *OX* since costs would fall more rapidly than prices and profits would mount. As long as this condition existed there could be no condition of equilibrium. This could not be obtained unless, and until, the supply curve turned upward and cut the demand curve from below.

Where the supply curve cut the demand curve from below and then extended above it, it might be thought at first that equilibrium would exist at the point of intersection or where

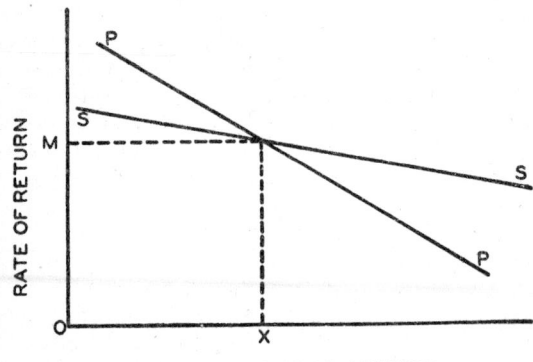

QUANTITY OF FACTOR OFFERED

Chart 91. Equilibrium when Negatively Sloping Supply Curve Cuts Negatively Sloping Marginal Productivity Curve from Below.

the quantity *OX* would be produced. For while the costs of units in excess of this quantity (*OX*) would be reduced, they would not be decreased as rapidly as the price per unit would fall. The industry as a whole would, therefore, lose even more heavily on all units produced in excess of *OX*, and it would seem from the graphic representation that these added units would therefore not be forthcoming and that equilibrium would be at the point of intersection.

But this is a hasty conclusion, which fundamentally rests on a confusion between the effects of an increase in production upon *an industry* and upon *a concern*. In the preceding paragraph, the implicit assumption was that a policy which had these evil effects for an industry as a whole would also have them for each concern when taken by themselves. This is a mistake. Where an industry is highly competitive, the supply is likely to come from either a multitude or at least a large number of plants where the relative contribution of each plant to the total produced is slight. It is this condition of atomistic competition which Cournot assumed and which we, following him, shall adopt. Let us first assume that the supply curve slopes downward in each firm and in such a fashion as to be a microcosm of that for industry as a whole. This condition would then mean in practice that each concern, taken by itself, would profit more from the reduction in unit costs which it would effect by increasing its output beyond its share of the supply (OX) than it would lose from the reduced price which its own addition to the total supply would entail.

This whole problem may be illustrated by the following example: Let us assume that at $1.00 per unit, there will be 1,000,000 units demanded and that the unit cost (including all items) of supplying their share of this quantity will be $1.00 for each and every concern. The quantity is supplied by 100 concerns which have each an output of 10,000 units. Now, let us assume that the elasticity of the demand for the product is unity, and that the elasticity of the supply (or average cost curve) is in the industry and in each plant — 0.10. Then a doubling in output to 2,000,000 units would halve the unit price to 50 cents, but would only reduce average unit costs by 10 per cent, to 90 cents. Such a doubling by the industry would therefore not increase the total gross receipts, which would remain at $1,000,000 (i.e., 2,000,000 × .50), but since total cost would increase to $1,800,000 (i.e., 2,000,000 × .90) there would be a net loss of $800,000 for the industry, or $8,000 for each firm.[8] An increase in output for the industry would, therefore, seem the road to ruin and a course which, if it had a collective will, would not be followed.

But under competition this collective will is lacking. Decisions are made by individual concerns which can consider only their own individual interests. An individual plant, by doubling its output, would cut its average cost by 10 per cent, to 90 cents, while its addition to the total supply would by itself raise this supply by only 1 per cent, or from 1,000,000 to 1,010,000 units. This addition of 1 per cent in the total quantity would, under the conditions of unit elasticity, cause a reduction of 1 cent in

---

[8] On the assumption that each firm doubles its output.

unit price, to a level of 99 cents. The total receipts of the firm would, other things being equal, rise to $19,980 (i.e., 20,000 × .99), and since its total costs would be $18,000, a net profit of $1,980 would result. This profit would, however, accrue on the assumption that other things were indeed equal. Thus each plant, unable to control the action of its competitors, is under such conditions driven to expand its output, although this action, when generalized, causes at least temporary ruin for the industry as a whole. With a negative supply curve of this type there is, therefore, no competitive point of equilibrium. The losses which are suffered will drive most of the firms into bankruptcy, and the ultimate result will be a tendency towards a monopoly to prevent such cut-throat competition from recurring.

It might be thought that there will be a similar lack of equilibrium in the case of labor. For both the demand (marginal productivity) and short-time supply curves are negatively inclined, and the situation would seem to be identical with that already analyzed in the case of commodities. But this does not follow. An increased quantity of commodities will be produced by plants because of the fact that costs will be reduced more than the sales price will be lowered. Indeed, with a myriad of producers, the influence on sales price will be negligible and the effects on costs will be virtually dominant. In the case of labor, however, the increased quantity would not be forthcoming unless the wage rate were of itself lowered. In this case, quantity is a function of price and not of the ratio of added cost, as is the case with commodities. But wages would be held up and cumulative disequilibrium largely prevented by the marginal productivity curve.

Thus, where the supply curve cuts the marginal productivity curve from above, as in Chart 90, then even though the supply price of labor for quantities beyond OX (the amount required at the point of intersection) would be less than the corresponding marginal productivities, nevertheless the competitive bidding of employers would fix wages at the points of marginal productivity and not at the supply prices. This would, in itself, cause the quantity of labor offered in excess of OX to decrease and hence for its marginal productivity to be raised still further. This would mean a further rise in wages and a still further decrease in the quantities of labor offered. It will thus be seen that even though the quantity of labor offered should exceed OX and the wage fall below OM, nevertheless this discrepancy between supply price and marginal productivity would operate to bring back both the quantity and the price of labor to these points, instead of carrying them ever farther away, as would be the case with commodities.

The question then presents itself whether the supply would be carried to a quantity less than OX and wages to a point higher than OM. The answer to this is found in the fact that when the supply curve cuts the marginal productivity curve from above, then at all points to the left of the intersection of the two curves the marginal productivity would be less than the supply price. This would mean that wages would, in consequence, be less than the nominal supply price for all quantities less than OX. But these lower rates of wages would call forth more units of labor which would lower wages still further, and so on. This process would again continue until the quantity of labor increased to OX and wages fell to OM. We thus obtain a determinate solution in the case of distribution where the supply schedule cuts the demand schedule from above and find the point of intersection to be that of equilibrium. This result is opposite to that which Cournot obtained in the case of commodities. Since in practise the short-run supply curve of labor and the marginal productivity curve of labor seem to be of the type indicated, this result is also of some importance.

Such would be the conditions under competition. If the employers were, however, so organized as to control the bids for labor made by individual members, they could take advantage of the negative supply schedules to force wages down below OM. By so doing they would force more labor to offer itself and cause longer hours to be worked. This would give an actual return to capital beyond that obtained from the initial advantage of monopoly bargaining power. This fact may help to explain the ability of strong organizations of employers in isolated labor markets to wring cumulative advantages from labor.

Let us now turn to where the negatively sloping supply curve cuts the demand curve from below, as in Chart 91. Do we have equilibrium here at the point of intersection? It is certainly true that at points to the right of OX, the marginal productivities, or competitive wages, would be less than the supply price. Consequently these added quantities would not be forthcoming, and the situation would not permanently move to the right of OX.

If any quantity of labor less than OX were, however, offered, the wage would be higher than the supply price. Consequently, the quantity of labor would decrease, and the productivity would rise still further. This process would be cumulative. We, therefore, get the interesting result that while there would be partial disequilibrium under such conditions of supply as Cournot dealt with in his system, it will be to the left of the point of intersection for labor, instead of to the right, as in the case of commodities.

If there were an employers' monopoly, their buying power could force wages down to a point where the quantity OX would be available. Wages might be forced still further and made less than marginal productivity. The more rapid decline of marginal productivity than of the scale of supply prices would, however, impose a check upon this tendency.

14. So far as the historical ratio of growth between capital and labor is concerned, it is apparent that the former has increased more rapidly than the latter. This fact largely accounts for the increase in real wages which occurred prior to the great depression which began in 1929. It is probable that the supply of land available for people of western European states increased more rapidly than their populations during the years from 1850 to 1925. This fact accounted also in part for the rising standard of living during the nineteenth century.

15. So far as the future is concerned, there promises to be annual net additions to capital for a long time to come. The total supply of capital, therefore, will continue to grow during that period. Population will, in all probability, continue to grow at a slower rate than that of capital, with the result that the marginal productivities of labor will continue to rise and those of capital to fall. This condition does not, however, take into consideration the possibility of great economic catastrophies, such as war and prolonged and recurrent business depressions, which may affect the economic position of labor very adversely. But the long-run tendencies, aside from the possibility of political and economic breakdown and assuming a general tendency towards equilibrium, would seem on the whole to be favorable to labor.

16. If we turn from the historical to the more purely economic long-run supply curves of labor, capital, and land, we come into far more shadowy territory. There seems to be no conclusive evidence that an increase in wages will, other things being equal, appreciably send up the birth rate or the net-

growth rate. There is, on the contrary, some direct, and still more inferential, evidence that the opposite may occur.

So far as the long-run supply curve of capital is concerned, it is probable, on grounds of deductive reasoning that, while (1) annual increments to the total supply of capital will continue unless the rate of interest falls to an abnormally low level, nevertheless (2) the rate at which the total supply of capital grows is in some degree a direct function of the rate of interest. An examination of the sources of capital would seem to indicate on *a priori* grounds that with other things equal more capital will tend to be saved at a higher, than at a lower rate of interest. It must frankly be confessed, however, that such statistical evidence as has been collected and interpreted furnishes no inductive support for this hypothesis and the whole problem needs to be attacked far more thoroughly and in a much more detailed fashion.

The supply of land would seem to have a slight positive elasticity.

If these tentative conclusions are correct, then, if and as the rate of wages increases because of the greater growth of capital, and as the rate of interest falls in consequence, we may expect a dampening off in the rate of growth of capital, unless the supply curve of savings moves equally to the right. Whether this will reach the point where the supply of capital as well as that of labor will cease to increase and we will move into the stationary state envisaged by Ricardo and Mill, is uncertain. For that is probably too far in the future to project our estimates.

17. The fact that the elasticity of the demand for labor seems to be between — 3.0 and — 4.0 indicates that where unemployment is caused by a wage rate which is higher than marginal productivity, a reduction of one per cent in the rate of wages should normally lead to an increase of 3 or 4 per cent in the volume of employment and hence to an increase in the total income of the workers of from 2 to 3 per cent. If wages are pushed up above the point of marginal productivity, the decrease in employment would normally be from three to four times as great as the increase in hourly rates so that the total income of the working class would be reduced in the ratio indicated above. It should also be noted that Pigou in his recent *Theory of Unemployment* arrives by almost purely deductive methods at an almost identical estimate of the elasticity of de-

mand for labor during periods of depression, namely that it is "probably not less than — 3.0." [9]

It does not follow however that the cause of unemployment is uniformly a wage which is in excess of marginal productivity. There are other causes of a seasonal, cyclical, and technological nature and in these cases a reduction in the wage rate need not invariably bring the greater expansion in employment.

[9] Pigou, A. C., *Theory of Unemployment*, p. 97.

STATISTICAL APPENDIX

TABLE I

INDEXES OF PHYSICAL PRODUCTION, 1899 = 100

Year	Food	Textiles	Leather	Iron and Steel	Non-Ferrous Metals	Lumber	Stone, Clay and Glass	Paper and Pulp	Chemicals	Manufacturing Weighted by Value Added in Manufacturing in 1923	Manufacturing Weighted by Number Employed
1899	100.0	100.0	100.0	100.0	100.0	100.0	100.0	100.0	100.0	100.0	100.0
1900	100.3	101.1	99.5	95.4	102.4	99.5	99.5	108.3	101.7	100.2	100.2
1901	122.2	102.6	105.0	117.3	113.2	99.0	113.4	116.7	113.7	111.5	109.5
1902	116.0	117.7	117.3	133.0	146.0	98.5	124.2	125.1	127.5	121.2	120.0
1903	122.7	118.2	118.7	128.8	142.6	98.0	119.4	133.5	135.0	123.2	120.6
1904	122.8	118.5	117.8	119.9	141.7	97.7	117.2	141.8	142.1	123.4	120.2
1905	138.9	131.8	131.6	164.3	164.2	103.6	134.1	151.5	161.0	142.3	139.3
1906	139.5	132.9	128.5	179.4	185.0	114.4	145.6	174.7	175.9	150.8	148.7
1907	129.4	134.3	115.5	181.0	162.2	120.3	143.0	189.5	179.9	149.5	149.1
1908	133.2	123.8	102.3	109.6	148.9	116.0	119.3	158.1	177.5	133.2	126.4
1909	141.1	151.4	126.7	174.3	193.0	129.0	155.0	190.7	194.7	160.3	158.3
1910	131.7	143.4	121.4	185.9	200.0	125.9	165.6	190.1	185.1	157.2	157.2
1911	138.4	132.5	118.0	162.4	201.8	118.6	160.6	196.7	203.7	155.5	150.7
1912	148.1	150.6	139.2	204.0	220.3	121.1	173.8	198.7	228.8	174.5	168.9
1913	150.2	158.0	127.2	214.3	229.1	115.6	183.5	236.9	235.9	180.1	176.3
1914	152.5	159.5	126.3	164.6	206.7	103.9	168.6	239.1	234.1	170.6	165.6
1915	169.1	164.4	121.2	211.7	257.7	99.0	182.4	243.9	253.8	186.8	181.4
1916	149.7	198.5	134.8	278.4	331.8	105.3	210.9	272.2	311.5	217.6	214.1
1917	158.0	186.7	156.9	275.3	321.0	96.4	199.3	270.3	326.5	218.5	210.8
1918	192.2	182.3	180.9	283.6	362.7	87.6	171.3	268.4	392.0	237.3	219.0
1919	188.7	164.7	144.5	231.5	318.5	94.0	148.6	273.2	331.1	209.7	203.4
1920	172.1	148.9	128.6	271.6	392.3	82.0	183.9	319.8	382.7	223.6	218.7
1921	176.4	159.5	123.1	131.0	211.8	75.1	138.6	255.2	312.9	180.6	166.5
1922	200.2	192.5	140.0	222.7	391.9	88.5	189.4	341.9	363.6	229.2	220.9
1923	210.6	202.5	152.6	303.7	400.3	103.5	231.2	374.6	414.2	260.3	253.7
1924	224.7	171.9	126.0	256.2	341.4	100.1	243.4	391.0	414.5	247.1	234.7
1925	219.6	196.5	135.0	304.4	421.7	106.8	266.1	417.4	465.6	274.2	261.5
1926	223.7	198.3	138.0	323.9	427.3	103.5	266.1	470.7	492.0	284.5	273.9

For intercensus years the index numbers have been obtained by interpolation (for method see Douglas, Paul H., *Real Wages in the United States*, Appendix F) using Day's unadjusted annual indexes of the physical volume of production: *Review of Economic Statistics*, 1923, p. 193; 1926, p. 148; *Journal of the American Statistical Association*, 1921, p. 557. Census figures were obtained from *The Growth of Manufactures 1899-1923*, Census Monograph VIII. The Manufacturing Production Index is a weighted average of the nine groups.

TABLE II

WHOLESALE PRICE INDEXES, 1899 = 100

Year	Food Excluding Bread[1]	Textiles[2]	Leather[3]	Iron and Steel[4]	Non-Ferrous Metals[5]	Lumber[6]	Stone, Clay and Glass[7]	Paper and Pulp[8]	Chemicals[9]	Manufacturing Weighed by Value Added in Manufacturing in 1923[10]	B. of L. St. All Commodity Index[11]	Manufacturing Weighted by Number Employed
1899	100.0	100.0	100.0	100.0	100.0	100.0	100.0	100.0	100.0	100.0	100.0	100.0
1900	106.5	111.7	100.0	105.2	94.2	107.4	102.8	121.2	101.2	105.8	107.5	107.5
1901	105.9	100.8	99.0	101.0	93.7	100.7	99.6	111.6	103.8	102.1	105.9	101.8
1902	111.7	103.6	102.8	101.5	74.4	109.5	96.4	114.0	106.7	104.6	112.8	104.2
1903	109.0	110.7	101.0	94.0	83.2	114.8	98.6	119.8	103.7	105.0	114.2	106.0
1904	113.2	110.9	100.6	79.0	80.6	116.6	84.2	124.6	103.7	103.0	114.4	103.0
1905	115.5	113.4	109.1	83.1	94.1	124.5	84.4	117.4	101.5	105.6	115.1	106.2
1906	111.9	123.1	116.8	90.1	114.0	141.8	91.4	109.2	94.7	109.8	118.4	113.0
1907	119.5	133.1	117.4	96.7	120.4	151.0	87.4	117.5	96.8	115.5	124.9	119.8
1908	123.1	114.9	112.6	88.8	81.5	143.0	76.0	116.3	98.2	108.6	120.5	110.1
1909	131.2	118.4	124.5	84.0	81.9	147.4	77.7	104.6	98.5	110.8	129.5	111.3
1910	136.1	122.4	121.9	85.3	82.5	149.9	80.5	104.6	101.1	113.3	134.9	113.6
1911	130.0	116.4	119.0	79.1	82.2	150.7	78.5	104.6	100.6	109.9	124.3	110.1
1912	140.0	116.8	130.6	78.2	101.7	157.3	75.7	108.1	99.5	113.5	132.4	113.6
1913	134.6	120.1	137.9	84.1	96.3	161.8	85.9	110.5	98.9	115.4	133.7	116.8
1914	135.6	114.5	143.5	72.8	82.7	149.5	78.1	108.3	100.4	111.5	130.5	109.9
1915	137.1	113.4	152.8	76.7	117.6	146.0	82.4	105.5	138.1	121.3	133.1	114.6
1916	158.7	147.6	189.1	130.1	173.5	165.0	102.0	165.6	198.2	160.5	163.8	153.6
1917	219.1	206.9	250.6	209.6	179.5	216.3	127.3	209.7	203.5	207.4	225.1	228.1
1918	249.7	287.6	254.5	174.4	156.4	250.2	153.9	198.5	224.8	231.4	251.5	228.9
1919	271.5	283.6	352.4	154.2	128.8	338.7	168.8	214.1	193.6	242.0	265.5	235.6
1920	288.1	345.5	346.8	186.3	128.1	495.0	197.8	338.2	203.1	284.8	295.8	290.3
1921	189.9	198.1	221.1	129.8	84.8	266.4	166.6	200.2	141.8	179.3	187.0	183.0
1922	183.6	210.1	211.7	116.4	90.5	296.9	157.6	170.4	123.7	176.1	185.2	181.3
1923	194.3	233.3	210.9	139.1	103.2	335.0	173.9	191.2	124.7	191.2	192.7	199.0
1924	190.8	223.7	205.5	129.8	100.7	297.6	165.6	187.3	121.9	182.8	187.9	188.2
1925	210.1	227.0	213.2	121.2	109.8	301.5	154.6	195.7	125.5	186.8	198.3	191.6
1926	209.6	209.6	202.4	118.6	108.3	299.7	155.2	186.0	123.3	180.2	191.6	184.7
1927	....	200.6	218.4	113.8	99.4	277.2	143.3	171.5	119.1	....	182.8	....
1928	....	201.9	246.4	112.6	101.1	270.1	141.5	166.3	117.8	....	....	....

[1] U. S. Bureau of Labor Statistics, Bulletin No. 543, p. 38, minus bread. [2] *Idem.* [3] *Ibid.*, Hides and Leather Products. [4] For 1913 to 1928 *ibid.*, p. 19; prior to 1913 a weighted index was computed using the eight most important products, the weights being the quantities marketed in 1919. [5] For 1913 to 1928, *ibid.*, p. 19; prior to 1913 a weighted index was computed using the six most important products, the weights being the quantities marketed in 1919. [6] For 1913 to 1928, *ibid.*, p. 22; prior to 1913 a weighted index was computed using seven kinds of lumber, the weights being the quantities marketed in 1919. [7] For 1899 to 1928 the index is a weighted average of brick, cement, lime, glass, plate and two kinds of window glass, the weights being the quantities marketed in 1919. [8] For 1913 to 1928, *ibid.*, p. 30; prior to 1913 the index is a weighted average of newsprint and wrapping paper, the weights being the quantities marketed in 1919. [9] For 1899 to 1928, *ibid.*, p. 38. [10] The index is a weighted average of the nine groups. [11] *ibid.*, p. 38.

TABLE III

Exchange Value = Ratio of Wholesale Prices to General Price Level: Nine Groups and Manufacturing

Price Relative

Value = All Commodity Index

Year	Food	Textiles	Leather	Iron and Steel	Non-Ferrous Metals	Lumber	Stone, Clay and Glass	Paper and Pulp	Chemicals	Manufacturing Weighted by Value Added in Manufacturing in 1923	Manufacturing Weighted by Number Employed
1899	100.0	100.0	100.0	100.0	100.0	100.0	100.0	100.0	100.0	100.0	100.0
1900	99.1	103.9	93.9	97.9	87.6	99.9	95.6	112.7	94.1	98.4	100.0
1901	100.0	95.2	93.5	95.4	88.5	95.1	94.1	105.4	98.0	96.4	96.1
1902	99.0	91.8	91.1	90.0	66.0	97.1	85.5	101.1	94.6	92.7	92.4
1903	95.4	96.9	88.4	82.3	72.9	100.5	86.3	104.9	90.8	91.9	92.8
1904	99.0	96.9	87.9	69.1	70.5	101.9	73.6	108.9	90.6	90.0	90.0
1905	100.3	98.5	94.8	72.2	81.8	108.2	73.3	102.0	88.2	91.7	92.3
1906	94.5	104.0	98.6	76.1	96.3	119.8	77.2	92.2	80.0	92.7	95.4
1907	95.7	106.6	94.0	77.4	96.4	120.9	70.0	94.1	77.5	92.5	95.9
1908	102.2	95.4	93.4	73.7	67.6	118.7	63.1	96.5	81.5	90.1	91.3
1909	101.3	91.4	96.1	64.9	63.2	113.8	60.0	80.8	76.1	85.6	85.9
1910	100.9	90.7	90.4	63.2	61.2	111.1	59.7	77.5	74.9	84.0	84.2
1911	104.6	93.6	95.7	63.6	66.1	121.2	63.2	84.2	80.9	88.4	88.6
1912	105.7	88.2	98.6	59.1	76.8	118.9	57.2	81.6	75.2	85.7	85.8
1913	100.7	89.8	103.1	62.9	72.0	121.0	64.2	82.6	74.0	86.3	87.4
1914	103.9	87.7	110.0	55.8	63.4	114.6	59.8	83.0	76.9	85.2	84.2
1915	103.0	85.2	114.8	57.6	88.4	109.7	61.9	79.3	103.8	90.7	86.1
1916	96.9	90.1	115.4	79.4	105.9	100.7	62.3	101.1	121.0	97.6	93.8
1917	97.3	91.9	111.3	93.1	79.7	96.1	56.6	93.2	90.4	91.7	101.3
1918	99.3	114.4	101.2	69.3	62.2	99.5	61.2	78.9	89.4	91.7	91.0
1919	102.3	106.8	132.7	58.1	48.5	127.6	63.6	80.6	72.9	90.6	88.7
1920	97.4	116.8	117.2	63.0	43.3	167.3	66.9	114.3	68.7	95.8	98.1
1921	101.6	105.9	118.2	69.4	45.3	142.5	89.1	107.1	75.8	95.6	97.9
1922	99.1	113.4	114.3	62.9	48.9	160.3	85.1	92.0	66.8	94.8	97.9
1923	100.8	121.1	109.4	72.2	53.6	173.8	90.2	99.2	64.7	99.3	103.3
1924	101.5	119.1	109.4	69.1	53.6	152.0	88.1	99.7	64.9	97.0	100.2
1925	106.0	114.5	107.5	61.1	55.4	158.4	88.1	98.7	63.3	94.0	96.6
1926	109.4	109.4	105.6	61.9	56.5	152.0	78.0	97.1	64.4	94.4	96.4
1927	.....	109.7	119.5	62.3	54.4	156.0	81.0	93.8	65.2	.....	.....
1928	.....	107.9	131.6	60.1	54.0	151.6	78.4	88.8	62.9	.....	.....

Derived from Table II.

TABLE IV

RELATIVE TOTAL VALUE PRODUCT FOR NINE GROUPS AND ALL MANUFACTURING

Year	Food	Textiles	Leather	Iron and Steel	Non-Ferrous Metals	Lumber	Stone, Clay and Glass	Paper and Pulp	Chemicals	Manufacturing Weighted by Value Added in Manufacturing in 1923	Manufacturing Weighted by Number Employed
1899	100.0	100.0	100.0	100.0	100.0	100.0	100.0	100.0	100.0	100.0	100.0
1900	99.4	105.0	92.5	93.4	89.7	99.4	95.1	122.1	95.7	98.6	100.2
1901	122.2	97.7	98.2	111.9	100.2	94.1	106.7	123.0	111.4	105.6	105.2
1902	114.8	108.0	106.9	119.7	96.4	95.6	106.2	126.5	120.6	111.2	110.9
1903	117.1	114.6	104.9	106.0	104.0	98.5	103.0	140.0	122.6	110.8	111.9
1904	121.6	114.8	103.5	82.9	99.9	99.6	86.3	154.4	128.7	108.2	108.2
1905	139.3	129.8	124.8	118.6	134.3	112.1	98.3	154.5	142.0	127.7	128.6
1906	131.8	138.2	126.7	136.5	178.2	137.1	112.4	161.1	140.7	137.8	141.9
1907	123.8	143.2	108.6	140.1	156.4	145.4	100.1	178.3	139.4	137.9	143.0
1908	136.1	118.1	95.5	80.8	100.7	137.7	75.3	152.6	144.7	113.9	115.4
1909	142.9	138.4	121.8	113.1	122.0	146.8	93.0	154.1	148.2	135.5	136.0
1910	132.9	130.1	109.7	117.5	122.4	139.9	98.9	147.3	138.6	132.0	132.4
1911	144.8	124.0	112.9	103.3	133.4	143.7	101.5	165.6	164.8	133.2	133.5
1912	156.5	132.8	137.3	120.6	169.2	144.0	99.4	162.1	172.1	144.7	144.4
1913	151.3	141.9	131.1	134.8	165.0	139.9	117.8	195.7	174.6	152.1	154.1
1914	158.4	139.9	138.9	91.8	131.0	119.1	100.8	198.5	180.0	141.1	139.4
1915	174.2	140.1	139.1	121.9	227.8	108.6	112.9	193.4	263.4	164.5	156.2
1916	145.1	178.8	155.6	221.0	351.4	106.0	131.4	275.2	376.9	209.0	200.8
1917	153.7	171.6	174.6	256.3	255.8	92.6	112.8	251.9	295.2	193.3	213.5
1918	190.9	209.3	183.1	196.5	225.6	87.2	104.8	211.8	350.4	200.8	199.3
1919	193.0	175.9	191.8	134.5	154.5	119.9	94.5	220.2	241.4	184.3	180.4
1920	167.6	173.9	150.7	171.1	169.9	137.2	123.0	365.5	262.9	209.5	214.5
1921	179.2	168.9	145.5	90.9	95.9	107.0	123.5	273.3	237.2	159.2	163.0
1922	198.4	218.3	160.0	140.1	191.6	141.9	161.2	314.5	242.9	209.4	216.3
1923	212.3	245.2	166.9	219.3	214.6	179.9	208.5	371.6	268.0	251.9	262.1
1924	228.1	204.7	137.8	177.0	183.0	158.6	214.4	389.8	269.0	227.7	235.2
1925	232.8	225.0	145.1	186.0	233.6	162.3	207.6	412.0	294.7	245.8	252.6
1926	244.7	216.9	145.7	200.5	241.4	161.5	215.5	457.0	316.8	258.6	264.0

Derived from Tables I and III.

508

TABLE V

Employment Index: Nine Industries and Manufacturing, 1899-1927

Year	Food	Textiles	Leather	Iron and Steel	Non-Ferrous Metals	Lumber	Stone, Clay and Glass	Paper and Printing	Chemicals	Manufacturing
1899	100.0	100.0	100.0	100.0	100.0	100.0	100.0	100.0	100.0	100.0
1900	100.9	104.8	97.3	101.0	112.8	99.5	97.6	112.1	99.7	102.9
1901	101.4	107.3	103.7	107.4	114.8	101.9	102.5	104.9	106.9	105.2
1902	105.7	115.4	102.9	124.5	122.8	111.2	120.6	138.8	114.5	116.1
1903	113.9	116.9	107.5	132.1	122.7	116.0	124.0	139.8	122.4	119.5
1904	113.4	113.8	102.8	111.9	112.5	110.7	117.7	124.3	119.7	113.8
1905	118.6	121.8	111.4	143.6	144.7	121.1	143.6	141.0	114.3	126.0
1906	118.8	125.7	118.9	176.1	163.1	132.5	153.4	146.5	116.2	134.2
1907	128.4	124.7	123.6	196.3	168.9	133.8	156.6	148.8	126.5	138.2
1908	123.6	119.5	112.7	122.1	135.3	124.1	129.5	136.9	149.6	125.5
1909	138.7	143.0	122.9	131.1	145.1	138.8	143.0	153.3	147.5	140.9
1910	135.6	138.7	126.0	162.3	162.8	141.0	153.7	181.4	160.3	147.1
1911	140.2	140.9	126.3	146.2	168.0	138.8	151.7	164.3	167.4	145.8
1912	158.1	147.0	137.4	156.7	178.5	145.7	146.3	158.8	173.2	152.2
1913	158.4	147.7	128.9	160.5	175.9	145.0	148.7	184.0	173.9	154.3
1914	168.8	150.3	123.3	132.7	154.7	128.1	141.3	170.3	168.4	147.5
1915	166.8	152.3	123.8	138.3	153.8	126.4	126.6	169.3	200.2	148.8
1916	182.1	159.2	144.4	186.7	203.7	137.6	138.6	187.3	247.4	167.3
1917	195.6	164.4	129.1	210.7	212.7	136.3	145.1	197.0	274.7	173.9
1918	212.2	160.7	127.4	216.3	198.8	127.1	117.6	193.5	295.7	171.2
1919	236.3	163.2	143.0	202.4	204.7	130.5	129.3	195.5	246.0	173.6
1920	220.2	162.1	129.6	219.4	224.6	126.1	132.3	213.5	245.5	173.8
1921	193.5	152.3	114.0	126.3	143.3	106.1	108.6	182.4	182.3	144.4
1922	198.9	160.4	127.7	153.8	171.1	133.0	127.7	193.0	189.2	159.4
1923	210.5	174.4	140.0	203.0	196.8	139.4	148.5	208.3	223.7	176.3
1924	208.4	158.7	125.3	185.5	177.1	136.9	147.3	210.0	210.9	167.1
1925	203.6	165.0	128.0	193.9	184.0	138.8	150.9	214.5	219.4	171.0
1926	206.2	164.5	128.3	203.0	190.6	138.2	155.7	221.8	228.6	173.6
1927	210.3	171.3	128.1	189.2	182.2	128.5	150.0	223.5	231.9	172.7

The manufacturing index is a weighted average of nine groups, the weights being the number employed in census years. For explanation see text, chapter VIII, pp. 180 ff.

TABLE VI

VALUE PRODUCT PER EMPLOYEE: NINE INDUSTRIES AND MANUFACTURING, 1899–1926

Year	Food	Textiles	Leather	Iron and Steel	Non-Ferrous Metals	Lumber	Stone, Clay and Glass	Paper and Printing	Chemicals	Manufacturing Weighted by Value Added in 1923	Manufacturing Weighted by Number Employed
1899	100.0	100.0	100.0	100.0	100.0	100.0	100.0	100.0	100.0	100.0	100.0
1900	98.5	100.2	95.1	92.5	79.5	99.9	97.4	108.9	96.0	95.8	97.4
1901	120.5	91.1	94.7	104.2	87.3	92.3	104.1	117.3	104.2	100.4	100.0
1902	108.6	93.6	103.9	96.1	78.5	86.0	88.1	91.1	105.3	95.8	95.5
1903	103.3	98.0	97.6	80.2	92.3	84.9	83.1	100.1	100.2	92.7	93.6
1904	107.2	100.9	100.7	74.1	88.8	90.0	73.3	124.2	107.5	95.1	95.1
1905	117.5	106.6	112.0	82.6	92.8	92.6	68.5	109.6	124.2	101.3	102.1
1906	110.9	109.9	106.6	77.5	109.3	103.5	73.3	110.0	121.1	102.7	105.7
1907	96.4	114.8	87.9	71.4	92.6	108.7	63.9	119.8	110.2	99.8	103.5
1908	110.1	98.8	84.7	66.2	74.4	111.0	58.1	111.5	96.7	90.8	92.0
1909	103.0	96.8	99.1	86.3	84.1	105.8	65.0	100.5	100.5	96.2	96.5
1910	98.0	93.8	87.1	72.4	75.2	99.2	64.3	81.2	86.5	89.7	90.0
1911	103.2	88.0	89.4	70.7	79.4	103.5	66.9	100.8	98.4	91.4	91.6
1912	99.0	90.3	99.9	77.0	94.8	98.8	67.9	102.1	99.4	95.1	95.2
1913	95.5	96.1	101.7	84.0	93.8	96.5	79.2	106.4	100.4	98.6	99.9
1914	93.8	93.1	112.7	69.2	84.7	93.0	71.3	116.6	106.9	95.7	94.5
1915	104.4	92.0	112.4	88.1	148.1	85.9	89.2	114.2	131.6	110.6	105.0
1916	79.7	112.3	107.8	118.4	172.5	77.0	94.8	146.9	152.3	124.9	120.0
1917	78.6	104.4	135.2	121.6	120.3	67.9	77.7	127.9	107.5	111.2	122.8
1918	90.0	130.2	143.7	90.8	113.5	68.6	89.1	109.5	118.5	117.3	116.4
1919	81.7	107.8	134.1	66.5	75.5	91.9	73.1	112.6	98.1	106.2	103.9
1920	76.1	107.3	116.3	78.0	75.6	108.8	93.0	171.2	107.1	120.5	123.4
1921	92.6	110.9	127.6	72.0	66.9	100.8	113.7	149.8	130.1	110.2	112.9
1922	99.7	136.1	125.3	91.1	112.0	106.7	126.2	163.0	128.4	131.4	135.7
1923	100.9	140.6	119.2	108.0	109.0	129.1	140.4	178.4	119.8	142.9	148.7
1924	109.5	129.0	110.0	95.4	103.3	115.9	145.6	185.6	127.5	136.3	140.8
1925	114.3	136.4	113.4	95.9	127.0	116.9	137.5	192.1	134.3	143.7	147.7
1926	118.7	131.9	113.6	98.8	126.7	116.9	138.4	206.0	138.6	149.0	152.1

Derived from Tables IV and V.

510

TABLE VII

INDEX OF MONEY WAGES: NINE GROUPS AND MANUFACTURING, 1899–1927[1]

Year	Food	Textiles	Leather	Iron and Steel	Non-Ferrous Metals	Lumber	Stone, Clay and Glass	Paper and Printing	Chemicals	Manufacturing[2]
1899	100.0	100.0	100.0	100.0	100.0	100.0	100.0	100.0	100.0	100.0
1900	....	104.6	98.7	104.4	100.5	106.1	103.2	100.0	105.0	103.6
1901	....	105.2	103.8	110.5	101.2	109.4	106.3	105.2	107.9	106.4
1902	....	111.5	105.8	114.0	107.1	115.5	110.5	105.3	109.8	110.9
1903	....	113.5	110.8	117.3	111.8	117.1	114.6	112.6	104.6	113.6
1904	113.0	109.1	111.7	109.4	112.5	122.3	117.8	113.6	111.5	113.6
1905	....	112.8	115.1	116.2	124.8[1]	115.9	121.9	114.5	108.5	115.3
1906	....	119.8	119.5	123.0	114.6	127.3	133.7	117.6	111.5	121.6
1907	....	127.4	125.1	127.9	115.0	128.0	129.9	118.5	122.5	125.8
1908	....	123.6	125.2	113.4	109.5	126.3	119.6	124.5	122.6	122.7
1909	127.8	126.1	126.4	126.9	121.5	127.1	126.5	126.6	126.6	126.4
1910	130.2	127.7	130.8	132.0	119.1	113.2	130.5	128.6	124.6	125.5
1911	132.8	132.4	134.2	131.5	119.3	117.8	130.7	130.7	127.1	128.5
1912	136.9	135.7	134.1	135.5	137.9	128.1	137.5	138.2	135.2	134.9
1913	142.1	142.7	140.8	151.4	140.2	144.6	147.2	144.6	146.2	144.1
1914	143.3	139.0	140.8	144.8	133.8	146.0	142.6	144.3	150.5	142.5
1915	138.7	142.8	141.1	132.5	131.5	143.5	134.9	144.9	151.1	141.1
1916	149.9	161.7	156.7	160.3	150.7	158.4	140.3	147.5	164.3	155.3
1917	168.4	188.5	176.8	209.8	164.7	180.7	161.9	155.6	189.2	177.7
1918	212.7	236.6	217.3	279.6	199.5	228.6	207.5	191.6	219.7	222.3
1919	252.5	284.5	267.7	307.6	234.7	273.9	252.1	233.5	267.7	265.6
1920	291.1	344.2	302.0	373.4	287.7	321.3	316.6	291.4	303.0	316.6
1921	279.8	293.0	276.3	271.6	245.7	272.3	280.8	282.1	275.2	278.6
1922	263.0	282.5	270.8	247.2	248.6	267.4	267.3	285.5	273.8	270.5
1923	278.1	306.8	278.8	300.9	286.2	287.8	294.3	292.8	290.1	292.0
1924	281.7	295.1	276.6	301.8	281.0	293.0	303.1	301.6	297.6	291.7
1925	285.6	308.0	278.8	306.6	274.2	296.1	305.8	310.7	302.9	297.8
1926	288.2	310.5	287.2	312.7	291.7	300.2	308.2	321.9	303.5	302.9
1927	295.0	316.0	285.8	310.9	283.2	305.9	309.5	326.5	306.8	306.1

[1] For explanation see text, chapter VIII, 2.
[2] 1899–1909 weighted average of eight groups only (no data for the food group). Weights are the number employed in census years.

TABLE VIII

Index of Real Wages: Nine Groups and Manufacturing, 1899–1926

Year	Food	Textiles	Leather	Iron and Steel	Non-Ferrous Metals	Lumber	Stone, Clay and Glass	Paper and Printing	Chemicals	Manufacturing[1]
1899	100.0	100.0	100.0	100.0	100.0	100.0	100.0	100.0	100.0	100.0
1900	....	101.8	96.1	101.7	97.8	103.3	100.5	97.4	102.2	100.9
1901	....	99.8	98.5	104.8	96.0	103.8	100.9	99.8	102.4	100.9
1902	....	103.1	97.9	105.5	99.1	106.8	102.2	97.4	101.6	102.6
1903	....	100.0	97.6	103.3	98.5	103.2	101.0	99.2	92.2	100.1
1904	100.7	97.2	99.6	97.5	100.3	109.0	105.0	99.2	92.2	101.2
1905	....	100.5	102.6	103.6	111.2	103.3	108.6	101.2	96.7	102.8
1906	....	103.1	102.8	105.9	98.6	109.6	115.1	102.0	96.0	104.6
1907	....	103.6	101.7	104.0	93.5	104.1	105.6	101.2	99.6	102.3
1908	108.7	105.1	106.5	96.4	93.1	107.4	101.7	96.3	104.3	104.3
1909	104.7	107.2	107.5	107.9	103.3	108.1	107.6	105.9	107.7	107.5
1910	103.4	102.7	105.2	106.2	95.8	91.1	105.0	105.7	100.2	101.0
1911	105.6	103.1	104.5	102.4	92.9	91.7	101.8	103.5	99.0	100.1
1912	106.2	104.6	103.4	104.5	106.3	98.8	106.0	101.8	104.2	104.0
1913	106.1	106.7	105.2	113.2	104.8	108.1	110.0	106.6	109.3	107.7
1914	104.8	102.9	104.2	107.2	99.0	108.1	105.6	108.1	111.4	105.5
1915	103.7	107.9	106.6	100.1	99.3	108.4	101.9	106.8	114.1	106.6
1916	96.6	111.8	108.4	110.9	104.2	109.5	97.0	109.4	113.6	107.4
1917	100.2	108.1	101.4	120.4	94.5	103.7	92.9	102.0	108.5	102.0
1918	105.0	111.5	102.4	131.8	94.0	107.7	97.8	89.3	103.5	104.8
1919	104.6	118.3	111.3	127.9	97.6	113.9	104.8	90.3	111.3	110.4
1920	117.0	123.6	108.5	134.1	103.3	115.4	113.7	97.1	108.8	113.7
1921	117.9	122.5	115.5	113.5	102.7	113.8	117.4	104.7	115.1	116.5
1922	122.5	126.7	121.4	110.9	111.5	119.9	119.9	117.9	122.8	121.3
1923	123.3	135.2	122.8	132.6	126.1	126.8	129.6	128.0	127.8	128.6
1924	122.2	129.2	121.1	132.1	123.0	128.3	132.7	129.0	130.3	127.7
1925	122.5	131.7	119.2	131.1	117.3	126.6	130.8	132.0	129.6	127.4
1926		132.0	122.1	133.0	124.0	127.6	131.0	136.9	129.0	128.8

[1] A weighted average of nine groups (for the years 1899–1908 of eight groups only). The weights are the number employed in census years.

Source: The indexes of Money Wages as given in Table VII divided by a Cost of Living Index (Douglas, Paul H., *Real Wages in the United States 1890–1926*, p. 60.)

TABLE IX

RELATIVE MOVEMENT OF REAL WAGES AND OF AVERAGE VALUE PRODUCTIVITY
PER EMPLOYEE IN MANUFACTURING, 1899–1926
(1899 = 100)

Year	Relative Real Wages (1)	Relative Average Value Productivity (2)	Relation of Average Value Productivity to Real Wages in Points[1] (3) = (2) − (1)	Percentage Deviation of Relative Value Productivity from Real Wages[2] $(4) = \dfrac{(2) - (1)}{(1)}$
1899	100	100	0	0
1900	101	96	−5	−4.9
1901	101	100	−1	−1.0
1902	103	96	−7	−6.8
1903	100	93	−7	−7.0
1904	101	95	−6	−5.9
1905	103	101	−2	−1.9
1906	105	103	−2	−1.9
1907	102	100	−2	−2.0
1908	104	91	−13	−12.5
1909	108	96	−12	−11.1
1910	101	90	−11	−10.9
1911	100	91	−9	−9.0
1912	104	95	−9	−8.7
1913	108	99	−9	−8.3
1914	106	96	−10	−9.4
1915	107	111	+4	+3.7
1916	107	125	+18	+16.8
1917	102	111	+9	+8.8
1918	105	117	+12	+11.4
1919	110	106	−4	−3.6
1920	114	121	+7	+6.1
1921	117	110	−7	−6.0
1922	121	131	+10	+8.3
1923	129	143	+14	+10.9
1924	128	136	+8	+6.2
1925	127	144	+17	+13.4
1926	129	149	+20	+15.5

[1] Sum of deviations in points *without* regard to sign $(\Sigma d) = 235$

Average deviation in points, *i.e.* $\dfrac{(\Sigma d)}{N}$ 235 ÷ 27 = 8.7 *without* regard to sign

Sum of deviations in points *with* regard to sign = + 3
Average deviation in points *with* regard to sign = 0.1

[2] Sum of deviations in percentages *without* regard to sign $(\Sigma d) = 212.0$
Average deviation in percentages *without* regard to sign $\dfrac{(\Sigma d)}{N}$ *i.e.* 212 ÷ 27 = 7.8

Sum of deviations in percentages *with* regard to sign = 9.8
Average deviation in percentages *with* regard to sign = 0.36

TABLE X

PROPORTION OF MALES IN EACH AGE GROUP GAINFULLY EMPLOYED IN
AMERICAN CITIES, 1920

	14 Years	15 Years	16 Years	17 Years	18–19 Years	20–24 Years	25–44 Years	45–64 Years	65 & Year Over
Atlanta, Ga..............	31.8	49.9	65.7	73.3	83.7	94.0	98.0	96.5	67.9
Baltimore, Md............	18.9	44.6	67.6	79.5	88.1	94.6	97.9	95.4	63.3
Boston, Mass............	13.7	33.4	54.4	70.4	82.2	90.9	98.0	95.4	62.6
Bridgeport, Conn.........	14.9	39.1	65.0	77.5	85.8	94.1	97.8	94.0	60.1
Buffalo, N. Y............	5.4	28.4	58.9	73.8	82.4	92.4	97.4	93.2	57.7
Chicago, Ill..............	13.7	38.9	63.9	76.4	85.9	93.5	98.1	95.1	59.6
Cincinnati, Ohio..........	4.2	29.8	61.4	77.6	85.6	93.0	97.5	94.3	60.1
Cleveland, Ohio..........	3.2	25.7	59.7	74.6	85.4	94.6	98.2	94.6	58.0
Columbus, Ohio..........	6.4	20.7	45.8	60.6	75.7	86.9	96.0	93.8	60.5
Dallas, Tex..............	15.5	34.4	49.5	65.7	79.3	92.1	98.0	95.0	62.4
Denver, Colo............	15.1	30.9	49.1	62.9	74.1	89.0	96.9	94.1	60.9
Detroit, Mich............	5.0	20.4	61.0	78.6	89.5	96.2	98.6	94.9	58.2
Fall River, Mass.........	52.7	72.9	80.9	86.5	90.1	94.3	98.4	94.2	55.6
Houston, Tex............	19.3	43.2	61.9	74.3	85.7	94.6	98.6	95.9	64.3
Indianapolis, Ind.........	17.1	38.6	63.5	74.3	84.5	93.2	98.0	94.9	63.6
Kansas City, Mo.........	10.6	29.1	52.1	65.8	78.7	91.7	97.5	95.3	63.6
Los Angeles, Cal.........	5.8	17.6	40.3	58.7	75.3	89.0	96.6	88.8	47.1
Louisville, Ky...........	14.1	32.3	63.5	77.6	87.5	95.6	98.3	95.7	63.6
Memphis, Tenn..........	17.2	36.8	58.5	70.6	84.4	93.6	97.6	96.2	67.1
Milwaukee, Wis..........	22.2	42.4	61.1	77.4	85.9	93.3	98.4	95.3	60.4
Minneapolis, Minn........	5.8	15.8	43.9	60.3	73.0	87.0	97.5	94.4	61.6
New Haven, Conn........	20.7	46.5	64.5	73.4	80.4	90.3	98.1	94.8	62.3
New Orleans, La.........	28.3	50.6	68.8	80.5	88.3	93.8	97.7	94.5	60.8
New York, N. Y.........	6.9	34.1	65.1	78.8	86.9	94.1	98.1	93.4	56.9
Newark, N. J............	14.2	41.7	66.8	77.0	85.5	95.1	98.2	94.9	61.8
Norfolk, Va..............	21.4	40.8	59.2	79.1	88.9	95.6	98.2	96.1	67.3
Omaha, Nebr............	8.3	23.8	50.3	67.0	80.0	92.1	97.7	94.4	59.8
Philadelphia, Pa..........	12.0	30.7	64.5	79.3	87.9	93.4	97.2	94.7	63.2
Pittsburgh, Pa...........	7.4	22.5	56.2	72.2	83.5	92.8	97.9	95.7	59.8
Portland, Ore............	12.9	23.2	45.3	58.1	71.3	86.2	97.6	95.5	50.8
Providence, R. I.........	28.0	52.0	67.2	75.7	84.5	91.9	98.0	94.9	61.3
Richmond, Va............	19.0	42.0	61.5	74.7	82.7	90.3	96.6	94.1	60.7
Rochester, N. Y.........	6.8	31.2	62.8	74.6	83.7	92.1	97.6	93.9	60.1
St. Louis, Mo............	20.8	48.6	70.7	80.0	87.2	93.3	97.9	95.8	64.9
St. Paul, Minn...........	5.8	19.3	53.4	67.1	79.3	90.1	97.8	95.2	61.8
Salt Lake City, Utah......	9.0	19.9	36.7	52.2	71.1	87.4	97.4	95.4	63.5
San Francisco, Cal........	6.6	21.3	48.7	72.8	85.8	92.2	97.7	93.3	56.4
Scranton, Pa.............	12.1	32.2	66.4	79.5	86.2	93.9	98.0	95.3	61.6
Seattle, Wash...........	11.4	25.6	42.9	57.0	69.6	85.5	96.9	94.5	61.4
Washington, D. C........	11.5	28.4	49.0	64.3	80.6	91.4	96.8	93.5	63.2

14th Census of the United States, Vol. IV, Table 19, p. 452.

TABLE XI

PROPORTION OF FEMALES IN EACH AGE GROUP GAINFULLY EMPLOYED IN AMERICAN CITIES, 1920

	14 Years	15 Years	16 Years	17 Years	18–19 Years	20–24 Years	25–44 Years	45–64 Years	65 Years Over
Atlanta, Ga...............	10.5	25.4	40.7	49.1	52.3	51.8	41.6	31.8	16.1
Baltimore, Md............	12.8	32.3	58.2	65.6	62.5	47.7	31.4	23.6	10.6
Birmingham, Ala.........	5.4	11.9	27.5	33.5	41.7	37.7	31.3	26.0	11.0
Boston, Mass.............	8.3	21.9	43.1	59.8	71.2	61.7	35.8	26.6	10.8
Bridgeport, Conn........	15.4	35.5	57.8	67.1	71.7	52.0	27.2	17.4	6.8
Buffalo, N. Y............	4.2	22.6	51.5	63.7	65.7	48.0	23.4	15.3	6.2
Chicago, Ill..............	10.9	31.0	57.9	70.0	71.7	54.2	28.4	18.2	6.8
Cincinnati, Ohio.........	0.7	4.2	39.2	57.5	64.2	50.9	31.1	23.1	9.3
Cleveland, Ohio..........	0.9	5.3	38.1	61.4	66.3	45.2	24.4	15.5	5.7
Columbus, Ohio..........	0.8	3.7	21.2	37.7	50.5	44.8	28.6	21.3	7.8
Dallas, Tex..............	5.0	17.2	31.0	43.1	54.0	49.7	36.2	23.3	7.7
Denver, Colo.............	6.3	17.1	30.9	43.6	51.4	48.1	30.7	22.0	8.5
Detroit, Mich............	2.0	13.0	47.2	62.9	60.7	41.0	21.9	15.0	5.6
Fall River, Mass.........	46.8	63.0	78.2	79.9	82.6	71.3	44.4	27.4	9.1
Houston, Tex............	6.0	15.2	29.1	40.0	48.8	43.8	33.4	23.6	10.9
Indianapolis, Ind........	9.0	23.7	44.4	52.1	56.3	44.9	28.4	21.2	8.2
Kansas City, Mo.........	3.9	12.6	31.4	45.8	53.1	48.1	32.3	21.3	7.2
Los Angeles, Calif........	1.5	7.0	22.6	36.8	45.8	43.6	32.5	22.9	7.7
Louisville, Ky...........	7.2	20.3	44.8	56.5	58.5	51.0	36.5	27.6	12.9
Memphis, Tenn..........	7.9	16.6	30.6	42.4	48.3	46.8	38.1	31.8	15.8
Milwaukee, Wis..........	16.6	35.9	52.6	68.7	73.1	54.6	25.8	15.6	5.7
Minneapolis, Minn.......	2.8	8.1	31.5	52.0	64.2	58.7	30.7	16.8	5.3
New Haven, Conn.......	15.8	33.2	54.9	63.5	69.9	56.0	28.3	20.2	8.9
New Orleans, La.........	11.1	25.2	38.3	48.6	50.2	42.2	33.7	27.2	13.6
New York, N. Y.........	4.5	27.0	58.6	73.8	75.0	56.2	29.3	19.8	8.3
Newark, N. J............	11.7	36.2	61.6	69.6	69.9	48.5	23.3	16.3	6.4
Norfolk, Va..............	6.3	18.0	30.8	41.7	49.1	44.8	34.6	28.7	12.2
Omaha, Nebr.............	2.8	14.2	35.9	50.7	58.4	51.5	29.6	18.0	5.3
Philadelphia, Pa.........	9.7	25.7	54.4	67.4	68.4	50.9	29.1	21.7	8.9
Pittsburgh, Pa...........	5.1	15.1	41.0	56.8	60.6	46.0	24.8	17.3	6.3
Portland, Ore............	1.9	7.2	26.6	41.6	52.6	48.6	30.2	20.6	6.0
Providence, R. I.........	25.2	43.8	60.6	68.3	73.3	61.6	35.4	24.0	9.0
Richmond, Va............	11.5	28.9	47.7	54.2	60.2	52.6	37.7	29.1	13.9
Rochester, N. Y.........	5.4	26.3	58.4	70.3	71.2	57.8	31.6	21.6	7.9
St. Louis, Mo............	12.8	36.5	57.8	66.4	64.8	50.6	30.5	21.5	9.3
St. Paul, Minn...........	2.5	11.4	41.8	60.2	68.0	57.9	30.0	16.5	5.3
Salt Lake City, Utah......	1.8	6.4	21.9	35.3	50.1	42.1	22.1	16.6	6.9
San Francisco, Calif......	1.7	9.4	31.6	48.8	59.6	53.1	33.7	22.9	8.0
Scranton, Pa.............	9.3	26.9	52.2	63.5	69.1	51.5	21.9	11.3	4.5
Seattle, Wash............	2.4	8.2	22.2	37.8	50.9	46.3	29.5	20.3	7.2
Washington, D. C........	4.5	14.1	35.9	50.6	65.8	68.7	52.4	37.5	15.7

14th Census of the United States, Vol. IV, Table 20, p. 454.

TABLE XII

PROPORTION OF NATIVE WHITES OF FOREIGN PARENTAGE, NEGROES AND FOREIGN BORN WHITES AND THE PROPORTION GAINFULLY EMPLOYED, IN 6 AGE GROUPS IN 38 AMERICAN CITIES, 1920

Females

	10-14			15-19			20-24		25-44		45-64		65 and over	
	z^1	x^1	u^1	z	x	u	z	x	z	x	z	x	z	x
Atlanta	33.0	3.4	3.1	35.0	45.2	2.3	38.3	51.8	36.8	41.6	33.1	31.8	29.0	16.1
Baltimore	15.4	2.9	20.6	21.2	57.1	17.0	26.7	47.7	31.3	31.4	31.2	23.6	35.8	10.6
Birmingham	39.4	1.9	5.4	43.2	32.3	3.7	47.6	37.7	46.0	31.3	42.2	26.0	37.4	11.0
Boston	9.1	1.7	50.7	16.5	54.0	44.7	28.9	61.7	48.7	35.8	53.5	26.6	51.3	10.8
Bridgeport	9.7	3.1	54.0	18.7	61.4	43.8	35.2	52.0	49.1	26.0	49.7	17.4	46.8	6.8
Buffalo	6.8	.9	38.1	11.5	54.1	36.6	17.5	48.0	31.0	23.4	41.6	15.3	54.6	6.2
Chicago	10.8	2.2	46.9	18.0	61.0	42.0	27.1	54.2	43.3	28.4	56.5	18.2	68.1	6.8
Cincinnati	9.4	.3	11.9	11.3	47.9	11.4	13.6	50.9	18.1	31.1	22.4	23.1	32.9	9.3
Cleveland	12.1	.3	47.2	21.3	49.1	37.7	32.6	45.2	45.3	24.4	52.3	15.5	61.9	5.7
Columbus	10.3	.2	8.8	12.0	34.2	8.4	14.4	44.8	16.5	28.6	16.5	21.3	23.0	7.8
Dallas	17.6	1.5	5.1	17.5	41.6	4.3	19.3	49.7	22.6	36.2	22.0	23.3	22.2	7.7
Denver	5.2	1.5	21.1	7.6	39.8	21.5	9.2	48.1	17.8	30.7	28.6	22.0	34.4	8.5
Detroit	15.2	.6	33.6	20.0	50.5	30.3	30.4	41.0	40.6	21.9	50.1	15.0	60.5	5.6
Houston	27.0	1.9	8.8	30.5	37.8	8.0	35.6	43.8	36.7	33.4	35.3	23.6	40.1	10.9
Indianapolis	12.5	2.1	6.3	12.4	47.7	5.8	14.4	44.9	17.5	28.4	17.6	21.2	25.8	8.2
Kansas City, Mo.	10.9	1.1	12.1	13.3	40.8	9.9	15.3	48.1	19.3	32.3	21.1	21.3	26.2	7.2
Los Angeles	12.0	.5	19.7	16.6	32.9	15.9	18.0	43.6	23.6	32.5	26.4	22.9	28.7	7.7
Louisville	14.9	1.8	5.1	16.3	49.0	6.2	20.8	51.0	24.1	36.5	24.8	27.6	39.6	12.9
Memphis	36.5	2.4	4.7	41.1	38.6	3.1	44.8	46.8	45.9	38.1	40.7	31.8	41.4	15.8
Milwaukee	6.9	3.1	34.4	10.5	61.5	35.0	12.5	54.6	26.4	25.8	45.2	15.6	71.3	5.7
Minneapolis	5.4	.7	38.3	8.8	47.0	29.6	12.4	58.7	26.2	30.7	44.1	16.8	54.1	5.3
New Haven	9.8	3.2	53.7	16.6	58.6	43.6	28.8	56.0	44.8	28.3	46.5	20.2	45.5	8.9
New Orleans	27.7	2.9	7.8	30.0	43.1	7.0	33.1	42.2	36.1	33.7	32.2	27.2	47.1	13.6

TABLE XII—Continued

PROPORTION OF NATIVE WHITES OF FOREIGN PARENTAGE, NEGROES AND FOREIGN BORN WHITES AND THE PROPORTION GAINFULLY EMPLOYED, IN 6 AGE GROUPS IN 38 AMERICAN CITIES, 1920

Females

	10–14			15–19			20–24		25–44		45–64		65 and over	
	z^1	x^1	u^1	z	x	u	z	x	z	x	z	x	z	x
New York	11.3	1.0	55.0	23.8	62.6	43.0	38.6	56.2	53.3	29.3	58.6	19.8	64.7	8.3
Newark	11.3	2.4	48.7	19.6	61.9	39.4	31.6	48.5	45.1	23.3	48.6	16.3	53.5	6.4
Norfolk	39.7	2.1	6.9	43.7	39.6	4.8	46.7	44.8	46.2	34.6	40.2	28.7	32.2	12.2
Omaha	9.0	.8	26.6	13.2	44.9	25.4	16.7	51.5	26.1	29.6	39.3	18.0	49.4	5.3
Philadelphia	11.9	2.0	35.7	19.9	57.6	29.4	29.2	50.9	38.8	29.1	39.5	21.7	41.0	8.9
Pittsburgh	9.5	1.1	36.0	14.5	47.5	32.7	22.7	46.0	34.7	24.8	40.2	17.3	46.5	6.3
Portland, Ore.	6.4	.6	18.3	9.2	37.4	17.3	10.4	48.6	19.1	30.2	28.2	20.6	34.0	6.0
Providence, R. I.	8.9	4.8	50.1	16.7	63.8	42.6	28.2	61.6	43.3	35.4	48.3	24.0	46.1	9.0
Richmond	31.2	2.8	3.7	35.1	51.7	2.3	37.6	52.6	37.3	37.7	32.1	13.9	37.0	13.9
Rochester	9.6	1.2	31.2	16.8	60.2	28.5	21.1	57.8	30.1	31.6	35.5	21.6	45.8	7.9
St. Louis, Mo.	11.3	2.8	16.9	14.4	58.9	14.4	17.2	50.6	23.5	30.5	28.2	21.5	52.7	9.3
St. Paul	6.1	.7	31.3	9.2	52.0	34.0	10.3	57.9	23.9	30.0	46.7	16.5	64.4	5.3
San Francisco	7.9	.6	32.3	12.7	43.6	28.9	16.6	53.1	28.8	33.7	39.7	22.9	60.6	8.0
Scranton	4.0	2.0	40.9	7.4	56.7	38.9	12.0	51.5	29.4	21.9	42.0	11.3	55.0	4.5
Seattle	8.2	.6	21.8	11.4	35.5	21.5	14.9	46.3	26.1	29.5	35.4	20.3	39.1	7.2

[1] x = Proportion Gainfully Employed; *14th Census*, Vol. IV, Table 20, p. 454.
z = Proportion of Negroes and Foreign Born Whites; *ibid.*, Vol. II, Tables 15 and 16, pp. 288 ff.
u = Proportion of Native Whites of Foreign Parentage; *idem.*

TABLE XIII

PROPORTION OF NATIVE WHITES OF FOREIGN PARENTAGE, NEGROES AND FOREIGN BORN WHITES AND THE PROPORTION GAINFULLY EMPLOYED, IN 6 AGE GROUPS IN 38 AMERICAN CITIES, 1920

Males

	10–14			15–19			20–24		25–44		45–64		65 and over	
	z^1	x^1	u^1	z	x	u	z	x	z	x	z	x	z	x
Atlanta	30.4	11.5	3.5	32.7	72.5	2.5	35.6	94.0	33.9	98.0	35.8	96.5	32.5	67.9
Baltimore	14.2	4.5	20.9	18.5	74.4	17.9	25.0	94.6	34.3	97.9	36.0	95.4	38.7	63.3
Birmingham	37.5	4.8	6.1	40.4	63.9	4.6	45.2	93.5	43.9	97.5	48.5	95.9	41.5	68.0
Boston	8.8	3.4	50.8	15.8	64.6	45.1	26.3	90.9	50.1	98.0	54.6	95.4	52.8	62.6
Bridgeport	9.9	3.4	55.0	19.6	70.9	42.3	32.5	94.1	55.5	97.8	54.4	94.0	50.6	60.1
Buffalo	6.7	1.4	38.6	11.1	65.5	36.7	17.8	92.4	37.4	97.4	46.0	93.2	58.7	57.7
Chicago	10.4	2.9	47.3	17.8	70.4	42.2	26.1	93.5	49.5	98.1	60.2	95.1	71.0	59.6
Cincinnati	8.6	1.8	11.6	10.7	68.8	12.1	13.6	93.0	20.7	97.5	28.2	94.3	48.0	60.1
Cleveland	11.7	1.4	47.3	20.6	66.6	38.1	32.3	94.6	58.2	98.2	58.1	94.6	66.2	58.0
Columbus	10.0	3.0	8.9	11.5	57.2	7.4	16.1	86.9	21.5	96.0	21.8	93.8	25.3	60.5
Dallas	15.9	5.5	5.7	18.4	63.5	5.0	20.6	92.1	23.6	98.0	27.7	95.0	26.3	62.4
Denver	5.2	4.8	21.6	8.0	59.2	20.7	11.5	89.0	21.1	96.9	31.6	94.1	39.3	60.9
Detroit	11.7	2.2	37.3	21.9	71.3	41.2	30.9	96.2	48.6	98.6	53.2	94.9	63.3	58.2
Houston	25.6	7.3	9.4	29.6	70.8	8.2	36.1	94.6	37.0	98.6	39.8	95.9	44.0	64.3
Indianapolis	11.9	6.9	6.2	12.6	70.5	5.5	14.9	93.2	19.6	98.0	21.0	94.9	27.3	63.6
Kansas City, Mo.	10.5	3.2	12.1	12.7	62.1	9.9	15.3	91.7	22.7	97.5	25.1	95.3	28.4	63.6
Los Angeles	12.1	2.6	19.6	16.7	55.0	15.8	19.8	89.0	27.9	96.6	31.3	88.8	32.9	47.1
Louisville	13.8	3.9	5.3	15.8	70.7	5.7	18.5	95.6	24.6	98.3	29.7	95.7	41.5	63.6
Memphis	34.6	6.1	5.5	40.2	68.5	3.7	41.5	93.6	43.3	97.6	44.7	96.2	46.0	67.1
Milwaukee	7.3	5.9	33.9	11.0	71.1	35.5	14.3	93.3	35.8	98.4	53.3	95.3	74.7	60.4
Minneapolis	5.6	2.5	32.3	9.1	54.0	34.8	14.0	87.0	34.6	97.5	49.5	94.4	55.8	61.6
New Haven	9.8	4.3	54.1	16.8	68.8	43.7	27.2	90.3	49.5	98.1	51.7	94.8	51.5	62.3
New Orleans	25.8	7.4	7.6	26.6	76.2	7.5	30.2	93.8	37.7	97.7	38.3	94.5	50.9	60.8

518

TABLE XIII—Continued

PROPORTION OF NATIVE WHITES OF FOREIGN PARENTAGE, NEGROES AND FOREIGN BORN WHITES AND THE PROPORTION GAINFULLY EMPLOYED, IN 6 AGE GROUPS IN 38 AMERICAN CITIES, 1920

Males

	10-14			15-19			20-24		25-44		45-64		65 and over	
	z^1	x^1	u^1	z	x	u	z	x	z	x	z	x	z	x
New York	11.1	1.5	55.3	22.5	70.6	43.7	34.6	94.1	57.1	98.1	62.5	93.4	67.9	56.9
Newark	11.0	3.1	39.4	19.2	71.5	38.8	28.4	95.1	50.1	98.2	54.4	94.9	57.8	61.8
Norfolk	36.9	7.6	7.3	42.7	74.5	5.7	45.2	95.6	48.3	98.2	45.9	96.1	37.4	67.3
Omaha	9.9	3.2	26.5	13.5	62.2	25.3	19.7	92.1	32.1	97.7	42.4	94.4	50.7	59.8
Philadelphia	11.3	2.6	36.3	18.6	70.7	30.1	27.1	93.4	42.5	97.2	43.9	94.7	43.9	63.2
Pittsburgh	9.1	1.8	36.6	13.8	63.7	32.3	23.6	92.8	41.2	97.9	47.4	95.7	52.4	59.8
Portland, Ore.	6.6	5.7	18.5	9.8	54.6	17.5	13.1	86.2	26.4	97.6	33.9	95.5	38.3	50.8
Providence	9.1	5.6	49.0	15.9	72.7	42.8	26.5	91.9	47.4	98.0	55.7	94.9	49.1	61.3
Richmond	29.4	5.8	4.0	30.8	69.7	3.0	35.9	90.3	36.5	96.6	35.9	94.1	29.0	60.7
Rochester	9.9	1.7	31.3	15.8	67.6	24.9	21.6	92.1	36.1	97.6	39.6	93.9	33.1	47.4
St. Louis, Mo.	10.4	4.6	17.6	13.8	75.2	14.7	17.3	93.3	28.2	97.9	35.5	95.8	55.0	64.9
St. Paul	5.4	2.0	30.2	9.0	61.1	34.7	12.5	90.1	31.0	97.8	51.6	95.2	68.5	68.5
San Francisco	7.8	2.2	32.3	11.6	67.8	23.8	19.0	92.2	37.5	97.7	46.0	93.3	63.5	56.4
Scranton	3.7	2.6	40.6	7.1	70.1	38.1	12.0	93.9	35.9	98.0	48.8	95.3	58.1	61.6
Seattle	7.9	4.8	22.3	11.0	54.2	20.6	16.8	85.5	34.2	96.9	40.5	94.5	43.0	61.4

[1] x = Proportion Gainfully Employed; *14th Census,* Vol. IV, Table 19, p. 452.
z = Proportion of Negroes and Foreign Born Whites; *ibid.,* Vol. II, Tables 15 and 16, pp. 288 ff.
u = Proportion of Native White of Foreign Parentage, *idem.*

TABLE XIV

CORRECTING THE AVERAGE MONEY WAGE IN MANUFACTURING FOR THE EFFECT OF WOMEN'S WAGES AND DIFFERENCES IN FOOD COST

	Wage Earners in Manufacturing [1]				Ratio of Female Earnings to Male Earnings	Col. 4 × Col. 5	Col. 6 Plus Col. 8 Denominator	Average Uncorrected Earnings	Earnings per Male Worker	Index A Costs of Food [3]	Earnings per Male Worker Corrected for Difference in Food Costs [3]
	Number		Proportion								
	Total	Males	Males	Females							
	1	2	3	4	5	6	7	8	9	10	11
Atlanta, Ga.	15739	11506	0.731	0.269	0.824	0.221	0.952	922	968	106.1	912
Baltimore, Md.	97814	68906	0.704	0.296	0.519	0.154	0.858	1054	1228	99.5	1234
Birmingham, Ala.	17264	16353	0.947	0.053	0.514	0.027	0.974	1152	1183	107.8	1097
Boston, Mass.	88759	57736	0.650	0.350	0.690	0.242	0.892	1086	1217	106.5	1143
Bridgeport, Conn.	42862	32219	0.752	0.248	0.528	0.131	0.883	1209	1369	105.1	1303
Buffalo, N. Y.	75899	64403	0.849	0.151	0.545	0.082	0.931	1261	1354	97.3	1392
Chicago, Ill.	403942	311051	0.770	0.230	0.529	0.122	0.892	1257	1409	95.1	1482
Cincinnati, Ohio	69680	51354	0.737	0.263	0.444	0.117	0.854	985	1153	94.9	1215
Cleveland, Ohio	157730	130840	0.830	0.170	0.444	0.075	0.905	1339	1480	99.9	1481
Columbus, Ohio	26751	22022	0.823	0.177	0.444	0.079	0.902	1158	1284	97.0	1324
Dallas, Tex.	7913	5926	0.749	0.251	0.597	0.150	0.899	1006	1119	104.4	1072
Denver, Colo.	16635	14216	0.855	0.145	0.581	0.084	0.939	1163	1239	96.4	1285
Detroit, Mich.	167016	145179	0.869	0.131	0.556	0.073	0.942	1470	1560	98.4	1585
Fall River, Mass.	37015	19335	0.522	0.478	0.690	0.330	0.852	824	967	105.0	921
Houston, Tex.	9860	8781	0.891	0.109	0.597	0.065	0.956	1055	1104	99.9	1105
Indianapolis, Ind.	49977	40559	0.812	0.188	0.390	0.073	0.885	1049	1185	97.2	1219
Kansas City, Mo.	22137	15798	0.714	0.286	0.437	0.125	0.839	1073	1279	97.9	1306
Los Angeles, Calif.	47118	38643	0.820	0.180	0.462	0.083	0.903	1170	1296	96.2	1347
Louisville, Ky.	29902	23883	0.799	0.201	0.312	0.063	0.862	966	1121	97.3	1152
Memphis, Tenn.	11963	10057	0.841	0.159	0.604	0.096	0.937	876	935	102.9	909
Milwaukee, Wis.	84222	63111	0.749	0.251	0.506	0.127	0.876	1068	1219	94.6	1289
Minneapolis, Minn.	38154	29393	0.770	0.230	0.583	0.134	0.904	1082	1197	91.2	1312
New Haven, Conn.	30874	21728	0.704	0.296	0.528	0.156	0.860	1018	1184	106.0	1117
New Orleans, La.	26641	18234	0.684	0.316	0.523	0.165	0.849	924	1088	98.0	1110

TABLE XIV—Continued

CORRECTING THE AVERAGE MONEY WAGE IN MANUFACTURING FOR THE EFFECT OF WOMEN'S WAGES AND DIFFERENCES IN FOOD COST

	Wage Earners in Manufacturing[1]				Ratio of Female Earnings to Male Earnings[2]	Col. 4 × Col. 5	Col. 6 Plus Col. 3 Denominator	Average Uncorrected Earnings	Earnings per Male Worker	Index A Costs of Food[3]	Earnings per Male Worker Corrected for Difference in Food Costs
	Number		Proportion								
	Total	Males	Males	Females							
	1	2	3	4	5	6	7	8	9	10	11
New York, N. Y.	638775	424558	0.665	0.335	0.545	0.183	0.848	1262	1488	104.0	1431
Newark, N. J.	86707	65254	0.753	0.247	0.558	0.138	0.891	1203	1350	104.2	1296
Norfolk, Va.	5119	3822	0.747	0.253	0.678	0.172	0.919	1169	1272	106.3	1197
Omaha, Nebr.	21304	17858	0.838	0.162	0.530	0.086	0.924	1278	1383	97.4	1420
Philadelphia, Pa.	281105	196903	0.700	0.300	0.457	0.137	0.837	1163	1389	102.2	1359
Pittsburgh, Pa.	83290	72796	0.874	0.126	0.457	0.058	0.932	1319	1415	102.6	1379
Portland, Ore.	26813	24143	0.900	0.100	0.474	0.047	0.947	1445	1526	96.5	1581
Providence, R. I.	53372	34619	0.649	0.351	0.724	0.254	0.903	996	1103	108.0	1021
Richmond, Va.	21759	15037	0.691	0.309	0.678	0.210	0.901	912	1012	103.5	978
Rochester, N. Y.	63792	44348	0.695	0.305	0.545	0.166	0.861	1085	1260	98.0	1286
St. Louis, Mo.	107919	76998	0.713	0.287	0.437	0.125	0.838	1006	1200	95.4	1258
St. Paul, Minn.	22649	16766	0.740	0.260	0.583	0.152	0.892	1079	1210	91.0	1330
Salt Lake City, Utah	6362	5133	0.807	0.193	0.511	0.099	0.906	1124	1241	94.7	1310
San Francisco, Calif.	48550	37784	0.778	0.222	0.462	0.103	0.881	1230	1396	96.1	1453
Scranton, Pa.	14467	8008	0.554	0.446	0.457	0.204	0.758	828	1092	101.5	1076
Seattle, Wash.	40843	37740	0.924	0.076	0.608	0.046	0.970	1552	1600	98.9	1618
Washington, D. C.	10482	9193	0.877	0.123	0.530	0.065	0.942	1258	1335	104.9	1273

[1] Source: *14th Census of U. S.*, Vol. IX, Table 6 of each section on the different states. (Average number employed by sex and age in cities of over 10,000.)
[2] U. S. Bureau of Labor Statistics, Bulletin No. 265, Table 6.
[3] Table XV-A.

521

TABLE XV

COMMODITIES INCLUDED IN THE BUDGETS WHICH WERE USED FOR
GEOGRAPHICAL INDEX OF THE COST OF LIVING, 1919

Food	Quantity	Food	Quantity
Beef Steak............lb.	66.1	Coffee..............lb.	39.3
Beef Roast........... "	59.9	Tea................. "	6.7
Beef Stew............ "	44.7	Onions............. "	65.5
Pork, Fresh.......... "	40.5	Beans (dried)........ "	23.4
Bacon............... "	17.0	Prunes............. "	10.3
Ham................ "	19.9	Raisins............. "	9.3
Mutton............. "	17.4	Milk (canned) 16 oz. can	62.2
Poultry............. "	23.4	Oleo...............lb.	16.7
Lard................ "	36.6	Nut Margarine...... "	4.5
Salmon (canned)...... "	8.8	Crisco............. "	10.2
Eggs...............doz.	61.2	Rolled Oats........ "	29.6
Butter..............lb.	67.5	Corn Flakes...8 oz. pkg.	5.9
Cheese.............. "	12.0	Cream of Wheat	
Milk (fresh)..........qt.	324.0	28 oz. pkg.	6.2
Flour (wheat).........lb.	260.1	Bread...............lb.	435.2
Rice................ "	32.1	Corn Meal.......... "	69.4
Sugar............... "	147.5	Potatoes............ "	709.2
Cabbage............ "	63.1	Macaroni........... "	20.6
Corn (canned)..No. 2 can	10.3	Beans (canned) No. 2 can	6.4
Tomatoes (canned) "	15.2	Peas (canned). "	9.7
Oranges...........doz.	6.5	Bananas..........doz.	10.0

Fuel and Light
Anthracite Coal...........ton 1.7
Bituminous Coal.......... " 2.6
Gas.............1000 cu. ft. 32.0

Rent
Rooms, houses.............. 5.0
Rooms, flats................ 4.5

Dry Goods
Blankets.................... .5
Sheets..................... 1.2
Cotton Goods...........yd. 130.0

TABLE XV-A

Geographical Indexes of the Cost of Living in 41 Cities, 1919

	Index A[1]	Index B[2]	Index C[3]
Atlanta	106.1	106.1	102.3
Baltimore	99.5	97.1	92.8
Birmingham	107.8	102.0	102.6
Boston	106.5	105.2	102.0
Bridgeport	105.1	103.6	110.1
Buffalo	97.3	101.1	99.3
Chicago	95.1	96.7	96.9
Cincinnati	94.9	92.6	96.1
Cleveland	99.9	98.3	101.3
Columbus	97.0	94.5	95.8
Dallas	104.4	103.1	107.4
Denver	96.4	100.5	97.4
Detroit	98.4	96.7	103.3
Fall River	105.0	103.1	95.7
Houston	99.9	100.7	102.5
Indianapolis	97.2	94.2	92.0
Kansas City, Mo.	97.9	99.7	99.8
Los Angeles	96.2	102.7	100.4
Louisville	97.3	96.6	96.3
Memphis	102.9	103.8	107.8
Milwaukee	94.6	94.3	91.6
Newark	104.2	103.3	101.7
New Haven	106.0	105.6	.....
New Orleans	98.0	100.8	100.3
New York	104.0	103.7	105.7
Norfolk	106.3	106.7	103.0
Omaha	97.4	101.9	102.5
Philadelphia	102.2	101.1	98.4
Pittsburgh	102.6	101.4	108.6
Portland	96.5	98.6	96.3
Minneapolis	91.0	95.2	97.4
Providence, R. I.	108.0	107.6	100.5
Richmond	103.5	100.8	96.9
Rochester	98.0	98.4	.....
St. Louis	95.4	95.8	101.5
St. Paul	91.0	.....	95.5
Salt Lake City	94.7	99.6	105.1
San Francisco	96.1	100.3	104.4
Scranton	101.5	100.6	93.2
Seattle	98.9	100.8	103.6
Washington	104.9	102.9	.....

[1] Index A is composed of the total Food Cost of the Standard Budget (the arithmetic mean 458.8 = 100)

[2] Index B is composed of Food Costs plus Light, Fuel and Dry Goods (the arithmetic mean 606.1 = 100)

[3] Index C is composed of Index B plus Rent (the arithmetic mean 790.5 = 100)

TABLE XVI

	Chicago	*Detroit*
Atlanta, Ga.	487	517
Baltimore, Md.	463	496
Birmingham, Ala.	445	478
Boston, Mass.	474	505
Bridgeport, Conn.	451	486
Buffalo, N. Y.	432	467
Chicago, Ill.	455	489
Cincinnati, Ohio.	453	486
Cleveland, Ohio.	434	470
Columbus, Ohio.	429	461
Dallas, Tex.	459	492
Denver, Colo.	441	474
Detroit, Mich.	431	467
Fall River, Mass.	516	544
Houston, Tex.	458	491
Indianapolis, Ind.	447	481
Kansas City, Mo.	448	481
Los Angeles, Calif.	431	465
Louisville, Ky.	473	505
Memphis, Tenn.	472	502
Milwaukee, Wisc.	451	486
Minneapolis, Minn.	443	477
New Haven, Conn.	456	489
New Orleans, La.	461	493
New York, N. Y.	457	492
Newark, N. J.	444	479
Norfolk, Va.	466	498
Omaha, Nebr.	442	478
Philadelphia, Pa.	455	487
Pittsburgh, Pa.	435	471
Portland, Ore.	436	469
Providence, R. I.	478	511
Richmond, Va.	471	501
Rochester, N. Y.	460	494
St. Louis, Mo.	463	495
St. Paul, Minn.	447	482
Salt Lake City, Utah.	416	450
San Francisco, Calif.	454	487
Scranton, Pa.	436	472
Seattle, Wash.	432	464
Washington, D. C.	507	535

For explanation see text Chapter XI, 5.

TABLE XVII

NATIVE WHITES OF FOREIGN PARENTAGE, FOREIGN-BORN WHITES, AND NEGROES
AS PERCENTAGES OF TOTAL POPULATION AND THE PERCENTAGE GAINFULLY
OCCUPIED AND ATTENDING SCHOOL IN FORTY-ONE CITIES

	Per Cent Foreign-born White[1]	Per Cent Negro[1]	Native White of Foreign Parentage[1]	Per Cent 15 Year Males Gainfully Occupied[2]	Per Cent Attending School 14 and 15 Years[1]
Atlanta, Ga.............	2.4	31.3	2.4	49.9	70.0
Baltimore, Md.........	11.4	14.8	15.9	44.6	69.4
Birmingham, Ala.......	3.4	39.3	3.7	28.1	79.4
Boston, Mass..........	31.9	2.2	31.8	33.4	82.8
Bridgeport, Conn......	32.3	1.6	32.8	39.1	76.7
Buffalo, N. Y.........	24.0	0.9	30.5	28.4	80.8
Chicago, Ill...........	29.8	4.1	32.9	38.9	72.9
Cincinnati, Ohio......	10.7	7.5	20.0	29.8	87.4
Cleveland, Ohio.......	30.1	4.3	30.9	25.7	86.4
Columbus, Ohio.......	6.8	9.4	10.2	20.7	86.8
Dallas, Tex...........	5.5	15.1	5.0	34.4	81.3
Denver, Colo..........	14.7	2.4	16.8	30.9	82.7
Detroit, Mich.........	29.1	4.1	24.9	20.4	88.8
Fall River, Mass.......	35.1	0.3	....	72.9	44.8
Houston, Tex..........	8.7	24.6	8.5	43.2	76.7
Indianapolis, Ind......	5.4	11.0	8.5	38.6	75.0
Kansas City, Mo......	8.4	9.5	10.8	29.1	82.5
Los Angeles, Calif......	19.4	2.7	15.1	17.6	90.3
Louisville, Ky.........	4.9	17.1	11.5	32.3	79.1
Memphis, Tenn........	3.6	37.7	4.7	36.8	75.0
Milwaukee, Wis........	24.1	0.5	33.4	42.4	88.1
Minneapolis, Minn.....	23.1	1.0	28.6	15.8	90.7
New Haven, Conn.....	28.1	2.8	33.7	46.5	69.3
New Orleans, La.......	6.7	26.1	10.8	50.6	68.0
New York, N. Y.......	35.4	2.7	33.3	34.1	78.0
Newark, N. J..........	28.2	4.1	32.2	41.7	70.0
Norfolk, Va...........	5.7	37.5	4.5	40.8	74.5
Omaha, Neb...........	18.5	5.4	21.6	23.8	85.7
Philadelphia, Pa.......	21.8	7.4	24.5	30.7	85.7
Pittsburgh, Pa.........	20.4	6.4	26.8	22.5	87.7
Portland, Ore.........	18.2	0.6	16.2	23.2	90.7
Providence, R. I.......	29.0	2.4	32.0	52.0	64.4
Richmond, Va.........	2.7	31.5	3.4	42.0	75.4
Rochester, N. Y.......	24.1	0.5	26.5	31.2	81.3
St. Louis, Mo.........	13.4	9.0	20.5	48.6	71.6
St. Paul, Minn........	22.0	1.4	29.9	19.3	88.5
Salt Lake City, Utah...	16.5	0.6	....	19.9	92.5
San Francisco, Calif....	27.7	0.5	24.8	21.3	87.2
Scranton, Pa..........	20.7	0.4	32.8	32.2	81.0
Seattle, Wash.........	23.4	0.9	17.3	25.6	86.2
Washington, D. C......	6.5	25.1	....	28.4	82.5

[1] 14th Census of U. S., Vol. III, Tables 10 and 11 for the respective states.
[2] Ibid., Vol. IV, Table 19, p. 452.

TABLE XVIII

SCHOOL ATTENDANCE IN DIFFERENT AGE GROUPS FOR FORTY-ONE CITIES

	14 and 15 Years		16 and 17 Years		18 and 19 Years	
	Males	Females	Males	Females	Males	Females
Atlanta, Ga............	70.0	77.0	34.3	40.2	14.2	10.4
Baltimore, Md..........	69.4	68.2	26.9	24.8	10.6	7.8
Birmingham, Ala.......	79.4	83.3	40.8	45.1	12.5	11.6
Boston, Mass..........	82.8	84.0	41.5	44.8	17.0	13.6
Bridgeport, Conn.......	76.7	72.9	26.5	28.4	9.9	7.2
Buffalo, N. Y..........	80.8	76.5	32.4	29.5	13.4	9.6
Chicago, Ill............	72.9	72.3	30.0	28.1	11.8	8.1
Cincinnati, Ohio.......	87.4	93.1	37.9	40.7	15.9	12.1
Cleveland, Ohio........	86.4	91.3	35.1	39.6	13.4	10.1
Columbus, Ohio........	86.8	91.0	47.2	54.6	18.8	19.2
Dallas, Tex............	81.3	84.7	43.5	48.6	16.4	12.4
Denver, Colo..........	82.7	84.7	47.9	54.1	22.7	19.8
Detroit, Mich..........	88.8	87.6	31.8	32.0	9.0	7.0
Fall River, Mass.......	44.8	45.9	22.1	21.1	12.8	10.1
Houston, Tex..........	76.7	81.7	37.0	43.3	11.8	10.2
Indianapolis, Ind.......	75.0	75.0	31.6	34.0	11.9	9.8
Kansas City, Mo.......	82.5	84.0	43.3	46.2	15.8	13.0
Los Angeles, Calif......	90.3	90.4	52.3	55.7	21.6	20.2
Louisville, Ky..........	79.1	77.7	28.4	32.3	9.4	9.8
Memphis, Tenn........	75.0	80.7	34.5	43.4	11.3	11.1
Milwaukee, Wis........	88.1	87.3	52.1	49.6	16.1	12.9
Minneapolis, Minn.....	90.7	90.4	50.1	51.7	24.3	17.8
New Haven, Conn......	69.3	72.1	31.7	35.7	15.4	11.0
New Orleans, La.......	68.0	72.6	27.2	33.1	8.6	8.9
New York, N. Y.......	78.0	78.3	27.7	26.3	10.7	7.1
Newark, N. J..........	70.0	70.2	25.7	24.6	10.1	6.6
Norfolk, Va............	74.5	80.7	33.7	42.9	9.6	10.9
Omaha, Nebr...........	85.7	87.3	40.5	47.4	14.8	13.7
Philadelphia, Pa........	85.7	83.5	30.2	30.0	9.7	7.7
Pittsburgh, Pa.........	87.7	83.3	36.6	37.0	14.7	11.0
Portland, Ore..........	90.7	91.6	54.1	57.9	25.9	20.5
Providence, R. I.......	64.4	65.5	31.5	32.0	14.6	11.1
Richmond, Va..........	75.4	74.3	34.3	36.3	13.1	11.5
Rochester, N. Y........	81.3	78.2	32.6	31.0	14.7	10.7
St. Louis, Mo..........	71.6	72.1	28.8	27.8	11.7	8.6
St. Paul, Minn.........	88.5	87.0	39.4	40.8	17.8	13.9
Salt Lake City, Utah....	92.5	92.7	63.7	64.1	25.0	22.5
San Francisco, Calif....	87.2	89.1	51.1	50.2	28.5	13.8
Scranton, Pa...........	81.0	79.1	26.8	32.8	10.0	9.8
Seattle, Wash..........	86.2	89.2	51.9	58.5	25.5	20.7
Washington, D. C.......	82.5	83.8	46.4	43.3	21.1	12.3

Source: *14th Census*, Vol. II, p. 1085 ff.

TABLE XIX

AVERAGE HOURLY MONEY-EARNINGS AND AVERAGE HOURS PER WEEK IN SEVENTEEN INDUSTRIES IN 1890, 1914, AND 1926

	1890		1914		1926		1914 Relative to 1890		1926 Relative to 1890	
	Earnings (Dollars)	Hours	Earnings (Dollars)	Hours	Earnings (Dollars)	Hours	Earnings	Hours	Earnings	Hours
1. Cotton	.097	62.6	.153	56.8	.328	53.3	157.7	90.7	338.1	85.1
2. Woolen	.121	60.0	.182	55.0	.491	49.3	150.4	91.7	405.8	82.2
3. Boots and Shoes	.169	58.9	.243	54.7	.528	49.0	143.8	92.9	312.4	83.2
4. Clothing	.143	55.7	.256	51.3	.750	44.3	179.0	92.1	524.5	79.5
5. Hosiery and Knit Goods	.113	61.3	.172	54.8	.441	51.4	152.2	89.4	390.3	83.8
6. Lumber	.150	65.2	.194	61.7	.361	58.1	129.3	94.6	240.7	89.1
7. Iron and Steel	.229	67.2	.298	65.5	.637	54.4	130.1	97.5	278.2	81.0
8. Slaughtering and Meat Packing	.174	60.1	.201	60.0	.494	49.7	115.5	99.8	283.9	82.7
9. Foundries and Machine Shops	.319	54.4	.413	49.6	.961	46.3	129.5	91.2	301.3	85.1
10. Building Trades	.341	51.3	.567	44.7	1.313	43.8	166.3	87.1	385.0	85.4
11. Granite and Stone	.405	48.7	.541	44.2	1.301	43.9	133.6	90.8	321.2	90.1
12. Book and Job Printing	.290	56.1	.451	47.9	1.037	44.2	155.5	85.4	357.6	78.8
13. Newspaper Printing	.448	49.2	.610	44.9	1.150	45.1	136.2	91.3	256.7	91.7
14. Planing Mills	.293	53.3	.404	48.6	1.027	45.0	137.9	91.2	350.5	84.4
15. Baking	.204	64.5	.342	52.5	.925	47.8	167.6	81.4	453.4	74.1
16. Coal Mining—Bituminous	.180	60.0	.323	51.6	.719	48.4	179.4	86.0	399.4	80.7
17. Unskilled Work	.148	59.7	.207	55.7	.433	53.6	139.9	93.3	292.6	89.8

Source: Douglas, Paul H., *Real Wages in the United States 1890-1926*, pp. 96, 101, 112, 114, 135, 150, 152.

527

TABLE XX

Relative Hours per Week and Relative Real Hourly Earnings, Fifteen Industries, 1890–1926

1890–99 = 100

Year	Cotton		Boots and Shoes		Clothing		Hosiery and Knit Goods		Woolens		Lumber		Iron and Steel		Slaughtering and Meat Pkg.		Bakers		Building		Planing Mills		Book and Job Printing		Newspaper Printing		Metal Trades		Granite and Stone		Payroll Industries		Union Mfg. Industries		All Mfg.	
	x	y	x	y	x	y	x	y	x	y	x	y	x	y	x	y	x	y	x	y	x	y	x	y	x	y	x	y	x	y	x	y	x	y	x	y
1890	101	98	100	95	100	95	101	102	101	97	100	101	100	103	100	101	101	96	101	102	96	101	101	95	101	97	100	97	102	96	100	99	101	95	101	95
1891	101	98	101	96	100	98	101	107	101	98	100	103	100	104	104	100	101	99	97	100	99	99	101	98	100	98	100	98	101	101	100	101	101	98	101	98
1892	101	98	100	98	100	98	100	100	101	99	101	101	100	104	100	100	100	98	99	101	100	98	100	100	98	100	100	98	101	100	100	104	100	98	100	98
1893	100	106	100	101	100	99	100	100	106	106	103	103	100	107	100	105	100	100	100	103	100	100	100	100	101	99	101	101	101	101	99	104	100	99	100	101
1894	98	102	100	100	100	100	100	100	106	98	101	101	101	99	100	100	100	95	101	102	100	95	100	104	99	100	100	102	101	101	99	99	100	102	99	102
1895	100	103	100	104	100	101	100	107	99	99	101	99	101	99	100	97	100	94	100	100	100	100	100	101	100	101	100	100	100	99	100	99	100	102	100	102
1896	100	101	100	101	100	100	100	100	98	98	103	96	101	101	97	100	98	101	99	99	101	101	100	100	101	100	101	99	99	99	100	100	99	100	100	101
1897	100	101	100	101	100	101	100	100	100	100	96	95	100	95	95	97	101	100	98	101	99	101	100	101	101	101	99	99	97	99	100	97	99	100	100	101
1898	99	101	100	101	100	99	100	95	99	98	98	96	100	99	93	99	101	101	99	98	99	101	97	103	98	102	99	100	97	99	100	99	99	99	99	100
1899	100	104	99	101	100	102	99	90	99	99	99	99	99	99	93	102	98	101	97	102	99	101	95	103	98	101	99	99	96	97	100	99	99	99	100	100
1900	100	97	98	98	100	97	98	95	99	104	98	98	100	103	91	99	96	99	97	105	99	101	94	103	95	103	98	99	94	101	98	100	98	98	99	101
1901	100	94	96	96	99	95	98	90	99	103	100	101	100	103	94	91	94	100	93	107	97	101	93	100	96	100	100	100	94	102	98	101	98	99	99	100
1902	99	102	97	97	98	99	99	98	99	102	99	98	100	106	94	94	96	102	92	108	97	102	93	103	96	99	99	99	94	103	98	98	98	96	98	100
1903	99	101	97	101	99	103	98	98	99	103	97	102	100	103	94	96	94	102	92	111	97	104	93	100	96	102	98	101	94	102	98	99	96	99	97	101
1904	99	101	97	103	98	101	98	105	99	108	97	102	99	100	92	96	93	104	92	114	97	104	92	106	95	99	95	101	94	103	98	101	96	100	97	101
1905	99	99	96	100	98	104	97	106	98	107	96	103	99	99	92	100	92	99	91	116	96	101	91	106	95	102	95	100	94	99	98	102	95	100	96	103
1906	98	112	96	100	98	101	97	112	98	105	96	103	99	99	90	88	91	107	91	116	96	103	90	104	93	98	94	96	94	99	98	100	95	97	96	102
1907	96	112	96	105	98	106	97	110	98	106	96	101	99	98	88	86	90	109	90	120	96	103	87	109	93	103	94	95	94	104	97	101	94	102	95	102
1908	96	112	96	100	98	102	95	103	96	102	96	102	99	99	86	89	90	117	91	121	96	103	86	107	93	103	93	95	93	98	96	101	93	94	95	100
1909	96	107	94	98	97	113	95	103	95	111	96	100	99	96	87	87	89	117	90	115	96	99	86	109	93	96	92	96	93	95	95	104	93	95	94	102
1910	94	116	94	102	92	115	92	114	93	108	95	100	97	97	86	87	84	117	90	118	96	98	86	108	92	97	92	97	92	100	95	106	92	95	94	102
1911	92	116	93	102	91	126	90	116	93	111	95	93	97	102	89	92	83	121	89	117	96	98	86	108	92	97	92	94	93	96	94	104	92	96	93	102
1912	92	118	93	102	91	129	90	126	92	122	93	101	97	100	92	124	82	124	89	124	96	102	82	112	92	100	92	94	93	98	94	106	91	98	93	104
1913	91	115	93	116	90	132	88	125	92	122	93	93	99	116	91	119	81	119	89	116	96	112	82	105	92	93	89	91	92	94	94	116	89	87	92	107
1914	91	121	93	127	90	128	87	122	92	131	90	101	99	123	80	102	79	110	88	118	88	110	81	120	91	79	87	100	92	79	91	116	87	89	90	104
1915	91	126	93	126	87	162	86	122	98	177	88	115	99	128	80	104	77	126	88	94	86	101	84	128	92	73	84	98	92	81	91	120	88	89	88	109
1916	91	130	91	130	84	166	85	133	98	185	89	95	94	123	80	97	74	147	87	103	86	96	83	131	91	73	83	94	92	84	86	135	85	92	86	113
1917	87	143	86	111	83	220	83	139	95	172	90	108	94	104	81	120	75	185	87	127	86	101	81	138	94	95	86	110	92	108	86	131	85	114	86	122
1918	84	148	83	125	83	222	84	159	98	186	90	108	94	116	81	122	74	191	87	137	86	141	80	145	92	100	86	114	91	115	85	134	86	119	86	124
1919	85	166	83	128	82	224	84	164	83	188	90	105	82	226	85	121	74	199	87	147	86	147	80	147	92	107	86	120	92	121	84	147	85	127	85	134
1920	85	165	83	124	80	218	84	165	83	178	90	105	81	225	83	121	75	202	87	150	86	145	80	145	93	107	86	123	92	142	84	145	85	133	85	133
1921	86	143	83	128	80	215	85	172	83	169	90	104	81	121	83	123	75	187	87	157	86	144	80	145	93	106	85	126	92	133	84	140	85	127	85	132

x = Relative Hours per Week; y = Relative Hourly Earnings; Source: Douglas, Paul H., *Real Wages in the United States, 1890–1926*, pp. 104, 118, 115, 120, 135, 186.

528

TABLE XXI

State	Males		Females	
	Hours	Earnings (Dollars)	Hours	Earnings (Dollars)
Alabama...................	7.6	0.423	5.7	0.290
Arkansas..................	7.5	0.300	...	....
California.................	7.3	0.577	7.2	0.270
Colorado..................	5.9	0.659	...	.....
Connecticut...............	8.4	0.509	7.5	0.301
Delaware..................	7.4	0.596	5.8	0.312
Florida...................	8.1	0.336	7.8	0.282
Georgia...................	7.5	0.306	7.6	0.249
Idaho.....................	5.0	0.510	...	.....
Illinois...................	7.4	0.623	7.5	0.325
Indiana...................	7.7	0.615	7.7	0.240
Iowa......................	7.5	0.538	7.1	0.258
Kansas....................	5.2	0.703	6.8	0.296
Kentucky..................	6.3	0.574	8.0	0.141
Louisiana.................	8.7	0.356	9.1	0.178
Maine.....................	8.8	0.471	8.4	0.296
Maryland..................	7.3	0.584	7.0	0.316
Massachusetts.............	8.2	0.416	7.4	0.318
Michigan..................	8.0	0.541	7.2	0.334
Minnesota.................	7.8	0.480	7.4	0.295
Mississippi................	6.7	0.308	...	.....
Missouri..................	7.7	0.541	7.4	0.246
Montana..................	6.2	0.462	...	.....
New Hampshire............	7.9	0.468	7.5	0.304
New Jersey................	8.2	0.529	7.4	0.327
New Mexico...............	5.9	0.671	...	.....
New York.................	8.3	0.542	7.5	0.327
North Carolina............	7.6	0.326	7.4	0.258
Ohio......................	7.7	0.622	7.2	0.295
Oklahoma.................	7.2	0.635	...	.....
Oregon...................	6.5	0.703	6.9	0.314
Pennsylvania..............	7.5	0.643	7.6	0.290
Rhode Island..............	8.7	0.493	8.3	0.374
South Carolina............	7.8	0.303	...	.....
Tennessee.................	7.1	0.409	7.9	0.222
Texas.....................	7.2	0.439	6.4	0.295
Utah.....................	5.4	0.818	...	.....
Vermont..................	8.4	0.458	7.3	0.330
Virginia..................	7.4	0.431	7.4	0.292
Washington...............	6.0	0.604	7.2	0.306
West Virginia.............	7.0	0.639	7.0	0.294
Wisconsin.................	8.7	0.472	7.9	0.263
Wyoming.................	4.9	0.852	...	.....

Source: *U. S. Bulletin of Labor Statistics*, No. 265, Table 6.

TABLE XXII

Industries	Males		Females	
	Hours Per Day	Earnings Per Hour (Dollars)	Hours Per Day	Earnings Per Hour (Dollars)
Automobiles.................	8.2	0.571	7.8	0.380
Boxes, paper................	8.3	0.384	7.5	0.242
Brick.......................	7.7	0.460	7.5	0.272
Cars.......................	7.8	0.698	...	.....
Chemicals..................	8.4	0.456	...	.....
Cigars.....................	7.8	0.446	7.6	0.326
Clothing, men's............	7.8	0.558	7.3	0.338
Clothing, women's..........	8.1	0.724	7.4	0.368
Anthracite Coal............	7.4	0.616	...	.....
Bituminous Coal............	5.5	0.723	...	.....
Confectionary..............	8.7	0.359	7.4	0.231
Electrical Machinery........	7.9	0.527	7.6	0.322
Foundries..................	8.2	0.545	7.1	0.333
Furniture..................	8.5	0.348	8.1	0.214
Glass......................	7.7	0.502	7.3	0.231
Hosiery and Underwear......	7.7	0.467	7.6	0.286
Iron and Steel.............	7.8	0.748	6.1	0.419
Leather....................	8.1	0.521	6.9	0.317
Logging....................	6.0	0.434	...	.....
Lumber....................	7.2	0.358	...	.....
Machine Tools..............	8.6	0.542	7.7	0.345
Other Machinery...........	8.2	0.599	...	.....
Millwork...................	8.1	0.401	...	.....
Overalls...................	7.1	0.583	6.7	0.305
Paper and Pulp.............	8.6	0.490	8.0	0.278
Pottery....................	7.1	0.646	6.8	0.324
Rubber....................	8.2	0.497	7.6	0.326
Silk.......................	8.0	0.456	7.8	0.335
Typewriters................	8.6	0.496	7.8	0.300

Source: *U. S. Bulletin of Labor Statistics*, No. 265, Table 5.

TABLE XXIII

AVERAGE FULL TIME HOURS PER WEEK AND AVERAGE HOURLY EARNINGS BY
STATES FOR SELECTED INDUSTRIES, 1926

State	Hosiery—Females		Hosiery—Males	
	Hours	Earnings (Dollars)	Hours	Earnings (Dollars)
Alabama and Louisiana.....	55.0	0.192	54.9	0.286
Georgia.................	55.0	0.229	55.0	0.348
Illinois.................	53.9	0.284	57.1	0.412
Indiana.................	49.5	0.415	50.3	0.713
Massachusetts............	48.0	0.323	48.7	0.449
Michigan................	50.4	0.352	53.3	0.563
New Hampshire and Vermont	48.3	0.355	48.5	0.495
New Jersey..............	47.1	0.506	48.5	1.268
New York...............	49.0	0.521	49.3	1.172
North Carolina...........	55.2	0.276	55.0	0.404
Ohio...................	49.9	0.330	51.4	0.586
Pennsylvania.............	50.2	0.442	52.4	0.829
Rhode Island.............	51.5	0.319	51.8	0.453
Tennessee...............	54.0	0.249	54.7	0.377
Virginia.................	52.1	0.216	52.8	0.347
Wisconsin...............	49.4	0.434	50.3	0.858

State	Hosiery and Underwear— Males and Females		Underwear Males		Underwear Females	
	Hours	Earnings (Dollars)	Hours	Earnings (Dollars)	Hours	Earnings (Dollars)
Connecticut.........	51.3	0.386	51.1	0.500	51.3	0.361
Georgia.............	55.1	0.258	58.0	0.229	56.7	0.189
Illinois.............	53.1	0.352	48.9	0.526	45.8	0.453
Indiana.............	49.2	0.489	50.2	0.500	47.6	0.355
Massachusetts.......	48.1	0.407	48.3	0.566	48.0	0.405
Michigan...........	51.5	0.330	51.7	0.477	51.8	0.294
Minnesota and Wisconsin........	49.4	0.533	50.1	0.517	48.5	0.413
New Hampshire and Vermont.........	48.9	0.390	49.6	0.482	49.4	0.354
New York..........	49.9	0.448	50.8	0.480	49.8	0.357
Ohio..............	50.0	0.370	51.8	0.431	49.5	0.344
Pennsylvania........	51.2	0.560	52.5	0.448	51.9	0.326
Rhode Island........	51.3	0.364	50.8	0.475	51.2	0.360
Tennessee..........	54.2	0.291	55.1	0.375	54.1	0.266
Virginia............	52.2	0.246	....	.....	....	.....
Alabama and Louisiana........	55.0	0.215	....	.....	....	.....
New Jersey..........	47.6	0.797	....	.....	....	.....
North Carolina......	55.2	0.328	....	.....	....	.....

Source: *U. S. Bureau of Labor Statistics Bulletin*, No. 452, Table 3.

TABLE XXIV

AVERAGE FULL TIME HOURS PER WEEK AND AVERAGE HOURLY EARNINGS BY
STATES FOR FOUNDRIES AND MACHINE SHOPS, 1925

State	Foundries		Machine Shop	
	Hours	Earnings (Dollars)	Hours	Earnings (Dollars)
Alabama.................	54.6	0.436	54.4	0.523
California...............	47.6	0.692	46.4	0.739
Colorado................	52.9	0.554	48.7	0.592
Connecticut..............	50.9	0.597	50.7	0.586
Georgia.................	56.1	0.376	54.2	0.429
Illinois..................	52.3	0.650	49.8	0.665
Indiana.................	50.7	0.609	53.0	0.544
Iowa....................	54.3	0.556	54.1	0.492
Kansas.................	53.4	0.506	54.5	0.529
Kentucky...............	51.2	0.529	50.9	0.484
Louisiana................	50.0	0.486	50.9	0.537
Maine...................	49.3	0.605	49.1	0.537
Maryland................	51.8	0.559	48.8	0.603
Massachusetts...........	48.9	0.682	49.3	0.609
Michigan................	50.6	0.636	51.6	0.600
Minnesota...............	54.8	0.565	50.7	0.575
Missouri.................	53.0	0.579	52.9	0.530
New Hampshire...........	49.5	0.640	50.0	0.604
New Jersey..............	51.9	0.604	49.7	0.635
New York...............	50.4	0.574	48.6	0.624
Ohio....................	53.3	0.610	50.8	0.587
Oregon..................	47.1	0.648	48.1	0.655
Pennsylvania.............	50.9	0.627	51.1	0.605
Rhode Island.............	51.3	0.614	51.2	0.560
Tennessee................	50.8	0.420	50.1	0.549
Texas...................	52.3	0.468	51.1	0.533
Washington..............	47.9	0.685	47.9	0.690
Wisconsin...............	52.0	0.610	51.3	0.583

Source: *U. S. Bureau of Labor Bulletin*, No. 422, p. 5, Table 2.

TABLE XXV

BIRTH, DEATH AND NET FERTILITY RATES FOR SWEDEN, 1750–1931

Year	Birth Rate per 1000	Death Rate per 1000	Net Fertility Rate per 1000	Year	Birth Rate per 1000	Death Rate per 1000	Net Fertility Rate per 1000
1750	36.391	26.864	9.527	1790	30.484	30.433	0.051
1751	38.680	26.182	12.498	1791	32.625	25.488	7.137
1752	35.908	27.339	8.569	1792	36.584	23.900	12.684
1753	36.123	24.027	12.096	1793	34.388	24.274	10.114
1754	37.218	26.331	10.887	1794	33.790	23.598	10.192
1755	37.517	27.379	10.138	1795	32.036	27.940	4.096
1756	36.121	27.660	8.461	1796	34.678	24.651	10.027
1757	32.611	29.917	2.694	1797	34.767	23.807	10.960
1758	33.415	32.367	1.048	1798	33.680	23.082	10.598
1759	33.619	26.274	7.345	1799	32.023	25.182	6.841
1760	35.699	24.782	10.917	1800	28.721	31.430	−2.709
1761	34.815	25.801	9.014	1801	30.040	26.080	3.960
1762	35.085	31.218	3.867	1802	31.716	23.708	8.008
1763	34.976	32.899	2.077	1803	31.358	23.768	7.590
1764	34.702	27.237	7.465	1804	31.902	24.866	7.036
1765	33.412	27.677	5.735	1805	31.726	23.483	8.243
1766	33.793	25.057	8.736	1806	30.750	27.512	3.238
1767	35.357	25.625	9.732	1807	31.157	26.218	4.939
1768	33.606	27.171	6.435	1808	30.392	34.850	−4.458
1769	33.055	27.149	5.906	1809	26.671	40.041	−13.370
1770	32.984	26.059	6.925	1810	32.947	31.566	1.381
1771	32.242	27.766	4.476	1811	35.302	28.806	6.496
1772	28.887	37.406	−8.519	1812	33.572	30.266	3.306
1773	25.522	52.446	−26.924	1813	29.744	27.367	2.377
1774	34.455	22.358	12.097	1814	31.195	25.075	6.120
1775	35.633	24.844	10.789	1815	34.768	23.588	11.180
1776	32.923	22.497	10.426	1816	35.322	22.660	12.662
1777	33.034	24.934	8.100	1817	33.402	24.253	9.149
1778	34.815	26.645	8.170	1818	33.827	24.367	9.460
1779	36.699	28.502	8.197	1819	32.986	27.360	5.626
1780	35.705	21.736	13.969	1820	32.971	24.456	8.515
1781	33.464	25.552	7.912	1821	35.443	25.566	9.877
1782	32.049	27.257	4.792	1822	35.878	22.594	13.284
1783	30.327	28.107	2.220	1823	36.833	21.017	15.816
1784	31.526	29.748	1.778	1824	34.556	20.774	13.782
1785	31.431	28.298	3.133	1825	36.491	20.540	15.951
1786	32.892	25.944	6.948	1826	34.836	22.606	12.230
1787	31.474	23.952	7.522	1827	31.295	23.051	8.244
1788	33.867	26.684	7.183	1828	33.608	26.737	6.871
1789	32.009	33.130	−1.121	1829	34.847	28.974	5.873

Year	Birth Rate per 1000	Death Rate per 1000	Net Fertility Rate per 1000	Year	Birth Rate per 1000	Death Rate per 1000	Net Fertility Rate per 1000
1830	32.906	24.082	8.824	1870	28.782	19.802	8.980
1831	30.489	26.005	4.484	1871	30.416	17.210	13.206
1832	30.860	23.379	7.481	1872	30.039	16.276	13.763
1833	34.107	21.743	12.364	1873	30.800	17.202	13.598
1834	33.735	25.679	8.056	1874	30.846	20.316	10.530
1835	32.668	18.553	14.115	1875	31.166	20.273	10.893
1836	31.836	19.972	11.864	1876	30.839	19.592	11.247
1837	30.842	24.647	6.195	1877	31.068	18.661	12.407
1838	29.373	24.101	5.272	1878	29.827	18.060	11.767
1839	29.488	23.557	5.931	1879	30.523	16.936	13.587
1840	31.435	20.353	11.082	1880	29.364	18.099	11.265
1841	30.334	19.417	10.917	1881	29.067	17.685	11.382
1842	31.654	21.059	10.595	1882	29.351	17.354	11.997
1843	30.777	21.453	9.324	1883	28.940	17.312	11.628
1844	32.155	20.274	11.881	1884	30.005	17.534	12.471
1845	31.452	18.834	12.618	1885	29.442	17.750	11.692
1846	29.943	21.828	8.115	1886	29.762	16.605	13.157
1847	29.584	23.685	5.899	1887	29.659	16.129	13.530
1848	30.335	19.680	10.655	1888	28.778	15.993	12.785
1849	32.843	19.840	13.003	1889	27.738	15.988	11.750
1850	31.890	19.791	12.099	1890	27.951	17.119	10.832
1851	31.737	20.718	11.019	1891	28.269	16.814	11.455
1852	30.694	22.698	7.996	1892	26.978	17.877	9.101
1853	31.366	23.663	7.703	1893	27.355	16.826	10.529
1854	33.496	19.758	13.738	1894	27.102	16.385	10.717
1855	31.748	21.446	10.302	1895	27.490	15.189	12.301
1856	31.469	21.771	9.698	1896	27.183	15.637	11.546
1857	32.429	27.577	4.852	1897	26.674	15.354	11.320
1858	34.773	21.692	13.081	1898	27.108	15.080	12.028
1859	34.992	20.133	14.859	1899	26.354	17.653	8.701
1860	34.825	17.653	17.172	1900	26.997	16.836	10.161
1861	32.566	18.472	14.094	1901	27.032	16.054	10.978
1862	33.383	21.400	11.983	1902	26.482	15.370	11.112
1863	33.618	19.335	14.283	1903	25.700	15.088	10.612
1864	33.613	20.250	13.363	1904	25.749	15.293	10.456
1865	32.815	19.358	13.457	1905	25.656	15.621	10.035
1866	33.110	19.980	13.130	1906	25.700	14.365	11.335
1867	30.834	19.643	11.191	1907	25.534	14.587	10.947
1868	27.472	20.984	6.488	1908	25.700	14.910	10.790
1869	28.248	22.270	5.978	1909	25.583	13.669	11.914

TABLE XXV—Continued

BIRTH, DEATH AND NET FERTILITY RATES FOR SWEDEN, 1750–1931

Year	Birth Rate per 1000	Death Rate per 1000	Net Fertility Rate per 1000	Year	Birth Rate per 1000	Death Rate per 1000	Net Fertility Rate per 1000
1910	24.662	14.040	10.622	1920	23.614	13.297	10.317
1911	23.994	13.797	10.197	1921	21.541	12.402	9.139
1912	23.799	14.193	9.606	1922	19.586	12.786	6.800
1913	23.162	13.649	9.513	1923	18.916	11.410	7.506
1914	22.876	13.838	9.038	1924	18.113	11.958	6.155
1915	21.593	14.674	6.919	1925	17.584	11.732	5.852
1916	21.216	13.560	7.656	1926	16.822	11.765	5.057
1917	20.912	13.390	7.522	1927	16.114	12.698	3.416
1918	20.311	18.010	2.301	1928	16.053	12.018	4.035
1919	19.757	14.457	5.300	1929	15.192	12.194	2.998
				1930*	15.360	11.700	3.660
				1931*	14.793	12.523	2.270

* Provisional.
Source: Computed from data given in the *Statistisk Årsbok for Sverige*.

TABLE XXVI
Birth, Death and Net Fertility Rates for Norway, 1801–1931

Year	Birth Rate per 1000	Death Rate per 1000	Net Fertility Rate per 1000	Year	Birth Rate per 1000	Death Rate per 1000	Net Fertility Rate per 1000
1801	27.695	27.556	0.139	1840	27.836	19.815	8.021
1802	27.573	24.900	2.673	1841	29.793	17.258	12.535
1803	28.914	24.599	4.315	1842	30.738	17.981	12.757
1804	27.737	23.200	4.537	1843	30.167	17.936	12.231
1805	29.235	20.361	8.874	1844	29.938	17.128	12.810
1806	29.589	20.659	8.930	1845	31.231	16.907	14.324
1807	29.017	22.084	6.933	1846	31.067	17.870	13.197
1808	26.875	26.404	0.471	1847	30.792	20.342	10.450
1809	22.187	35.289	−13.102	1848	29.745	20.476	9.269
				1849	32.044	18.325	13.719
1810	26.325	26.802	0.477	1850	30.951	17.221	13.730
1811	26.680	24.735	1.945	1851	31.868	17.100	14.768
1812	29.061	21.262	7.799	1852	31.021	17.934	13.087
1813	25.647	28.923	3.276	1853	31.977	18.330	13.647
1814	24.148	22.145	2.003	1854	34.245	16.034	18.211
1815	29.926	19.678	10.248	1855	33.433	17.151	16.282
1816	35.093	19.328	15.765	1856	32.194	16.898	15.296
1817	32.462	17.663	14.799	1857	33.009	17.108	15.901
1818	30.768	19.048	11.720	1858	33.483	16.068	17.415
1819	31.902	19.702	12.200	1859	34.753	17.033	17.720
1820	33.307	18.906	14.401	1860	33.253	17.166	16.087
1821	34.720	20.453	14.267	1861	30.700	19.514	11.186
1822	32.942	19.464	13.478	1862	32.078	19.977	12.101
1823	33.943	17.732	16.211	1863	32.740	18.875	13.865
1824	32.474	18.461	14.013	1864	31.864	17.798	14.066
1825	34.339	17.431	16.908	1865	31.914	16.606	15.308
1826	34.849	18.466	16.383	1866	31.733	17.052	14.681
1827	32.023	17.979	14.044	1867	30.072	18.468	11.604
1828	31.800	19.407	12.393	1868	29.511	18.313	11.198
1829	33.635	19.359	14.276	1869	28.906	17.150	11.756
1830	32.309	19.721	12.588	1870	29.167	16.233	12.934
1831	30.969	19.783	11.186	1871	29.321	16.879	12.442
1832	29.901	18.474	11.427	1872	29.965	16.670	13.295
1833	30.707	20.337	10.370	1873	29.855	16.968	12.887
1834	31.700	22.435	9.265	1874	30.989	18.341	12.648
1835	32.640	19.485	13.155	1875	31.532	18.785	12.747
1836	29.414	19.240	10.174	1876	31.549	18.856	12.693
1837	28.702	20.774	7.928	1877	31.712	16.879	14.833
1838	27.762	19.890	7.872	1878	31.471	15.958	15.513
1839	26.676	21.622	5.054	1879	32.125	15.107	17.018

TABLE XXVI—Continued
BIRTH, DEATH AND NET FERTILITY RATES FOR NORWAY, 1801–1931

Year	Birth Rate per 1000	Death Rate per 1000	Net Fertility Rate per 1000	Year	Birth Rate per 1000	Death Rate per 1000	Net Fertility Rate per 1000
1880	30.908	16.187	14.721	1907	26.322	14.318	12.004
1881	30.047	17.013	13.034	1908	26.299	14.225	12.074
1882	30.609	18.641	11.968	1909	26.747	13.563	13.183
1883	30.969	16.957	14.012				
1884	31.632	16.625	15.007	1910	25.795	13.511	12.284
1885	31.499	16.454	15.045	1911	25.707	13.198	12.509
1886	30.876	16.261	14.615	1912	25.336	13.476	11.860
1887	31.387	16.197	15.190	1913	25.046	13.277	11.769
1888	30.381	17.265	13.116	1914	25.122	13.461	11.661
1889	29.638	17.757	11.881	1915	23.611	13.382	10.229
				1916	24.228	13.841	10.387
1890	30.420	18.008	12.412	1917	25.059	13.605	11.454
1891	30.758	17.700	13.058	1918	24.567	17.154	7.413
1892	29.582	17.876	11.706	1919	22.672	13.762	8.910
1893	30.338	16.457	13.881				
1894	29.606	16.898	12.708	1920	26.144	12.766	13.378
1895	30.396	15.641	14.755	1921	23.975	11.496	12.479
1896	29.954	15.202	14.754	1922	23.116	12.022	11.094
1897	30.038	15.349	14.689	1923	22.509	11.579	10.930
1898	30.327	15.286	15.041	1924	21.046	11.249	9.797
1899	29.930	16.758	13.172	1925	19.485	11.032	8.453
				1926	19.313	10.765	8.548
1900	29.693	15.846	13.847	1927	17.822	11.149	6.673
1901	29.847	14.999	14.848	1928	17.674	10.806	6.868
1902	29.222	13.918	15.304	1929	17.270	11.480	5.790
1903	28.617	14.795	13.822				
1904	27.919	14.316	13.603	1930	17.370	10.410	6.960
1905	27.117	14.749	12.368	1931	16.730	10.740	5.990
1906	26.773	13.655	13.118				

Source: *Statistisk Årbok för Kongeriket Norge.*

TABLE XXVII
Birth, Death and Net Fertility Rates for Denmark, 1800–1931

Year	Birth Rate per 1000	Death Rate per 1000	Net Fertility Rate per 1000	Year	Birth Rate per 1000	Death Rate per 1000	Net Fertility Rate per 1000
1800	29.914	28.454	1.460	1840	30.419	20.989	9.430
1801	31.088	27.711	3.377	1841	29.737	19.826	9.911
1802	32.185	23.222	8.963	1842	30.064	20.154	9.910
1803	33.091	22.530	10.561	1843	29.805	19.284	10.521
1804	32.230	23.729	8.501	1844	30.340	19.338	11.002
1805	32.792	23.249	9.543	1845	30.634	19.440	11.194
1806	30.200	22.332	7.868	1846	30.069	21.498	8.571
1807	30.994	22.935	8.059	1847	30.579	21.705	8.874
1808	30.647	25.231	5.416	1848	30.621	21.077	9.544
1809	29.272	25.054	4.218	1849	30.976	22.365	8.611
1810	30.348	22.692	7.656	1850	31.438	19.123	12.315
1811	30.505	24.369	6.136	1851	30.075	18.439	11.636
1812	29.782	26.960	2.822	1852	33.167	19.568	13.599
1813	29.108	22.846	6.262	1853	31.624	24.964	6.660
1814	30.400	24.708	5.692	1854	32.701	18.415	14.286
1815	34.074	21.645	12.429	1855	31.894	19.972	11.922
1816	32.936	20.661	12.275	1856	32.366	18.721	13.645
1817	32.806	19.003	13.803	1857	32.896	21.758	11.138
1818	32.096	18.872	13.224	1858	33.194	23.177	10.017
1819	32.499	19.482	13.017	1859	33.560	20.294	13.266
1820	31.496	20.877	10.619	1860	32.611	20.189	12.422
1821	32.072	24.045	8.027	1861	31.647	18.361	13.286
1822	33.738	20.313	13.425	1862	30.855	18.292	12.563
1823	32.589	17.657	14.932	1863	30.922	18.142	12.780
1824	31.312	18.569	12.743	1864	30.093	23.164	6.929
1825	31.262	19.236	12.026	1865	31.158	22.989	8.169
1826	31.408	21.135	10.273	1866	32.003	20.724	11.279
1827	29.206	20.039	9.167	1867	30.270	19.847	10.423
1828	30.261	23.560	6.701	1868	30.978	19.225	11.753
1829	29.637	28.790	0.847	1869	29.324	19.010	10.314
1830	28.924	25.306	3.618	1870	30.351	19.013	11.338
1831	29.725	30.124	−0.399	1871	30.103	19.411	10.692
1832	27.034	26.270	0.764	1872	30.325	18.360	11.965
1833	32.262	23.263	8.999	1873	30.779	18.634	12.145
1834	33.044	23.529	9.515	1874	30.861	19.960	10.901
1835	31.694	22.935	8.759	1875	31.883	21.037	10.846
1836	30.464	22.309	8.155	1876	32.623	19.728	12.895
1837	30.012	21.730	8.282	1877	32.261	18.678	13.583
1838	29.782	20.012	9.770	1878	31.593	18.449	13.144
1839	28.969	20.511	8.458	1879	31.865	19.659	12.206

TABLE XXVII—Continued
BIRTH, DEATH AND NET FERTILITY RATES FOR DENMARK, 1800–1931

Year	Birth Rate per 1000	Death Rate per 1000	Net Fertility Rate per 1000	Year	Birth Rate per 1000	Death Rate per 1000	Net Fertility Rate per 1000
1880	31.686	20.363	11.323	1907	28.206	14.146	14.060
1881	32.153	18.281	13.872	1908	28.573	14.645	13.928
1882	32.325	19.244	13.081	1909	28.239	13.097	15.142
1883	31.776	18.434	13.342				
1884	33.320	18.331	14.989	1910	27.511	12.855	14.656
1885	32.497	17.823	14.674	1911	26.691	13.443	13.248
1886	32.380	18.114	14.266	1912	26.645	13.021	13.624
1887	31.741	18.194	13.547	1913	25.582	12.483	13.099
1888	31.464	19.537	11.927	1914	25.574	12.533	13.041
1889	31.182	18.512	12.670	1915	24.196	12.814	11.382
				1916	24.373	13.374	10.999
1890	30.462	18.989	11.473	1917	23.656	13.198	10.458
1891	30.951	20.025	10.926	1918	24.120	12.987	11.133
1892	29.624	19.493	10.131	1919	22.598	13.019	9.579
1893	30.786	19.000	11.786				
1894	30.383	17.575	12.808	1920	25.408	12.940	12.468
1895	30.260	16.948	13.312	1921	23.992	11.024	12.968
1896	30.473	15.650	14.823	1922	22.245	11.876	10.369
1897	29.759	16.571	13.188	1923	22.296	11.294	11.022
1898	30.228	15.466	14.762	1924	21.787	11.240	10.547
1899	29.694	17.261	12.433	1925	20.992	10.827	10.165
				1926	20.491	11.035	9.456
1900	29.658	16.814	12.844	1927	19.575	11.565	8.010
1901	29.736	15.754	13.982	1928	19.593	11.005	8.588
1902	29.223	14.616	14.607	1929	18.561	11.224	7.337
1903	28.721	14.667	14.054				
1904	28.944	14.102	14.842	1930	18.719	10.778	7.941
1905	28.392	14.995	13.397	1931	18.031	11.376	6.655
1906	28.512	13.535	14.977				

Source: *Danmarks Statistik, Statistisk Aarbog.*

TABLE XXVIII
Birth, Death and Net Fertility Rates for England and Wales, 1850–1932

Year	Birth Rate per 1000	Death Rate per 1000	Net Fertility Rate per 1000	Year	Birth Rate per 1000	Death Rate per 1000	Net Fertility Rate per 1000
1850	33.402	20.769	12.633	1892	30.541	19.036	11.505
1851	34.247	21.975	12.272	1893	30.767	19.174	11.593
1852	34.286	22.408	11.878	1894	29.625	16.599	13.026
1853	33.277	22.882	10.395	1895	30.341	18.720	11.621
1854	34.080	23.538	10.542	1896	29.798	17.148	12.650
1855	33.807	22.688	11.119	1897	29.679	17.436	12.243
1856	34.534	20.550	13.984	1898	29.290	17.518	11.772
1857	34.347	21.746	12.601	1899	29.129	18.249	10.880
1858	33.575	23.032	10.543				
1859	35.042	22.441	12.601	1900	28.747	18.228	10.519
				1901	28.511	16.914	11.597
1860	34.369	21.239	13.130	1902	28.543	16.253	12.290
1861	34.614	21.627	12.987	1903	28.483	15.458	13.025
1862	35.018	21.451	13.567	1904	28.104	16.344	11.760
1863	35.329	23.013	12.316	1905	27.341	15.300	12.041
1864	35.532	23.785	11.747	1906	27.228	15.470	11.758
1865	35.479	23.282	12.197	1907	26.457	15.108	11.349
1866	35.322	23.459	11.863	1908	26.823	14.845	11.978
1867	35.559	21.801	13.758	1909	25.815	14.623	11.192
1868	35.959	21.964	13.995				
1869	34.892	22.325	12.567	1910	25.060	13.502	11.558
				1911	24.348	14.584	9.764
1870	35.302	22.947	12.355	1912	23.988	13.384	10.604
1871	35.036	22.622	12.414	1913	24.091	13.795	10.296
1872	35.803	21.340	14.463	1914	23.784	13.981	9.803
1873	35.447	21.040	14.407	1915	23.038	15.901	7.137
1874	36.036	22.197	13.839	1916	22.675	14.671	8.004
1875	35.376	22.726	12.650	1917	19.544	14.590	4.954
1876	36.437	20.940	15.497	1918	19.476	17.983	1.493
1877	35.960	20.263	15.697	1919	19.545	14.232	5.313
1878	35.629	21.566	14.063				
1879	34.701	20.742	13.959	1920	25.853	12.515	13.338
				1921	22.404	12.105	10.299
1880	34.286	20.558	13.728	1922	20.445	12.757	7.688
1881	33.905	18.876	15.029	1923	19.741	11.582	8.159
1882	33.657	19.560	14.097	1924	18.839	12.214	6.625
1883	33.272	19.536	13.736	1925	18.275	12.158	6.117
1884	33.420	19.565	13.855	1926	17.779	11.616	6.163
1885	32.852	19.204	13.648	1927	16.650	12.334	4.316
1886	32.840	19.521	13.319	1928	16.723	11.661	5.062
1887	31.850	19.073	12.777	1929	16.251	13.444	2.807
1888	31.272	18.161	13.111				
1889	31.143	18.221	12.922	1930	16.300	11.400	4.900
				1931	15.800	12.300	3.500
1890	30.244	19.547	10.697	1932*	15.300	12.000	3.300
1891	31.434	20.216	11.218				

* Provisional.
Source: *Statistical Abstract for the United Kingdom.*

TABLE XXIX
Birth, Death and Net Fertility Rates for France, 1801–1931

Year	Birth Rate per 1000	Death Rate per 1000	Net Fertility Rate per 1000	Year	Birth Rate per 1000	Death Rate per 1000	Net Fertility Rate per 1000
1801	32.800	27.700	5.100	1840	27.900	23.700	4.200
1802	33.000	27.700	5.300	1841	28.500	23.200	5.300
1803	32.500	31.200	1.300	1842	28.500	24.000	4.500
1804	31.300	31.000	0.300	1843	28.200	23.100	5.100
1805	31.600	28.800	2.800	1844	27.500	22.000	5.500
1806	31.400	26.800	4.600	1845	27.900	21.100	6.800
1807	31.800	27.600	4.200	1846	27.300	23.200	4.100
1808	31.300	26.500	4.800	1847	25.400	23.900	1.500
1809	32.000	25.000	7.000	1848	26.500	23.600	2.900
				1849	27.700	27.400	0.300
1810	31.800	24.900	6.900	1850	26.800	21.400	5.400
1811	31.600	26.100	5.500	1851	27.143	22.333	4.810
1812	30.100	26.200	3.900	1852	26.838	22.548	4.290
1813	30.500	26.400	4.100	1853	25.865	21.963	3.902
1814	33.900	29.800	4.100	1854	25.670	27.646	−1.976
1815	32.500	26.000	6.500	1855	25.082	26.072	−0.990
1816	32.900	24.500	8.400	1856	26.419	23.227	3.192
1817	31.800	25.300	6.500	1857	26.019	23.753	2.266
1818	30.600	25.300	5.300	1858	26.751	24.125	2.626
1819	32.900	26.100	6.800	1859	28.017	26.955	1.062
1820	31.700	25.400	6.300	1860	26.200	21.402	4.798
1821	31.700	24.300	7.400	1861	26.884	23.180	3.704
1822	31.700	25.300	6.400	1862	26.552	21.666	4.886
1823	31.200	24.000	7.200	1863	26.894	22.489	4.405
1824	31.600	24.500	7.100	1864	26.614	22.763	3.851
1825	31.000	25.900	5.100	1865	26.515	24.304	2.211
1826	31.400	26.500	4.900	1866	26.434	23.237	3.197
1827	30.800	24.900	5.900	1867	26.389	22.700	3.689
1828	30.500	26.200	4.300	1868	25.676	24.055	1.621
1829	30.000	25.000	5.000	1869	25.737	23.452	2.285
1830	29.900	25.000	4.900	1870	25.511	28.306	−2.795
1831	30.300	24.600	5.700	1871	26.606	34.780	−8.174
1832	28.600	28.500	0.100	1872	26.757	21.967	4.790
1833	29.500	24.700	4.800	1873	26.080	23.275	2.805
1834	29.800	27.800	2.000	1874	26.176	21.434	4.742
1835	29.900	24.500	5.400	1875	25.944	23.054	2.890
1836	29.200	22.300	6.900	1876	26.193	22.600	3.593
1837	28.000	25.300	2.700	1877	25.488	21.640	3.848
1838	28.500	24.200	4.300	1878	25.188	22.551	2.637
1839	28.200	22.700	5.500	1879	25.064	22.477	2.587

TABLE XXIX—Continued
BIRTH, DEATH AND NET FERTILITY RATES FOR FRANCE, 1801–1931

Year	Birth Rate per 1000	Death Rate per 1000	Net Fertility Rate per 1000	Year	Birth Rate per 1000	Death Rate per 1000	Net Fertility Rate per 1000
1880	24.526	22.875	1.651	1907	19.672	20.157	−0.485
1881	24.874	22.001	2.873	1908	20.122	18.902	1.220
1882	24.796	22.225	2.571	1909	19.517	19.147	0.370
1883	24.774	22.217	2.557				
1884	25.345	23.210	2.135	1910	19.584	17.778	1.806
1885	24.267	21.966	2.301	1911	18.737	19.570	−0.833
1886	23.884	22.508	1.376	1912	18.915	17.453	1.462
1887	23.506	22.028	1.478	1913	18.758	17.656	1.102
1888	23.051	21.882	1.169	1914[1]	17.875	18.778[2]	−0.903
1889	22.946	20.718	2.228	1915[1]	11.594	18.490[2]	−6.896
				1916[1]	9.528	17.504[2]	−7.976
1890	21.836	22.838	−1.002	1917[1]	10.535	17.929[2]	−7.394
1891	22.595	22.869	−0.274	1918[1]	12.169	22.001[2]	−9.832
1892	22.311	22.833	−0.522	1919[1]	12.618	19.312	−6.694
1893	22.790	22.604	0.186				
1894	22.264	21.229	1.035	1920[3]	21.263	17.117	4.146
1895	21.723	22.187	−0.464	1921	20.688	17.666	3.022
1896	22.473	20.040	2.433	1922	19.272	17.443	1.829
1897	22.199	19.406	2.793	1923	19.087	16.693	2.394
1898	21.745	20.873	0.872	1924	18.693	16.842	1.851
1899	21.790	20.983	0.807	1925	18.935	17.430	1.505
				1926	18.757	17.448	1.309
1900	21.280	21.935	−0.655	1927	18.178	16.509	1.669
1901	22.003	20.145	1.858	1928	18.162	16.455	1.707
1902	21.646	19.496	2.150	1929	17.713	18.019	−0.306
1903	21.131	19.262	1.869				
1904	20.879	19.423	1.546	1930	18.100	15.700	2.400
1905	20.583	19.636	0.947	1931	17.400	16.300	1.100
1906	20.556	19.877	0.679				

[1] Data refer to 77 départements.
[2] Civilian population only.
[3] 90 départements.
Source: *Statistique générale de la France: Mouvement de la Population.*

TABLE XXX
Birth, Death and Net Fertility Rates for:
(a) Germany, 1871–1931
(b) Prussia, 1816–1930

(a) Germany, 1871–1931

Year	Birth Rate per 1000	Death Rate per 1000	Net Fertility Rate per 1000	Year	Birth Rate per 1000	Death Rate per 1000	Net Fertility Rate per 1000
1871	34.496	29.584	4.912	1902	35.050	19.431	15.619
1872	39.438	28.977	10.461	1903	33.836	19.971	13.865
1873	39.653	28.253	11.400	1904	34.062	19.558	14.504
1874	40.078	26.721	13.357	1905	32.947	19.802	13.145
1875	40.557	27.574	12.983	1906	33.072	18.187	14.885
1876	40.898	26.346	14.552	1907	32.250	18.017	14.233
1877	40.006	26.416	13.590	1908	32.055	18.063	13.992
1878	38.850	26.240	12.610	1909	31.048	17.173	13.875
1879	38.885	25.622	13.263				
				1910	29.810	16.195	13.615
1880	37.613	26.016	11.597	1911	28.622	17.301	11.321
1881	37.029	25.455	11.574	1912	28.265	15.568	12.697
1882	37.235	25.741	11.494	1913	27.453	15.004	12.449
1883	36.589	25.861	10.728	1914	26.827	19.049	7.778
1884	37.038	25.973	11.065	1915	20.367	21.366	−0.999
1885	37.038	25.687	11.351	1916	15.203	19.169	−3.966
1886	37.046	26.175	10.871	1917[1]	13.539	19.971	−6.432
1887	36.890	24.185	12.705	1918[1]	13.872	24.045	−10.173
1888	36.568	23.726	12.842	1919[1]	20.041	15.555	4.486
1889	36.385	23.669	12.716				
				1920[1]	25.880	15.097	10.783
1890	35.727	24.350	11.377	1921[1]	24.980	13.770	11.210
1891	37.011	23.400	13.611	1922[1]	22.636	14.196	8.440
1892	35.729	24.100	11.629	1923	20.776	13.753	7.023
1893	36.758	24.592	12.166	1924	20.221	12.078	8.143
1894	35.864	22.290	13.574	1925	20.458	11.787	8.671
1895	36.101	22.144	13.957	1926	19.293	11.538	7.755
1896	36.296	20.832	15.464	1927	18.146	11.824	6.322
1897	35.967	21.319	14.648	1928	18.368	11.484	6.884
1898	36.112	20.547	15.565	1929	17.730	12.600	5.130
1899	35.844	21.452	14.392				
				1930	17.500	11.100	6.400
1900	35.616	22.060	13.556	1931	16.000	11.200	4.800
1901	35.734	20.651	15.083				

[1] Years of territorial changes; after 1922 the data refer to the present territory.
Source: *Statistisches Jahrbuch für das Deutsche Reich.*

TABLE XXX—Continued
BIRTH, DEATH AND NET FERTILITY RATES FOR:
(b) PRUSSIA, 1816–1930

Year	Birth Rate per 1000	Death Rate per 1000	Net Fertility Rate per 1000	Year	Birth Rate per 1000	Death Rate per 1000	Net Fertility Rate per 1000
1816	44.000	28.200	15.800	1856	36.400	27.800	8.600
1817	43.900	29.700	14.200	1857	40.600	30.100	10.500
1818	43.800	29.700	14.100	1858	41.700	29.600	12.100
1819	45.600	31.000	14.600	1859	42.100	27.800	14.300
1820	44.100	27.000	17.100	1860	40.600	25.600	15.000
1821	44.700	25.500	19.200	1861	39.600	27.200	12.400
1822	43.800	27.400	16.400	1862	39.100	26.400	12.700
1823	42.800	27.300	15.500	1863	41.500	28.000	13.500
1824	42.700	26.900	15.800	1864	41.700	28.200	13.500
1825	43.500	27.200	16.300	1865	41.200	29.200	12.000
1826	42.900	29.000	13.900	1866	41.100	35.900	5.200
1827	39.500	29.400	10.100	1867	38.600	28.100	10.500
1828	39.800	29.700	10.100	1868	38.600	29.000	9.600
1829	38.900	30.500	8.400	1869	39.700	28.100	11.600
1830	38.700	30.400	8.300	1870	40.200	29.000	11.200
1831	37.800	35.600	2.200	1871	35.300	30.200	5.100
1832	37.000	32.300	4.700	1872	41.500	31.100	10.400
1833	40.900	31.500	9.400	1873	41.500	29.800	11.700
1834	41.800	31.900	9.900	1874	42.100	27.700	14.400
1835	39.500	28.200	11.300	1875	42.800	28.600	14.200
1836	40.200	27.400	12.800	1876	42.700	27.400	15.300
1837	40.000	31.500	8.500	1877	41.700	27.400	14.300
1838	40.200	27.900	12.300	1878	40.500	27.500	13.000
1839	40.000	29.900	10.100	1879	40.800	26.400	14.400
1840	40.100	28.600	11.500	1880	39.700	27.300	12.400
1841	39.600	27.800	11.800	1881	38.600	26.500	12.100
1842	41.300	28.800	12.500	1882	39.200	27.000	12.200
1843	39.500	29.000	10.500	1883	38.600	27.200	11.400
1844	40.300	26.100	14.200	1884	39.200	27.300	11.900
1845	41.200	27.600	13.600	1885	39.400	27.100	12.300
1846	39.300	29.700	9.600	1886	39.400	27.800	11.600
1847	36.200	31.800	4.400	1887	39.400	25.500	13.900
1848	35.700	33.500	2.200	1888	39.100	24.400	14.700
1849	42.800	30.900	11.900	1889	38.800	24.700	14.100
1850	41.600	28.000	13.600	1890	38.100	25.500	12.600
1851	40.800	26.900	13.900	1891	39.300	24.300	15.000
1852	40.000	33.100	6.900	1892	37.700	24.800	12.900
1853	38.900	30.800	8.100	1893	38.900	25.600	13.300
1854	38.100	29.400	8.700	1894	38.000	23.100	14.900
1855	36.000	32.100	3.900	1895	38.300	23.200	15.100

TABLE XXX—Continued

BIRTH, DEATH AND NET FERTILITY RATES FOR:

(b) PRUSSIA, 1816–1930

Year	Birth Rate per 1000	Death Rate per 1000	Net Fertility Rate per 1000	Year	Birth Rate per 1000	Death Rate per 1000	Net Fertility Rate per 1000
1896	38.400	22.100	16.300	1914	27.700	19.100	8.600
1897	38.100	22.400	15.700	1915	21.000	22.000	−1.000
1898	38.300	21.400	16.900	1916	16.000	19.000	−3.000
1899	37.800	22.700	15.100	1917	14.400	20.600	−6.200
				1918	14.600	25.200	−10.600
1900	37.500	23.100	14.400	1919	20.300	15.900	4.400
1901	36.200	20.500	15.700				
1902	35.500	19.200	16.400	1920	25.800	15.400	10.400
1903	34.400	19.700	14.700	1921	24.900	13.600	11.300
1904	34.700	19.200	15.400	1922	23.200	14.500	8.700
1905	33.500	19.600	13.900	1923	21.200	13.900	7.200
1906	33.700	17.900	15.800	1924	20.800	12.200	8.600
1907	33.000	17.800	15.200	1925	20.900	11.800	9.100
1908	32.700	17.900	14.800	1926	19.600	11.600	8.000
1909	31.700	17.000	14.800	1927	18.400	11.900	6.500
				1928	18.600	11.500	7.100
1910	30.500	16.000	14.600	1929	17.900	12.600	5.300
1911	29.400	17.200	12.200				
1912	28.900	15.500	13.400	1930	17.500	10.900	6.500
1913	28.200	14.900	13.300				

Source: *Statistisches Jahrbuch für den Freistaat Preussen.*

TABLE XXXI

Birth, Death and Net Fertility Rates for Switzerland, 1871–1931

Year	Birth Rate per 1000	Death Rate per 1000	Net Fertility Rate per 1000	Year	Birth Rate per 1000	Death Rate per 1000	Net Fertility Rate per 1000
1871	28.973	27.618	1.355	1902	28.509	17.051	11.458
1872	29.783	22.156	7.627	1903	27.370	17.394	9.976
1873	29.678	22.718	6.960	1904	27.324	17.528	9.796
1874	30.393	22.267	8.126	1905	26.922	17.578	9.344
1875	31.844	24.039	7.805	1906	26.853	16.631	10.222
1876	32.799	24.140	8.659	1907	26.223	16.441	9.782
1877	32.037	23.461	8.576	1908	26.387	15.819	10.568
1878	31.332	23.298	8.034	1909	25.500	16.099	9.401
1879	30.549	22.563	7.986				
				1910	25.039	15.127	9.912
1880	29.649	21.919	7.730	1911	24.185	15.789	8.396
1881	29.849	22.429	7.420	1912	24.142	14.167	9.975
1882	28.878	21.949	6.929	1913	23.229	14.345	8.884
1883	28.520	20.434	8.086	1914	22.408	13.761	8.647
1884	28.272	20.207	8.065	1915	19.456	13.270	6.186
1885	27.744	21.252	6.492	1916	18.971	13.038	5.933
1886	27.782	20.661	7.121	1917	18.538	13.712	4.826
1887	27.858	20.199	7.659	1918	18.728	19.341	−0.613
1888	27.690	19.882	7.808	1919	18.641	14.197	4.444
1889	27.614	20.313	7.301				
				1920	20.942	14.442	6.500
1890	26.621	20.947	5.674	1921	20.805	12.749	8.056
1891	28.194	20.635	7.559	1922	19.603	12.923	6.680
1892	27.687	19.045	8.642	1923	19.362	11.785	7.577
1893	27.931	20.089	7.842	1924	18.763	12.504	6.259
1894	27.348	20.114	7.234	1925	18.436	12.163	6.273
1895	27.288	19.187	8.101	1926	18.216	11.733	6.483
1896	28.063	17.802	10.261	1927	17.440	12.341	5.099
1897	28.253	17.689	10.564	1928	17.318	11.960	5.358
1898	28.458	18.265	10.193	1929	17.029	12.447	4.582
1899	28.955	17.651	11.304				
				1930	17.242	11.586	5.656
1900	28.581	19.275	9.306	1931	16.725	12.109	4.616
1901	29.045	17.966	11.079				

Source: *Statistisches Jahrbuch der Schweiz.*

TABLE XXXII
BIRTH, DEATH AND NET FERTILITY RATES FOR ITALY, 1862–1931

Year	Birth Rate per 1000	Death Rate per 1000	Net Fertility Rate per 1000	Year	Birth Rate per 1000	Death Rate per 1000	Net Fertility Rate per 1000
1862	37.988	31.064	6.924	1898	33.517	22.936	10.581
1863	39.014	31.069	7.945	1899	33.873	21.888	11.985
1864	37.928	29.570	8.358				
1865	38.490	29.928	8.562	1900	32.998	23.771	9.227
1866	34.644	25.974	8.670	1901	32.516	21.980	10.536
1867	36.551	34.165	2.386	1902	33.428	22.238	11.190
1868	35.316	30.484	4.832	1903	31.742	22.428	9.314
1869	36.999	27.739	9.260	1904	32.876	21.159	11.717
				1905	32.673	22.003	10.670
1870	35.571	28.904	6.667	1906	32.137	20.911	11.226
1871	35.820	29.058	5.762	1907	31.698	20.896	10.802
1872	37.966	30.780	7.186	1908	33.666	22.765	10.901
1873	36.421	30.092	6.329	1909	32.744	21.670	11.074
1874	34.967	30.396	4.571				
1875	37.813	30.793	7.020	1910	33.290	19.852	13.438
1876	39.340	28.911	10.429	1911	31.525	21.414	10.111
1877	37.132	28.427	8.705	1912	32.375	18.152	14.223
1878	36.317	29.181	7.136	1913	31.692	18.746	12.946
1879	37.944	29.834	8.110	1914	31.069	17.941	13.128
				1915	30.476	20.364	10.112
1880	33.955	30.839	3.116	1916	24.013	19.661	4.352
1881	38.099	27.635	10.464	1917	18.854	18.612	0.242
1882	37.148	27.564	9.584	1918	17.649	32.144	−14.495
1883	37.237	27.601	9.636	1919	21.410	18.790	2.620
1884	39.003	26.923	12.080				
1885	38.568	26.936	11.632	1920	32.037	18.853	13.184
1886	36.966	28.724	8.242	1921	30.568	17.555	13.013
1887	38.931	27.993	10.938	1922	28.925	16.943	11.982
1888	37.538	27.508	10.030	1923	28.191	15.946	12.245
1889	38.262	25.572	12.690	1924	28.420	16.754	11.666
				1925	27.782	16.785	10.997
1890	35.811	26.315	9.496	1926	27.199	16.905	10.294
1891	37.174	26.115	11.059	1927	26.942	15.761	11.181
1892	36.058	26.178	9.880	1928	26.165	15.757	10.408
1893	36.478	25.156	11.322	1929	25.112	16.025	9.087
1894	35.480	24.975	10.505				
1895	34.896	25.045	9.851	1930	26.700	14.090	12.610
1896	34.771	24.063	10.708	1931	24.900	14.710	10.190
1897	34.741	21.932	12.809				

Source: *Annuario Statistico Italiano.*

TABLE XXXIII
Trend Ratios of Indexes of Real Wages, Birth Rates, and
Net Growth Rates in England and Wales, 1861–1912

A. 1861–1877
Trend Ratios of

Year	Real Wages	Birth Rates	Net Growth Rates
1861	92.0	99.0	105.0
1862	93.0	100.0	107.0
1863	99.0	100.0	99.0
1864	108.0	101.0	96.0
1865	109.0	101.0	98.0
1866	105.0	101.0	94.0
1867	94.0	100.0	105.0
1868	92.0	101.0	106.0
1869	97.0	98.0	95.0
1870	101.0	100.0	93.0
1871	105.0	99.0	93.0
1872	104.0	100.0	103.0
1873	108.0	99.0	103.0
1874	110.0	101.0	99.0
1875	109.0	99.0	91.0
1876	106.0	101.0	107.0
1877	101.0	100.0	107.0

B. 1878–1912

Year	Real Wages	Birth Rates	Net Growth Rates
1878	96.0	101.0	101.0
1879	93.0	99.0	100.0
1880	96.0	99.0	100.0
1881	97.0	99.0	109.0
1882	96.0	100.0	105.0
1883	98.0	100.0	102.0
1884	93.0	101.0	105.0
1885	93.0	101.0	104.0
1886	93.0	101.0	102.0
1887	97.0	99.0	99.0
1888	99.0	98.0	102.0
1889	102.0	99.0	101.0
1890	106.0	97.0	86.0
1891	102.0	102.0	91.0
1892	97.0	100.0	93.0
1893	98.0	102.0	94.0
1894	99.0	99.0	105.0
1895	101.0	102.0	94.0
1896	104.0	100.0	102.0
1897	103.0	101.0	98.0
1898	103.0	100.0	96.0
1899	106.0	100.0	87.0

TABLE XXXIII—Continued

TREND RATIOS OF INDEXES OF REAL WAGES, BIRTH RATES, AND NET GROWTH RATES IN ENGLAND AND WALES, 1861–1912

B. 1878–1912
TREND RATIOS OF

Year	Real Wages	Birth Rates	Net Growth Rates
1900	106.0	99.0	85.0
1901	104.0	99.0	93.0
1902	102.0	101.0	102.0
1903	100.0	102.0	109.0
1904	97.0	101.0	99.0
1905	97.0	101.0	104.0
1906	99.0	101.0	103.0
1907	100.0	99.0	102.0
1908	93.0	102.0	109.0
1909	94.0	100.0	104.0
1910	98.0	99.0	111.0
1911	104.0	97.0	96.0
1912	105.0	97.0	105.0

For explanation see text, chapter XV.

TABLE XXXIV

LINK RELATIVES OF CAPITAL GROWTH AND INTEREST RATES FOR THE
UNITED KINGDOM

Year	Link Relatives of Absolute Increments of Capital	Link Relatives of Percentage Rates of Growth of Capital	Link Relatives of Consol Yields
1865	. . . . .	. . . . .	100.6
1866	. . . . .	. . . . .	101.8
1867	107.0	103.0	94.7
1868	100.0	97.1	99.1
1869	102.2	100.0	100.9
1870	116.0	112.1	100.3
1871	133.0	127.0	99.7
1872	109.7	106.4	100.3
1873	96.2	92.0	100.0
1874	98.7	93.5	100.0
1875	89.4	86.0	98.8
1876	41.5	40.5	98.8
1877	82.1	80.0	99.7
1878	132.6	133.3	100.0
1879	123.0	118.8	97.8
1880	88.0	84.2	99.0
1881	151.5	150.0	98.4
1882	95.0	95.8	99.7
1883	95.8	91.3	99.0
1884	128.6	128.6	100.3
1885	94.9	92.6	101.7
1886	103.6	100.0	98.7
1887	102.6	100.0	99.0
1888	107.6	104.0	92.2
1889	95.3	92.3	103.3
1890	109.9	108.3	101.4
1891	78.2	76.9	100.7
1892	86.5	85.0	99.0
1893	104.4	100.0	98.2
1894	78.7	76.5	97.5
1895	105.4	107.7	95.2
1896	126.9	121.4	95.4
1897	87.9	88.2	98.8
1898	89.7	86.7	101.2
1899	110.3	107.7	103.6
1900	102.3	107.1	107.4
1901	88.6	86.7	105.8
1902	96.2	92.3	99.7
1903	118.7	116.7	94.5
1904	104.5	107.1	102.9
1905	135.5	133.3	98.2
1906	124.6	120.0	101.8
1907	121.7	116.7	104.9
1908	101.0	100.0	97.6
1909	90.7	89.3	102.8
1910	. . . . .	. . . . .	103.4

TABLE XXXV

LINK RELATIVES OF CAPITAL GROWTH AND INTEREST RATES FOR THE
UNITED STATES

Year	Link Relatives of Percentage Rates of Growth of Capital	Link Relatives of Absolute Increments of Capital	Link Relatives of Average Bond Yield
1880	.....	.....	100.0
1881	.....	.....	89.0
1882	117.4	127.7	98.3
1883	101.0	111.3	103.8
1884	56.9	62.3	98.1
1885	86.2	91.1	97.5
1886	106.0	111.9	92.7
1887	245.3	258.3	100.0
1888	1.5	2.1	101.1
1889	2400.0	2000.0	92.2
1890	60.4	63.7	103.2
1891	179.3	184.3	103.7
1892	61.5	64.7	101.1
1893	112.5	114.6	99.2
1894	52.8	55.1	99.5
1895	.....	.....	94.2
1896	.....	.....	98.5
1897	80.0	82.6	98.8
1898	171.9	177.2	94.9
1899	63.6	68.1	96.9
1900	142.9	145.7	100.6
1901	168.0	177.6	100.0
1902	35.7	38.5	100.6
1903	210.0	215.8	106.1
1904	71.4	76.8	104.5
1905	151.1	156.8	98.3
1906	132.4	141.1	101.2
1907	96.7	105.7	104.5
1908	37.9	41.3	101.9
1909	103.0	104.6	98.6
1910	79.4	84.1	102.8
1911	159.3	163.7	101.6
1912	97.7	101.2	100.3
1913	83.3	87.2	102.1
1914	88.6	90.3	104.1
1915	122.6	128.6	101.7
1916	89.5	92.4	97.6
1917	126.5	130.2	106.0
1918	86.0	89.9	106.4
1919	56.8	57.9	102.2
1920	76.2	76.7	104.8
1921	62.5	67.5	101.2
1922	180.0	180.8	90.4
1923	.....	.....	99.8
1924	.....	.....	100.7
1925	.....	.....	100.4

For explanation see text, chapter XVIII.

BIBLIOGRAPHY

BIBLIOGRAPHY

The following references may be of some value to the student of wage theory who wishes to pursue the subject further.

The vast majority of the works cited have been used in the preparation of this work and the references represent those books and articles in the English, French, German, and Italian languages which the author believes to be most helpful.

It is not, however, a complete or definitive bibliography of the subjects listed, since this would require one or more volumes in itself.

To help the student, the books and sources have been classified under the following eight main headings with subdivisions under each:

    I. The General Theory of Distribution.
    II. The Theory of Wages.
    III. The Theory of Production.
    IV. The Long-Time Supply of Labor.
    V. The Short-Run Supply of Labor.
    VI. The Movement of Money and Real Wages.
    VII. The Theory of Interest.
    VIII. The Probable Supply Curve of Capital.

I. THE GENERAL THEORY OF DISTRIBUTION

1. Classical

Anderson, James: *An Enquiry Into the Nature of the Corn Laws.* Edinburgh, 1777. 60 pp.

Anderson, James: *Observations on the Means of Exciting a Spirit of National Industry.* Dublin, S. Price, etc., 1779. 2 vols.

Bagehot, Walter: *Economic Studies.* Edited by Richard Holt Hutton. 2d edition. London and New York, Longmans, Green & Co., 1888. 215 pp.

Bastiat, Frederic: *Harmonies of Political Economy.* Translation from the French by Patrick James Stirling. London, J. Murray, 1860–1870. 2 vols.

Bastiat, Frederic: *Harmonies Economiques.* 10 ed. Paris, Guillaumin et Cie, 1893, 660 pp.

Bastiat, Frederic: *Capital et Rente.* Paris, Guillaumin et Cie, 1849. 60 pp.

Bonar, James: *Malthus and His Work.* New York, Macmillan Co., 1885, 432 pp.

Cairnes, J. E.: *Some Leading Principles of Political Economy Newly Expounded.* New York, Harper & Bros., 1874. 421 pp.

Cairnes, J. E.: *Essays in Political Economy.* London, Macmillan & Co., 1873. 371 pp.

Cannan, Edwin: *A History of the Theories of Production and Distribution in English Political Economy from 1776–1848.* 3d edition. London, P. S. King & Son, 1924. 422 pp.

Cannan, Edwin: *A Review of Economic Theory.* London, P. S. King & Son, 1929. 448 pp.

Child, Josiah: *A New Discourse of Trade.* To which is added a short treatise of interest. 5th edition. Glasgow, R. & A. Foulis, 1751. 184 pp.

Hume, David: *Essays and Treatises on Several Subjects.* London, Printed for T. Cadell (etc.), 1770. 4 vols.

Lauderdale, James Maitland: *An Inquiry Into the Nature and Origin of Public Wealth.* 2d edition. Edinburgh, A. Constable & Co., 1819. 465 pp.

Longfield, Mountifort: *Lectures on Political Economy.* Dublin, W. Curry, Jr., & Co., 1834. 267 pp.

McCulloch, J. R.: (Article) "Political Economy" in *Encyclopædia Britannica.* 4th edition supplement, 1823.

McCulloch, J. R.: *The Principles of Political Economy.* London, A. Murray & Son, 1870. 360 pp.

McCulloch, J. R.: *Notes of Mr. McCulloch's Lecture on the Wages of Labour and the Condition of the Labouring People. . . .* Bradford, printed by Inkersley, 1825. 16 pp.

Malthus, Thomas Robert: *Principles of Political Economy.* 2d edition. London, W. Pickering, 1836. 446 pp.

Marcet, Mrs. Jane: *Conversations on Political Economy.* 3d edition. London, Longman, Hurst, etc., 1819. 486 pp.

Mill, James: *Elements of Political Economy.* 3d edition. London, H. G. Bohn, 1844. 304 pp.

Mill, John Stuart: *Principles of Political Economy.* Ashley edition. New York and London, Longmans, Green & Co., 1909. 1013 pp.

Quesnay, François: *Oeuvres économiques et philosophiques.* Francfort S/M, J. Baer et Cie, 1888. 814 pp.

Ricardo, David: *Works Including Principles of Political Economy, High Price of Bullion, Proposal for an Economical and Secure Currency,* etc. Edited by J. R. McCulloch. London, J. Murray, 1888. 584 pp.

Say, Jean-Baptiste: *Traité d'Économie Politique.* Paris, Guillaumin et Cie, 1841. 640 pp. English translation by C. R. Princep. New American edition, Philadelphia, J. B. Lippincott Co., 1855. 488 pp.

Senior, N. W.: *Political Economy.* 6th edition. London, Charles Griffin & Co., 1872. 231 pp.

Sidgwick, Henry: *The Principles of Political Economy.* 2d edition. London and New York, Macmillan Co., 1887. 595 pp.

Smith, Adam: *The Wealth of Nations.* Edwin Cannan's edition. London, Methuen & Co., [1904.] 2 vols.

Torrens, Robert: *An Essay on the External Corn Trade.* London, printed for Longman, Rees, etc., 1826. 416 pp.

Walker, Francis A.: *Political Economy.* New York, Henry Holt, 1887. 537 pp.

West, Sir Edward: *Price of Corn and Wages of Labour.* London, J. Hatchard & Son, 1826. 150 pp.

2. Austrian

Aftalion, Albert: "Les Trois Notions de la Productivité et les Revenus," *Revue d'Économie Politique,* Tome XXV, 1911, pp. 145–184 and 345–369.

Böhm-Bawerk, Eugen von: "The Austrian Economists" *Annals of the American Academy of Political and Social Science,* Vol. I, 1891, pp. 361–384.

Clark, J. B., and Giddings, Franklin Henry: *The Modern Distributive Process.* Boston, Ginn & Co., 1888. 69 pp. See especially *The Natural Rate of Wages* by F. H. Giddings.

Clark, John Bates: "Distribution as Determined by a Law of Rent," *Quarterly Journal of Economics,* Vol. V, pp. 289–318.

Clark, John Bates: "The Statics and the Dynamics of Distribution," *Quarterly Journal of Economics,* Vol. VI, pp. 111–119.

Clark, John Bates: "The Law of Wages and Interest," *Annals of the American Academy of Political and Social Science,* Vol. I, 1890, pp. 43–65.

Clark, John Bates: *The Philosophy of Wealth. Economic Principles Newly Formulated.* Boston, Ginn & Co., 1894. 236 pp.

Clark, John Bates: *Essentials of Economic Theory as Applied to Modern Problems of Industry and Public Policy.* New York, Macmillan Co., 1907. 566 pp.

Clark, John Bates: *The Distribution of Wealth, A Theory of Wages, Interest and Profits.* New York and London, Macmillan Co., 1902. 445 pp.

Engländer, Oskar: "Karl Mengers Grundsätze der Volkswirtschaftslehre" *Schmollers Jahrbuch,* Vol. LI, 1927, pp. 371–401.

Fetter, Frank Albert: *Economics.* New York, Century Co., 1915–1916. 2 vols.

Jevons, William Stanley. *The Theory of Political Economy.* 4th edition. London and New York, Macmillan Co., 1911. 339 pp.

Kleinwächter, F. von: "Die Lehre vom Grenznutzen and das sogenannte Zurechnungsproblem der Wiener Nationalökonomischen Schule," *Jahrbücher für Nationalökonomie und Statistik,* Vol. 114, 1929, pp. 97–133.

Macvane, S.: "The Austrian Theory of Value," *Annals of the American Academy of Political and Social Science*, Vol. IV, pp. 348-377.

Mayer, H.: "Zurechnung," *Handwörterbuch der Staatswissenschaften*, Vol. VIII, pp. 1206–1228 (4th edition, 1928) and "Verteilung," *Ibid.*, pp. 675–678.

Menger, Karl: *Grundsätze der Volkswirtschaftslehre.* 2d edition. Wien, Holder-Tichler-Temsky, etc., 1923. 335 pp.

Mitchell, W. C.: "Wieser's Theory of Social Economics," *Political Science Quarterly*, Vol. XXXII, pp. 95–118.

Montemartini, G.: "Über die Theorie der Grenzproductivität," *Zeitsch. f. Volksw. Sozialpol. u. Ver.*, Vol. VIII, pp. 467–503.

Philippovitch, Eugen von: *Grundriss der Politischen Oekonomie.* Tübingen, J. C. B. Mohr, 1893–1907. 2 vols.

Schumpeter, Joseph: "John Bates Clark, Essentials of Economic Theory as Applied to Modern Problems of Industry and Public Policy," *Zeitsch. f. Volksw. Sozialpol. u. Ver.*, Vol. XVII, pp. 653–659.

Schumpeter, Joseph: "Das Rentenprincip in der Verteilungslehre," *Schmollers Jahrbuch*, 1907, Vol. XXXI, pp. 31–65 and pp. 591–634.

Schumpeter, Joseph: "Professor Clark's Verteilungstheorie," *Zeitsch. f. Volksw. Sozialpol. u. Ver.*, Vol. XV, pp. 325–333.

Schumpeter, Joseph: *Das Wesen und der Hauptinhalt der theoretischen Nationalökonomie.* Leipzig, Duncker & Humblot, 1908. 626 pp. See also H. Mayer in *Zeitsch. f. Volksw. Sozialpol. u. Ver.*, Vol. XX, pp. 181–209.

Wieser, Friedrich von: *Natural Value.* Translated by W. Smart. London and New York, Macmillan Co., 1893. 240 pp.

Wieser, Friedrich von: *Über den Ursprung und die Hauptgesetze des Wirtchaftlichen Werthes.* Wien, A. Hölder, 1884. 214 pp.

Wieser, Friedrich von: "The Theory of Value [A Reply to Professor Macvane]." *Annals of the American Academy.* Vol. II, pp. 600–629. 1892.

Wieser, Friedrich von: "The Austrian School and the Theory of Value," *Economic Journal*, Vol. I, pp. 108–121.

Wieser, Friedrich von: *Social Economics.* Translated by A. Ford Hinrichs. New York, Greenberg, [1927.] 470 pp.

3. Mathematical

Allen, R. G. D.: "The Foundation of a Mathematical Theory of Exchange," *Economica*, 1932, No. 36, pp. 197–225.

Amoroso, Luigi: *Lezioni di Economica Matematica.* Bologna, N. Zanichelli, 1921. 478 pp.

Amoroso, Luigi: "Contributo alla teoria matematica della dinamica economica," *R. accad. d. Lincei Rendic. classe di Sci. fis. Ser. 5,* Vol. XXI, part I, pp. 259–265, 341–345.

Amoroso, Luigi: "L'Applicazione della Matematica alla Economia Politica," *Giornale degli Economisti,* Vol. XL, 1910, pp. 57–63.

Antonelli, Etienne: *Principes d'Économie Pure.* Paris, Marcel Rivière, 1914. 206 pp.

Barone, Enrico: *"Grundzüge der Theoretischen Nationalökonomie.* Translated by Hans Staehle. Bonn, Kurt Schroeder Verlag, 1927. 275 pp.

Barone, Enrico: "Studi Sulla Distribuzione," *Giornale degli Econ.,* February and March, 1896. pp. 107–155, 235–252.

Boven, Pierre: *Les Applications Mathématiques a l'Économie Politique.* Lausanne, F. Rouge et Cie, 1912. 204 pp.

Bowley, A. L.: *The Mathematical Groundwork of Economics.* Oxford, Clarendon Press, 1924. 98 pp.

Cassel, Gustav: *Fundamental Thoughts in Economics.* London, T. F. Unwin, 1925. 159 pp.

Cassel, Gustav: *The Theory of Social Economy.* Translated by Joseph McCabe. New York, Harcourt, Brace & Co., 1924. 2 vols.

Conrad, Otto: "Der Zusammenbruch der Grenznutzentheorie, eine Auseinandersetzung mit Joseph Schumpeter," *Jahrbücher für Nationalökonomie und Statistik,* Vol. 129, pp. 481–528.

Cournot, Antoine Augustin: *Researches into the Mathematical Principles of the Theory of Wealth.* Translated by N. T. Bacon. New York, Macmillan Co., 1897, in Economic Classics. 171 pp.

Cournot, Antoine Augustin: *Recherches sur les Principes Mathématiques de la Théorie des Richesses.* Paris, 1838. 198 pp.

Cunynghame, Sir Henry H. S.: *A Geometrical Political Economy.* Oxford, Clarendon Press, 1904. 128 pp.

Edgeworth, Francis Y.: *Mathematical Psychics.* London, C. Kegan Paul & Co., 1881. 150 pp.

Edgeworth, Francis Y.: *Papers Relating to Political Economy.* London, Macmillan & Co., 1925. 3 vols.

Edgeworth, Francis Y.: "The Theory of Distribution," *Quarterly Journal of Economics,* Vol. XVIII, pp. 159–219.

Evans, Griffith Conrad: *Mathematical Introduction to Economics.* New York. McGraw-Hill Book Co., 1930. 177 pp.

Fisher, Irving: *Elementary Principles of Economics.* New York, Macmillan Co., 1912. 514 pp.

Fisher, Irving: *Mathematical Investigation in the Theory of Money and Prices.* 1892. (Reprinted in 1926 by the Yale University Press, New Haven.) 126 pp.

Frisch, Ragnar: *New Methods of Measuring Marginal Utility.* Tübingen, J. C. B. Mohr, 1932. 142 pp.

Gossen, Hermann Heinrich: *Entwicklung der Gesetze des Menschlichen Verkehrs.* New edition. Berlin, R. L. Prager, 1889. 277 pp.

Jevons, W. Stanley: *The Theory of Political Economy.* London, Macmillan & Co., 1888 (3d edition). 296 pp.

Kühne, Otto: *Die Mathematische Schule in der Nationalökonomie.* Berlin, 1928, W. De Gruyter & Co.

Lampe, A.: "Schumpeter's System und die Ausgestaltung der Verteilungslehre," *Jahrbücher für Nationalökonomie und Statistik,* Vol. 121, 1923, pp. 417–444 and 513–546.

Moore, Henry L.: *Synthetic Economics.* New York, Macmillan Co., 1929. 186 pp.

Moret, Jacques. *L'Emploi des Mathématiques en Économie Politique.* Paris, M. Giard & E. Brière, 1915. 271 pp.

Morss, Noel: "The Distribution Equilibrium under the Specific Productivity Theory," *Quarterly Journal of Economics,* Vol. XLI, pp. 349–352.

Pantaleoni, Maffeo: *Principii di Economia Pura.* 2d edition. Firenze, G. Barbera, 1894. 376 pp.

Pareto, Vilfredo: *Cours d'Économie Politique.* Lausanne, F. Rouge, Paris, Pichon [etc.] 1897. 2 vols.

Pareto, Vilfredo: *Manuel d'Économie Politique.* Paris (2d edition.) 1927, Marcel Giard. 695 pp.

Pareto, Vilfredo: "La Courbe de la Répartition de la Richesse." (Extrait du recueil public par la faculté de droit de l'université de Lausanne à l'occasion de l'exposition nationale suisse.) Genève, 1896. pp. 373–387.

Sanger, C. P.: "Recent Contributions to Mathematical Economics," *Economic Journal,* Vol. V, pp. 113–128.

Schultz, Henry: "The Italian School of Mathematical Economics," *Journal of Political Economy,* Vol. XXXIX, pp. 76–85.

Schultz, Henry: "Frisch on the Measurement of Marginal Utility." *Journal of Political Economy.* (February, 1933) Vol. XLI, pp. 94–110.

Schumpeter, Joseph: "Das Grundprinzip der Verteilungstheorie," *Archiv für Sozialwissenschaft und Sozialpolitik,* Vol. XLII, p. 22.

Schumpeter, Joseph: "Bemerkungen über das Zurechnungsproblem," *Zeitsch. f. Volksw. Sozialpol. u. Ver.,* Vol. XVIII, pp. 79–132.

Schumpeter, Joseph: *Das Wesen und der Hauptinhalt der Theoretischen Nationalökonomie.* Leipzig, Duncker & Humblot, 1908. 626 pp.

Walras Léon: *Études d'Économie Sociale.* Lausanne, F. Rouge, 1896. 464 pp.

Walras, Léon: *Éléments d'Économie Politique Pure.* 2d edition. Lausanne, F. Rouge, etc. 523 pp.

Walras, Léon: *Études d'Économie Politique Appliquée.* Lausanne, F. Rouge, 1898. 499 pp.

Wicksell, Knut: *Über Wert, Kapital und Rente nach den neueren Nationalökonomischen Theorien.* Jena, G. Fischer, 1893. 143 pp.

Wicksell, Knut: *Vorlesungen über Nationalökonomie.* Jena, G. Fischer, 1913–28. Theoretischer Teil. First vol.

Wicksteed, Philip H.: *The Common Sense of Political Economy, including a Study of the Human Basis of Economic Law.* London, Macmillan & Co., 1910. 702 pp.

Wicksteed, Philip H.: *An Essay on the Coördination of the Laws of Distribution.* London, Macmillan & Co., 1894. 56 pp.

Wicksteed, Philip H.: *The Alphabet of Economic Science.* London and New York, Macmillan Co., 1888. 142 pp.

Zawadzki, Wl.: *Les Mathématiques Appliquées à L'Économie Politique.* Paris, Marcel Rivière. 1914. 331 pp.

4. Neo-Classical

Bye, Raymond T.: *Principles of Economics.* New York, Alfred A. Knopf, 1924. 508 pp. Chap. XVII. (Distribution.)

Cannan, E.: *Wealth; a Brief Explanation of the Causes of Economic Welfare.* London, P. S. King & Son, 1914. 274 pp.

Cannan, E.: "The Division of Income," *Quarterly Journal of Economics,* Vol. XIX, pp. 341–369.

Carver, Thomas N.: "The Marginal Theory of Distribution," *Journal of Political Economy,* Vol. XIII, pp. 257–266.

Carver, Thomas N.: *The Distribution of Wealth.* New York, Macmillan Co., 1908. 290 pp.

Carver, Thomas N.: *Principles of Political Economy.* Boston and New York, Ginn & Co., 1919. 588 pp.

Carver, Thomas N.: "Clark's Distribution of Wealth," *Quarterly Journal of Economics,* Vol. XV, pp. 578–602.

Commons, John R.: *The Distribution of Wealth.* New York and London, Macmillan Co., 1905. 258 pp.

Fetter, Frank A.: *The Principles of Economics.* New York, Century Co., 1904. 610 pp.

Flux, A. W.: *Economic Principles.* 2d edition. New York, E. P. Dutton & Co., 1923. 305 pp.

Knight, Frank H.: *Risk, Uncertainty and Profit.* Boston and New York, Houghton Mifflin Co., 1921. 381 pp.

Knight, Frank H.: "Economics at Its Best," *American Economic Review,* Vol. XVI, pp. 51–58.

Marshall, Alfred: *Principles of Economics.* 6th edition. London, Macmillan & Co., 1910. 871 pp.

Marshall, Alfred: "Distribution and Exchange," *Economic Journal,* Vol. VIII, pp. 37–59.

Pigou, Arthur Cecil: *The Economics of Welfare.* 2d edition. London, Macmillan & Co., 1924. 783 pp.

Robinson, Joan: *The Economics of Imperfect Competition.* London, Macmillan Co., 1933. 352 pp.

Seager, Henry R.: *Principles of Economics.* 3d edition. New York, H. Holt & Co., 1923. 698 pp.

Taussig, F. W.: *Principles of Economics.* 3d edition. New York, Macmillan Co., 1928–1930. 2 vols.

Taylor, Fred Manville: *Principles of Economics.* 8th edition. New York, Ronald Press, 1921. 577 pp.

Young, A. A.: "Pigou's Wealth and Welfare," *Quarterly Journal of Economics,* Vol. XXVII, pp. 672–686.

5. Institutionalist

Anderson, Benjamin M.: *Social Value, A Study in Economic Theory, Critical and Constructive.* Cambridge, Riverside Press, 1911. 204 pp.

Burns, E. M.: "Does Institutionalism Complement or Compete with 'Orthodox Economics'?" *American Economic Review,* Vol. XXI, pp. 80–87.

Clark, J. M.: "Economic Theory of an Era of Social Readjustment," *American Economic Review,* Vol. IX, supplement, pp. 280–290.

Clark, J. M.: "Economics and Modern Psychology," *Journal of Political Economy,* Vol. XXVI, pp. 1–30 and 136–166.

Commons, John R.: *The Distribution of Wealth.* New York and London, Macmillan Co., 1905. 258 pp.

Copeland, M. A.: "Economic Theory and the Natural Science Point of View," *American Economic Review,* Vol. XXI, 1931, pp. 67–79.

Edie, Lionel Danforth: *Principles of the New Economics.* New York, Thomas Y. Crowell Co., 1922. 525 pp.

Edie, Lionel Danforth: "Some Positive Contributions to the Institutional Concept," *Quarterly Journal of Economics,* Vol. XLI, pp. 405–440.

Hadley, Arthur T.: *Economics, an Account of the Relations Between Private Property and Public Welfare.* New York, G. P. Putnam's Sons, 1899. 496 pp.

Hadley, Arthur T.: "Some Fallacies in the Theory of Distribution," *Economic Journal,* Vol. VII, pp. 477–486.

Hamilton, Walter H.: "The Institutional Approach to Economic Theory," *American Economic Review,* Vol. IX, supplement, pp. 309–324.

Hobson, J. A.: *The Economics of Distribution.* New York, Macmillan Co., 1900. 361 pp.

Hobson, J. A.: "The Law of the Three Rents," *Quarterly Journal of Economics,* Vol. V, pp. 263–288.

Hobson, J. A.: "The Subjective and the Objective View of Distribution," *Annals of the American Association of Political and Social Science*, Vol. IV, pp. 378–403.

Hobson, J. A.: "Marginal Units in the Theory of Distribution," *Journal of Political Economy*, Vol. XII, pp. 449–472.

Hobson, J. A.: "Neo-Classical Economics in Britain," *Political Science Quarterly*, Vol. XL, 1925, pp. 337–383.

Jaffé, William: *Les Théories Économiques et Sociales de Thorstein Veblen.* Paris, M. Giard, 1924. 187 pp.

Knies, Karl: *Die politische Ökonomie vom Standpunkt der geschichtlichen Methode.* Braunschweig, C. A. Schwetschke & Sohn, 1883. 533 pp.

Laughlin, J. Laurence: "Hobson's Theory of Distribution," *Journal of Political Economy*, Vol. XII, pp. 305–326.

Leroy-Beaulieu, Paul: *Essai sur la Répartition des Richesses et sur la tendance à une moindre inégalité des conditions.* 4th edition. Paris, Guillaumin et Cie, 1897. 630 pp.

Patten, Simon H.: "The Theory of Dynamic Economics." Publications of the University of Pennsylvania, *Political Economy and Public Law Series*, Vol. III, No. 2, Philadelphia, 1892.

Roscher, Wilhelm G. F.: *Principles of Political Economy.* Translated by John Lalor. Chicago, Callaghan & Co., 1878. 2 vols. Vol. II. Book III on Distribution. Chap. III on Wages.

Schmoller, Gustav: *Grundriss der Allgemeinen Volkswirtschaftslehre.* Leipzig, Duncker & Humblot, 1900–1904. 2 vols.

Veblen, Thorstein. *The Place of Science in Modern Civilization.* New York, B. W. Huebsch, 1919. 509 pp.

6. General

Berry, Arthur: "The Pure Theory of Distribution." Report of *British Association for the Advancement of Science*, 1890, pp. 923–924.

Broda, E.: "Die Lösungen des Zurechnungsproblems," *Zeitsch. f. Volksw. Sozialpol. u. Ver.*, Vol. XX, 353 pp.

Carey, Henry Charles: *Principles of Political Economy.* Philadelphia, Carey, Lea & Blanchard, 1837–1840. 3 vols.

Carey, Henry Charles: *Manual of Social Science;* being a Condensation of the Principles of Social Science. Kate McKean, 1865. Philadelphia, H. C. Baird. 548 pp.

Davenport, Herbert Joseph. *Value and Distribution,* a critical and constructive study. Chicago. University of Chicago Press, 1908. 582 pp.

Davenport, Herbert Joseph: "Non-Competing Groups," *Quarterly Journal of Economics*, Vol. XL, pp. 52–81.

Davenport, Herbert Joseph: *The Economics of Enterprise.* New York, Macmillan Co., 1913. 544 pp.

Devas, Charles Stanton: *Political Economy*. London, New York, etc., Longmans, Green & Co., 1920. 672 pp. Book III Distribution.

Diehl, Karl: Gibt es ein allgemeines Ertragsgesetz für alle Gebiete des Wirtschaftslebens?" *Jahrbücher für Nationalökonomie und Statistik.* Vol. 120, pp. 1–32.

Diehl, Karl: "Zurechnungstheorie und Verteilungslehre," *Jahrbücher für Nationalökonomie und Statistik*, Vol. 131, pp. 641–687.

Gide, Charles: *Political Economy*. Translation from the 3d edition of the "Cours d'Économie Politique." Boston, New York, etc., D. C. Heath & Co., 1914. 762 pp.

Hawtrey, Ralph George: *The Economic Problem*. London and New York, Longmans, Green & Co., 1925. 417 pp.

Hayek, Friedrich A. von: "Bemerkungen zum Zurechnungsproblem," *Jahrbücher für Nationalökonomie und Statistik*, Vol. 124, pp. 1–18.

Jennings, Richard: *Natural Elements of Political Economy*. London, Longman, Brown, etc. 1855. 275 pp.

Landry, A.: "On the Returns of Productive Agents and on the Productivity of Capital in Particular," *Quarterly Journal of Economics*, Vol. XXIII. pp. 557–592.

Lederer, Emil: *Grundzüge der Ökonomischen Theorie*. Tübingen, Mohr, 1922. 184 pp.

Lexis, Wilhelm: *Allgemeine Volkswirtschaftslehre*. Berlin and Leipzig, B. G. Teubner, 1910. 259 pp.

Liefmann, R.: "Zurechnung und Verteilung," *Schmollers Jahrbuch*, Vol. XLVIII, 1924. pp. 439–471.

Liefmann, R.: "The Chief Problem of Economic Theory. Note on Prof. Kleene's review of Liefmann's Grundsätze der Volkswirtschaftslehre," *Quarterly Journal of Economics*, Vol. XXXVI, pp. 335–342.

List, Friedyrich: *The National System of Political Economy*. Translated by Sampson S. Lloyd. New edition with an introduction by J. Shield Nicholson. London, Longmans, Green & Co., 1904. 366 pp.

Longfield, Mountifort: "Lectures on Political Economy," *London School of Economics and Political Science*. No. 8 in a series of reprints of scarce tracts in economics and political science. 267 pp.

Macfarlane, Charles William: *Value and Distribution*. Philadelphia, J. B. Lippincott Co., 1899. 317 pp.

Martin, P. W.: *The Flaw in the Price System*. London, P. S. King & Son, 1924. 109 pp.

Mohrmann, Warthold: *Dogmengeschichte der Zurechnungslehre*. Jena, G. Fischer, 1914. 110 pp.

Monroe, Arthur Eli: *Value and Income.* Cambridge, Harvard University Press, 1931. 286 pp.

Nicholson, Joseph Shield: *Elements of Political Economy.* New York and London, Macmillan Co., 1903. 538 pp. Book II on Distribution.

Pierson, Nikolaas Gerard: *Principles of Economics.* Translation by A. A. Wotzel. London and New York, Macmillan Co. 1902–1912. Esp. Chaps. IV and VI.

Rufener, Louis August: *Price, Profit and Production;* principles of economics. Boston and New York, Houghton Mifflin Co., 1928. 842 pp.

Sargant, William Lucas: *Recent Political Economy.* London, 1867. 213 pp.

Schumpeter, Joseph: *Das Wesen und der Hauptinhalt der theoretischen Nationalökonomie.* Leipzig, Duncker & Humblot, 1908. (Esp. part II, Ch. II, and part III.) 626 pp.

Smart, William: *The Distribution of Income.* London, New York, Macmillan Co., 1899. 341 pp.

Stucken, Rudolf: "Gibt es ein allgemeines Ertragsgesetz für alle Gebiete des Wirtschaftslebens?" *Jahrbücher für Nationalökonomie und Statistik,* Vol. 123, pp. 636–652. Reply to K. Diehl's article in Vol. 120, p. 1 *ff.*

Truchy, Henri: *Cours de'Économie Politique.* 2 vols. Paris, 1919. Libraire de la Société du recueil Sirey.

Watkins, George Pendleton: *Welfare as an Economic Quantity.* Boston and New York, Houghton Mifflin Co., 1915. 191 pp.

II. THE THEORY OF WAGES

1. The Marginal Productivity Theory

Adriance, Walter M.: "Specific Productivity," *Quarterly Journal of Economics,* Vol. XXIX, pp. 149–176.

Aftalion, A.: "Les trois notions de la Productivité et les Revenus," *Revue d'Économie Politique,* Tome XXV, 1911, pp. 145–184 and pp. 345–369.

Barone, Enrico: "Studi Sulla Distribuzione," *Giorn. degli Econ.,* February and March, 1896, Vol. XIII, pp. 105–155, 235–252.

Böhm-Bawerk, Eugen von: *The Positive Theory of Capital.* Translation by William Smart. New York, Macmillan Co., 1891. 428 pp.

Carver, T. N.: "The Theory of Wages Adjusted to Recent Theories of Value," *Quarterly Journal of Economics,* Vol. VIII, pp. 377–402.

Clark, John Bates: *The Distribution of Wealth; a theory of wages, interest and profits.* New York and London, Macmillan Co., 1902. 445 pp.

Clark, John Bates: "Possibility of a Scientific Law of Wages." Publication of the *American Economic Association*, Vol. IV, No. 1, 1889, pp. 39–69.

Clark, John Bates: "The Law of Wages and Interest," *Annals of the American Academy of Political and Social Science.* Philadelphia, Vol. I, pp. 43–65.

Clark, John Bates: "Surplus Gains of Labor," *Annals of the American Academy of Political and Social Science.* Vol. III, pp. 607–617.

Clark, John Bates: "The Dynamic Law of Wages," *Yale Review*, Vol. VII, pp. 375–382.

Downey, E. H.: "The Futility of Marginal Utility," *Journal of Political Economy.* Vol. XVIII, No. 4 (April, 1910), pp. 253–268.

Gossen, Hermann Heinrich: *Entwicklung der Gesetze des menschlichen Verkehrs.* New edition. Berlin, R. L. Prager, 1889. 277 pp.

Hicks, J. R.: "Marginal Productivity and the Principle of Variation," *Economica*, 1932, No. 35, pp. 79–88. See also H. Schultz's reply in No. 37 and Mr. Hicks' rejoinder.

Hicks, J. R.: *The Theory of Wages.* London, Macmillan & Co., 1932. 247 pp.

Jevons, W. Stanley: *The Theory of Political Economy.* London, Macmillan & Co., 1888. 3d edition. 296 pp. Esp. Chap. V.

Liefmann, R.: "Das Gesetz des Ausgleichs der Grenzerträge," *Jahrbücher für Nationalökonomie und Statistik,* Vol. 108.

MacVane, S. M.: "Böhm-Bawerk on Value and Wages," *Quarterly Journal of Economics,* Vol. V, pp. 24–43.

Montemartini, Giovanni: *La teorica della produttività marginali,* Pavia, Tip. Fratelli Fusi, 1899. 230 pp.

Moore, Henry L.: *Laws of Wages, an Essay in Statistical Economics.* New York, Macmillan Co., 1911. 196 pp.

Padan, R. S.: "J. B. Clark's Formulæ of Wages and Interest," *Journal of Political Economy,* Vol. IX, pp. 161–190.

Schultz, Henry: "Marginal Productivity and the General Pricing Process," *Journal of Political Economy,* Vol. XXXVII, No. 5, pp. 505–551.

Schultz, Henry: "Marginal Productivity and the Lausanne School— a Reply," *Economica*, 1932, No. 37, pp. 285–296.

Schumpeter, Joseph: "Das Grundprinzip der Verteilungstheorie," *Archiv für Sozialwissenschaft und Sozialpolitik,* Vol. XLII, pp. 1–88.

Soule, George: "The Productivity Factor in Wage Determinations," *American Economic Review,* Vol. XIII, supplement No. 1, pp. 129–140.

Strigl, Richard: Angewandte Lohntheorie. *Wiener Staatswissenschaftliche Studien,* Neue Folge Band IX. Leipzig und Wien, Franz Deuticke, 1926. 170 pp.

Thünen, J. H. von: *Der Isolierte Staat.* Rostock, 1842 and 1850. (Reprinted by G. Fischer Jena, 1930). 678 pp.

Wicksell, Knut: *Über Wert Kapital und Rente nach den neuen Nationalökonomischen Theorien.* Jena, G. Fischer, 1893. 143 pp.

Wicksell, Knut: *Vorlesungen über Nationalökonomie auf Grundlage des Marginalprinzipes.* Translation by M. Langfeldt. Jena, G. Fischer, 1913–28. 2 vols.

Wood, Stuart: "A New View of the Theory of Wages," *Quarterly Journal of Economics,* Vol. III, pp. 60–86 and pp. 462–480.

Wood, Stuart: "Theory of Wages, Contributions to the Wage Question." *Publication of the American Economic Association,* Monographs V. 4, No. 1, pp. 1–35, 1889. The price of a given amount of labor is the same as the price paid for the use of such amount of capital as would replace the laborer in those employments where labor and capital are interchangeable and where either can be used to equal advantage.

Wood, Stuart: "A Critique of Wages Theories," *Annals of the American Academy,* Vol. I, pp. 426–461.

2. The Equilibrium Theory

Amonn, Alfred: *Das Lohnproblem. Gefahren der Lohnsteigerungen.* Berlin, Junker & Dünnhaupt Verlag, 1930. 56 pp.

Antonelli, E.: *La théorie de l'échange sous le régime de la libre concurrence.* Paris, 1914. 206 pp. (Second Part.)

Bagge, Gösta: *Arbetslönens Reglering Genom Sammanslutnigar.* Stockholm, 1917. 483 pp.

Barone, Enrico: "Studi sulla Distribuzione," *Giornale degli Economisti,* Vol. XII, pp. 107–155 and pp. 235–252.

Cassel, Gustav: *The Theory of Social Economy.* Translation by Joseph McCabe. New York, Harcourt, Brace & Co., 1924. 2 vols.

Cournot, A.: *The Mathematical Principles of the Theory of Wealth.* Translation by Bacon. New York, Macmillan Co., 1897. 209 pp.

Hicks, J. R.: "Edgeworth, Marshall, and the Indeterminateness of Wages," *Economic Journal,* Vol. XL, pp. 215–231.

Jenkin, Fleeming: "The Graphic Representation of the Laws of Supply and Demand and Their Application to Labour." In *Papers of Fleeming Jenkin.* London, Longmans, Green & Co., 1887. Vol. II, pp. 76–107.

Pareto, Vilfredo: *Manuel d'Économie Politique.* Translation by Alfred Bonnet. 2d edition. Paris, Marcel Giard, 1927. 679 pp. Chap. V.

Schumpeter, J.: *Das Wesen und der Hauptinhalt der theoretischen Nationalökonomie.* Leipzig, Duncker & Humblot, 1908. 626 pp.

Smith, Adam: *Wealth of Nations.* McCulloch edition. Edinburgh, Adam & Charles Black, 1863. Book I, Chap. VIII. 669 pp.

Valk, William L.: *The Principles of Wages.* London, P. S. King, 1928. 139 pp.

Walras, Léon: *Éléments d'Économie Politique Pure.* Paris, F. Pichon, 1926. 487 pp. Section IV, Production.

Wicksteed, P. H.: *An Essay on the Coördination of the Laws of Distribution.* London, Macmillan & Co., 1894. 56 pp.

Zawadzki, Wl.: *Les Mathématiques appliquées a l'Économie Politique.* Paris, Marcel Rivière et Cie, 1914. 331 pp. Chap. V.

3. The Subsistence Theory

Cantillon, Richard: *Essai sur la nature du commerce en général.* Traduit de l'anglois. A Londres, chez F. Gyles, dans Holborn.

Lassalle, Ferdinand J.: *Arbeiterlesebuch.* Berlin, Allg. Deutsche Assoz. Buchdruckerei, 1878. 72 pp.

Lassalle, Ferdinand J.: *Kapital und Arbeit.* (Herr Bastiat-Schulze v. Delitzsch, der ökon. Julian.) Berlin, T. Glocke, 1893. 259 pp.

Lassalle, Ferdinand J.: *What is Capital?* Freely translated from Chap. IV of F. Lassalle's "Herr Bastiat-Schultze v. Delitzsch," by F. Keddell. New York, Intern. Publ. Co., 1899. 28 pp.

Lassalle, Ferdinand J.: *The Working Man's Programme.* Translated by E. Peters. London, The Modern Press, 1884. 59 pp.

Locke, John: *Consequence of the Lowering of Interest and Raising the Value of Money.* In works of J. Locke, Vol. V, New edition. London, printed for T. Tegg, etc., 1823.

McCulloch, J. R.: *A Treatise on the Circumstances Which Determine the Rate of Wages and the Condition of the Labouring Classes.* 2d edition. London, G. Routledge & Co., 1854. 117 pp.

Malthus, Thomas Robert: *An Essay on the Principle of Population.* Reeves & Turner, 1878, 8th edition. London. 551 pp. (Book III, Chap. XIII of Increasing Wealth as It Affects the Condition of the Poor).

Malthus, Thomas Robert: *Principles of Political Economy.* London, William Pickering, 1836. 446 pp. (Book I, Chap. IV of The Wages of Labour.)

Ricardo, David: *Principles.* (Gonner, editor.) London, George Bell & Sons, 1903. 455 pp. (Chap. V on Wages.)

Smith, Adam: *Wealth of Nations.* (McCulloch, editor.) Edinburgh, Adam & Charles Black, 1863. 634 pp. Book I, Chap. VIII of the Wages of Labour.

Torrens, Robert. *An Essay on the External Corn Trade.* London. Printed for Longman, Rees, etc., 1826. 416 pp. (p. 57 *ff.* on Wages.)

Turgot, A. R. J.: *Reflections on the Formation and Distribution of Wealth.* Translated from the French. London, J. Good, 1793. 122 pp.

4. The Wages-Fund Theory

Böhm-Bawerk, Eugen von: *The Positive Theory of Capital.* Translated by William Smart. New York, Macmillan Co., 1891. 428 pp. (For wages fund, see Book 4, sec. 4.)

Cairnes, J. E.: *Some Leading Principles of Political Economy Newly Expounded.* New York, Harper & Bros., 1874. 421 pp. (Part II on wages.)

Jäger, O.: "Die Lohnfonds-Theorie." *Zeitsch. f. Volksw. Sozialpol. u. Ver.,* Vol. X, pp. 145–162.

Kleene, G. A.: *Profit and Wages, a Study in the Distribution of Income.* New York, Macmillan Co., 1916. 171 pp.

Longe, Francis Davy: *F. D. Longe on the Wages-Fund Theory,* 1866. Baltimore, The Lord Baltimore Press, 1904. 72 pp.

Longe, Francis Davy: *A Critical Examination of Mr. George's "Progress and Poverty" and Mr. Mill's "Theory of Wages."* London, Simpkin & Marshall, etc., 1883. 58 pp.

McCulloch, J. R.: *A Treatise on the Circumstances Which Determine the Rate of Wages and the Condition of the Labouring Classes.* 2d edition. London, G. Routledge & Co., 1854. 117 pp.

McCulloch, J. R.: *Principles of Political Economy.* London, A. Murray & Son, 1870. p. 327 *ff.* (wage fund arithem. example). 360 pp.

Marcet, Mrs. Jane: *Conversations on Political Economy.* 3d edition. London, Longmans, Hurst, etc., 1819. 486 pp. (pp. 117, 118, and 130.)

Mill, John Stuart: *Principles of Political Economy.* W. J. Ashley, editor. London, Longmans, Green & Co., 1909. 1013 pp. Book II, Chaps. XI–XIV.

Perry, Arthur L.: *Elements of Political Economy.* 9th edition. New York, Scribner, Armstrong & Co., 1873. 501 pp.

Senior, Nassau William: *Political Economy.* 6th edition. London, Charles Griffin & Co., 1872. 231 pp. (Proximate Causes Deciding the Rate of Wages, p. 154 *ff.*)

Senior, Nassau William: *Three Lectures on the Rate of Wages, Delivered Before the University of Oxford, 1830.* 2d edition. London, John Murray, 1830. 62 pp.

Taussig, F. W.: "The Wages-Fund Doctrine at the Hands of German Economists," *Quarterly Journal of Economics,* Vol. IX, pp. 1–25.

Taussig, F. W.: *Wages and Capital, an Examination of the Wages-Fund Doctrine.* New York, D. Appleton & Co., 1896. 329 pp.

Taussig, F. W.: "Capital, Interest and Diminishing Returns," *Quarterly Journal of Economics*, Vol. XXII, pp. 333–363.

Thompson, J. G.: "Present Work and Present Wages." *Quarterly Journal of Economics*, Vol. XXIV, pp. 515–535.

Thornton, William Thomas: *On Labour; Its Wrongful Claims and Rightful Dues; Its Actual Present and Possible Future.* 2d edition. London, Macmillan & Co., 1870. 499 pp.

Walker, Francis A.: "The Wage-Fund Theory," *North American Review*, Vol. 120, p. 94 *ff*.

Walker, Francis A.: *The Wages Question.* New York, Henry Holt, 1891. 428 pp.

West, Sir Edward: *Price of Corn and Wages of Labour.* London, J. Hatchard & Son, 1826. 150 pp.

5. The Bargain Theory

Barnett, George E.: "Chapters on Machinery and Labor," *Quarterly Journal of Economics*, Vol. XXXIX, pp. 337–356, and pp. 544–574.

Barnett, George E.: "The Stonecutters' Union and the Stone Planer," *Journal of Political Economy*, (May, 1916.) Vol. XXIV, 417–444.

Barnett, George E.: "Introduction of the Linotype," *Yale Review*, November, 1904. Relation between introduction of machinery and trade-union policy.

Böhm-Bawerk, Eugen von: *Control or Economic Law.* An essay. Translated by John Richard Mez. Eugene, Oregon, 1931.

Bunting, J. B.: *Is Trade Unionism Sound?* A suggestion for outflanking the power of capital. London, Benn Brothers, 1922. 98 pp.

Commons, John R., and Associates: *History of Labour in the United States.* 2 vols. New York, Macmillan Co., 1926.

Commons, John R.: "Wage Theories and Wage Policies," *American Economic Review.* Vol. XIII, Supplement No. 1, pp. 110–117.

Coon, S. J.: "Collective Bargaining and Productivity," *American Economic Review*, Vol. XIX, pp. 419–427.

Davidson, John. *The Bargain Theory of Wages.* New York and London, G. P. Putnam's Sons, 1898. 319 pp.

Frain, H. La Rue: "Some Factors Affecting the Bargaining Power of the Workers in the Glass Bottle Industry," *American Economic Review*, Vol. XVII, pp. 429–447.

Garrett, S. S.: "Wages and the Collective Wage Bargain," *American Economic Review*, Vol. XVIII, pp. 670–683.

Hobson, John A.: *The Economics of Distribution and the Science of Wealth.* New York, Macmillan Co., 1900. 361 pp.

Hutt, W. H.: *The Theory of Collective Bargaining.* London, P. S. King & Son, 1930. 112 pp.

Jevons, William Stanley: *The State in Relation to Labor.* London, Macmillan & Co., 1887. 116 pp. (Trade unionism cannot increase the wages of labor as a group. He does not recognize inequality of bargaining power.)

Landauer, Carl: *Grundprobleme der funktionellen Verteilung des Wirtschaftlichen Wertes.* Jena, G. Fischer, 1923. 253 pp. (especially pp. 1–67 Bargain Theory.)

Nicholson, J. S.: "Capital and Labor: Their Relative Strength," *Economic Journal,* Vol. II, pp. 478–490.

Phillippovitch, Eugen von: *Grundriss der Politischen Ökonomie.* Tübingen, J. C. B. Mohr, 1893–1907. 2 vols.

Pigou, A. C.: "Wage Policy and Unemployment," *Economic Journal.* Vol. XXXVII, pp. 355–368.

Rowe, J. W. F.: *Wages in Practise and Theory.* London, Routledge, 1928. 277 pp.

Stockett, Joseph Noble: *The Arbitral Determination of Railway Wages,* Boston and New York, Houghton Mifflin Co., 1918. 198 pp.

Truchy, Henri: *Cours d'Économie Politique.* Paris, 1921. 2 vols.

Tugan-Baranowsky, M. T.: *Soziale Theorie der Verteilung.* Berlin, J. Springer, 1913. 82 pp.

Webb, Sidney and Beatrice: *Industrial Democracy.* London and New York, Longmans, Green & Co., 1897. 2 vols.

Weber, Adolf: *Der Kampf zwischen Kapital und Arbeit.* Tübingen, J. C. B. Mohr, 1910. 579 pp.

6. The Efficiency Theory

American Economic Association: *The Adjustment of Wages to Efficiency;* three papers read before the American Society of Mechanical Engineers, 1889, 1891, 1895, by H. R. Towne, F. A. Halsey, and F. W. Taylor.

Ansiaux, Maurice: *Heures de Travail et Salaires.* Paris, F: Alcan, 1896. 299 pp.

Batten, Edward: *A Fair Wage; being reflections on the minimum wage and some economic problems of today.* London, I. Pitman & Sons, 1923. 90 pp.

Bauer, Wilhelm: *Die wirtschaftliche Bedeutung hoher Löhne.* Heidelberg, Weiss, 1932. 80 pp.

Beardsley, Charles, Jr.: "The Effect of an Eight Hours' Day on Wages and the Unemployed," *Quarterly Journal of Economics,* Vol. IX, pp. 450–459.

Bigge, George E.: "Wage Rates and the Use of Machinery," *American Economic Review,* Vol. XVII, pp. 675–680. Discusses Hayes' article.

Bowie, J. A.: "A New Method of Wage Adjustment in the Light of the Recent History of Wage Methods in the British Coal Industry," *Economic Journal*, Vol. XXXVII, pp. 384–394.

Brentano, Lujo: *Hours and Wages in Relation to Production*. Translated by Mrs. William Arnold. London, S. Sonnenschein & Co., 1894. 143 pp

Brentano, Lujo: *Über das Verhältnis von Arbeitslohn und Arbeitszeit zur Arbeitsleistung*. 2d edition. Leipzig, Duncker & Humblot, 1893. 103 pp.

Clay, Henry: "Unemployment and Wage Rates," *Economic Journal*, Vol. XXXVIII, pp. 1–15.

Cohen, Joseph L.: *Family Income Insurance, a Scheme of Family Endowment by the Method of Insurance*. London, P. S. King & Son, 1926. 47 pp.

Copley, F. B.: *Frederick W. Taylor, Father of Scientific Management*, New York and London, Harper & Bros., 1923.

Douglas, Paul H.: *Wages and the Family*. Chicago, University of Chicago Press, 1925. 290 pp.

Edgeworth, F. Y.: "Equal Pay to Men and Women for Equal Work," *Economic Journal*, Vol. XXXII, pp. 431–457.

Fawcett, Millicent Garrett: "Equal Pay for Equal Work," *Economic Journal*, Vol. XXVIII, pp. 1–6.

Graham, Frank D.: "Relation of Wage Rates to the Use of Machinery," *American Economic Review*, Vol. XVI, pp. 434–442.

Hammond, M. B.: "Wages Boards in Australia," *Quarterly Journal of Economics*, Vol. XXIX. I. Victoria, pp. 98–148; II. Outside Victoria, pp. 326–339; III. Organization and Procedure, pp. 339–361; IV. Social and Economic Results, pp. 563–630.

Hammond, M. B.: "The Regulations of Wages in New Zealand," *Quarterly Journal of Economics*, Vol. XXXI, pp. 404–446.

Hayes, Gordon H.: "The Rate of Wages and the Use of Machinery," *American Economic Review*, Vol. XIII, pp. 461–465.

Heaton, H.: "The Basic Wage Principle in Australian Wage Regulation," *Economic Journal*, Vol. XXXI, pp. 309–319.

Johnson, Alvin S.: "The Effect of Labor-Saving Devices upon Wages," *Quarterly Journal of Economics*, Vol. XX, pp. 86–109. The beneficence or maleficence of product multiplication turns upon the combining proportions of capital and labor in the industry concerned.

Lees Smith, H. B.: "Economic Theory and Proposals for a Legal Minimum Wage," *Economic Journal*, Vol. XVII, pp. 504–512.

Moore, Henry L.: "The Efficiency Theory of Wages," *Economic Journal*, Vol. XVII, pp. 571–579.

Murphy, H. M.: *Wages and Prices in Australia: on labour laws and their effects, also how to prevent strikes*. Melbourne and Sydney, George Robertson & Co., 1917. 144 pp.

Portus, G. V.: "The Development of Wage Fixation in Australia," *American Economic Review*, Vol. XIX, pp. 59–75.

Rathbone, Eleanor F.: "The Remuneration of Women's Service," *Economic Journal*, Vol. XXVII, pp. 55–68.

Rathbone, Eleanor F.: *The Disinherited Family; a plea for direct provision for the costs of child maintenance through family allowances*. London, G. Allen & Unwin, 1927. 345 pp.

Schoenhof, Jacob: *The Economy of High Wages; an inquiry into the cause of high wages and their effect on methods and cost of production*. New York, G. P. Putnam's Sons, 1893. 414 pp.

Schulze-Gaevernitz, G.: *Der Grossbetrieb ein wirtschaftlicher und sozialer Fortschritt*. Leipzig, Duncker & Humblot, 1892. 281 pp. (A study of the cotton industry which shows how an increase in wages, if accompanied by technical progress, is compatible with the industrial prosperity of the country.)

Sells, Dorothy M.: *The British Trade Board System*. London, P. S. King & Son, 1923. 293 pp.

Tawney, R. H.: *The Establishment of Minimum Wage Rates in the Chain-Making Industry Under the Trade Boards Act of 1909*. London, G. Bell & Sons, 1914. 157 pp.

Tawney, R. H.: *The Establishment of Minimum Rates in the Tailoring Industry Under the Trade Boards Act of 1909*. London, G. Bell & Sons, 1915. 274 pp.

Thompson, Herbert Metford: *The Theory of Wages and its Application to the Eight-Hour Question and Other Labour Problems*. London and New York, Macmillan Co., 1892. 140 pp.

Tozer, John: "Mathematical Investigation of the Effect of Machinery on the Wealth of a Community in Which It Is Employed and on the Fund for the Payment of Wages," Cambridge Philos. Trans., Vol. VI, pp. 507–522.

U. S. Bureau of Labor Statistics: *Family Allowances in Foreign Countries*. Bulletin No. 401. Washington, Government Printing Office. 1926.

Vibart, Hugh H. R.: *Family Allowance in Practice*. London, P. S. King & Son, 1926. 237 pp.

7. The Exploitation Theory

Boucke, Oswald F.: *Principles of Economics*. New York, Macmillan Co., 1925. 2 vols.

Bray, J. F.: *Labour's Wrongs and Labour's Remedy*. No. 6 in a series of reprints of scarce tracts in economic and political science. London, London School of Economics, 1931.

Bukharin, N. and Preobrazhensky, E.: *The A. B. C. of Communism*. London, 1922. 422 pp.

Cassel, Gustav: *Das Recht auf den vollen Arbeitsertrag*. Göttingen, Vandenhoeck & Ruprecht, 1900. 168 pp.

George, Henry: *Progress and Poverty*. New York, J. W. Lovell Co., 1882. 410 pp.

Gonner, E. C. K.: *The Social Philosophy of Rodbertus*. New York, Macmillan Co., 1899. 210 pp.

Marx, Karl: *Capital*. (Charles H. Kerr, editor.) Translated from the third German edition by S. Moore and E. Avelling. Chicago, C. H. Kerr & Co., 1915. (3 vols.) Vol. I.

Marx, Karl: *Value, Price and Profit*. Chicago, C. H. Kerr & Co., 1908. 128 pp.

Marx, Karl: *Wage-Labor and Capital*. Translated by Harriet E. Lothrop. New York, New York Labor News Co., 1902. 60 pp.

Marx, Karl, and Engels, F.: *Communist Manifesto*. Chicago, C. H. Kerr & Co., 1912. 64 pp.

Menger, Anton: *The Right to the Whole Produce of Labour*. Translated by M. E. Tanner with an introduction by H. S. Foxwell. London and New York, Macmillan Co., 1889. 271 pp.

Oppenheimer, Franz: *Der Arbeitslohn*. Jena, 1926. 74 pp.

Oppenheimer, Franz: *Das Grundgesetz der Marx'schen Gesellschafts-lehre*. Berlin, G. Reimer, 1903. 148 pp. (Chap. II on exploitation theory.)

Owen, Robert Dale: *The Life of Robert Owen Written by Himself*. London, E. Wilson, 1857–1858. 2 vols.

Rodbertus-Jagetzow, Karl: *Zur Beleuchtung der sozialen Frage*. Berlin, Puttkammer & Mühlbrecht, 1899. 2 vols.

Rodbertus-Jagetzow, Karl: *Overproduction and Crises*. Translated by Julia Franklin, London, S. Sonnenschein & Co., 1898. 140 pp.

Rodbertus-Jagetzow, Karl: *Neue Briefe über Grundrente, Renten-prinzip und Soziale Frage*. Karlsruhe, G. Braun, 1926. 398 pp.

Rodbertus-Jagetzow, Karl: *Das Kapital*. Edited by Th. Kozak. Berlin, Puttkammer & Mühlbrecht, 1884. 315 pp.

8. General

Arndt, Paul: *Lohngesetz und Lohntarif*. Frankfurt am Main. Universitätsbuchhandlung, 1926. 201 pp.

Bonar, James: "The Value of Labor in Relation to Economic Theory," *Quarterly Journal of Economics*, Vol. V, pp. 137–164.

Brentano, Lujo: *Über J. H. von Thünen's naturgemässen Lohn und Zinsfuss im isolierten Staat*. Göttingen, Universitätsbuchdruckerei von E. A. Huth, 1867.

Burns, Eveline Mabel: *Wages and the State*. London, P. S. King & Son, 1926. 443 pp.

Carey, Henry Charles: *Essay on the Rate of Wages, with an Examination of the Causes of the Difference in the Condition of the Labouring Population Throughout the World*. Philadelphia, Carey, Lea & Blanchard, 1835. 255 pp.

Carver, Thomas N.: *The Theory of Wages Adjusted to Recent Theories of Value*. Boston, G. H. Ellis, 1894. 28 pp.

Carver, Thomas N.: *The Present Economic Revolution in the United States*. Boston, Little, Brown & Co., 1925. 270 pp. Increasing ownership of capital by wage earners is obliterating the distinction between the capitalistic and wage-earning class.

Cobb, Charles W.: "Some Statistical Relations Between Wages and Prices," *Journal of Political Economy*, Vol. XXXVII, pp. 728–736.

Commons, John R: *The Distribution of Wealth*. London, Macmillan & Co., 1893. 258 pp.

Conrad, Otto: *Lohn und Rente*. Leipzig und Wien, F. Deuticke, 1909. 256 pp.

Cornélissen, Christian: *Traité Général de Science Économique*. Tome Deuxième: Théorie du Salaire et du Travail Salarié. Paris, Marcel Giard, 1926. 704 pp.

Crook, James W.: *German Wage Theories, a History of Their Development*. Columbia University Studies. Vol. IX, No. 2, 1898. 113 pp.

Dane, Edmund: *Wages and Labour Costs—a statement of the economic laws and theory of wages*. London, Macmillan & Co. 1927. 194 pp.

Davenport, Herbert Joseph: "Wage Theory and Theories," *Quarterly Journal of Economics*, Vol. XXXIII, pp. 256–297.

Dobb, Maurice H.: *Wages*. New York, Harcourt, Brace & Co., 1928. 169 pp.

Dobb, Maurice H.: "A Sceptical View of the Theory of Wages," *Economic Journal*, Vol. XXXIX, pp. 506–519.

Feis, Herbert: "Organization, Distribution and Wages," *American Economic Review*, Vol. IX, pp. 468–481.

Feis, Herbert: *A Collection of Decisions Presenting Principles of Wage Settlement*. New York, H. W. Wilson Co., 1924. 452 pp.

Friday, David: *Profits, Wages, and Prices*. New York, Harcourt, Brace & Co., 1920. 256 pp. (Chaps. VI and VII.)

Furniss, Edgar S.: *The Position of the Laborer in a System of Nationalism*. A study in the Labor Theories of the Later English Mercantilists. Boston and New York, Houghton Mifflin Co., 1920. 260 pp. Chaps. II–IV. Doctrines of Employment and Importance of the Laboring Class. Chap. VII. Mercantile Tneories of Wages (subsistence cost theory).

Giddings, Franklin H.: "The Natural Rate of Wages," *Political Science Quarterly*, Vol. II, pp. 620–637.

Graham, William: *The Wages of Labour*. London and New York, Cassell & Co., 1921. 165 pp.

Grier, Lynda: "The Meaning of Wages," *Economic Journal*, Vol. XXXV, pp. 519–535.

Hamilton, Walton: "A Theory of the Rate of Wages," *Quarterly Journal of Economics*, Vol. XXXVI, pp. 581–625. Discussion of how real wages are to be raised.

Hamilton, W. H., and May, Stacy: *The Control of Wages*. New York, George H. Doran Co., 1923. 185 pp.

Hollander, Jacob H.: "The Residual Claimant Theory of Distribution," *Quarterly Journal of Economics*, Vol. XVII, pp. 261–279.

Kleene, G. A.: "The Supply Price of Labor," Note in *Quarterly Journal of Economics*, Vol. XXXII, pp. 400–404.

Knapp, G. F.: *Zur Prüfung der Untersuchungen Thünen's über Lohn und Zinsfuss im isolierten Staat*. Braunschweig, F. Vieweg und Sohn, 1865. 35 pp.

Komorzynski, J.: "Von Thünen's Naturgemässer Arbeitslohn," *Zeitsch. f. Volksw. Sozialpol. u. Ver.*, Vol. III, p. 27.

Magruder, Mary Lanier: *Wages*. New York and London, Harper & Bros., 1924. 308 pp.

Marschak, Jakob: *"Die Lohndiskussion."* Tübingen, 1930, J. C. B. Mohr (Paul Siebeck). 32 pp.

Milnes, Nora: *The Economics of Wages and Labour*. London, 1926, P. S. King & Son, Ltd. 197 pp.

Mises, L.: "Die Wirtschaftsrechnung im Sozialistischen Gemeinwesen." *Archiv für Sozialwissenschaft und Sozialpolitik*, Band 47.

Moore, Henry L.: "Von Thünen's Theory of Natural Wages," *Quarterly Journal of Economics*, Vol. IX, pp. 291–303, and Vol. IX, pp. 388–408.

Patten, Simon N.: "President Walker's Theory of Distribution," *Quarterly Journal of Economics*, Vol. IV, pp. 34–49.

Polier, Léon: *L'idée du juste salaire; essai d'histoire dogmatique et critique*. Paris, V. Giard & E. Brière, 1903. 388 pp.

Robbins, Lionel: *Wages*. London, Jarolds, 1925. 94 pp.

Robertson, D. H.: "Wage-Grumbles" in his *Economic Fragments*. London, P. S. King & Son, 1931. 267 pp.

Rowe, John Wilkinson Foster: *Wages in Practice and Theory*. London, G. Routledge & Sons, 1928. 277 pp.

Schmoller, Gustav: "Die Lohntheorie." *Schmollers Jahrbuch*. Vol. XXXVIII (1914), pp. 1705–1736.

Schumacher, M.: *Uber J. H. von Thünen's Gesetz vom Naturgemässen Arbeitslohne*. Rostock, 1869. 84 pp.

Torrens, R.: *A Letter to Lord Ashley on the Principles Which Regulate Wages* . . . London, Smith, Elder & Co., 1844. 80 pp.

Torrens, R.: *On Wages and Combination*. London, Longmans & Longman, 1834. 133 pp.

Walker, Francis A.: "The Doctrine of Rent and the Residual Claimant Theory of Wages," *Quarterly Journal of Economics*. Vol.

V, pp. 417–437. See also *Quarterly Journal of Economics*, Vol. IV, S. N. Patten and F. B. Hawley on Residual Theory.

Walker, Francis A.: *Political Economy*. 3d edition. New York, H. Holt & Co., 1888. Part IV, esp. Chaps. V and VI—Wages.

Walker, Francis A.: *The Wages Question*. New York, H. Holt & Co., 1891, 428 pp. See also *Quarterly Journal of Economics*, Vols. IV and V for S. N. Patten's and F. B. Hawley's Criticism and Walker's Reply.

Wallis, Percy and Albert: *Prices and Wages; an investigation of the dynamic forces in social economics*. London, P. S. King & Son, 1921. 456 pp.

Wicksell, Knut: "Kapitalzins und Arbeitslohn," *Jahrb. f. National-ökonomie und Statistik*, 3 Folge, Bd. VI, pp. 852–874.

Wolkoff, Mathieu: "Le salaire naturel d'après M. de Thünen," *Journ. des écon.*, 2d series, Vol. X, pp. 263–270.

Wolkoff, Mathieu: "Nouvelles observations au sujet de l'ouvrage de M. de Thünen sur le salaire naturel," *Journal des écon.*, 2d series, Vol. XVI.

Zwiedineck-Südenhorst, Otto von. *Lohnpolitik und Lohntheorie.* Leipzig, Duncker und Humblot, 1900. 410 pp.

Zwiedineck-Südenhorst, Otto von: "Lohntheorie und Lohnpolitik," *Handwörterbuch der Staatswissenschaften*. 4th edition, Vol. VI (1925), pp. 396–426.

III. THE THEORY OF PRODUCTION

1. The Theory of Production

Bullock, Charles J.: "The Variation of Productive Forces," *Quarterly Journal of Economics*, Vol. XVI, pp. 473–513.

Byé, M.: *Les Lois des Rendements Non Proportionelles*. Paris. Sirey, 1928. 553 pp.

Carver, Thomas N.: "The Universal Law of Diminishing Returns. Another Comment." Note in *Quarterly Journal of Economics*, Vol. XVII, pp. 335–336.

Chapman, S. J.: "Laws of Increasing and Decreasing Returns in Production and Consumption," *Economic Journal*, Vol. XVIII, pp. 52–59.

Clark, C. G.: "Statistical Studies Relating to the Present Economic Position of Great Britain," *Economic Journal*, 1931, Vol. XLI, pp. 343–369.

Clark, John Bates: "A Universal Law of Economic Variation," *Quarterly Journal of Economics*, Vol. VIII, pp. 261–279.

Clark, J. M.: "Inductive Evidence of Marginal Productivity," *American Economic Review*, Vol. XVIII, 1928, pp. 449–467.

Cobb, Charles W.: "Contour Lines in Economics," *Journal of Political Economy*, Vol. XXXVII, pp. 225–229.

Cobb, Charles W.: "Production in Massachusetts Manufacturing, 1890–1928," *Journal of Political Economy*, Vol. XXXVIII, pp. 705–707.

Davenport, Herbert Joseph: *The Economics of Enterprise*. New York, Macmillan Co., 1913. 544 pp.

Douglas, Paul H., and Cobb, C. W.: "A Theory of Production," *American Economic Review*, Supplement, Vol. XVIII, No. 1, pp. 139–165.

Mixter, C. W.: "The Variation of Productive Forces. A Comment." Note in *Quarterly Journal of Economics*, Vol. XVII, pp. 332–334.

Oparin, D. I.: "Das theoretische Schema der gleichmässig fortschreitenden Wirtschaft als Grundlage einer Analyse ökonomischer Entwicklungsprozesse." *Weltwirtschaftliches Archiv*, Band 32, Heft 2. Especially p. 423 *ff.*

Schultz, Henry: "Marginal Productivity and the Lausanne School— A Reply," *Economica*, 1932, No. 37, pp. 285–296. See also Mr. Hicks' article in No. 35, and his rejoinder in No. 37.

Schultz, Henry: "Marginal Productivity and the General Pricing Process," *Journal of Political Economy*, Vol. XXXVII, pp. 505–551.

Watkins, G. P.: "A Third Factor in the Variation of Productivity: The Load Factor," *American Economic Review*, Vol. V, pp. 753–786.

West, Sir Edward: *The Application of Capital to Land*. Hollander edition, 1815. [Baltimore, The Lord Baltimore press, 1903]. 54 pp. The necessity of having recourse to land inferior tends to make labor less productive in the process of improvement.

Wolman, Leo: "The Theory of Production," *American Economic Review*, Vol. XI, (March, 1921). pp. 37–56.

Wunderlich, Frieda: *"Produktivität.* Jena, G. Fischer, 1926. 358 pp.

Zawadzki, Wladyslaw: *Esquisse d'une Théorie de la Production*. Paris, M. Rivière, 1927. 177 pp.

2. The Facts of Production

Bowley, Arthur Lyon: *The Division of the Product of Industry; an analysis of material income before the war*. Oxford, Clarendon Press, 1919. 60 pp.

Bowley, Arthur Lyon: *The Change in the Distribution of the National Income, 1880–1913*. Oxford, Clarendon Press, 1920. 27 pp.

Burns, Arthur F.: "The Measurement of the Physical Volume of Production," *Quarterly Journal of Economics*, Vol. XLIV, pp. 242–262.

Day, Edmund E., and Woodlief, Thomas: *The Growth of Manufactures, 1899–1923*. Census Monograph VIII. Washington, Government Printing Office, 1928.

Day, Edmund E.: "An Index of the Physical Volume of Production," *Review of Economic Stat.*, 1921, pp. 19–23; 1920, pp. 246–259, 287–300, 309–337, 361–367. *Ibid.*, 1924, pp. 193–204.

Douglas, Paul H., and Tolles, N. A.: "A Measurement of British Industrial Production," *Journal of Political Economy*, Vol. XXXVIII, pp. 1–28.

International Labor Office: *Enquête sur la Production Rapport général.* Paris, Berger-Leorault, 1923–1925. Five vols.

King, Willford I.: *Is Production Keeping Pace with Population?* Bankers Statistics Corporation, Special Service, Vol. II, No. 19, August, 1920.

Kuczynski, Jürgen: *Wages and Labor's Share in the Value Added by Manufacture.* Washington, D. C., American Federation of Labor, 1928. 224 pp. Gives the wages, number employed, value added, percent which goes to labor and relatives for census years, all manufacturing groups.

League of Nations: *The Course and Phases of the World Economic Depression.* Geneva, 1931. 339 pp.

League of Nations: *Memorandum on Production and Trade.* 1925 to 1929–1930. Geneva, 1931. 139 pp.

London and Cambridge Economic Service: Monthly Bulletins and Supplements.

Massachusetts: *Annual Report of the Statistics of Manufactures.* Department of Labor and Industry.

Matthews, Ada M.: "The Physical Volume of Production in the United States for 1924," *Review of Economic Statistics*, July, 1925, pp. 208–216.

Maxwell, W. Floyd: "The Revised Index of the Volume of Mining," *Review of Economic Statistics*, 1929, pp. 68–109.

Maxwell, W. Floyd: "The Physical Volume of Production in the United States for 1925," *Review of Economic Statistics*, 1926. pp. 144–152 for 1926; *ibid.*, 1927, pp. 142–150.

Michell H.: "An Index of the Physical Volume of Production in Canada," *Review of Economic Statistics*, 1927, pp. 69–73.

Ogburn, William F., and Jaffé, William: *The Economic Development of Post-War France—A Survey of Production.* New York, Columbia University Press, 1929. 613 pp.

Procopovitch, S. N.: "The Distribution of National Income," *Economic Journal*, Vol. XXXVI, pp. 69–82. England, Prussia, United States, Australia. Discussion of methods, etc.

Rowe, J. W. F.: "An Index of the Physical Volume of Production," *Economic Journal*, Vol. XXXVII, pp. 173–187.

Standard Statistics Co., "Standard Daily Trade Service." *Annual Statistical Bulletin.*

Svenska Handelsbanken. *Index.* Stockholm, Sweden (monthly bulletin).

U. S. Department of Commerce, Bureau of the Census: *Biennial Census of Manufactures*. Washington, Government Printing Office.

U. S. Department of Commerce: *Survey of Current Business* (Annual Supplement). Washington, Government Printing Office.

IV. THE LONG-TIME SUPPLY OF LABOR

1. The Theory of Population

Alison, Archibald: *The Principles of Population*. Edinburgh, W. Blackwood & Sons, 1840. 2 vols.

Bertheau, Charles: *Essai sur les Lois de la Population*. Paris, Chevalier-Marescq et Cie, 1892. 480 pp.

Bertillon, Jacques: "La Natalité selon le Degré d'aisance," *Bulletin de l'Institut International de Statistique, XI*, Rapports et Mémoires No. 9. pp. 163–176. A pioneer study in the relative fecundity of different social classes.

Beveridge, Sir William: "Population and Unemployment," *Economic Journal*, Vol. XXXIII, pp. 447–475.

Bonar, James: *Theories of Population from Raleigh to Arthur Young; lectures delivered in the Galthonian laboratory, University of London, under the Newmarch Foundation, 1929*. London, G. Allen & Unwin, 1931.

Bonar, James: *Malthus and His Work*. New York, Macmillan Co., 1924. 432 pp.

Booth, David: *A Letter to the Rev. T. R. Malthus. Being an answer to the criticism on Mr. Godwin's work on population*. London, Longman, Hurst, Rees, etc., 1823. 124 pp.

Bourdon, J.: "Is the Increase in the Population a Real Danger for the Food Supply of the World?" *Proceedings of the World Population Conference, 1927*, pp. 111–113.

Brentano, Lujo: "The Doctrine of Malthus and the Increase of Population During the Last Decades," *Economic Journal*, Vol. XX, pp. 371–393.

Brownlee, J.: "The Use of Death Rates as a Measure of Hygienic Conditions," *Medical Research Council, Special Report*, No. 60, 1922. Section IX.

Brownell, J. L.: "The Significance of a Decreasing Birth Rate," *Annals of American Academy of Political and Social Science*, Vol. V. pp. 48–89.

Cady, George Johnson: "The Early American Reaction to the Theory of Malthus," *Journal of Political Economy*, Vol. XXXIX, pp. 601–632.

Carr-Saunders, A. M.: "Differential Fertility," *Proceedings of the World Population Conference, 1927*, pp. 130–143.

Carr-Saunders, A. M.: *The Population Problem; a study in human evolution*. Oxford, Clarendon Press, 1922. 516 pp.

Carr-Saunders, A. M.: *Population.* London, Oxford University Press. H. Milford, 1925. 111 pp.

Connor, L. R.: "Fertility of Marriage and Population Growth," *Journal of the Royal Statistical Society,* Vol. LXXXIX, pp. 553–566.

Cox, Harold: *The Problem of Population.* New York and London, G. P. Putnam's Sons, 1923. 244 pp.

Dalton, H.: "The Theory of Population," *Economica,* Vol. VIII, pp. 28–50.

Dalton, H.: "A New Contribution to the Population Problem," *Economica,* Vol. III, No. 8, pp. 122–132.

Darwin, Leonard: "Eugenics in Relation to Economics and Statistics," *Journal of the Royal Statistical Society,* Vol. LXXXII, pp. 1–27 (1919), and discussion, pp. 27–33.

Darwin, Leonard: "Population and Civilization," *Economic Journal,* Vol. XXXI, pp. 187–195.

Doubleday, Thomas: *The True Law of Population, shown to be connected with the food of the people.* London, G. Peirce, 1847. 278 pp.

Drysdale, Charles R.: *The Population Question According to T. R. Malthus and J. S. Mill.* London, William Bell, 1878. 94 pp.

Dublin, Louis I.: "The Statistician and the Population Problem," *Journal of American Statistical Association,* Vol. XX, pp. 1–12.

Dublin, Louis I., and Lotka, A. J.: "On the True Rate of Natural Increase," *Journal of American Statistical Association,* Vol. XX, (1925), pp. 305–339.

Dumont, Arsène: *Dépopulation et Civilisation.* Paris, Lecrosnier et Babé, 1890. 520 pp.

East, E. M.: "Food and Population," *Proceedings of the World Population Conference,* Geneva, 1927; edited by M. Sanger, pp. 85–92. See also discussion, pp. 92–128.

East, E. M.: *Mankind at the Crossroad.* New York, London, C. Scribner's Sons, 1926. 360 pp.

Elster, L.: "Bevölkerungslehre und Bevölkerungspolitik. Das Bevölkerungsproblem," 1924. *Handwörterbuch der Staatswissenschaften,* 4th edition, pp. 735–825. (Two articles on population. Very good.)

Ensor, George: *An Inquiry Concerning the Population of Nations, containing a refutation of Mr. Malthus' Essay on Population.* London, E. Wilson, 1818. 502 pp.

Everett, Alexander Hill: *New Ideas on Population: with remarks on the theories of Malthus and Godwin.* Boston, O. Everett, 1823. 125 pp. Increase in population brings its own remedy in increased productivity through division of labor and increased skill.

Fairchild, Henry P.: "Optimum Population," *Proceedings of the World Population Conference*, Geneva, 1927, editor, G. M. Sanger, pp. 72–85.

Field, James Alfred: *Essays on Population.* Chicago. University of Chicago Press, 1931. 440 pp.

Gini, Corrado, Nasu, Shirodi, Kuczynski, and Baker: *Population.* 1930. Chicago, University of Chicago Press. 312 pp.

Godwin, W.: *Of Population: an inquiry concerning the power of increase in the numbers of mankind, being an answer to Malthus' essay on that subject.* London, printed for Longman, Hurst, etc. 1820. 626 pp.

Gonnard, René: *Histoire des Doctrines de la Population.* Paris, Nouvelle Librairie Nationale, 1923. 352 pp.

Grahame, James: *An Inquiry into the Principle of Population; including an exposition of the causes and the advantages of a tendency to exuberance of numbers in society.* Edinburgh, A. Constable & Co., 1816. 332 pp.

Gray, Simon: *The Happiness of States.* London, J. Hatchard & Son, 1819. 672 pp. Population regulates subsistence.

Gray, Simon: *Gray Versus Malthus.* The principles of population and production investigated, discussed by George Purves (pseud.). London, Longman, Hurst, etc., 1818. 496 pp.

Griffith, Grosvenor Talbot: *Population Problems of the Age of Malthus.* Cambridge, University Press, 1926. 276 pp.

Hart, Hornell: "Familial Differential Fecundity," *Journal of American Statistical Association*, Vol. XX, pp. 25–30.

Hazlitt, Wm.: *A Reply to the Essay on Population, by the Rev. T. R. Malthus.* In a Series of Letters. London, Longman, Hurst, etc., 1807. 378 pp. Argues that there is no limit to subsistence until the earth's surface is occupied and intensive culture resorted to.

Hiller, E. T.: "A Culture Theory of Population Trends." *Journal of Political Economy*, Vol. XXXVIII, pp. 523–550.

Himes, Norman E.: "McCulloch's Relation to the Neo-Malthusian Propaganda of His Time: An Episode in the History of English Neo-Malthusianism," *Journal of Political Economy*, Vol. XXXVII, pp. 73–86.

Hotelling, Harold: "Differential Equations Subject to Error and Population Estimates," *Journal of American Statistical Association*, Vol. XXII, pp. 283–314.

Jarrold, Thomas: *Dissertations on Man, Philosophical, Physiological and Political; in answer to Mr. Malthus' "Essay on the Principle of Population."* London, Cadell & Davis, etc. 1806. 367 pp. (Optimistic, upholding Godwin.)

Keynes, John Maynard: *The Economic Consequences of the Peace.* New York, Harcourt, Brace & Howe, 1920. 298 pp.

Knibbs, George Handley: *The Mathematical Theory of Population.* Melbourne, McCarron, Bird & Co., 1917.

Knibbs, Sir George Handley: *The Shadow of the World's Future.* London, E. Benn, Ltd., 1928. 131 pp.

Kraft, Louis: *Bevölkerungs Probleme.* Tübingen, Mohr, 1917. A discussion of over- and under-population.

Kuczynski, R. R.: *The Balance of Births and Deaths.* Vols. I and II, 1928 and 1931. Washington, Brookings Institution. 140 pp. and 170 pp.

La Loggia, E.: "Teoria della Populazione," *Giornale degli Economisti,* Vol. VII, pp. 391–416 and 488–520.

Leroy-Beaulieu, P.: *La Question de la Population.* Paris, F. Alcan, 1913. 512 pp.

Leroy-Beaulieu, P.: "The Influence of Civilization on the Movement of Population," *Journal of Royal Statistical Society,* Vol. LIV, 1891, pp. 372–384.

Lloyd, William Forster: *Two Lectures on the Checks to Population.* Delivered at the University of Oxford, 1833. London, Roake & Varty, etc., 1837.

Malthus, Thomas Robert: *First Essay on Population, 1798,* edited by James Bonar. London, Macmillan & Co., 1926. 396 pp. (especially Chaps. XI and XVI).

Malthus, Thomas Robert: *An Essay on the Principle of Population.* London, Reeves & Turner, 1888, 9th edition. 551 pp.

Mixter, C.: "Letters of Rae (1796–1872) to Mill on the Malthusian Doctrine of Population," *Economic Journal,* Vol. XII, pp. 112–120.

Mombert, Paul: *Bevölkerungslehre.* Jena, Gustav Fischer, 1929. 495 pp. First part contains a historical review and discussion of Malthus. Second part, discussion of possibility of population growth, relation to food supply, over-population, etc.

Nitti, F. S.: *La Population et le Système Social.* Paris, V. Giard & E. Brière, 1897. 276 pp. First book, history of population theories; Second book, his theory rejects Malthusian pessimism.

Nitti, F. S.: *Population and the Social System.* London, Swan, Sonnenschein & Co., 1894. 192 pp.

Oppenheimer, Franz: *Weltprobleme der Bevölkerung.* Leipzig. Deutsche wissensch. Buchhandl., 1929. 71 pp.

Owen, Robert Dale: *Moral Physiology, a Brief and Plain Treatise on the Population Question.* 8th edition. London, E. Truelove, 1832. 88 pp. (Neo-Malthusian—artificial restriction of size of families.)

Patten, Simon N.: "A New Statement of the Law of Population," *Political Science Quarterly,* Vol. X, pp. 44–61.

Pearl, R.: *Studies in Human Biology.* Baltimore, Williams & Wilkins Co., 1924. 653 pp

Pearl, R.: *The Biology of Death.* Philadelphia and London, J. B. Lippincott Co., 1922. 275 pp.

Pearl, R., and Reed, L. J.: "On the Mathematical Theory of Population Growth," *Metron.*, Vol. III, No. 1, 1923.

Pearl, R., and Reed, L. J.: "A Further Note on the Mathematical Theory of Population Growth," *Proceedings of the National Academy of Science,* Vol. VIII, pp. 365–368.

Pearl, R., and Reed, L. J.: "On the Rate of Growth of the Population of the U. S. Since 1790 and Its Mathematical Representation," *Proceedings of the National Academy of Science,* Vol. VI, pp. 275–288.

Pearl, R.: *The Biology of Population Growth.* New York, Alfred A. Knopf, 1926.

Place, Francis: *Illustrations and Proofs of the Principle of Population: including an examination of the proposed remedies of Mr. Malthus and a reply to the objections of Mr. Godwin and others.* London, Longman, Hurst, etc., 1822. 280 pp. (Study of immigration into America.)

Plummer, Alfred: "The Theory of Population," *Journal of Political Economy,* Vol. XL, pp. 617–637.

Quetelet, Adolphe: *Sur l'Homme et le Développement de ses Facultés.* Paris, Bachelier, 1835 (2 vols.). (Book I Chaps. I–IV on births, Chaps. V and VI on deaths, and Chap. VII on population growth.)

Ravenstone, P.: *A Few Doubts as to the Correctness of Some Opinions Generally Entertained on the Subjects of Population and Political Economy.* London, J. Andrews, 1821. 474 pp.

Reuter, Edward Byron: *Population Problems.* Philadelphia, London, etc., J. B. Lippincott Co., 1923. 338 pp.

Ricardo, David: *Letters of David Ricardo to Thomas Robert Malthus, 1810–1823.* Edited by James Bonar. Oxford, Clarendon Press, 1887. 251 pp.

Rickards, George K.: *Population and Capital.* London, Longman, Brown, Green, etc., 1854. 259 pp.

Robbins, L.: "The Optimum Theory of Population." In Gregory and Dalton's *London Essays in Economics,* 1927, p. 103. (Contains a summary of Cannan's theory.)

Robertson, D. H.: "A Word for the Devil," *Economica,* Vol. III, No. 9, pp. 203–208.

Rossiter, William S.: "The Adventure of Population Growth," *Journal of American Statistical Association,* Vol. XVIII, pp. 561–574.

Sadler, Michael T.: *The Law of Population: A Treatise in Six Books; in disproof of the superfecundity of human beings and developing of the real principle of their increase.* London, John Murray, 1830. 2 vols.

Sanger, Margaret: *Problems of Overpopulation.* New York, American Birth Control League, 1926. 208 pp.

Sanger, Margaret (editor): *Proceedings of the World Population Conference, Geneva, 1927.* London, E. Arnold & Co., 1927. 383 pp.

Senior, Nassau William: *Two Lectures on Population, Delivered Before the University of Oxford, 1828, to which is added a correspondence between the author and T. R. Malthus.* London, Saunders & Otley, 1829. 90 pp. (Most interesting is the appendix—correspondence with Malthus.) Senior states that food has increased faster than population. (See p. 77.)

Smissen, Edouard van der: *La Population, les causes de ses progrès et les obstacles qui en arrêtent l'essor.* Bruxelles, Société Belge de librairie, 1893. 561 pp. Book I, Historical summary of changes in Population; Book II, Malthus; Book III, Population problems in the nineteenth century.

Spengler, Joseph J.: "Comparative Fertility of the Native and Foreign-born Women in New York, Indiana and Michigan," *Quarterly Journal of Economics,* Vol. XLV, pp. 460–483.

Spengler, Joseph J.: "Fertility in Providence, R. I.," *American Journal of Sociology,* November, 1932, pp. 377–397.

Spengler, Joseph J.: "Has the Native Population of New England Been Dying Out?" *Quarterly Journal of Economics,* Vol. XLIV, pp. 639–662.

Stangeland, C. E.: *Pre-Malthusian Doctrines of Population,* New York, Columbia University Press. 1904. 356 pp.

Stevenson, T. H. C.: "The Fertility of Various Social Classes in England and Wales from the Middle of the Nineteenth Century to 1911," *Journal of the Royal Statistical Society,* Vol. LXXXIII, pp. 401–432, and discussion, pp. 432–444.

Stevenson, T. H. C.: "The Vital Statistics of Wealth and Poverty," *Journal of the Royal Statistical Society,* Vol. XCI, 1928, pp. 207–220, and discussion, pp. 221–230.

Tandler, Julius: "Psychology of the Fall in the Birth Rate," *Proceedings of the World Population Conference,* Geneva, 1927. Edited by M. Sanger, pp. 208–212.

Thomas, Dorothy Swaine: *Social Aspects of the Business Cycle.* London, George Routledge & Sons, New York, E. P. Dutton & Co., 1925. 217 pp. (Studies in Economic and Political Science edited by the London School of Economic and Political Science.) Chap. III, Marriage and the Business Cycle; Chap. IV, Births and the Business Cycle; Chap. V, Death and the Business Cycle, pp. 79–112. Statistical analysis of data referring to England and Wales and U. S.

Thompson, W. S.: "Population Facts for the United States and their Interpretation," *Journal of American Statistical Association*, Vol. XVIII, pp. 575–587.

Thompson, W. S.: "Size of Families from which College Students Come," *Journal of American Statistical Association*, Vol. XX, pp. 481–495.

Thompson, W. S.: "Population," *American Journal of Sociology*, Vol. XXXIV, pp. 3–15 and pp. 959–975.

Verhulst, P. F.: "Notice sur la loi que la population suit dans son accroissement," *Correspondance mathématiques et physique publiée par A. Quetelet*, Tome X, 1838, pp. 113–121.

Verhulst, P. F.: "Recherches mathématiques sur la loi d'accroissement de la population," *Nouveaux mémoires de l'Académie Royale des Sciences et Belles Lettres de Bruxelles*, Tome XVIII, 1845, pp. 1–38, and Deuxième mémoire sur la loi d'accroissement de la population, *Ibid.*, Tome XX, 1847, pp. 1–32.

Verrijn-Stuart, M. C. A.: "Natalité, Mortinatalité et Mortalité enfantine selon le degré d'aisance dans quelques villes et un nombre de communes rurales dans les Pays-Bas," *Bulletin de L'Institut International de Statistique*, Tome XIII, 1903, pp. 357–368.

Weyland, John: *The Principles of Population and Production as They Are Affected by the Progress of Society, with a View to Moral and Political Consequences.* London, Baldwin Cradock & Joy, 1816. 493 pp. (The natural tendency of population rises with the state of society.)

Whelpton, P. K.: "Differentials in True Natural Increase," *Journal of American Statistical Association*, Vol. XXIV, pp. 233–249.

Willcox, W. F.: "The Nature and Significance of the Changes in the Birth and Death Rates in Recent Years," *Publications of American Statistical Association*, Vol. XV, pp. 1–15.

Willcox, W. F.: "The Expansion of Europe in Population," *American Economic Review*, Vol. V, pp. 737–752.

Willcox, W. F.: "Population and the World War: a Preliminary Survey," *Journal of American Statistical Association*, Vol. XVIII, pp. 699–712.

Wolf, J.: "Une Nouvelle loi de la population," *Revue d'Economie Politique*, Vol. XVI, pp. 499–514. See also Oppenheimer's criticism, *ibid.*, Vol. VII, pp. 333–355.

Wolfe, A. B.: "Economic Conditions and the Birth-Rate After the War," *Journal of Political Economy*, Vol. XXV, pp. 521–541.

Wolfe, A. B.: "Is There a Biological Law of Human Population Growth?" *Quarterly Journal of Economics*, Vol. XLI, pp. 557–594.

Wright, Harold: *Population.* New York, Harcourt, Brace & Co., 1923. Cambridge Economic Handbooks. By increasing the productivity of labor and restricting the birth-rate, the population problem can be solved.

2. The Facts of Population Movements

A. United States

Crum, F. S.: "The Birth-Rate in Massachusetts, 1850–1890," *Quarterly Journal of Economics*, Vol. XI, pp. 248–265.

Dublin, Louis I., and Lotka, Alfred J.: "On the True Rate of Natural Increase as Exemplified by the Population of the United States, 1920," *Journal of American Statistical Association*, 1925, Vol. XX, pp. 305–339.

Dublin, Louis I., and others: *Population Problems in the United States and Canada*. Boston and New York, Houghton Mifflin Co., 1926. 318 pp.

Dublin, Louis I., and Lotka, Alfred J.: "The Present Outlook for Population Increase," *Studies in Quantitative and Cultural Sociology*. American Sociological Society, 1930, Vol. XXIV, pp. 106–114.

Dublin, Louis I., and Lotka, Alfred J.: "The True Rate of Natural Increase of the Population of the United States, Revision on Basis of Recent Data," *Metron*, 1930, Vol. VIII, No. 4, pp. 107–117.

Hill, Joseph A.: "Comparative Fecundity of Women of Native and Foreign Parentage in the United States," *Journal of American Statistical Association*, Vol. XIII, pp. 583–598.

Hooker, R. H.: "Correlation of the Marriage Rate with Trade," *Journal of Royal Statistical Society*, Vol. LXIV, 1901, pp. 485–492.

Johnson, Stewart: "The Relation between Large Families, Poverty, Irregularity of Earnings and Crowding," *Journal of Royal Statistical Society*, Vol. LXXV, 1912, pp. 539–550.

Kuczynski, R. R.: "The Fecundity of the Native and Foreign Born Population in Massachusetts," *Quarterly Journal of Economics*, Vol. XVI, pp. 1–36 and pp. 141–186.

Lotka, Alfred J.: "A Natural Population Norm," *Journal of the Washington Academy of Sciences*, 1913, Vol. 111, pp. 241–248.

Lotka, Alfred J.: "The Stability of the Normal Age Distribution," *Proceedings of National Academy of Sciences*, 1922, Vol. VIII, pp. 339–345.

Lotka, Alfred J.: "The Progressive Adjustment of Age Distribution to Fecundity," *Journal of the Washington Academy of Sciences*, 1926, Vol. XVI, pp. 505–513.

Lotka, Alfred J.: "The Relation Between Birth Rate and Death Rate in a Normal Population and the Rational Basis of an Empirical Formula for the Mean Length of Life Given by William Farr," *Journal of American Statistical Association*, Vol. XVI, pp. 121–130.

Ogburn, W. F., and Thomas, Dorothy S.: "The Influence of the Business Cycle on Certain Social Conditions," *Journal of American Statistical Association*, Vol. XVIII, pp. 324–340.

Ogle, William: "On Marriage Rates and Marriage Ages with Special Reference to the Growth of Population," *Journal of Royal Statistical Society*, Vol. LIII, 1890, pp. 253–280, and discussion, pp. 280–289.

Reed, L. J. "Time Changes in the Number of Gainfully Employed Men and Women in the United States in Relation to Population Growth." *Proceedings of the International Population Union, Problems of Population* edited by G. H. L. F. Pitt-Rivers, London, George Allan & Unwin, 1932. 378 pp.

Rossiter, W. S.: *Increase of Population in the United States, 1910–1920*. Washington, Government Printing Office, 1922.

United States Department of Commerce, Bureau of Census. Bulletins on Birth Statistics and Mortality Statistics.

Thompson, Warren S. and Whelpton, P. K. *Population Trends in the United States*. New York and London, McGraw-Hill Book Co., 1933. 415 pp.

Thompson, Warren S. and Whelpton P. K. "The Population of the Nation," in *Recent Social Trends*, Vol. I, pp. 1–58.

Whelpton, P. K.: "Differentials in True Natural Increase," *Journal of American Statistical Association*, 1929, Vol. XXIV, pp. 233–249.

Whelpton, P. K.: "Population in the United States, 1925–1975," *American Journal of Sociology*, Vol. XXXIV, pp. 253–270.

Whelpton, P. K.: "Population Trends in Differentials of True Increase and Age Composition," *American Journal of Sociology*, 1930, Vol. XXXV, pp. 870–880.

Willcox, W. F.: "The Nature and Significance of the Changes in the Birth and Death Rates in Recent Years," *Publication of the American Statistical Association*, Vol. XV, pp. 1–16.

B. Great Britain

Andréadés, Andreas M.: *La Population anglaise avant, pendant et après la grande guerre*. Ferrara, A. Neppi & Co., 1922. 147 pp.

Baines, Sir J. Athelstane: "The Recent Trend of Population in England and Wales," *Journal of Royal Statistical Society*, Vol. LXXIX, 1916, pp. 399–417.

Beveridge, Sir William: "Mr. Keynes' Evidence for Over-Population," *Economica*, Vol. IV, No. 10, pp. 1–20.

Bowley, A. L.: "Birth and Population in Great Britain," *Economic Journal*, Vol. XXXIV, pp. 188–192.

Bowley, A. L.: *Numbers Occupied in the Industries of England and Wales, 1911 and 1921*. December, 1926, London, The Executive Committee of London and Cambridge Economic Service. 1926.

Bowley, A. L.: *Occupational Changes in Great Britain, 1911 and 1921.* London, The Executive Committee of London and Cambridge Economic Service, May, 1926.

Bowley, A. L.: *Estimates of the Working Population of Certain Countries in 1931 and 1941.* Submitted to the Preparatory Committee for the International Economic Conference. Geneva, League of Nations, 1926.

Cannan, Edwin: "The Probability of a Cessation of the Growth of Population in England and Wales During the Next Century," *Economic Journal,* Vol. V, December, 1895, pp. 505–515. Estimated growth of population.

Cannan, Edwin: "The Changed Outlook in Regard to Population, 1831–1931," *Economic Journal,* Vol. XLI, pp. 519–532.

Census of England and Wales, 1911: "Fertility of Marriage," Vol. XIII.

Connor, L. R.: "Fertility of Marriage and Population Growth," *Journal of Royal Statistical Society,* Vol. LXXXIX, May, 1926, pp. 553–566.

De Jastrzebski, T. T. S.: "Changes in the Birth Rate and in Legitimate Fertility in London, 1911–1921," *Journal of Royal Statistical Society,* Vol. LXXXVI, 1923, pp. 26–45, and discussion, pp. 46–58. (Greater decrease among poorer classes than among the well-to-do.)

Dunlop, James Craufurd: "The Fertility of Marriage in Scotland: a census study," *Journal of Royal Statistical Society,* Vol. LXXVII, 1914, pp. 259–288, and discussion, pp. 288–299. See also Vol. LXXVIII, 1915, pp. 35–54.

Elderton, Ethel Mary: *Report on the English Birthrate.* London, Dulan & Co., 1914.

England and Wales: *Annual Report of the Registrar-General of Births, Deaths, and Marriages in England and Wales.*

Great Britain: National Council of Public Morals, National Birth Rate Commission; First Report: *The Declining Birth Rate; Its Causes and Effects,* 1916; Second Report: *Problems of Population and Parenthood,* 1920; Fourth Report: *Youth and the Race,* 1923.

Newsholme, Arthur, and Stevenson, T. H. C.: "The Decline of Human Fertility in the United Kingdom as Shown by Corrected Birth Rates," *Journal of Royal Statistical Society,* Vol. LXIX, 1906, pp. 34–87, and discussion, pp. 133–147.

Newsholme, Arthur: *The Elements of Vital Statistics.* 3d edition. London, Swan, Sonnenschein & Co., 1899. Including also discussion of methods of constructing life-tables.

Sharpe, F. R., and Lotka, A. J.: "A Problem in Age Distribution," *London, Edinburgh, and Dublin Philosophical Magazine,* 1911, 6 series, Vol. XXI, pp. 435–438.

Sydenstricker, E., and Notestein, F. W.: "Differential Fertility According to Social Class," *Journal of American Statistical Association*, Vol. XXV, pp. 9–32. A study of 69,620 native white married women under forty-five years based upon the U. S. Census returns of 1910.

Thompson, Warren: "Britain's Population Problem as Seen by an American," *Economic Journal*, Vol. XXXVI, pp. 177–191.

Welton, Thomas A.: "On the Death Rates in Various Parts of England and Wales in 1913," *Journal of Royal Statistical Society*, Vol. LXXIX, 1916, pp. 37–54. See also note in Vol. LXXX, 1917, pp. 521–528.

Welton, Thomas A.: "On the Birth Rates in Various Parts of England and Wales in 1911, 1912, and 1913," *Journal of Royal Statistical Society*, Vol. LXXIX, 1916, pp. 18–36. See also note in Vol. LXXX, 1917, pp. 521–528.

Yule, G. U.: "On the Changes in the Marriage and Birth Rates in England and Wales during the Past Half Century; with an Inquiry as to Their Probable Causes," *Journal of Royal Statistical Society*, Vol. LXIX, 1906, pp. 88–132. See also discussion, pp. 135–147.

Yule, G. U.: "The Growth of Population and the Factors which Control It," *Journal of Royal Statistical Society*, Vol. LXXXVIII, 1925, pp. 1–58. Discussion on the Laws of Population, T. H. C. Stevenson, pp. 63–90.

Yule, G. U.: *The Fall of the Birth Rate*. Cambridge, University Press, 1920. 43 pp.

C. Germany

Bortkiewicz, L. von: "Die Sterbeziffer und der Frauenüberschuss in der Stationären und in der Progressiven Bevölkerung," *Bulletin de l'Institut International de Statistique, 1911*, Vol. XIX, 1 session, part II, pp. 63–138.

Fischer, Eugen: Report on Muckermann's Studies of the Differential Fertility Within Certain Social Groups in Germany. *Proceedings of the International Population Union*, edited by G. H. L. F. Pitt-Rivers. London, G. Allen & Unwin, 1932, pp. 106–111.

Germany: Statistik des Deutschen Reichs; Statistisches Jahrbuch für das Deutsche Reich. Wirtschaft und Statistik.

Prussia: Statistisches Jahrbuch für den Preussischen Staat.

Rubin, Marcus, and Westergaard, Harald: *Statistik der Ehen auf Grund der Socialen Gliederung der Bevölkerung*. Jena, Gustav Fischer, 1890. Data refer to Denmark; analysis of marriages and births of different social classes.

Statistik des Deutschen Reichs: "Die Bewegung der Bevölkerung in den Jahren, 1925–1927." Vol. 360, pp. 52–57, 206.

Statistik des Deutschen Reichs: "Die Bevölkerung des Deutschen Reichs nach den Ergebnissen der Volkszählung, 1925." Vol. 401, Part II, pp. 669–673.

D. France

Bertheau, Charles: *Essai sur les lois de la Population.* Paris, Chevalier-Maresq et Cie, 1892. 480 pp.

Bertillon, Jacques: *La Dépopulation de la France, ses consequences, ses causes, measures à prendre pour la combattre.* Paris, Felix Alcan, 1911. 346 pp.

France: *Annuaire Statistique; Statistique de la France; Statistique du Movement de la Population.* Statistics for 90 departments in *Statistique de la France, 1925.*

Husson, Raoul: "Natalité et accroissement de la population en France et à l'étranger avant et après la guerre," *Bulletin de la Statistique générale de la France, 1931,* Vol. XX, pp. 245–298.

Ogburn, W. F., and Jaffé, William: *The Economic Development of Post-War France.* New York, Columbia University Press, 1929. 613 pp.

Schone, Lucien: *Histoire de la Population française.* Paris, Arthur Raisseau, 1893. 428 pp.

E. Canada

Canada: *The Canadian Yearbook.*

Kuczynski, R. R.: *Birth Registration and Birth Statistics in Canada.* Washington, Brookings Institution, 1930. 219 pp.

Quebec: *Statistical Yearbook of Quebec.*

F. Other Countries

Allen, G. C.: "The Population Problem in Japan," *Economica,* Vol. VI, p. 170.

Austria: Österreichisches Statistisches Handbuch. Statistisches Handbuch für die Republik Österreich.

Denmark: Danmarks Statistik, Statistik Aarbog.

Edin, Karl Arvid: "Fertility in Marriage and Infantile Mortality in the Different Social Classes in Stockholm from 1919–1922," *Proceedings of the World Population Conference, Geneva, 1927.* Edited by M. Sanger, pp. 205–208.

Edin, Karl Arvid: "The Fertility of the Social Classes in Stockholm, 1919–1929," *Proceedings of the International Population Union.* Edited by G. H. L. F. Pitt-Rivers. London, George Allen & Unwin, 1932, pp. 91–101.

Italy: Movimento della Popolazione. Annuario Statistico Italiano.

Kuczynski, Robert Réné: *The Balance of Births and Deaths.* New York, Macmillan Co., 1928 (2 vols.). Very valuable statistical material for all European countries. Contains data on births and birth rates, fertility tables, population for practically all European countries.

Niceforo, A.: "The Development of the Population in Italy," *Proceedings of the World Population Conference*, Geneva, 1927. Edited by M. Sanger. pp. 59–70.

Norway: *Statistisk Arbok.*

Sweden: *Statistisk Arsbok*, especially 1931. p. 35 *ff*.

Switzerland: *Statistisches Jahrbuch der Schweiz.*

Sydenstricker, Edgar: "Population Statistics of Foreign Countries," *Journal of American Statistical Association*, Vol. XX, pp. 80–89.

Szulc, Stefan: "Les mesures de l'accroissement naturel de la population," *Revue Trimestrielle de Statistique de la République Polonaise*, 1930, Vol. VII, pp. 1–16.

3. General

Baines, J. A.: "The Recent Growth of Population in Western Europe; an Essay in International Comparison," *Journal of Royal Statistical Society*, Vol. LXXII, pp. 685–713.

Beveridge, Sir William: "The Fall of Fertility Among European Races," *Economica*, Vol. V, pp. 10–27.

Edge, Major P. Granville: "Vital Registration in Europe," *Journal of Royal Statistical Society*, Vol. XCI, 1928, pp. 346–379.

Farr, W.: *Vital Statistics* (Memorial Volume). London, The Sanitary Institute etc., 1885.

Greenwood, Major: "The Vital Statistics of Sweden and England and Wales; an Essay in International Comparison," *Journal of Royal Statistical Society*, Vol. LXXXVII, 1924, pp. 493–531, and discussion, pp. 532–543.

Kiaer, A. N.: *Statistische Beiträge zur Beleuchtung der Ehelichen Fruchtbarkeit*. Christiania, J. Dybwad, 1903. Statistics of the fertility of marriages for all European countries, United States, Argentine, Brazil.

Kuczynski, R. R.: *Fertility and Reproduction*. New York, Falcon Press, 1932. 94 pp. Methods of measuring the balance of births and deaths.

Lotka, Alfred J.: "Studies on the Mode of Growth of Material Aggregates," *American Journal of Science*, Vol. 174, 1907, pp. 199–216.

Pitt-Rivers, G. H. L. F.: *Problems of Population*. Being the report of the proceedings of the second general assembly of the International Population Union. London, George Allen & Unwin, Ltd., 1932, 378 pp.

Stevenson, T. H. C.: "The Vital Statistics of Wealth and Poverty," *Journal of Royal Statistical Society*, Vol. XCI, 1928, pp. 207–220, and discussion, pp. 221–230.

Wolfe, A. B.: "The Population Problem Since the World War: a Survey of Literature and Research," *Journal of Political Economy*, Vol. XXXVI, pp. 529–559, pp. 662–685; *ibid.*, Vol. XXXVII, pp. 87–120.

V. THE SHORT-RUN SUPPLY OF LABOR

1. Theory

Bagge, Gösta: *Arbeitslönens Reglering Genom Sammanslutningar.* Stockholm, 1917. 483 pp. (Esp. pp. 427–465).

Böhm-Bawerk, Eugen von: "The Ultimate Standards of Value," *Annals of American Academy of Political and Social Science*, Vol. V, pp. 149–208.

Bowley, A. L.: "Wages and the Mobility of Labour," *Economic Journal*, Vol. XXII, pp. 46–52.

Brentano, Lujo: *Hours and Wages in Relation to Production.* Translated by Mrs. W. Arnold. London, S. Sonnenschein & Co., 1894. 143 pp.

Chapman, S. J.: "Hours of Labour," *Economic Journal*, Vol. XIX, pp. 353–373.

Children's Bureau, U. S. Dept. of Labor: "Trend of Child Labor in the United States, 1920–1923," *Monthly Labor Review*, Vol. XVII, No. 3, September, 1923, pp. 671–675.

Douglas, Paul H.: "Personnel Problems and the Business Cycle," *Administration*, Vol. IV, July, 1922, pp. 15–28.

Douglas, Paul H.: "Absenteeism in Labor," *Political Science Quarterly*, Vol. XXXIV, December, 1919, pp. 591–608. (*Esp. pp. 596–604.*)

Eckler, A. Ross: "Occupational Changes in the United States," *Review of Economic Statistics*, 1930, pp. 77–89. Shift in numbers away from those who produce material goods to production of services.

Frain, H. LaRue: "The Relation Between Normal Working Time and Hourly and Weekly Earnings" (note), *Quarterly Journal of Economics*, Vol. XLIII, pp. 544–550.

Furniss, Edgar S.: *The Position of the Laborer in a System of Nationalism.* Boston and New York, Houghton Mifflin Co., 1920.

Hadley, Arthur Twining: *Economics.* New York, G. P. Putnam's Sons, 1902. 496 pp.

Harrod, R. F.: "Notes on Supply," *Economic Journal* (1930), Vol. XL, pp. 232–241.

Hart, Hornell: *Fluctuations in Unemployment in Cities of the United States, 1902–1917.* Cincinnati, Ohio, Helen S. Trounstine Foundation, 1918.

Jennings, Richard: *Natural Elements of Political Economy.* London, Longman, Brown, Green, etc., 1855. 275 pp.

Jevons, H. Stanley: *Essays on Economics.* London and New York, Macmillan Co., 1905. 280 pp.

Jevons, W. Stanley: *The Theory of Political Economy.* 3d edition. London, Macmillan & Co., 1888. 296 pp.

Jones, J. H.: "The Present Position of the British Coal Trade," *Journal of Royal Statistical Society,* Vol. XCIII, 1930, pp. 1–53. See also discussion, pp. 54–63.

Knight, Frank H.: *Risk, Uncertainty and Profit.* Boston and New York, Houghton Mifflin Co., 1921. 381 pp.

Marshall, Alfred: *Principles of Economics.* 6th edition. London, Macmillan & Co. 1910. Book VI, Chaps. IV and V. 871 pp.

Patten, Simon Nelson: *The Theory of Dynamic Economics.* Publications of the University of Pennsylvania Political Economy and Public Law Series, Vol. III, No. 2. Philadelphia, 1892.

Reinsch, Paul S.: *Colonial Administration.* New York and London, Macmillan Co., 1905. 422 pp.

Robbins, Lionel: "The Economic Effects of Variations of the Hours of Labor," *Economic Journal,* Vol. XXXIX, pp. 25–40.

Robbins, Lionel: "On the Elasticity of Demand for Income in Terms of Effort," *Economica,* Vol. X (1930) pp. 123–129.

Robertson, D. H.: "Economic Incentives," *Economica,* Vol. I, pp. 230–245.

Seager, Henry R.: *Principles of Economics.* 3d edition. New York, H. Holt & Co., 1923. 698 pp.

Smith, Adam: *Wealth of Nations.* (McCulloch, editor.) Edinburgh, A. & C. Black, 1863. 634 pp. Book I, Chap. VIII.

2. Sources and Facts

Census of England and Wales, 1911, Vol. X., Cd. 7018.

Clark, V. S.: "Labor Conditions in Java," *U. S. Bureau of Labor Bulletin, No. 58* (1905), pp. 906–954.

Clark, V. S.: "Labor Conditions in the Philippines," *United States Bureau of Labor Bulletin, No. 58* (1905), pp. 721–905.

Connor, L. P.: "On Certain Aspects of the Distribution of Income in the United Kingdom in the Years 1913 and 1924," *Journal of Royal Statistical Society,* Vol. XCI, 1928, pp. 50–66. See also discussion, pp. 67–78.

Douglas, Paul H.: *Real Wages in the United States.* Boston and New York, Houghton Mifflin Co., 1930. 682 pp. Esp. Part II and bibliography.

International Labour Review, Geneva. Statistics of Real Wages— Statistics Showing Movements in the General Level of Wages, Vol. XX, pp. 113–125, 1929; Vol. XXI, pp. 117–127, 1930.

Kuczynski, R. R.: *Arbeitslohn und Arbeitszeit in Europa und Amerika, 1870–1909.* Berlin, 1913, Julius Springer. 817 pp.

Ross, F. A.: School Attendance, Census Monograph No. 5.

Simiand, François: *Le Salaire, L'Évolution Sociale et La Monnaie,* 3 vols. Paris, Felix Alcan, 1931–1932. 586 pp., 620 pp., 152 pp., and charts.

Simiand, François: *Le Salaire des Ouvriers des Mines de Charbon en France; contribution à la théorie économique du salaire.* Paris, É. Cornély et Cie, 1907. 520 pp.

U. S. Bureau of Labor Statistics: Wages and Hours of Labor. Bulletins, Wages and Hours of Labor Service No. 1–15.

U. S. Bureau of Labor Statistics: Wages and Hours in Foundries and Machine Shops, 1925, Bulletin No. 422. in Hosiery and Underwear Industries, 1926; Bulletin No. 452.

U. S. Bureau of Labor Statistics: Bulletin No. 265. Industrial Survey in Selected Industries in the United States, 1919.

U. S. Bureau of the Census: Thirteenth Census of the United States (1910). Vol. IV, pp. 71–73. Fourteenth Census of U. S., Vol. VIII, pp. 222–238, and Vol. IV.

Weyl, Walter E.: "Labor Conditions in Porto Rico," *U. S. Bureau of Labor Bulletin, No. 61* (1905), pp. 723–856.

Weyl, Walter E.: "Labor Conditions in Mexico," *U. S. Bureau of Labor Bulletin, No. 38* (1902), pp. 1–94.

VI. THE MOVEMENT OF MONEY AND REAL WAGES

1. *United States*

Brissenden, Paul F.: "Earnings of Factory Workers, 1899 to 1927," *Census Monograph X,* Washington, 418 pp.

Douglas, Paul H.: *Real Wages in the United States.* Boston and New York, Houghton Mifflin Co., 1930. See also bibliography.

Douglas, Paul H.: "The Movement of Real Wages and Its Economic Significance," *Supplement to American Economic Review,* March, 1926, Vol. XVI, No. 1, pp. 17–53.

Gunton, George: *Wealth and Progress, a Critical Examination of the Wages Question.* New York, D. Appleton & Co., 1891.

Hansen, Alvin H.: "Factors Affecting the Trend of Real Wages," *American Economic Review,* Vol. XV, pp. 27–42, and note on p. 294.

Hansen, Alvin H.: "The Buying Power of Labor During the War," *Journal of American Statistical Association,* Vol. XVIII (March, 1922), pp. 56–66.

Hansen, Alvin H.: "The Best Measure of Real Wages," *American Economic Review Supplement No. 1,* Vol. XVI, pp. 5–16.

Heer, Clarence: *Income and Wages in the South.* Chapel Hill, University of North Carolina Press, 1930. 68 pp.

Johnson, Alvin: "Real Wages° and the Control of Industry," *American Economic Review*, Vol. XVI, supplement, No. 1, pp. 54–58.

Jones, F. W.: "Real Wages in Recent Years," *American Economic Review*, June, 1917, pp. 319–330.

Lubin, Isador: *Miners' Wages and the Price of Coal.* Institute of Economics, Series 1924. New York, McGraw-Hill Book Co., 1924.

Maher, Amy G.: *Wage Rates, Earnings and Fluctuation of Employment*, Ohio, 1914–1926. Information Bureau on Women's Work, Toledo, 1928.

National Industrial Conference Board: *Wages and Hours in American Industry.* New York, National Industrial Conference Board, 1925. 199 pp.

National Industrial Conference Board: *The Economic Status of the Wage-Earner in New York and Other States, 1928.* See also *Wages in the United States, 1928.*

National Industrial Conference Board: *Wages, Hours and Employment in American Industries*, July, 1914, January, 1924.

Nearing, Scott: *Wages in the United States*, 1908–1910. New York, Macmillan Co., 1911.

Report Massachusetts Special Commission on the Necessaries of Life. Boston, 1925, 1927, 1928.

Rubinow, I. M.: "Recent Trend of Real Wages," *American Economic Review*, Vol. IV. pp. 793–818.

Thompson, J. G.: "Present Work and Present Wages," *Quarterly Journal of Economics*, Vol. XXIV, pp. 515–535.

Wolfers, Arnold: *Amerikanische und Deutsche Löhne*, 1930. Berlin, Julius Springer. 139 pp.

2. Great Britain

Andrews, Irene Osgood: *Economic Effects of the War upon Women and Children in Great Britain.* Preliminary Economic Studies of the War. Carnegie Endowment for International Peace. New York, Oxford University Press, 1918.

Bowley, Arthur Lyon: *Prices and Wages in the United Kingdom, 1914–1920.* Oxford, Clarendon Press, 1921. 228 pp.

Bowley, Arthur Lyon and Wood, G. H.: "Statistics of Wages in the United Kingdom During the Last Hundred Years." Parts I–XIV, *Journal Royal Statistical Society*, Vols. LXI–LXIX.

Bowley, Arthur Lyon: "Changes in Average Wages (Nominal and Real) in the United Kingdom Between 1860–1891," *Journal of Royal Statistical Society*, Vol. LVIII, 1895, pp. 223–278.

Bowley, Arthur Lyon: *A New Index-Number of Wages.* London and Cambridge, Economic Service (1929).

Bowley, Arthur Lyon: "Comparison of the Changes in Wages in France, the United States, and the United Kingdom, from 1840–1891," *Economic Journal,* Vol. VIII, pp. 474–489.

Bowley, Arthur Lyon: "Comparison of the Rates of Increase of Wages in the United States and in Great Britain, 1860–1891," *Economic Journal,* Vol. V, pp. 369–383.

Bowley, Arthur Lyon, and Hogg, M. H.: *Has Poverty Diminished?* London, P. S. King & Son, 1925. 236 pp.

Bowley, Arthur Lyon: *Livelihood and Poverty.* London, G. Bell & Sons, 1915. 222 pp.

British Board of Trade (Labour Dept.): "Wages and Hours of Labour: Reports on Changes of Wages and Hours of Labour in the United Kingdom." See especially cd. 8975, 1562, 7635, 309, and 7080.

British Board of Trade (Labour Dept.): "Earnings and Hours Enquiry in the United Kingdom." Textiles cd., 4545; building, etc., cd., 5086; agriculture cd., 5460; railway cd., 6053; clothing cd., 4844; public utilities cd., 5196; engineering cd., 5814; and miscellaneous cd., 6556.

Chapman, Sydney John: *Work and Wages in Continuation of Lord Brassey's "Work and Wages" and "Foreign Work and English Wages."* London, New York, Longmans, Green & Co., 1904–1914.

Clark, Colin: *The National Income, 1924–1931.* London, Macmillan & Co., 1932. 167 pp. Esp. Chap. V, Wages.

Fawcett, Henry: *The Economic Position of the British Labourer.* Cambridge and London, Macmillan & Co., 1865. 265 pp.

Florence, P. Sargant: "A Statistical Contribution to the Theory of Women's Wages," *Economic Journal,* Vol. XLI, pp. 19–37.

Giffen, Sir Robert: *Essays in Finance.* 2d series. New York, G. P. Putnam's Sons, 1886.

International Labour Review, Vol. XII, 1925, pp. 74–82. Reports and Enquiries. Hours of Labour and Overtime Rates of Pay in the Principal Industries in Great Britain.

Page, William: *Commerce and Industry; a historical review of the economic conditions of the British Empire from the Peace of Paris in 1815 to the declaration of war in 1914 based on parliamentary debates.* London, Constable & Co., 1919. 2 vols.

Pigou, A. C.: "Prices and Wages from 1896–1914," *Economic Journal,* Vol. XXXIII, pp. 163–171. Concludes that increased food supply and higher prices did not produce any material setback to real wages.

Rowe, J. W. F.: "Wages in the Cotton Industry, 1914–1920," *Economic Journal,* Vol. XXXIV, pp. 200–210.

Rowe, J. W. F.: *Wages in the Coal Industry.* London, P. S. King, 1923.

Wood, Frances: "The Course of Real Wages in London, 1900–1912," *Journal of Royal Statistical Society*, Vol. LXXVII, 1913–1914, pp. 1–55, and discussion, pp. 56–68.

Wood, George H.: "The Statistics of Wages in the United Kingdom During the Nineteenth Century," *Journal of Royal Statistical Society*, Vol. LXXIII, Cotton Industry; Part XV, pp. 39–58. Part XVI, pp. 128–163; Part XVII, pp. 283–315; Part XVIII, pp. 411–434; Part XIX, pp. 585–626.

Wood, George H.: "Real Wages and the Standard of Comfort Since 1850," *Journal of Royal Statistical Society*, Vol. LXXII, 1909, pp. 91–103.

Wood, George H.: "Stationary Wage-Rates," *Economic Journal*, Vol. II, pp. 151–156.

Wood, George H.: "The Course of Average Wages Between 1790 and 1860," *Economic Journal*, Vol. IX, pp. 588–592.

Wood, George H.: "Changes in Average Wages in New South Wales, 1823–1898," *Journal of Royal Statistical Society*, Vol. LXIV, pp. 327–335 and pp. 661–676.

3. Germany

Bresciani-Turroni, C.: "The Movement of Wages in Germany During the Depreciation of the Mark and After Stabilization," *Journal of Royal Statistical Society*, Vol. XCII, 1929, pp. 374–414. See also discussion, pp. 414–427.

Germany: Wirtschaft und Statistik; Reichsarbeitsblatt; Lohn und gehaltserhebungen vom February, 1920. (Statistik des Deutschen Reichs, Band 293.)

Schmoller, Gustav: "Die Tatsachen der Lohnbewegung in Geschichte und Gegenwart." *Schmollers Jahrbuch*, Vol. XXXVIII, pp. 525–556.

Wolfers, Arnold: *Amerikanische und Deutsche Löhne.* Berlin, Julius Springer, 1930. 139 pp.

4. Other Countries

Anderson, George: *Fixation of Wages in Australia.* Melbourne, Macmillan & Co., 1929. 568 pp.

International Wage Comparisons: Documents arising out of conferences held at the International Labour Office, 1929 and 1930, convened by the Social Science Research Council of New York. Manchester, Manchester University Press, 1932. 262 pp.

International Labour Review, Geneva. Statistics of real wages.

Italy: Indici del Movimento Economico Italiano, Vol. I–IV. La Vita Economica.

Ogburn, W. F. and Jaffé, W.: *The Economic Development of Postwar France.* New York, Columbia University Press, 1929. 613 pp.

Richardson, J. H.: "International Comparisons of Real Wages," *Journal of Royal Statistical Society*, Vol. XCIII, 1930, pp. 398–423. See also discussion, pp. 423–441.

Simiand, François: *Le Salaire, l'Évolution Sociale et la Monnaie*. 3 vols., Paris, Felix Alcan, 1932.

VII. THE THEORY OF INTEREST

Ansiaux, M.: "Le Phénomène de l'Intérêt et son Explication," *Revue de l'Institut de Sociologie Bruxelles*, 1921–1922. Deuxième année, Tome I, pp. 47–57.

Bilgram, H.: "The Interest Controversy," *Quarterly Journal of Economics*, Vol. V, pp. 375–377.

Bilgram, H.: "Analysis of the Nature of Capital and Interest," *Journal of Political Economy*, Vol. XVI, 1908, pp. 129–151.

Bilgram, H.: "Comments on the 'Positive Theory of Capital'," *Quarterly Journal of Economics*, Vol. VI, pp. 190–206.

Böhm-Bawerk, Eugen von: *Capital and Interest*. London, Macmillan & Co., 1890, 431 pp.

Böhm-Bawerk, Eugen von: *The Positive Theory of Capital*. Translated by William Smart. London, Macmillan & Co., 1891, 428 pp.

Böhm-Bawerk, Eugen von: "Zur neuesten Literatur über Kapital und Kapitalzins," *Zeitschrift für Volkswirtschaft, Sozialpol. u. Ver.*, Vol. XV, pp. 443–461.

Böhm-Bawerk, Eugen von: "Eine dynamische Theorie des Kapitalzinses," *Zeitsch. f. Volksw. Sozialpol. u. Ver.*, Vol. XXII, 1913, pp. 1–62 and pp. 640–656.

Böhm-Bawerk, Eugen von: "The Positive Theory of Capital and Its Critics," *Quarterly Journal of Economics*, Vol. IX, pp. 113–131 and 235–256; Vol. X, pp. 121–155.

Böhm-Bawerk, Eugen von: "Capital and Interest Once More," *Quarterly Journal of Economics*, Vol. XXI, pp. 1–21; and pp. 247–282.

Böhm-Bawerk, Eugen von: "The Origin of Interest," *Quarterly Journal of Economics*, Vol. IX, pp. 380–387. Reply to Mr. Clark's article, Vol. IX, pp. 257–278.

Böhm-Bawerk, Eugen von: *Kleinere Abhandlungen über Kapital und Zins*. Wien und Leipzig, Holder-Tichler-Temsky, A. G., 1926. 585 pp.

Bortkiewicz, L. von: "Der Kardinalfehler der Böhm-Bawerkschen Zinstheorie." *Schmollers Jahrbuch*, 1906, Vol. XXX, pp. 943–972.

Bortkiewicz, L. von: "Zur Zinstheorie," *Schmollers Jahrbuch*, Vol. XXX, pp. 1288–1303.

Brown, Harry G.: "The Marginal Productivity Versus the Impatience Theory of Interest," *Quarterly Journal of Economics*, Vol. XXVII, pp. 630–650.

Brown, Harry Gunnison: *Economic Science and the Common Welfare.* Columbia, Missouri, Lucas Brothers, 1926. 273 pp. esp. Part II; Chaps. III and IV.

Cannan, Edwin: The Determination of the Rate of Interest in *An Economist's Protest.* pp. 285–298. London, P. S. King & Son, Ltd., 1927. 438 pp.

Carver, Thomas Nixon: *The Distribution of Wealth.* New York, Macmillan Co., 1904. 290 pp.

Carver, Thomas Nixon: "The Place of Abstinence in the Theory of Interest," *Quarterly Journal of Economics,* Vol. VIII, pp. 40–61. See also note in Vol. XVIII, pp. 142–145.

Carver, Thomas Nixon: "Clark's Distribution of Wealth," *Quarterly Journal of Economics,* Vol. XV, pp. 578–602.

Cassel, Gustav: *The Theory of Social Economy.* New York, Harcourt, Brace & Co., 1924. 2 vols.

Cassel, Gustav: *The Nature and Necessity of Interest.* London, Macmillan & Co., 1903. 188 pp.

Chapman, S. J.: "Must Inventions Reduce the Rate of Interest?" *Economic Journal,* Vol. XX, 1910, pp. 465–469.

Child, Sir Josiah: *A New Discourse of Trade.* 5th edition. Glasgow, R. & A. Foulis, 1751. 184 pp. To which is added a treatise of interest.

Clark, John Bates: *Distribution of Wealth.* New York, Macmillan Co., 1899. 445 pp.

Clark, John Bates: "The Origin of Interest," *Quarterly Journal of Economics,* Vol. IX, pp. 257–278. See also Böhm-Bawerk's reply, p. 380.

Conrad, Otto: "Böhm-Bawerks Kritik der sozialistischen Zinstheorie," *Zeitsch. f. Volksw. Sozialpol. u. Ver.,* Vol. XX, Wien, 1911, pp. 699–729.

Conrad, Otto: "Kapitalzins," *Jahrbücher für Nationalökonomie und Statistik,* Vol. XC, pp. 325–359. Discussion of theories of interest; advances his monopoly-gain theory.

Davenport, H. J.: *Value and Distribution.* Chicago, University of Chicago Press, 1908. 582 pp.

Davenport, H. J.: "Interest Theory and Theories," *American Economic Review,* Vol. XVII, pp. 636–656.

Davies, George R.: "Factors Determining the Interest Rate," *Quarterly Journal of Economics,* Vol. XXXIV, pp. 445–461.

Diehl, K.: "Zur Kritik der Kapitalzinstheorie von Böhm-Bawerk," *Jahrbücher für Nationalökonomie und Statistik,* Vol. 105, 1915, pp. 577–607.

Fetter, Frank A.: "Interest Theories, Old and New," *American Economic Review,* Vol. IV, pp. 68–92.

Fetter, Frank A.: *Economic Principles.* New York, Century Co., 1915. 523 pp.

Fetter, Frank A.: "Interest Theory and Price Movements," *American Economic Review, Supplement,* Vol. XVII, pp. 62–105. Especially Part I. Historical Stages in the Conception of the Interest Problem.

Fetter, Frank A.: "The 'Roundabout Process' in the Interest Theory," *Quarterly Journal of Economics,* Vol. XVII, pp. 163–180.

Fetter, Frank A.: "Clark's Reformulation of the Capital Concept" in *Economic Essays Contributed in Honor of John Bates Clark.* New York, Macmillan Co., 1927, pp. 136–156.

Fisher, Irving: "The Impatience Theory of Interest," *American Economic Review,* Vol. III, pp. 610–618.

Fisher, Irving: *The Theory of Interest, as determined by impatience to spend income and opportunity to invest it.* New York, Macmillan Co., 1930. 566 pp. A revision of *The Rate of Interest* published in 1907.

Fisher, Irving: *The Rate of Interest, its Nature, Determination and Relation to Economic Phenomena.* New York, Macmillan Co., 1907. 442 pp.

Fisher, Irving: "A Reply to Critics," *Quarterly Journal of Economics,* Vol. XXIII, pp. 536–541.

Fisher, Irving: "Capital and Interest: Reply to Professor Veblen," *Political Science Quarterly,* Vol. XXIV, pp. 504–516.

Flux, A. W.: "Irving Fisher on Capital and Interest," *Quarterly Journal of Economics,* Vol. XXIII, pp. 307–323.

Friday, David: *Profits, Wages and Prices.* New York, Harcourt, Brace & Howe, 1920. 256 pp.

Giddings, F. H.: "The Growth of Capital and the Cause of Interest," *Quarterly Journal of Economics,* Vol. V, pp. 242–248.

Gonner, E. C. K.: "Some Considerations About Interest," *Economic Journal,* Vol. XVIII, pp. 42–51.

Gonner, E. C. K.: *Interest and Savings.* New York, Macmillan Co., 1906. 172 pp.

Graziani, Augusto: "Capitale e Interesse," *Società Reale di Napoli,* 1925, pp. 33–92.

Green, D. I.: "The Cause of Interest," *Quarterly Journal of Economics,* Vol. V, pp. 361–365. Criticism of Böhm-Bawerk and Giddings.

Hadley, Arthur T.: "Interest and Profits," *Annals of the American Academy,* Vol. IV, pp. 337–347.

Hawley, F. B.: "The Fundamental Error of Kapital und Kapitalzins," *Quarterly Journal of Economics,* Vol. VI, pp. 280–307.

Heinze, Gerhard: *Statische oder dynamische Zinstheorie?* Versuch einer kritischen Beleuchtung der Cassel'schen und Schumpeter'schen Zinstheorie. Leipzig, A. Deichert, 1928. 165 pp.

Hoag, Clarence Gilbert: *A Theory of Interest.* New York, Macmillan Co., 1914. 228 pp.

Jevons, W. Stanley: *Theory of Political Economy*. 3d edition. London, Macmillan & Co., 1888. 296 pp.

Kleene, G. A.: "The Income of Capital," *Quarterly Journal of Economics*, Vol. XXVI, pp. 313–340.

Knight, Frank H.: *Risk, Uncertainty and Profit*. Boston and New York, Houghton Mifflin Co., 1921.

Knight, Frank H.: "Neglected Factors in the Problem of Normal Interest," *Quarterly Journal of Economics*, Vol. XXX, pp. 279–310. (Supply and demand of capital.)

Knight, Frank H.: "Professor Fisher's Interest Theory: a case in point," *Journal of Political Economy*, Vol: XXXIX, pp. 176–210.

Knight, Frank H.: "Interest" in the *Encyclopedia of the Social Sciences*, Vol. VIII, pp. 131–143.

Kotany, L.: "A Theory of Profit and Interest," *Quarterly Journal of Economics*, Vol. XXXVI, pp. 413–453.

Landry, A.: "On the Returns of Productive Agents and on the Productivity of Capital in Particular," *Quarterly Journal of Economics*, Vol. XXIII, pp. 557–592.

Landry, A.: "Irving Fisher: The Rate of Interest," *Revue d'Economie Politique*, 23 anneé, 1909 (Bulletin Bibliographique), pp. 156–159.

Landry, A.: *L'Intérêt du Capital.*" Paris, V. Giard and E. Brière, 1904. 367 pp.

Lavington, F.: "Uncertainty in Its Relation to the Rate of Interest," *Economic Journal*, Vol. XXII, pp. 398–409.

Lowrey, Dwight M.: "The Basis of Interest," *Annals of the American Academy of Political and Social Science*, Vol. II, pp. 629–652.

McGown, A. F.: "The Nature of Interest and the Causes of its Fluctuations," *Quarterly Journal of Economics*, Vol. XXXI, pp. 547–570. Capital yields interest, because a given product can be turned out with less labor with the aid of capital than without its aid.

Molinari, G. de: "Le Fondement et la Raison d'être de l'intérêt du capital," *Journal des Économistes*, Paris, Vol. LIV, pp. 321–339.

Monroe, A. E.: "Investment and Saving: A Genetic Analysis," *Quarterly Journal of Economics*, Vol. XLIII, pp. 567–603. Saving and interest.

Mourre, B.: "Le cause des variations du taux de l'intérêt," *Revue d'Économie Politique* (Paris). Vol. XXXVIII (1924), pp. 45–65.

Oswalt, H.: "Zur Zinstheorie," *Schmollers Jahrbuch*, Vol. 31, pp. 1281–1288.

Pareto, Vilfredo: *Cours d'Économie Politique*. Lausanne, F. Rouge, 1896 and 1897. First vol., 430 pp.; second vol., 426 pp.

Rae, John: *The Sociological Theory of Capital*. New York, Macmillan Co., 1905. 485 pp.

Ricci, U.: "La Teoria dell' Astinenza," *Giornale degli Economisti,* Vol. XXXVII, pp. 295–310 and 511–536. Deals also with Cairnes and Senior's abstinence theory.

Sax, Emil: *Der Kapitalzins.* Berlin, Julius Springer, 1916. 249 pp.

Schmoller, Gustav: *Grundriss der Allgemeinen Volkswirtschaftslehre.* Leipzig, Verlag von Duncker & Humblot, 1908. 2 vols.

Schumpeter, Joseph: "Eine dynamische Theorie des Kapitalzinses," *Zeitsch. f. Volksw. Sozialpol. u. Ver.,* Vol. XXII, pp. 599–639 (1913).

Seager, Henry R.: "The Impatience Theory of Interest," *American Economic Review,* Vol. II, pp. 834–851. See also comment on I. Fisher's article in Vol. III, p. 610. *American Economic Review,* Vol. III, p. 618.

Smart, William: "The New Theory of Interest," *Economic Journal,* Vol. I, pp. 675–687.

Taussig, F. W.: "Capital, Interest and Diminishing Returns," *Quarterly Journal of Economics,* Vol. XXII, pp. 333–363.

Veblen, Th.: "Fisher's Rate of Interest," *Political Science Quarterly,* Vol. XXIV, pp. 296–303.

Walker, Francis A.: "Dr. Boehm-Bawerk's Theory of Interest," *Quarterly Journal of Economics,* Vol. VI, pp. 399–416.

Walras, Léon: *Éléments d'Économie Politique Pure.* Lausanne, F. Rouge, 1900. 491 pp.

Webb, Sidney: "The Rate of Interest and the Laws of Distribution," *Quarterly Journal of Economics,* Vol. II, pp. 188–208 and 469–472.

VIII.   THE PROBABLE SUPPLY CURVE OF CAPITAL

1. Theories

Bastiat, Frédéric: *Capital et rente.* Paris, Guillaumin et Cie, 1849. 60 pp.

Bilgram, Hugo: "Analysis of the Nature of Capital and Interest," *Journal of Political Economy,* Vol. XVI, 1908, pp. 129–151.

Böhm-Bawerk, Eugen von: *Capital and Interest.* A critical history of economical theory translated by William Smart. London and New York, Macmillan Co., 1890. 431 pp.

Böhm-Bawerk, Eugen von: *The Positive Theory of Capital.* Translated by William Smart. London, Macmillan & Co., 1891. 428 pp.

Böhm-Bawerk, Eugen von: "The Positive Theory of Capital and Its Critics," *Quarterly Journal of Economics,* Vol. IX, pp. 113–131 and pp. 235–256; Vol. X, pp. 121–155.

Böhm-Bawerk, Eugen von: "The Nature of Capital: a Rejoinder," *Quarterly Journal of Economics,* Vol. XXII, pp. 28–47.

Böhm-Bawerk, Eugen von: "The Function of Saving." Translated from the German by Henry R. Seager. *Annals of the American Academy,* Vol. XVII, pp. 454–466.

Böhm-Bawerk, Eugen von: "Capital and Interest Once More: I. Capital vs. Capital Goods," *Quarterly Journal of Economics,* Vol. XXI, pp. 1–21; II. A Relapse to a Theory of Productivity, pp. 247–282.

Böhm-Bawerk, Eugen von: "Zur neuesten Literatur über Kapital und Kapitalzins," *Zeitsch. f. Volksw. Sozialpol. u. Ver.,* Vol. XV, pp. 443–461, and Vol. XVI, pp. 1–38.

Böhm-Bawerk, Eugen von: "Einige Strittige Fragen der Kapitalstheorie," *Zeitsch. f. Volksw. Sozialpol. u. Ver.,* Vol. VIII, pp. 105–146, 365–399, 553–601.

Böhm-Bawerk, Eugen von: "Gegenbemerkungen zu Professor Clark's Replik betreffend, 'Das Wesen des Kapitals,'" *Zeitsch. f. Volksw. Sozialpol. u. Ver.,* Vol. XVI, pp. 441–457.

Bonar, James: "The Positive Theory of Capital," *Quarterly Journal of Economics,* Vol. III, pp. 336–351.

Bowley, Arthur Lyon: *A Short Account of England's Foreign Trade in the Nineteenth Century, Its Economic and Social Results.* 3d edition. New York, C. Scribner's Sons, 1905. 165 pp.

Bowley, Arthur Lyon, and Stamp, Sir Josiah: *The National Income, 1924. A comparative study of the income of the United Kingdom in 1911 and 1924.* Oxford, Clarendon Press, 1927. 59 pp.

Bowley, Arthur L.: *Division of the Product of Industry.* Oxford, Clarendon Press, 1919. 60 pp.

Bowley, Arthur L.: *The Change in the Distribution of the National Income, 1880–1913.* Oxford, Clarendon Press, 1920. 27 pp.

Cairnes, J. E.: *Some Leading Principles of Political Economy Newly Expounded.* New York, Harper & Bros., 1874 (p. 80 *ff.* on supply of capital). 421 pp.

Cannan, Edwin: "What Is Capital?" *Economic Journal,* Vol. VII, pp. 278–284. A reply to Mr. I. Fisher's article in Vol. VI, p. 509.

Carver, Thomas N.: "Automatic Saving and the Rate of Accumulation," *Quarterly Journal of Economics,* Vol. XXXVIII, pp. 347–351.

Cassel, Gustav: *The Theory of Social Economy.* New York, Harcourt, Brace & Co., 1924. 654 pp.

Cassel, Gustav: *The Nature and Necessity of Interest.* London, Macmillan & Co., 1903. 188 pp.

Chiozza-Money, Leo Giorgio: *Riches and Poverty.* London, Methuen & Co., 1906. 338 pp.

Clark, Colin: *The National Income, 1924–1931.* London, Macmillan & Co., 1932. 167 pp.

Clark, John Bates: "Über das Wesen des Kapitals," *Zeitsch. f. Volksw. Sozialpol. u. Ver.*, Vol. XVI, pp. 426–440.

Clark, John Bates: "The Genesis of Capital," *Yale Review*, Vol. II, pp. 302–315.

Clark, John Bates: *Capital and Its Earnings.* Publication of American Economics Association, Vol. III, 2, 1888. 69 pp.

Clark, John Bates: "Concerning the Nature of Capital: A Reply," *Quarterly Journal of Economics*, Vol. XXI, pp. 351–370.

Clark, John Bates: *Distribution of Wealth.* New York, Macmillan Co., 1899. 445 pp.

Crum, William Leonard: *Corporate Earning Power.* Stanford Press, 1929. 342 pp.

Davenport, H. J.: *Value and Distribution.* University of Chicago Press, 1908. 582 pp.

Dewing, A. S.: *The Financial Policy of Corporations.* New York, Ronald Press, 1926. 5 vols.

Epstein, Ralph C.: "Statistical Light on Profits, as Analyzed in Recent Literature," *Quarterly Journal of Economics*, Vol. XLIV, pp. 320–344.

Epstein, Ralph C.: "Industrial Profits in 1917," *Quarterly Journal of Economics*, Vol. XXXIX, pp. 241–266.

Fetter, Frank A.: "Recent Discussion of the Capital Concept," in *Economic Essays* contributed in honor of John Bates Clark, pp. 136–156. New York, Macmillan Co., 1927.

Fetter, Frank A.: *Economic Principles.* New York, Century Co., 1915. 523 pp.

Fetter, Frank A.: "Recent Discussion of the Capital Concept," *Quarterly Journal of Economics*, Vol. XV, pp. 1–45. Criticism of B. B.

Fisher, Irving: "Senses of 'Capital'," *Economic Journal*, Vol. VII, pp. 199–213. The Rôle of Capital in Economic Theory, *Ibid.*, pp. 511–537.

Fisher, Irving: "What Is Capital?" *Economic Journal*, Vol. VI, pp. 509–534. See Cannan's reply in Vol. VII, p. 278.

Fisher, Irving: "A Reply to Critics," *Quarterly Journal of Economics*, Vol. XXIII, pp. 536–541.

Fisher, Irving: "Professor Fetter on Capital and Income," *Journal of Political Economy*, Vol. XV, pp. 421–434.

Fisher, Irving: *The Theory of Interest.* New York, Macmillan Co., 1930. 566 pp.

Fisher, Irving: "Capital and Interest: Reply to Professor Veblen," *Political Science Quarterly*, Vol. XXIV, pp. 504–516.

Fisher, Irving: *The Nature of Capital and Income.* New York, Macmillan Co., 1906.

Flux, A. W.: "Irving Fisher on Capital and Interest," *Quarterly Journal of Economics*, Vol. XXIII, pp. 307–323.

Foster, William T., and Catchings, Waddill: *Profits*. Boston and New York, Houghton Mifflin Co., 1925. 465 pp.

Friday, David: *Profits, Wages and Prices*. New York, Harcourt, Brace & Howe, 1920. 256 pp. Esp. Chap. IV.

Giddings, F. H.: "The Growth of Capital and the Cause of Interest," *Quarterly Journal of Economics*, Vol. V, pp. 242–248.

Giddings, F. H.: "The Theory of Capital," *Quarterly Journal of Economics*, Vol. IV, pp. 172–206. See also correspondence, pp. 81 and 346.

Gilbert, Chester Garfield, and Pogue, J. E.: *America's Power Resources; the economic significance of coal, oil and water power*. New York, Century Co., 1921. 326 pp.

Gonner, Edward C. K.: *Interest and Saving*. New York, Macmillan Co., 1906. 172 pp.

Graziani, Augusto: *Capitale e Interesse*. Società Reale di Napoli, 1923. 62 pp.

Hadley, Arthur T.: "Interest and Profits," *Annals of the American Academy of Political and Social Sciences*, Vol. IV, pp. 337–347.

Hawley, F. B.: "The Fundamental Error of 'Kapital und Kapitalzins,'" *Quarterly Journal of Economics*, Vol. VI, pp. 280–307.

Hawley, F. B.: "The Controversy About the Capital Concept," *Quarterly Journal of Economics*, Vol. XXII, pp. 467–475. For a criticism, see Böhm-Bawerk in *Quarterly Journal of Economics*, Vols. IX and X.

Hayek, F. A. von: "A Note on the Development of the Doctrine of Forced Saving," *Quarterly Journal of Economics*, November, 1932, Vol. XLVII, No. 1, pp. 123–133.

Hoag, Clarence Gilbert: *A Theory of Interest*. New York, Macmillan Co., 1914. 228 pp.

Hobson, C. K.: *The Export of Capital*. New York, Macmillan Co., 1914. 264 pp.

Johnson, Alvin S.: "Influences Affecting the Development of Thrift," *Political Science Quarterly*, Vol. XXII, pp. 224–244.

Jurisch, K. W.: "Die Abhängigkeit zwischen Kapital und Zinsfuss," *Vierteljahrsschrift für Volkswirtschaft*, Band. XCI, pp. 1–38.

Keynes, J. M.: "A Note on the Long-Term Rate of Interest in Relation to the Conversion Scheme." *Economic Journal*, Vol. XLII, pp. 415–423.

King, Willford I.: "The Net Volume of Saving in the United States," *Journal of American Statistical Association*, Vol. XVIII, pp. 455–470.

King, Willford I.: *The National Income and Its Purchasing Power*. New York, National Bureau of Economic Research, Inc., 1930. 394 pp.

Knauth, Oswald W.: "The Place of Corporate Surplus in the National Income," *Journal of American Statistical Association,* Vol. XVIII, pp. 157–166.

Knight, Frank H.: "Neglected Factors in. the Problem of Normal Interest," *Quarterly Journal of Economics,* Vol. XXX, pp. 279–310.

Kotany, L.: "A Theory of Profit and Interest," *Quarterly Journal of Economics,* Vol. XXXVI, pp. 413–453.

Landry, Adolphe: *L'Intérêt du Capital.* Paris, V. Giard et E. Brière, 1904. Bibliothèque Internationale d'Économie Politique. 367 pp.

Landry, Adolphe: *Manuel d'Économique.* Paris, 1908. V. Giard et E. Brière. 889 pp.

Landry, Adolphe: "On the Returns of Productive Agents and on the Productivity of Capital in Particular," *Quarterly Journal of Economics,* Vol. XXIII, pp. 557–592.

Macvane, S. M.: "The Theory of Business Profits," *Quarterly Journal of Economics,* Vol. II, pp. 1–36. Criticism of F. A. Walker's article in Volume I, pp. 265–288. See also Mr. Walker's reply in Vol. II, pp. 263–296.

Macvane, S. M.: "Capital and Interest," *Quarterly Journal of Economics,* Vol. VI, pp. 129–150.

Mill, John Stuart: *Principles of Political Economy.* Ashley edition. London, Longmans, Green & Co., 1909. Book II, Chap. XV, Of Profits. 1013 pp.

Mitchell, Waldo F.: *The Uses of Bank Funds.* Chicago, University of Chicago Press, 1925. 181 pp.

Mixter, Charles W.: "Böhm-Bawerk on Rae," *Quarterly Journal of Economics,* Vol. XVI, pp. 385–412.

Monroe, A. E.: "Investment and Saving: a genetic analysis," *Quarterly Journal of Economics,* Vol. XLIII, pp. 567–603.

Moulton, Harold G.: "Commercial Banking and Capital Formation," *Journal of Political Economy,* Vol. XXVI, pp. 484–508, 638–663, 705–731, 849–881.

Oppenheimer, Franz: *Wert und Kapitalprofit.* 3d edition. Jena, 1926. 79 pp.

Padan, R. S.: "J. B. Clark's Formulae of Wages and Interest," *Journal of Political Economy,* Vol. IX, pp. 161–190.

Patten, Simon N.: "The Fundamental Idea of Capital," *Quarterly Journal of Economics,* Vol. III, pp. 188–203.

Rae, John: *Sociological Theory of Capital; being a complete reprint of the New Principles of Political Economy, 1834.* Edited by Charles Whitney Mixter. New York, London, Macmillan & Co., 1905. 485 pp.

Ramsey, F. P.: "A Mathematical Theory of Saving," *Economic Journal,* Vol. XXXVIII, pp. 543–559.

Ricardo, David: *Principles*. (Gonner, editor.) London, George Bell & Sons, 1903. 455 pp. Chap. VIII on Profits.

Rickards, George K.: *Population and Capital*. London, Longman, Brown, etc., 1854. 259 pp.

Seltzer, Lawrence H.: "The Mobility of Capital," *Quarterly Journal of Economics*, Vol. XLVI (May, 1932), pp. 496–508.

Senior, Nassau William: *Political Economy*. 6th edition. London, Charles Griffin & Co., 231 pp. Sections on instruments of Production and Distribution of Wealth.

Sloan, Lawrence H.: *Corporation Profits*. New York, Harper & Bros., 1929. 365 pp.

Soule, George: *The Accumulation of Capital*. New York, League for Independent Democracy, 1924. 19 pp.

Spahr, Charles Barzillae: *The Present Distribution of Wealth in the United States*. New York, Boston, T. Y. Crowell & Co., 1896. 184 pp.

Stamp, Josiah C.: *British Incomes and Property: the application of official statistics to economic problems*. London, P. S. King & Son, 1916. 537 pp. Chapter XI deals with the national capital. General observations on Giffen's method.

Stamp, Josiah C.: *Studies in Current Problems in Finance and Government*. London, P. S. King & Son, 1924. 342 pp. Especially chapter on profits and wages.

Stehman, Jonas Warren: *The Financial History of the American Telephone and Telegraph Co*. Boston and New York, Houghton Mifflin Co., 1925. 339 pp.

Tuttle, C. A.: "The Real Capital Concept," *Quarterly Journal of Economics*, Vol. XVIII, pp. 54–96.

Tuttle, C. A.: "The Fundamental Notion of Capital Once More," *Quarterly Journal of Economics*, Vol. XIX, pp. 81–110.

Veblen, Thorstein: "On the Nature of Capital," *Quarterly Journal of Economics*, Vol. XXII, pp. 517–542, and Vol. XXIII, pp. 104–136.

Walker, Francis A.: "The Source of Business Profits," *Quarterly Journal of Economics*, Vol. I, pp. 265–288. See also MacVane's criticism in Vol. II, pp. 1–36, and Walker's reply in Vol. II, pp. 263–296.

Webb, Sidney: "The Rate of Interest and the Laws of Distribution," *Quarterly Journal of Economics*, Vol. II, pp. 188–208 and 469–472.

Wicksell, Knut: "Kapitalzins und Arbeitslohn," *Jahrbücher für Nationalökonomie und Statistik*, Vol. LIX, pp. 852–874.

Wolfe, A. B.: "Savers' Surplus and the Interest Rate," *Quarterly Journal of Economics*, Vol. XXXV, pp. 1–35.

2. The Growth of Capital

Douglas, Paul H.: "An Estimate of the Growth of Capital in the United Kingdom, 1865–1909," *Journal of Economic and Business History,* Vol. II, No. 4, August, 1930.

Giffen, Sir Robert: *The Growth of Capital.* London, G. Bell & Sons, 1889. 169 pp.

King, Willford Isbell: *The Wealth and Income of the People of the United States.* New York, Macmillan Co., 1915. 278 pp.

Leven, Maurice: *Income in the Various States, its sources and distribution 1919, 1920 and 1921.* New York, National Bureau of Economic Research, 1925. 306 pp.

National Bureau of Economic Research. *Income in the United States, its amount and distribution, 1909–1919.* 2 vols. New York, National Bureau of Economic Research, 1921.

Stamp, Josiah C.: "An Estimate of the Capital Wealth of the United Kingdom in Private Hands," *Economic Journal,* Vol. XXVIII, pp. 276–286.

Stamp, Josiah C.: *Wealth and Taxable Capacity.* London, P. S. King & Son, 1922. 195 pp.

U. S. Department of Commerce—Bureau of the Census: *Estimated National Wealth, Computed as Part of the Decennial Report on Wealth, Public Debt and Taxation, 1922.* Washington, Government Printing Office, 1924.

U. S. Department of Commerce—Bureau of the Census: *Special Report on Wealth, Debt and Taxation, 1904.* Washington, Government Printing Office, 1907.

U. S. Department of Commerce—Bureau of the Census: *Estimated Valuation of National Wealth, 1850–1912.* (Part of the Report on Wealth, Debt and Taxation, 1913.) Washington, Government Printing Office, 1915.

U. S. Department of Commerce—Bureau of the Census: *Biennial Census of Manufactures.* Washington, Government Printing Office.

U. S. Department of Commerce—Bureau of the Census: *Commercial Valuation of Railway Operating Property in the United States,* 1904. Special Bulletin No. 21. Washington, Government Printing Office, 1905.

U. S. Department of Commerce—Bureau of the Census: *Census of Electrical Industries, 1902, 1907, 1912, 1917, 1922 and 1927.* Including Telegraphs, Telephones, Street Railways and Electric Light and Power Stations.

U. S. Federal Trade Commission: *National Wealth and Income,* 69th Congress, 1st Session, Senate Document No. 126. 1926.

U. S. Geological Survey: *Mineral Resources of the United States.* 1921. 2 vols.

3. *The Actual Rates of Interest*

Burgess, W. Randolph: "Factors Affecting Changes in Short Term Interest Rates," *Journal American Statistical Association.* Vol. XXII, 1927, pp. 195–201.

Fisher, Irving: "The Rate of Interest After the War," *Annals of American Academy of Political and Social Sciences,* Vol. LXVIII, 1916, pp. 244–251.

Fisher, Irving: *The Theory of Interest.* New York, Macmillan Co., 1930, especially appendix to Chap. XIX, p. 520 *ff.*

Friday, David: *Profits, Wages and Prices.* New York, Harcourt, Brace & Howe, 1920, 252 pp. Chap. V.

Giffen, Robert: "Accumulations of Capital in the United Kingdom in 1875–1885," *Journal of Royal Statistical Society,* Vol. LIII. 1890, pp. 1–35.

Grimes, John Alden, and Craigue, William Horace: *Principles of Valuation.* New York, Prentice-Hall, Inc., 1928. 274 pp.

Kock, Karin: *A Study of Interest Rates,* Stockholm Economic Studies. London, P. S. King & Son, 1929. 264 pp.

Lavington, F.: "Short and Long Rates of Interest," *Economica,* 1924, No. 12, pp. 291–303.

Lévy, R. G.: "Du Taux Actuel de l'Intérêt," *Journal des Économistes,* Vol. XXXVII, 5e série (1899) pp. 321–338; Vol. XXXVIII, 5e série (1899) pp. 19–31.

Loutchitch, Leonidas J.: *Des Variations du Taux de l'Intérêt en France de 1800 à nos jours.* Paris, F. Alcan, 1930. 167 pp. (Statistical study on interest rates in France.)

Macaulay, F. R.: "The Construction of an Index Number of Bond Yields in the United States, 1859 to 1926." *Journal American Statistical Association,* March, 1926, pp. 27–39.

MacDonald, Robert A.: "The Rate of Interest Since 1844," *Journal of Royal Statistical Society,* Vol. LXXV, 1912, pp. 361–400, and discussion, pp. 401–411.

Mackenroth, Gerhard: "Period of Production, Durability and the Rate of Interest in the Economic Equilibrium." *Journal of Political Economy,* Vol. XXXVIII, pp. 629–659.

Persons, Warren M., and Frickey, Edwin: "Money Rates and Security Prices," *Review of Economic Statistics,* Vol. VIII, No. 1. (January, 1926), pp. 29–46.

Review of Economic Statistics. Vol. 17, June, 1907, pp. 213–220. Rates on U. S. Treasury Certificates (issued 1920–1921); Discount Rates (Bank of England and open market) in London. Bank Rates of discount charged in selected money markets; Changes in Central Bank Rates in World Monetary Centers.

Riefler, W. W.: *Money Rates and Money Markets in the United States.* New York and London, Harper & Brothers, 1930. 259 pp.

Standard Statistics Company. *Annual Statistical Bulletin.*

CHARTS

TABLES

TABLES IN APPENDIX

INDEX

INDEX

Aldrich Committee Report, 119, 121.

Algeria, comparison of actual population growth with values computed from the Pearl-Reed formula, 331; graphic representation of population growth, 336.

Arbitration, effect on wages, 93.

Austria, birth rates of various economic classes in Vienna, 402; length of population cycle, 342; net reproduction rate, 378.

Automobile Industry, hourly wages and standard hours per week, 311 ff., 530.

Aves, Ernest, effect of trade board rulings in Australasia, 76.

Bagehot, Walter, mobility of capital, 70 n.

Baking, correlating real hourly wages with standard hours per week, 305, 306, 527, 528.

Balakshin, S., world power resources, 108 n.

Bargaining Power, effect on supply curves, 248 ff., 493; of capital and labor, 90 ff.; theories, 77 ff.

Barone, Enrico, marginal productivity analysis, 38.

Belgium, length of population cycle, 342.

Berle, Adolf A., the modern corporation, 449 n.

Bertillon, Jacques, birth rates of different economic classes, 402, 403, 405.

Besant, Annie, Neo-Malthusian movement, 390.

Birth Rate, corrected for abnormal age composition, 375 ff.; correlated with real wages, England and Wales, 384 ff., Massachusetts, 395 ff.; in different countries, 352 ff., 533 ff.; of different social classes, 402 ff., 413 ff.; trend ratios correlated with real wages, England and Wales, 391 ff., 548, Massachusetts, 396 ff.; see also population and fertility.

Böhm-Bawerk, Eugen von, criticism of Marx's theory of profits, 43 n.; theory of capital, 431 ff., 456; theory of value based on demand curves alone, 97 n.

Boldrini, Marcello, differential fertility in Italy, 406 n.

Bonnet, C. E., employers' association in United States, 77 n.

Book and Job Printing, real hourly wages correlated with standard hours per week, 305, 306, 527, 528.

Boots and Shoes, real hourly wages correlated with standard hours per week, 305, 306, 527, 528.

Bowley, A. L., distribution of National Income in Great Britain, 221, 222, 490; estimated increase in real wages in Great Britain, 410, 411.

Bradlaugh, Charles, Neo-Malthusian movement, 390.

Brownlee, T., effect of standard of living on fertility, 348.

Brentano, L., effect of standard of living on population growth, 349, 350, 351; efficiency theory of wages, 72.

Bresciani-Turroni, C., distribution of income in Germany, 222, 490.

Brissenden, P. F., employment systems, 78 n.

Building Industry, hourly wages correlated with standard hours per week, 305, 306, 527, 528, 530.

Bulkly, M. E., effect of Trade Boards Act, 75.

Burgdörfer, F., differential birth rate in Germany, 418, 419.

Burns, Arthur F., Index of Physical Production, 103 n.

Cairnes, T. E., average pain cost of saving, 57 n.; concept of supply curves of factors, 230, 423, 425 ff.; labor reduced to common units of sacrifice, 15; non-competing groups, 52.

Canada, distribution of National Income, 490; estimated elasticity of marginal productivity curve of labor and capital, 491; movement of population, 369 ff.; real wages compared with power used, 109.

Cannan, E., principle of diminishing increment, 316.

Capital, assumptions of marginal productivity theory regarding, 69 ff.; breaking up the combined dose of labor and, 30 ff.; cost index, New